A Spectacular Secret

A Spectacular Secret

Lynching in American Life and Literature

JACQUELINE GOLDSBY

The University of Chicago Press   Chicago and London

JACQUELINE GOLDSBY is associate professor of English at the University of Chicago.

The University of Chicago Press, Chicago 60637
The University of Chicago Press, Ltd., London

Printed in the United States of America

15 14 13 12 11 10 09 08 07 06   1 2 3 4 5
ISBN: 0-226-30137-0 (cloth)
ISBN: 0-226-30138-9 (paper)

Library of Congress Cataloging-in-Publication Data

Goldsby, Jacqueline Denise.
A spectacular secret : lynching in American life and literature / Jacqueline Goldsby.
p. cm.
Includes bibliographical references and index.
ISBN 0-226-30137-0 (cloth : alk. paper)—ISBN 0-226-30138-9 (pbk. : alk. paper)
1. Lynching—United States—History. 2. United States—Race relations. 3. Lynching—United States—Historiography. 4. Lynching in literature. 5. American literature—History and criticism. I. Title.

HV6457.G65 2006
364.1′34—dc22   2005026551

♾ The paper used in this publication meets the minimum requirements of the American National Standard for Information Sciences—Permanence of Paper for Printed Library Materials, ANSI Z39.48–1992.

In memory of my mother

One is really at a loss for words in dealing with the subject of lynching. The horrible wickedness of it is so plain, and so gigantic, that only one conclusion is possible; and comment falls so short of the terrible reality as to constitute an anticlimax. It is hard to stretch the imagination so far as to realize these deeds belong to our day and land. JAMES F. MORTON, "THE CURSE OF RACE PREJUDICE"

Contents

Illustrations

Introduction

Reading a poem led me to write this book. Or better said, I was inspired by reading a poem aloud and hearing in its cadences a call to rethink my understanding of literary and cultural history's relation to one another as fields of academic inquiry. Because Gwendolyn Brooks's lynching ballads indelibly shaped the chapters that follow, it is helpful if I here trace how one of those poems transformed my understanding of lynching's significance to the African American past and to the trajectories of American life as experienced today.

Then off they took you, off to jail,
A hundred hooting after.
And you should have heard me at my house.
I cut my lungs with laughter,
    Laughter,
    Laughter,
I cut my lungs with laughter.[1]

The "Ballad of Pearl May Lee" begins with this plunge into danger: over the course of the poem, the speaker's lover Sammy is arrested then kidnapped from jail, "wrapped... around a cottonwood tree" (l. 83), and burned to death by the "hundred hooting" white men that constitute the lynch mob. Sammy's crime? Rape—a charge made after what the poem's speaker, Pearl May Lee, believes was her lover's consensual tryst with a white woman:

Say, she was white like milk, though, wasn't she?
And her breasts were cups of cream.

In the back of her Buick you drank your fill.
Then she roused you out of your dream.
In the back of her Buick you drank your fill.
Then she roused you out of your dream. (ll. 61–66)

The vicious tumult of these three imagined scenes—Sammy's death march, Pearl May Lee's house of bitter mirth, and the sexual fervor in the back of the white woman's car—is anchored by the aural symmetries of Pearl May Lee's oration. Repeating herself two and three times over (by doubling and trebling lines and stanzas), she beats down her hurt with the metrical foot of the iamb, using the elements of poetic form to redress the pain of Sammy's betrayal. The tightly tuned rhyme scheme ("after" paired with "laughter"; "cream" matched with "dream"), together with the alliteration within and between lines ("A *h*undred *h*ooting after," "*b*reasts," "*b*ack," and "*B*uick") constrain the fury of the poem without confining it, making the poem's turns of events all the more memorable to the reader.

Remarkably, though, the ruthlessness of Sammy's white paramour and the mob's sadism meets its match in Pearl May Lee's rage, a tonal congruity I found disturbing. Pearl May Lee seeks a sarcasm beyond mere bitterness, one that sounds disdainful itself because Sammy's choice to risk his life implies her inability to satisfy his needs as a lover. Since Sammy's first tryst limns her memory of his death, irony becomes Pearl May Lee's shield against despair:

You paid for your dinner, Sammy boy,
And you didn't pay with money.
You paid with your hide and my heart, Sammy boy,
For your taste of pink and white honey,
    Honey,
    Honey,
For your taste of pink and white honey. (ll. 95–101)

Hearing the ferocity of the poem's speaker, "Pearl May Lee" led me to ask different questions about the history of anti-black lynching in the United States. Where scholarly studies usually focus on the 3,417 African American victims of white mob violence between 1882 and 1968, Brooks's poem turned my attention to the lovers, wives, children, sisters, brothers, friends, and extended kin who survived lynching's violence.[2] How did communities remain or become that—communities—in the face of mob assaults? How did the living cope not only with the brutal losses of their loved ones but with the fact of their own survival? Indeed, what did it mean to be "spared" lynching's way of death? Using African American newspapers or actual survivors' oral histories as primary sources, I could address these questions more directly, perhaps.[3] Listening carefully to "Ballad of Pearl May Lee," however, I realized that untold histories of lynching were possible to conceive, ones that conventional sources might in fact obscure from view.

First published in *A Street in Bronzeville* (1945), the ballad presents a figure who presumably lives in Chicago, which is to say that she represents the history of lynching summarized by the "push-pull" thesis that is meant to account for the Great Migration: mob murders "pushed" black southerners to leave the region while the allure of social and economic opportunity in the North "pulled" African Americans away from Dixie.[4] Pearl's flight to safety is not an act of protest against southern white supremacy, though, because the poem refuses to be magnified by the hope of resistance that the "push-pull" paradigm promotes. Instead, she seethes over Sammy's rejection of her "dark meat" (l. 38), not to damn the psychology of white racism so much as to hold black people (and, specifically, black men) accountable for the system of caste politics we internalize and use to subjugate black women as sex objects. Or, as Pearl May Lee puts this point, "Yellow was for to look at, / Black for the famished to eat" (ll. 40–41).

The narrowed scope of Pearl's anger suggested to me that her predicament was an event in need of a history broad enough to redefine lynching as a practice of racial domination. For instance, her sexual jealousy, a sentiment that no woman-authored, anti-lynching stage dramas admit into their telling, emerges surreptitiously in the ballad's cousin—namely, the blues. As Adam Gussow suggestively argues, the laments for lost loves and empty beds that abound in blues women's songs can be read as memorials to the black men lost to lynch mob murders.[5] But the sharp edge of Pearl May Lee's laughter slashes the page with an angry sorrow that needs a name of its own, one that neither the blues nor feminist critiques of lynching develop in their analyses of the violence.[6] Thus, when she insists upon her prospects for freedom—"Oh, dig me out of my don't despair / Pull me out of my poor-me / Get me a garment of red to wear. / You had it coming surely" (ll. 1–4)—I was challenged to imagine where Pearl's desire for the world might lead in an interpretation of lynching's effects beyond the instance she represents. Surely, black women widowed by lynch mobs must have felt such rage somewhere, sometime, in which case Pearl's fictional experience does not lie irrevocably outside the realm of the possible. On the contrary, the poem points toward the historical through the force of its literary form.

Notably, the poem is written as a ballad, a genre that—in its common or folk form—narrated events of popular concern for working-class audiences in particular. Sung by traveling poets in public, communal settings, ballads were crafted to be easily recalled by listeners who, in turn, adapted the poems to reflect their personal interests or local mores.[7] According to *The Princeton Encyclopedia of Poetry and Poetics,* what made ballads malleable was their impersonal approach to storytelling. The poem's narrator "seldom allows his own subjective attitude toward the events to intrude. Comments on motives are broad, general, detached" (62). Though Brooks only wrote about lynching in the ballad mode, she did so in rebellious ways. For instance, "Pearl May Lee" personalizes the event of Sammy's murder in every possible way; elongating the usual four-line stanza to seven, the poem's construction draws attention to itself as a non-anonymous piece. Why break the genre's codes so deliberately? Brooks's clear affinity with ballad aesthetics co-existed with her obvious skepticism toward it, a dissonance which gives rise to the cultural commentary offered through the poem's form.

When I read "Pearl May Lee" aloud, I envision Brooks's protagonist in her Chicago kitchenette apartment, naming the ballad for herself and reciting its lines to proclaim the salience of her experience of Sammy's murder against the history and sociology of lynching as it was understood in 1945.[8] For me, then, the "Ballad of Pearl May Lee" evoked a different set of questions that influenced the argument and methods of this book. What kind of evidence could literature offer to a history of lynching's violence? And more precisely, what histories of lynching could the aesthetic forms of literary depictions reveal that we did not already know?

Written and published throughout the century that lynching became a racialized form of punishment, a rich canon of literary sources points toward another way of understanding the oppressive force of the practice. By reading history *out* of literary texts instead of *into* them, I glean accounts of lynching's "life"—its formation, meaning, and significance as a social practice—that identify the material and psychic forces in addition to racism that allowed the violence to remain unchecked in American society and under-interrogated in American cultural criticism. Thus, in the chapters that follow, debates over the federal powers of the nation-state; struggles to confer citizenship rights to women, people of color, and immigrants; the growing hegemony of secularized science and technology over the domains of public and private life; the rise of corporate-monopoly capitalism; and the confusions brought on by the abundance of mass culture—in short, America's emergence into modernity at the start of the twentieth century—orient my analyses, because the literary works I analyze narrate lynching as congruent with these transformations. More precisely, the narrative forms of these texts suggest this relation, and I follow the leads their genres prompt, weaving together close textual analysis with conventional historical sources to explain how and what literature bears witness to in its depictions of lynching's violence.

Shifting our attention to cultural formations beyond the South and structures of legitimation besides racism that made the violence both possible and tolerable as a social practice, I argue that lynching's relation to modernity consolidated its repressive force with the long-lasting effects historians and cultural critics usually attribute to the manifestly racist sources and aims of the practice. This reformulation is most sharply encoded in the book's central theme, that of lynching's "cultural logic," a term I have carefully chosen and one that has several interpretive facets. The first is, frankly, rhetorical. For long enough, we have stressed both the local and irrational dimensions of lynching in our analyses of the violence.[9] By shifting our perspective to lynching's "logic," I ask that we conceive of anti-black mob murders as a networked, systemic phenomenon indicative of trends in national culture. Consequently, I mean to think more broadly about why lynching emerged when it did, why it persisted for so long, and what instrumental purposes the violence served over time. Put another way, why lynching thrived amid American progress and abundance (as opposed to southern provincialism and impoverishment) is a riddle that I address in this book, one that the concept of "cultural logic" allows me to explore.

Thus, the second reason I speak of lynching's cultural logic is to adopt the critical posture of Gwendolyn Brooks's ballad as my own, to challenge the prevailing definitions of lynching's oppressive functions and cultural effects. Arguments that stress the regionalism of the violence rather than its national scope or that hold lynching to be symptomatic of racism's supposedly "eternal" hatreds cede too much ground for substantive materialist analysis to evolve, precisely because such hypotheses imply the violence is largely resistant if not immune to historical change. For this reason I don't turn to models premised on scapegoating, purity taboos, or identity politics. These approaches, I believe, limit analysis rather than further it insofar as they are unable to readily admit when change occurs that alters what the violence means. For instance (as I discuss in chapter 6), the lynching of Emmett Till in 1955 was, like any other lynching of an African American, heinous, needless, and awful. And yet his murder initiated a chain of events that transformed modern racial politics in America. How do accounts that stress the racial etiquette of the South as the locus of the case's importance allow us to conceive the "progress" his murder created? Ever since, Till's alleged wolf whistle directed toward a white woman has focused public debate about the case, entrenching us in the long, inexorable history of social taboos against interracial desire in the South. But do America's anxieties about miscegenation best explain why Till's is the murder we remember most readily? What does it mean that his death organizes how at least two generations of Americans know the history of lynching? How do the answers to those questions clarify what lynching does and means as a tactic of racist terrorism? Similarly, for Stephen Crane to write *The Monster* when he did (1898) and how he did ("under the spur of great need") was, as chapter 2 shows, a remarkably self-serving act on Crane's part; and yet it is precisely because Crane "forgets" to depict the lynching on which his novella is based in any explicit way that we're made privy to how northern white liberals' indifference—cultivated through the economics of corporate-monopoly capitalism and the aesthetics of realist fiction writing, as the literary history of Crane's novella shows—supplemented the negrophobia we're all familiar with as the driving impulse behind lynching murders.

In my definition and use of the term, then, the "cultural logic" of lynching enabled it to emerge and persist throughout the modern era because its violence "fit" within broader, national cultural developments. This synchronicity captures why I refer to lynching as "spectacular": the violence made certain cultural developments and tensions visible for Americans to confront. On the other hand, because lynching's violence was so unspeakably brutal—and crucially, since the lives and bodies of African American people were negligible concerns for the country for so long a time—cultural logic also describes how we have disavowed lynching's normative relation to modernism's history over the last century. Hence, I speak of lynching's "secrecy" as an historical event.[10]

I turn to literature to trace this dynamic and its consequences because, I believe, literature is particularly responsive to historical developments we cannot bear to admit shape the course of our lives. This, for me, has been the lesson and challenge of the "Ballad of Pearl May Lee": how, through the provocative uses of genre, does literature imagine for us the histories we cannot admit we need to know? For the purposes of this study, then, cultural logic operates on two levels at once. First, it traces how the operations of racism fit into and sustain a historical milieu not as an ever-present norm, but as a process the unfolding of which cannot be fully predicted in advance. Second, it guides my turn to literature and genre because fictive discourse models how cultural logic works: we choose works that "fit" with our interests, but find our deepest pleasures from those that disavow an exact coherence with the real world. Chapters 2–5 of this book define lynching's cultural logic through particular case studies. My hope is that these build on one another, each demonstrating from different but complementary angles of approach how the "fit" and "disavowal" that characterized the violence across time multiplied lynching's power to oppress to more insidious degrees that we have cared to know.

Insofar as my argument depends on analyzing literary forms as registers or archives of lynching's history, the book is not exempt from the processes and tensions described in the following chapters. I have no doubt that my argument emplots the violence as much as any other text I explore. Thus, I should explain my turn to narrative biography and the length of the chapters throughout the book. As I deploy it, life-writing encompasses people, things (newspapers, novellas, novels, and photographic apparatuses), and ideas (literary genres and movements) not to privilege personal experience as incontrovertibly "true" or self-evidently significant. I mean instead to suggest how, through the individual instance, personal circumstance meets the public sphere's developments to reveal history in all its contradictions and complications. Biography is particularly important when studying lynching because our tendency has been to regard the murders as one and the same event (i.e., an act of racial domination) that literally look the same way every time (dead bodies hanging from trees; burnt corpses atop pyres; shot bodies sprawled on the ground; bloated bodies dredged from rivers). Biography protects against my homogenizing the murders I examine, requiring instead that I produce accounts that hone in on select events while reflecting systemic forces that, in turn, help us understand specific cases and their relation to (as well as their differences from) one another.

Since lynching's cultural logic functions best when it conceals how the violence fit into a given historical milieu, each biography narrated in the chapters is a "secret" one—a history we don't know as well as other "major" figures, events, and processes that have come to characterize the period I study. For this reason, the chapters tend to run long; the little-known stories I tell require lengthy explication. For instance, since Ida B. Wells is routinely omitted from histories of Progressive-era journalism, I analyze her craftsmanship in chapter 2 as I narrate the innovations that modernized news writing during the 1890s and 1900s. Similarly, because Stephen Crane's critics stress his life history as an urban observer in New York City and New Jersey's Asbury Park, in chapter 3 I treat at some length Crane's relation to Port Jervis, his hometown in upstate New York, the cultural history of which is important to the lynching that occurred there and that inspired Crane's novella *The Monster.*

I could abbreviate my argument by directly engaging the established scholarship more than I do, but I have chosen to consign those debates to the book's endnotes, thus preserving the storytelling style that characterizes the text of the chapters. This is important because what we know about lynching has settled into narrative molds that are hard to break apart so that we might ask other kinds of interpretative questions. "It's a southern phenomenon." "The Klan did it." "Poor white trash did it." "The rape myth is a lie." "Lynching maintained white supremacy." "The murders aimed to keep black people subordinate, in their place." The best way to enlarge on this array of accounts while interrogating their claims and conclusions is, I think, to involve the reader in other narratives sufficiently long to prompt one to rethink *what* is known about lynching and to reconsider *how* one knows it. Knowing what I'm trying to accomplish, then, I hope readers will persevere in working their way through the chapters.

Thinking biographically matters to me for a fourth reason: it has enabled me to remember life in the midst of lynching's death toll—the lives of the men, women, and children killed; the lives of the writers who confronted the catastrophes and the anxiety and fear they caused; the lives of the texts that bear witness to this violence in and across time. Life must be asserted in the face of the attempt to suppress public discourse that lynching murders encouraged. Ever mindful of the caveat that "to articulate the past historically does not mean to recognize it 'the way it really was.'... It means to seize hold of a memory as it flashes up at a moment of danger," I assume that my biographical accounts are as volatile as Walter Benjamin suggests, the better to discern both the "flash"-strength and "moment of danger" that life-stories encompass.[11] And yet a sad conundrum that has made lynching's history difficult to comprehend frustrated me as well. Protest movements didn't stop the violence.[12] For that reason, writing biography led me to adopt a point of view signaled throughout this book by a carefully chosen pronoun—namely, "we." Who is included in that circle of reference and why do I draw it so ambiguously?

Using "we" has prompted me to imagine my relation to those who came before me in this history. I speak of "us" in these pages because there have been moments during my research for this book that I've felt distanced from the people and events I write about not only because of time, culture, and circumstance, but also because lynching's cruelties are so great as to have often exceeded my own interest in coming to understand them as an object of knowledge. This is, after all, a topic that should not exist for me or anyone else to write about. The murders I narrate in the chapters that follow should not have happened. Writing "we" has enabled me to look as fully as I can at the flash of danger this history presents, to be outraged when necessary, and to be self-aware of my own limitations as I learned what I needed but sometimes didn't want to know to write this book.

Another mode of collective understanding has been crucial to this book. Thinking and writing interdisciplinarily offered the best approach for me to respond to the issues posed by the literature I study here: what cultural formations other than southern white supremacy explain lynching's ebb and flow with the tides of American life? Given lynching's cultural logic—its capacity to reproduce and even mimic social structures while seeming distant, strange, and disavowable to us because its violent excess is directed against black people—how should we understand the dimensions of racism, class division, and gender difference that the murders unquestionably reproduced and reinforced? Do identity politics summarize all there is to know about the violence? Probing after lynching's meanings this way is not to dispute the scholarship that proves mob murders' instrumentality as a tactic of racist repression. Nor do I take issue with the statistical evidence of reported mob murders that map lynching to have been a largely southern phenomenon. Indeed, I draw heavily from such studies in the chapters that follow.

But I want to be clear what this book is not about. I do not treat the role of the Ku Klux Klan or its subsidiary terrorist cells in any substantive way. Nor do I dwell on the gender politics of the rape myth. Negrophobes have little say in my argument since I'm more concerned with the normalization of lynching's violence rather than its demonization (which also explains why I don't feature literature as a mode of "resistance").[13] In short, because the history I propose to tell follows from works of imaginative literature (rather than the other way around), this book charts a genealogy that often mirrors but more frequently departs from the knowledge we already possess.

Nonetheless, in writing this book I have benefited from an upsurge in recent years of public interest in lynching's history. In the effort to "educate the general public of the injustices suffered by people of African Heritage in America, and to provide visitors with an opportunity to rethink their assumptions about race and racism," America's Black Holocaust Museum in Milwaukee, Wisconsin, was founded in 1988 by James Cameron, who survived a lynch mob's attack in 1930.[14] Since the museum's opening, Americans have begun to acknowledge publicly the losses that lynching has exacted from black families, black communities, and our common life as a nation. Survivors of lynching murders and race riots in Tulsa, Oklahoma; Rosewood, Florida; Duluth, Minnesota; Moore's Ford, Georgia; and Scottsboro, Alabama have mobilized to demand reparations from state governments for the destruction of life, property, and opportunity the assaults in those locales caused.[15] On the popular front, the editors of *Time* magazine declared "Strange Fruit," Billie Holiday's incomparable elegy for lynching victims, the "Song of the Century" at the end of the year 2000, while the first year of the new millenium began with an equally astonishing event. Mounted first at Manhattan's Roth-Horowitz Gallery and then at the New York Historical Society for almost a year, the "Without Sanctuary" photograph exhibit revived what its owners, James Allen and John Littlefield, called "Lynching Photography in America."[16] Adding to these acts of remembrance, scholarly investigation about lynching has gained new momentum, with no fewer than ten books devoted to the topic published within the last five years.

How should we understand this upsurge of public interest? Surely it marks what Michel Rolphe Trouillot calls the "production of history": "What we are observing here is archival power at its strongest. The power to define what is and what is not a serious object of research and, therefore, of mention."[17] This moment is deeply and importantly humanist, though, because people and the politics they make are defining this moment as much as any institution's power. We are witnessing instead, I think, how language names what counts as significant and worthy of collective memory. Although the term "lynching" has been part of America's lexicon of violence since the late-eighteenth century, the range and types of violence referred to by the term vary widely, as I discuss in chapter 1.[18] Despite the word's imprecision, and despite the fact that black people were "lynched" in any number of ways (hanging, shooting, stabbing, burning, dragging, bludgeoning, drowning, and dismembering), similar atrocities that occurred in the course of race riots aren't called "lynching," nor are they factored into established inventories of lynching's death toll.[19] Hundreds of murders and assaults occurred under the regimes of convict lease labor and debt peonage too, the accounts of which often describe what we would consider lynchings. Like the rapes of black women by white men, however, those atrocities aren't considered part of lynching's history.[20]

Put another way, a complex history of racial violence is concealed by our increasingly restricted use of the term "lynching." Like an archive, the word functions to *denominate* the violence, ordering and fixing its meanings in ways that delimit our capacities to interpret it.[21] For that reason, I use "lynching" interchangeably with "murder," "anti-black mob violence," and "lynching's violence." Ultimately, though, to produce a history of lynching attentive to its constitution and operations through language, we need to invent a new name for the violence. What the word(s) might be, I cannot claim to know. But I can suggest where we might begin our search. As the nation's unlistened-to history, I am sure the word exists where Ralph Ellison assures us American literature works its power best: indelibly, at the "lower frequencies." There, the lives lost to us and made invisible by lynching and its cultural logic are waiting for us to listen.

ONE

A Sign of the Times: Lynching and Its Cultural Logic

History, like trauma, is never simply one's own. . . . History is precisely the way we are implicated in each other's traumas.
CATHY CARUTH, *UNCLAIMED EXPERIENCE: TRAUMA, NARRATIVE, AND HISTORY*

A chronicler who recites events without distinguishing between major and minor ones acts in accordance with the following truth: nothing that has ever happened should be regarded as lost for history.
WALTER BENJAMIN, "SOME THESES ON THE PHILOSOPHY OF HISTORY"

On February 1, 1893, a black man named Henry Smith was arrested in Paris, Texas, for raping and murdering a three-year-old white girl, Myrtle Vance. Smith was taken into custody after being tracked down by a search posse some two thousand members strong; so large a group was thought to be needed because the suspect had bolted out of the state for Arkansas, where he was eventually captured. On his return to the small town located in the northeastern corner of Texas, a thunderous tribunal of ten thousand spectators, many of whom had been ferried to the scene of the crime by specially arranged railroad junkets, met up with Smith to kill him.

First paraded around the business district for those "thousands in the city who wanted to see the fiend of fiends and monster of monsters," Smith was carted off to a clearing just beyond the city limits of Paris. There, atop a scaffold bearing a placard entitled "Justice," the dead child's father exacted the vengeance he had been waiting for. With fire-stoked iron rods Henry Vance burned the black man's arms, legs, chest, back, and mouth. Then, to complete his deed, Vance set all of Smith's body aflame as final punishment for his daughter's murder. "And so did death come to Henry Smith," one commentator wrote in 1893.[1]

When death came to Henry Smith, it was no clandestine affair. As local resident J. M. Early bragged: "If we, locally speaking, [had] been an insignificant moiety of a great nation with no other notoriety than suspected sturdiness, we are so no longer. Wherever print is read, wherever speech is the vehicle of thought, the people of Paris [Texas], of the United States of America, are now geographically located, and for moral stamina and worth, are known."[2] In newspapers around the country, front-page headlines spread word of the events in Paris, Texas. From Chicago to New York City, Philadelphia, Washington, D.C., Atlanta, and Kansas City—even to London—did the mob's grisly feat come to be known.[3] The town photographer J. L. Mertins copyrighted and deposited as many as twelve images with the Library of Congress (ensuring the pictures' having an archival home in that national repository). Another technophile preserved the event in an equally astonishing way: a sound recording of Henry Smith's trial by fire was made, copies of which—like Mertins's photographs—were reprinted and sold throughout the nation (see fig. 1.1).[4]

Later that year another black man, Samuel Burdett, encountered these records of Henry Smith's lynching in Seattle. "Whiling away an hour seeing the sights" in the city he called home, Burdett came upon a crowd "that was attending some sort of entertainment." "Curious," he approached the group, threading his way to the front "where a man was mounted on a stand or platform of some sort." At the center of the circle, Burdett clearly saw that the attraction was not an impromptu theatrical performance or a street-corner oration, but a carefully planned display of the newest technology America had to offer in 1893. An exhibit "for civilized citizens to enjoy according to their individual relish for the awful—for the horrible," Burdett recalled in anguish, the presentation "consisted of photographic views, coupled with phonographic records of the utterances of a negro who had been burned to death in Paris, Texas, a short time before."[5] Mounted on easels and placed in chronological order, the photographs tracked the Paris lynching from the discovery of Myrtle Vance's corpse to the capture, torture, and cremation of Henry Smith. Adjacent to these images was a gramophone with several

Figure 1.1. Paris, Texas photographer J. L. Mertins sought to obtain the copyright for "Little Myrtle Vance Avenged" by depositing this image along with eleven other photographs chronicling the lynching murder of Henry Smith in 1893. Mertins's efforts to assert intellectual property rights were in vain, since bootleg copies of the series circulated across the country from Seattle to Philadelphia and were used in early cinematic adaptations of the murder. (Photo courtesy of the Library of Congress, Prints and Photographs Division, LC-USZ62-29285.)

listening devices—what we would today recognize as headsets. As its disc plate spun, listeners could hear a recording of the confrontation between Myrtle Vance's father and the child's alleged assailant.[6]

This remarkable combination of sight and sound intrigued Burdett, who "had never heard or seen such a thing." "Like the others who were there" on that street corner in Seattle, he "took up the tubes of the phonographic instrument and placed them to [his] ears." What Burdett then saw and heard profoundly unnerved him; gripped by guilt nearly a decade later, he described the moment: "Oh, horror of horrors! Just to hear that poor human being scream and groan and beg for his life, in the presence and hearing of thousands of people, who had gathered from all parts of the country about to see it."[7] Printed on the page, Burdett's torment is clear. The clichéd exclamation ("Oh, horror of horrors!") sounds out his struggle to find language to express his encounter. Underscored by his compound phrasing ("scream *and* groan *and* beg"), Smith's cries press on the reader's ears, forcing us to imagine the agony of both black men. However, as his prose also demonstrates, it is unclear who horrifies Burdett more: the mob that watched the murder in Paris, Texas, or the entranced audience of onlookers in Seattle.

Certainly Burdett did not share the Texans' reasons for wanting to see Henry Smith killed; as a member of the International Council of the World, he was an avid anti-lynching activist.[8] Nonetheless, his interest in witnessing something new, something novel, something modern—his own admission of being "curious" "like the others"—enticed him to look at the photographs and to listen to the sound recording of Henry Smith's murder. And for that reason, the function of the audio-visual display confused Burdett's perception of his relation to the murder scene. Was viewing the simulation a way to protest the lynching, or did watching amount to a vicarious act of complicity with the southern mob? How different could Seattle and Paris, Texas, be if the deaths of black people were openly sought out as public events worth seeing and without the risk of legal reprisal? These questions, raised by Henry Smith's murder and by Samuel Burdett's anguished memories of his place in the crowd, suggest we should reexamine the history of lynching in America, to explore more broadly why mob violence was indeed a "horror of horrors" for African Americans and how mechanisms of modernity served to mediate the public's experience of the violence at the turn of the nineteenth century.

Henry Smith's murder and Samuel Burdett's encounter with it were not unusual in their day. The United States during the 1890s saw the numbers of vigilante murders of African Americans soar to unprecedented heights. In the year that Smith was lynched, 103 blacks died at the hands of white mobs. During the period 1882–1930 (the years, scholars agree, when the most reliable lynching statistics were kept), 3,220 African American men, women, and children were murdered by lynch mobs.[9] Though the majority of these murders occurred in the Deep South, anti-black mob violence spread to far western states like Colorado, midwestern states like Illinois and Minnesota, and northeastern states like Pennsylvania and New York.[10] And as the lynching of Henry Smith demonstrates, mass-media representations of the violence extended the borders of southern lynchings as well. Indeed, the national press kept such a steady watch over the violence that, in 1903, William James worried about the effect it might have on the country's collective soul: "The hoodlums in our cities are being turned by the newspapers into as knowing critics of the lynching game as they long have been of the prize-fight and football." The Harvard philosopher's remarks appeared in *Literary Digest,* one of the genteel magazines that devoted editorial space to debates about the practice of lynching in late nineteenth-century American society.[11] Book-length studies also stirred the air of public commentary. Lynching apologists such as Phillip Alexander Bruce, Frederick L. Hoffman, and Robert W. Shufeldt published their best-selling books and monographs with reputable establishments, while anti-lynching activists such as T. Thomas Fortune, Mary Church Terrell, and Kelly Miller relied on an earnest and growing black publishing industry to carry their words of protest to African American readers across the nation during these crucial decades.[12]

The word "lynching," however, did not always refer to the summary, extralegal executions of African Americans by groups (larger than three) of self-appointed public authorities.[13] As one commentator noted in 1900, the "modern application" of the term, "with its deeds of wild lawlessness or ruthless murder," misrepresented the word's earlier use.[14] After the Revolutionary War but before the Civil War, lynching referred to the nonlethal, corporeal punishment of white men by semiregular public authorities in frontier societies.[15] Public lashing, tar-and-feathering, and riding the rail were the usual penalties meted out to Tory loyalists, horse and livestock thieves, bank robbers, or adulterers who threatened to disturb the peace in just-established communities. What distinguished "lynch law" between the 1780s and 1850s were its statelike aspirations to govern, since "upright and ambitious frontiersmen wished to re-establish the values of a property-holder's society." For this reason, lynch mobs during these decades were also noted for their decorum and restraint—hence, the other oft-used term for pre-Civil War vigilantism, "regulators"—in dispensing punishment to outlaws and wrongdoers.[16]

But all this is true only of lynch-law justice as applied to white men. For African Americans who transgressed the laws and customs of their plantation societies, the master's and mistress's lash often stopped short of regulators' apocryphal thirty-nine strokes, the better to inflict more damaging pain; slave narratives published during and about this period are replete with scenes of torture and whippings that demonstrate how economizing corporeal punishment maximized its brutal effects. Similarly, African Americans who disturbed the peace by plotting to overturn the slave regime were summarily executed under the auspices of the state but in conspicuously unrestrained demonstrations of the law's power, as the examples of the 1714 and 1741 New York City conspirators, Gabriel Prosser (1800), Denmark Vesey (1822), and Nat Turner (1831) attest.[17] During the antebellum era, then, it is clear that the term "lynching" referred to something different than what we now understand that term to mean. Furthermore, the practices of punishment designated by the word evolved over time as well. If, however, what always distinguishes lynching is its extralegal status, the word "lynching" potentially misidentifies the range and aims of punishments targeting African Americans precisely because the state routinely allowed extreme, and often lethal, measures of discipline to be exacted on them.

By all accounts, though, the racialization of lynching—the near-exclusive targeting of African American people for punishment by white vigilante mobs—took clear shape during the era of Reconstruction.[18] Marked by an "increased harshness" that generally involved the killing of black people, "the word 'lynch' has come to be a synonym for 'murder' or mistreatment of a Negro, South as well as North," essayist Walter Fleming observed in 1905. Lynching's lethal turn made it an especially heinous tactic of social control at the end of the nineteenth century.[19] First, the "modern" practice was crucial to the restoration of the Confederacy's power. The terrorist campaigns waged by the Ku Klux Klan during its first incarnation between 1867 and 1871—the Klan's infamous "night rides" and race riots—accomplished southern Democrats' goals to oust northern Republicans from leadership positions across the region and to intimidate African Americans from casting ballots in local, state, and national elections.[20]

Though scholars agree that the reestablishment of "Redeemer" governments in the former Confederate states enabled the practice of anti-black lynching to thrive, African Americans were terrorized and murdered with impunity because they had been excluded from the legal and moral frameworks that defined national citizenship at the end of the nineteenth century.[21] Paradoxically, the U.S. Supreme Court's rulings in the *Slaughterhouse* (1873), *Cruikshank* (1876), *Civil Rights* (1883), and *Plessy* (1896) cases made emancipated blacks more vulnerable to mob assault from any and all quarters, precisely because these new laws and public policies conceded the point that made lynching an actionable crime.[22] By nullifying African Americans' rights of citizenship and, with them, the affirmative duty to protect black people from unjust harm, the federal government effectively granted mobs a license to kill. For instance, since the 1870 Force Bill and the 1871 Ku Klux Klan Act allowed federal courts jurisdiction over cases involving racial violence against blacks, either one could have been cited as precedents to criminalize lynching as murder; they were not.[23] Between 1901 and 1934, anti-lynching activists vigorously argued that the Fourteenth Amendment's due process clause ensured alleged black criminals the right to fair trials in competently administered courts. However, each time federal anti-lynching legislation was introduced (in 1901, 1921, 1922, and 1934) Congress rejected those bills on the grounds that such a law would violate the constitutional ideal of protecting states' rights.[24] Though contemporary commentators insisted otherwise—"no definition has ever been attached to 'lynch law' that does not plainly indicate that its operation is wholly without, and, indeed, in opposition to, the established laws of government," Howell Featherston argued in 1900—by the end of the nineteenth century there was nothing *extra*legal about the mob murders of African Americans.[25] Lynching functioned as a tool of domination meant to coerce (and not rough-handedly correct), to deny (and not merely restrict), and to subjugate (not only banish or dispatch) black people, depriving them of the political, economic, social, and cultural opportunities promised by emancipation.

Lynching's trajectory from its antebellum roots to its (then) modern-day practice disturbed contemporary observers who debated its place and function in late-nineteenth-century American society. "The barbarities and atrocities [of lynching] . . . almost beggar description and hardly find parallel in the world today and have been seldom matched or surpassed in the world's history," Winthrop Sheldon lamented in 1906.[26] But more than a decade earlier, in 1892, Frederick Douglass had observed the very same thing—white lynch mobs that struck out with "frantic rage and extravagance." For more than ten years the most violent excesses of mob rule had been tolerated as if they were a commonplace affair:

> Not a breeze comes to us from the late rebellious states that is not tainted and freighted with Negro blood. In its thirst for blood and its rage for vengeance, the mob has blindly, boldly, and defiantly supplanted sheriffs, constables and police. It has assumed all the functions of civil authority. It laughs at processes, courts, and juries, and its red-handed murderers range abroad unchecked and unchallenged by law or by public opinion. If the mob is in pursuit of Negroes who happen to be accused of crime, innocent or guilty, prison walls and iron bars afford no protection. Jail doors are battered down in the presence of unresisting jailers, and the accused, awaiting trial in the courts of law, are dragged out and hanged, shot, stabbed or burned to death, as the blind and irresponsible mob may elect.[27]

Even the unreconstructed southern novelist Thomas Nelson Page was awestruck by the sweep of lynching's violence: "Over 2,700 lynchings in eighteen years are enough to stagger the mind," he wrote. "Either we are relapsing into barbarism, or there is some terrific cause for our reversion to the methods of medievalism."[28]

The atrociousness of anti-black lynchings left the African American scholar Kelly Miller nearly speechless because he, unlike Page, identified with the sufferings of black lynch victims and was enraged at how lynching's death sentence could extend to any African American. "Such fiendish practice outrages human feeling, and hurts the heart of the world," the sociologist cried.[29] The nation's callous disregard for the mortal danger under which African Americans lived was indeed widespread. Religious denominations were divided in reaction to the violence. For instance, the southern branches of the Methodist church refrained from public censure of anti-black lynch mobs while the northern branches issued their first repudiation of the practice in 1900.[30] Nor did U.S. presidents use their bully pulpits to the fullest advantage of anti-lynching politics. As Winthrop Sheldon reminded readers of *Arena* in 1906, "no reference . . . of any practical importance has ever been made to the subject [of lynching] by any of our Presidents in their annual messages [to Congress]," a silence that not even Franklin D. Roosevelt would break.[31] In what was perhaps the most egregious display of governmental neglect to at least acknowledge the problem, President William McKinley steadfastly refused to condemn the Wilmington, North Carolina race riots of 1898 despite such pleas from African Americans as the following:

> We have suffered, sir . . . since your accession to office . . . from the hate and violence of people claiming to be civilized, but who are not civilized, and you have seen our sufferings. . . . Yet you have at no time and on no occasion opened your lips on our behalf. . . . Is there no help in the federal arm for us, or even one word of audible pity, protest, and remonstrance? Black indeed we are, sir, but we are also men and citizens.[32]

Where a pogrom like the Wilmington riot galvanized black activists, other violent outbreaks so overwhelmed African Americans that they were traumatized into a seeming complaisance. Ida B. Wells recalled the black community's response to the Springfield, Illinois race riots of 1908 with sad bitterness:

> As I wended my way to Sunday School that bright Sabbath day, brooding over what was still going on at our state capital, I passed numbers of people parading in their

Sunday finery. None of them seemed to be worried by the fact of this three days' riot going on not less than two hundred miles away.[33]

While it may be that some African Americans of the day were motivated to at least appear unperturbed by lynching murders (recall Samuel Burdett's being lured by the technology that enabled him to "witness" Henry Smith's murder), such demeanor lends credence to Winthrop Sheldon's observation in 1906 that "this indifference is by no means confined to the South." Rather, a malaise was "almost the country over":

The American citizen, as he partakes of his morning roll and coffee and reads in his newspaper the sickening account of the latest lynching tragedy, is moved for the time being with a thrill of horror. He lays his paper aside, goes to his daily work, becomes absorbed in the business of money-making, and—that is the end of it. The incident is closed. It is only a few days' sensation and soon forgotten.[34]

We have all but forgotten how varied and complex were the debates about lynching at the turn of the nineteenth century. This is because scholarly studies have unwittingly polarized our understanding of the violence as it was inflicted on African American communities. For instance, we have stressed the politics of negrophobia in our analyses of lynching because, despite its instrumental effects in maintaining social hierarchies, racism—at bottom, we believe—is stirred by deep, irrational hate.[35] And yet, as the observations by Kelly Miller, Ida B. Wells, and Winthrop Sheldon suggest, African Americans' trauma and white Americans' apathy allowed lynching to thrive as much as did white southerners' much-studied antipathy. Understanding the politics of hurt, shame, and indifference (rather than fear, rage, and obsession) might help explain why anti-lynching movements never succeeded in criminalizing anti-black mob murders. Furthermore, as Sheldon hints, such a study should examine how "the business of money-making" urged white Americans to be "thrilled" with horror at the news of lynching in one moment, only to "forget" the murders in the next. What, then, becomes the proper economic context to interpret lynching: southern impoverishment or northern abundance?

Scholars, however, have tended to close off such promising routes of interpretation. Typically, historians, sociologists, psychologists, and literary critics analyze lynching in one (or a combination) of three ways: as a phenomenon peculiar to the South and its regimes of white patriarchal supremacy in economic and electoral politics; as the murderous fulfillment of Freudian sexual pathologies; or as the perverse but decisive culmination of "making" whiteness and masculinity the nation's ideals of citizenship. As rich as it is, however, the historiography has institutionalized the perception that lynching means less to the central processes defining American life and culture because the violence is, we presume, best understood as regional and aberrant.[36] Regarded as a "southern" problem, lynching confirms the extent of rural "backwardness" compared with urban sophistication. It reifies the feudalistic power dynamics of agrarian politics against the hierarchical instabilities produced by technologically driven industrialization. Lynching lays bare the neuroses shaping the ideologies of white supremacy against the humanism of democratic liberalism. However, the lynching murders of Mexicans and Chinese in the West, Southwest, and far North ought to be a first clue that we need to develop sustained analyses that posit lynching to evince more than the South's economic provincialism or its perverse will to racial dominance. Moreover, the ever-lurking symbols of American progress deployed in the mob murders of African Americans (hanging victims from electric street light poles or suspension bridges; using newly invented cameras to take and sell photographs of the murders; playing football with victims' corpses) denies us refuge in the presumption that lynchings were always retrograde, atavistic displays of racial aggression.[37]

To be sure, writing about lynching during the pivotal decades of its racial transformation was as divisive as the scholarship describes. Indeed, the all-too-familiar demonization of black men as inherently criminal, rapacious "fiends," "brutes," "imps," and "beasts" no doubt stirred the foment that caused the numbers of anti-black lynchings to rise so high at the start of the twentieth century.[38] I am interested in exploring another history of lynching, however, one that examines those strands of public discussion that have yet to be accounted for in our now-familiar paradigms of analysis. In the chapters that follow, I turn to representations of lynching across various print and visual media, to read the depictions of the violence from the inside out, as it were. That is, rather than read history *into* such literary texts, I read history *out* of them to discern how American writers understood the meanings of lynching and its effects as a tactic to subjugate black people.

Consider, for instance, the rhetoric about lynching's "contagious" potential. From the 1890s to the 1920s, observers vividly characterized anti-black mob murders as an addictive practice, a "habit" that could spread uncontrollably around the country like a communicable disease. "A plague worse than cholera is upon us," the editors of the *Nation* warned, while another essayist fretted how the "mania" spawned "mock lynchings":

> A mob of lynchers is seldom content with the death of the immediate victim. Very often . . . in the wake of a lynching [blacks] . . . are beaten, shot at, and driven from their homes; their houses are burned to the ground and their property destroyed, in order to intimidate and terrorize the entire neighborhood.[39]

The reign of terror described here was always news for African American newspapers to report, as I discuss in chapter 2. What is worth noting in this account is the author's designation of such pogroms as "*mock* lynchings." In today's parlance, we would call this repetition of the crime "copycatting." But the question we must ask is why anti-black lynchings coincided with the era in national life when "mock" experience was becoming more commonplace, when cultural production and experience was increasingly organized around serial processes and events? We have preferred to understand the increasing reenactments of lynching murders as evidence of the depths of white supremacy's power and white southerners' "rage for order," to recall historian Joel Williamson's striking phrase. But contemporary observers at the turn of the nineteenth century linked lynching's reproducibility to other cultural processes that were not necessarily "southern" concerns. Many echoed Samuel Burdett's complaint that lynching modeled the politics of U.S. imperialism at its worst: "The butchery of a bound and tied human being can occur here where men volunteer as soldiers to go to Cuba or to Manila to aid the oppressed, as we say."[40] Similarly, others argued that lynching's "epidemic" spread throughout an increasingly borderless world, citing anti-Semitic violence in Russia and genocidal atrocities in the African Congo and in Turkey.[41] Some worried that lynching's global "outbreaks" would inevitably double back to destroy white Americans themselves: "Let this mob spirit continue unbridled, and the victims will not always be Negroes. When a howling, blood-thirsty, unreasoning mob starts into stringing up white men without a hearing, lynching will not be viewed with such complaisance," the usually pro-lynching *Atlanta Constitution* opined.[42]

In adopting the vocabulary of epidemiology to explain the virulence of lynching's popularity and, as importantly, its protean capacities to transform itself into other modes—what I call its "mass appeal" in chapter 4—these writers expressed deep concern for the national-global (rather than regional-local) scope of the violence. Using metaphors of "continuums" and "reproducibility" also gave voice to their need to comprehend lynching's power to oppress black people as a symptom of the country's (then) present course of development rather than as an atavism of a long-ago past. Indeed, as I read such essays, the language of contagion suggests that lynching's sustainability was evidence not only of racism's force but also of mass culture's impact on American society at the end of the nineteenth and start of the twentieth centuries. However, we have neglected to investigate these lines of argument, even though the sources implore us to do just that. "As this is not by any means a mere skin disease but one which afflicts the social organization in its most vital parts, it [lynching] is certainly worthy of careful study," Edwin Maxey urged, while Edward L. Pell advised that "lynch law as an epidemic will never be suppressed by ignoring the conditions which keep the atmosphere infected with the germs of the lynching fever."[43]

What "conditions" of national life might we then study to learn what kept the "lynching fever" high? Recalling the example of Henry Smith, since his murder occurred in the same year as the devastating financial panic of 1893, perhaps lynching reflected deep need and want: need for a scapegoat onto which the mob could project its frustrations over the wants created by the unstable and unpredictable cotton market.[44] Though important to investigate, an account that focuses solely on the social effects of impoverishment, split labor markets, or the psychology of projection and denial seems incomplete in light of the cultural and technological riches used to stage Smith's murder. How, for instance, are we to understand the mob's use of the railroad to create a crowd of strangers to watch the event; what kind of a public sphere was being instituted through this lynching in Paris, Texas? And then there is the riddle posed by the audio-visual record of the event: the synchronized photo-sound montage that Samuel Burdett experienced in Seattle resembles in function (if not form) the kinetoscope Thomas Edison introduced to the nation and the world in 1888. How are we to assess what appears to be a remarkable convergence between lynching and the advent of motion pictures?[45] Indeed, occurring three months before the opening of the World Columbian Exposition in Chicago, the lynching of Henry Smith joined together a brutal display of racially charged force with the nation's emblems of technological achievements; consequently his murder affects our sense of historical time for the era as a whole. The convergence of violence and cultural advances does not repudiate our notions of "modern" progress; their intersections appear to confirm and specify them. Toward what end? And with what effects with respect to lynching's power to oppress African American people?

In this book I argue that lynching thrived at the turn of the new century not because the violence was endemic to the South's presumed retrograde relation to the developments that constituted modernity in America. Rather, I contend that anti-black mob murders flourished as registers of the nation's ambivalences attending its nascent modernism, which we can see on many cultural fronts.[46] First, lynching was not as aberrant a practice as we now think. In the years when anti-black lynchings reached their peak (between 1882 and 1922), the violence was part of a cultural milieu that saw westward expansion and the completion of the transcontinental railroad bring about the Plains Indians Wars of the 1870s and 1880s. Nativist vigilantism against the influx of immigrants from southern and eastern Europe in the Northeast and the entry of the Chinese into the West during the 1890s and 1900s created a lethal synergy with anti-black mob violence. Because labor strikes were often deadly conflicts of interest, workers' battles with corporate bosses were often compared with lynching as twinned symptoms of modernization's distemper. For example, A. P. Dennis depicted the 1904 miners' strike in Ludlow, Colorado in the following way:

> Here, as in other parts of the country, men were brutally beaten for the sole reason that they were working for their living in pursuance of the liberty guaranteed them by the constitution. A day seldom passes without its grim record of mob violence in some part of the country—violence which deprives some human being of "life, liberty, or property" without due process of law.[47]

Indeed, America at the turn of the nineteenth century edged toward modernity with such aggressive brio that the parallels between the "backward" practice of lynching and the steps we have welcomed as progress seem hard to ignore. The "strenuous life" extolled by "Rough Rider" Theodore Roosevelt as the coming century's new model of masculinity—epitomized by the hard-hitting pursuits of bare-knuckle boxing, football, and hunting—venerated hand-to-hand combat and killing of wildlife as leisure pastimes.[48] Industrial innovation resulted in American workers toiling long hours over complicated machinery that caused severe physical injuries and even deaths. Though urban cities expanded so rapidly because of immigration and migration, the impoverished conditions of slum tenements exposed millions of Americans to disease, crime, and vice. Even the food that graced a family's table (if there was enough to buy and serve) was infected by the processes of industrial production that promised to deliver many goods for less money; the slaughter of meat, as Upton Sinclair famously revealed in *The Jungle* (1905), symbolized how brutal business enterprise could be.[49] Finally, the Civil War, which staggered the nation but transformed it into a more perfect union of states, gave way to World War I, in which torpedo-launching submarines, bomb-dropping airplanes, and long-range-firing machine guns initiated the reorganization of the globe that would continue throughout much of the twentieth century.

When lynching became murderous at the end of the nineteenth century, African Americans were its main victims, but the aggression that characterized lynching's violence was common to the country during that time. With the parallels between lynching and these cultural contests so omnipresent, observers pondered whether lynching thrived not in spite of but because of modernity's effects on the public's temperament. "These horrors—the rapings, the lynchings, the burnings—are not ancient history, they are the products of American life in the closing decades of the nineteenth century," Atticus G. Haygood noted in his 1893 essay about Henry Smith's murder, "The Black Shadow across the South."[50] Like Frederick Douglass, who spent the last years of his life contemplating whether the "changed" and "altered times" of the late nineteenth century were a salient factor in the political causes and effects of the violence, Georgia's governor William T. Northen also wondered whether the violence stemmed from sources beyond the society and culture of the South. "These things amaze me and are not to be accounted for upon any theory with which I have been familiar heretofore. It behooves us all to seriously consider a proper solution of the difficulties that surround us," Northen explained to a friend.[51] Perhaps sociologist John Franklin Crowell best summarized in 1894 the state of cultural affairs I wish to examine: "Most people are really at a loss to account for the existence of any such thing as a lynching. They cannot imagine a condition of society which would make such a movement possible, much less rational or necessary."[52]

In the chapters that follow, I explore anti-black lynchings as a phenomenon symbolic of its time. Moreover, I argue that its power to oppress African Americans was intensified by its relations to cultural developments we ordinarily categorize as "modern."[53] The dizzying pace of progress in the late nineteenth century left the nation confused about its prospects and uncertain of the outcomes of these processes. Americans' preoccupation with establishing new standards for national identity and citizenship; our anxieties about the purchasing power of money and the systems through which capital would come to regulate our social exchanges; our disquiet over the emergence of blacks and women as autonomous participants in civic life; our desire to know whether, in the era of secularized, incorporated power and mass culture, our fates would ever be under our full control again—all these social dilemmas, I argue, are crucial contexts in which we should contemplate the meanings and effects of lynching's violence.

Following the interpretive lead suggested by John Franklin Crowell and others, I seek out what other factors beside southern racism and the political economy of white supremacy made lynching "necessary and rational"—what I call "culturally logical"—in American life as the nineteenth century drew to a close. In my view, a paradox concerning lynching's history at the end of that century remains unaddressed. On the one hand, anti-black mob murders intersected quite frequently with the technologies and temperament at work in national cultural developments. On the other hand, lynching's relation to modernity's evolution in the United States has been persistently disavowed. My category of "cultural logic" helps provide a two-fold response to this paradox.

First, I use the term to refer to lynching's synchronicities or its fit with developments in national society and culture. As I have already noted, contemporary observers regarded lynching as an "American crime" and a "national shame," but they were also flummoxed by lynching's place in history, calling it "new" and "savage," "old" and "strange," an "invention" and a "tradition" all at once. This response, which Raymond Williams defines as the dialectic between "residual" and "emergent" cultural forms, does not confuse the point of describing lynching as culturally logical. On the contrary, Williams's theory helps specify the utility of my concept. Rather than emphasizing the ways in which lynching is separate from its contemporary milieu, using the term "cultural logic" allows me to investigate lynching's connections to the past and present in order to distinguish between its causes and contexts more readily.[54] Put another way (and to explain a second key word in my argument), "culturally logical" is akin to how Guy Debord defines the function of "spectacles" in modern social life: "The spectacle cannot be understood either as a deliberate distortion of the visual world or as a product of the technology of mass dissemination of images. *It is far better viewed as a weltanschauung that has been actualized, translated into the material realm—a world view transformed into an objective force.*"[55] If, as Debord contends here, spectacles are more than image events, lynching can be understood as an articulation of the social world's organization at any given point in time. But my further point is that the social world to which lynching refers is not just that of the South but, as Debord points out, the *weltanschauung* of the nation. I understand cultural logic, then, as a matrix that informed and, in turn, was formed by the violence. Because of its reciprocal capacity, an appeal to cultural logic counters those arguments that characterize the violence as anomalous, aberrant, local, and anti-modern.

What is more, lynching fit within the flow of American history for as long as it did because its cultural logic allowed us to disavow its connections to national life and culture. This second operation contributes to lynching's status as a cultural secret. We ignore lynching's possible relations to American modernity partly as a matter of preference (progress simply cannot be that awful or disempowering), but primarily because it is possible for us to do so. And here, racism returns from the repressed that my definition of cultural logic might be said to effect, since my argument depends on this presumption: once African Americans became the majority targets of lynching's violence—and because African Americans lacked the legal, civic, and moral authority to repel mob assaults on their collective lives—the history of those deaths could be marginalized from our conventional accounts of the formation and meaning of modernity in American life.[56] Or, as Michael Rogin observes about such "motivated forgetting": "That which is insistently represented becomes, by being normalized to invisibility, absent and disappeared."[57] Throughout this study, then, I argue that lynching worked as a strategy of terrorism and racial domination precisely because it was more than a highly visible and cruel ploy for power on the part of southern whites against the civil rights and aspirations of black people. Lynching thrived as a social practice at the turn of the nineteenth century because, to the degree that the violence could be integrated "secretly" into the new regimes and routines of American life, the death toll of African American lynch victims could be both shocking and ordinary, unexpected and predictable, fantastic and normal, horrifying and banal—which is how Samuel Burdett, during a Sunday's stroll in Seattle—encountered and experienced the lynching of Henry Smith.

Since, as Toni Morrison reminds us, "it requires hard work *not* to see" racism's many faces, lynching's cultural logic has been hard for us to discern.[58] Lost to us because it has sustained the secrets of lynching's power to oppress so well for so long a time, the cultural logic of the violence also reveals how it seals itself off from scrutiny—if, that is, we

Figure 1.2. Dehumanizing images of African American men often fueled the arguments of lynching's apologists, who claimed that "black beasts" deserved death in order to safeguard white women from the threat of rape. This political cartoon, which helped incite the Wilmington (North Carolina) race riot of 1898, suggests that white male defenders of anti-black mob violence actually feared political miscegenation more: rising up from the "fusion ballot box," the sharp-taloned demon reaches for the white male electorates of the Republican and Populist parties. Though meant to convince North Carolinians that "Negro Rule" would end in the sexual "mongrelization" of the white race, this image shows instead how belittled white men imagined themselves to be by the prospects of emancipated African Americans. (Reprinted with permission of the North Carolina Collection, University of North Carolina Library at Chapel Hill.)

know where to look for the fit and are determined to see the connections once we find them.

Consider, for instance, two political cartoons from 1898 and 1906. Figure 1.2 depicts a black man in the guise of an incubus, a mythological bird of prey that, legend purports, had sexual intercourse with women while they slept.[59] This iconography was the centerpiece of the North Carolina Democrats' campaign to regain control of the state legislature, prompting the infamous Wilmington race riots. As historian Glenda Gilmore astutely observes, the heavy-handed symbolism of gargantuan black beasts terrorizing defenseless white women traded on long-standing sexual stereotypes of African American men as unruly, insatiable carnal creatures. But beneath the false propaganda was a subtle ploy to stigmatize the ascent of black politicians to electoral power in the state. The miscegenation that North Carolina Democrats feared most was not the erotic coupling of black men and white women but the "fusion politics" that joined black voters with the Republican and Populist parties into power blocs that controlled the state's government.[60] This distortion—what historian Martha Hodes aptly calls "the sexualization of politics"—incontestably led to the Wilmington riots as well as to hundreds of anti-black lynching murders at the turn of the nineteenth century.[61] This I do not doubt.

I do wonder about the visual resemblances between the image of the incubus and that in the cartoon shown in figure 1.3. Here, the heads of the nation's major corporations have metamorphosed into vultures roosting atop the decrepit crypt of a bank, looking to fatten themselves on the poverty of white workers.[62] Neither of these images was uncommon, which is why they impress me as both striking and related. How should we understand the shared graphic vocabulary that likens black men and corporate moguls to dark, malevolent, bestial birds who stalk belittled white women and men? The argument that African Americans' economic ambitions and achievements spurred lynching murders is well known and, again, empirically correct. Less understood, these illustrations suggest, is the extent to which the market motives of mob violence were determined by the nation's turn to corporate capitalism as much as by southern agribusiness's racist political economy.[63]

The same holds true for the most-often-cited explanation of lynching after the rape of white women—namely, the argument that legal delays spurred mobs to dole out "rough justice." Countless lynchings began and ended with jailhouse raids and courtroom "rescues," but not because the law was "too slow." Rather, southern lynch mobs—like millions of other Americans—distrusted judicial and political administrations *per se,* and sought to counter the effects of living under centralized systems of power that were increasingly deaf to the needs of individuals and blind to the concerns of the community (see figures 1.4 and 1.5).[64] As one apologist explained in 1895: "In this free country, where we frown upon all forms of arbitrary power . . . the public has naturally lost all confidence in the administration of justice in criminal cases," because, another observed, "to the people of our republic the semblance of national authority—the authority which stands back of the elemental guarantees of our government—is not a familiar sight. . . . The machinery of our Government moves noiselessly; it is in effect invisible."[65]

Lynching dramatized just how (in)visible the processes of governance could be, precisely because the law was rarely invoked by the nation (or its states) to prosecute anti-black mob murders as crimes. "A guilty Negro could no more extricate himself from the meshes of the law in the South than he could slide from the devil-fish's embrace or the anaconda's

Figure 1.3. Feared and resented by the American public because of their predatory powers, U.S. corporations—here figured as the nation's largest trusts—were often symbolized by dark, monstrous figures, not unlike the bestial imagery associated with African American men by pro-lynching advocates. (Photo courtesy of the Library of Congress, Prints and Photographs Division, LC-USZ62-06363.)

Figures 1.4 and 1.5. The growth of bureaucratic systems in government, economics, and the law at the turn of the nineteenth century fed nightmarish visions of Americans being crushed by large-scale, distant powers and diminished by impersonal routine and process. In this cultural milieu, lynching was defended as a practice meant to restore popular sovereignty and states' rights. (Photos courtesy of Library of Congress, Prints and Photographs Division, LC-USZ62-26205, LC-USZ62-49513.)

coils," Mary Church Terrell fumed in her 1904 essay "Lynching from a Negro's Point of View."[66] Indeed, the refusal to accord black defendants their rights of due process was perfected by the cultural logic that saw lynchings exceed the number of legal executions between 1885 and 1900, with the effect of legitimizing capital punishment's revival as an exercise of state-sanctioned violence.[67] Lynching coexisted with state-sanctioned death sentences because mob murders offered an alternative to the inefficiencies and anti-humanitarianism of bureaucratized power. But for that same reason, lynching was easy to disavow as a practice that helped shape modern definitions of federalism and twentieth-century American jurisprudence because the murders were so uncivilized.[68]

Appealing to political cartoons, nonfiction essays in newspapers and magazines, and, in the chapters that follow, novels, poems, and photographs (together with writers' diaries, correspondence, and manuscript drafts), it is not by accident that I have located lynching's cultural logic in various forms of writing and visual representation. As a literary historian, the archives I feel compelled to explore are those that house

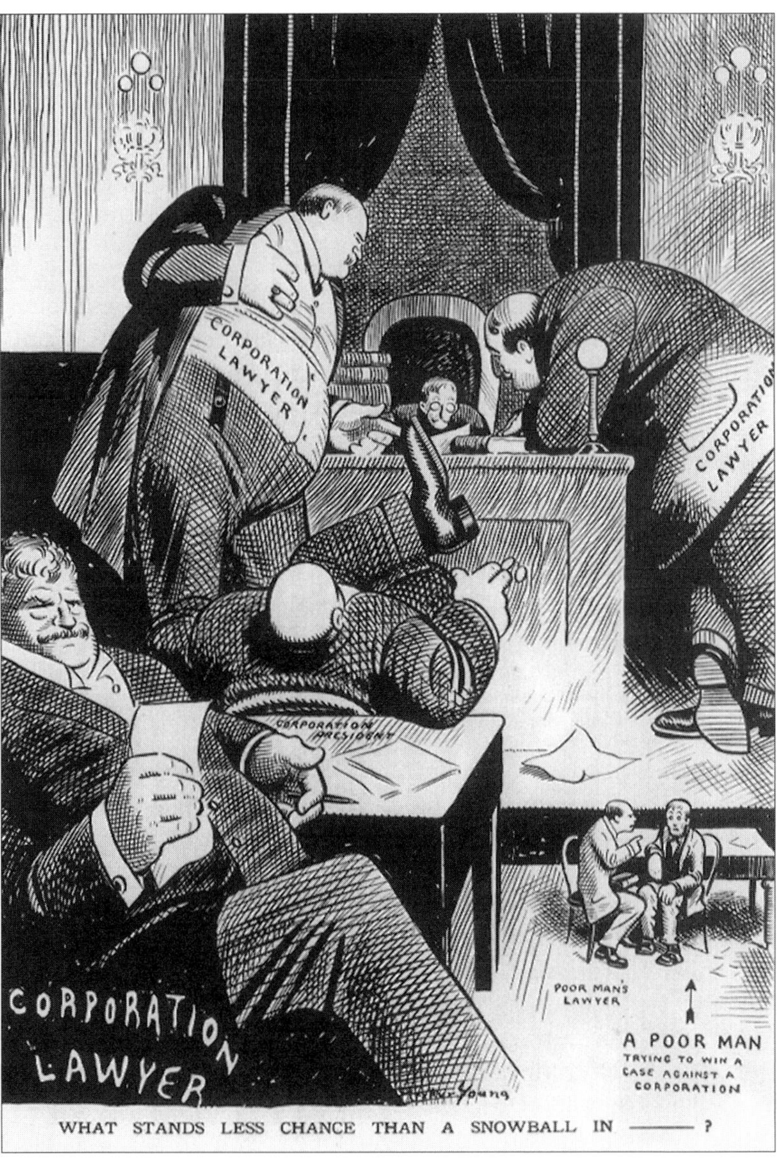
CORPORATION LAWYER
CORPORATION LAWYER
CORPORATION PRESIDENT
CORPORATION LAWYER
POOR MAN'S LAWYER
A POOR MAN
TRYING TO WIN A CASE AGAINST A CORPORATION
WHAT STANDS LESS CHANCE THAN A SNOWBALL IN ——— ?

Figure 1.5.

artifacts chronicling the craft of print culture, but my choice of sources reflects more than my disciplinary bias. My focus bears witness to the overwhelming evidence that writing and visual representations were vital means through which Americans encountered lynching's violence and labored to make sense of its meanings. In the periodical press alone there were at least three hundred articles on the topic published between 1882 and 1922.[69] Indeed, the newspaper coverage of the violence is so staggering that no scholar has published a systematic survey (let alone a comparative analysis) of the daily and weekly news reports of anti-black lynching murders. The best solution critics have managed (myself included) has been to track specific murder cases or follow the media's record in select states. Reading through the national news discourse about lynching over a century's time would most likely generate a book of its own.

The role of the graphic arts in cultivating public discussion about lynching is also surprisingly expansive. It is eminently more manageable to study, though, not least because the broad-stroked pictures of political cartoons are easier to discern amid the welter of writing in newspapers and magazines. Throughout the book I reproduce some of them for their remarkable capacity to envision lynching's cultural logic, along with the recently organized Allen/Littlefield Collection of American Lynching Photographs. My analyses in the chapters that follow, however, put the greatest stock in the evidence culled from literature as generally understood. Like its startling frequency in the archives of newspapers, magazines, political cartoons, and photography, lynching's violence—especially that kind directed against African American people—haunts the writing of Thomas Dixon, Thomas Nelson Page, Albion W. Tourgée, Kate Chopin, Ellen Glasgow, Owen Wister, Mark Twain, Theodore Dreiser, Frances E. W. Harper, Pauline E. Hopkins, Alice Dunbar-Nelson, Sutton E. Griggs, Paul Laurence Dunbar, and Charles W. Chesnutt, to survey the canon before World War I. Because literature has no particular obligation to represent history in a straightforward fashion, it is freer to respond to history's events and influences, especially those we cannot bear to admit shape the content and course of our lives. To recall John Franklin Crowell's point, literature imagines for us the grounds on which we might be able to envision the sociohistorical conditions that made lynching culturally logical—a practice whose fit and place in time could be disavowed through our habits of thinking about it.

For these reasons, I pay close attention in particular to writers' uses of literary form; I have found that genres and their representational conventions leave rich and surprising evidence of authors' perceptions of lynching's violence. For instance, why does Claude McKay write "The Lynchers" as a Petrarchan sonnet? Why does the elegy's mode of address appeal to Paul Laurence Dunbar and Angelina Weld Grimké in "The Haunted Oak" and "Tenebris" (and, further, how might we link their resignification of trees to the most renowned instance of lynching's anti-pastoralism, Lewis Allan's "Strange Fruit" and Billie Holiday's incomparable rendition of it)? What was so demanding about lynching as a poetic subject that Richard Wright would turn away from the concentrated lyricism of haiku (his preferred mode of writing poetry) to the Whitmanian-length lines that abound in "Between the World and Me"? And to recall the example of Gwendolyn Brooks in the introduction, why did she write sonnets to protest war (her magnificent "Gay Chaps at the Bar" sequence), but when confronting the violence of lynching (a task she took on five times) she turned always to the ballad?[70]

I ask comparable questions about prose narrative and visual works in the following chapters. But whether the texts I study are poetry or prose, ballads or sonnets, one-act plays or novels, the question literature raises for the study of lynching's cultural logic is this: what historicizing authority do literary genres possess such that they enable authors to comprehend lynching's violence in ways that conventional histories might not allow or encourage them to do?[71]

The very effort to recreate the violence as narrative in a news article, novel, short story, poem, play, photograph, stereograph, film, or video suggests, I believe, how an author perceived lynching as a social force within the storytelling structures of a given medium. Put another way, as Wai-Chee Dimock argues in *Residues of Justice: Literature, Law, and Philosophy,* genre can be an expression of cognition—of the ways people actively make meaning of the world.[72] More than just a set of "styles," genre aesthetics express historically contingent principles, methods, and techniques by which artists and their publics define what constitutes a work of art, how that work is to be produced, and why they are committed to creating (or supporting) it. An author's sense and pursuit of craft can, therefore, contain within its discursive structures knowledge of social and cultural history that, in turn, informs the fictive world depicted in a literary text or artifact. Fictive discourse can resist an author's impulse to chronicle the violence as an accurate account, though, because any literary form creates certain aesthetic demands that can trump the imperatives of rendering politics and history "correct" or "right." Genre's capacity to address itself to history but to resist being reduced to real life—or, that is, genre's mediation between the world of the text and the world of real history—makes it receptive to analysis of lynching's cultural logic.

A significant but untold dimension of lynching's force as a tactic of white supremacy derives from its capacity not just to terrorize but to traumatize survivors into silence, leaving gaps of knowledge in its wake. Or, as Toni Morrison's *Beloved* asks regarding the abyss created by slavery: how do we and how can we speak about unspeakable acts? What language can be summoned to give life to events that should have never happened? Unlike the actual murders and social histories of lynching, literary depictions often leave the residue of its ineffability—its secrecy—in their formal structures. Thus, I seek out the gaps and silences within the literary narratives as evidence of how lynching's cultural logic operates and how its dynamics extend lynching's power to oppress.

Not every novel, short story, stage drama, poem, or photograph depicting lynching approaches the task of historicizing the violence this way. Works that principally thematize the violence are not highlighted in the following chapters. These include short stories such as Charles W. Chesnutt's "Po' Sandy," "Dave's Neckliss," and "The Sheriff's Children," as well as Theodore Dreiser's "Nigger Jeff" (1901). By the same token, novels like Chesnutt's *The Marrow of Tradition* (1901), Pauline Hopkins's *Contending Forces* (1900), and Thomas Dixon's abhorrent classic *The Clansman* (1905) do not find their way into my main argument either.[73] Nor do Mark Twain's or Angelina Weld Grimké's fiction, precisely because they engage the dynamics that make lynching's cultural logic so hard to trace. For this reason, it may be helpful here to briefly discuss salient examples of Twain's and Grimké's work as counterexamples to my principal argument and of the way I read history out of literary texts.

Twain's famously staged lynching scenes in *The Adventures of Huckleberry Finn* (1884), *A Connecticut Yankee in King Arthur's Court* (1889), and *Puddn'head Wilson* (1894) are conspicuously cast as allegories meant to criticize the nation's long-standing tolerance of racial violence, but as these scenes unfold they turn into narrative digressions that only go to diminish the point of Twain's including them at all. For instance, as soon as the Duke and Dauphin are chased away by the mob ready to tar and feather them for their swindles and scams, Huck and Jim shove out on their raft farther south down the Mississippi River, leaving the con artists—and any questions their murders may have posed for the novel's critique of racial injustice—stranded and soon forgotten. Similarly, since the Negro Tom Driscoll would have been lynched for murdering his white foster father at the time of *Puddn'head Wilson*'s publication, Twain turns that threat from tragedy into farce by having Driscoll booted out of a temperance rally by the mob that despises him. Set in the antebellum south, the novel ends with Driscoll's being "sold down the river," which is its own kind of death sentence to be sure, but one differently inflected (and inflicted) than the violence of lynching.

Twain's obvious ambivalence toward historicizing both operations of lynching's cultural logic in his novels—the fit and the disavowal—emerges most fully in *Connecticut Yankee*. Technocrat Hank Morgan's return to sixth-century England turns late-nineteenth-century America's claims to be modern and civilized into material for chilling satire; the brutality of machine guns, dynamite, and electricity never seemed so sure as when Morgan deliberately unleashes their power to massacre the horse-charging, lance-bearing, armor-clad medieval knights in the novel's final chapter, "The Battle of the Sand Belt." But when Twain's Yankee loses his way in a forest and comes upon a grove of hanged bodies, the unnerving display of ancient feudal power breaks the novel's allegorical promise to hold democracy accountable for its crimes of excess. In 1889, the year the novel was published, fifty-eight African Americans were reported murdered by lynch mobs. However, because Hank Morgan insists that the mass hangings he discovers symbolize the fate of "poor whites" in the slave South—and because there is no omniscient narrator's voice to contest Morgan's analogy (as in *Puddn'head Wilson*)—the novel suppresses the full history of modernity's indebtedness to racial violence.[74]

Nonetheless Twain's weak grasp on lynching as a novelistic subject remains instructive. His seeming failures to make his allusions to lynching sustain his narrative designs—or, that is, his use of narrative techniques to render anti-black mob violence inarticulable as a textual event—reveal how lynching's cultural logic obscures what we presume to be the proper milieu to interpret the murders. In my reading, these novels' entanglements with the law, eugenics, mass culture, and mechanized warfare would therefore serve as the historicist contexts in which we might analyze lynching's functions in the text, functions that might prompt us to question the viability of Twain's references to lynching's "real" world politics.

Angelina Weld Grimké's short fiction resists narrating lynching's fit with the cultural times so intensively that, on a first reading, her prose seems (like Twain's) to archive how African Americans disavowed the power of lynching's cultural logic.[75] Structured around the dualisms of rural/urban, south/north, savage/civilized, white/black, "Blackness" (n.d.) and "Goldie" (1920) pose staunch arguments that cast lynching as inexorably anti-modern. In "Blackness" (the draft version of "Goldie"), Grimké locates the violence in the rural South and provides copious narrative detail depicting the region. As the protagonist recounts his arrival home—Victor Forrest is a college graduate who lives in a northern city—he notices the railroad's decaying infrastructure: the train pulls up to a "crude wooden station" where the interior is illumined by "lamplight" held by the cruel, white station master who taunted the protagonist as a boy. Indeed, the train ride south is likened to the Middle Passage of slavery (232–46), a regression signaled by the protagonist's walk home. Though it is pitch dark, Forrest knows exactly how to reach the road because nothing had changed since his last time there: "Even in the dark I knew everything was just as I had left it ten years ago" (236).

The story's disavowal of lynching's relation to the culture of modernity that Forrest represents occurs through Grimké's adoption of the gothic genre. When the protagonist arrives at his sister's home only to find the house ransacked and destroyed, he is devastated not only by what he sees but also by what he cannot feel: "his hand stretched out before, he started forward again. This time, after only a couple of steps, his hand came in contact with the housefront. He was feeling his way along, cautiously still, when all of a sudden his fingers encountered nothing but air" (299). In this void of emptiness, Victor calls out for his sister and brother-in-law, but his voice sounds out the alienation that has haunted him ever since he stepped off the train: "It seemed to him, *somebody else* called out" (299; emphasis added). When he gathers the courage to cross the doorway into the wreckage of his sister's life (which is to say, the brutality of her death), Victor becomes completely estranged from himself, as if his body is no longer his own. "This other person who seemed, somehow, to have entered his body, moved forward" (299), opens the door to the backyard, and encounters "two terribly mutilated swinging bodies" hanging lifeless above "a tiny unborn child, its head crushed in by a deliberate heel" (302).

In submitting this version of the story to *Atlantic Monthly* for publication, Grimké most likely thought that the magazine's audience of white, middle-class readers would find the gothic fictionalization of Mary Turner's murder more bearable to contemplate.[76] When compared to the depiction of lynching that drives the stage drama *Rachel* (1916), the stakes of "Goldie's" account become clear and are a sobering surprise. In her play (staged in noncommercial venues for predominantly black audiences in New York, Philadelphia, and Boston), Grimké meticulously links lynching to its supports in modern American culture—schools, urbanization, housing, and employment.[77] The character Tom Loving bitterly sums up his chances as a socially dead man:

> Today we colored men and women—everywhere—are up against it. Every year, we are having a harder time of it. In the South they make it as impossible as they can for us to get an education. We're hemmed in on all sides. Our one safeguard—the ballot—in most states, is taken away already, or is being taken away. Economically, in a few lines, we have a slight show—but at what a cost! In the North, they make a pretence of liberality: they give us the ballot and a good education, and then—snuff us out. Each year, the problem just to live, gets more difficult to solve. (53)

In the published text, these eloquent connections are paired with the characters' halting, broken speech in a disorienting way. For every cogently stated soliloquy or dialogue exchange there are passages full of ellipses, dashes, unfinished statements, and unusually dense stage directions that convey in print what the actors' speech and body language were meant to project to the theater audience: the severity with which lynching's violence depletes the capacity of language to narrate history coherently.[78] When read against the modernist aesthetics of *Rachel*'s script, the gothic twists to "Goldie" (the moralizing bifurcations, the brutalized corpses discovered in the many-chambered house, the protagonist's mind warping before the reader's eyes) archive Grimké's divided expectations for her reading audiences, which is to say that her appeals to genre delineate just how limited on both sides of the color line was the public's knowledge about lynching.

Grimké's example brings me back to the case with which I began this discussion—the lynching murder of Henry Smith and Samuel Burdett's encounter of the audio-visual reenactment of the event. Burdett's memoir, *A Test of Lynch Law,* confirms how historically suggestive narrative forms of writing about lynching could be. We know that Burdett agonized over his presence in the Seattle crowd that day; during the eight-year lag between that event in 1893 and the publication of his memoir in 1901, he admits that "the things seen and heard [at the exhibit] have haunted the writer from that day to this."[79] Given the traumatic impact of that experience, Burdett remained firm in his refusal to profit from the sale of his memoir, suggesting that the very act of writing about the murder placed him in a complex moral dilemma. Aiming to "engage the attention of our busy people long enough to scan this little pleader for money," Burdett certainly did not want to reconstruct the trap that lured him to look at the audio-visual display of Henry Smith's murder (11). Nonetheless, his pamphlet's low price—like the nickel fee he paid to watch and hear Smith die—threatened to place the booklet on a par with the filmic reproduction of the murder, insofar as both were commercial commodities. Thus, Burdett printed *A Test of Lynch Law* from his own funds and relied on readers' donations to recover his publishing costs. And to add value to the booklet's cheap price, Burdett closed the volume with a short story that fictionalized Smith's murder, to imagine an outcome that could restore his own and his readers' faith in democratic justice.

In his fictionalized version of Smith's lynching, the mob that murdered Joe Taylor (a "half-breed Negro" living in Coalburg, a town in the "state of Anarky") is arrested and brought to trial somewhere in "the West" (19). The prosecuting attorney is a maverick loner hired to try the case on behalf of the state. A plain-speaking cowboy gifted with legal genius, Mr. Bowman pledges to win a conviction of the murderers for their heinous deed, and the plot unfolds as the cowboy-lawyer investigates the lynching. Remarkably, readers are spared the gruesome details about Joe Taylor/Henry Smith's death by torture; rather Burdett emphasizes the capture and indictment of the mob's leaders. If moral relief comes with this shift in emphasis, confusion surfaces too, because the trial's change of venue and the fictional story's surprise ending countermand the memoir's ethics in significant ways.

Anticipating the argument justifying mob vigilantism in Owen Wister's best-selling novel *The Virginian* (1901), Burdett's narrator romanticizes the West as a just setting for the law's retribution because the region is unspoiled by racism's corrosive, divisive effects. Unfailingly scrupulous, Westerners like Bowman "had the courage of [their] convictions under any and all circumstances. When he went into a case, he went in soul as well as body; and besides that, he was an untiring worker for whatever cause he undertook" (49). Seeming to forget that pathfinders like Bowman often undertook the campaigns of violent racial conflict that made the West a mythic site of national renewal—the warfare waged by the United States to annex Native American tribal lands and Mexico's northernmost territory—the narrator nevertheless retains this utopian vision to underscore the indeterminacy of the murder's setting: Joe Taylor's murder does not happen in the South; "Anarky" could be anywhere in the United States.

And yet, in "A Test of Lynch Law," the West persists as a venue for (rather than a refuge from) the reproduction of racial violence, precisely because Burdett cannot resist the seductions of the short story's formal brevity. Once the mob leaders are captured and their trial date is set, the reader assumes that the story's climax will occur in court and a denouement will follow that scene. This anticipated chain of events, however, breaks. Once the lawyer-protagonist outlines his case against the mob, the text stops abruptly at the close of Bowman's opening argument. The narrator then interjects that the interrogation and cross-examinations of witnesses, and the state and defense counsels' final summations are to come in a subsequent serial installment to which readers can subscribe for one dollar (53). Though he justly decries the selling of Henry Smith's murder as a form of leisure entertainment—"Here we are selling the dying groans and pitiful pleadings for mercy of a man as he suffers that awful agony of having his eyes burned out one at a time with hot irons. Think of it!" (19)—Burdett's proposed serial novel buys into that very system of trade. After *A Test of Lynch Law* condemns the mass marketing of lynching as popular entertainment, how, then, are we to understand the text's contradictions of its own stated purposes? How does Burdett's resistance to closure vis-à-vis the short story's form mediate the meaning of lynching's violence for his reading public, and with what implications for our understanding of anti-black mob murders generally?

———

To pursue this line of argument, I trace lynching's genealogy across the modern era by referencing select mob murders and reading them concurrently with the production of lynching narratives across a wide range of literary sources. My principal chapters (2–5) focus on the turn of the nineteenth century (1882–1922) because these were the decades when the violence raged utterly unchecked across the nation. Three authors are central to my discussion: Ida B. Wells-Barnett, Stephen Crane, and James Weldon Johnson. A fourth, Gwendolyn Brooks, anchors the book's concluding sixth chapter, which contemplates how the late nineteenth century's cultural logic took shape in twentieth century American life. Since, as I noted earlier, visual representations played a vital role in organizing lynching's cultural logic, I devote a chapter to lynching photography as well.

Each of the following chapters follows a similar pattern of argument. I begin with cultural biography, describing and analyzing an author's encounter with lynching in the context of a social shift that is not stereotypically "southern" but that concerned the nation as a whole. In the course of this discussion, I also chronicle the author's entry into the vocation of writing and the development of his or her aesthetic principles as a writer, noting how the author comes to link an understanding of history, lynching, and literature into critical (though not always commensurate) relation to one another. By weaving together the author's personal and professional lives this way (or, in the case of lynching photography, by tracing the genealogies of the medium's technologies and common camera styles), I use narrative history to gauge the "fit" between lynching and its cultural milieu as intimately as possible.

For this reason I offer my authorial choices as representative rather than as idiosyncratic. Being writers gave Wells, Crane, Johnson, and Brooks no greater claim to safety from lynching; in fact, they all had a personal encounter with the violence that either nearly killed them or unnerved them to their cores. Because of their commitments to literary craft, what they did possess was an especially keen capacity to search for language that could articulate the meaning of lynching, not only for their individual lives, but for the common public's as well. "No pen—no tongue can fully portray these horrors," many magazine writers and pamphleteers on both sides of the color line lamented.[80] The struggles of Wells, Crane, Johnson, and Brooks to imagine what they knew about lynching and why (which I trace through their private writings and draft manuscripts of the texts I feature) are no different than our own then or now, except that their artistry leaves us with a rich record of teachings from which we may learn.

To receive those lessons, my discussions in the chapters that follow each deliberately shifts away from narrative history to the mode of close textual analysis. The second half of each chapter focuses on the writing in which the author's encounter with lynching finds fullest expression: Wells's anti-lynching pamphlets; Crane's novella *The Monster*; Johnson's novel *The Autobiography of an Ex-Colored Man*; and Brooks's poem "The Last Quatrain of the Ballad of Emmett Till." Chapter 5 on lynching photography follows this model since, as with literature, I assume that photographs, stereographs, and postcards figure lynching differently because each medium implies distinctive aesthetic requirements for practitioners to negotiate. Freed to move beyond the presumption that the images document the violence accurately, I therefore consider how the imperatives of visual literacy—what it means to see, and how technologies of seeing organized American social life and knowledge—reinforced the scope of lynching's power to oppress.

Thus, with each chapter I examine a different phenomenal field to define lynching's cultural logic. Ida B. Wells's long career as the nation's leading anti-lynching activist is elucidated through the professionalization of the nation's news corps and the secularization of American life at the turn of the nineteenth century. Stephen Crane's shock at the lynching that occurred in his hometown in upstate New York and his decision to publish *The Monster* as a belated response draws the ascendance of corporate capitalism and the passive aggression of white Americans' indifference into the folds of lynching's history. James Weldon Johnson's multiple encounters with lynching led him to fret about the ease with which lynching's death wish spread throughout the country; his life story and writings about the violence boldly name the consolidation of mass cultural production as a key development that enabled lynching to thrive. Finally, once photography gained both the technological capacity and cultural credibility to rival writing's power as a medium of historical knowledge, the transformation of visual experience from the end of the nineteenth century across the twentieth sheds important light on the history of lynching's cultural logic and its continued effects in our national life.

Lynching bridges the fields of history and literary studies because it is itself an act and a sign, a literal thing and a symbolic representation to which the violence refers. Or, as Toni Morrison has remarked, lynching is a "metaphor of itself."[81] However, as I have suggested, lynching's cultural logic changes over time, and does so (in part) as forms of mediation refashion the representation of the violence. If, as I contend in this book, our experience of lynching depends on the forms through which we have come to know the violence, the very different writing styles practiced by Ida B. Wells, Stephen Crane, James Weldon Johnson, and Gwendolyn Brooks can teach us how to conceptualize lynching's oppressive effects more broadly.

At the end of this study, we are still left to confront the most perplexing legacy of all about the violence: why does lynching, which we must at the very least acknowledge was a horrifically long chapter in our nation's life, remain so tightly held a secret in American cultural studies? What is so hard to fathom about lynching's past that we resist the many lessons it presents? Precisely because the work of literature is to imagine what we otherwise cannot know and say about our lives, literary accounts of lynching can help us confront the consequences of limiting our knowledge to the manifest meanings of the violence. And so, in addition to archiving a "new" or an "other" history of lynching, this literature can model for us how we might learn to live with lynching's past instead of remaining unconsciously mired in it.

TWO

Writing "Dynamitically": Ida B. Wells

Creating a new culture does not only mean one's own "original" discoveries. It also, and most particularly, means the diffusion in a critical form of truths already discovered, their "socialization" as it were, and even making them the basis of vital action, an element of co-ordination and intellectual and moral order. For a mass of people to be led to think coherently and in the same coherent fashion about the real and present world, is a philosophical event.

ANTONIO GRAMSCI, *THE PRISON NOTEBOOKS*

To be a woman in such an age carries with it a privilege and an opportunity never implied before. But to be a woman of the Negro race in America, and to be able to grasp the deep significance of the possibilities of . . . crisis, is to have a heritage, it seems to me, unique in the ages.

ANNA JULIA COOPER, *A VOICE FROM THE SOUTH*

The front-page news in the *Memphis Weekly Appeal-Avalanche,* the *Memphis Daily Scimitar,* and the *Memphis Commercial-Appeal* during the weeks of March 1892 enraged Ida B. Wells because she knew the lead stories were untrue. What had come to be known throughout the city as the "lynching at the Curve" did not involve the deaths of "negro desperadoes," as these papers purported.[1] Wells knew Thomas Moss, Calvin McDowell, and Henry Stewart to be honest, peaceable men. In fact, she was the godmother of Moss's infant daughter. The trio's crime, however, was a serious cultural offense: they broke the unwritten law that prohibited black men from competing with whites for economic dominance in the southern marketplace. Moss,

McDowell, and Stewart had started a business, the People's Grocery Company, at the curve in the electric trolley line that serviced the African American community living beyond the city limits of Memphis. For several years that area had been served by just one merchant, a white man named W. H. Barnett. But the rail line provided an opportunity to challenge Barnett's monopoly. Land was cheap outside of Memphis, so Moss, McDowell, and Stewart pooled their assets together to open their store. An immediate success, the People's Grocery Company broke Barnett's hold over the district's shopping options, a development the white store owner did not favor at all.[2]

A child's game gone wrong brought this economic conflict to a crucial breaking point. When a group of white boys lost a round of marbles to their black playmates, the children quarreled and the black boys won the ensuing fisticuffs. The father of one of the losers retaliated on his son's behalf by flogging one of the winners. Accompanied by a group of supporters, the black child's parent beat the white man who had attacked his son. With W. H. Barnett's support, the white father filed charges against the entire group of black men, but since the People's Grocery Company served as a social center for the community at the Curve, Moss, McDowell, and Stewart became involved in the dispute too. When the court case was dismissed, the white men vowed revenge, threatening to "clear out" the black-run store. Deciding to protect themselves and their property, the black merchants rallied a group of neighboring friends and residents to keep armed watch over the business.

At this point, the Memphis sheriff intervened and arrested the three partners for inciting a riot. But Moss, McDowell, and Stewart did not survive their arrest. Rousted from their cells by an armed mob of white men, they were taken by train to the wasteland outside the Memphis city limits. There, the competition between the People's Grocery Store and W. H. Barnett came to an end. The mob lined up before the three, aiming their gun and rifle barrels at the men. "Tell my people to go west . . . there is no justice for them here," Thomas Moss was reported to have said. Fulfilling the prophecy of Moss's dying words, the mob fired away. McDowell's eyes were blown out of their sockets. Moss and Stewart's heads and necks were "horribly shot" through by the fusillade of gunfire.[3]

Given the circumstance of the murders, Wells resented the capacity of the Memphis press to dominate public discussion of this lynching. "The [Memphis] daily papers . . . helped to make this trouble by fanning the flames of racial prejudice," she bristled, observing that one journal in particular exploited the commercial possibilities of the incident. As she recalled dryly, "one of the morning papers held back its edition in order to supply its readers with the details of [the] lynching" (*Crusade,* 56, 50). While the practice of "scooping" or providing "extra" coverage of emergency crises and disasters was not uncommon in 1890s journalism—crime and murder stories had been popular with the American public since the mid-nineteenth century and tabloid-style reports were a sure boost for sales—it did not go unnoticed by Wells that the Memphis press did more than sensationalize this lynching.[4] The reporting strategies and publishing tactics of these newspapers functioned to "create" rather than "report" the event, their accounts in this way aiding and abetting the murders. This, to Wells, was an egregious abuse all too characteristic of the "malicious and untruthful white press."[5] The pages of the *Memphis Free Speech* were, by contrast, devoted to rallying the black public to protest the murder. At her editor's desk, Wells wrote columns urging African Americans to boycott the new trolley car lines and to stop shopping at Memphis stores. In others, she echoed Thomas Moss's dying words and called on black residents to leave Memphis and migrate west, which they did in business-crippling numbers.[6] Wells's final editorial about the murder was also her most daring statement, however, and she nearly paid for it with her own life.

Infuriated with how the Memphis media obscured the economic causes of the lynching, Wells decried the violence in no uncertain terms. "Nobody in this section of the country believes the old threadbare lie that Negro men rape white women," she began in her editorial. "If Southern white men are not careful, they will over-reach themselves and public sentiment will have a reaction; a conclusion will then be reached which will be very damaging to the moral reputation of their women" (*SH,* 17). This challenge to the long-vaunted sexual chastity of southern white women provoked the *Memphis Commercial Appeal* to denounce Wells as a "wench" and a "would-be martyr" who did not write her own news copy. The *Memphis Daily Scimitar* went so far as to issue this death threat against Wells: "If the negroes themselves do not apply the remedy without delay it will be the duty of those whom he has attacked to tie the wretch who utters these calamities to a stake at the intersection of Main and Madison Sts. [*sic*], brand him in the forehead with a hot iron and perform upon him a surgical operation with a pair of shears" (*SH,* 18).[7]

While the hate and threatened violence of this statement are horrifying, the confusion underlying this call to shears is significant too. Presuming that the "wretch" who authored the *Free Speech*'s editorial was one of the newspaper's male copublishers, the *Scimitar* endorsed the "surgical operation" of a symbolized castration as proper punishment.

This was accomplished quite efficiently and without delay. The business elites of Memphis met at the Cotton Exchange Building to decide how to stop Wells's growing influence over the city's black residents. Adopting the *Scimitar*'s opinion as its own, this mob of department store merchants, bankers, and lawyers razed the offices of the *Free Speech*. Destroying the paper's printing equipment and trashing its stock of supplies, the corporate scions of Memphis forced Wells into exile from the South for the rest of her life.[8]

The lynching at the Curve and the "threadbare lie" editorial are canonical events in Ida B. Wells's political career. The murders of her friends and her own close call with death were, as a recent biographer observes, a "conversion experience" that propelled Wells to lead the nation's anti-lynching movement from 1892 to 1909.[9] And as cultural historians and feminist theorists have long argued, Wells's career as a journalist in Memphis foreshadowed the exposés to come, which radically revised public debates about lynching as a tool of racial, gender, and class domination.[10] For instance, Wells conclusively showed that the charge of rape so often levied to justify lynching on ideological grounds was empirically untrue, and she used this statistical evidence to suggest how the public's belief in this myth secured the subordination of white women, black women, and black men to white patriarchal authority. Wells also proposed an equally controversial hypothesis to explain the selective targeting of African Americans by white lynch mobs: with the end of chattel slavery eliminating the economic incentive to protect black laborers' lives as a market asset, white men were free to control the capital they once owned—the bodies of black men, women, and children—through the destructive violence of lynching. To speak about consensual sex between interracial romantic partners and to suggest that violent excess was endemic to capitalist economies were daring, defiant pronouncements for a black woman to make in public and in print at the turn of the nineteenth century. However, it is arguably true that Wells's exchanges with the Memphis press in this instance (like her most famous anti-lynching writings) were calculated to shock readers as much as the editorials in the white press fueled her own anger. For when read as part of the media milieu of the 1890s, the threadbare editorial itself was drenched in the yellow ink of sensationalized reporting tactics. Or, to put this point another way, the importance we attribute to Wells's anti-lynching activism is partly due to her interest in the changing culture of

American journalism, because her newswriting style led her toward the radical positions she espoused.

As this chapter shall show, the power of Wells's insights into lynching's cultural logic and the violent response elicited by her writings ultimately followed from her decision to heed the advice of Frederick Douglass: "tell a story" that would reveal how the "forms of the charge"—or the narrative structures used by the popular press—depicted lynching in ways that made the violence tolerable to the American public.[11] Wells's arguments were seditious not simply because of what she said, but because she framed those propositions in terms that challenged her readers to recognize how the styles of news writing shaped what they knew about lynching. Highlighting her commitment to write about anti-black mob violence in the self-reflexive manner that Douglass encouraged, I argue that Wells's formal experiments with the craft of journalism made her critique of lynching as revelatory in her time as it continues to be for us today. Indeed, her styles of news writing link lynching to the "great human experiment" that the threadbare lie editorial performs so effectively on the page: freedom's secularizing influence upon American life as the nineteenth century turned into the twentieth.[12]

Though we usually associate the secularization of American society with developments that span the course of the nineteenth century, but that do not include lynching, the narrative form of the threadbare lie editorial suggests otherwise.[13] The liberties Wells takes in that column's blunt, direct address were unprecedented coming from a black woman. The social transformations that made her career in journalism possible—the emancipation of African Americans from slavery, the liberation of women from Victorian-era gender roles, and the ascendance of American newspapers as central arbiters of historical knowledge in public life—allow us to examine how those modes of secularized progress paradoxically helped create the milieu in which lynching thrived before World War I. Reading her personal diaries and memoir for clues to establish lynching's relation to secularization at the end of the nineteenth century, I begin this chapter by reexamining Wells's life history in Memphis prior to the murder of her friends at the Curve. The sources reveal Wells to have been an ambitious woman who, like so many "New Women" of the 1880s, rebelled against the strictures of domesticity. And yet, as a recently emancipated slave, Wells was attracted to the legitimizing aura that traditional codes of gender conduct offered to "New Negroes." As I demonstrate, her struggles to fulfill the opportunities and demands posed by these two movements reveal how strife-causing liberation could be, particularly for an African American woman coming of age in the late-nineteenth-century South. Recognizing that gender and racial emancipation set long-standing definitions of subjectivity, agency, and identity in flux, Wells resolved to make these developments central to her analysis of lynching because, as she came to realize in the 1880s and 1890s, it was the newness and unregulability of freedom itself that stirred mobs' violent unrest. Read in this context, Ida B. Wells's life history gauges the fit between lynching and post-emancipation identity politics by more complex terms than we have considered before.

As much as her experience of freedom in her private life, the meaning and practice of prose writing in late-nineteenth-century American culture also shaped Wells's understanding of secularization's role in lynching's cultural logic, especially in view of how she transformed herself from an amateur into a professional author during those fin-de-siècle decades. By taking her decision to write for newspapers instead of publishing novels as culturally significant (a vocational change of heart chronicled in her diaries and memoir), and in probing the literary history that compelled Wells to make that choice, I return to her apprentice years in the profession to explore how her analysis of lynching depended on her keen appreciation for late-nineteenth-century journalism's expanded hegemony as a curator of public knowledge. Using the journalism manuals of her time as cues, I argue that *Southern Horrors* (1893) tropes on the death-coaxing allure of what was known as the autobiographical "stunt"; *A Red Record* (1895) exploits the credibility of sociological empiricism; *Lynch Law in Georgia* (1899) discloses the fabrications involved in wire reporting; and *Mob Rule in New Orleans* (1900) ponders the inuring effects of serialized investigations. As each pamphlet demonstrates, news writing was quite varied at the turn of the nineteenth century, its styles less fixed and more pliable than we often appreciate.[14] Narrated in any of these four modes (apart from any racist intention a journalist may have had), the most broadly reported lynching could be normalized into a routine, habit-forming reading event, so long as the genre conventions detailing the murder remained transparent to the reader's eye. Calling attention to journalism's capacities to mask the effects of its narrative forms, Wells's pamphlets parody then-emerging genres of news writing in order to show how those styles—together with the professional practices that characterize them—shaped the public's knowledge of lynching.

Wells's parodies are particularly remarkable, though, because they offer such a stark contrast to the nineteenth-century tradition of that literary practice. Read separately or together, her pamphlets do not caricature their "host" modes for the purpose of satirizing them to the point of dysfunction. Rather, Wells repeats but remodels the conventions of each genre to recuperate news writing's value as an ethically motivated source of public power.[15] For this reason alone, Wells's pamphlets are literary landmarks because they anticipate one of the definitive interventions that characterize modernist art forms: her parodic techniques enact the "self-referentiality by which art reveals its awareness of the context-dependent nature of meaning."[16] However, because Wells adopts this tactic to confront the nation's appetite for the atrocity of racial violence, American literary history delivers to us news about lynching that, in Ida B. Wells's time, was not fit to print. More than a complaint against the news media's racism, Wells's pamphlets imagine lynching's oppressive force to derive from narrative's capacity to mediate what could be known about the violence and how freely we might think of lynching as historically significant. Thus, like the testaments offered by her life and literary career, Wells's pamphlets constitute a starting point for exploring how forms of progress in early-modernist America sanctioned the proliferation of racial violence.

Being Modern in Memphis

Ida B. Wells's coming of age led her to think about lynching and writing as she did because that journey—which, as she records it in her private diaries and public memoir, seemed so particular, singular, and individual to her—was exemplary of the nation's cultural history at the end of the nineteenth century.[17] For instance, the first decade of Wells's life was, in her view, "indistinct," her adolescence "a kind of butterfly existence."[18] She recalls her childhood with such idyllic calm because her family, like those of many emancipated slaves, labored hard to balance the newfound opportunities and dangers that came with being freed people. On the one hand, from the time she was born in 1862, Wells was cocooned with five siblings in Holly Springs, Mississippi, in the home built by her carpenter-father and tended for by her Methodist-teaching mother. On the other hand, during the 1870s, African Americans lived under the threat of race riots and home-wrecking night rides; in one of Wells's earliest memories from those "butterfly years," she recalls "hear[ing] the words Ku Klux Klan long before I knew what they meant" (*Crusade,* 9).[19] However, what Wells experienced as protective enmeshment—her mother's Bible teachings and her father's newspaper reading—became, when her parents died in 1878, riven by conflicts that symbolized how the political legacies of one era in American life changed into a new social order.[20]

After her parents' deaths, Wells experienced another setback in having to stop her schooling at Rust University in order to care for her surviving siblings. Carrying this load for nearly ten years, Wells greeted her twenty-fifth birthday full of remorse and self-derision for being "intellectually lacking." Praying for divine guidance, she ached to know what her future would bring:

> There is nothing for which I lament the wasted opportunities as my neglect to pick up the crumbs of knowledge that were in my reach. Consequently I find myself at this age as deficient in comprehensive knowledge as the veriest school-girl just entering the higher course. I heartily deplore the neglect. God grant that I may be given firmness of purpose sufficient to essay & *continue* its eradication! Thou knowest I hunger and thirst after righteousness and knowledge. O, give me the steadiness of purpose, the will to acquire both. Twenty-five years old today! May another 10 years find me increased in honesty and purity of purpose and motive![21]

With emancipation coming the year after her first birthday, Wells could lament her lack of a vocation—what she refers to here as her low stores of "purpose and motive"—because she grew up knowing herself to be a "Negro" who was not a dehumanized object of property. Given that Wells's desires to be autonomous and literate would have been illegal in the first half of the nineteenth century, it is remarkable that she does not blame society for her weak efforts to remain "steady" with her educational goals. Instead, Wells feels that "comprehensive knowledge" could raise her life chances above those of the "veriest school girl" because she knows that the culture at large—and particularly African Americans—increasingly valued educational attainment and college training as the mark of distinction between the laboring and middle classes.[22] As she saw the world that twenty-fifth birthday, she alone bore the responsibility to satisfy her "hunger" for "righteousness and knowledge" because she had the cultural means to do so.

Having a choice but letting the chance go untested; understanding herself to have a will and the right to act upon it; being ambitious for change but resisting the "steadiness of purpose" that emancipation demanded—these all lead Wells to pray in this and the many other diary entries addressed to her God. But if her worries seem like those of any other Christian who struggled to reconcile piety with the ways of the material world, they were not. For African Americans like Wells, this age-old tension was enormous to contemplate because, as religious historian Evelyn Brooks Higginbotham explains:

> During the closing decades of the nineteenth century, the church became the most influential force for collective self-help and self-determination in the black community. Since the time of slavery, the church had provided an emotional and spiritual bulwark against individual demoralization and defeat. In the 1880s and 1890s—at a time of disfranchisement, segregation, and rampant racial violence—the church came increasingly to represent an ideological and social space for articulating group needs and implementing programs for their fulfillment. The black church constituted an arena in which poor, racially oppressed men and women assembled, freely voiced their opinions, and exhibited a sense of national community.[23]

With the black church fusing together the sacred and secular in these ways, piety was more than a spiritual outlook for Wells. It was a politicized disposition, insofar as choosing the correct path to salvation advanced the social fortunes of "an oppressed . . . national community." Black women were especially trained to regard their life chances in these terms. "Duty-bound to teach the value of religion, education, and hard work," Higginbotham observes, "the women of the black Baptist church . . . equated public behavior with individual self-respect and with the advancements of African Americans as a group."[24] Wells's twenty-fifth birthday caused her such anxiety, then, because she was torn between her desire to honor God and her "will to acquire" a bountiful life—or, that is, Wells's commitment to uplift the race was at odds with her desire to do for self.

Wells wrote this diary entry in Memphis, Tennessee, where she and her siblings moved after their parents' death. Memphis was a wise decision on Wells's part because it was a thriving hub of commerce and culture during the 1880s and 1890s.[25] Cotton was exported to global textile markets from the city's shipping ports, while lumber, grain, and livestock were routed across the South and Midwest by ten different railroad companies and steamship firms. Foodstuffs and consumer goods easily made their way from northern manufacturers to the city's wholesale dealers, whose sales prowess earned Memphis bragging rights as the fifth largest market in the country. Flush with capital, the city kept pace with the latest technologies in transportation and communication. The electric streetcar system that figured in the lynching at the Curve started running in 1890, while telephones linked the city's homes and businesses into a grid that routed information more rapidly than ever before. Marking a decisive recovery from the city's deadly and destructive race riot in

1866, all of these developments advanced Memphis's reputation as the "Chicago of the South."[26]

Compared to Wells's former home in rural Mississippi, African Americans prospered in Memphis, another sign that the city had recovered from the cataclysm of 1866. Streaming in from western Tennessee, eastern Arkansas, and northern Mississippi, black manual laborers were able to land better paying jobs on the levees, steamship lines, and lumber yards.[27] Because real estate investors, doctors, and lawyers served the niche markets created by the black working class, a bourgeoisie emerged to help assert the community's commanding presence in Memphis politics. Comprising almost one-half of the population (44 percent), African Americans swung elections toward candidates sympathetic to civil rights issues throughout the 1880s.[28] This confidence girded the elaborate infrastructure of the city's black public sphere as well. Three newspapers catered to black readers; several churches ministered to the community's spiritual needs; seven public schools and one normal institute trained the city's black youth; and a host of fraternal organizations, political, literary, and social clubs, militias, burial associations, and secret societies gave the thirty thousand black residents of Memphis ample reason to feel as though their presence was vital to the city's operations.

Wells led an active life in this milieu. With her earnings as a teacher (a well-paying and prestigious post for a black woman), she was able to sate her appetite for books, writing in her diaries about fiction she bought and read.[29] She frequented the city's theaters to watch touring companies perform dramas and operas, inspiring her life-long devotion to the stage.[30] Judging from her diary entries, though, the temples of urban culture Wells attended most often were Memphis's department stores. Much like the heroine of Theodore Dreiser's *Sister Carrie,* Wells followed the siren song of fashion. When clothes, trinkets, and other luxuries whispered her name, she answered, unable to "resist the impulse" to buy cloaks, purses, hats, pins, and cabinet photographs of herself, even as those purchases sunk her into debt. "My expenses are transcending my income; I must stop," she reprimanded herself in her diary one Sunday, only to find herself two weeks later succumbing to "spend[ing] money in frolic."[31]

One of those "southern middle-class African Americans... determined to have unmediated access to the increasing variety of products, from first-class train travel to ready-made clothes and moving pictures that their money enabled them to buy," Wells frequently fought off creditors seeking payments on overdue bills.[32] Though this personal experience no doubt led to her later calls for economic boycotts to protest lynching, before 1892 she felt ambivalent toward consumerism as a source of political power. Worried about her inclinations "to be drawn into something else expensive and profitless against [her] will,"[33] Wells wrote time and again in her journal about urban delights that tempted her away from the safety of known norms.[34] Parties, shopping, taking pictures, dating, theater, travel, fame, ambition—in short, material abundance, economic and political freedom, and sexual desire—rivaled and tested religion's teachings of "right" conduct in the social world Wells inhabited:

> With me, my affairs are at one extreme or the other. Just now there are three in the city who, with the least encouragement, would make love to me; I have two correspondents in the same predicament—but past experience will serve to keep me from driving them from me. I am enjoying existence very much now; I don't wonder longer, but will enjoy life as it comes. I am an anomaly to my self as well as to others. I do not wish to be married but I do wish for the society of the gentlemen.[35]

"Enjoying existence . . . as it comes" was a radical path for Wells to take. As historian Patricia A. Schecter observes, "the intimate world of Memphis' aspiring black middle class placed its own demands on female composure and comportment."[36] However manageable the city may have been, the black community was hedged in both by the structures of racism and by its own rules of social engagement; thus, Wells's ambitions—particularly because she was a woman—were likely to cause conflict.

Living in Memphis when they did, as they did, Wells and her suitors were New Negroes, the generation of African Americans who faced the extraordinary task of reinventing the definitions of black gender identity that had been misshapen by the slave past.[37] As historians and feminist critics have shown, the antebellum era's ideals of masculinity and femininity contradicted the meanings of gender as African Americans experienced them.[38] On plantations black men were just as likely to perform domestic work as black women were to toil in the fields, reversing the dominant cultural division of men's and women's labors into public (male) and private (female) domains. Unable to marry legally, the roles of husband and wife, or father and mother, were ones black men and women inhabited precariously, since their families could be separated by sales or rental agreements and their children counted as stock in their masters' property inventories. In slavery and freedom, African Americans embraced the complexities of their gender identities, but a new code of conduct emerged at the end of the nineteenth century that promised to liberate blacks by holding them accountable to the social mores from which they had been excluded under slavery. New Negroes, this ethos held, should aspire to the traditional bourgeois norm where black men led the community's life in public, while black women were to bear children and cultivate pious, disciplined, intellectually rich homes. Although it challenged the legacy of stereotypes that demeaned African Americans as impious, unchaste, lascivious, illiterate, undisciplined, homeless chattel, the New Negro credo threatened to limit the place of black women in the movement toward modernity and full freedom because it idealized black men as the symbol of racial emancipation.[39]

Being expected to serve the race without challenging black men's authority in public was a compromise Ida B. Wells was unwilling to make, however. By her own admission, she lacked "an obedient disposition . . . extreme tractableness & [an] easily controlled . . . ladylike refinement."[40] Understanding herself to be possessed of "tempestuous, rebellious, hard headed willfulness," Wells found it impossible to hide her light under a bushel for anyone—especially black men:

> I have never stooped to underhand measures to accomplish any end & I will not begin at this late day by doing that that my soul abhors; sugaring men, weak, deceitful creatures, with flattery to retain them as escorts or to satisfy a revenge, and I earnestly pray My Father to show me the right & give me the strength to do it because it is right, despite temptations. I shall pray for Mr. G[raham] & all the others who have formed themselves in league against a defenseless girl, that they may see the light & the injustice done me & that I may bear it meekly, patiently.[41]

Wells was enraged when several of her suitors, frustrated by her rejections of their sexual advances, started rumors accusing her of being a tease ("playing with edged tools") and a "heartless flirt."[42] Though the first to admit her eagerness for romantic adventure ("I do not wish to be married but I do wish for the society of the gentlemen"), Wells insisted on the right to determine her sexual and gender conduct for herself, rather than being guided by the rules New Negroes would have imposed on her.[43] As history would have it, at the end of the nineteenth century, when Wells found these norms both enabling and frustrating, those same structures were eroding in the lives of white men and women.

Beginning in the 1880s and cresting during the 1890s and 1900s, white Americans were challenged by the secularization of their households. The rapid expansion of corporate-monopoly capitalism increased opportunities for work, education, and leisure for men and women of all classes. With the blurring of what had earlier been separate domains dividing the sexes, a generation of New Women strode into the halls of academe, through the lobbies of government, onto the shop floors of factories, and behind the desks of corporate businesses.[44] Though their paychecks reflected less earnings than the wages paid to men, these women spent their money on pastimes that widened their usual domains and habits. They paid rent for apartments shared with other women and used their leftover "pin money" to buy fashionable clothes and to promenade about town with their friends. Largely understood to be a social development rooted in the North—because there, we suppose, modernity took strongest hold through advancements in industry, education, commerce, and government—New Women transformed the contours of southern life as well. The delicate *belles dames* mythologized in the region's discourse of womanhood were, in record numbers, moving to cities, working in factories and textile mills, and living on their own. As the twentieth century got underway, many attended normal schools and colleges to start careers as teachers, while others became active in the public affairs of the Women's Christian Temperance Union and United Daughters of the Confederacy.[45] As an upshot of these changing roles, southern white women called white men's political leadership into question. For example, Georgia's Rebecca Latimer Felton spared no man's feelings—including the revered Confederate loyalists'—when she ridiculed southern farmers for pursuing economic policies that saddled the region with debt during the 1880s and 1890s. "'It makes a veteran like myself smile to hear you prate about foreign trade or the tariff, silver and gold, metallic conferences and war with Spain as an excuse for depression in business and low prices,'" she smirked.[46] Though exceptional in its blunt candor, Felton's rebuke was symptomatic of the broader discontent felt by the droves of women who chose to work outside the home and join reform movements that implicitly criticized how the south's male leadership handled the region's affairs.[47]

North and South, then, New Women and New Negroes heralded how modernity's social encroachments—in the forms of industrialization, urbanization, and commercialization—changed what had been sacrosanct understandings about the place of women and black people in nineteenth-century America. Simply put, it was traditionally understood that they were not to hold positions or lead lives of public consequence, nor were they to unseat white men from their perches of power. However, between the freedoms that African Americans and white women assumed were theirs to claim and an economy whose booms and busts seemed to cycle on beyond anyone's control, white men in the South and the North could no longer claim unrivaled authority to govern over these new developments in national life. In the South this meant, as Joel Williamson observes, that "[white] men found themselves less and less able to provide for their women in the accustomed style, and there seemed to be no promise to the end of the decline."[48] To make matters worse, newly empowered women like Felton bitterly reminded them of their failures in public. The tensions were as sharp in the North, where "middle-class [white] men worried that they were losing control of the country," as Gail Bederman points out. Heading settlement homes, staffing government agencies, occupying college faculties, and joining labor unions, New Women helped transform how business was conducted in nearly every sector of public life.[49] "Between 1880–1920," Bederman explains, "white middle class men's beliefs that they were the ones who should control the nation's destiny" no longer held sway. Challenged by infidels on each side—heretical New Women and damnable emancipated blacks—white men could recover their lost sense of authority through violence. In the perceived breach of tradition, lynching could be culturally logical because "the manliness of the lynch mob" promised to fulfill white men's hopes to recover their social dominance.[50]

During the 1880s, 1890s, and 1900s, when New Negroes and New Women rivaled white men for cultural power, the reports of anti-black mob lynchings were as widespread and frequent as they would ever be,[51] quite often coded by two kinds of vocabularies: the language of generational change and the lexicon of medieval conquest. The "new issue" of African Americans rejected the codes of subservience honored by the "old negro" who, "without parade stand for good order, and do what they can to repress lawlessness among their people," Thomas Nelson Page wistfully argued in 1904.[52] The modern black man respected no such limits at all. "'He grows more bumptious on the street, more impudent in his dealings with white men; and then when he cannot achieve social equality as he wishes, with the instinct of the barbarian to destroy what he cannot attain to [*sic*], he lies in wait . . . and assaults the fair young girlhood of the South,'" the *Atlanta Journal* cried out in the weeks leading up to that city's cataclysmic race riot in 1906.[53]

As black activist Mary Church Terrell noted, "No language is sufficiently caustic, bitter, and severe to express the disgust, hatred, and scorn with which southern gentlemen . . . cal[l] the 'New Issue,'" but the discourse that proved most malleable for the purpose of legitimating lynching's violence and concealing its relation to the politics of cultural change was that of medieval ritual.[54] Figuring white lynch mobs as the chivalrous guardians of both white women's virtue and national culture, apologists for lynching, North and South, narrated the murders as battles waged against depraved black "beasts," "imps," and "monsters" that white mobs valiantly slew. Burning and dismembering the "fiends" purged the world of a blasphemous presence; white maidens—symbolic of the nation's purity—were rescued from sexual assault by killing these black foes.

Cast as a chivalric drama, lynching appealed as a tactic to restore patriarchal power on both sides of the Mason-Dixon line not simply because it offered white men (and those white women who preferred the privileges that the status quo provided them) the chance to put "uppity" blacks and unruly white women in their proper subordinate places. Rather, the allusions to the medieval past created a time lag in which the jolts caused by these new social arrangements might be understood and redefined. Lynching was culturally logical, then, because the violence dramatized how fully different freedom was from what Americans—white and black, men and women, North and South—had known before. At the same time, lynching murders veiled their importance to this shift precisely because the violence was so "ancient" and "uncivilized."

For Ida B. Wells, witnessing lynching's emergence at this historical juncture determined the direction her life and work would take. As a New Negro, she was expected to channel her energies in ways that stifled her because she was a woman. Though living as a New Woman made it possible for her to harbor ambitions that New Negro politics would not endorse as her "true" purpose, that ideal left Wells in a cultural lurch too, because she could neither financially afford nor emotionally bring herself to quit "the society of the gentlemen" like her white contemporaries pledged themselves to do.[55]

When understood in the context of these transformations and not through the experience of her friends' murder at the Curve in 1892, Wells's lifelong commitment to anti-lynching activism makes clearer sense.[56] Having been maligned for transgressing African Americans' social standards of decency, she had personally experienced the indignities of being "misrepresented"—and by black people—in public discourse. Wells knew what it was like to be falsely punished for following one's sexual desires in "improper" ways. Though it is clear that her later analyses of lynching's sexual politics follow from these early years in Memphis, Wells's struggle to define her autonomy as a black woman proved to be crucial to the other modern movement that made her career in anti-lynching politics possible as well. Since writing about lynching was the way Wells chose to protest the practice, exploring the extent to which her literary career was wholly indebted to lynching allows us to examine the role of news writing in perpetuating lynching's cultural logic.

Making Novel Choices

Wells first worked as a teacher in Memphis, a job she found "confining," "monotonous," and "boring."[57] Since classrooms limited her to the kind of political leadership that "true" race women were encouraged to assume—nurturing, cultivating, and mothering African Americans to take part in the coming modern era—Wells looked to the city of Memphis and its arenas of black cultural production to rethink what her life calling ought to be. An enthusiastic member of her church's lyceum, Wells volunteered to keep the group's minutes, a task at which she proved to be quite skilled; she would soon apply those talents for the city's black teachers' association. In 1891 she was elected secretary and then editor of the association's newsletter, a post that brought her great satisfaction (*Crusade,* 22–23). Her success at—but more, her pleasure in—writing for the public soon prompted Wells to consider journalism as a vocation.

Home to three black-owned newspapers, Memphis was an ideal place for Wells to explore this possibility. Because it was undercapitalized (though not impoverished), the black press operated under a code of cooperation that encouraged writers, editors, and publishers to pool their labors in the interests of cultivating a wider readership.[58] Thus, in the course of her apprenticeship as a journalist, Wells wrote for as many as ten different newspapers, starting with the Baptist-run *Living Way* in 1883 and nondenominational papers in at least eight other cities.[59] According to the *Indianapolis Freeman,* Wells progressed impressively, rising from "'a mere insignificant, country-bred lass into one of the foremost among the female thinkers of the race to-day.'"[60] Indeed, her resumé confirms this ringing endorsement of her abilities. In 1887 she addressed the National Afro-American Press Convention's annual meeting and in 1889 was elected to serve as the group's secretary.[61] By 1892 Wells had delivered two major speeches about the state of the field ("Woman in Journalism" in 1887 and "The Requirements of Southern Journalism" in 1892). She had also joined the ranks of newspaper ownership, purchasing a managing share of the *Memphis Free Speech and Headlight* in 1889.[62]

One way to account for Wells's quick ascent is as evidence of the progressive edge to New Negro politics, where gender equity characterized the "civic partnerships" between black women and black men.[63] However, the article that secured her journalistic status suggests another interpretation of Wells's rise to prominence in the field, one that links her difficulties conforming to black gender norms to the prose style and narrative forms she would eventually craft to write about lynching. In 1891 Wells published a controversial editorial in the *Memphis Free Speech and Headlight,* attributing the inadequate facilities and instructional resources of the city's black schools to a social scandal involving the city's school board. White male supervisors were romantically involved with various black female teachers "whose mental and moral characters were not the best," Wells charged. Convinced that "such a condition deserved criticism," she published her opinion but refrained from signing it, because "such a protest coming from a man . . . would be heeded" over one lodged by a woman. However, when the paper's co-owner, J. L. Fleming, "refused to father" the comment by publishing it under his name, Wells let the statement appear without any attribution. Gaining fame as the most active writer on the *Free Speech*'s small staff, Wells could not conceal her role in the controversy for long. As she recounts it, the editorial "created a sensation," prompting the school board to dismiss Wells from her teaching post.[64]

In her memoir, Wells justified publishing the article by claiming the exposé taught black parents about the municipal power structure in Memphis and how patronage politics had compromised their children's learning. At the moment of its publication, though, the report committed a serious breach of decorum because New Negro political etiquette discouraged discussion about sexuality in public. Determined to enter the twentieth century free of the tainted legacy created by racist stereotypes, "respectable" race men and race women avoided the topic of sex in public debates—if the matter needed to be discussed at all.[65] But sex was not marginal to the Memphis school board scandal so far as Wells was concerned. Sex was endemic to the controversy itself precisely because the liaisons she reported were common knowledge within the city's black communities; the novel breakthrough of Wells's editorial was to protest them openly as a kind of political graft. In her opinion, the barter of sexual favors for public positions of power was the heresy to decry, not her writing about this political economy. Indeed, the scandal revealed how intricately linked matters of state governance could be to the practices of sex—or, that is to say, how the spheres of public and private life were becoming increasingly enmeshed in the modern age.[66]

Being ousted from her classroom post was itself not too troubling for Wells; it made it possible to devote her energies to journalism full-time. Harder to bear was the black reading public's response to her editorial. As Wells recalled it, "the worst part of the experience was the lack of appreciation shown by the parents. They simply couldn't understand why one would risk a good job, even for their children" (*Crusade,* 37). This reproach no doubt taught Wells a valuable professional lesson. Since black women could not "mother" stern, controversial, "worldly" opinions for public debate without risk of retribution, Wells would have to "father" her prose. Or, as the *New York Age*'s T. Thomas Fortune would later put it when praising Wells, she would have to write "more as a man," with firm, vigorous resolve in graphic, frank language about the pressing issues of the time (*Crusade,* 33).

For Wells, however, there was no need for her to "write like a man" either to pursue her career or to earn public acclaim. The ranks of black women journalists may have been small at the end of the nineteenth century but they were hardly thin; during the years of Wells's apprenticeship (1883–92), eighteen other black women published regularly throughout the black press.[67] Furthermore, given that fiction writing had become a popular endeavor for black women authors in the 1890s, Wells could have aimed for the success of Frances E. W. Harper, Pauline E. Hopkins, Victoria Earle Matthews, or Anna Julia Cooper, all of whom excelled at producing news articles, essays, novels, and short stories that were highly politicized and widely read by the black reading public. But Wells refused to adopt her female peers' impassioned but restrained styles of writing. Rather, as her failed efforts to coauthor a novel with a man reveal, Wells preferred hard-hitting, blunt-sounding prose, features that later would capture how the fluidity of gender roles, racial identities, and genre forms—or, that is, the threat of modern society's formlessness—enabled lynching to surge unchecked.

Writing "Dynamitically"

In the early spring of 1886 Wells took up the project of authoring a novel with her favorite suitor, Charles Morris, a journalist who lived in Louisville, Kentucky. Morris proposed this venture in their correspondence, suggesting that Wells write two books, one on her own and the other in collaboration with him. The plan made Wells nearly swoon in her diary entry of January 28, 1886: "The stupendous idea of writing a work of fiction causes me to smile in derision of myself at daring to dream of such a thing."[68] According to her diaries, Wells finished outlines for both novels but the completed manuscripts never materialized.[69] "Not much attracted" to Morris's ideas for their jointly authored work, Wells declined to proceed because her beau's plan was "too much on the style of other novels—rather sensational."[70] But she quit her own project too, because she could not resist that same tendency.

As she recounts their plots, Wells's novels were based on three extraordinary cases from the docket of the Memphis County Court. One involved the strange extremities that marked daily life for black people in the South: a young black girl was tried and sentenced to hard labor at the county workhouse for defending herself when a white girl pushed her out of a walk path. In the second trial, a white man was denied a marriage license because his fiancée was black; by cutting the woman's fingers and sucking her blood, he proclaimed himself black too. The man obtained the license. But on learning of the ruse, the man's family had him arrested for breaking antimiscegenation laws. The third case that intrigued Wells involved another interracial couple. The pair had schemed to obtain a valid marriage license by having a white friend stand in for the bride at the court clerk's office, and then to use the certificate to relocate legally to another state. When their ruse was discovered, officials charged the pair with fraud.[71] That a walk outdoors could result in a minor's incarceration; that a man's legal status and very identity turned on the ingestion of a few drops of another's blood; that a couple could remain in good stead with the state as long as it disobeyed the state's edicts—the absurdities of any one of these courthouse dramas were rich with storytelling promise. And yet, Wells could not manage the task. She abandoned writing her novel because she could not transform these episodes into a sustained work of prose fiction. Why not, and what does her failure tell us?

Wells was the first to admit and contemplate her failure. Novel writing was not her forte because, as she understood it, the requirements of fictive discourse exceeded her capacities of expression. "Today witnessed my first essay in story-writing; I have made a beginning," she noted in her diary on the first of September 1886. "I know not where or when the ending will be. I can see and portray in my mind all the elements of a good story but when I attempt to put it on paper my thoughts dissolve into nothingness."[72] Calling her first effort at writing fiction an "essay," Wells manifestly meant that her scrapped attempt was a "try." But as a mode of writing, the "essay" signals Wells's recognition of a literary form that (like the novel) is topically capacious but imaginatively demanding, and which (unlike her try at novel writing) she evinced abundant skills at producing. Her diary entries show her to be a supple expository writer fond of nimble wordplay ("I would very much like to go but fear I can't spell able," she quipped in rejecting one suitor's entreaties); drolly humorous ("the inevitable baby is there with all the habits peculiar to all babyhood," she remarked about a recently married friend's child); unabashedly direct ("Went to service yesterday morning & found a very slender, puerile-looking, small specimen of humanity occupying the pulpit," she reflected upon a visiting minister's sermon);

and deeply appreciative of subtlety ("I certainly enjoy [Charles Morris's letters] because there is always something interesting & couched in such chaste and apt language I am instructed and entertained and amused," she enthused over her dear beau's correspondence).[73] Wells's diary also chronicles her efforts to sculpt her prose into persuasive, pleasing forms:

> Finished & at last mailed off to the A.M.E. Church Review on the 24th, my article on "Our Young Men" not because I was satisfied with it or thought it worthy of publication by reason of the lucid exposition and connected arrangement, but as a trial to get the opinion of others. I never wrote under greater strain, but kept at it until it was finished, anyhow. I think sometimes I can write a readable article & then again I wonder how I could have been so mistaken in myself. A glance at all my "brilliant?" productions pall on my understanding; they all savor of dreary sameness, however varied the subject, and the style is monotonous. I find a paucity of ideas that make it a labor to write freely & yet—what is it that keeps urging me to write notwithstanding all?[74]

Since she knew the depths of her talents at writing expository prose, Wells thus judged her "essays" at fiction lacked by comparison (see figure 2.1).

This self-assessment illuminates the diary entry that follows Wells's announcement of her novel's end. On September 4, 1886, Wells exults over a different "essay" she published in a Kansas City newspaper:

> Wrote a dynamitic article to the G[ate] C[ity] P[ress] almost advising murder! My only plea is the pitch of indignation to which I was carried by reading an article in the home papers concerning a great outrage that recently happened in Jackson Tenn. A colored woman accused of poisoning a white one was taken from the county jail and stripped naked and hung up in the courthouse yard and her body riddled with bullets and left exposed to view! O my God! can such things be and no justice for it? The only evidence being that the stomach of the dead woman contained arsenic & a box of "Rough on Rats" was found in this woman's house, who was a cook for the white woman. It may be unwise to express myself so strongly but I cannot help it & I know not if capital may not be made of it against me but I trust in God.[75]

In this diary entry (the closest transcription we have of her no longer extant news article) Wells writes in awe of the murder scene and what it implies. Two women are dead. One by poisoning, the other by hanging and nearly inconceivable mutilation. Mystery haunts the precipitating event: did the arsenic found in the white woman's stomach match the ingredients in "Rough on Rats"? If she committed the crime, why would the black cook kill her employer? If innocent, who was the murderer—or was this a case of suicide? Wells's later defense of her graphic depictions of

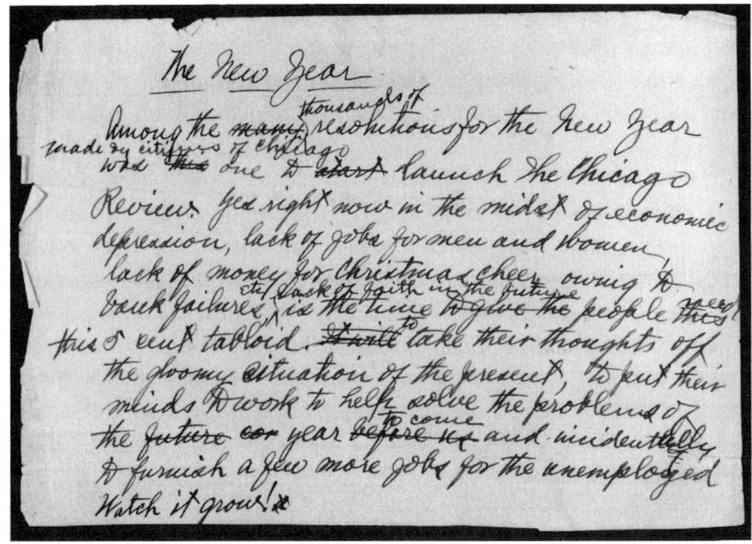

The New Year

Among the ~~many~~ thousands of resolutions for the New Year made by citizens of Chicago was ~~the~~ one to ~~start~~ launch The Chicago Review. Yes right now in the midst of economic depression, lack of jobs for men and women, lack of money for Christmas cheer owing to bank failures, lack of faith in the future etc, is the time to ~~give the people this~~ [illegible] this 5 cent tabloid. ~~It will~~ to take their thoughts off the gloomy situation of the present, to put their minds to work to help solve the problems of the ~~future~~ ~~cor~~ year ~~before us~~ to come and incidentally to furnish a few more jobs for the unemployed. Watch it grow!

Figure 2.1. As this handwritten draft attests, Ida B. Wells labored diligently to craft her news writing. (Ida B. Wells Papers, box 5, folder 2. Reprinted with permission by Special Collections Research Center, University of Chicago Library.)

lynchings would echo this first one: "However revolting these lynchings [were], . . . the wildest efforts of my imagination [could not] manufacture one to equal their reality."[76] And yet, for Wells, the "great outrage" of this case is the prolonged display of the victim's nude, bullet-ridden body in Jackson's courthouse square, her shock signaled by the exclamation points and question mark on her diary page. Deprived of due process and a fair trial, the black woman was killed and mutilated not only as a sign of rebuke to the state, but to the God Wells herself implores for justice: "can such things be and no justice for it?"[77]

Faced with such horrific brutality, Wells would write in kind; her "dynamitic article . . . almost advises murder!" However, by likening her prose to those explosives hurled by anarchists in Chicago (indeed, the Haymarket Riots and trial had occurred not long before this lynching), Wells admits in this diary entry that her desire to write about the case stems from her ambition to break conformity to the cultural style of protest expected of her as a New Negro woman.[78] Where female peers like Anna Julia Cooper, Frances E. W. Harper, and Victoria Earle Matthews published intense but refined essays and fiction about mob violence, Wells cultivated a "simple, plain and natural . . . way without any long-drawn doctrine or finely spun theology or rhetoric."[79] Thus in this diary entry she trained her attention toward (and not away from) the gross minutiae of both death scenes: the bullet holes bored through the lynch victim's nude body; the dissected stomach of the poisoned woman's corpse; the brand name of the arsenic used in the first crime. Though she sought God's blessing to justify this essay, Wells was equally motivated by a selfish—or, we could say, secular—commitment to stir the public's interest in the case.

Though obviously indignant over this murder case, she also sounds pleased by the prospects of violating the gendered expectations for "race women" activists and finding a prose style that would distinguish her among her journalism peers. By being a woman and "almost advising murder"—or, that is, by "fathering" this article and calling for such a bold response—Wells claims the mantle of masculine authority to achieve a level of public visibility otherwise beyond her reach.[80]

Thus, with her first published essay about lynching, Wells professed her faith in the power of news writing as the scripture by which black people might save their lives. After all, her own news reading led Wells to write about this case. She was "*carried by reading* an article in the home papers" to a "pitch of indignation." Fired by that zeal, she wrote her article and sent it to Kansas City, spreading the bad news of this event like a gospel. For Wells, accounts of lynching murders needed to be professed and heard throughout the nation. This commitment explains why journalism best suited her "dynamitic" style. Unlike novels, newspapers depended on time-sensitive modes of writing and reading—an hour-to-hour, day-by-day, week-to-week devotion—that, if cultivated in the right ways, might loosen lynching's fit within modernity.

Lynching and the New(s) Way of Knowing the World

Even had she not demonstrated such a strong preference and aptitude for writing essays, Ida B. Wells was right to consider journalism a means to the ends she hoped to achieve for two reasons. First, at the end of the nineteenth century, news reporting came to rival fiction writing as a viable literary career. Journalists increasingly committed to the idea of craft, understanding themselves to be creative writers and considering their prose styles to be akin to art forms.[81] Second, if the African American press by the 1890s had become nominally modernized, mainstream newspapers in metropolitan America—the white press—had transformed into "an immense social institution of overwhelming capabilities" whose scale of operation and influence no doubt inspired Wells's work in the field.[82] Technological advances in printing equipment for both text and visual images, upgrades in transportation networks, electrification of communication lines through telegraph and telephone lines, along with increased revenues from advertising resulted in faster, cheaper, and more widely spread circulation of newspapers in urban centers like New York, Chicago, St. Louis, Boston, and San Francisco.[83] This concentration of resources and readers probably explains why, when she was forced to flee Memphis following the lynching at the Curve in 1892, Wells chose not to go "west" as Thomas Moss advised. Nor did she settle in Philadelphia or Washington, D.C., where Frances E. W. Harper and Frederick Douglass offered her refuge (*Crusade,* 58, 72–75). Rather, Wells relocated to New York City because it was where American journalism was modernizing itself most dramatically. To raise an effective anti-lynching movement through the mass media, Wells would not only have to write from journalism's epicenter to maximize her access to those technologies, she would also have to refine her "dynamitic" prose style in order to expose journalism's role in knowledge production, one whose aesthetic forms helped cultivate the climate in which lynching thrived.

Most scholars of lynching agree that mainstream newspapers (especially in the South but in the North and West as well) tended to condone the violence through editorial comment and strategic publishing protocols.[84] First, when covering the murders after they had taken place, information-based reporting and opinion essays often praised the vigilantes as peacekeepers against outbreaks of black criminality and violence.[85] As a second strategy (used in the case of Henry Smith's murder in Paris, Texas and as late as 1934 in the case of Claude Neal in Florida), newspapers frequently published the plans for lynchings in advance, thereby encouraging the mob's ranks to grow.[86] A third kind of report extended the reach of the mob's assault by using the most graphic descriptions of the murders to restage the lynchings in as much detail as possible. Spread across a front page or crowding an inside page with a series of long columns, these reports were impossible to ignore.[87] Though the journalistic coverage ostensibly was meant to inform the public about the incident, these accounts actually compounded the violence by turning readers into both voyeurs and victims. Trapped into looking at or urged to glance away from the text, the public's interest was always defined within the circumference of the mob's will to power.[88]

A fourth journalistic pattern—the shortened wire reports telegraphed across the country by the Associated Press networks—had a different effect. Not unlike lynching postcards (which sought to codify the event into a portable "view"), wire news accounts of lynching diminished the violence to a point of inconsequence. Often lining the margin of an inside page, these bulletin accounts figured lynching as but a small detail, a routine occurrence in the course of the everyday. As filler for a blank space on the news page, the story then served as its own kind of grave, a place to bury and cover over what would otherwise be an empty spot. A final strategy echoed the fourth one and enabled newspapers to exercise their most subtle form of influence: the discretionary power of silence. By not publishing, and in effect suppressing, reports of lynching, newspapers fostered the belief that the violence bore no lasting significance, a suggestion that also worked to add to the death count.

Insofar as late-nineteenth-century newspapers relied heavily on sensationalized reporting to attract a mass readership, lynching was arguably no more nor less important a topic to cover. Paradoxically, the hyperbole of tabloid news prose created this leveling effect, because the copious exaggeration of coarse detail turned what were properly social, political, and economic conflicts into spectacles erupting from the realm of irrational, private scandal. Headlines that blared out "Desperado Burned to a Crisp" or "Negress Taken From Jail & Riddled With Bullets" all but obscured how the lynchings might be articulations of the social stresses and cultural anxieties raised by the occasions of emancipated black people and women enjoying their newfound freedoms in public life.[89] However, Wells's news account of the Jackson, Tennessee case was "dynamitic" precisely because it embraced the sensational itself: "advising murder" required nothing less than language charged with the fury of "indignation." Put another way, the structural conditions and formal imperatives of news writing—as much as any content that news reports and editorials might convey about the violence—shaped lynching's meanings and effects in ways that specified the work Wells felt called to do.

The distinctness of Wells's approach becomes clear when we situate her writing in relation to the work of her black peers.[90] Editors and reporters like T. Thomas Fortune of the *New York Age,* John Mitchell Jr. of the *Richmond Planet,* William Monroe Trotter of the *Boston Guardian,* Calvin Chase of the *Washington Bee,* Edward Copper of the *Indianapolis Freeman,* Alexander Manly of the *Wilmington Daily Record,* Josephine St. Pierre Ruffin of the Boston-based *Woman's Era,* and freelancer John Edward Bruce waged vigorous campaigns of counterterrorism through newsprint. Arguing against white vigilantism and championing the maligned character of black lynch victims, for instance, they labeled white mobs and state officials with the language of Darwinist degeneracy so often affixed to African Americans: "brutes," "fiends," and "uncivilized."[91] Unlike mainstream newspapers, though, black journals covered the whole spectrum of lynching offenses, whether murders had occurred or not. For the African American press, lynching was a chronic crisis that required regular surveillance rather than the spasmodic attention paid it by the white press, whose inconsistent coverage made of the violence an estranging event, indistinguishable from any other of its kind.

Black newspapers contextualized lynching's public significance by designing page layouts to maximize the murders' range of reference. Coverage of lynchings was rarely front-page page news; that space was reserved for headlining the achievements, debates, contests, and commerce with the larger world that affirmed black life. Placed inside the inner leaves of black newspapers, reports of lynching deaths took up a greater number of columns, comprising as much as two full pages of print and visual text. In the *Richmond Planet,* statistical tables enumerated the loss of life every week for the entire duration of the paper's forty-five year run (1884–1929). During the 1890s, advertisements for Marlin Repeating Rifles and Double Action Revolvers appeared on the opposite page, tacitly inviting readers to arm themselves against lynching's violence.[92] Case reports not only focused on instances resulting in death but also featured incidents in which, incredibly, victims managed to survive. They also highlighted the pogroms that often preceded or followed the lynching murders as well.[93] Just as often, efforts at restoration and repair were reported, describing the recovery of lynching victims' bodies, the funeral and burial rituals, and the fundraising campaigns mounted to aid surviving families.[94] In the *Indianapolis Freeman,* a newspaper widely recognized as the first black paper to print half-tone illustrations in its weekly editions, anti-lynching political cartoons delivered a ringing blow to reports about mob murders. Set prominently at the top half or midsection of the paper, these hand-drawn images made no uncertain claims about lynching's relation to central developments in national life (see figure 2.2).

These journalistic strategies, however, worked only insofar as they depended on the writing styles and idioms of the mainstream press. Headlines in black newspapers also screamed with the language of sensationalized invective: "Butchered in a RACE WAR/White Residents of a Georgia Town Exterminate Colored People/TEN COLORED MEN KILLED. . . ."[95] Detail-rich, suspense-laden opening paragraphs riveted readers' attention to atrocious scenes of violence:

> Three hundred armed men, with faces masked, surround a jail just at the darkest hour before the dawn while the inmates are sleeping heavily. They move with caution and as an organized body. The jailer is quietly seized and quickly overpowered. His keys are

Figure 2.2. The first illustrated African American newspaper, the *Indianapolis Freeman*, routinely published political cartoons that explicitly linked lynching to developments defining modern life and politics. "The Ways of the Heathern" appeared December 23, 1905.

taken from him, the heavy doors unlocked and before eight colored sleeping within were awaken [*sic*] their cells are filled with strange figures and they are seized and carried out into the night.[96]

The same techniques used to demonize African Americans and mobilize public opinion in support of lynch mobs were, as these examples suggest, flexible enough for black journalists to reverse the rhetoric of excoriation. Though Wells certainly supported these tactics (and, as we shall soon see, was quite adept at using them), her "dynamitic" writing style strongly suggests that she understood the form of news writing differently from her peers. Given how she understood her failure at fiction, Wells was equipped to explore how the role of time in journalism—or, that is, the ephemerality of the news—structured lynching's meanings as a knowable event.

As Richard Grant White observed in his 1870 essay "The Morals and Manners of Journalism," newspaper editors and reporters enjoyed unrivaled power to shape the public's perception of the world because of the time frame in which news texts worked on readers' consciousness. "In a quarter of an hour," White argued, a report or an editorial could "give [readers'] minds a bias from which they could never recover."[97] In an era when the pace of progress was so dizzying, news writing's social role became clear: to still this flux by naming, describing, analyzing, and then physically aligning sociohistorical change into columnar spaces that imparted a sense of cohesion, certainty, and constancy to public life. The titles of many American newspapers evince this purpose. They supplied "chronicles," "ledgers," "records," and "dispatches" filed from the fronts of history. They shone like "stars" or stood firm like sturdy "posts" and stalwart "tribunes." By the 1890s, newspapers were culturally positioned to do the work the Bible had once performed as the arbiter of meaning in daily life. The corporate headquarters of newspapers in New York and Chicago blended the architectural grandeur of medieval churches with the modern impulse toward skyscraping design, vesting their offices with the aura of towering, sanctified authority. With the extension of their publication schedule to the weekend, newspapers became important devotional texts on the most sacred of days, the Sunday Sabbath. Posing their power to bestow meaning as both timeless yet very much about the day, newspapers served as a bulwark against which the unruliness of the world could be measured and contained.[98]

The key to news writing's secularizing force, though, was White's exemplary fifteen minutes, or what Benedict Anderson calls "simultaneity": the consensus of meaning produced when people in different places read the same text at the same time.[99] At the end of the nineteenth century, however, commentators described journalism's production of history using another construct. Since American newspapers were also believed to be "so unsteady and unruly a thing . . . whose main object in life is apparently that of being different today than it was yesterday," the ephemerality of news writing and news reading was vividly important to secularizing knowledge and producing newspapers' historicist effects.[100] For at the end of Grant's fifteen minutes, the newspaper was discarded or traded away. That newspapers were never meant to be saved or archived implies that the knowledge they imparted as texts was as evanescent as time itself.[101]

Unlike books, which have a tangible durability that encourages their collection, newspapers' artifactual fragility not only compressed reading into ever-shorter periods of time; their disposability reinforced newspapers' growing authority as the archives of public history. The punctuality of news writing and reading—its "dynamitic" potential—is distinct from the timelessness of fictive discourse, which seeks to suspend a reader's sense of duration, the better to seduce the reader into the world of its text. Or, as Wells realized when she quit writing her novel: "I know not where or when the ending will be. . . . When I attempt to put it on paper my thought dissolves into nothingness."

This continuum of fiction writing's readiness to "dissolve into nothingness," on the one hand, and news writing's capacity to blast its subjects into "dynamitic" shards, on the other, explains why, unlike her black peers, Wells's most important writings about lynching were not published in newspapers but printed and distributed as pamphlets. With a storied pedigree dating back to the nation's revolutionary era, the medium proved equally transformative in Wells's hands because pamphlets perfectly embodied the flux of historical time as part of their rhetorical force. For Wells, anti-lynching debates were to be fought not only over what she often called the politics of "misrepresentation": countering wrong facts and bad arguments with accurate information and morally just opinions. More profoundly, Wells's pamphlets intimate that her interests lay as much with exposing the formal structures and modes of news discourse to the reading public, to show how journalism's professional premises and aesthetic strategies organized what was possible to be known in public debates about the violence.

Wells's pamphlets critiqued the habits of thought implicit in journalism's narrative conventions by parodying news writing's most popular modes at the turn of the nineteenth century. The autobiographical "stunt," the sociological treatise, the wire report, and the serial investigative story each valorized a particular trope as an emblem of journalistic certitude: eyewitness testimony, hard-boiled statistics, telegraphed dispatches, and expertly sleuthed "clews" all functioned in these genres as gauges of authentic facts and material evidence. Wells deployed these modes by repeating their signature tropes but then using them differently from their prescribed functions. This self-reflective, or "dynamitic," approach allowed Wells to expose how journalism's genres of representation were premised on knowledge constructs that, chillingly, valorized the deaths of black people as an acceptable symbol of news writing's achievements. Read as a collective canon, Wells's pamphlets archive how, as American journalism turned modern at the end of the nineteenth century, newspapers abided by and abetted the murders of black people as the sum (rather than the price) of their ambitions.[102]

Stunted Knowledge: The (Dis)pleasures of Reading in Southern Horrors

On October 5, 1892, "the greatest demonstration ever attempted by race women for one of their number" was held at Manhattan's Lyric Hall.[103] A capacity crowd came to hear Ida B. Wells recount the "southern horrors" that had driven her away from Memphis earlier that year. The third such lecture Wells had delivered since fleeing the South, this rally in New York City surpassed the previous two in Washington, D.C. and Philadelphia in its stunning tribute to Wells's importance as a news writer of national renown. "The arrangements for that meeting were perfect," she recalled. "An electric light spelled 'Iola,' my pen name, at the back of the platform. The programs were miniature copies of the *Free Speech*." The organizers also presented Wells with $500 along with a gold brooch "made in the shape of a pen, an emblem of [her] chosen profession" (*Crusade,* 79–80).

The dazzling glare of her pseudonym burning behind her in bright electric lights; the jeweled pin engraved with "Mizpah" (Hebrew for "lookout") clasped in shining place on her dress; the hundreds of dollars raised to fund the publication of her lecture as a pamphlet to be distributed nationally—in the midst of this public acknowledgment of her achievements Wells was overcome with grief.[104] Gripped by a "loneliness and homesickness for the days and friends that were gone," she started to cry, quite likely because she felt ambivalent about being fêted for writing about lynching murders (*Crusade,* 79–80). After the tearful lecture, Wells was congratulated by one man who stated that her willingness to display her emotions was a more "effective" way to "convince cynical and selfish New York of the seriousness of the lynching situation than anything else [she] could have done." Wells was stunned: how had black northeasterners come to be so "selfish" that her openly shedding tears should be the most "effective" way to persuade them to take lynching "seriously"?

Though public displays of grief were not the way Wells intended to launch her national career as an anti-lynching journalist, her emotional breakdown and the literary history of its racial underpinnings best characterize her first pamphlet parody *Southern Horrors: Lynch Law in All Its Phases* (see figure 2.3; cited as *SH*). Rightfully assuming that African

SOUTHERN HORRORS.

LYNCH LAW

IN ALL

ITS PHASES

MISS IDA B. WELLS,

Price, - - - Fifteen Cents.

THE NEW YORK AGE PRINT,

1892.

Figure 2.3. Prominently displayed on the title page of *Southern Horrors*, Ida B. Wells's portrait signaled that her first anti-lynching pamphlet was autobiographical. After this visual introduction, Wells proceeds to parody the genre to critique how news-writing made lynching a socially tolerable practice. (Title page photo courtesy of the Manuscripts, Archives, and Rare Books Division, the Schomburg Center for Research in Black Culture, New York Public Library, Astor, Lenox, and Tilden Foundations.)

Americans' news-reading skills were in special flux—black literacy rates were skyrocketing just as news writing genres were emerging that were particularly compelling to read—Wells crafted *Southern Horrors* to foreground two styles that might encourage the ennui of black readers.[105] Linking together the antebellum slave narrative with a modern mode called the "stunt," Wells troped on their shared autobiographical impulses and mutual signature symbol—namely, the body in distress—to explore how each idealizes and racializes pain as a redemptive sign of authenticity or truth. Legitimizing the harm done to black bodies as an extreme (but readily available) encounter with the "real" in daily life, these genres, *Southern Horrors's* parody suggests, depended on a death wish that heightened the public's tolerance for reports of lynching to such a degree that even African Americans could become indifferent to mob violence.

Hence, *Southern Horrors* opens by juxtaposing two incongruent images between its cover and the pamphlet's preface. Inside, following the elegant line-engraved portrait of Wells, is a depiction of her defilement by language: "It is with no pleasure I have dipped my hands in the corruption here exposed," she confesses in the preface, but "somebody must show that the Afro-American race is more sinned against than sinning, and it seems to have fallen to me to do so" (*SH,* 14–15). Instead of washing her hands of the world's grime as a proper lady would do, she dips her pen into the well to write about lynching's crimes, a gesture that steeps her in "corruption." Placed under siege, she does not take pen to hand for the joy of self-expression or the challenge of intellectual discovery. Nor does she voluntarily select her topic; it "fell upon" her, a "sinful" burden to bear. She writes reluctantly, with "no pleasure." Fouled by the text as a condition of its existence, Wells's only hope for self-renewal is to "give the world a true, unvarnished account of the causes of lynch law in the South" (*SH,* 14). Accordingly, the reader must prepare for a narrative whose credibility depends, the preface suggests, on the degree to which the writer's body can withstand physical danger.

Consequently, the preface's first paragraph informs the reader that Wells was directly threatened by the violence about which she writes. "The greater part of what is contained in these pages was published in the *New York Age* June 25, 1892, in explanation of the editorial which the Memphis whites considered sufficiently infamous to justify the destruction of my paper the *Free Speech,*" the pamphlet announces (*SH,* 14). This start marks *Southern Horrors* as an autobiographical-eyewitness narrative, but one whose authority proceeds from the writer's vulnerability to the violence of lynching. Since mob murder is the threat Wells escaped and still courts with these revelations, to win the reader's trust she places her own life in jeopardy once again by forsaking her *nom de plume*—"Iola"—and publishing her actual name beneath her woodcut portrait. An odious exchange to generate narrative interest, the equation of her mortality with the authenticity of the pamphlet's report is nullified by the cover portrait. That image of Wells—young, confident, lovely, and assured; looking away from the viewer so as to remain uncaptured by our gaze—creates the discursive space wherein the pamphlet's parody occurs.

African American readers of *Southern Horrors* would have been primed to these cues because of their long-standing familiarity with autobiographical narrative. Though they may not have read every slave narrative published before the Civil War, black people were immersed in rich oral traditions about historical figures and family genealogies from that time, while the 1890s launched a veritable boom in life writing through newspaper, magazine, and book profiles of "men of distinction," "homespun heroines," and "masterminds" of the race. Thus, for *Southern Horrors* to have a second preface from the country's most famous autobiographer, Frederick Douglass, was a strategic coup that served three functions at once. First, an endorsement from African America's most heroic ex-slave no doubt boosted *Southern Horrors*'s sales.[106] Second, by vouching for Wells's skill as a prose writer, Douglass urged black readers to regard *Southern Horrors* as an evolution of the slave autobiography and to trust Wells's modern update as a true account. "Her faithful papers on the lynch abomination has . . . no work equal to it in convincing power," Douglas praised (*SH*, 15).[107] Third, Douglass's prefatory letter models the ways in which the racialized legacies of the fugitive slave narrative necessarily compromised the history of lynching Wells felt compelled to tell.

Casting her in the role he struggled not to prototype during his writing career—the black autobiographer recounting personal experience in the most transparent terms possible—Douglass directed Wells to use artifice as she saw fit. "You give us what you know and testify from actual knowledge. You have dealt with the facts with cool, painstaking fidelity and left those naked and uncontradicted facts to speak for themselves" (*SH*, 15). In the first sentence, Douglass seems to valorize the idea of Wells's vulnerability to violence, for one source of her narrative's "convincing power" flows from her "actual knowledge" of lynching's threat. The second testament, however, distinguishes between two categories of evidence and testimony in *Southern Horrors* that, as Douglass glosses them, call the truth of Wells's claims into question.

First are facts that can be "dealt with." Others are "left . . . to speak for themselves," because they are "naked and uncontradicted." Classifying Wells's knowledge in these terms, Douglass suggests if facts that are "dealt with" cannot "speak for themselves," they must be made to speak. They cannot be "left naked," to extend Douglass's conceit, they must be clothed. With her writing now figured as a function of fashion, Douglass then invokes the language of connoisseurship to describe Wells's talent at argument: she handles either kind of fact "with cool, painstaking fidelity." "Fidelity" is a cagey complement for Douglass to pay because the word refers neither to the essence nor the constitution of truth *per se*. Defined in the *Oxford English Dictionary* as the "strict conformity to truth or fact of a description [or] translation," "fidelity" indicates narrative achievement—a quality of tone instead of a kind of form. Having revised his own autobiographies no less than three times over the course of the nineteenth century, Douglass no doubt understood the import of fidelity's effect. His preface therefore reminded readers that *Southern Horrors* could derive its power as a "truthful" narrative as much from its insistence on style as from the facts Wells cites to prove her claims.

And indeed, Wells picks up the gauntlet thrown down by Douglass:

> This statement is not a shield for the despoiler of virtue, nor altogether a defense for the poor, blind, Afro-American Sampsons who suffer themselves to be betrayed by white Delilahs. *It is a contribution to truth, an array of facts,* the perusal of which it is hoped will stimulate this great American Republic to demand that justice be done though the heavens fall. (*SH,* 14; emphasis added)

The word "array" amplifies "fidelity's" rhetorical power precisely because its allusion to arrangement suggests that Wells does not define facts as timeless or self-evident phenomena. As her pun suggests, the "truth" that facts embody exists within an ordered display that writing allows her to manipulate. She therefore calls for close "perusal" of the rest of *Southern Horrors* because by paying critical attention to the pamphlet's allusions to narrative forms, African American readers could discern how news writing's representational practices might be deeply perilous to their own lives.

For this reason, *Southern Horrors* parodied another mode of life writing that venerated a death wish against black people: the autobiographical "stunt."[108] Beginning in the 1870s and peaking in the 1890s, this news-writing style became a popular fad in American journalism. The stories of reporters taking on heroically improbable missions enthralled news readers who enjoyed having their daily chronicles "spiced" with tales of risk, intrigue, adventure, and danger.[109] Reporters like Nellie Bly, Stephen Crane, and David Graham Phillips became national celebrities for traveling around the world in eighty days, slumming in vice districts, infiltrating the corridors of power inside the United States, and living to write their stories. Characterized by a "straight-shooting style" and an exhilarating "slapdash air," stunt reports made gripping news copy because they reveled in the attention to detail that autobiographical narrative allowed.[110] This emphasis on first-person, participant-observer experience resulted in "self-centered" reports that valorized personal witness over expert opinion. Indeed, as Jean Marie Lutes argues in her study of the genre, the stunt's appeal lay largely in the triumph of popular wisdom over the official knowledge of bureaucratized power and authority.[111]

The stunt was a tactic that the capital-hungry black press used as eagerly as its white counterparts. For instance, the *Boston Guardian*'s irrepressible William Monroe Trotter shall forever be remembered as the notorious upstart who, in 1903, shouted down Booker T. Washington at a public meeting when the Wizard of Tuskegee was at the height of his influence.[112] John Mitchell Jr., the "Fighting Editor" and publisher of the *Richmond Planet,* shocked readers throughout Virginia's state capitol when he announced in a column that he would duel members of a lynch mob that had recently murdered a black man.[113] Wells planned no less daring events during her apprentice years in Memphis. In 1883, she caused quite a disturbance when she was forced to give up her first-class seat and take a place in the "colored" section of a train bound from Shelby County, Tennessee; the lawsuits she filed and won were topics for several news reports that she filed with *The Living Way* newspaper.[114] Likewise, Wells's editorials encouraging African Americans to boycott Memphis businesses and to migrate west were stunts by definition because they created news for Wells to report, but with this difference: reading them inspired black people to rethink and act beyond what the prevailing common sense told them was the right response to the lynchings at the Curve.

If, according to historians of journalism, stunt reporting was primarily an urban mode of news writing, its practice by the black press suggests that rural America was equally dangerous and complex, precisely because the genre brought with it the threat of actual bodily injury and death for black journalists who dared write in its vein. John Mitchell Jr. may have intimidated the lynch mob he challenged to battle, but magazine editor J. Max Barber barely escaped Atlanta alive because he dared to publish critical accounts of the 1906 riots in *The Voice of the Negro*.[115] For publishing his version of Wells's "threadbare lie" editorial, Alexander Manly's *Wilmington Record* in North Carolina was destroyed during that city's cataclysmic riot of 1898.[116] And R. C. O. Benjamin's body was an archive of racial violence: he was shot at, caned, and beaten up by whites who opposed his pamphlets protesting lynching. Citing his wounds as evidence of his authority to write, yet refusing to refer to himself in the first person, Benjamin ironically invoked the emblem that made the stunt worthwhile in the first place: "These episodes and the hair breadth escapes of Mr. Benjamin from death are related in order that the reader might form an opinion as to his competency to write a book upon the inconsistencies of the prejudiced Southerner and the deviltry they [*sic*] perpetrate upon the race."[117] In the world of black journalism at the end of the nineteenth century, staging autobiographical stunts not only ran the risk but required—when it came to reporting about lynching—that literal or symbolic violence be done to black writers in order to authenticate those narratives as "real."

Southern Horrors parodies the stunt's tendencies toward excess to reveal how those impulses might, for better or worse, skew the public's interest in lynching as a newsworthy subject. First, exploiting the genre's interest in personal experience and colloquial prose, Wells indulges in a syntax all her own. With great brio, she jostles between southern white dialect and standard English, squeezing them both between quotation marks to disparage the "honah" of white women, the reliability of the "leading citizens" of the South, and the morality of America as the "land of liberty" (*SH,* 19, 30, 31). Freed from the usual rigors of editorial correction that governed stunt news writers, Wells writes like the anarchist her "dynamitic" sensibility urged her to be. "One by one the Southern States have legally (?) disfranchised the Afro-American," she asserts in one passage. In another she asks, "the truth remains that Afro-American men do not always rape (?) white women without their consent" (*SH,* 19, 29). Rather than pose these claims as grammatically correct queries, Wells scrambles the order of these and many other sentences in *Southern Horrors* to reflect the form of her argument itself.[118] For in addition to questioning (if not exclaiming against) the legality of rape charges brought against black male victims of lynch mobs, Wells's oddly placed asides provoke the reader into an engagement with text as to its meaning. Faced with these imploding sentences, the reader must decode them into intelligible statements, a translation that calls attention to the structures of news writing that would otherwise conceal the composition of these claims *as* claims. Leaving evidence of her own thinking in the text this way, Wells parodies the stunt as a writing style weakened by the very features—its valorization of personal experience and colloquial expression—that constituted its appeal.

Southern Horrors parodies the stunt's limitations in a second way by testing its standards of credible evidence. The greatest misperception about lynching, that the violence was just punishment for the crime of rape, was directly attributable to journalists' violating the profession's standard for reporting news of that class of crime. According to Edwin L. Shuman, author of the best-selling primer *Steps into Journalism* (1894), incidents of "rapes, abortions, or seductions" were not to be submitted "except when persons of marked importance were involved," in which case journalists were to "be careful to give only facts that are in proof through judicial proceedings. Send nothing on as mere rumor."[119] Because rumor and innuendo formed the basis of countless reports of rape that ended with the mob murders of black men, *Southern Horrors* turns that high-minded standard on its head by reveling in the self-authorized claims that stunt reporting allowed.

Wells argued that alleged rapes involving black men and white women were, more often than not, instances of consensual love affairs that, because they violated the social taboos and legal rulings against miscegenation, became subject to extralegal punishment. "There are thousands of such cases throughout the South, with the difference that the Southern white men in insatiate fury wreak their vengeance without intervention of law," she complained (*SH,* 21). This charge was heretical, but Wells broke all canons of propriety with her second indictment. "Notorious for their preference for Afro-American women," white men were the worst offenders because it was not illegal for them to rape black women. "At the very moment . . . civilized whites were announcing their determination 'to protect their wives and daughters'" from black male sexual predators, white men stalked black women fearlessly because, as Wells angrily observed, "when the victim is a colored woman it is different" (*SH,* 26). These, of course, are crucial arguments for Wells to address and she does so in a bleak-humored chapter titled "The Black-White of It." If we remember to "peruse" the claims she makes in these pages, however, they become all the more daring given the methods she uses to prove her points. Wells "arrays" her facts into an order that turns the stunt's preference for autobiographical witness against itself by indulging the inherent limitations of personal knowledge as a reliable archive.

Perusing *Southern Horrors*'s citational rhetoric, it is stunning to note how cavalierly Wells describes her evidence. About one case of consensual adultery, she writes: "*In the winter of 1885–6* the wife of a practicing physician in Memphis, in good social standing *whose name has escaped me,* left home, husband and children, and ran away with her black coachman" (*SH,* 21; emphasis added). While the "winter of 1885-6" can refer to any number of months between November and March, it hardly bothers Wells that she cannot remember the family's name. That information "escapes" her and, crucially, she feels no pressure to research it. By the stunt's standards of proof, it would not matter whether Wells accurately pinpointed names, dates, or places in her report. She can rely on either "thousands" (*SH,* 21) or "hundreds" (*SH,* 25) of examples to support her arguments, because the stunt's autobiographical focus grants her the license to be as rigorous or idiosyncratic as she prefers. Though powerful and moving, personal testimony ultimately reflected the writer's bias, and this was perhaps the chief limitation to the stunt as an historical archive. With the reporter appointed to be the sole source and arbiter of what constituted "real" experience, the "truth" of the matter was then restricted to the references she selected. Whatever else occurred beyond the ambit of the reporter's interest did not, for the stunt's purpose, exist. Given the stunt's narrative conventions, whole areas of history could be rendered unremarkable and not worth knowing. The evidence Wells marshals to document the rape of black girls or women by white men best measures this effect of *Southern Horrors*'s parodic force: disturbingly, there is none. Wells lists no newspaper accounts of the four cases she discusses (*SH,* 26–28), not even from the black press. Nor does she claim personal relationships to the victims as authority for her statements. Refusing to disclose her sources, Wells lets these elisions stand as testimony to the stunt's power to mediate how acts of racial violence were archived as public history in the first place.[120]

Thus does *Southern Horrors* propose why news coverage of lynching was so terrifying to read and yet necessary to write. If it was not critically reimagined to surpass its limitations, life writing could justify the threats of pain, danger, and death that African Americans faced every day. After all, there was nothing truer than death, and both slave narratives and stunts routinely broached that limit as a feature of their storytelling appeal. With black suffering ascribed a status of narrative normalcy in both genres, its racialization set a crucial cognitive process in motion, one that helped legitimize lynching's violence as both a narrative subject and an historical event. Because racism devalued black citizenship and with it the loss of black life, lynchings could occur with impunity, while news accounts of mob murders served as the vicarious encounter with death that the slave narrative and stunt attempted but never fulfilled.

If it seems odd that Wells directed such a parody to an African American audience, we must remember that blacks were avid newspaper readers and cherished autobiography as, perhaps, the genre that honored their lives and ambitions with the full measure of dignity they deserved. Black Americans needed to understand these genres more critically so that they might know that lynching was not an inexorable condition against which no life-affirming steps could be taken. Parodying the stunt one final time, *Southern Horrors* ends with a call for "Self-Help," in which Wells outlines a bold set of proposals for black activism. Readers could stage a "bloodless revolution" (*SH,* 40) through consumer boycotts and labor strikes, or they could follow her most notorious plan: to provide "a Winchester rifle . . . a place of honor in every black home," using the weapon "for that protection which the law refuses to give" (*SH,* 42). Just as radical, Wells challenged African Americans to "rally a mighty host to the support of their journals, [to] enable them to do much in the way of investigation" (*SH,* 43). And given the cases that she lists as needing explanation, much writing needed to be done.[121] In the meantime, *Southern Horrors* accomplished quite a lot on its own, for the pamphlet delivered what it promised its "perusers": a way to reimagine history that might encourage African Americans to create new habits of thinking that would safeguard their lives.

The Sacrifice of Science: Lynching and the Limits of Objectivity in A Red Record

Because *Southern Horrors* addressed African-American readers, the white press ignored it. "For nearly a year I had been in the North, hoping to spread the truth and get moral support for my demand that those accused of crimes be given a fair trial and punished by law instead of by mob," Wells complained. "Only in one city—Boston—had I been given even a meager hearing, and the press was dumb. I refer, of course, to the white press, since it was the medium through which I hoped to reach the white people of the country, who alone could mold public opinion" (*Crusade,* 86). To reach past the "dumb" white press to the readers whose interests it organized, Wells engineered an event that ranks as one of the most important stunts in the history of American journalism: her anti-lynching "crusade" waged in Britain between 1893 and 1895.[122] She lectured across England and Scotland to packed meeting halls and followed those public appearances with letters to the editors of those countries' newspapers, summarizing her speeches and answering the complaints of skeptics and critics. In person, she struck a powerful figure; Wells was roundly praised in the British press for her "singular refinement" at the lectern, the "absence of rhetoric" in her arguments, and the "cautious and unimpassioned" tone of her talks (*Crusade,* 147, 150).[123] Wells also reprinted *Southern Horrors* to sell at her lectures. Retitled *United States Atrocities,* the British edition turned the acronym "U.S.A." into a damning statement that expanded lynching's "horrors" beyond the South, equating the nation's identity with the practice of racial violence.

Wells's British tour galvanized press coverage on both sides of the Atlantic because those lectures proposed a startling revision of lynching's history: southern whites were the uncouth, lawless brutes that wantonly assaulted "weak and defenseless" African Americans. Retracing the steps of fugitive slaves who sought political aid for their cause in London, Wells called on the British to intervene in its former colony's affairs once again because the United States lacked the moral and cultural sophistication to control the racial anarchy in its midst. As she wrote to the *Birmingham Daily Post* (England):

> America cannot and will not ignore the voice of a nation that is her superior in civilization. The pulpit and press of our own country remains silent on these continued outrages and the voice of my race thus tortured and outraged is stifled or ignored wherever it is lifted in America in a demand for justice. It is to the religious and moral sentiment of Great Britain we now turn. These can arouse the public sentiment of America so necessary for the enforcement of law. (*Crusade,* 100)

By soliciting the aid of "civilized" Europeans to discipline the "savage" whites of America, Wells so aroused the wrath of her countrymen that her work could no longer be ignored. While British newspapers expanded coverage of her speeches to debate her claims, the white American press monitored Wells's activities for the opportunity to malign her personally and dispute her accusations. The "slanderous, nasty-minded mulattress" had no business trying to set a foreign power against American interests; the "mulattress missionary" needed to pack her bags and return to face the punishment she justly deserved, the *New York Times* railed.[124] Because she had chosen to lecture in Liverpool and Manchester—two ports that received Dixie cotton for sale before, during, and after the Civil War—"southern conspiracy theorists linked Wells with 'northern capitalists' and 'western bondholders' bent on sabotaging economic and foreign immigration to the region," according to one biographer.[125] Planned to maximize her impact on political debates and public policy about lynching in the United States, Wells's crusade deployed the technique of the stunt to perfection. Her analysis of lynching reached the broadest possible public, forcing white people in the United States and across Europe to regard lynching as a crisis of global significance.[126]

The pamphlet that followed from Wells's crusade abroad was not concerned with the stunt, however, but with the style that incited the antagonism of her American detractors, on the one hand, and impressed Wells's British supporters, on the other. I refer here to the less subjective mode of analysis captured by the pamphlet's title: *A Red Record: Tabulated Statistics and Alleged Causes of Lynching in the United States, 1892–1893–1894.*[127] In this work, Wells parodies the discourses of American social sciences (particularly sociology) to explore how paradigms of objectivity and empiricism functioned to produce and reinforce white Americans' simultaneous rage for and disinterest in lynching as a crisis of national concern. "Tabulated" statistics besotted the pages of late-nineteenth-century American newspapers, calculating the growth of the nation toward its manifestly modern destiny. *A Red Record* takes close measure of this sensibility to insist on counting lynching murders as one of those developments, but does so by defining the limits to the positivist faith that such statistical thinking encouraged.[128] Focusing on the inuring effects of quantifying lynching into symbols of aggregate, "objective" data—numbers, tables, and records—the pamphlet links lynching's cultural logic to the very orders of proof so vital to the authority of scientific rationalism in American life.

It is not surprising that Wells should have been attuned to the newfound importance of empiricism to national politics given that she wrote and published *A Red Record* in Chicago, the city that was to American sociology what Manhattan was to American journalism: the intellectual hub of the field's development at the turn of the nineteenth century.[129] Like newspapers, social science research promised to distill the chaotic flux of modern life into orderly accounts; like news-writing genres, social science methodologies structured the public's common sense about what constituted order at all. "The millions have fragmentary knowledge of social relations and they are trying to transmute that meager knowledge into social doctrine and policy," Albion Smalls observed in the inaugural issue of the *American Journal of Sociology* in 1895. Certain that trained academics could fill these gaps, Smalls urged his colleagues to "reduc[e] all available pertinent facts about the past and present human association to generalized knowledge, which shall indicate both direction and means of improvement."[130] At a time when social phenomena seemed overwhelmingly interdependent—why, for instance, was gold more valuable than silver for domestic monetary policy and did that difference encourage foreign immigration into the country?—empirical analysis promised to show otherwise inscrutable forces to be contingent developments that could be managed through rational planning.[131]

During the 1880s and 1890s, social scientists and reformers published their research findings and opinions in newspapers, pamphlets, and magazines for a public overwhelmed by the dizzying developments of modern life. Not least among these unsettling conditions was the unclearly dubbed "race problem," whose need for "direction and means of improvement" led social scientists to choose lynching as one of the field's earliest test cases for data collection and analysis.[132] Appropriately, then, Wells addressed her second pamphlet to "the student of American sociology" (*RR,* 140) because *A Red Record* attempts to fulfill Smalls's directive by organizing "all available pertinent facts" about lynching's "past and present" to explain why the violence occurred, to account for its relation to other social phenomena, and to propose a "direction and means of improvement."[133]

Notably, this pamphlet does not mention the longest-standing "race science" of the nineteenth century—anthropology—even though that discipline was arguably a better target for critique.[134] Wells parodies sociological discussions instead, precisely because the discipline's hold on the white imagination was not as firm and the statistics that made its methods seem valid were potentially more malleable. The seeming neutrality of numbers, together with the detached, objective-sounding tone of social science writing, encouraged the public to regard empirical data as a nonpartisan account of the problems such research describes. Wells recognized the utility of statistical thinking: by measuring the aggregates of lynching's trends, she could marshal empirical evidence to support her critiques of the violence. However, because they condense the complex and tangled histories of social encounters gone awry into an abstraction of mere numbers, statistics (and the habits of thought numeracy promoted) reduced lynching's violence to a cultural naught, wherein the tallied losses of black life fail to measure any other condition but their own privation. Therefore, *A Red Record* parodies the overspecialization of knowledge that empiricism, as a method that also informs the ethos of news writing, generated as well.

On opening *A Red Record,* no pictorial image greets the reader. Unlike *Southern Horrors*'s flattering portrait of Wells on the title page, *A Red Record*'s cover and front matter are filled only with print text. By removing evidence of her body from the text, Wells recalls the death wish her first pamphlet exhumed from the genres of the slave narrative and stunt, but in *A Red Record* this empty space evinces the loss Wells entails by switching to yet another mode of news writing. If she turned to sociology because its empiricism enjoyed a cultural purchase she wished to acquire, the protocols of proof that would enhance Wells's credibility with a white audience also required that she act disinterestedly toward an issue she cared passionately about. The title, *A Red Record: Tabulated Statistics and Alleged Causes of Lynchings in the United States, 1892–1893–1894,* is numbing for the reader precisely because it is so controlled. Lacking the exclamatory brevity of *Southern Horrors: Lynch Law in All Its Phases* (with a headline phrasing any newsboy could have easily shouted out on a busy street corner), *A Red Record* bespeaks white readers's voyeuristic desire to distance themselves from the "southern horrors" of lynching in order to learn about them. Thus does the tonal repose of *A Red Record*'s full title single out the readership Wells meant to parody with her writing.

Exchanging *Southern Horrors*'s parody of intense subjectivity for one that dissembles a rigorously removed objectivity, *A Red Record* begins its discussion with aloof formality:

> The student of American sociology will find the year 1894 marked by a pronounced awakening of the public conscience to a system of anarchy and outlawry which had grown during a series of ten years to be so common, that scenes of unusual brutality failed to have any visible effect upon the human sentiments of the people of our land. (*RR,* 140)

Where her first pamphlet began with the tumult of Wells's account of her editorial duels with the Memphis press, here her dispassion is both visible and audible to the reader's eye and ear; the language of this passage gives voice to the restrained "refinement" that captivated Wells's audiences in Britain. If the cool tone of this introduction sounds more masculine than feminine, however, that is because *A Red Record* parodies the patriarchal voice of rational objectivity to examine its limitations as much as to claim its authority for this particular work.[135]

Relieved of the need to feel, Wells proceeds without affect:

> These pages are written in no spirit of vindictiveness, for all who give the subject consideration must concede that far too serious is the condition of that civilized government in which the spirit of unrestrained outlawry constantly increases in violence, and casts its blight over a continually growing area of territory. We plead not to the colored people alone, but for all victims of the terrible injustice which puts men and women to death without form of law. (*RR,* 149–50)

By apparently divesting her self-interests so fully, Wells's version of objectivity actually allows her to make a series of partisan accusations in this passage. White Americans, she charges without vindictiveness, cannot "concede" lynching's immorality by considering the physical harm done to African Americans as fellow rights-bearing citizens; whites reflect instead on the problem in terms of the political damage done to "the condition of government." Following these abstractions, Wells does not refer to lynching by name. It is "the subject" that deserves the public's "consideration," "unrestrained outlawry" that threatens to spread like "blight," and "the terrible injustice which puts men and women to death without form of law." But the equipoise of Wells's diction actually captures how narrow-minded liberal thinking could be, for the very language that allows white readers to entertain Wells's argument as impartial frees them from protesting lynching first and foremost on behalf of the lives of black people.

Wells's use of evidence, though, targets this temperament and its consequences for critique. The idiosyncratic array of rumors, newspaper reports, and personal testimony cited in *Southern Horrors* is consolidated in *A Red Record* by a single source of information: the annual compilation of lynching statistics published by the *Chicago Tribune*. Since 1882 that newspaper had developed "a specialty of the compilation of numbers touching upon lynching," Wells explains, and its data were widely regarded as credible because the statistics were based on reported cases of mob murders across the country.[136] Referring only to cases "vouched for" by the paper, Wells reasons that *A Red Record* will "be safe from the charge of exaggeration":

> The purpose of the pages which follow shall be to give the record which has been made, not by colored men, but that which is the result of compilations made by white men, of reports sent over the civilized world by white men in the South. Out of their own mouths shall the murderers be condemned. (*RR,* 150)

No sooner does Wells refuse the authority of black witnesses to serve as reliable documentary sources than she judges the culprits of mob violence to be "murderers," and hints unsubtly at journalism's complicity (if not collusion) with the practice—"out of [the] mouths" of published news reports comes the evidence Wells cites.

Wells therefore devotes the entire second chapter of *A Red Record* to reprinting the *Tribune*'s data. "Lynch Law Statistics" dutifully collates the alleged offenses, names, places, and death dates for the victims of mob murders during the year 1893 in what appears to be the layout style of the

Tribune's annual report. Removed from the busy pages of the newspaper to the singular focus of Wells's pamphlet, these same charges read quite differently. Instead of a ledger of misdeeds done and punished, Wells's version of the *Tribune*'s table details how arbitrary mob violence actually was. Black people were murdered for felony crimes and misdemeanor transgressions alike, all without due process of court trials. They were killed, too, for breaking the *de facto* laws of white supremacy: "insulting whites," "race prejudice," and "turning state's evidence" (*RR*, 150–57). Set in a larger typeface than the *Tribune*'s harder-to-read font, the twenty-eight "alleged causes" that Wells identifies loom large on the page, urging white readers to contemplate what these categories imply about their knowledge of lynching.

Precisely because the categories themselves invite the math, Wells tallies the cases and discovers two important trends in 1893. Though murder and rape were the most frequent charges against black lynching victims that year, the forty-four killings and thirty-nine rapes those men allegedly committed were each less than one-half of the 159 mob deaths that year. These data lead Wells to conclude: "The facts contended for will always appear manifest—that not one-third of the victims lynched were charged with rape, and further that the charges made embraced a range of offenses from murders to misdemeanors" (*RR*, 156–57). The reliability of the finding, however, is undermined by the impact of the empirical evidence. Because the *Tribune*'s necrology tables were organized according to the victims' alleged crimes, the murdered dead appear buried beneath the banner of the accusations lodged against them:

Suspected Robbery
Dec. 23, unknown Negro, Fannin, Miss.

Assault
Dec. 25, Calvin Thomas, near Brainbridge, Ga.

Attempted Assault
Dec. 28, Tillman Green, Columbia, La.

Incendiarism
Jan. 23, Patrick Wells, Quincy, Fla.; Feb. 9, Frank Harrell, Dickery, Miss.; Feb. 9, William Filder, Dickery, Miss. (*RR*, 151)

Arrayed in this manner (to recall Wells's theory of facts in *Southern Horrors*), the name of the crime, not the name of the person murdered, determines how the reader initially encounters the data. Presented this way, the victims' deaths—and lives—become unremarkable. With nothing to compel readers to linger on the names, even the significance of the murder dates is of no concern. Because readers could easily overlook these points, Wells observes later in the pamphlet how the Christmas season does not stop lynch mobs from their murderous attacks, and that two men were lynched on the same day in Dickery, Mississippi (*RR*, 239).

As Wells parodies it here, sociology's empiricism uncovers a main support to lynching's cultural logic: white Americans' disinterest in the deaths of black people. Merged into a lumpen mass, counted once as a ritual to begin the New Year, the men named in the *Tribune*'s lists can be easily forgotten precisely because this information does not communicate what their deaths might have meant. For as many different names that are included in the *Tribune*'s charts over the years, there are as many histories that would explain each murder, histories that might clarify lynching's meanings beyond defining the violence through the categories of crime. But the *Tribune*'s quantitative display makes those individual histories unavailable for public knowledge because the lives lived—and lost—become interchangeable with one another. Every murder case is the same as the next so long as the lynchings are reductively grouped in this tabular form.

To counter this effect of the *Tribune*'s data, chapters 3–6 of *A Red Record* reformats the necrology tables in two ingenious ways. First, Wells devises her own classificatory model. Rather than sorting victims by the crimes they allegedly committed, she accounts for them using a scheme that stresses the crimes committed by the lynch mobs. "Lynching Imbeciles," "Lynching Innocent Men," "Lynched for Anything or Nothing," and the "History of Some Cases of Rape" are the rubrics used to reevaluate the murders indexed by the *Tribune*. Second, using this typology, Wells measures the cost exacted by empiricism's standards of proof by narrating the histories of select cases. With their names, dates, and locations of death as her sources, Wells traces twenty-one lynchings to their original news sources, excerpting from those reports graphic descriptions of the torture endured by the men. Indeed, the work of mobs' murderous hands is especially visible because Wells juxtaposes two of these narratives with visual illustrations of lynching murders, to draw attention to the limitations of her own writings as a "re(a)d" record.[137] Calling attention to the forms through which the white reading public had become accustomed to perceive lynching as an event of public note, Wells proves that lynch mobs were the perpetrators of crime and this much more: when conceived not as writing's *a priori* justification but instead as its conditional complement, empiricism allows Wells to recuperate the deaths of lynching's black victims as histories full of meaning that reason cannot deny.[138]

Wired Text, Weird Truth: The Fiction of Lynching in Lynch Law in Georgia

Judging from the response to Wells's British lecture tour and the publication of *A Red Record,* white Americans finally began to acknowledge the threats lynching posed to national life. For all the malicious slurs they hurled at Wells, both northern and southern newspapers routinely invoked the pamphlet's statistical analysis of rape as if Wells's calculations were a long-accepted axiom of truth. Anxious to deflect Wells's censure that lynching made the United States "uncivilized," politicians took action; between 1893 and 1897, nine state governments introduced anti-lynching laws that held local officials and municipalities legally liable for mob murders that occurred under their jurisdiction.[139] Praise for these achievements flowed from her sister club women, who heralded Wells's work as heroic, while her fellow male journalists adopted her method of empiricist argument for their own work.[140] However, other black leaders responded fractiously to Wells's return from overseas. J. L. Fleming, Wells's former copublisher of the *Memphis Free Speech,* denounced her "fire-eating speeches," blaming her for stoking racial tensions without securing federal protections from the threat of lynching for southern blacks. Julia Ringwood Coston, editor of *Ringwood's Afro-American Journal of Fashion,* decreed that "mercurial persons" such as Wells were unfit to lead protest movements on behalf of the race. And Howard University's Kelly Miller dismissed Wells's efforts as marginal to the mainstream of African American thought: "All colored people do not sanction Miss Wells [*sic*] fiery flings at the South."[141] Coming from both sides of the color line, this criticism left Wells "physically and financially bankrupt":

> I felt that I had done all that one human being could do in trying to keep the matter before the public in my country and in trying to find that righteous public sentiment which would help put a stop to these terrible lynchings. I had gone from the Atlantic to the Pacific in this endeavor. . . . Thus it seemed to me I had done my duty. (*Crusade,* 238)

Insofar as *A Red Record* pointed national debates about lynching in more hopeful directions, Wells had done her duty indeed. The exchange she hoped that *Southern Horrors* might generate was brought about with her second pamphlet, not because white Americans agreed with her work, but because the parodic force of her writing transformed the terms and structure of public discourse about lynching so markedly. The hard-won success of *A Red Record* made Wells's third pamphlet a particularly bitter project, though, because the murders that led her to publish *Lynch Law in Georgia* clarified how the medium of news writing could be continually outmatched by the malevolence with which racism expressed itself.[142] On March 16, 1899 in Palmetto, Georgia, a mob of reportedly two hundred white men stormed the makeshift jail cell where nine black agricultural laborers were imprisoned for allegedly setting their boss's farm on fire. On the eve of the trial, the mob shot the "Palmetto Nine" to death in a gross display of its own firepower. Four months later, Sam Hose, a tenant farmer accused of murdering his landlord and raping that man's wife, was tortured and burned to death in Newnan, Georgia, after which a nearly inconceivable atrocity followed: Hose's bones and organs were pickled and sold in a local butcher shop. Georgia's cataclysm came to its grisly end that summer when Elijah Strickland, a neighbor of Hose's, was accused of serving as his accomplice and was put to death by hanging and mutilation as well.[143]

The violence of these murders stunned Wells. Struggling to contain her rage, *Lynch Law in Georgia* first insists that the reader "Consider the Facts," a preface in which Wells rails against "these savage demonstrations" that seek to "teach the Negro in the South that he has no rights that the law will enforce" (*LL,* preface). In the absence of legal due process, the press must act as the arbiter of truth, Wells argues, because news writing and newspapers were ethically obligated to promote rational thinking about social crises like lynching:

> In dealing with all vexed questions, the chief aim of every honest reporter should be to ascertain the facts. No good purpose is subserved either by concealment on the one hand or exaggeration on the other. "The truth, the whole truth, and nothing but the truth," is the only sure foundation for just judgment. (*LL,* preface)

Exaggeration, however, best describes the *Atlanta Constitution*'s coverage of these murders. During the two-week manhunt for Sam Hose, for instance, the newspaper ran lengthy, front-page accounts that eagerly tracked the mob's search and endorsed the lynchers' cause by posting a $500 reward for Hose's capture. According to historian Mary Louise Ellis, "in the first two weeks after the lynching, virtually every editor in the state published a response to the events at Newnan [the site of Sam

Hose's murder]. The smaller (weekly) papers filled their columns with excerpts of those editorial comments and also reprinted sympathetic views from journalists outside the state."[144] Significantly, Ellis notes, those recycled editorials emphasized the alleged rape of Mattie Cranford over the murder of her husband Alfred, as this column from the *Constitution* exclaimed:

> The wife was seized, choked, thrown upon the floor, where her clothing soaked up the blood of her husband and ravished! Remember the facts! . . . Remember the slain husband, and, above all, remember that shocking degradation which was inflicted by the black beast, his victim swimming in her husband's warm blood as the brute held her to the floor! Keep the facts in mind! When the picture is painted [by critics of lynching] of the ravisher in flames, go back and view that darker picture of Mrs. Cranford outraged in the blood of her murdered husband![145]

A perfect example of the folk pornography inspired by lynching, the circulation of salacious news reports and editorials also exemplifies the seductive allure of wire reporting in late-nineteenth-century American journalism. For precisely that reason, *Lynch Law in Georgia* parodies this practice of news writing in order to demystify how its narrative techniques diminished the public's capacity to regard lynching as a deeply "vexed question" about the trajectories of modern American life.

Wire reporting was not new to American newsrooms in 1899; as early as 1848, newspapers began using telegraphs to transmit copy from distant locales to the city-based headquarters of major papers across the country.[146] However, by the time Wells published *Lynch Law in Georgia,* wire reporting had radically transformed how news gathering, writing, and publishing occurred. For a high-priced fee, newspapers subscribed to receive telegraphed copy from wire services like the Associated Press, which hired field correspondents ("stringers") to file news reports from across the nation. Once these writers telegraphed or phoned their stories to the main news office, a desk journalist revised the stringer's report for an editor who approved the final copy for publication.[147]

The segmentation of the news writing process was an unprecedented innovation, not least because the division of creative labor into stringing, rewriting, and editing channeled the practice of making judgment calls away from relying on a hunch toward resorting to an established "house style." This reorganization also meant in theory that wire reporting promised to synchronize the availability of the news to the broadest possible reading public.[148] In contrast, the production schedules for Wells's pamphlets usually lagged behind established news cycle routines, a fact that calls attention to wire reporting's creation of information hierarchies whereby certain locales knew more about the world than other places. As a first look into how this system worked, *Lynch Law in Georgia* reprises Wells's signal gesture from *A Red Record,* granting the empiricist authority of white news sources. "That the awful story of . . . slaughter may not be considered overdrawn" (*LL,* 2), she claims to reprint excerpts from the reports of Royal Daniel, a staff correspondent for the *Atlanta Journal* (*LL,* 2).[149]

Like any metropolitan paper, the *Journal's* accounts of the Georgia murders were manufactured through the three-stage assembly process before Daniel's copy appeared in the home paper or was transmitted across the wire news market. Since this process concealed its operations behind the bureaucratized routines of the newspaper's production, Wells's pamphlet parodies this system by tracking the evolution of the story as a function of time. Splicing together Daniel's columns into a continuous feed of text, Wells reprints them without referencing either a calendar or the *Journal's* publication schedule. Daniel's dateless reports mark time's passing nonetheless because each account changes perceptibly, showing when he likely revised information gathered at the murder scene into the chilling narrative that concludes his series of reports. Though the blurring of news and fiction writing was an obvious concern for Wells, *Lynch Law* reads as if she were equally unnerved by the stark choice this method of reporting implied: as news "sung over the wires" (as the profession called it), lynching could be understood as a high point in a day's history or as inconsequential to the meaning of any given day.

On the pamplet's page, Wells's transmission of Daniel's report divides into three clear parts, starting with a dispatch that conforms exactly to the model the Associated Press (AP) prescribed for its correspondents: "When the news is of extraordinary character, or very sensational, file at once a bulletin of one hundred words, and await instructions before sending details. . . . A story should be told as briefly as consistent with an intelligent statement of the facts. The news should be given in the first paragraph, details following."[150] According to Wells, Daniel's initial bulletin read as follows:

> A mob of more than 100 desperate men, armed with Winchesters and shotguns and pistols and wearing masks, rode into Palmetto at 1 o'clock this morning and shot to death four Negro prisoners, desperately wounded another and with deliberate aim fired at four others, wounding two, believing the entire nine had been killed. (*LL,* 1)

Fifty-three words long, this summary not only meets the AP manual's specifications, it reveals the most important feature of wire reporting's prose style. Withholding the causal details about the murder (Exactly how was the execution performed? Why did this massacre shooting occur?), this report prioritizes the news over the story, notably placing the climax of the event—the lynchings—first. This method, known in 1890s journalism as the "inverted pyramid," reversed the established conventions of storytelling because "the reporter tells his story briefly in one paragraph and then goes back and tells it all over again in a more detailed way."[151]

And more details do follow this lead, like jottings from a reporter's field notebook:

> Last night nine Negroes were arrested and placed in the warehouse near the depot. The Negroes were charged with the burning of the two business blocks here in February.
>
> At 1 o'clock this morning the mob dashed into town while the people slept.
>
> They rushed to the warehouse in which the nine Negroes were guarded by white men.
>
> The door was burst open and the guards were ordered to hold up their hands.
>
> Then the mob fired two volleys into the line of trembling, wretched, and pleading prisoners, and to make sure of their work, placed pistols in the dying men's faces and emptied the chambers. (*LL,* 2)

These details are followed by more notes about the trial date, the demeanor of the mob ("the men did their work orderly and coolly"), and the posture of the black men as they were shot ("the nine Negroes were tied with ropes and were helpless"). Finally, a roster of the dead, a catalog of the survivors' injuries, and a status report on the murder's aftermath finish the section.

In the third phase of Daniel's report—the rewriting stage—these details assume a new form. According to Wells's reprint, the notes merge into a seamless but highly plotted narrative that unmistakably embellishes the initial report's bare outline of the murder. "It was just past the hour of midnight. The guards were sleepy and tired of the weary watch and the little city of Palmetto was sound asleep, with nothing to disturb the midnight hour or to interrupt the crime that was about to be committed," Daniel's next column read (*LL,* 3). Crafted to create a state of suspense rather than to impart information, Daniel's revision shows strong signs of "rehashing . . . a previous news story . . . to give a new twist to old facts in order to bring them nearer to the present time."[152] For instance, this exchange occurs just before the shooting begins:

> The Negroes, helpless, tied together with ropes, begged for mercy, for they saw the cold gun barrels, the angry and determined faces of the men, and they knew it meant death—instant death to them.
>
> "Oh, God, have mercy!" cried one of the men in his agony. "Oh give me a minute to live." The cry for mercy and the prayer for life brought an oath from the leader and derisive laughter from the mob.
>
> "Stand up in a line," said the man in command. "Stand up and we will see if we can't kill you out; if we can't we'll turn out" (*LL,* 14).

What began as a compact news bulletin narrated from some physical distance away becomes, by this third edition, an intimate "scene of carnage and death" (*LL,* 6) in which Daniel's seeming proximity to the scene is so close that it reads as if he were an eyewitness to the murder, interviewed a mob participant, or even faked the account.[153] In 1899, though, the liberties taken in reporting this dialogue were in perfect accord with "one of the most valuable secrets of the profession at its present stage of development." For as Edwin L. Shuman instructed wire writers, "truth in essentials, imagination in non-essentials is considered a legitimate rule of action in every [news] office. The paramount object is to make an interesting story."[154]

Collating Daniel's columns to filter through the pamphlet like a wire conduit—and, more ingeniously, positioning herself as Daniel's editor—Wells exposes why wire reporting's misrepresentation of lynching murders was more complex than readers might suppose. The time that elapsed between editions of newspapers made it possible for journalists like Daniel to rewrite reports without calling attention to their process of revision.[155] When reprinted in Wells's booklet, though, the transformations come into focus for what they were: a depiction of lynching that biases the reader's response to the murders. This prejudice occurs most clearly through the narrative's point of view, which shifts from eliciting at least a nominal concern for the "helpless Negroes" to inciting the reader's wonder at the white mob's power.

Characterized more fully than the nine black prisoners, the white mob members are "angry-determined" as they curse and laugh "derisive[ly]" at their victims' pleas for mercy. Their distinction as a group is honed to an even finer point once their leader speaks. Taunting the black men with a cruel bargain for freedom—if the nine can elude the fusillade of bullets, the mob will "turn out," sparing them from death—the commander asserts a textual presence that extends to the rest of his charges. Compared to the white men's vocal and physical prowess, the black men cry the voice of the abject. To enhance this effect, Daniel makes two significant revisions before his final story as Wells reprints them. First, he invents scores more mob members. Where the usually rabid *Atlanta Constitution* scaled back its initial report of one hundred lynchers to twenty, Daniel stuck with the larger number, the better to imagine the sweep of the mob's force.[156] "In an instant," the mob swarmed into the warehouse premises, "seem[ing] to come up through the floor and through the walls, so rapidly did they fill the room" (*LL,* 3). Before this supernatural vision, the murdered bodies of the black men all but disappear. This is a remarkable revision for Daniel to make, because his first report features each victim's name and specifies his injury. Though indexed in the "details" that accompanied the *Journal*'s first bulletin, this acknowledgment at least lent some textual dignity to the African Americans' deaths.[157] By the end of the revised story, however, each black man and his particular wounds merge into one image of nameless "Negroes" whose "streams of blood were dyeing red the floor and spreading out in pools" (*LL,* 6). Figured as an orgy of spontaneous death, the wire report of these lynching murders not only makes the loss of nine black lives incidental to the history of this event, it effectively functions to absolve the mob of its culpability.

That Wells called her writing technique in *Lynch Law in Georgia* "reprinting" underestimates the strategy's parodic power. Hardly reductive and not at all mimetic in its goals and effects, her style of quotation penetrates the illusion of ephemerality that the daily (dis)appearance of newspapers created. Day by day, report by report, the murders of the Palmetto Nine changed focus and shifted in meaning as information about the lynchings was distilled to produce Royal Daniel's sequence of stories. Taking full advantage of the pamphlet's autonomy as a discursive space, Wells parodied wire writing's protocols to test the system's limits as a source to document history. For, as the murders of the Palmetto Nine, Sam Hose, and Elijah Strickland made clear, African Americans could live or die, ignobly or not, because of how journalists practiced their craft.[158]

Serial Killing: Mob Rule in New Orleans

Despite its bleak critique, *Lynch Law in Georgia* maintained the recuperative outlook that parody can generate. "[I write] in the belief that there is *still* a sense of justice in the American people . . . that . . . will *yet* assert itself," Wells declared at the pamphlet's start (*LL,* preface; emphasis added). One year later, her publication of *Mob Rule in New Orleans* (1900) put Wells's faith in the power of parody to a harder test.[159] No sooner had she published *Lynch Law in Georgia* and become "engaged on a work not yet finished" than she was "interrupted" and left Chicago to investigate the pogrom incited by Robert Charles's one-man war against the New Orleans police department in July 1900. Quarreling with policemen who harassed him to leave a street stoop, Charles shot at the four officers, killing one and wounding the others. A citywide-wide manhunt ensued, and for nearly a week Charles miraculously staved off the entire police force with dazzling—and deadly—marksmanship.[160] The riot's maelstrom must have stirred Wells's memories of her own near-death escape from Memphis just eight years before, because she invokes the language of her church-based faith to reaffirm her belief in journalism's social power:

> We do not believe that the American people who have encouraged such scenes by their indifference will read unmoved these accounts of brutality, injustice, and oppression. We do not believe that the moral conscience of the nation—that which is highest and best among us—will always remain silent in the face of such outrages, *for God is not dead, and His Spirit is not entirely driven from men's hearts.* (*MRNO,* 255; emphasis added)

In this passage from *Mob Rule's* preface, Wells's plea for a sacralized ideal of public discourse signals a retreat from the deliberately secular tone of her earlier pamphlets. She had reason to despair not just over Charles's death but also over her freelance writing career, because unlike her other pamphlets (all of which enjoyed substantial measures of public interest if not popular sales support), *Mob Rule* was self-published on the thinnest of budgets. Wells candidly admits to having "no funds" and to being "entirely dependent upon contributions from friends . . . in carrying on the work" of printing and distributing the booklet (*MRNO,* 256). Having rejected the centralized organization and profit motives of newspapers for so long, Wells was confronted with the political consequences of her professional choice. A lynching murder like Robert Charles's required maximum access to resources and technology to canvass crime scenes, but by 1900 Wells lacked the financial and cultural capital necessary to keep pace with the supersaturated coverage that metropolitan dailies could provide to the public.

Turning to the mainstream press as her primary source once again, Wells "freely" cites the reports published in the *New Orleans Picayune* and *Times-Democrat* to reconstruct the events leading to Charles's death, but does so to make a different parodic point. Highlighting the New Orleans papers' better-funded capacities to mount an exhaustive but biased serial investigation of Charles's murder, *Mob Rule* is Wells's most "dynamitic" pamphlet precisely because her parody turns the critical lens back onto her own news-writing practice. Though she decries the monopoly effects of the *Picayune* and *Times-Democrat*'s serial coverage, Wells critiques their tactics by counterpoising them against her own. Probing the limitations of both sets of tactics, she contemplates whether a new form of news writing might be possible, one that would encourage readers to support an alternative press, on the one hand, and on the other to regard lynching murders as the paradox they were—an intolerable act worth reading about.

Judging from their page layouts, New Orleans's daily newspapers devoted considerable resources to covering Robert Charles's incredible duel with the police. Full-length, illustrated reports dominated the front page and inner leaves of the *Picayune* and *Times-Democrat* during the weeks of July 1900, and both papers extended their influence beyond Louisiana by dispatching wire reports to news outlets around the country.[161] Wells remarked on the impressive scope of this work, seeming to compliment the *Picayune* and *Times Democrat* for providing "the most *minute* details of the week's disorder" (*MR,* 254; emphasis added). "*Minute*" tips her parodic hand, however. Finely wrought, painstakingly collected information that would explain Charles's deadly uprising did not follow from headlines that blared "Two Police Victims of an Assassin's Weapon," or from advertisements offering "$250 REWARD" for the "capture, dead or alive . . . of the negro murderer ROBERT CHARLES."[162] Since such invectives characterized these newspapers' coverage throughout the crisis, Wells's pun implies that the city's knowledge about the case and its causes were as deep as a minute was long.

Doubling the meaning of time and depth this way, Wells opens herself to critique, however, because her word play points to the structural restrictions she faced by choosing not to join a newspaper staff.[163] In Wells's view, New Orleans competitors "were in the best position to trace the record" of the riot not simply because they lived at its epicenter, but because they had "all the resources at their command" to cover the event in a comprehensive way. Compared with Wells's self-publishing enterprise, these daily newspapers were a mammoth concentration of labor and wealth. In 1895, *A Red Record* successfully challenged both the U.S.

and the British media's hegemony over public discourse about lynching; but by 1900, the monopoly power wielded by urban newspapers proved harder to break. Pamphleteering afforded Wells editorial liberties she clearly deemed priceless, but in five years' time the value of her practice plummeted to lows from which it could not recover. Writing when mass-media publications in the United States succeeded only through large print runs funded not by loyal subscribers but through steep advertising fees, Wells's plan for distributing *Mob Rule*—"Those who would like to assist in the work of disseminating these facts, can do so by ordering copies, which are furnished at greatly reduced rates for gratuitous distribution" (*MRNO,* 256)—had become a naïve wish, one that was politically expensive to maintain.

Investigating the murder of Robert Charles on her own, Wells could not keep pace with the *Picayune* and *Times-Democrat,* which had assigned several reporters to cover various sectors and angles of the event. Since both papers published their accounts as the crisis immediately unfolded (instead of weeks or months after the fact, as Wells had to do) their staggered publishing schedules (the *Picayune* was sold morning and night; the *Times-Democrat* in the evening) allowed them to keep a round-the-clock vigil over the case. For Wells, the situation as it stood mocked her efforts to cover Charles's case. Dwarfed by the *Picayune* and *Times-Democrat*'s *de facto* cartel, she hurled back her usual stone but with a curve, citing the white press reports interchangeably as one undifferentiated source. More than a defense of her own methods of investigation, though, *Mob Rule in New Orleans* reprises the reprinting strategy of *Lynch Law in Georgia,* holding both Wells herself and the New Orleans dailies accountable for exploiting news-writing tactics that may very well have alienated the public from wanting to know (much less take action against) the full consequences of allowing lynching's violence to proceed unchecked.

For both Wells and the New Orleans dailies, Robert Charles's case was unquestionably newsworthy. How could a single black gunman shoot one white policeman dead, kill and wound twenty-seven other officers, and hold the city's entire police force at bay for a week? For an America that had just defeated Spain in a war that made the Unites States colonial lords over "our little brown brothers" in Cuba and the Philippines, Charles's insurrection was astonishing. The *Picayune* and *Times-Democrat* therefore covered this event and Wells herself admitted, "in the frenzy of the moment, when a dozen men lay dead, . . . it was natural for a prejudiced press and for citizens in private life to denounce [Robert Charles] as a desperado and murderer." How to cover the case and toward which social ends news reports would lean were the issues at stake. Or as Wells considered, "sea depths are not measured when the ocean rages, nor can absolute justice be determined while public opinion is lashed into fury" (*MRNO,* 308–9). For these reasons, the dailies' decision to mount an extended serial investigation was a reasonable way to quell the public's fury because that format aimed, over time, to track issues in depth. Serial news writing, however, poses certain intellectual and ethical risks that, when left unchecked (as *Mob Rule in New Orleans* parodies them), could inure readers to a case study like Charles's.

The practice of extending news reports of a particular event beyond one day was not new to American journalism, given the precedents set by serialized fiction during the mid-nineteenth century. What was distinctive about the genre by 1900 was the variety of its modes: stunts, political exposés, war dispatches, travelogue sketches, and wire reports often ran for long-term cycles in newspapers and mass-market magazines.[164] In this regard, Wells's parody of wire reports becomes particularly instructive as a counterexample; the initial one-hundred-word bulletin or an elaborated rewrite was meant to be consumed in a single reading session as a discrete account. With wired reports, one installment was to suffice. As one journalism manual explained, since any subsequent accounts are "for the benefit of those readers who have not read the previous story," every single one "must be complete and clear in itself."[165]

Where wire reporting fostered a fragmented literacy, serial news coverage cultivated reading as a habit-forming desire best fulfilled once the entire run of stories concluded. Robert Charles's lynching fulfilled this narrative covenant exactly. The citywide manhunt readily lent itself to stories that the *Picayune* and the *Times-Democrat* printed around the clock. With so many men swarming the streets, Charles eluding capture, and "Negroes" being "hunted all night" by white posses numbering at least 350 men strong, both papers illustrated the series with line-engraved drawings, creating *dramatis personae* that made the stories easier to follow.[166] The police officers killed by Charles were memorialized in a portrait in the *Picayune*'s edition of July 25, 1900; Charles was prominently pictured in both papers looking quite dignified. Suited in a coat and necktie, face and moustache freshly barbered, head topped with a tasteful bowler, Charles looked like a most peaceable New Negro.[167] That, though, was the great mystery the dailies' serials aimed to solve. "It is only natural that the deepest interest should attach to the personality of Robert Charles. What manner of man was this fiend incarnate? What conditions developed him? Who were his preceptors? . . . These are questions involving one of the most remarkable psychological problems of modern times," the *Times-Democrat* mused in its July 25, 1900 report titled "The Making of a Monster" (*MRNO,* 305).

Wells reprints these installments in *Mob Rule* to show how the series format allowed Charles's "accusers [to] *g[i]ve full license to their imagination* and [to] distort the facts they had obtained, in every way possible, to prove a course of criminality, which the records absolutely refuse to show" (*MRNO,* 302; emphasis added). One in particular raised her concern: accompanying the police during a search of Charles's abandoned apartment, reporters from the *Picayune* and *Times-Democrat* proudly proclaimed to have discovered "clews" that provided "a complete index to the character of the man." Pamphlets describing Bishop Henry M. Turner's back-to-Africa movement, empty cocaine bottles, bullet molds, and soiled books were, to these observers, signs that Charles was a "desperado," an "arch-fiend," and a "monster" whose sole aim was to bring about "the discomfiture of the white race" (*MRNO,* 305).[168] To Wells, whose investigation was neither sanctioned nor aided by the police, these same items suggested different motives. His booklets on Bishop Turner's emigration movement were not proof of Charles's irrational antipathy toward whites, but were evidence of his hopes for the prospects for black liberation (*MRNO,* 309–11). These reading materials, along with his "well-worn text-books" and "well-filled copy books" led her to conclude that Charles was an intellectual who coveted industry and self-improvement, spending "the hours after days of hard toil" increasing his literary skills (*MRNO,* 310). To double check her surmises against other independent sources, Wells expanded her research to interview Charles's friends and business associates, "clews" the *Picayune* and *Times-Democrat* failed to follow. They all recalled Charles to be "a law-abiding, quiet, industrious, peaceable man" (*MRNO,* 314).[169]

That the evidence in Charles's apartment yielded such disparate judgments about his life is, of course, Wells's point and recalls the lesson of *A Red Record*'s parody: the necessity to name empiricism's potential and limits as a truth-defining discourse. Given Wells's frankly expressed frustration with her own pamphlet's lack of resources, *Mob Rule*'s parody invites speculations concerning Wells's methods of work. What kind of serial might she have published with the resources enjoyed by the nation's major papers? Perhaps Wells and her team of stringers would have fanned out across the city tracing the swath of destruction cut by the posses searching for Charles. These mobs of white men and boys stormed through black neighborhoods harassing, beating, and killing scores of innocent men and women.[170] Wells might have followed a report on the dead, injured, or missing with another that related the experiences of survivors. Or, perhaps, she could have featured the story of Melby Dotson, whose waking dream is a case study in the psychology of terrorism. Soon after Charles's murder, Dotson was traveling by rail through Baton Rouge. He fell asleep and into a nightmare in which he was being lynched. As he struggled to free his neck from the mob's rope, Dotson cried out so loud that the conductor came to his aid. Awakening to find himself being grabbed and shouted at by a white man, Dotson shot and killed the conductor. Horrifically, Dotson's nightmare came true. Arrested for murder, he was kidnapped from his jail cell by a lynch mob and hung to death from a telephone pole.[171]

Wells did not write such a series, though. Without a newspaper staff to direct, the work could not be done. Given her decision to publish as a freelance pamphleteer, and because of the limited resources available for her work to survive in that medium, parody was an important tool for Wells's critique of lynching. But since the subtleties of her pamphlets also allowed readers to disavow what she would have them know about the violence, parody limited the range of social change her readers might undertake, beginning with the act of reading her work. "If the reader can do no more," she pleads at *Mob Rule*'s close, "he can pass this pamphlet onto another, or send to the bureau addresses of those to whom he can order copies mailed" (*MRNO,* 256).

Facing Facts

On January 1, 1902, Wells wrote a revealing letter to political activists in Chicago. As chair of the city's Afro-American League's Anti-Lynching Bureau, it was her job to sum up the year's work and to set the group's agenda for the term to come. As Wells viewed them, the bureau's prospects looked bleak. Not only had lynchings continued—135 were recorded by the *Chicago Tribune* in 1901—their severity remained horrific. Six people had been burned alive that year. What stirred Wells's worry most, though, was the public's indifference to this news. "Time was when the country resounded with denunciation and horror of burning a human being by so called Christian and civilized people," she reminded the League:

> The newspapers were full of it. The last time a human being was made fuel for flames it was scarcely noticed in the papers editorially. And *the chairman of your bureau finds it harder every year to get such matter printed. In other words, the need for agitation and*

publication of facts is greater than ever, while the avenues thro [sic] *which to make such publications have decreased.*[172]

The "time" Wells recalls so keenly was, most likely, those years when her first two pamphlets and British crusade transformed national debates and state policies about lynching. Those achievements, significant as they were, lasted less than a decade. If this lament to the Anti-Lynching Bureau sounds dispirited, that is because Wells's letter marks the end of her own political effectiveness.[173]

Critically, though, she links her waning authority to the problem of writing and publishing news without recourse to commercialized domains. By virtue of its massification, the nation's media effectively blocked "avenues" of discourse that "agitators" like Wells used to reform the public's common sense about lynching. This, after all, was why she went to such lengths to publish pamphlets. Each booklet invited readers to join an alternative economy that valued knowledge not as a market commodity but as a moral commitment to examine how newspapers defined what mattered as history. And yet, her report to the Anti-Lynching Bureau repeated the same hard fact she was forced to confess in her preface to *Mob Rule in New Orleans:* "Although the chairman [Wells] has determined to issue a periodical, there are absolutely no funds in the treasury to pay postage, much less the printer." Writing and publishing noncommercial journalism had become impossible for Wells to sustain economically. Worse was the prospect that, without her pamphlets, a mode of comprehending lynching's violence stood to be lost as well.

As experiments in narrative forms, Wells's pamphlets suggest that the textual effects of news-writing styles were as much the cause of racist reports about lynching as were the anti-black politics of any given journalist or newspaper.[174] In Wells's hands, the narrative structures and practices of the stunt, the empirical treatise, the wire report, and serial investigation vindicated the violence done to black people, because in each of those genres the threat of death authenticated what could be known as news at all. This presumption held true for both the mainstream and black press, so long as African American journalists relied uncritically on these same genres in the name of modernizing the profession. That news writing and news reading could engender such complicities with lynching's violence is unnerving, but it is the threat that each of Wells's pamphlets cautions against.

Parody spared Wells the cost of making this mistake. The self-reflexive critique characteristic of her pamphlets allowed her the necessary distance to recognize news writing's knowledge-shaping structures and, thus, to avoid compromising her political intentions as an anti-lynching activist. For that reason, "dynamitic" writing could not be abandoned as a means of struggle to end the practice of lynching. The mob murders of African American people had to be checked as a problem not simply of wrong, racist action but of misformed cognition and thought, a point Wells underscored in her letter to the Anti-Lynching Bureau: "We can only change public sentiment and enforce laws by educating the people, giving them the facts."

The facts of modernity taught Ida B. Wells what she needed to know about lynching and American journalism both, given her life stories in Memphis, New York, London, and Chicago. Her desire to be a new kind of black woman—stirred by her appetites for material pleasure, comfort, and delight; driven by her intellectual ambitions; devoted to spiritual reflection and commitment—led her to encounter the contradictions of modern freedom in the most profound ways. To be able to love as one chose (or not); to pursue a vocation that suited one's interests and skills best without regard for tradition's demands; to cultivate the impossible-to-predict needs that turn individual decisions into the collective actions of history—the trajectory that led Wells to her career in journalism primed her understanding that freedom and desire were, alone and together, two of the most radicalizing forces in American politics at the end of the nineteenth century.

Indeed, as the most intimate conduit of knowledge, desire was one of the most unregulated realms of experience anyone could inhabit. All kinds of unprecedented developments—both good and bad—could follow from the actions of fully free people, as African American and feminist histories about Wells's time make clear. For this reason, the personal liberties claimed by New Negroes and New Women were no less important to the secularization of American life than the increased authority accorded to science and technology, economics and the market, politics and the art of governance. And as Wells's literary career attests, newspapers were vital to this revolution because they opened new worlds for black and female readers to join and belong. Unsettling the traditional prerogatives of white men's social authority so thoroughly, these changes helped spur the revival of the "ancient" rite of lynching. Returning to the traditions of the past, white men believed killing black people would safeguard them against the threats that racial and gender emancipation might bring.

However, with their all-too-frequent participation in and defense of lynching's violence, white women chose more often than not to buy into the riches of unfreedom.[175] And, by 1902, black people had turned a tin ear to Wells's voice, judging from her second complaint to the Anti-Lynching Bureau:

> Nowhere does [an] apathetic condition prevail to a greater extent than within the membership of the Anti-Lynching Bureau. When the Bureau was first organized three years ago, it was thought that every man, woman, and child who had a drop of Negro blood in his veins and every person else who wanted to see mob law put down would gladly contribute 25 cents per year to this end. There were upwards of 300 responses to the first appeal, [but] less than 50 per cent renewed at the end of that year.

Wells's frustration is explicable; beneath it lie chagrin and embarrassment too. Why would African Americans not contribute to a cause meant to protect and save their lives? However, Wells's tally of the bureau's ledgers underestimated the power of her critique's scope. Because if she was right—if black life was so precariously dependent on the fears of white women as well as the anxiety-ridden animus of white men; if the common sense of white people could not conceive that the mob murders of black people were unjust and needed to be stopped—then black people were not (and, maybe worse, could not be) free, and their efforts to inform themselves about the nation's news implicated them in the violence that threatened them on so many sides. Indeed, it must have been daunting for Wells's African American readers to absorb her message. Perhaps the Anti-Lynching Bureau's membership rolls and publication funds plummeted so low by 1902 because the truth about lynching as Wells knew it was more than sobering. It was traumatizing.

And yet, much of what we now routinely claim to know about lynching is due to Wells.[176] Her empirical refutation of the rape myth—popularized by *A Red Record*—has never been disputed since 1895. And so many of the NAACP's anti-lynching tactics were indebted to Wells, from its near single-minded focus on the violence until the 1940s, its publication of pamphlet-exposés, its use of private undercover detectives to investigate lynching murders, to its organization of women members into "anti-lynching crusades."[177]

If, with the passing of time, Wells's protest tactics became political common sense, that may be because her sense of history's unfolding at the turn of the nineteenth century was so acute—perhaps more acute—than her contemporaries could stand. Every pamphlet Wells published was written in the wake of lynch murder(s); worse yet, and despite her efforts, black Americans remained at risk. But the prospects of changing how the nation regarded those losses and threats—the chance to teach people to read news as history they could remake to "deal justly with any man or cause" (*MRNO,* 309)—gave Wells reason to write. Without a renewed conception of the world that allowed such violence to occur, all the facts she could gather would not save anyone from the politically desolate future that lynching foretold.

THREE

"The Drift of the Public Mind": Stephen Crane

It is easy for men to discount and misunderstand the suffering or harm done to others. Once accustomed to poverty, to the sight of toil and degradation, it easily seems normal and natural; once it is hidden beneath a different color of skin, a different stature or a different habit of action and speech, all consciousness of inflicting ill disappears.

W. E. B. DU BOIS, *BLACK RECONSTRUCTION IN AMERICA, 1860–1880*

Forgetting is not secondary; it is not an improvised failing of what has first been constituted as memory. Forgetfulness is a practice.

MAURICE BLANCHOT, *THE WRITING OF DISASTER*

The charge was the usual one, but the circumstances were, by all accounts of those who witnessed and reported the event, bizarre. Robert Lewis, the African American coachman at the Delaware House hotel in Port Jervis, New York, was accused of raping a white woman, twenty-year-old Lena McMahon. According to witnesses, this assault occurred outdoors, at the noon hour, on June 2, 1892, atop a grassy knoll overlooking the Neversink River. A group of "colored boys" were fishing at the water's edge and a group of "several young girls"—white—were eating lunch beneath a tree when "a mulatto about 5 feet, 7 inches high and weighing about 170 pounds, put in an appearance and brutally outraged [McMahon] in sight of the girls and colored boys before mentioned," a local paper reported.[1]

A posse rallied together quickly to capture Lewis, who fled north toward the town of Hugenot, where he was caught trying to cross the Delaware Canal. News of his alleged crime and capture raced by telegraph and telephone lines between Port Jervis and Otisville, so that by the time the posse returned to deliver Lewis to the police stationed at the Port Jervis jail, a crowd of five hundred filled the width of Ball Street and soon seized Lewis, who "was nearly frightened to death and trembled like a leaf all the way into town."[2]

Lewis was right to be terrified because once the wagon stopped his life came to a prolonged, brutal end. Dragged through the town at the end of a rope fastened around his neck, Lewis was beaten and kicked by mob members so severely that "the man was practically dead before he was hung upon the tree." According to the *Richmond Planet,* "the scene was appalling beyond description. The yells of the man could be heard for blocks and his distorted and agonized features could be plainly seen under the glare of a neighing [*sic*] electric light."[3] At the sturdily limbed maple tree that marked the intersection of Sussex and Main Streets, Lewis's sufferings only increased. Before the Baptist Church and across the street from the home of Orange County jurist William Howe Crane, Lewis was hung not once but twice. Since the mob's leaders failed to knot the rope precisely enough, Lewis was strangling slowly to death, so he was lowered to the ground in order to adjust the noose. He was then pulled up towards the tallest branches of the tree, where he was left for more than an hour.[4] Two thousand residents watched Lewis die this way, braving a "severe storm with thunder and lightning" that broke out that night. "So great was their [the mob's] desire to avenge the assault on the young woman" that "nobody, not even the women, cared" that the weather had turned foul, the *New York World* reported.[5]

What made the murder of Robert Lewis one of the most vexing lynchings of the 1890s was, partly, its locale. Situated at the conjunction of three northeastern states (New York, New Jersey, and Pennsylvania), Port Jervis enjoyed unprecedented levels of prosperity during the post-Civil War years, making it doubly unlikely for a lynching murder to occur there. Moreover, the town was not vexed by "battle fatigue" or the "romance of reunion," two other cultural tensions historians sometime point toward to explain lynching's violence. Though Port Jervis lost its share of men in the Civil War, the townsfolk did not "wave the bloody flag" (as the saying went) either decrying or embracing black emancipation as the war's outcome. Nor did the town pledge its allegiance to the idea of federalism by demonizing African Americans as unruly enemies of the nation-state.[6]

For these reasons, the town's spot on the national map is infamous since it was one of the twelve sites where lynching murders occurred in the North before World War I.[7] At the time of Lewis's murder, however, the press paid curious attention to this point. The rarity of the case and the town's proximity to New York City prompted the metropolitan newspapers in Manhattan to take front-page notice, but leading papers in the southern and African American press barely mentioned the event. For the *Atlanta Constitution,* Lewis's alleged crime could have been hyped as proof that the rape charge was no myth and was likely to thrive in the more racially tolerant North, but the paper did not openly gloat over this case. Instead, the editors opted to run a single digest of "Northern and Southern Comment," all of which concurred with the *Philadelphia Press*'s lament: "it is useless to denounce such violence in the South if it is to be encouraged in the North."[8] For the black press, Lewis's murder proved that lynching had no regional bounds and was indeed a national threat to all black Americans. However, two renowned papers, the *Richmond Planet* and *Indianapolis Freeman,* relied on the one "special" wire report that they each published a month after the murder.[9] If this paucity of comment is remarkable, the meager coverage of Lewis's murder becomes clear when we consider the most unusual development that occurred during the lynching.

Before he was killed, Lewis made a startling accusation to his captors. Lena McMahon's suitor, a white man named Peter Foley, "set him up" to rape the woman.[10] Just as stunning is that Lewis's confession was widely believed to be true. "The general regret" that pervaded Port Jervis following the lynching only deepened once news of Lewis's confession elicited more details about Foley's suspicious role in the alleged rape. "If many of the mob who lynched Lewis could have had their way Foley would have been hanged, for the general opinion seems to be that he [Foley] was responsible for the negro's assault on Miss McMahon," a local paper concluded.[11] "Thursday June 2d marks one of the most disgraceful scenes that was ever enacted in Port Jervis, if not in Orange County," the *Port Jervis Evening Gazette* bemoaned and "greatly lament[ed]" the mob's "crime" as much as "that of the wretch who fell victim to the fury of the populace."[12] The *Port Jervis Union* sounded deeply contrite in its editorial, expressing despair over the mob's violence rather than outrage at the seriousness of Robert Lewis's alleged crime. "The magnitude of this disgrace is keenly felt. We mourn like a stricken household," the *Union* declared. Hoping for reconciliation, the paper asked the nation's forgiveness, assuring America that the townsfolk would "purify ourselves as if by fire."[13] Putting a blunter point on the town's *mea culpas,* the father of Lena McMahon declared Foley's guilt in these unsparing terms: "He is the nigger that ought to have been hung!"[14]

That the people of Port Jervis came to accept Robert Lewis's explanation hardly warrants our acclaim; his brutal beating and murder at the hands of the mob were not a slate one could wipe clean. Nonetheless, it is significant that the town's animus shifted away from Lewis and toward Foley; as Ida B. Wells argued so forcefully in her pamphlet *Southern Horrors* (*SH,* see chapter 2) the charges of rape levied against black men were deemed to be self-evident and always true. "This cry has had its effects," she wrote in her first pamphlet. "It has closed the heart, stifled the conscience, warped the judgment and hushed the voice of the press and pulpit on the subject of lynch law throughout this 'land of liberty'" (*SH,* 30). In Port Jervis, however, a black suspect's testimony led to a coroner's inquest and laid the groundwork for McMahon's family to bring criminal charges against Foley for his role in the alleged rape.[15]

For a black man to accuse a white man of perfidy in a case of sexual assault and to have his claim taken seriously was a remarkable event in the annals of lynching's history at the turn of the nineteenth century. Still, Wells was not impressed by this development. More questions were raised at the coroner's inquest than were answered, and Peter Foley was found not guilty in the larceny trial brought against him. For these reasons, Wells exhorted African Americans to fund one of its own newspapers to investigate the case more thoroughly:

> At the preliminary examination, it developed that [Peter Foley] had been a suitor of the girl's. She had repulsed and refused him, yet had given him money and he had sent threatening letters demanding more.
>
> . . . Why should she yield to his demands for money if not to prevent him from exposing something he knew? It seems explainable only on the hypothesis that a *liaison* existed between the colored boy and the white girl, and the white man knew of it. The press is singularly silent. Has it a motive? We owe it to ourselves to find out. (*SH,* 43)

Remarkably, though, Wells misjudged the "motives" at issue in this case. First, the news coverage in Port Jervis did not try to conceal the probability that a consensual liaison precipitated the entire cycle of violence, from the alleged rape of Lena McMahon to the lynching of Robert Lewis. Where the New York City dailies covering the case (the *World, Tribune,* and *Times*) remained comparatively "silent" on this issue, the weekly papers in Port Jervis actively questioned the sexual relations that may have led Foley, McMahon, and Lewis into contact with one another.[16]

Resisting the "frenzy of the moment" that Wells decried in the New Orleans media coverage of Robert Charles's murder, the press corps in Port Jervis maintained the social composure she believed professional journalists owed the public when reporting cases of lynching. Only the first news report (published immediately after the alleged assault and lynching) referred to Robert Lewis in derogatory terms, with two sparingly used epithets: the rape was "fiendish" and Lewis was a "brute."[17]

In keeping with her own interests in the sexual politics of lynching and the press's strategies of structuring the public's common sense about the violence, Wells presumed that the love triangle in question involved a heterosexual relationship between Robert Lewis and Lena McMahon, with Peter Foley figuring as the jealous rival. Instead, Lewis's confession implied a more devastating—and modern—transgression, for the most illicit consensual arrangement of all was the interracial homosocial alliance between himself and Foley. As the *New York World* surmised, "The lynching of the negro Bob Lewis, which took place here nearly two weeks ago, is producing new and unsuspected features as the story is being investigated by authorities with a view to what was underneath."[18] Indeed, what could have inspired Foley to ask or otherwise encourage Lewis to rape Lena McMahon? What conflict could there have been between them for Foley to have felt that McMahon merited such punishment? Why would Lewis have served Foley's goals: was the black man so devoid of autonomy, agency, and morality that he could not refuse Foley's proposal? What were the reasons for and terms of the agreement between these two men? What kind of trust and shared interests existed between them to conclude such a deal?

Sociologists like Georg Simmel and Gustave Le Bon were concerned with the life choices people made in the rapidly changing contexts of "crowded" living at the turn of the nineteenth century; and as historian Lisa Duggan reminds us, late-nineteenth-century American psychiatry was "obsessed" with studying situations and events in which individuals lost or ceded self-control and will power to others.[19] We could certainly investigate what lay "underneath" the compact between Foley and Lewis (together with the mob's violence) in either of those discipline's terms. The intimacies presumed by the men's plan (as well as the acts of violence done to Lewis in the course of the lynching murder) also suggest we could look beneath their agreement to trace how this instance of violence intersected with the pivotal development that defined sexology as a modern science, the designation of homosexuality as a new social identity.[20] However, I choose to map the subterranean forces that drove the violence in Port Jervis as a problem about money, or, more precisely, about the meanings of money in the market society of late-nineteenth-century America. This approach emerges from the most acutely observed and discerning account of Lewis's murder—namely, Stephen Crane's novella *The Monster.*

The Art of Fiction and the History of an Event

A more unlikely writer could not have responded to Ida B. Wells's call to investigate the murder of Robert Lewis, but Stephen Crane had his own reasons for publishing *The Monster.* In 1897—five years after the murder had occurred—Crane was desperate to sell a story lucrative enough to fend off creditors who were ready to force him into bankruptcy.[21] However, once the proceeds from the novella were banked and distributed to pay his debts, Crane faced the ire of his hometown community in Port Jervis, who felt he had betrayed their long-standing trust by disclosing the shameful event of Robert Lewis's murder to public scrutiny once again.[22] Remote but prosperous, small-sized but grand-minded in its aspirations for urbanity and sophistication, the fictional setting of *The Monster* resembles Port Jervis so closely that when the novella was first published in 1898, Crane's fans in upstate New York no doubt knew that "Whilomville" was not just any American town. Crane had trained his spotlight onto their world and most shameful moment, something that the town's residents did not want to be revealed to the nation in the pages of a renowned magazine.[23]

A haunting tale about the limited capacities of money to correct moral debts and fulfill ethical obligations; a gripping account of the tyrannies of mob rule and the necessity of individual courage when tested, literally, under fire—Crane's novella draws explicitly from the public record of Robert Lewis's lynching murder for the details of its plot but leaves out its telltale sign: there is no lynching as such in *The Monster.* Henry Johnson, the black servant to the white Trescotts, is horribly burned and disfigured while trying to rescue his employer's son from a blaze that engulfs the family's home. The story details the aftermath of this tragedy as young Jimmie's father and the residents of Whilomville debate whether and how to care for the injured man. Through Crane's storytelling, the deliberate murder of Robert Lewis becomes a disabling injury that accidentally befalls Henry Johnson; in fiction the black man survives his ordeal whereas, as an historical event, Robert Lewis died a brutal, ignoble death. Why, then, did the residents of Port Jervis find *The Monster* to be such an outrage? Why, to put the point more directly, did the reading public of Port Jervis accord fiction the power to hold it accountable for Robert Lewis's murder in 1892?

Whether anyone else ever discerned the novella's source or not, *The Monster* would link Port Jervis to the lynching of Robert Lewis in perpetuity, asserting the town's complicities with (if not responsibility for) the violence time and again through the kind of renewable knowledge that literature provides. Unlike the substantive but evanescent comprehension that newspapers produce as common sense, literature constitutes knowledge differently because, first, the text persists in the world as a physical, material artifact—we do not tend to discard or destroy books the way we dispose of newspapers. Second, literature is not a thing but, rather, an idea that readers strive to understand though can only possess incompletely, because literature is, in its aims and at its end, speculative. Yet readers since the novella's publication have avoided exploring *The Monster*'s possible connections to lynching, ostensibly because there is no lynching *per se* in the text.[24] Nonetheless, there is no reason why readers could not imagine Henry Johnson's plight to be implicated with lynching's history in American life at the turn of the nineteenth century. After all, African American victims of mob violence were often maligned and dehumanized by the epithet that is the novella's title: black men, more than any other social group during the 1890s, were demeaned as "monsters" to be burned to death for their criminal deeds against white people. Indeed, by the time *The Monster* first appeared in the August 1898 issue of *Harper's Magazine,* the Wilmington, North Carolina, race riot had introduced the incubus as the newest icon demonizing black masculinity, while the burning of Sam Hose in April 1899 followed the book publication of Crane's late masterwork by just two months. Indeed, any of the 1,134 lynchings reported between 1882 and 1899 might have prompted readers to think of anti-black mob violence as the historicist context for *The Monster*'s fictive concerns.[25] That critical connection was never made in Stephen Crane's time, however, nor would it be for more than a century.[26]

Lynching: An Embarassment of Riches

This contest over the right to know the history of Robert Lewis's murder certainly vexed the relationship between Stephen Crane and Port Jervis; as we will see, Crane paid a steep price for exploiting the literary value of this event against the town's expectation of a native son's loyalty and trust. However, it is precisely this clash of values among the moral, market, and narrative economies shaping the worlds of Stephen Crane and Port Jervis that links the murder of Robert Lewis (and those like it) to a broader set of cultural formations than, *prima facie,* the lynching seems to suggest. I intend in this chapter to ask how Stephen Crane's disputes with his creditors, publishers, and hometown led him to write *The Monster* when he did and as he did. This requires exploring the intricate relations between lynching and money, writing and money, lynching and writing, and writing and history, with the aim of explaining how they networked into a set of cultural practices that legitimized lynching's violence in late-nineteenth-century America.

The chapter begins this exploration by linking the murder of Robert Lewis to the anxieties gripping not just Port Jervis, but all of America as the nation made its epochal transition into corporate-monopoly capitalism. Port Jervis harbored grand ambitions to join this economic movement, but the lynching of Robert Lewis threw that plan into crisis because the violence brought forward the anxieties and incapacities endemic to this new order of living. The worry over losing independence to remote and distant centers of power; the fear of being divided against one's neighbor in the competition for scarcer resources; the mistrust of the enlarged systems of governance required to make this new social engine run—these, I argue, were the unvoiced tensions lurking beneath the surface of Port Jervis's monied calm, and they erupted fiercely in the manner that Lewis was put to death. Thus, this chapter evaluates how lynching fit into and made sense within the idea of value promoted by the economy of corporate-monopoly capitalism.

Because Stephen Crane encountered this lynching directly, the chapter focuses on his response in two ways. Crane was deeply affected by the murder of Robert Lewis and frequently referenced the event in his earliest writings, his news dispatches from New Jersey's Asbury Park, and his famous "Tenderloin Sketches" of the Lower East Side in Manhattan. Surveying these works of journalism, I argue that Crane's long-standing interest in depicting scenes of urban indifference to human suffering can be traced back to the murder of Robert Lewis in Port Jervis. Thus, I contend, Crane's initial forays into writing realism (along with the signature tropes that critics have come to associate with his aesthetics) were importantly influenced by the violence of lynching. These early writings contain within them their own crisis of meaning, however, because the murder consistently appears and disappears in these writings as the event to which the stories refer but do not depend on to produce a sense of narrative completion. These textual effacements of Lewis's death are important to mark not only because the stories based on it were meant for public consumption as "news." These sketches are, in fact, models of disavowal that archive the will of white readers (and the means at their disposal) to remain insensible about lynching's impact on the course of their lives.

Written and published seven years after the murder of Robert Lewis, *The Monster* refines this practice of indifference into a more fully realized politics, the better for Crane to historicize how, at the end of the nineteenth century, the apathy of northern whites like himself was as crucial to lynching's persistence as southern whites' long-noted antipathy toward African Americans. Turning to his unpublished contracts and private communiqués, I explore how his own financial binds led Crane to produce *The Monster* as a particularly marketable story. The publishing process and aesthetic premises of realist fiction allowed him to remake Robert Lewis's lynching into an event without a past and a commodity to be traded at will. These same archival sources show, however, that this was a vexing power for Crane to exercise because of his own exploitation by this very same system. Unraveling the complicated identifications that Crane asserted to exist between himself and black sharecroppers (but not Robert Lewis), I argue that as both a narrative and literary artifact, *The Monster* reveals to us how corporate-monopoly capitalism sanctioned white Americans' indifference to the mortal violence done to black people in the name of making large-scale systems—be they cities and towns, states and nations, economies and markets, or even novellas and novels—run.

Indeed, deploying realism's craft the way that Port Jervis hoped its post-lynching inquests would divert further interest in Robert Lewis's murder, *The Monster* labors methodically to commit its black protagonist to a textual death that releases us from thinking about how, over the course of the story, we are led to care less about Henry Johnson's fate. Thus, the second half of the chapter considers what this "drift of the public's mind" in the narrative implies for lynching's cultural logic in society.[27] As I read the novella, *The Monster* narrates the violence done to Henry Johnson as an accidental injury and then plots the black man's recovery in such a way as to devalue it against the greater narrative emphasis paid to Johnson's white protector, Doctor Ned Trescott. Whether Crane cared more (or less) about Robert Lewis we can only know through the best evidence *The Monster* provides—the novella's transfiguration of the lynching as the burning away of Henry Johnson's face. That moment, steeped in the history of Lewis's murder, all but dares the reader to think of the scene as anything but a trope for the necessary effacements produced by fiction writing. And yet, the brilliance of what we now know to be Crane's slip of memory tells us this and something more. Because the accident of Johnson's burning involves an exquisite eruption of "description" as Roland Barthes defines that term—the irreducible sign of the "real" in realist fiction—I end the chapter by studying this scene, and asking why Crane's depiction of the lynching brings us closer to understanding Robert Lewis's death by, paradoxically, distancing us from the actual historical event. For that reason, I conclude, Crane's elision of the murder is not just a bad, flawed, or "racist" choice, because the novella predicts the history of the future of lynching's cultural logic all too well. The novella's literary history archives how easily it was then, has been, and continues to be for white Americans to remember to forget the violence done to black people in the name of progress and achievement.

A Tale of Two Cities: Port Jervis, New York

A "well-built" town with "broad streets, fine sidewalks, trolley cars, electric lights, telephones connecting it with all the surrounding county, and all the other modern conveniences," Port Jervis, New York was a place where fortunes and ambitions knew no limits at the turn of the nineteenth century.[28] Located at the juncture of New York, New Jersey, and Pennsylvania, the town could afford to build its infrastructure using the newest modern technologies because it was a "busy center of population and industry" (PJ, 1). Its residents worked at well-paying jobs in some eighty-two factories. Unlike southern towns of comparable size, the industries of Port Jervis manufactured finished rather than raw products, which diversified the town's economy and strengthened it (though not perfectly) against the market fluctuations that made agrarian-based, single-crop economies so precarious during the 1890s and 1900s.[29] Another foundation lending support to Port Jervis's wealth was its transportation systems. The Erie Railroad and the Delaware and Hudson Canal paid out over $1 million in wages to laborers who routed shipments of luxury goods (glass, silver plating, silk, gloves, shoes, and shirts) and anthracite coal out of the Pennsylvania mines to New York City, Trenton, Boston, and Chicago. Instead of uprooting the town's economic networks (which often took place in the wake of railroad development in piedmont counties of the South), the Erie line consolidated Port Jervis's wealth. The constant circulation of goods and payments kept dollars flowing into the registers of local stores, businesses, and banks, infusing the town with an "air of prosperity" (PJ, 1–2) that it maintained from the end of the nineteenth century through the first two decades of the twentieth.[30]

Those who breathed easiest in this monied atmosphere were the elites of Port Jervis's industrial class (the owners and managers of its factories, railroad, and canal); its entrepreneurial-proprietor class (restaurateurs, hoteliers, and landlords of rental homes and real estate); and its resident professional class (physicians, lawyers, bankers, ministers, and journalists). Where the Bourbon elites of the New South were, according to C. Vann Woodward, "intellectually malnourished" since they devoted themselves so wholly to "material achievement" in order to match and surpass "the standard of competition set by their Northern counterparts," the patriarchs of Port Jervis welcomed and embraced metropolitan culture, arranging for it to be delivered upstate.[31] They hired architects from New York City to design and build their homes. Their children attended public schools whose curricula were "fully abreast of the times" (PJ, 9). Well-stocked with books and magazines, its free library was so heavily used by town residents that it was quickly approved for building funds from Andrew Carnegie's national program of library construction at the start of the twentieth century.[32] Three opera houses served as year-round venues for traveling theatrical troupes that "furnish[ed] a high order of drama and spectacles" for the town (PJ, 10). D. W. Griffith shot his early Biograph films nearby.[33] The white working class settled everywhere around the elites' enclave on East and West Main Streets, while one hundred or so African Americans resided in the southernmost section of town, near "the old hills."[34] Looking through a lens of optimism, the businessmen who profiled the town's growth boasted: "It is well not to be misled by the name 'village' to infer that Port Jervis is a mere country hamlet" (PJ, 1–2). Instead, these boosters explained, the town should be regarded as a citadel of national culture:

> The social life of the town is animated by the best spirit of progressive American life. The culture and art of refined leisure, and broad, intelligent acquaintance with the world are not wanting; graduates of leading universities and thoroughly trained professional men maintain the intellectual tone, and the progress of wealth and elegance adds those touches and amenities of splendid luxury which give zest and life to so many social movements. (PJ, 18)

A "country town" that saw itself evolving into a "thriving city," Port Jervis was a place in transition. Moving from one ideal of communal life to another, one social system to another, one political status to another, one cultural outlook to another—Port Jervis was (in the opinion of its business elites), on the brink of great change. Indeed, because of its prosperity, the town's entry into "progressive American life" poised it to experience what Alan Trachtenberg calls "the incorporation of America," the "traumatic," "wrenching" shifts "regarding the meaning of prevalent ideas, . . . regarding the identity of the individual, the relation between public and private realms, and the character to the nation."[35]

Shepherding a community through this transformation perhaps struck Reverend Jonathan Townley Crane as a ministerial challenge when, in the spring of 1878, he was assigned to serve as pastor of the Drew Methodist Church in Port Jervis. A studious cleric who used his pulpit to denounce the dangers of "popular amusements" that the wage-earning classes enjoyed during their leisure time—alcohol, gambling, and prostitution filtered through some eighty saloons—Reverend Crane found an active field of work in this "zesty" town.[36] Stephen Crane was seven years old when his father relocated the family to upstate New York, but they all moved away when, in 1880, Reverend Crane died unexpectedly. Though Mary Crane eventually chose Asbury Park, New Jersey as the family's permanent home, Stephen did not forsake his connections to Port Jervis. He visited the town frequently between 1883 and 1896 because his oldest brother remained there during the town's boom years.[37] Stephen's sojourns back and William's choice to stay are worth examining because the brothers' perceptions of the town's wealth help pinpoint why such an "enlightened, moral, intelligent, and progressive community" (PJ, 1) erupted so furiously in the summer of 1892, its "trained professional men" and sturdy working class killing Robert Lewis in a nearly unfathomable brutal way.

A lawyer by training, William Howe Crane made a strategic choice when he decided not to accompany his mother and siblings to New Jersey.[38] The high-finance but seasonal economy of a resort town like Asbury Park probably seemed impenetrable to an outsider like William, especially when Port Jervis was open to him as a "desirable place for profitable permanent investment of capital" (PJ, 2).[39] Seizing every opportunity, William insinuated himself into the businesses and bureaucracies that made Port Jervis prosper. A commanding lecturer at the Young Men's Literary Society, a venerable member of the county bar association, a popularly elected jurist to the county court, a policy-eager member of the school district and Free Library, William enjoyed a wide scope of political power upstate.[40] Perhaps the most telling example of William's identification with modern corporate-monopoly capitalism was his bold plan to establish the Hartwood Club, an exclusive hunting lodge and preserve located in the woods of Sullivan County.

Putting his legal skills and political contacts to efficient use, he organized a group of family and friends to purchase a tract of land to found the retreat. To that initial parcel, William added more lots by arranging the purchase of acreage from families who had fallen behind on their tax payments. By the time the Hartwood Park Association applied to be incorporated in 1893, William in four years' time had amassed more than five thousand acres of land for the club's use. To make the enterprise truly cost efficient, William took advantage of New York State's newly enacted statutes that exempted nonprofit syndicates from property taxes.[41] Creating the Hartwood Club as a social and financial shelter for himself and his family and friends, William skillfully managed his wealth as the nation's corporate-monopoly capitalist economy allowed, thereby sparing himself the worry that big city opportunities were passing him by.[42]

For William Crane, Port Jervis stoked his ambitions to be a self-made man of the coming century. For his brother Stephen, the town was his special refuge when the pressures of monied life in New York City and the Jersey Shore became too much for him to bear. The diversions that drew crowds by the tens of thousands to Asbury Park—the ocean, boardwalk, and beaches; the vendors, games, and contests; the concerts, parades, and revivals—left Crane longing for the primeval outdoors where he could lead the "strenuous life" Teddy Roosevelt urged young, virile white men to pursue at the nineteenth century's end. This need became particularly urgent once Stephen published *The Red Badge of Courage* in 1895 and was overwhelmed by the public's interest in him.[43] Rather than embrace his novel's success and the celebrity status Manhattan wanted to give him, Crane fled from both back to Port Jervis. "I couldn't breathe in that accursed tumult," he complained to one friend. In the woods of Sullivan County and William's Hartwood Club there were trails to ride horseback, lakes to fish, and forest groves to hunt, and Crane returned home throughout the year for extended visits, usually in late summer and early fall.[44] Preferring upstate New York's natural beauty to public fame, Stephen rejected the kind of authority that William labored so diligently to accrue.

It meant a great deal to the people of Port Jervis that Stephen spent his early boyhood as their neighbor and, as he grew famous, not only maintained his ties to the community but, more flattering, found Port Jervis inspiring for his literary work. For instance, the town took great pride in *The Red Badge of Courage* because Stephen, in the course of gathering source material, interviewed local veterans of the Orange County Blossoms brigade who had fought at Chancellorsville.[45] But his earlier work had impressed them as much. The "Sullivan County Tales" (1892)—a series of comic short stories based on his adventures with local friends in the nearby woods and lakes—was Stephen's first success in writing fiction.[46] An early satire of small-town American journalism, "The Pike County Puzzle" (1894) did not irk local journalists as it could have; they, in fact, praised Stephen's "satiric genius" and contributed to the project by letting Crane use the printing press of the *Port Jervis Union* to perfect the "Puzzle's" conceit of being an actual newspaper.[47] In a show of remarkable solidarity, Port Jervis extended its resources and moral support to Stephen again when he used the pages of the *Evening Gazette* to criticize Theodore Roosevelt (then police commissioner of New York City) for leading the purge of prostitutes from Manhattan's so-called Tenderloin district.[48] For the son of a Methodist minister and an evangelical temperance activist to crusade on behalf of urban sex workers was a daring stand for Stephen to take in 1896; for a small town in upstate New York to endorse such a protest was not shocking so much as revelatory of how deeply entwined both Stephen and Port Jervis remained with older ideas of an "incorporated" community at the start of the twentieth century.

The refuge Stephen found in Port Jervis was not, however, how William perceived the town's value. For the elder brother, Port Jervis served as a modern corporate trust, a shield behind which he could amass and control his wealth without outside scrutiny.[49] Between Stephen and the town, the antebellum idea of trust—the close-knit intimacies of scaled-down, person-to-person interactions based on loyalty and reciprocity—kept them in balanced touch with each other.[50] The different character of the brothers' alliances to their hometown becomes clear in light of Stephen's dealings with William during his trips to Port Jervis. The eldest brother always hosted the younger when he arrived each summer, letting Stephen board at his family's home; for his part, and as his star rose in national literary circles, Stephen made sure to invite William to attend celebrity events with him.[51] Though Stephen never paid for his brother's hospitality, he did not hesitate to ask William for money—especially after he moved to New York City and was struggling to earn his living as a writer. Embodied in the person of brother, Port Jervis was another source of trust to Stephen—a trust fund—full with capital ready for his asking. But while William's wealth prompted Stephen to ask for financial aid when pressed by his debts, William understood those requests as business deals. The money was never a gift but always a loan Stephen was liable to repay.[52]

The brothers' competing notions of wealth, care, and debt help explain the divided temper of Port Jervis itself, and why the town's economic ambitions made the lynching of Robert Lewis possible. By its own measures, Port Jervis thrived like a central city, "animated . . . by the best spirit of progressive American life" (PJ, 18). However, given its slow-growing population (nine thousand in 1890; eleven thousand in 1900) and geographic locale in rural upstate New York, Port Jervis was only a town, and no amount of self-congratulatory boosting could change that demographic fact.[53] Though the town categorically fit historian Robert Wiebe's description of "island communities" (one of the thousands of small, self-sustaining towns tucked away in America's hinterlands at the end of the nineteenth century), Port Jervis fed on the energies that animated the larger metropolitan world.[54] Facilitated by its robust economy, the town continued "steadily moving forward with the general advance of the country" (PJ, 11).[55] Confronted with the conflicts any diverse community might face in its daily life, Port Jervis did not need to be officially recognized as a city to believe it was one. As cultural historian Richard Ohmann explains, since "the city was the main locus of production and power" in late-nineteenth-century national life, "the idea of urbanity figured centrally in people's understanding of what their world had become."[56] But Port Jervis's self-understanding was split between two models of thinking about social relations and obligations (to recall Thomas Haskell's theory of American economic history), for which the lives of Stephen and William can serve as standards for measure.[57]

On one scale, the town's standard of living implied a strong embrace of William's ethos. With the business elites championing industrial development financed by the pursuit of investment capital and robust consumer consumption, the town's middle and working classes contributed their fair share of support by their labor and by spending their wages throughout the town and region. Since what was good for the market was good for the polis, too, the town's business leaders marveled that "the same methods and principles which have given success to . . . the energetic merchants" were also used by the town council, which worked with "great efficiency [typical of] corporate management" (PJ, 16). Gauged by Stephen's relation to the town, however, "great efficiency" compromised the town's traditional models of incorporated community, wherein economic development was fostered through culturally bound, locally determined ties of intimacy, dependency, reciprocity, and emotional trust.

Put another way, the moral economy of Port Jervis was at odds with its fiscal culture. The spirit of capitalism embodied by Stephen and William reflected the same faith but different denominations: the younger's commitment to personal loyalty and craft-oriented, subsistence-level wealth harkened back to the culture of mercantile-entrepreneurial capitalism of the pre-Civil War nineteenth century, while the elder's zeal for acquiring capital and managing institutional bureaucracies embraced the styles of late-nineteenth-century, corporate-monopoly capitalism. This tension between the Cranes' worldviews was an earlier version of the crisis Rebecca Latimer Felton decried in her fiery 1897 speech "Woman on the Farm," for she predicted that violent havoc would follow from rural Georgia's expanding interest in corporate-financed agribusiness. Specifically, she warned—and, indeed, threatened with great malevolence—that lynchings would proceed unchecked ("a thousand a week if necessary") if white men abandoned their home farms to cut deals with venture capitalists.[58] It is neither eerie nor uncanny that Felton's prediction of events in Georgia would have earlier erupted in New York. For as the differences between the Crane brothers and the murder of Robert Lewis make clear, the development of corporate-monopoly capitalism in the town had not reconciled the contradictions between the old and new economies. It made utter sense that in 1892, at the height of Port Jervis's prosperity and in the course of its "progressive" stride forward into the twentieth century, Robert Lewis was brutally murdered for the very reasons that Stephen and William Crane found the town to be such a congenial retreat.

The Rage of Indifference: Understanding the Lynching of Robert Lewis

As I discussed in chapter 1, the boom–bust cycles that made the 1870s, 1880s, and 1890s tumultuous but flush years for the growth of corporate-monopoly capital also created conditions of grinding poverty and pervasive violence across the nation, especially in the South. Because urbanization and industrialization there depended on outside capital and federal regulation (particularly in the forms of construction bonds, venture finance, coinage policy, and favorable tariff rates), the region functioned as a colony of corporate-monopoly capital, a power-driven relation that often erupted with the lynching murders of African Americans. Unlike southerners, who believed the region had been forced into a way of life it did not want—who, as I argue in chapter 2, believed that the region had been raped by the penetration of corporate-monopoly capital into their home economies—Port Jervis enjoyed unprecedented prosperity because of the market's new forms. In its efforts to position itself as a hub of regional economic development, Port Jervis was like those economies Martin J. Sklar describes in *The Corporate Reconstruction of American Capitalism,* a juncture where "big city" metropolitan money was strategically allied with "smaller hinterland capital" to build market conduits that served the interests of the ruling elites in both realms.[59] Though the town's market economy was not at all on par with its principal trading partners, it still did not resemble Newnan, Georgia's, where Sam Hose and the Palmetto Nine were murdered by mobs in 1899; or Coatesville, Pennsylvania's, where Zachariah Walker was burned to death in 1912; or Marietta, Georgia's, where Leo Frank was lynched in 1915. In Port Jervis capital investment was not perceived to have come from afar or from "foreign" or outside sources. Capital did not impose itself *en masse,* neither unsettling traditional relations of authority and agency, nor setting the stage for conflicts and violence to break out among the constituencies of the local community. Why, then, amid this abundance, was Robert Lewis lynched?[60]

Consider the violence that provoked Lewis's murder: the alleged rape of Lena McMahon. The alliance between Lewis and Peter Foley seems improbable. One man was white, the other black. One claimed to be a member of corporate-monopoly capitalism's professional-managerial class (Foley presented himself in Port Jervis as an insurance sales agent), the other was a laborer-servant in the leisure industry (Lewis was the livery driver at Port Jervis's finest hotel).[61] However, for the acquaintanceship between Foley and Lewis to have evolved into a deal that resulted in two grave crimes does not defy but, rather, defines the social good that contracts and labor could be said to produce. By turning the notions of trust, duty, reciprocity, obligation, and authority on their heads, Foley and Lewis's agreement actually specified how destructive and morally bereft contracts could be as a basis for social action or personal conduct.

If his captors' testimony is to be believed, Lewis had agreed with Foley that the white man's sexual partners were his for the taking; as Seward B. Horton claimed at the coroner's inquest, "Foley told him if he wanted a piece go down and get it [;] she would kick a little but never mind that."[62] Coupling their interests in what was surely a strange confederacy, Foley and Lewis evinced a callous disregard for the person and rights of Lena McMahon, whose consent to their deal was irrelevant to the men's proxy plan. Equally disturbing, though, is the premise of agency to which the men's agreement appeals. Effectively confusing the will of one for the other, each man denied his role in the violence, allowing the impersonal structure of their incorporation to shield them from individual responsibility for the assault on McMahon. Symptomatic of the idea of agreement that the market economy could conceivably allow, Foley and Lewis's conspiracy revealed how the boundaries defining the relations between the self and culpability were shifting so profoundly that only egregious acts of violence—committed with equally astonishing degrees of indifference—could mark this transition.[63]

The citizens of Port Jervis acted comparably at the lynching of Robert Lewis. On the one hand, the mob's descent to wanton violence was remarkable. A crowd of nearly two thousand surged forward and "took possession" of Lewis. He was already bound by his hands and feet when unidentified members of the crowd fastened a noose around his neck, handling him "most savagely." This wild abandon was hardly uncontrolled or without purpose, though. In what could only be a deliberate act of defiance, the crowd rigged the rope to hoist Lewis's body up high not simply for the crowd to see, but to rise above the churches nearby and the home of county judge William Howe Crane, two visible pillars of community order—religion and the law.

The murder proceeded swiftly because Judge Crane was so ineffective as an authority figure. As he testified at the coroner's inquest, he had been reading at home when his servant "told [him] they were going to hang a nigger on our front tree."[64] Threading his way to the trunk of the tree, Crane succeeded in snatching the rope from the mob's leaders, a struggle he described to the panelists as follows:

> A man dove down in front of me and shoved me one side and attempted to rope around negro's neck I picked up rope and jerked it away from him[.] Then there ensued a scuffle for the rope[.] The next I saw of it, it was over the branch of the tree[.] I sprang to the tree and caught hold of the rope and tried to pull it down but there were too many on end of rope[.] Then some one caught hold of me and jerked me back. I turned and saw Dr. Illman. He said there is no use, Judge, we will only get hurt. The crowd gave a surge and I flew in the street with the crowd I turned toward the tree but seemed to be a dense body of men about it. The negro was hanging. I turned away and went home.[65]

On this account, Crane's individual effort was dwarfed by the "dense body of men" whose will to kill was so strong that he, the town's arbiter of the law, could not check it. It took a "negro hanging" for the judge to recognize that the town's corporate power vested itself as much in violence as it did in his hands.

Since, like William Crane, others "turned away and went home," the coroner's inquest quickly turned into a "farce," as one local paper complained, because so many witnesses were unwilling to identify the faces of those who killed Robert Lewis.[66] One member of the search posse, S. H. Horton, testified that he was "too busy watching his house to recognize anyone in the crowd." Sol Carley, who was also part of the group that arrested Lewis, claimed only to have known one man in the crowd; as Carley testified, once done with his job he "went home, leaving the negro in the middle of the mob."[67] Though police officer Simon S. Yaples named seven men who participated in the beating and hanging of Lewis, his word did not persuade the coroner's jury to issue a ruling that might authorize a criminal trial.[68] As witness after witness swore under oath that the members of the mob were unknown to them, Port Jervis realized its dream of being a modern metropolis. Like a city teeming with millions, no one in the crowd at Lewis's lynching knew anyone else.

The witnesses' anonymity to one another is doubly remarkable since six of the witnesses called were people whose powers of observation should have been particularly keen: Dr. Sol Von Etten (the examining physician of Lena McMahon and Robert Lewis), Patrick Collier (the undertaker who removed Lewis's body from the scene of the crime), Sherwood Rightmeyer (editor of the *Port Jervis Index*), and W. T. Doty (editor of the *Orange County Farmer*). Despite wrestling with the murderers hand-to-hand, Judge Crane named only one mob leader with any certainty, while that man, Raymond Carr, asserted that he did not "recogniz[e] a lyncher" at all.[69] The working-class men called to testify—John Doty, John Haney, Patrick Collier, Edward Carrigan, Patrick Salley, John Kinsella, William Bonar, John Feldman, and Lewis Avery—experienced memory lapses too, vaguely recalling those who played a pivotal role in the mob's violence.[70] This display of collective amnesia can be interpreted as an assertion of racial solidarity across class lines. But for a town that boasted of its efficient, business-oriented style of government (PJ, 16), the collapse of its judicial bureaucracy during the town's worst public crisis is the more revealing political development. "The machinery of justice in Orange County is not equal to the emergency," the *New York Morning Advertiser* declared, while the *New York Times* cajoled that "the only conclusion . . . this jury can come to, it seems, according to the evidence is that Lewis was the only one on the rope and that his death must have been self-inflicted."[71]

As I pointed out in chapter 1, the resistance to "regular processes" of bureaucratized authority were, at this time, rife throughout the nation. The expanded powers of the federal government together with the hierarchical styles of corporate control threatened the autonomy of individuals and local communities (ironically, the Port Jervis coroner's inquest was held in the "corporation room" of the Superior Court). Yet the imposition of legalistic or rule-bound routine—the deep impersonality of process *qua* process—fostered the wish (and chance) for Americans to be "relieved . . . of personal responsibility" for the very outcomes those systems produced.[72] Nowhere did this loophole claim more lives than in the South, where legal procedures and institutional structures girded the void in which lynching thrived. The failure of the coroner's inquest to find criminal fault in Robert Lewis's murder proved that the law could move "too slow" in the North as well, resulting in the same deadly outcome.

Perversely, the town's indifference toward Lewis only intensified after his death and manifested itself in strange signs of violence. The first target was the murder site; the *Port Jervis Gazette* reported that "men, women, and children have hacked the tree on which the hanging occurred until it looks as if a cyclone had struck it. Bits of the rope were cut up and distributed among the crowd of morbid relic seekers."[73] Port Jervis was home to many avid gardeners who took care to protect the town's tree trunks from damage. That these same people would "hack away" and destroy what at other times they nurtured was remarkable for the latent destructiveness turned against the social order of which they were a part.[74] In another macabre show of force, "hundreds of people" showed up at the local mortuary to attack Robert Lewis's body yet again. Barging their way to the casket where he lay on view during a memorial service organized by his family and the town's black community, the crowd desecrated Lewis's corpse. "Strips of clothing were cut from the body, and some relic hunters even cut the hair from the negro's head," the *Port Jervis Union* reported, adding that "the crowd had to be shut out entirely, as Mr. Carley [the undertaker] said that the negro would have been carried off piecemeal otherwise."[75] And one man did exactly that. Ed Geisenheimer, a local hotelier, obtained the dead man's shoes and a piece of the rope used to kill him. According to the *Union,* Geisenheimer "rented" these effects to Worth's Museum in New York City for "the modest sum of $5 per week."[76]

What these relic seekers wanted, as I argue in chapter 5, stems from the same weaknesses that white people sought to deny by acquiring and trading lynching photographs and postcards: the wish to exert mastery over an experience they could not fully claim to possess. However, given the particular circumstances of Robert Lewis's murder, the commodification of the mementos taken from his body signified that "the progress of wealth and elegance" endowed Port Jervis with a kind of power that had consequences for which its residents were not yet fully prepared. That is why stamping out "negro inferiority" or controlling black men's alleged lust for white women were never the town's central anxieties about this case. Rather, coming to terms with the social estrangement that followed from the town's prosperity drove Port Jervis to such lengths as the lynching and its aftermath. More than a chance, freakish occurrence, the conspiracy of rape linking Lewis to Peter Foley, the heinous manner of Lewis's death, and the inquiry into the men's pact forced Port Jervis to confront how the economy that guided its entry into the modern age simultaneously ratified acts of extreme violence as the basis of its social order.

In the end, though, the people of Port Jervis chose to disavow the consequences of this event in the course of the town's history, preferring instead to acknowledge the social miracles they believed money could perform. "It is best for us all to be silent," counseled Jonathan Crane's successor at the Drew Methodist Church, the Reverend Dominic Taylor. Residents carried out this pastoral suggestion and turned the 1890s into the most profitable decade in the town's history.[77] Since no direct evidence was discovered to corroborate Lewis's charge of conspiracy, the district attorney could not prosecute Peter Foley for his role in the matter. With the witnesses' testimonies leaving too few leads to follow, there was no mandate to obtain indictments against the mob's leaders at the coroner's inquest. The coroner's jury therefore found (as so many southern investigations concluded) that Robert Lewis died "being hanged by a person or persons unknown."[78]

Sketching Lynching's Past

Stephen Crane undoubtedly knew about the lynching of Robert Lewis. During the last weeks of May 1892, he journeyed upstate and was likely at the Hartwood Club or fishing on Orange County's lakes when the murder took place on June 2.[79] Since the train back to Asbury Park stopped at Port Jervis, he would have had at least two opportunities to learn about Lewis's death. Given his close friendships and connections to the local press, Crane could easily have read the *Union* and *Gazette*'s coverage of the case or overheard residents gossiping about the papers' reports because "the town was still excited and groups of people were on every corner" discussing the lynching.[80] Or, perhaps, he discussed the event with William. Even had his brother refused to talk about the incident (or if Stephen had somehow not heard the rumors or seen the news reports in Port Jervis), Crane could not have missed the front-page coverage of the lynching in the downstate dailies. The stories and editorials published in the *New York Tribune* undoubtedly caught Stephen's attention, because Robert Lewis's murder coincided with the first significant achievement of Crane's literary career. Between February and July 1892, the *Tribune* published a series of his humorous sketches of local life in and around Sullivan County, a collection of stories now known as the "Sullivan County Tales." Had he read the June installments of his fiction series, Crane could hardly not have noticed the extensive reports about the lynching in his former hometown.[81]

Claiming that Stephen Crane knew early on about Robert Lewis's murder is one thing; tracking and judging how this lynching influenced Crane's literary career is quite another, and requires speculation about Crane's social interests and practice of his craft. But such evidence exists and, further, strongly suggests that the murder broadened Crane's understanding of literature and lynching's cultural logic. For instance, critics have long observed that a tonal shift occurs in Crane's journalism from the early 1890s but have resisted putting forward any reason to explain the marked invective that suffuses these works.[82] The "Sullivan County Tales"—all written before July 1892—read nothing like Crane's news reports about Asbury Park, which were written and published after Lewis's murder. Where his mirthful short stories gently mock a group of well-meaning but dim-witted hunters confronting nature's cosmic forces in the woods of upstate New York, the Asbury Park dispatches are notable for their open disdain toward the pretensions of bourgeois civility and the crass materialism of popular culture.[83] Could it be that the Port Jervis lynching soured Crane's mood? If so, can we then say that Robert Lewis's murder shaped Crane's critique of American abundance and honed his talents at irony? And further, what does that relation and literary technique teach us about the history of lynching as Crane understood it?

Consider this passage from an oft-cited work from this period, "Parades and Entertainments":

> The parade of the Junior Order of United American Mechanics [. . .] was a deeply impressive one to some persons. There were hundreds of the members of the order, and they wound through the streets to music of enough brass bands to make furious discords. It probably was the most awkward, ungainly, uncut, and uncarved procession that ever raised clouds of dust on sun-beaten streets. (*Works,* vol. 8, 521)[84]

This unflattering portrait of a nationally prominent labor union led to Crane's dismissal from his post as a stringer for the *New York Tribune,* and ever since critics have interpreted this Asbury Park sketch as the launch of Crane's professional career and as indicative of his ambivalence regarding the limitations of mass political movements.[85] It is arguable, however, that Crane's fierce rebuke of this parade lands its punch so squarely because of its resonance with the lynching that occurred in Port Jervis less than one month before. Upstate, thousands "wound through the streets," their yells and cries sounding like "enough brass bands to make furious discords." Upstate, the mob was, by the town's own admission, "the most awkward, ungainly, uncut, and uncarved procession that ever raised clouds of dust on sun-beaten streets." For this vocabulary of dissent to be potentially interchangeable with the scene of violence in Port Jervis suggests that the lynching may have served Crane as a lexicon to judge the developments that defined the world in which he lived. If watching the mechanics' march reminded Crane of Robert Lewis's lynching, "Parades and Entertainments" deserves even more credit as cultural critique, because the sketch then proposes (starting with the plurals in its title) that lynching's social sources were conceivably related to the conditions that made America's playgrounds of wealth possible.

Crane's hometown comes under damning scrutiny through the proxy of Asbury Park in another famous report, "On the Boardwalk." Narrating the scene of the beach all awhirl on opening day, Crane narrows his view to a resort patron engrossed by thoughts of his financial prowess, making him a spectacle of opulence and blindness at once:

> The average summer guest here is a rather portly man, with a good watch chain and a business suit of clothes, a wife, and about three children. He stands in his two shoes with American self-reliance and, playing casually with his watch chain, looks at the world with a clear eye. He submits to the arrogant process of some of the hotel proprietors with a calm indifference; he will pay fancy prices for things with great unconcern[. . . .] He enjoys himself in a very mild way and dribbles out a lot of money under the impression that he is proceeding very cheaply. (*Works,* vol. 8, 516–17)

Read as a text without a particular past (save the moment of the writer's encounter with the man in Asbury Park), this portrait confirms Crane's long-standing disrespect for bourgeois authority. However, published just two months following Robert Lewis's murder on August 14, 1892, this passage recalls the summer resort that was Crane's other home. Port Jervis also billed itself as a retreat where businessmen could spend their summer vacations and "look at the world with a clear eye." The scions of Port Jervis may as well have vacationed in Asbury Park since they yielded so readily to an "arrogant process . . . with a calm indifference" when they watched the mob kill Robert Lewis. Indeed, the businessman's desire to spend his wealth on things with "unconcern" recalls how the lynching and the inquiries that followed in Port Jervis were themselves "cheap proceedings."

No doubt knowing of William's failed effort to stop the lynching and aware that the members of his brother's class could not successfully prosecute the mob's leaders, Crane probably had Port Jervis's professionals in mind when he wrote:

> The bona fide Asbury Parker is a man to whom a dollar, when held close to his eye, often shuts out any impression he may have had that other people possess rights. He is apt to consider that men and women, especially city men and women, were created to be mulcted by him. (*Works,* vol. 8, 522)

In a deft, subtle pun, Crane associates the power of the dollar to eclipse the rights of others with the verb "mulcted." Monied Americans like "the bona fide Asbury Parker" believe they can *fine* others to sustain their status since issuing penalties in accordance with established laws is a legitimate way to acquire what they want. The second definition of "mulcted" in the *Oxford English Dictionary*—to deprive or divest of—implies that expropriating the rights of others is another strategy the Asbury Parker uses to shore up his claims to wealth. Viewing dollars "close to [their] eye[s]," the leaders of Port Jervis staged the coroner's inquest in part to keep hold over the "city men and women" on whom Port Jervis depended for its capitalist aspirations. As a local paper reported, recognizing "what the lynching will mean to the town, hardly anyone can be found now among the town's leading citizens who justifies the action of the mob."[86] However, the "bona fides" of the lawyers, doctors, business managers, and journalists were tarnished when these men took the stand only to "shut out any impression" of the men who lynched Robert Lewis. Admitting his social impotence as if it were a heroic trait, William's testimony was, perhaps, the most incriminating in this regard. Perhaps Stephen wrote contemptuously about the world of Asbury Park because its culture of wealth and excess took on new meaning in light of the violence done to the "mulcted" body of Robert Lewis.

That Crane wanted to explore lynching's possible sources in national culture is an intriguing conclusion we might draw from another landmark moment in his early news-writing career. Since "Parades and Entertainments" left him without regularly paid work, Crane wanted to resume reporting but in a different locale. In the late summer months of 1892, he applied to work for the American News Service, requesting assignments that would have sent him to the Deep South.[87] Because he was dispatched instead to Nebraska (from where he traveled to Mexico), critics have overlooked Crane's initial impulse to test his skills at regional writing by observing American life below the Mason-Dixon line. Perhaps the episode has been ignored in biographical studies of Crane because it was a lost chance. But since his request followed directly after being fired from the *Tribune* for "Parades and Entertainments"—and if the caustic tone and anticorporate critique of the Asbury Park sketches were motivated by Crane's recollection of the Port Jervis lynching—why not suppose that Crane specifically sought writing assignments from the Deep South because he wanted to study that part of America where lynching was widespread? What could southern culture teach him about northern race relations? And what kinds of reports might Crane have written if the American News Service had honored his first request?

Again, we cannot answer these questions directly because Crane never covered the South for that news service. Remarkably, though, the most precise study of the Port Jervis lynching emerges in one of Crane's most northern sketches, "When a Man Falls, a Crowd Gathers" (1894). The event of this report is stark but simple: an elderly man drops unconscious in the streets of Manhattan's Lower East Side and a "crowd gathers" to watch him suffer through an epileptic fit. But Crane's report draws so freely from the news accounts of Robert Lewis's murder that the sketch reads like a reprise of Port Jervis's violent spasm in June 1892:

> It was as if an invisible hand had reached up from the earth and had seized him by the hair. He seemed dragged slowly, relentlessly backward, while his body stiffened convulsively, his hands clenched, and his arms swung rigidly upward. A slight froth was upon his chin. Through his pallid half-closed lids could be seen the steel-colored gleam of his eyes that were turned toward all the bending, swaying faces and in the inanimate thing upon the page yet burned threateningly, dangerously, shining with a mystic light, as a corpse might glare at the live ones that might seem to trample it underfoot. (*Works,* vol. 8, 522)

Several crucial details in this passage recall the torture Robert Lewis endured in the streets of Port Jervis: the "seizure by the hair" to fit the noose about his neck; the slow drag "relentlessly backward" to bring Lewis to the hanging tree; the kicks and blows that "trampled him under foot" and rendered him an "inanimate thing" and, twice over, a "corpse." In Crane's sketch, the physician, policeman, and "tall German" who fend off the crowd to aid the Italian man could easily be surrogates for Dr. W. H. Illman, Officer Simon Yaples, and Judge William Crane, who performed the same roles when the mob raged through the streets of Port Jervis.

Their recollections of the mob's fatal onslaught on Lewis are echoed in another riveting passage in Crane's sketch:

> When a man struck another match and in its meagre light the doctor felt the skull of the prostrate one to discover if any wound or fracture had been caused by his fall to the stone sidewalk, the crowd pressed and crushed again. It was as if they anticipated a sight of blood in the gleam of the match and they scrambled and dodged for position. (*Works,* vol. 8, 348).[88]

Where William Crane's and Dr. Illman's efforts to get Lewis to the hospital proved futile, in Crane's sketch an ambulance does arrive to transport the Italian man to a hospital. Paradoxically, as this difference confirms, the premise of "When a Man Falls" echoes Lewis's murder so closely that the allusions imply that the lynching models the critique of urban indifference the sketch builds toward.

Like Lewis, whose race made his the most memorable face in Port Jervis, the Italian man's ethnicity and language (both body and verbal) distinguish him in this cityscape crammed full of people: "The man and boy conversed in Italian, mumbling the soft syllables and making little quick egotistical gestures. They walked with the lumbering peasant's gait, slowly, blinking their black eyes at the passing show of the street" (*Works,* vol. 8, 345). Segregated from the world in such visceral terms, the old man becomes hypervisible in the text because the reader views the scene of suffering at a remove. As the Italian's body clenches in pain, however, the crowd's "spell of fascination" is not the reader's own; we see this moment unfold through the narrator's eyes. While the crowd's visual attention hones in on the man near death, our sightline pulls back with Crane's to take in this panorama:

> The loaded street-cars jingled past this scene in endless parade. Occasionally, from where the elevated railroad crossed the street there came a rhythmical roar, suddenly began and suddenly ended. Over the heads of the crowd hung an immovable canvas sign. "Regular dinner twenty cents." (*Works,* vol. 8, 347)

While humans struggle to live and die with dignity, the world of modern commerce follows its "endless parade," oblivious to the Italian man's crisis. "Loaded" trolley cars are full of people who "jingle" past his emergency. With the "roar" of the elevated railroad drowning out the man's cries to keep its schedule, the system negates how precious little time remains for the man to regain consciousness. Set in the streets of Manhattan, the story's re-vision of the Port Jervis lynching implies that anti-black violence is a commanding force shaping Americans' experience of urbanization and immigration, not as a backlash reaction to these developments but as illustrative of the transformations themselves. This link between lynching and modernization is figured in this scene by the sobering funereal trope at its center. Though the sign above the crowd promises relief from bodily want and expiration—twenty cents will buy a "regular dinner"—the message conveyed by the canvas banner is less delectable than it seems. "Hanging immovabl[y]" in the air as did Robert Lewis after the mob's second pull of the lynch rope, the advertisement's still-life appearance likens it to a shroud, covering the scene inside the meaning of death. Like a cheap meal, Crane's imagery suggests, not only an Italian but a black man's life can be claimed, easily consumed, digested, and used as energy to continue not only the work of living but the process of writing as well. For both the arts of literary representation and the acts of making history were, as Crane envisioned them, structured by the system the railroads symbolized: the world of corporate-monopoly capitalist development.

Crane's writings from this early period are neither mysterious nor anomalous if work like "Parades and Entertainments," "On the Boardwalk," and "When a Man Falls, a Crowd Gathers" are read as his attempts to comprehend the relevancy of the murder of Robert Lewis to his common sense about the world taking shape around him. Indeed, in these works, the cultural developments that lynching portends (together with the accountability to state power that lynching thwarts) lay the foundations for what would evolve into the signal concerns of Crane's fiction. The anomie of city life and mass culture, together with the deaths and delusions fostered by state-sanctioned violence, figured as the upturned face, the outsized crowd, and the unpredictable force of nature: these tropes of Crane's "modern" mind are, arguably, traceable to the lynching murder of Robert Lewis. That event was so far-reaching in its implications that Crane could only imagine American history and his craft as a writer anew in its wake.[89] As powerful as these allusions to the Port Jervis lynching are, however, none of these sketches explicitly cites Robert Lewis's murder as its source. Why, then, does Crane ignore the very history that his sketches seem to narrate? Why does he actively disavow lynching's importance as the source of these writings' social power?

Best appreciated for its swift, penetrating observations, the sketch was a mode that was never meant to be comprehensive in its range of reference.[90] As its name hints, the sketch's strength was its capacity for underdevelopment or, that is, the plenitude of feeling reaped from the writer's indulging his subjective point of view. Necessarily incomplete, sketches were also by definition indirect, and for Crane these formal requirements were amenable to his idea of how writing occurred and history could be known. "By such small means does the real writer suddenly flash out in the sky above those who are always doing rather well," he believed.[91]

However, lynching's material absence from Crane's early news sketches suggests how white Americans—and particularly those in the liberal North—could turn a blind eye toward the murders in their midst. To the extent that news sketches were provisional histories at best (in fact, since their provisionality defined their literariness as such), readers could safely claim they did not know and could not know the full range of details about the topic of a given report. Because Crane's works were exclusionary in this way, "Parades and Entertainments" or "When a Man Falls, a Crowd Gathers" model how late-nineteenth-century news writing narrowed the boundaries within which lynching could be understood as newsworthy and as history, just as Ida B. Wells's parodies predicted.[92]

A work of fiction published near the end of his life allowed Crane the opportunity to confront the consequences of his sketches' effects and to think more deeply about how integral lynching was to the history of his time. Conceived "under the spur of great need," Crane composed and published *The Monster* (1898) when he was in desperate debt to various creditors in England and his publishers in the United States.[93] His correspondence and literary contracts reveal that he refused to edit *The Monster* because its length as a novella promised to absolve him of financial debts that were crippling his life and career. With the story's commercial value riding on Crane's readiness to trade on the death of Robert Lewis, *The Monster*'s narrative form can therefore enlarge our view of the economic forces that sustained lynching on a national level. Drawing on literary histories of American publishing's economic reorganization at the end of the nineteenth century, I argue that Crane's account of lynching in *The Monster* sheds light on how the rise of corporate-monopoly capitalism—as much as the exploitative labor relations under southern sharecropping—stunted American political feeling in ways that allowed lynching to flourish. Indeed, the artistic license that distinguishes Crane's work suggests not only how the moral economy of corporate-monopoly capitalism hardened the hearts of white Americans toward the violence of lynching, *The Monster*'s narrative form bears witness to the market's power to shape public memory into modes that devalued the deaths of black people, thus making lynching culturally logical and, so, easier for white Americans to tolerate.

A Matter of Life and Debt

In 1893—just one year after Robert Lewis had been lynched and the same year that Henry Smith was murdered in Paris, Texas—the economic shift that had generated such prosperity and violence in Port Jervis had taken hold in the world of literature.[94] Inspired by the syndicates, conglomerates, monopolies, trusts, and cartels that were revolutionizing the national economy, publishers like Irving Bacheller, S. S. McClure, Joseph Pulitzer, William Randolph Hearst, and Frank Doubleday adapted the tactics of Andrew Carnegie, Cornelius Vanderbilt, and John Rockefeller to manage their newspaper, magazine, and book companies in similar fashions. Manufacturing, distributing, and selling books in line with the vertical model of corporate production, postbellum publishers sold more books with greater profit than ever before.[95] Treating writers as "brains futures" and literature as "capital," firms like S. S. McClure's managed the work of art by this proposition: "Today we are a nation of corporate employees: directly or indirectly the corporation controls our living. And, as the corporation grows greater and greater, fewer and fewer men control them, and our individual lives with them."[96]

Accordingly, the very idea of what constituted writing and how it was best practiced began to change.[97] "Fiction factories" churned out the dime novels and story papers that an increasingly literate public loved to read. Metropolitan newspapers and mass-market magazines relied on expansive staffs of journalists to generate the headline stories that sold hundreds of thousands of those publications. To maximize the efficiency of literary production across these media, publishers paid writers by the word and preferred work that could be easily franchised as serials. As a commodity traded like any other on the market, literature no longer partook of the antebellum *zeitgeist* in which authorship and publishing were considered moral callings that authors and entrepreneurs heeded—either to express themselves or to serve God. In the 1890s, writing became a form of labor increasingly subject to the cultural grammar of the market.

On the one hand, as the career of Ida B. Wells makes clear, this secularization of authorship widened the range of American writers and writing. On the other hand, the industrialization of literary creativity doomed a writer like Stephen Crane, who, in every way and by all accounts, was a misfit in this new economic order.[98] "Making his simple little place" in the business of professional writing proved to be insurmountably difficult for him, partly because he refused to adopt the work ethic that was evolving into the industry's standard.[99] Compared to

Figure 3.1. Exploited by U.S. publishers throughout his career, Stephen Crane believed he had "come a cropper" and, as this allusion and his novella *The Monster* provocatively suggest, likened his fate as a writer to that of African American laborers who were often lynched for challenging the predatory contracts they were forced to make with their employers. (Photo courtesy of the Stephen Crane Collection, Syracuse University Library, Special Collections Research Center.)

the iron dedication of Wells (or, as we shall see, the calculated steadfastness of James Weldon Johnson), Crane was a regular slouch (see figure 3.1). "As a matter of truth I am very lazy, hating to work, only taking up a pen when circumstances drive me," he admitted to the editor of *Critic* magazine.[100] Meeting deadlines—the logistical key to a publisher's manufacturing schedule, sales, and cash flow—vexed Crane because his writing process was painstakingly slow. "I am often inexpressibly dull and uncreative and these periods often last for days," he explained to S. S. McClure, unconcerned with how the industry's hardest-driving publisher regarded this comment.[101] Throughout his career, Crane's inconstant efforts puzzled both efficiency-minded editors and his fellow writers who, despite their respect for his literary gifts, viewed him as haplessly inept at the business demands of writing.[102]

For instance, Henry James was so prolific during his later years partly because he hired a secretary who typed his dictated drafts for daily revision. Signing an exclusive contract with Harpers and Brothers not only guaranteed William Dean Howells that his work would see the light of print, that deal also assured him of advances on a regular basis. Mark Twain, who often tried noncommercial methods to distribute his books, incorporated himself as a business enterprise in 1894 to immunize him from the risks he faced developing new technologies for printing his work.[103] Crane, on the other hand, abandoned using his typewriter as soon as he purchased it, refused to work with one publisher consistently, and avoided learning the intricacies of contract and copyright laws, preferring a division of labor between himself and his agent that often placed the two at odds with one another. "If I was a business man, I would not need a business man to conduct my affairs for me," Crane snapped when his agent Paul Reynolds advised him not to sell his work without consulting with him first.[104]

As much as his poor business sense, Crane's aesthetic leanings placed him at odds with the publishing industry's new cultural demands. Favoring authors who wrote long fiction that cultivated book-buying readerships over time, publishers depended most on novels to boost their earnings and profit margins. Novel writing (defined by the industry's minimum standard of one hundred thousand words), however, was Crane's weakness if we judge his achievements with *Maggie* (1893), *The Red Badge of Courage* (1895), and *The Third Violet* (1896).[105] When offered the chance to reap more money from the best-selling *Red Badge* by writing novel-length sequels like it, Crane groused to a friend: "I am engaged in rowing with people who wish me to write more war-stories. Hang all war-stories."[106] But his facility with short stories and sketch writing for newspapers and magazines generated only unsteady income for Crane. Not realizing that his writing's value would decrease the more widely his work was available, Crane published so frequently in daily and monthly publications that his pay rate plummeted to a miserable 6.5 cents per word for his journalism and a paltry 2.7 cents per word for his fiction.[107] Indeed, costly mistakes like these led one publisher to remind Crane in no uncertain terms just what kind of literature the market would not bear: "We really [do] not care for [a] volume of short stories at all, and feel that we should lose money in its publication,—simply because it *is* a volume of short stories, and will not make a popular volume at best."[108]

Though Crane's repeated failures to master the corporate economy's rules of business belie our received history of him as a *wunderkind* of modern American literature, the broken arc of his career leads us unexpectedly back to the history of lynching and Robert Lewis's murder particularly. In the correspondence and unpublished sketches that follow from the summer of 1892 but that precede the publication of *The Monster* in 1898, Crane surmised that his poverty as an author subjected him to the lynch-like force of publishing's corporate power, an identification that transforms how we might conceive the political economy that gave rise to and sustained lynching as a viable, popular practice during Crane's lifetime.

For instance, in his private correspondence, Crane complained that publishers and critics were singularly brutish in their dealings with him, and he described himself as being overpowered by hordes that wanted to flay him and his work as the condition of his reputation, good and bad. "You don't know how that damned city tore my heart out by the roots and flung it under the heels of its noise," Crane remarked as the favorable reviews of *Red Badge of Courage* mounted. "On Friday it had me keyed to the point where I was no more than a wild beast and I had to make a dash."[109] To editor Ripley Hitchcock, Crane squirmed: "Before God, when these people set their fingers in my hair, it is a wonder that I escape with all my clothes. My only chance is to keep away from them," he wrote about one encounter with a publisher.[110] And from England the roar sounded louder, as he noted to his brother William: "There seem so many of them in America who want to kill, bury, and forget me purely out of unkindness and envy and—my own unworthiness, if you choose."[111]

These allusions to lynching are developed in even starker terms in an unpublished allegory drafted in 1892, "In the Country of Rhymers and Writers."[112] In it, "Little Mary Laughter" has fallen into a Rip Van Winkle-like cultural slumber and wakes up to an apocalyptically changed world. Gone are the peach trees whose fruit and shade pampered her as a child; instead, the story tells us, Mary finds herself standing "on paper ground under a paper tree while a brook of ink babbled noisily at her feet." As Rudolph Alphonso Moaner (a poet "fantastically clothed in the paper leaves of newspapers and magazines") escorts Mary to meet the country's leader, King Publico, the pair is stopped by the "Critical Guards" (*Works,* vol. 10, 100). Mary and the poet watch helplessly as the monarch's police force terrorizes and beats other travelers "unmercifully" and with "lusty blows," robbing their victims of the manuscripts they are trying to deliver to the king (ibid., 101). For Crane to regard the commercialization of literature as a world-changing event and, further, to figure that transformation as a lynching ritual could be read as an act of "love and theft," the kind of appropriation of black cultural expression that minstrel performers staged for white male working-class audiences throughout the nineteenth century.[113] But it is equally noteworthy that Crane projects himself to be a lynching victim in these writings. After all, what is there to "love" about having one's heart ripped out of one's chest? Why steal into the culture's apparent death wish for racial others—what advantage could Crane affirm by imagining himself to be subject to lynching's violence as well?

To be sure, Stephen Crane was no great champion of African American people. He claimed none as friends or colleagues, nor was supporting African Americans' civil rights a cause for him the way it was a political commitment for, say, Mark Twain. More often than not, Crane crossed the color line in the ways approved by the racism of the time: he boasted in private about his sexual taste for black prostitutes, and he routinely published work that dredged up negative stereotypes of black ineptitude.[114] However, Crane's struggles to negotiate fair contracts with his publishers (exacerbated by his free-fall into irremediable consumer debt) taught him how inflated the wages of whiteness could be. As collateral for a cash advance he sorely needed, Crane proposed in 1897 an irresistible offer to his most exacting publisher: for $700 he granted S. S. McClure the right of first refusal to consider his short fiction before trying to sell his work on the open market.[115] Crane believed he had gained an upper hand with this agreement because all he had to do (or so it seemed) was produce one or two stories that McClure would approve for syndication, at which point the debt would be paid. However, the "Scotch ass" prevailed.[116] Their pact not only granted McClure near-exclusive control over the publication of Crane's work, it also allowed the publisher to drive down Crane's asking price for his stories, because the $700 debt-ceiling encouraged the wily businessman to minimize his bids. Once Crane realized that this monopoly threatened his livelihood, he protested to his agent that "[McClure] seems to calculate on controlling my entire output. . . . Get me out of the ardent grasp of S. S. McClure Co."[117]

Just as he understood Port Jervis differently from his money-minded brother William, Crane failed to regard McClure's offer as the profit-hungry publisher posed it. Demonstrating loyalty was not McClure's impetus for making their deal; cultivating Crane's liability to his company was the publisher's goal. Crane did not recognize this distinction, though, because he trusted McClure in the traditional sense of corporate deal-making. "McClure's claim on the story was one which I gave him through courtesy and honor—no other," Crane insisted to his agent.[118] To the firm, however, Crane's offer was an impersonal opportunity for it to acquire a long-term property. Thus, McClure paid no heed when

Crane complained: "I have delivered to you over 25000 words against my debt, but I don't see myself any better off than had I asked you to wait until I got damned good and ready to pay."[119]

Crane's assertion is stunning because his plight, as he imagines it, resembles those exchanges studied by historians of the Deep South, where African American tenant farmers, sharecroppers, and debt peons pled to white landowners and field bosses for their pay at the end of harvest season. "Wage labor, sharecropping, and indentured contracts were all calibrated to limit freedom of movement and/or alternative employment," historian Thomas C. Holt writes about black laborers in the late-nineteenth-century South, a point searingly made by the *Richmond Planet* newspaper in 1892: "If a white man employ[s] a Negro to work and in turn refuse[s] to pay him the poor Negro dare not ask for his hard earned wages, or his employer will shoot him down at will or call in a posse at midnight, to hang him from a tree."[120] So far as Crane was concerned, his words—like the cotton bales packed, the tobacco leaves stripped, the sugar cane cut, and the turpentine barreled—were weighed on scales rigged to cheat him out of his due as well. For that reason, Crane believed the fate of black men mirrored his own: he had "come a cropper"—a sharecropper.[121] And if "In the Country of Rhymers and Writers" is the autobiographical allegory it appears to be, it was not hard for Crane to imagine suffering the ultimate penalty paid by black farm laborers who contested their contracts and pay rates; he, too, risked the threat of being lynched. Indeed, the historical lesson to be drawn from Crane's identification with the dangers faced by black workers is that contracts, for him and them, were double-edged instruments of social control. On one side, written agreements could regulate the power imbalances between the parties involved. On the other side, contracts could be used to coerce socially weak people to perform duties that exploited them and offered little if no recourse for relief.[122] In Crane's experience, contracts were statements of aggression, and he was not wrong to note how the failed promise of such agreements could encourage lynchings to occur.

Crane's deep insecurities about his fate in the modern corporate marketplace and the kind of society that economy promoted led him to write *The Monster,* and to do so in an unusual way. A highly planned piece of writing, the novella is perhaps his most disciplined effort. In July 1897, he conducted an inventory of his stock in trade—his prose—cataloguing his writing according to its publication status and word count.[123] Aware of his debt to McClure, Crane likely used this index to determine the kind of work that would relieve it. Based on his market rate, a short story would not have garnered enough to repay the loan in full, while a novel-length work (of a hundred thousand words or more) would have overtaxed his efforts. Figuring his labor value in this way, Crane's index calculated the literary form *The Monster* needed to take: a long prose fiction piece—not a novel, but a novella—that could appear in both magazine and book venues in two major markets, America and England.[124] At 20,675 words long and with an asking price of precisely $700, Crane reasoned that he could effectively end his debt to S. S. McClure. "The American rights alone of 'The Monster' ought to pay them easily, minus your commission. No; perhaps it wouldn't pay them fully but it would pay them a decent amount of it," he told his agent.[125]

That the success of Crane's plan depended on his crafting a story that his agent could readily sell is precisely the issue, though. But the narrative economy of *The Monster* does more than appropriate specific details of Robert Lewis's lynching murder as so much literary capital. With two deft but unnerving moves—turning *The Monster*'s white protagonist into the novella's principal focal point, and describing the deliberate murder of Robert Lewis as the accidental burning of the black dandy Henry Johnson—Crane cultivates the reader's indifference toward the suffering of both black men. The story's form of telling acts as "the monster" because, like his early news sketches, the indirect allusions to the Port Jervis lynching are mediated by two genre-specific tactics: Crane's use of an omniscient narrator who selectively processes the action of the story to marginalize the reader's interest in the experience of Henry Johnson's hurt, and Crane's style of description (as opposed to narration) that renders the violence done to the black protagonist as incidental to the text. Because these structural features follow from Crane's self-consciously crafted efforts to conclude his debt to S. S. McClure, I read *The Monster* in two ways as well: first, as a meditation on the violence that corporate-monopoly capitalism promotes; and second, for the politics of disavowal that realist fiction writing modeled as evidence of white Americans' indifference to the mortal dangers under which African Americans lived.

Lynching's Focal Points

Trundling along with his toy wagon, young Jimmie Trescott scoots about the front yard of his home, making believe he is a train. "Little Jim was, for the time, engine number 36, and he was making the run between Syracuse and Rochester," the narrator of *The Monster* tells us.[126] So fully does he will himself into this fantasy that the boy not only supposes he is the train, Jimmie imagines in his mind that he is locomotion, or movement itself: "He was fourteen minutes behind time, and the throttle was wide open" (*Monster,* 430).

Opening with one of his usual ploys, Crane, for whom play does more than occasion moments of levity or fun, begins *The Monster* with a game. Where, in Louisa May Alcott's *Little Women,* days and days (and with them, chapters and chapters) of game-playing enliven the world of the March sisters by enclosing them from society that much more securely, the impromptu football matches in *The Red Badge of Courage,* the king of the hill contest in *Maggie,* and the poker duel in "The Blue Hotel" enmesh us in the weave of history more tightly. Through the banalities of their aims, rules, and objects of play, games restate large-scale philosophies of society and culture in Crane's fiction, eliciting histories that might otherwise remain unknown to us. Since "things frequently happen in or as a game which establishes structure, tension, [and] a narratable state of events," this start to *The Monster* therefore invites the reader to suppose that world-shaping forces can move through local backyards.[127] Jimmie's fantasy recalls how railroads ushered the timetables and spatial maps of corporate-monopoly capitalism into the daily routines of small-town rural America and transformed the nation into the physically unified state it always aspired to be.

With the outcome of Jimmie's play, though, the game turns on this history too: that modernity requires violence, specifically the violence directed at cultural others, as the price of its achievements. Hastening his pace to keep on schedule, the wagon veers "around the curve" in the imagined train's track and plows into reality—his father's prized flower bed—where his wagon's wheel destroys a peony. Wanting to repair this damage without being noticed, Jimmie's tries to "resuscitate" the flower, fixing its "hurt spine" (*Monster,* 9). His effort fails, though, leaving him so worried about his fate that he finds himself without words to explain his fault: "It seemed that the importance of the whole thing had taken away the boy's vocabulary," the narrator observes, somewhat condescendingly (*Monster,* 10).

Jimmie's anxiety about destroying the flower is not ill-placed because the peonies are the prideful symbol of his family's wealth, and crushing the one mars the display of prosperous order that his father labors to maintain. Cutting, clipping, and watering his garden with fastidious care—"the doctor was shaving this lawn as if it were a priest's chin" (*Monster,* 9)—the physician Ned Trescott hardly seems a force of vengeful anger. But to Jimmie, the lawn mower powered by his father's hands is a "whirring machine" that symbolizes the physical punishment he fears is his due: "sweet, new grass blades spun from the knives" the narrator intones, suggesting a more cutting penalty is to come (*Monster,* 9).[128] The boy is spared physical punishment, though, because his father psychically chastens Jimmie, subjecting him to "disciplinary intimacy," a hands-off method that inculcates children into the rules of order by requiring them to punish themselves:

> "Well, Jimmie," [his father] said slowly, "I guess you had better not play train anymore today. Do you think you had better?"
>
> "No, sir," said Jimmie.
>
> During the delivery of the judgment the child had not faced his father, and afterwards he went away, with his head lowered, shuffling his feet (*Monster,* 10).[129]

Exceedingly polite and nonthreatening, this end to the train game would have the reader believe that, in the world of the Trescotts, disorder and reproval are eminently narratable because unruliness and discipline—or, that is, violence and punishment—are ultimately benign. However, by focusing on the destructiveness of the game in light of breaking the flower, Jimmie cannot fully atone for his act because his father exempts him from admitting his specific wrongdoing. Though Jimmie leaves the scene burdened by his guilty conscience (signaled here by his lowered head and shuffling feet), he has been freed from having to claim responsibility for the damage he has caused, a release ensured by his father's mangled speech. Mixing his use of the imperative, conditional, and subjunctive verb tenses in their exchange, Dr. Trescott confuses the relation between causes and effects, teaching his son (in a moment that becomes the novella's leitmotif) that his actions and their consequences can be effaced by the very disciplinary authorities that would have him admit his wrongful behavior.

Jimmie's trouble foreshadows his father's own, as Ned Trescott soon faces a grander version of his son's dilemma. When a fire breaks out in the Trescott home, Henry Johnson, the family's black servant, rescues Jimmie from perishing in the flames but, as a result, suffers horrific burns that destroy his face. The arc of this story enacts the principle of disavowal that Jimmie's train game makes narratable since, like the flower Jimmie destroys and is permitted not to remember, Henry Johnson's maimed condition mires Ned Trescott in deep wells of moral angst over the enormity of Johnson's sacrifice. As the story develops, however, the black man's presence in the text ceases to structure the telling of it. The narrator's attention shifts away from Johnson's experience of his injury to center on Trescott's quest to protect the servant from the town's ugly urge to banish him from the community.[130] As we are led not to see and, worse, not to feel remorse for our disinterest in Johnson's effacement from the text, "the question of how narrators are positioned, the space they occupy, how they came to be positioned there, and what kind of power, authority, and vision their positioning affords them" becomes imperative to address.[131] By diminishing the reader's concern for the violence done to Johnson, *The Monster*'s narrative structure models how arbitrarily social value is defined and with it, how readily African Americans could be killed both in real history and in the world of literary texts.

The black servant and white employer first appear in *The Monster* as narrative rivals, though, because Jimmie Trescott seeks consolation from Henry Johnson after his father's chastisement. Feeling "some kind of desire to efface himself" (*Monster,* 11) and to forget the confusion caused by his father's reaction, the white boy regards the black man with some measure of deference. According to the narrator, the two are "pals" who share a worldview: "In regard to almost everything in life they seemed to have minds precisely alike" (*Monster,* 11). Mocking Jimmie's bond with Johnson, the narrator insists on the black man's intellectual inferiority not because he is convinced of Johnson's mental impotence, but because the narrator seeks to preempt the force that the black man does, in fact, wield. For as the scene unfolds, Johnson acts on a self-regard that exceeds both young Jimmie's understanding and that of the narrator-text:

> For instance, it was plain from Henry's talk that he was known to be a light, a weight, and an eminence in the suburb of the town, where lived the larger number of the negroes, and obviously this glory was over Jimmie's horizon; but he vaguely appreciated it and paid deference to Henry for it *mainly because Henry appreciated it and deferred to himself.* (*Monster,* 11; emphasis added)

The narrator belittles the world that Johnson inhabits and to which Jimmie unknowingly "defers" by figuring black "eminence" in caricatured terms. The suburb where Johnson is "a light, a weight" (in a not-so-subtle pun) the narrator dubs "Watermelon Alley" and populates the place with broad-smiling, back-flipping, shuffling, and groveling black minstrels.[132] Whetting a late-nineteenth-century white readership's taste for black buffoonery, the narrator's vision of Johnson and the story's other African American characters is meant to be the reader's own, or to become the reader's own, by virtue of the narrator's knowledge of this world and the vantage point from which he issues such pronouncements. Sounding full of power and certainty, his estimation of Johnson's stature seeks to define or focalize the terms of the reader's interest as well. The narrator goes to such lengths, though, precisely because he is intimidated by the prospect of representing Johnson, whose worldview his omniscience cannot predict or control.

Recounting how Johnson prepares for his Saturday night on the town, the narrator begins condescendingly but then reluctantly defers to Johnson's self-authoring techniques:

> After Johnson had taken supper in the kitchen, he went to his loft in the carriage-house and dressed himself with much care. No belle of a court circle could bestow more mind on a toilet than did Johnson. On second thought, he was more like a priest arraying himself for some parade of the church. As he emerged from his room and sauntered down the carriage-drive, no one would have suspected him of ever having washed a buggy. (*Monster,* 13)

Infiltrating—indeed, penetrating—Johnson's zones of privacy, the narrator's textual authority appears to be confirmed in this scene, his omniscience marked by this forcible access to Johnson's private quarters and his observations of the black man in feminized terms. From the woman's traditional realm of the kitchen, the servant is tracked, surveilled, and domesticated as he moves to his loft. Dressing himself with the "care" and "mind" of a "belle of a court circle," Johnson goes through his motions unaware of the narrator's snide insinuation that he commands only a limited range of social authority.

But this slight does not hold for long, because as the black man acts, the narrator is compelled to revise his account with a "second thought" about his initial description. Changing his opinion—comparing Johnson's grooming ritual to a priestly sacrament instead of a woman's "toilet"—the narrator begrudgingly grants Johnson this gendered measure of respect because, as this passage reads, the black man's style of dress produces an unexpected, startling effect: "No one would have suspected him of ever having washed a buggy." Able to separate conventional forms from their functions and meanings, Johnson fashions a way to represent himself that the narrator cannot control. Astonished by this display of power, the narrator further admits that the "change" he notices "was somewhere far in the interior of Henry" (*Monster,* 13). The indeterminacy of this declaration (how far inside does this power and its meanings lie?) points toward another social and narrative order, one where Johnson's person and style can remain impervious to a centralized power's reach.

And indeed, when Johnson starts his evening stroll through downtown Whilomville, white men debate the effect of his aesthetic, but with no obvious impact on Johnson's sense of himself. Those loitering on the street ridicule the confidence of Johnson's gait by rudely likening his stride to a cakewalk, while others waiting for their shave and haircuts at Reifsnyder's barber shop follow suit by saluting Johnson with a racist epithet: "The coon is coming!" (*Monster,* 14). Stunned by the black man's "graceful form" (*Monster,* 14), the men argue whether the handsome flâneur is, in fact, Johnson: "I bait you any money that vas not Henry Johnson! . . . That man vas a Pullman-car porter or someding" (*Monster,* 15), the German shop owner marvels. Ceding Johnson's dominance as a man of fashion ("'That was Henry Johnson all right. Why he dresses like that when he wants to make a front! He's the biggest dude in town—anybody knows that"' [*Monster,* 15]), Reifsynder's clients give up the power that the narrator refuses to relinquish as the text's arbiter of taste. Setting himself apart from the group's judgment, the narrator nonetheless remains enthralled by Johnson's self-possessed authority: "Henry was not ruffled in any way by these quiet admonitions and complements. In reply he laughed a supremely good-natured, chuckling laugh, which nevertheless expressed an *underground complacency of superior metal,*" the narrator observes in awe (*Monster,* 14; emphasis added).

As a black man, however, and as the Trescott's family servant, Johnson is socially positioned to be subordinate to the wishes and whims of white people. The narrator addresses him as befits that status, referring to Johnson as "Henry Johnson," then "Henry," then variably as "Johnson," and finally—once he has been maimed by the fire—he ceases to be a person at all: the narrator calls him a "thing" and "it."[133] Further, the narrator reports Johnson's speech in the estranging, misspelled codes of dialect. Because his voice then reads and sounds like Jimmie Trescott's dialogue, Johnson is marked as childlike. With neither a stable patronymic nor a reliable tongue to signal his importance, Johnson's vacuousness compels him to regard Dr. Ned Trescott as his focal point of power, a relation the narrator rationalizes by likening it to nature's order. The doctor was due deference "on all points of conduct" because Johnson's "complete and unexpressed understanding" was that Ned Trescott was "the moon" (*Monster,* 11).

The narrator's investment in disavowing Henry Johnson's authority (and, with it, his narrative significance to the text's development) becomes unmistakably clear in the scene that mobilizes the story's main drama: the fire that engulfs the Trescotts' home. The plotting of the moment is crucial because Johnson's role in it turns the fire from an accident to a form of punishment. When the emergency bell sounds, the fire alarm's first knell is heard—or so we are told—on and around the town square. Johnson, at that point, has strolled past the barbershop and finished visiting his sweetheart, Bella Farragut, in a scene of minstrel mirth that continues the narrator's erosion of Johnson's authority (*Monster,* 15–16). For the next two chapters, Johnson does not figure in the text, as the narrator highlights the local fire companies' race to fight the blaze. Then, suddenly, Johnson appears at the fire: cutting through the crowds of firefighters and onlookers comes "one man who ran with almost fabulous speed. He wore lavender trousers. A straw hat with a bright silk band was held half crumpled in his hand" (*Monster,* 21). Johnson goes nameless here not because he moves so quickly, but because the narrator has lost sight of him in the story's plot. Though the narrator's cross-cutting between these scenes is formally astute—cinematic, even—the technique marginalizes Johnson from the center of the novella's plot, thus creating a gap wherein the black man naturally disappears as a function of the narrator's superior sense of form.

But Johnson asserts his textual authority by committing the story's most narratively significant act. Thrusting his way ahead of the fire chief and past the "babbled" (*Monster,* 21) cries of Jimmie's mother, Johnson bravely rushes into the house to save his "pal." To counter Johnson's display of freedom and will—for this is the moment in realist fiction where a story's protagonist becomes heroic (or not) by virtue of the choices he makes—the narrator's indifference toward Johnson becomes manifestly punitive as the scene unfolds.[134] First, the narrator discredits Johnson's courage by attributing his action to the feminizing effects of racial subordination. Johnson's familiarity with the floor plan, for instance, is linked to his servile status: "He plunged past [Mrs. Trescott] and disappeared, taking the long-familiar routes among these upper chambers, *where he had once held office as a sort of second assistant house-maid*" (*Monster,* 21; emphasis added). Next, the narrator can hardly contain his spite when he recounts how Johnson locates Jimmie. The "terror-stricken negro, all tousled with wool scorching" scoops up the dazed boy from his bed, "as if the whole affair were a case of kidnapping by a dreadful robber chief" (*Monster,* 77). As if turning Johnson's heroics into minstrelized farce is not enough, the narrator proceeds to emasculate him a third time by staging the rescue as a tableau of domestic sentimentalism. Clutching his arms around Johnson's neck but confused as to who it was that held him, Jimmie "called twice in muffled tones, 'Mam-ma! Mam-ma!'" letting out a "gorgeous bawl" (*Monster,* 77). With the white boy's trust in the

African American's courage and intelligence now neutered, the narrator completes Johnson's dehumanization by likening his desperation to bestiality. As he gropes to find his way out of the burning home, Johnson "paws" along the halls (*Monster,* 22) and "cries out in a howl" (*Monster,* 23) when he sees the stairway full of flames. When, before that impasse, Johnson "submit[s], submit[s] because of his fathers, bending his mind in a most perfect slavery to this conflagration" (*Monster,* 23), the narrator calls on the science of eugenics to dismiss the fear Johnson rightfully feels.

The main drama of *The Monster* takes place after the fire and Johnson's injury: from this point forward the themes of debt and obligation, restitution and remembrance emerge as the novella's focal concerns. But the price of this ticket is high. Johnson suffers irreparable damage to his face, rendering him a shadow of the man whose splendid artifice rivaled the narrator's powers at the start of the text. What reads like an accident, then, serves as a surreptitious punishment, one that the narrator never admits because his omniscience endows him with the right to exchange—and, so, to occlude from view and knowledge—Johnson's suffering for other narrative subjects.[135]

For instance, chronicling the town's immediate reaction to the fire, the narrator reports the news coverage of the incident:

> The morning paper announced the death of Henry Johnson. It contained a long interview with Edward J. Hannigan, in which the latter described in full the performance of Johnson at the fire. There was also an editorial built from all the best words in the vocabulary of the staff. The town halted in its accustomed road of thought, and turned a reverent attention to the memory of this hostler. In the breasts of many people was the regret that they had not known enough to give him a hand and a life when he was alive, and they judged themselves stupid and ungenerous for this failure. (*Monster,* 30)

This report of the *Morning Tribune*'s obituary is remarkable for how it thwarts the reader's concern for Henry Johnson's recovery from his wounds. Rather than call attention to the newspaper's mistake and then attend substantively to Johnson's experience of social death (a choice of emphasis that characterizes *The Autobiography of an Ex-Colored Man,* as we shall see in chapter 4), the narrator devotes fourteen of the novella's chapters to the breast-beating of the town's residents. Frightened by his maimed face (a sight worsened by the thick layers of white gauze that make him resemble a cyclops), the residents of Whilomville quickly turn from mourning Johnson's mistaken death to mocking, taunting, and shunning him because of his injuries, and for long stretches of narrative time we follow Johnson's persecution by the increasingly hostile community. As critics have long argued, these vignettes expose the cruelties of the town's racism and prejudice against disability, showing Whilomville to be more "monstrous" than Johnson ever could be. However, the crosscuts between these scenes of the townsfolk's angst create the same effect as the novella's punishment of Johnson at the fire. No longer a part of the reader's meaning-making concern, Johnson becomes marginal to—precisely because he is the spectacle of—the story of his own textual death.

The defining instance of this exchange of narrative interest occurs during Ned Trescott's great debate with Judge Denning Hagenthorpe. At the end of an evening meal, the physician and the jurist ponder the ethics of keeping Henry Johnson alive, each man presenting the bold arguments such a conversation would encompass. Hagenthorpe cautions Trescott not to commit the Frankensteinish "blunder of virtue" by reviving his servant. "You are performing a questionable charity in preserving this negro's life," the judge argues, calling strongly for Trescott to give up his savior complex (*Monster,* 31). Countering Hagenthorpe's complaint, the doctor charges that the town's prejudice (rather than his benevolence) will determine Johnson's fate. Notably, the men can spar like this because Johnson is not with them: "At dinner, away from the magic of the unwinking eye" (*Monster,* 31), they feel free to speak as they do. However, the vigor of their debate weakens considerably when the discussion raises Trescott's "real mental perturbation" (*Monster,* 53):

> "Well, what would you do? Would you kill him? [Trescott] asked, abruptly and sternly.
>
> "Trescott, you fool," said the old man, gently.
>
> "Oh, well, I know Judge, but then—" He turned red, and spoke with new violence: "Say, he saved my boy—do you see? He saved my boy."
>
> "You bet he did," cried the judge, with enthusiasm. "You bet he did." And they remained for a time gazing at each other, their faces illuminated with memories of a certain deed.
>
> After another silence, the judge said, "It is hard for a man to know what to do." (*Monster,* 33)

Once Trescott utters the word that would sanction Henry Johnson's murder ("kill"), what had been a source of conflict moments before collapses into a muddle of half-formed thoughts the men cannot articulate. Indeed, their language (or, more accurately, their lack of it) all but eviscerates the history of Johnson's injury and the violence done to him by the fire. Rather than recant his earlier position, Judge Hagenthorpe protests "gently" that Johnson "ought" to be allowed to die of natural causes. Trescott's refusal to seize on Hagenthorpe's hypocrisy turns their dialogue into a spectacle of worried impotence that commands the reader's interest and concern. This shift completes the displacement of Johnson's story as narratively significant because Hagenthorpe's final judgment suggests that "knowing what to do"—more than the pain Henry Johnson suffers—becomes the most important focal point in the story's telling. Thus, the white men's guilt drives the narrative forward.

This direction ironically exhausts itself, however, through the narrator's lavish attention to Trescott's role in Johnson's rehabilitation and care. Presuming the doctor's remedies are self-evidently just and good, the narrator's account demonstrates how the damage done in the interests of benevolence can itself be monstrous. Having tended Johnson back from death, Trescott finds someone else to conduct his moral vigil, arranging for a local black man, Alek Williams, to lodge Johnson in his home at the rate of $5 per week. The narrator takes great care to describe Trescott and Johnson's journey to this new refuge, once again using dialogue to legitimize what Trescott "knows to do." To the doctor's gentle promises of kind care and frequent visits, Johnson replies nonsensically: "'No, 'deed! No she! Alek Williams don' know a hoss! 'Deed he don't. He don' know a hoss from a pig.' The laugh that followed was like the rattle of pebbles" (*Monster,* 33). Confused that Trescott wants to replace him with Williams as the family coachman, Johnson rambles on incoherently, exasperating Trescott but convincing the reader that the doctor's plan to hire Alek Williams as Johnson's caretaker is best.

And yet the more the narrator describes this exchange, the more morally opaque Trescott's offer becomes:

> At the end of three miles the mare slackened and the doctor leaned forward, peering, while holding tight reins. The wheels of the buggy bumped often over out-cropping bowlders [*sic*]. A window shone forth, a simple square of topaz on a great black hill-side. Four dogs charged the buggy with ferocity, and when it did not promptly retreat, they circled courageously around the flanks, baying. A door opened near the window in the hill-side, and a man came and stood on a beach of yellow light. (*Monster,* 34)

Placing Johnson in these rough environs, Trescott effectively segregates him from his life in Whilomville and through that distance (in effect, if not by intention) increases the chances of avoiding contact with his servant altogether. Trescott performs this repudiation with high-minded finesse, though, bravely enduring the long ride into the countryside and defending Johnson from Williams's initial shock on seeing his old friend's injuries: "He gasped for a second, and then yelled the yell of a man stabbed in the heart" (*Monster,* 35).[136]

But the intensity of Williams's fright suggests how ill informed he was about the work he agreed to do. Believing his wealth has solved everyone's needs—Johnson gets to recuperate in a culturally familiar place; Alek Williams receives much-needed cash to support his family; and the doctor, like a good liberal reformer, gets to take care of so many poor black people and be rid of them all at the same time—Trescott violently insists that Williams accept the job as he defines it. Shouting at Williams—"You old black chump! You old black—shut up! Shut up! Do you hear?"—Trescott orders the black man and his wife to obey his command: "I've brought Henry for you to take care of, and all you've got to do is to carry out what I tell you" (*Monster,* 35). Indeed, Williams's poverty precludes him from rejecting Trescott's offer outright, while Johnson's injury makes him dependent on the doctor's medical skills and political clout to enable his recovery. That neither black man has a choice in his fate is figured by the odd phrase used to describe their view of one another: Johnson and Williams greet "front to front" instead of "face to face." Of all that "front" could mean, the American definition captures the black men's predicament because they are, in this moment, "a person, organization, etc. that serves as a cover for subversive or illegal activities." However, while certainly dominating, Trescott's control is not complete, because he himself is a front for both the narrator's machinations of the plot and the other dominating force that legitimizes these narrative operations of the novella itself: the cultural hegemony of corporate-monopoly capitalism and its theories of contract.

Trescott's care for Henry Johnson is, arguably, a contract of the antebellum sort, one reflecting that era's ideals of locally constituted, intimately defined collective life, with one man aiding another in need. As depicted in the text, though, the deal breaks down precisely because this agreement allows Trescott to exploit his racial and class power against Johnson's self-interest. Staying with Alek Williams is not Johnson's preference at all; but the doctor wants his servant to live apart from him. For this reason, what the narrator treats as the ramblings of a demented, diminished man are, in fact, Johnson's sage insights into the history his predicament recalls. He rightfully asks why should he stay with a man who "don' know a hoss from a pig" because he recognizes that with Williams, he would assent to Trescott's view of him as the chattel African Americans once were. Refusing this deal in the antebellum way, Johnson escapes from captivity, his fugitive flight evidence that, under slavery,

African Americans were the objects, rather than the makers, of legally binding contracts.

In the case of Alek Williams, Trescott rigs their agreement to his complete satisfaction because, as a poor black man, Williams has no leverage to bargain equally in their negotiations. Burdened by the freedoms of emancipation—married with a large family to support and a wage laborer with no ready prospects for work—Williams desperately needs the money Trescott is willing to pay. When he does protest (not to the doctor but to his boss's surrogate, Judge Hagenthorpe), Williams makes clear why the promise of money makes the contract exploitative: "What er man oughter git fer this kinder wuk is er salary. Yesseh . . . fer this kinder wuk er man oughter git er Salary"(*Monster,* 38). Arguing that he be compensated fairly for his labor, this poor black man understands that social charity is no longer a moral imperative but a business enterprise in late-nineteenth-century America. As long as their deal is conceived as an act of compassion rather than a market-based service, Williams's work is calculated according to its moral worth instead of rated by its capital value. Whether dealing with Henry Johnson, who is figuratively his slave, or with Alek Williams, whose emancipation is nominal at best, Trescott can neglect the rights of either because they both are black.

Trescott's willingness to use both Hagenthorpe and Williams as his business fronts and his financial capacity to move Johnson about according to his will therefore link the doctor's mastery over his world not to the moon but to the dominion enjoyed by modern corporate bosses. Such ambition is certainly possible in Whilomville insofar as the town's affinities with new ideals of money are ingrained into the texture of the place. For instance, the sun sits high above the town, its light "sprinkl[ing] through the lilac bushes" and "pour[ing] great coins" of brightness onto the homes below (*Monster,* 31). If nature recreates money's forms in this town, capital reproduces culture's effects, as gaslit shop windows warm the streets with a "radiance" that attracts residents out of their homes and into the public square, where they fashion bonds of "chumship" with one another (*Monster,* 14).[137] The ease with which Whilomville turns against Johnson, however, suggests the fragility of these intimacies, his burned-away face simultaneously "fronting" and effacing the aggression that modern corporate-monopoly capitalism makes possible. Turning the issue of Johnson's care into a problem of market-share management, the town launches an economic boycott against Trescott's medical practice to hasten Johnson's banishment from their midst. Consolidating the grassroots complaints into a more bureaucratic operation, a delegation of the town's business elites propose the option of deeding Johnson "a little no-good farm up beyond Clarence Mountain" (*Monster,* 63) or funding his stay in a state-run asylum. Though Trescott believes he resists both challenges ("Nobody can attend to him [Johnson] as I do myself," he insists [*Monster,* 63]), he has reneged on his promise to Johnson all along, because the town's laissez faire ethic is, ultimately, his own.

Thus, as much as it is a tasteful gesture to make the injured man appear less odious (and less obvious) to the town, when Trescott heeds the Whilomville sheriff's suggestion to use "a—er—mask, or some kind of veil" (*Monster,* 49) to conceal Johnson from the public's view, the "heavy crêpe" material (*Monster,* 52) masks Trescott's own desire to be rid of Johnson himself. While readers after 1903 might interpret the "veil" following W. E. B. Du Bois's sense of the term, in the 1890s the trope had a less metaphysical meaning. "Veils" (like "fronts") referred to corporate tactics of creating shell companies to shield the full range of their activities and profits from public interference.[138] Obscuring Trescott's role in Johnson's marginalization, and in that process blinding the reader to the structures controlling Johnson's fate, the veil therefore conceals the narrator's power to construe the novella's ending so that the story's conclusion cannot be read for what it enacts: the full effacement of black people from the structure and meaning of the plot.

Having resolved to withstand the protests raging against him, Ned Trescott finds his wife at home distraught and in tears. Shunned by friends who refuse to attend her weekly tea party, Grace becomes a target of the town's boycott too, this one led by the wives of the business elites, who use their social capital to extort Mrs. Trescott to betray her loyalties to her husband's cause. Importantly, Alek Williams's wife endured the same derision when her family was coerced into taking in Johnson; however, the black woman's discomfort is belittled by the text, given how the narrator exaggerates their ostracism through a scene of burlesque comedy that makes their pain forgettable (*Monster,* 35–39). Though parallels could be easily drawn between Grace Trescott's and Mary Williams's predicaments, they are effaced in favor of focalizing the white woman's shame and hurt as most deserving of the reader's empathy. Reifying the value of white suffering through the diminishment of black pain, the narrator fulfills the prophecy of the novella's opening scene by destroying yet another peon(y) and eluding responsibility for it once again.

Thus the narrator indulges his indifference toward black life and death freely in the novella's final scene. As Trescott comforts his sobbing wife, the couple sits before a fire in the family's parlor, an exquisite miniature version of the inferno that destroyed Henry Johnson's life. Warmed by the tasteful blaze and in its glow, Trescott contemplates Grace's loss of face, which becomes, in the narrator's elegy for it, the injury in most need for repair:

> The wind was whining round the house, and the snow beat aslant upon the windows. Sometimes the coal settled with a crumbling sound, and the four panes of mica flashed a sudden new crimson. As he sat holding her head on his shoulder, Trescott found himself occasionally trying to count the [tea] cups. There were fifteen of them. (*Monster,* 65)

Sheltered from the outside world, the Trescotts's conjugal solidarity is rendered as an image that leaves no place for Henry Johnson to return to this text. For the teacups—all "fifteen of them"—rivet the doctor's and the reader's focus to the idea of the family's lost prominence, together with the property rights ("fifteen of them") that financed the Trescott's social status. In this enumeration of money's power, Henry Johnson becomes an expendable figure, which the narrator's tone of resignation makes not only bearable but essential to the novella's drama.

The Real Monster

Cultivating the reader's disinterest in Henry Johnson was both easy and necessary for Stephen Crane to do. Easy because he could exploit the rampant racism of the era to justify his authorial choices; as Theodore Roosevelt once advised him, "it was more normal" for white protagonists to "come out on top" when vying for narrative dominance with characters of color.[139] And necessary because he had to craft a work that would accrue earnings sufficient to ease his financial debt. Normalizing the claims of white supremacy in these ways, the market could bear Crane's focus on Trescott as the novella's protagonist.

And yet, *The Monster* is so unlike Crane's previous work that the novella calls its own formal premises into question. Crane's view of American life in *The Monster*—from the types of flowers Ned Trescott grows in his garden (peonies) to the architectural style of his house (Queen Anne); from the net worth of the town's leading businessman ($400,000) to the train route Jimmie Trescott travels in his fantasy (the Number 14 Syracuse-Rochester line); from the scheduled time of Grace Trescott's weekly teas (Wednesdays) to the delivery schedule for the town's mail (Saturday afternoon)—differs drastically from the technique he used in his novels to describe the battlefields of Chancellorsville or the streets of Manhattan's Lower East Side. Where *The Red Badge of Courage* disoriented readers because it was not "a single carefully composed painting, serious, finished, scrupulously studied, but rather scores and scores of tiny flashlight photographs, instantaneous, caught, as it were on the run"—and though its cross-cutting between scenes creates its own kind of havoc in the text—*The Monster*'s chapters do unfold more slowly and neatly in chronological time.[140] The aloof irony and isolated settings that distinguish Crane's fiction often estranged his contemporaries from his work, but present-day critics embrace *The Monster* as one of his most engaging works ever.[141] That the normative structures of literary realism emerge so fully in *The Monster* does not herald an achievement on Crane's part, though. Instead, the novella's conventionalities bear within them the terrors of the era's history that Robert Lewis's murder revealed to Crane six years earlier. Indeed, precisely because the Port Jervis lynching is its cultural secret, *The Monster* depicts that event as unreal, the better to convey the social chaos that Lewis's murder itself represented. Thus the transformation of the Port Jervis lynching into Henry Johnson's burning requires a second reading, one that interrogates the aesthetic economy that would allow Crane to elide the murder from the story in the name of representing it as a "real" thing.

While his place in the realist canon has long been debated by critics, Crane himself believed that he belonged to that school of writing.[142] When called on to explain his literary methods and models, Crane proudly identified William Dean Howells and Hamlin Garland as his "literary fathers," acknowledging that their example was vital to his development as a writer.[143] Wanting to "write plainly and unmistakably so that all men (and some women) might read and understand" the world and their place in it, Crane's authorial ethics resonated with his mentors' credo that literature was uniquely able to instruct the reading public about the vicissitudes of daily life.[144] Realist aesthetics, however, harbored within them two paradoxes that, given how he chose to confront them, forced Crane to the margins of the movement and, with him, the kinds of narrative subjects that could be known and represented in the genre's discourse.

The first conceptual dilemma involved what it meant to write (as Crane put it) "plainly and unmistakably," or as William Dean Howells expressed it in "Novel-Writing and Novel Reading" (1899):

After all [. . .] when the artist has given his whole might to the realization of his ideal, he will only have an *effect* of life. We start in our novels with something we have known of life, that is with life itself; and then we go on and imitate what we have known of life. If we are very skillful and very patient we can *hide the joint.* But the joint is always there and on one side of it are real ground and real grass and on the other side the painted images of ground and grass.[145]

The emphases here are Howells's, who stresses the losses writing realist fiction entails. "We start in our novels with something we have known of life, that is with life itself," he declares, but the realist writer develops techniques of "imitation" to conceal how representing the material world and social history occurs. Creating the "effect of life" by "hiding the joint" becomes the standard of skill in Howellsian realism: to this effort the artist "give[s] his whole might." But the accomplishment of artifice, however pleasing and persuasive it might be, aggrieves Howells because "real" history resists the domain of the fictive text. "The joint is always there" between history and literature, reminding the novelist that the world as he knows it cannot fully be what it is as art.

The predicament that Howells laments is for Roland Barthes the *sine qua non* of realist fiction.[146] Description shapes and animates the "effect of life" because that technique makes the author's imagined version of the world familiar in the text. However, Barthes argues that central details and principal characters do not impart this sense of existential certainty. Rather, the marginalia of a story (Howells's "ground" and "grass") limit the realm of the real in realist fiction because seemingly extraneous bits generate the feel of verisimilitude in the text.[147] Seeming scraps and husks of information—the lather coating Reifsnyder's client's faces, the mare that needs tying up when Trescott delivers Johnson to Alek Williams's home, the name of the newspaper that misreports Johnson's death in the fire—add the degrees of "thickness" that allow readers to immerse themselves in the social domains of the text.

This immersion is possible because description differs from narration in one crucial respect: where narrative organizes a story and its elements, description "has no predictive mark" and so, according to Barthes, does not demand that movement or change occur in a story[148] Indeed, unlike narration, description operates most effectively to the degree it appears to do nothing to leverage its importance in the text. "This shows that the 'real' is supposed to be self-sufficient, that it is strong enough to belie any notion of 'function,'" Barthes explains.[149] Suspending the sign-making power of language by assuring readers that things are as they appear on the page, description can function this way because it purges language of its connotative capacities. Making the "real" in realism take hold, "the reality effect" produces "the basis of that unavowed verisimilitude which forms the aesthetic of all the standard works of modernity."[150]

Read in this light, the description of Henry Johnson and his maimed face function throughout *The Monster*'s "reality effect" as the signifier whose lack of referential power produces not only the sense of the real but the value and meaning of the real in the text. As I argued earlier, the harm that befalls Henry Johnson makes Ned Trescott's experience worth narrating; what Barthes makes clear is that the doctor's moral angst becomes the focus of the story instead of the black man's existential crisis because the narrator describes Johnson's condition instead of narrating it, thus figuring the violence done to Johnson to be the novella's "unavowed" source of verisimilitude. For the descriptions of Henry Johnson to derive their significance from their lack of narrative value suggests that violent harm, injury, and death should be inflicted on black people in realist fiction to tell and sell stories that satisfy readers' interests. In this way, *The Monster*'s invocation of racial violence is a frightening display of description's rhetorical function.

The Monster is not the first instance where descriptions of African Americans at or near death exert such clarifying force in Crane's prose work.[151] As I discussed earlier, the Asbury Park and New York Tenderloin sketches resonate sharply with Robert Lewis's lynching. And Crane's deservedly praised masterwork "The Open Boat" also depends on the history of a black man's death to develop its much-admired concern for the obligations that humans in need owe one another.[152] What distinguishes *The Monster* from these works is that, by 1898, Crane's financial needs led him to recognize how realist fiction mystified the social threats that African Americans withstood in actual life, particularly the violence of lynching.

One of Henry James's most famous ideas, the "sacrifice of relation" that characterized realist fiction, compelled authors to resist history's claims because "ugly facts, so stated and conceived, by no means constitut[e] the whole appeal" of historical events.[153] Rather, history could provide "motives" whose options were immeasurable and best determined by an unfettered imagination:

> The very source of interest for the artist [. . .] resides in the strong consciousness of his seeing all for himself. He has to borrow his motive, which is certainly half the battle; and this motive is his ground, his site and foundation. But after that he only lends and gives, only builds and piles high, lays together the blocks quarried in the deeps of his

imagination and on his personal premises. He thus remains all the while in intimate commerce with his motive, and can say to himself [. . .] that he alone has the *secret* of the particular case, he alone can measure the direction to be taken by his developed data.[154]

Because "he alone" discerns the narrative potential of historical events, the realist author also becomes the principal archivist of history itself, since the writer "has the *secret* of the particular case." That is not to say, however, that readers are wholly unaware of the author's stores of facts, because the "secret" of realism's narrative appeal does not lie in the author's ability to sequester his sources from critical scrutiny. Rather, as Catherine Gallagher and Stephen Greenblatt suggest, realism attracts (and more important) sustains readers' attention through the text's capacity to "disclose the open secret of [its] fictionality."[155]

In this way, according to Gallagher and Greenblatt, realist fiction does not offer mimetic reflections of the world but instead poses estimations of history as the basis of its appeal. Entering the "territory of speculation" opened up by these texts, readers seek risk and uncertainty when they turn to fiction to know the real:

In literature we self-consciously savor the fact that [according to Marx, in *Das Capital*] "the productions of the human brain appear as independent beings endowed with life." Our awareness that a literary work is entirely invented only enhances our wonder at its utility. Affirming nothing, denying nothing [. . .], the literary is the perfect consort of doubt. It indulges feigned acts of faith but requires only that we suspend our *dis*belief. [. . .] Literature, we might say, is not a relief from disbelief [. . .], but rather a particular way of enjoying it.[156]

Instead of documentary certainty, description's reality effect produces a state of enchantment, drawing readers into a zone of wonder where our critical faculties are poised between two epistemological states: knowing the world (however imperfectly) as it materially exists, on the one hand, and on the other, enjoying the processes of how the world is rendered cognizable to us in the fictive text. Realist fiction is most edifying not when all of a story's elements line up exactly with their historical antecedents, but when the fictive account is equally commonplace and unique, actual and speculative, believable and illusory. Rendering the "distinction between imagining and recalling" to be possibly "irrelevant," the state of suspense that realism generates is profound not for the knowledge of the material world its writings might promote, but for the indifference toward history that its fictions, by definition, require.[157]

Stephen Crane's great gift was that he recognized these paradoxes as enabling conditions of the realist project. Instead of following Howells's ideal that the artifice of representation must be invisible, but eschewing James's Olympian view of the novelist's authority, Crane heeded Emily Dickinson's credo—"Perception of an object costs / Precise the Object's loss"—by cultivating a writing style that all but exposed realism's "jointed" narrative seams to view. But *The Monster* puts so few of those strategies into action. Crane's usually stilted sentence structures, color-laden imagery, hyperbolic metaphors, aloof and (often) mocking irony, and flat characters do not sustain the novella's narrative except in one place, the scene where the lynching of Robert Lewis might be said to occur—the destruction of Henry Johnson's face. There, like the return of the repressed, Crane's style comes back in furious form. By reclaiming his usual literary style at this crucial moment, Crane's description of the burning posits a new history of lynching's violence, one that recognizes the destructive consequences of realist (dis)belief on the lives of black people generally speaking, and regarding the death of Robert Lewis in particular.[158]

The Fire Next Time

In *The Monster*'s penultimate scene, where Crane could have chosen to depict Lewis's lynching, he instead stages a tableau where his practice of writing realism is directly implicated in the violence done to both black men, Lewis and Henry Johnson. Because of this passage's significance, I quote it at length:

> An orange-colored flame leaped like a panther at the lavender trousers. This animal bit deeply into Johnson. There was an explosion at one side, and suddenly before him there reared a delicate, trembling sapphire shape like a fairy lady. With a quiet smile she blocked his path and doomed him and Jimmie [. . . .] Swifter than eagles, [. . .] her talons caught in him as he plunged past her. Bowing his head as if his neck had been struck, Johnson lurched forward, twisting this way and that [. . . .]
>
> [He] had fallen with his head at the base of an old-fashioned desk. There was a row of jars upon the top of this desk. For the most part, they were silent amid this rioting, but there was one which seemed to hold a scintillating and writhing serpent.
>
> Suddenly the glass splintered, and a ruby-red snake-like thing poured its thick length out on top of the old desk. It coiled and hesitated, and then began to swim a

languorous way down the mahogany slant. At the angle it waved its sizzling molten head to and fro over the closed eyes of the man beneath it. Then, in a moment of mystic impulse, it moved again, and the red snake flowed directly into Johnson's upturned face. (*Monster,* 24)

Critics have been dazzled by this scene, calling it a moment of "writerly extravagance," "rococo in the extreme," and a "postrealist fantasy" among other things.[159] It is certainly a *tour de force* of Crane's way with a pen—the excessive hyperbole, the overdrawn personification, the fortified pathetic fallacy, the saturated color field. It should also be clear, however, how this passage depends on the lynching of Robert Lewis for its rhetorical force. The man-hungry fire-as-panther may be the Port Jervis mob; the sapphire lady whose talons prove lethal may be Lena McMahon; the twists and turns of Henry Johnson's neck may refer to Robert Lewis's death throes. But what seems like a surplus of signification is description in the extreme: none of these details "do" anything to compel the narrator's focus on Henry Johnson as the central figure in the novella. The extravagance of Crane's prose did pay off in a different realm, though; as I have shown, such elaborately worded passages kept *The Monster*'s word count high and, with it, Crane's asking price for the manuscript as close to the $700 he needed to end his debt with S. S. McClure. Thus, precisely because the verbal riches of this description fail to sustain our attention to the great bodily harm done to Henry Johnson or Robert Lewis, the passage narrates Crane's role as a writer in cultivating lynching's irrelevance to the plot in an astoundingly honest way.

Johnson falls unconscious in Ned Trescott's private office, a secret laboratory where the doctor conducts "scientific experiments" apart from his caseload of human patients. Realism was supposed to bring the discipline of scientific inquiry to the act of imaginative writing; in this setting we are also in a writer's workshop, the place to which the realist author retreats to prepare his manuscripts. Conspicuously absent from his desk, though, the writer can return to this scene, take it up as his subject, and still not claim to know the truth revealed by the raging fire because the body of Henry Johnson is positioned out of the author's sight. On that vulnerable spot at the base of the desk, writing will happen, but violently: the jars lining the desktop are "silent amid [the] rioting" of the fire; the bottles full of acid-ink are poised to do damage in order to advance the author's craft.

However, the well that bursts—the "one which seemed to hold a scintillating and writhing serpent"—belongs to none other than Stephen

Crane himself, if we read this line anagrammatically as critic Michael Fried suggests.[160] Noting Crane's tendency to inscribe his initials into the phrasings of his texts, Fried might decode this line to find those letters in "*sc*intillant," and if "writhing" puns on "writing," the phallic serpent doubles as a pen and the whole phrase reads: "the one which seemed to hold a writing pen was Stephen Crane." The ink on Crane's desk, though, is animated by vengeance. The "ruby-red, snake-like thing" descends slowly down the table, an awful herald of how Crane's language, burning like acid, destroys what it touches. However, because "there is a difference," Kierkegaard suggests, "between writing on a blank sheet of paper, and bringing to light by the application of a caustic fluid a text which is hidden under another text," we cannot easily denounce Crane for veiling the lynching-as-burning.[161] To do so would be to forfeit the stunning critique of lynching's cultural logic that *The Monster*'s description of the violence offers. For Crane's recovery of his repressed writing style not only suggests why texts get hidden under other texts in the first place, his turn at self-parody teaches us how realist fiction can be indifferent to the history of its subjects. *The Monster's* description of the burning scene therefore enacts why—because realist fiction was a commodity like any other for sale on the corporate marketplace—the violence of lynching was too real for white Americans to understand.

The Price of Remembrance and the Cost of Silence

Squeezing out all he could of the novella's market value, Crane worked diligently to place *The Monster* in no fewer than three venues between 1898 and 1900.[162] Interestingly, though, each reprinting of *The Monster* deepened the novella's critique of lynching because the other stories published with it reinforced the clarity of the Crane's historicist vision.

For the 1899 collection published by Harpers and Brothers in the United States, Crane insisted that *The Monster* appear with "The Blue Hotel," which explicitly depicts and moralizes about the vigilante murder of a white man.[163] The 1901 London edition paired *The Monster* and "The Blue Hotel" again, along with "Twelve O'Clock," "Moonlight in the Snow," and "Manacled." These previously unpublished works concern the lynching-style murders of white men in the American West, and each quite explicitly links the deaths to corporate-monopoly development.[164] When read separately, the allusions to lynching in these stories invoke no cross-racial tensions. However, when bound into one text with *The*

Monster, the stories cry out for comparison because Crane's persistent interest in lynching as a literary trope tests the reader's willingness to contemplate the meaning of the violence from one instance to the next. In this way, the book-length editions reprise Jimmie Trescott's games but with this difference: reading the volumes as purposefully ordered sequences becomes a most serious form of play, urging us to regard—or not—the resonances between the volumes' other stories about lynching and *The Monster*'s depiction of Henry Johnson's plight.

But Crane's plan to publish the novella as one of *The Whilomville Stories* in 1900 reveals most of all how much was at stake with *The Monster*'s interpretation of lynching's cultural logic. In May 1898, Crane had a fresh manuscript to sell, a brief piece he called "His New Mittens." He instructed Paul Reynolds, his American-based literary agent, to deliver the work to Harper and Brothers as part of his contract for this new collection of fiction.[165] Able and tempted to sell these short stories individually to various buyers, Crane reminded his British agent that his contract with Harper restricted that option; but even more, the conceptual integrity of the project—to create a series of related stories about "boy life" in a small town—compelled them to reconsider their marketing strategy because Crane prioritized *The Monster* as the narrative center of *The Whilomville Stories*. "Harper's, in one sense, has the book rights to this series," Crane explained, "but this is mainly based upon an artistic reason—the fact that I do not think it is correct to separate the stories (Harper's have [*sic*] the rights to 'The Monster')."[166]

The "artistic reason" for keeping the collection intact might have been that *The Monster* was to be the cornerstone of Whilomville's social history. What slavery was to Faulkner's Yoknapatawpha County, the lynching-burning could have been to the boys and people of this northern town: the event that structured how the residents inhabit and know the world. Crane's vision remains lost to us; he died before *The Whilomville Stories* were published. And William Howe Crane, flexing his power as executor of Stephen's literary estate, not only censored the novella from the collection's first edition, he created his own front to conceal *The Monster*'s historical source.[167] According to his daughter, Edna Crane Sidbury, William explained to her that Henry Johnson's character was not based on the coachman Robert Lewis but on another local African American, a coal hauler named Levi Hume. Having survived a form of cancer that had eaten away the flesh of his face, Hume was "an object of horror" whose plight inspired Stephen's story, so William declared.[168] Since Sidbury's account first appeared in 1926, critics have accepted it as *The Monster*'s social origin, making the novella's literary history so much easier to conceive and tell.[169] However, William's disavowal of Stephen's interest in Robert Lewis's murder suggests how white Americans chose then (and often do now) to believe that lynching's violence did not—and does not still—shape the meaning of their lives. As William consoled Edna with the story of Port Jervis's black bogeyman, white Americans gladly accept arguments that cast lynching to be an anomalous danger, a culturally illogical symptom of the south's neurotic racism and antiquated politics, instead of being a manifestation of the social developments that made the nation prosper.

Unlike Ned Trescott—or his brother William and the town of Port Jervis—Stephen Crane viewed his capacity to do good (and bad) frankly. "To keep close to my honesty is my supreme ambition. I, however, do not say that I am honest. I merely say that I am as honest as a weak mental machinery will allow," he once explained.[170] As we have seen, one reason why Crane wrote *The Monster* was to buy his way out of his debtor's contract with his American publisher, and his need to earn money influenced his telling of the tale the way he did. To make financial capital from the lynching of Robert Lewis, Crane had to forget the details of the murder and exclude them from the text or else, he reasoned (and probably correctly) the story would not have sold.

Apart from its commodification by the market's notions of value, however, literary realism as an aesthetic practice requires a comparable—and compatible—sacrifice of relation that corroborates lynching's cultural logic as well. Omniscience and description deplete as much as they lend or explain in *The Monster* because Crane uses both techniques to cultivate the reader's indifference toward the violence done to Henry Johnson. Whether in health or near death, the narrator enlarges and diminishes the black man's significance to the text in the most perverse way: the more injuries Johnson sustains, the better Ned Trescott's angst is realized as the novella's preferred interest. The apathy that omniscience and description sanction thus proves to be historically instructive the way common sense and parody shed light on lynching's history in Ida B. Wells's anti-lynching pamphlets. Because in their own "weak" and "honest" ways, Crane's capitulations to the formal and commercial imperatives of realist writing gauge the lengths to which white Americans were willing to go in order to disavow the central importance of lynching's violence either to the nation's progress or to their daily lives.[171] Reading *The Monster* should lead us to rethink the forms that writing and contemplating history assume, and the kind of cultural work that literature can be expected to do in history's wake.

For these reasons, we can call the lynching of Robert Lewis and the mob murders like his an "American" phenomenon, not simply because he and those others were killed in places like Port Jervis, New York; Coatesville, Pennsylvania; Omaha, Nebraska; Detroit, Michigan; Wilmington, Delaware; Duluth, Minnesota; Marion, Indiana; and Cairo, Illinois. Rather, as the literary history of *The Monster* suggests, lynching was embedded in and made possible by the practices, institutions, and discourses that shaped the country's common life. Indeed, *The Monster* is a deeply prophetic and disturbing work because it presages the future of lynching's cultural logic. For instance, the lynching murder of Robert Lewis, together with *The Monster*'s fictionalization of it, clarifies Ida B. Wells's theory about the long-range economic implications of the violence. As she argued in *A Red Record,*[172] lynching was a symptom of capitalist development. Under slavery (that is, mercantile-industrial capitalism) black bodies were a capital investment to be protected; in freedom, as wage labor, the incentive to protect black lives was undercut, making the deaths of black people an expendable cost (*RR,* 140–41). Enmeshed as it was in a town where the contradictory ideals and practices of corporate-monopoly capitalism governed market society, the murder of Robert Lewis in Port Jervis and Stephen Crane's description of it refines Wells's proposition in this stunning way: lynching was culturally logical not because black people lacked value *per se,* but because they were regarded as surplus. Safeguarding the standing of black people as persons (much less citizens) was an expendable notion, a fungible commitment that could be—and was, lynching proves—spent without regard for the consequences.

This expression of racism made it nationally expedient to sustain the South's economic underdevelopment and, because of that neglect, to place the life prospects of black people in constant jeopardy. We know the undemocratic outrages of disfranchisement best: poll taxes, literacy tests, grandfather clauses, segregated buses, and divided water fountains. And we also know that funding this oppression was the super-exploitation that occurred in the places where black people worked. In the fields as sharecroppers, debt peons, and convict lease laborers, as well as in northern factories as strikebreakers, African Americans were systematically abused in ways that perfected their social death in the nation's public sphere. The literary history and narrative form of *The*

Monster archive the ways in which abundance, not scarcity, produced the apathy necessary for lynching to thrive in as many guises as it did, precisely because Crane's subjugation to corporate-monopoly capitalism's instrument of inequity—the contract—primed him to recognize just how many sacrifices that relation required.

FOUR

Lynching's Mass Appeal and the "Terrible Real": James Weldon Johnson

It is characteristic that not only a man's knowledge or wisdom, but above all his real life—and this is the stuff that stories are made of—first assumes transmissable form at the moment of his death.

WALTER BENJAMIN, "THE STORYTELLER"

Protest is an element of all art, though it does not necessarily take the form of speaking for a political or social program. It might appear in a novel as a technical assault against the styles which have gone before.

RALPH ELLISON, "THE WORLD AND THE JUG"

The news came as a shock. In June 1938, James Weldon Johnson and his wife had been visiting friends in Maine and were on their way home to Great Barrington, Massachusetts, when, while crossing a railroad trestle, a train slammed into their car, killing Johnson and wounding his wife severely.[1] The mourners who gathered at Salem Methodist Episcopal Church in Harlem were stunned by the sudden loss of their friend and colleague, for if the manner of Johnson's death was tragic, the timing of it, too, was certainly unjust. Having quietly mentored the generation of poets and novelists who came of age during the Harlem Renaissance, Johnson had finally earned his chance to shine: in 1931, he resigned from his post as executive director of the National Association for the Advancement of Colored People (NAACP) to accept a Julius G. Rosenwald fellowship at Fisk University. There, he assumed the Adam Spence Chair of Creative Writing in the Department of English, the first African American to hold that kind of prestigious post in the U.S. academy.[2] But now, the sanctuary filled with grief for a life so brutally ended, though the mourners surely wept as well for the volumes of work that would remain undone.

Johnson's stature as an author could hardly not have been on the mourners' minds: put to rest wearing his "working clothes"—his beloved smoking jacket (a splendid coat of red silk that fit him well) and a pair of dark trousers—Johnson clasped a copy of *God's Trombones* to his chest.[3] First published in 1927, these "sermons in verse" were indeed an achievement worthy of posthumous celebration. Through their flawless weaving of sound and sense, poems like "The Creation" and "Go Down Death" made Johnson's dream of black vernacular culture's expressive power become a reality. With them he was able to

> find a form that [would] express the racial spirit by symbols from within rather than symbols from without[; to find] a form that [was] freer and larger than dialect, but which still [held] the racial flavor; [to produce] a form [that] express[ed] the imagery, the idioms, the peculiar turns of thought, and the distinctive humor and pathos, too, of the Negro, but which [was] also capable of voicing the deepest and highest emotions and aspirations, and allow[ing] the widest range of subjects and widest scope of treatment.[4]

And yet, literary critics since his death have embraced Johnson's first and only novel, *The Autobiography of an Ex-Colored Man,* to commemorate his contributions to the African American and American literary canons.[5] That book had launched Johnson's literary career in 1912 and revived it in 1927, and had extended the formal boundaries of black fiction writing in unprecedented directions. But it was not the literary achievement Johnson wanted to be remembered for, if we take the last rite of his funeral seriously. Regardless of how accomplished today's readers now find it to be, it was not as the author of *The Autobiography of an Ex-Colored Man* that Johnson was mourned in 1938; rather mourners sympathetically reenacted what had been Johnson's own rage and grief regarding two incidents that nearly ended his life early on in his writing career—his encounters with lynching at the start of the twentieth century.

Although he directed the NAACP's anti-lynching campaign for fifteen years between 1916 and 1931, Johnson never publicly acknowledged that the assaults he suffered led him to join this protest movement or to write *The Autobiography of an Ex-Colored Man.* W. E. B. Du Bois first disclosed this secret to the world during his testimonial remarks at Johnson's resignation dinner from the NAACP in 1931.[6] Addressing the crowd of well-wishers, Du Bois delivered a shocking tribute to his colleague's activism when he divulged that "Mr. Johnson . . . was once nearly lynched in Florida, and quite naturally lynching to him, despite all obvious excuses and explanations and mitigating circumstances, can never be less than a terrible real."[7] With the audience riveted to hear more, Du Bois recounted the details of this "stern experience," a harrowing incident dating back to 1901 when Johnson was nearly beaten to death by a squad of National Guardsmen.[8]

As he lay on the ground being pummeled by the squadron's fists, feet, and gun butts, Johnson was forced to the very edges of psychic and social consciousness where, Du Bois explained, "the color line [was] no mere myth nor wild phantasmagoria of bitter souls." Fulfilling Du Bois's prophecy about racism's centrality to modern American life, this encounter "never allowed [Johnson] to mistake Life for the enjoyment of Life." Rather, the assault steeled Johnson to accept lynching as his "terrible real," a force which clarified the ways in which literal, violent enactments of racial power demarcated the boundaries between experience ("Life") and its aesthetic expressions (the things "enjoyed" from Life). Or, as Du Bois stated this point more sardonically: "[Johnson] may smile over aspects of [lynching], but it can never be a mere joke."

In one respect, Du Bois clearly aimed to suggest that this incident inspired Johnson's social work with the NAACP. By appealing to this rhetoric of authenticity, Du Bois sought to ratify Johnson's authority as a black man to direct what was then the organization's most important political campaign—its crusade for federal anti-lynching legislation. Just as remarkably, though, Du Bois's disclosure depends on allusions to American literary history for its rhetorical force. Indeed, his identification of Johnson's "terrible real" suggests that Du Bois—himself a novelist of measured renown—also meant for his tribute to explain lynching's influence on Johnson's aesthetic sensibilities as well. Punning on William Dean Howells's now much maligned claim in "Criticism and Fiction" (1891) that American literature—specifically, American realism—should "concern [itself] with the more smiling aspects of life . . . and seek the universal in the individual rather than social interests," Du Bois leveled a devastating critique against the nation's literary politics. In its emphasis on the quotidian and commonplace, the genre could embrace (and did, in local color and regionalist fiction) the varieties of experience across American communities. However, as Nancy Glazener and Kenneth Warren have shown, "high realism's" aspirations to heighten and refine readers' taste produced the discriminatory effect of eliding the racial crises endemic to the "social interests" of late-nineteenth-century America from the genre's discursive purview.[9] Du Bois's canny allusion implied that Johnson's experience with lynching positioned him to comprehend which of the pressures shaping contemporary African American life had been suppressed in realism's accounts of the nation's entry into modernity.[10] Johnson's writings about lynching not only deserved tribute as contributions to a more broadly conceived realist canon, Du Bois's remark urged. As his "terrible real," Johnson's narrative figurations of the violence would create their own kind of "moral spectacle," one that would expose realism's aesthetic and ethical limits to scrutiny and thus hold the genre accountable to the social world it purported to describe.[11]

And indeed, when one considers the whole of Johnson's literary *oeuvre,* the most striking feature about those works is how frequently lynching occurs, almost as if Johnson could not write without depicting or at least mentioning the violence.[12] For example, his autobiographical memoir *Along This Way* (1933) reads like a road map of the course lynching followed during the first two decades of the twentieth century, with sixteen such murders (including his own close calls) woven into the narrative of Johnson's lifetime.[13] In another nonfiction work, *Black Manhattan* (1930), Johnson links the emergence of Harlem as a center of black settlement and the development of black musical theater to the practice of lynching. The mob murders of blacks that occurred during the slave uprisings of 1714 and 1741, the Draft Riots of 1863, and the race riot of 1900 (along with the Silent Protest March against Lynching in 1917) serve as the cornerstones that found this pioneering study's periodization scheme. As Johnson scripts it, the theater of violence in New York's streets casts blacks' success on the Broadway stage in a sober light, illuminating an unstated premise of the book; in *Black Manhattan,* the practice of lynching measures the achievements of African American cultural production as art's social referent.[14] Johnson's debut verse collection, *Fifty Years and Other Poems* (1917), foreshadows *Black Manhattan*'s thesis by strategically placing lynching as the locus of narrative sensation and thematic unity within the text. Framed between the stately nationalist anthems and whimsical "jingles and croons" that open and close *Fifty Years* is a tightly woven sequence of poems—"O, Southland!," "The Black Mammy," "Father, Father Abraham," "Fragment," "The White Witch," and "Mother Night." These fierce lamentations of loss, betrayal, failure, and isolation climax with "Brothers," a poem whose highly stylized use of dashes recalls Emily Dickinson's spellbinding hymns as a lynch victim is burned to death.[15]

But it is the narrative form of *The Autobiography of an Ex-Colored Man* that captures Johnson's most sophisticated understanding of lynching's "terribly real" power as both an historical act and literary trope. This chapter exhumes those meanings and their implications from the double burial the novel has undergone since its initial publication in 1912: its explicit repression at Johnson's funeral in 1938 as a memorable achievement, and its tacit suppression since that time as a realist novel in American literary history.[16] To do so, I invite us to become "intimate" with Johnson's life history, the composition of the text, and some speculations about novel theory along the lines that Henry James suggests in his preface to *The Princess Cassamassima:*

> Intimacy with a man's specific behavior, with his given case, is desperately certain to make us see it whole—in which event arbitrary limitations of our vision lose whatever beauty they may have on occasion pretended to. What a man thinks and what he feels are the history and character of what he does; on all of which things the logic of intensity rests. Without intensity where is vividness, and without vividness where is presentability?[17]

As the event that was his "given"—as Johnson's "terrible real"—it should not surprise readers that the lynching scene that brings *The Autobiography of an Ex-Colored Man* to its climax is the novel's most "vividly" presented act. But on what premises does the scene's "logic of intensity" rest? What critical approaches will allow us to understand Johnson's "specific behavior" in the instance of this novel's composition, and how can our judgments "make us see [the novel] whole" again? Indeed, what does that "whole" consist of, interpretively speaking, and what consequences does it imply for our understanding not only of the novel's but of lynching's relation to American literary and cultural history?

This chapter addresses these questions from two angles of approach. First, I offer an account of Johnson's life and literary career before *The Autobiography of an Ex-Colored Man*'s initial publication in 1912, examining the novel's composition in light of evidence that critics persistently ignore: Johnson's memoir *Along This Way,* his unpublished correspondence, his personal pocket diaries, and his surviving manuscript drafts of the novel. These sources reveal that Johnson faced the threat of lynching on more than one occasion during his life. I argue that Johnson, profoundly traumatized by those near-death encounters, became (in Judith Butler's words) "passionately attached" to the violence as the sign and condition of his existence as a black man coming of political and creative age in Progressive-era America. However, lynching's presentability in *The*

Autobiography of an Ex-Colored Man does not depend on the empirical fact that Johnson endured versions of the violence repeatedly. Rather, by exploring recent theories about traumatic woundings and their narrative effects, I contend that the ways in which lynching oriented Johnson's self-knowledge and his relation to the world explain the scene's centrality to the novel and its vivid intensity in the text. My account of the novel's composition not only challenges what we presume the subject of fiction to be and mean, it also sheds new light on the nature of lynching's power to oppress. As we shall see, lynching was so "terrible" for Johnson because it determined the limits of what could be socially known and fictively figured as "real."

To put this point another way, Johnson's passionate attachment to lynching and its vivid depiction in *The Autobiography of an Ex-Colored Man* suggest that we can infer the meaning of the violence from the imperatives of fiction writing as Johnson practiced them in this novel. To do so, the second half of the chapter turns to the novel's narrative structure, and asks how the text's realist features fashion an account of American cultural history that casts lynching's meanings in a startling new light. Our common understanding of lynching's violence no longer holds sway in *The Autobiography of an Ex-Colored Man* because, in Johnson's plot, lynching is not simply a symptom of southern white supremacy's regressive character. Nor is the violence antithetical to industrially driven modes of progress. Indeed, as we saw in chapter 3 regarding Stephen Crane's *The Monster,* the political economy of the redeemed South does *not* explain why lynching occurs in Johnson's novel. Rather, *The Autobiography of an Ex-Colored Man* locates lynching's deadly, dominating impulses at the core of one of the central developments supposed to have transformed the nation's life for the better—the consolidation of mass cultural production in late-nineteenth- and early-twentieth-century America.[18]

In much the same ways that Johnson himself did, the ex-colored man encounters lynching's violence in shocking ways and nearly everywhere in the world that he travels. The labor, goods, services, things, people, and memories that make the novel's social world materially palpable and inhabitable to the narrator all bear the mark of lynching's violence on them. The recurrence of the violence and its ubiquity—much like Johnson's own encounters with lynching—are signs that the protagonist was traumatized by those contacts, to be sure. But because of its perverse plenitude, lynching also functions as a trope for the consequences of American abundance (as much as southern impoverishment), given its myriad figurations in the text. Infinitely reproducible, the violence reveals how mass cultural production harbors within it a death wish that, as Johnson imagines it, most readily exacted itself on the bodies and life prospects of black people. In the novel, the narrator repeatedly recalls scenes of racial violence to certify how the social world is made and organized, and to authenticate cultural processes whose operations are either invisible to the public's eye as "natural" or lie beyond the public's understanding altogether. Under these conditions lynching's popularity and persistence, its mass appeal, stems from its power to specify not where life and death begin or end, but how the realm of the "real" could be extended without limit or concern for the people, communities, and life worlds it consumed in its wake. This dimension of its violence made lynching so terrible and intractable a politic for the NAACP to counteract, which is why, as Du Bois appreciated, Johnson turned to the realist novel as a social form that could possibly prove this point.

The Horror Complex

Once W. E. B. Du Bois disclosed the story of his "terrible real" to the public, James Weldon Johnson ended his silence on the incident by writing an account of it in his memoir *Along This Way* (1933).[19] After graduating from Atlanta University in 1897, Johnson returned to his hometown in Florida where he pursued several lines of work at once—founding and editing the nation's first daily black newspaper, practicing law, and composing musical scores for the Broadway stage—in an effort to settle on a profession that would befit an enterprising race man (*ATW,* 137–40).[20] His fast track took a detour in May 1901, when a fire raged across Jacksonville. With many of the city's vital buildings destroyed, the governor declared martial law and ordered the National Guard to patrol the streets. Since the sizeable African American district was especially hard hit, the disaster that ensued became headline news in the nation's black press. A journalist covering the story for the *Washington (D.C.) Bee* asked Johnson for an interview, no doubt because the former editor and prominent community leader would have been an informative source for the *Bee*'s correspondent.[21]

Johnson carefully navigated the rubble-strewn streets on his way to the interview, but after arriving at Riverside Park and meeting there the very fair-complexioned journalist, he made a crucial mistake. Johnson was spotted by a group of whites then passing by in a trolley car who took instant notice of a black man leading an apparently white woman into a secluded grove of trees. These vigilant citizens immediately called out to a squad of National Guardsmen patrolling the area to investigate the suspicious tryst. The state's troopers trailed the journalists into the park's wooded area where they found the two sitting calmly on a bench overlooking the river. Enraged by this scene of illicit intimacy, the guardsmen cornered Johnson against a fence:

> They surge around me. They tear my clothes and bruise my body; all the while calling to their comrades, "Come on, we've got 'im! Come on, we've got 'im! Come on, we've got 'im!" And from all directions these comrades rush, shouting, "Kill the damned nigger! Kill the black son of a bitch!" (*ATW*, 167)

However much Johnson attempts to control the frenzy described in this passage, fear and despair, rage and disbelief smolder beneath his terse phrases. Even his efforts to strike back at the guardsmen by mocking their slang and curses are thwarted by the force of the assault on Johnson's memory. Because until this moment—and only with this moment—*Along This Way* had been narrated in the past tense. Writing in retrospect nearly three decades later, Johnson cannot find the language to partition off the incident as a mere past event while preserving its transformative effect. Instead, writing's porousness enables the moment to persist as an event Johnson feels and recognizes in the present. The depiction of the guardsmen as they "surge," "tear," "bruise," and "rush" against his body is such that the past and present become indistinguishable. Suspending time's movement forward, the threat of lynching (as Johnson recalls it) marks history's prospect of change.

Miraculously, Johnson did survive this moment. When the National Guard's ranking officer reached the park, he ordered that Johnson be arrested and the prisoner was marched to the troop's headquarters to be formally charged with abducting a white woman. Johnson maintained his bearing throughout this phase of his ordeal because he knew the story he would get to tell: the white damsel whose purity he placed in jeopardy was, in fact, a black woman. Correctly surmising that this revelation would set him free, Johnson also believed that this denigration of his character and of black women's sexuality were habits of mind encouraged by popular fiction's forms. "I was already anticipating the burlesque finale to this melodrama—melodrama that might have been tragedy—and I disliked spoiling any of the effects," he quipped (*ATW*, 168).[22]

Following his release from custody, however, Johnson did not experience liberty as relief. "For weeks and months the episode with all of its implications preyed on my mind and disturbed me in my sleep," he admitted while describing how terribly real the assault proved to be:

> I would wake often in the night-time, after living through again those few frightful seconds, exhausted by the nightmare of a struggle with a band of murderous, blood-thirsty men in khaki, with loaded rifles and fixed bayonets. It was not until twenty years after, through work I was then engaged in, that I was able to liberate myself completely from this horror complex. (*ATW,* 170)

The work that freed Johnson from his "horror complex" was the lobbying drive he led to introduce the NAACP-backed Dyer Federal Anti-Lynching Bill to Congress in 1921 and 1922.[23] Until that time he lived in fear of those "few frightful seconds," waking from the nightmare of the brutal beating for nearly twenty years. That the assault's emotional toll lasted longer than Johnson's physical injuries maps a geography of hurt worth tracing because, as we now know, traumatic wounds injure the mind as much as the body in devastating ways.

It is commonly understood that trauma involves "an overwhelming experience of sudden or catastrophic events." But, as Cathy Caruth explains in her incisive analysis of its phenomenology, trauma also inflicts an equally insidious injury: the victim's inability to fully register the damage that has occurred.[24] Because traumatic events usually take place without warning, they create a "breach in the mind's experience of time, self, and the world," she observes (4). Shutting down and blocking out the stimuli that hurt, the psyche shields the victim from being deluged with pain. However, the perceptual gap that results becomes its own source of woe insofar as the void in memory is filled by "the often delayed, uncontrolled repetitive appearance of hallucinations or other intrusive phenomena" (11). Enmeshed in cycles of remembering and forgetting, survivors of trauma cannot fully grasp what occurred to them in the first place, because their response to their injury is belated, surfacing only after the wounding event. Haunting the survivor's familiar bounds of experience, trauma can only be known indirectly, which is why it hurts even more. Or as Caruth stresses: "Trauma consists not only in having confronted death but in *having survived, precisely, without knowing it*" (64).

The evidence for Johnson's trauma manifested itself in his willfully induced silence about the assault. Deciding that he could not confide in his parents, Johnson refused to tell them what had happened. He divulged this secret to his brother only on the condition that Rosamond not reveal it to anyone (*ATW,* 170). In the 1920s, Johnson's interest in psychoanalysis (what he referred to as the "sex factor" in American racial politics) might have led him to therapy that would let him "talk" his way toward a cure for his affliction.[25] But Freud's interpretation of dreams had yet to have much impact on American medicine in 1900, so that by depriving himself of the chance to speak openly about the death threat, Johnson caught himself in an impossible predicament. The National Guard's failure to complete its murderous aim trapped him, in Caruth's words, "between the unbearable nature of [the] event and the unbearable nature of [his] survival" (7), because to be *nearly* lynched was *not* to be spared his life. The knowledge of that condition burdened Johnson with the awful weight of contemplating whether his own murder could have provided a perverse kind of closure to his "horror complex." Since wishing for death in these terms had to be one of the unspeakable "implications" that "preyed" on Johnson's mind during those long years after the assaults, what words could he summon to legitimate his own annihilation?

But as Saidiya V. Hartman, Thomas C. Holt, and J. William Harris remind us, the threat of physical annihilation was neither an unexpected nor a rare event in the lives of black people during the nineteenth and twentieth centuries. In the country and the city; in the fields, private homes, and factories; in the courthouse and at the ballot box; in the railroad car and at the clothing store—and as Johnson learned so painfully, at the end of a gun butt and a closed fist in a city park—African Americans constantly had to contend with death and life-denying social threats as they moved about in their public lives.[26] Thanks to the stringent codes of Jim Crow segregation in established law and popular custom, the "stage of sufferance" (to recall Hartman's apt phrase) was set and played on so regularly that, for the generation of African Americans who came of age after Emancipation, freedom routinely involved demeaning, brutalizing, and, with the practice of lynching, lethal encounters with the state, its white citizen-operatives, and its apparatuses.[27]

"The majority of the violence committed against the freed in the aftermath of slavery was incited by charges of unbecoming conduct, which included one's dress, demeanor, movement through public space, tone of voice, and companions," Hartman observes in *Scenes of Subjection,* a point verified by anti-lynching activists in the 1890s and early 1900s.[28] "Displease by look, word, or deed, a white man . . . and if he so desires, before nightfall, your property is likely to be reduced to ashes, and the owner a mangled corpse," Laura Arnold argued to a group of black women activists in Charlotte, North Carolina in 1901.[29] The normalization of violence as a means to punish self-possessed or ambitious African Americans made Kelly Miller nervous with worry: "Almost every reflecting Negro of my acquaintance is growing prematurely gray" for fear that the "vicarious load" of reading about lynching murders would be theirs to bear directly.[30] Always alert to the trends defining the violence, Ida B. Wells noted that "Negroes are lynched for 'violating contracts,' 'unpopularity,' 'testifying in court,' and 'shooting at rabbits.' Only Negroes are lynched for 'no offense,' 'unknown offense,' offenses not criminal, misdemeanors, and crimes not capital."[31] As these testimonies attest, lynching was traumatizing not because it was an anomalous or exceptional form of violence, as Caruth's model suggests, but precisely because white mobs murdered black people any day and every day.[32]

As a journalist, Johnson kept close tabs on these routines of racism, paying the extra expense of subscribing to a news wire service to ensure that Jacksonville's *Daily American* published the most accurate accounts of the threats faced by African American communities (*ATW,* 137). An avid news reader, he meticulously pasted reports of lynchings in his private scrapbooks, a habit he maintained all of his life.[33] This suggests how keenly Johnson felt about the lack of evidence documenting his own encounter with lynching. Imagine his hurt when, in 1901, eighty-six mob murders were reported in the national press and Johnson had no written proof of his own assault since the National Guard commander's dismissal of his case left no paper trail or news reports to save.[34] One of the countless African Americans who survived such near-misses and kept silent about them, Johnson confronted what makes racial trauma so hard to overcome: "the way violence becomes neutralized and the shocking becomes readily assimilated to the normal."[35]

The Jacksonville assault did not thwart Johnson's ambitions, though; like the many thousands of African Americans who protested lynching by leaving the South, Johnson departed Florida permanently afterward.[36] Seeking his chance for fame in Manhattan, he teamed with his brother Rosamond and fellow vaudevillian Bob Cole to produce phenomenally successful lyrics for the Broadway stage. This celebrity brought him to the attention of Booker T. Washington, who recruited Johnson into his political machine by nominating him for a post with the U.S. Consular Service in 1906. On the strength of the "wizard of Tuskegee's" recommendation, Johnson served two tours of duty as a diplomat during Theodore Roosevelt's tenure in the White House.

For his first assignment at Puerto Cabello, Venezuela, Johnson's goals were certain and clear. He wanted to earn a comfortable salary in a respectable line of work to support him and his wealthy bride-to-be Grace Nail. Soon into his term, though, Johnson's political aspirations began to grow. Wanting to influence U.S. foreign policy in a setting he believed to be more in keeping with his talents, he energetically sought promotion to a post in Europe.[37] Between 1908 and 1912, Johnson repeatedly applied for transfers, but each time his bids to move to the French locales of Nice, St. Etienne, and Berne were denied. Ironically, the only posts left open to him for advancement lay in the southernmost reaches of the Americas: his first tour of duty in Venezuela was extended two years and in 1910, Johnson was shipped to Corinto, Nicaragua, where he served efficiently but unhappily until his resignation in 1912.[38]

An appointment to the nation's diplomatic corps would have satisfied any number of black men anxious to prove their worth to a public convinced of their intellectual deficiencies and moral degeneracy. But for a college-educated "aristocrat of color" like Johnson, being treated as unworthy or average was an unbearable rejection; he was convinced that his training and talent were sufficient for him to successfully compete for a place within the ranks of America's cultural elites.[39] His inability to scale this wall of discrimination was a source of deep humiliation for Johnson. Friends and colleagues around the country knew what the hoped-for promotion meant to him as word of his possible transfer had started to spread among Atlanta University's alumni. Meanwhile, Booker T. Washington's network of political machinists geared up to lobby Theodore Roosevelt to transfer Johnson to western Europe, widening the circle of onlookers.[40] In letters to his wife, Johnson urged her to begin taking French lessons, scolding her sweetly when she did not write to him in the language.[41] When each of the European posts was assigned to a white diplomat, Johnson was more than embarrassed by the turn of events. "To say that I was bitterly disappointed would be putting it mildly," he confessed to his wife. "It [the denials] took the run out of me for a while."[42]

Having the "run" sapped from him meant that Johnson could not sleep, nor did he have an appetite for food, and began losing weight. He confided these symptoms to one person—his wife, Grace.[43] His reaction to being rejected by the Consular Service echoes his response to the National Guard's assault because the two incidents exacted what was for Johnson a comparable toll. As a black man living in the southern United States he was not supposed to keep social company with white women; as a black man seeking to administer U.S. foreign policy abroad, he was found to be unfit to work alongside white men as their intellectual equal.[44] In both instances, the racial hierarchy was reaffirmed because black criminality and black achievement were equivalent transgressions in the white supremacist imagination. As historian Glenda Gilmore reminds us (and as the portrait of Johnson reproduced in figure 4.1

Figure 4.1. Along with Ida B. Wells, James Weldon Johnson was central to anti-lynching activism in U.S. politics before the 1930s, not least because on two separate and different kinds of occasions he faced life-threatening assaults by federal government agencies. Lynching's infiltration into higher forms of national culture is the subject of Johnson's 1912 novel, *The Autobiography of an Ex-Colored Man*. (Photo courtesy of the Library of Congress, Prints and Photographs Division, Visual Materials from the NAACP Records, LC-USZ62-36618. Permission to reprint granted by Dr. Sondra Kathryn Wilson, executor of the estate of James Weldon Johnson.)

intimates), "the black lawyer, doctor, preacher, or teacher"—to which we could add the African American journalist and diplomat—"represented someone out of his or her place. The danger lay not in their numbers, but in the aspirations they inspired in their fellow African Americans and the proof they gave to the lie of inherent African inferiority."[45]

It may seem to some, however, that the physical beating he endured at the hands of the National Guard bears too little resemblance to the psychic belittlement he underwent in his association with the Consular Service. But nearly losing his life and failing to win a job promotion were very much alike, given the aggressive tactics directed against black federal employees under the White House administrations (Taft and Wilson) Johnson served. The racial policy that blocked Johnson's promotion path also resulted in ruthlessly slashing black employees from the federal government's personnel rosters (in direct violation of the Pendleton Civil Service Act of 1866), often harassing them until they were forced to leave their posts.[46] These onslaughts were well publicized in the African American press; as political cartoonist Lorenzo Harris sketched the problem for the NAACP's *Crisis* magazine, African Americans regarded government protocols to be as brutal in method as much as in intent and effects (see figure 4.2). Thus, the National Guardsmen's fists and bayonets were not that different from the Consular Service's bureaucratized tactics of subjugation. The cabled memos and confidential meetings, the politely conducted discussions and covertly aggressive correspondence, the rigidly detailed requirements and seemingly limitless delays engineered by his superiors wore Johnson's patience down to the point where his letter of resignation may as well have stated what he was coerced to tell his captors in Jacksonville: "I am your prisoner" (*ATW,* 167).[47]

The pivotal role that writing played in each assault clarifies why, for Johnson, the incidents were intimately tied together. In Jacksonville, no evidence of his fateful encounter with the National Guard was ever entered as part of the public record, while the paper trail of communiqués between Johnson and the Consular Service documents a war of wills whose severity was obscured by the language of formal civility exchanged by both parties.[48] The surfeit of archival evidence in the latter instance brings into sharp relief the dearth of written evidence for what transpired in the former case, precisely because in both instances the state used writing (or the lack of it) to obscure what transpired between Johnson and his antagonists. As forms of punishment, then, the beating and the rejection may as well have been near lynchings, since for Johnson the consequences of one event coincided so closely with the other. Attacked by units that symbolized the modernization of the federal government's

Figure 4.2. This political cartoon from the pages of *Crisis* magazine confirms James Weldon Johnson's worst perception of his battles with the U.S. Consular Service: that the federal government's political protocols not only discriminated against African Americans, but were meant to brutalize them as part of such routines and processes. (The author wishes to thank the Crisis Publishing Co., Inc., the publisher of the magazine of the National Association for the Advancement of Colored People, for the use of this material first published in the June 1915 issue of *Crisis*.)

purpose and structure (the National Guard was established in 1877 to protect the property rights of corporations as a national security interest, while the Consular Service expanded its ranks after 1900 to manage the expansion of the U.S. empire across the Americas and in the Pacific), Johnson learned firsthand that lynching's cultural logic was potentially boundless, a death wish without apparent limit.[49]

Impassioned Politics

Johnson relived his "soul murders" when he returned to the United States after his resignation from the Consular Service in 1912.[50] Recruited by W. E. B. Du Bois and Joel E. Spingarn, Johnson joined the newly formed NAACP in 1916, serving first as a national field secretary and then as the policy chief of its anti-lynching campaign.[51] Each post required Johnson to speak and write about lynching so often that his political visibility soared above that of Ida B. Wells, leading Spingarn (the organization's president) to marvel that Johnson "was actually and spiritually present at every outbreak of racial violence that occurred throughout America."[52] And yet, Johnson pursued this commitment without revealing his past encounters or admitting that he might have personal investments in the work. In his voluminous speeches and essays, he addressed lynching as a danger to which he was conceivably vulnerable as a black man from the South but from which he was effectively exempt given his stature as a renowned politician living in the North.[53] Why would Johnson imagine his safety in such self-abnegating terms? Why would he lock himself in the double bind of both speaking out against but remaining silent about the terrors that "preyed upon" and "disturbed" him for twenty years?

Acting as if his work with the NAACP had nothing to do with either the Jacksonville assault or his abjection in the Consular Service, Johnson may have been trapped within the cycles of traumatic forgetting Caruth describes. For, as he argued in a 1927 essay (though notably eliding any reference to his own experience), "no one can take part in a lynching or witness it and remain thereafter a psychically normal human being."[54] His persistent immersion in anti-lynching politics suggests it might be more apt to claim that Johnson was, as Judith Butler argues in *The Psychic Life of Power,* "passionately attached" to the violence.[55] Under this theory of trauma's effects, Johnson would attach himself to lynching because the experience importantly formed his agency, purpose, and being in the world. If it seems paradoxical (or masochistic) that Johnson's self-understanding be tethered to threats that jeopardized his life, Butler explains why trauma so often results in this sort of identification:

> What does it mean to embrace the very form of power—regulation, prohibition, suppression—that threatens one with dissolution in an effort, precisely, to persist in one's own existence? It is not simply that one requires the recognition of the other and that a form of recognition is conferred through subordination, but rather that *one is dependent on power for one's very formation, that that formation is impossible without dependency, and that the posture of the adult subject consists precisely in the denial and reenactment of this dependency.* (9; emphasis added)[56]

The tension between dependency and disavowal that characterizes passionate attachments certainly plots the trajectory of Johnson's political career. Where Caruth contends that trauma involves the impossibility of knowing the wounding event as a stable referent, the intrinsic dependency on pain is the pivot of trauma's knowledge claim as Butler describes it. James Weldon Johnson certainly enacted this relation as

Butler predicts. On the one hand, he willfully took public stands against the racist social structures and cultural practices that sought to keep him "in his place." On the other hand, he denied that his encounters with lynching motivated those same protests against the world's racial order. Nonetheless, Butler's model of trauma and its public consequences presumes two possibilities that do not necessarily occur in the formation of black subjectivity, assumptions that Johnson's encounters with lynching call into question.

First, people of color in the United States may very well want to claim a relation to power that precedes their condition of subordination in the United States.[57] But those entanglements with power—whether benign or malignant, life-giving or lethal—do not diminish the significance of having the harm one suffers being recognized as injurious. Whether by the "other" who inflicts it or through public policy that redresses loss on behalf of the state, the refusal by power in all its forms—the state, its agencies, and its ideal (white) citizen-subjects—to sanction the social woundings that racial subjects experience as "real" is the defining problematic of racial trauma.[58] For instance, despite Johnson's and the NAACP's concentrated efforts, lynching was not outlawed by the federal government until 1968, and then not as its own legislative principle but as a rider appended to the civil rights bills signed into law by Lyndon B. Johnson.[59] Black families courageous enough to file civil lawsuits for the wrongful deaths of their murdered kin won negligible verdicts for their losses: juries awarded as little as $2 in damages in these rare court cases.[60]

The extent of the actual and symbolic affront expressed by these court decisions becomes clear when compared to lynching murders involving foreign nationals. Between 1887 and 1901, the U.S. government paid reparations totaling $24,301 to the Italian and $440,499.39 to the Chinese governments as indemnity restitution for victims of mob violence.[61] The asymmetries of these awards suggest that Sharon Holland is right to ask: "When 'living' is something to be achieved and not experienced, and figurative and literal deaths are very much a part of the social landscape, how do people of color gain a sense of empowerment?"[62] James Weldon Johnson's near-death encounters were never recognized by the state and its agencies, a refusal that requires us to shift the terms of our analysis of lynching as an exercise of racial power. Institutionalizing indifference as public policy, lynching perfected passionate attachment's dynamic of dependence because the violence could be (as the examples of both Johnson and Stephen Crane suggest) so readily denied as an event of social consequence.

The trauma that follows in lynching's wake limits (if not deprives) black subjects' stores of an essential resource they need to repel power's force; it is the subversive energies of disavowal that make resistance to power possible. How, though, can one disavow a condition that is not regarded as such? In Butler's view, at any given moment the relations between powerful and powerless, dominator and dominated, can be transformed in potentially liberatory ways because when the weak claim the conventions of power's rule for themselves, power becomes "ambivalent" and therefore incapable of total domination.[63] In that context, however, parody requires cunning of the highest order because the parodist must use the master's tools to dismantle the master's house, all the while being cognizant of the structural inequities that make the ruse necessary in the first place.[64] As did Ida B. Wells, we might try to imagine parody functioning to expose power's abuses in a different but equally compelling way. This mode would reconfigure lynching's violence and its forms of expression not simply to turn power against itself, but to recognize and archive the less visible harm that lynching inflicts as a history that can be narrated and, hence, known. Or, as Butler suggests:

> A significant and potentially enabling reversal occurs when power shifts from its status as condition of agency to the subject's "own" agency (constituting an appearance of power in which the subject appears as the condition of its "own" power). How are we to assess that becoming? Is it an enabling break, a bad break? (Ibid.)

As far as his relationship to national government was concerned, Johnson's contacts with state power turned out to be "bad breaks." However, it is important to remember—and this is a biographical detail that critics inexplicably forget—that when Booker T. Washington arranged his initial Consular Service appointment in 1906, Johnson brought with him the draft manuscript of the novel he had begun that year, *The Autobiography of an Ex-Colored Man*. Hoping that his diplomatic post would serve as a writer's retreat, Johnson wrote solemnly but enthusiastically to his best friend: "I am gaining power to adjust the various experiences of my whole life to their relative places of importance."[65] And indeed, that Johnson managed during those same years to finish the novel, place it with a publisher, and return to the United States with a cult hit on his hands suggests that, with respect to his literary career, it proved to be an "enabling break" for him to have composed *The Autobiography of an Ex-Colored Man* in the wake of his encounters with lynching. As we shall now see, Johnson's turn to fiction writing prepared him to conceive of lynching as a "terribly real" instance of the death wish lying in wait for black people within national culture and its modern styles of power.

Lynching and the Ends of Art

Fortuitously, because the manuscript drafts of *The Autobiography of an Ex-Colored Man* have survived—along with the diaries and correspondence Johnson kept while he worked on the novel in Venezuela and Nicaragua—we can surmise how his encounters with lynching enveloped the novel's composition. For instance, on the cover page of the book's working draft, written in Johnson's hand beneath "The Autobiography of an Ex-Colored Man" is a neat column that reads "St. Etienne, France/ St. Etienne, France/ St. Etienne, France/St. Etienne, France/ St. Etienne, France/St. Etienne, France/St. Etienne, France."[66] Whether these mnemonic phrases expressed Johnson's enthusiasm, sorrow, or rage over the chance held out but denied to him we may never know for sure. But the inscription graphically confirms how assiduously he thought about the promotion, how intensely he brooded over the opportunity, and how profoundly the State Department's affront haunted the writing of the novel.

Another startling draft passage demonstrates the extraordinary will Johnson summoned to recreate the National Guard's assault into a literary scene. The pages where the novel's climactic lynching occurs are nearly indecipherable and difficult to read: Johnson's usually steady penmanship suddenly warps, leaving a messy trail of stricken and rewritten phrases across the yellow legal pad. Trying to render the narrator's horrified but studied detachment from the violence apparently taxed Johnson's imaginative energies, because the left-hand margin of the page records him venting incoherently: "That 'it' the great example in of the world in democracy was yet the civilized it not only the state in which a human being could be burned alive."[67]

To endow lynching with a power and meaning that extended beyond his own traumatic encounters was possible for Johnson to contemplate because the ends of art as he envisioned them allowed for such relief. He suggested as much when he recalled *The Autobiography of an Ex-Colored Man's* significance in his development as a writer. "The story developed in my mind more rapidly than I had expected that it would; at times, outrunning my speed to get it down," he explained. "The use of prose as a creative medium was new to me; its latitude, its flexibility, its comprehensiveness, the variety of approaches it afforded for surmounting technical difficulties gave me a feeling of exhilaration, similar to that which goes with freedom of motion" (*ATW,* 238). The diaries he kept between 1910 and 1912 tell us more precisely why novel writing proved to be so liberating for Johnson, for in his diary entries he links his musings about fictive discourse to the meaning of lynching as related social practices.

Laced with embittered and derisive commentary, these private writings reflect his battles with the Consular Service. Johnson traduces the mores of Victorian sentimentalism to the point where emotional forthrightness, spiritual piety, behavioral transparency and, above all, respectability cease to matter as attainable ideals. Feeling duped because he had actually believed his fellow diplomats respected him and his talent, Johnson lost his faith in language, declaring he would henceforth reject a man's word as a truth bond. "Generally believe less than you hear, [n]ever more than you can see," he instructed himself. Enraged that his training and achievements did not shield him from racial affronts, Johnson bitterly noted in another diary entry that "the open counterfeit which [*sic*] some white people treat the better class of colored is the sincerest complement they could pay."[68] Rife with disillusioned statements such as these, Johnson's personal notebooks point toward an important development in his worldview. In this same diary, in an "essayette," he also declared aesthetic allegiance to a cagey concept of authenticity he called "Art":

> Art is not and should not be Life, but it should be so like Life as to excite wonder, admiration, and pleasure and to stir the deeper emotions by its verisimilitude. It must always force the exclamation "How *like* life!" It should never call up the doubt "Is this Art or Life?" In fact, the very essence of the pleasure derived from Art grows out of the wonder that Art could create a thing so like Life. If we learn that the thing really is Life the wonder ceases, and with it, the greater part of the pleasure.[69]

Reminiscent of Henry James in "The Art of Fiction" (1884) or Hamlin Garland's "The Productive Conditions of American Literature" (1894), Johnson argues for a theory of realist representation that prizes ambiguity and confusion over mimetic accuracy. However, when read against his diaries' angry recognition of lynching's world-shaping power, the duplicities of Art's forms are not innocently wondrous but quite politically shrewd. Art can recover the "real" history that lynching threatens to eclipse.

"Nineteenth-century realist fiction makes most sense when it is viewed as an attempt to deal with situations which involve partial knowledge and continual approximation, and in which history, existing on a continuum with our other forms of experience and being, can be known and represented with varying degrees of accuracy," Harry E. Shaw tells us in *Narrating Reality*.[70] As Johnson's essayette suggests, to speak of realism's appeal was not to claim readers are beguiled by some mystical presumption of transparent correspondence, because the "real" in fictive discourse is never direct or complete. Rather, the reader "reveals" or judges what is or is not "real" about the text's depiction of its world; "realism's basic impulse [is to put] things into juxtaposition and [to lead] the reader to imagine the web of relations that connects them," as Shaw observes (221). Realism depends, in other words, not solely on acts of interpretation so much as on a "habit of mind" (4) that poises the author and reader to be collaborators in the making of the text. For Johnson's reader to put Shaw's point as a question— "Is this Art or Life?"—asserts that history in realist fiction is refracted through language rather than represented transparently by it. In that case, history in realism cannot be understood as being metaphoric. The "Art" of realism that Johnson calls for requires another rhetorical register, a different "habit of mind" to conceive historical reference and its fictive forms: namely, metonymy.

"Tropes select certain phenomena and ask the mind to perform a range of procedures with them . . . according to which we may select and organize experience," Shaw explains (107). Where metaphors organize perception through comparisons that work precisely to the degree that they leave no visible trace of the relations they assert, metonyms operate through a process of substitution in which we have to determine the whole of which the metonym is a part. Where metaphors encourage us to suspend judgment, metonyms urge us to discern relations and to draw conclusions, an activity that puts us in close touch with history's concatenation of time, persons, and events, the significance of which we can never know in advance.[71] This distinction between literary figures of speech helps explain why realism's theory of historical reference shows up in the same diary that Johnson kept throughout his ordeal with the Consular Service. For him, lynching was not a metaphor of his delimited citizenship rights as an African American. The varied ways in which he was brought close to death made lynching terribly real to him as a metonym, or, that is, as a problem of interpreting the most obvious part of lynching's meaning—its manifest racism—in relation to the larger but less visible structures that concealed lynching's mutability from view. However, discerning these connections could be the work of Art since, as Johnson argued, Art's pleasure "derive[s] from . . . the wonder that Art could create a thing so like Life" but "never call up doubt 'Is this Art or Life.'" With the difference between Life and Art blurred to this degree, Johnson could turn to fiction's forms as a way to reclaim history (and himself) from the destructive force of lynching's violence.

Lynching and the Politics of the Novel(ty) Form

This need to have *The Autobiography of an Ex-Colored Man* archive lynching's history as a function of aesthetic form Johnson spoke of in terms of the novel's craft. As he exulted to his wife Grace:

> I wrote the book to be taken as a true story, and it is proven that I am sufficiently a master of the technical art of writing to make it impossible for even so keen a critic as the one on the [*New York*] *Times* to say that the story is *not* true....
>
> But in it all, the absolute secrecy of the authorship must be maintained. You can see the importance of this from the *Times* review; as soon as it is known that the author is a colored man who could not be the character in the book, interest in it will fall. There must always be in the reader's mind the thought that, at least, it may be true.[72]

Just as he bade Rosamond to keep quiet about his beating at the hands of the National Guard and enjoined Grace's silence about the depths of his humiliation before the State Department, Johnson demands the same secrecy about his novel's authorship, partly because he hoped its success would deliver a redemptive blow in his battles against the federal government.[73] Thoroughly limned with the memories of both assaults, the novel's critical success bestowed one clear victory: Johnson had discovered that the power of novel writing lay specifically in creating artifice, a discursive rhetoric that, as he intimates to Grace, was not permitted to black writers in 1912. "The secrecy of [his] authorship had to be maintained," because for Johnson to seize hold of fictive discourse the way he did was a highly arrogant act, given the racial politics governing American novel writing during the nineteenth century.[74]

To be sure, fictive or anonymously authored autobiographies were not unprecedented. However, for an African American writer to deceive the public in the ways Johnson aimed to do was uncommon, given the value of truth telling in African American biographical literature.[75] From the enormously popular antebellum slave narratives to the "race literature" eagerly read by New Negroes during Johnson's day, African American life writing was compelling fare in great part because of its "corporeality"—that is, the ways in which black authors were expected to offer their bodies as proof of their narratives' claims of authenticity. Frederick Douglass's 1845 *Narrative* and Harriet Jacobs's *Incidents in the Life of a Slave Girl* (1861) are now regarded as paradigmatic texts in this mode, because in each of them the act and meaning of writing becomes inextricable from tropes depicting violence done to their (and others') bodies. The occasion of Douglass's recollecting his escape from bondage is a riveting one, not least because of the image he summons for it: wedging a pen inside the gashes lining his frostbitten foot, he links his quest for freedom to the arts of representation in order to remind us that the threat of death was a fundamental condition for black authorship. Harriet Jacobs understood that she could gain a sympathetic response from northern middle-class matrons so long as she disclosed her sufferings as a "slave girl" in body-based terms. However, by abstracting the prurient allure of her sexual abuse into figures of language—it is no coincidence that her master's physical assaults occur primarily as linguistic events and often in writing—Jacobs's tactics draw attention to how pervasive and potentially crippling the aesthetic demands of corporeality could be.

Cultural studies of anti-slavery politics tell us that the iconography of the black slave in painful distress, so plentiful and persuasive a symbol in abolitionist rhetoric, functioned as a political ideal to mobilize the antebellum masses to humanitarian action.[76] However, once race and the depiction of physical pain became forged as an essential condition for African American writing of the "real," a literary aesthetic was established that conferred narrative value on the wounded or otherwise defiled black body as the expressive medium of authentic knowledge and experience. This habit of mind (which, as I argued in chapter 2, Ida B. Wells parodies so intelligently in *Southern Horrors*) accounts for the critical and popular success enjoyed by the two works said to have inspired Johnson's own: Booker T. Washington's *Up from Slavery* (1901) and W. E. B. Du Bois's *The Souls of Black Folk* (1903). These fierce political rivals shared the reading public's approbation for their autobiographies because their narratives whetted this hunger for black suffering. The Tuskegee Wizard's rise from the degradations of slavery was reflected in the self-image he promoted of his fastidious (almost maniacal) personal hygiene; while Du Bois's "veil" memorialized how segregation restricted his access to the public sphere, the death-linked connotations of the funereal shroud reminding the reader of the socially dead body in which his brilliant mind was trapped. That Johnson felt constrained by this literary genealogy is not only clear in his letter to his wife but is unmistakably noted in his diaries' rejections of both Du Bois and Washington as desirable literary models: "B.T. Wash ought to have been a field hand. Du Bois a house servant. . . . " Johnson wrote privately to himself.[77] Johnson, however, follows through on the hidden implications of his novel's title by excising the narrator's body from the text, defining the protagonist's presence through the man's consciousness and voice. When the novel opens with this cryptic declaration—"I know that *in writing* the following pages I am divulging the great secret of my life"—Johnson turns toward

Melville before him ("Call me Ishmael") and anticipates Ellison after him ("I am an invisible man") to insist not just on the primacy of language but on the valences of print culture as the narrative's referent. Without his protagonist's body to focus the reader's interest, Johnson (like Ida B. Wells and Stephen Crane) recognized the political dead end of valorizing anti-black violence as evidence of the "real" at narrative work.

As an admirer of the "formless forms" of Walt Whitman's verse (*ATW,* 159) it seems exactly right that the "loose bagginess" of the novel (as Henry James would have it) appealed to Johnson for the purposes of *The Autobiography of an Ex-Colored Man* as an "Art" project. Precisely because its narrative structure cannot be fully predicted in advance (unlike the sonnets, ballads, and hymns he wrote), the novel was an apt medium in which Johnson could fathom the enormity of lynching's crime. A "change-obsessed literary form" that "abstract[s] from the flow and fury of existence . . . [those] patterns which are abiding, and re-creates them in the forms of artistic models that can be controlled and imbued with the personal values of the writer, down to even the last punctuation mark," the novel could bear witness to the metonymic complexities of the violence.[78] Since his own encounters taught him that lynching was both variable and ephemeral, Johnson had to conceive his novel as a self-reflexive exercise that paid scrupulous attention to the book's construction as fictive text.

In this regard, Johnson anticipated Mikhail Bakhtin's challenge to artists who work in the novel mode—to laugh at the predicament the violence posed for him and to the world at large:

> It is precisely laughter that destroys . . . any hierarchical (distancing and valorized) discourse. . . . Laughter has the remarkable power of . . . demolish[ing] fear and piety before an object, before a world, making of it an object of familiar contact and thus clearing the ground for an absolutely free investigation of it. Laughter is a vital factor in laying down that prerequisite for fearlessness without which it would be impossible to approach the world realistically[79]

Few novels of its day were as fearless as *The Autobiography of an Ex-Colored Man;* only Paul Laurence Dunbar's *The Sport of the Gods,* Stephen Crane's *Maggie,* Mark Twain's *Puddn'head Wilson,* Charles Chesnutt's *Marrow of Tradition,* and Edith Wharton's *Custom of the Country* match the lack of piety that Johnson displays before the "object" his novel attempts to represent. But to laugh at lynching does not mean to belittle its import and consequences. As Ida B. Wells demonstrated so well, parody can allow an author room to reform a subject by turning it "upside down, inside out, [and] peer[ing] at it from above and below . . . examin[ing] it freely and experiment[ing] with it."[80]

In writing his novel, though, Johnson wrestled with a subject that had "experimented" with him. How could a novelist turn lynching into an idea that, as Johnson understood all too well, not only thwarted speech but threatened to eclipse the very possibility of narration at all? *The Autobiography of an Ex-Colored Man* explores this dilemma boldly, posing the relation between history and fictive discourse—the realm of the real—to be one that can explain the cultural sources of lynching's power to oppress at the turn of the nineteenth century. Conceived as Johnson's theory of "Art" suggests (and laughing at it as much as he can), lynching becomes so "like Life" that in *The Autobiography of an Ex-Colored Man* it is not seen any differently than whatever else the novel imagines in its worldview, including the making and writing of the novel itself.

Johnson chose an obscure, conservative press in Boston whose limited printing capabilities would later enhance the book's status as a rare collector's item. He cajoled his family to act as press agents for the book in New York and Washington, D.C., generating much needed word of mouth to urge sales carefully upward. He hired a press clipping service to monitor the book's reception in the nation's newspapers, since these opinions would help keep the book at play in the marketplace.[81] In fact, once prospects for the book's critical acclaim and profit margins seemed sure, Johnson changed his given name—James William—for a more marketable one, James Weldon: "My name is so absolutely commonplace that it amounts to a handicap," he decided. "The Weldon gives it a little distinctiveness, and makes it a good deal more of a literary 'trademark,'" he argued to his college confidante George A. Towns.[82] From the seductions of its fake first-person narration to the rich and discreet appearance of the text itself (cloth-bound in maroon leather with gold lettering on the front cover and spine), Johnson deliberately styled his novel to parody publishing's modern protocols.

If these maneuvers seem as crass as Stephen Crane's financial gamesmanship surrounding the publication of *The Monster,* Johnson's commodification of *The Autobiography of an Ex-Colored Man* reveals the social threat that lynching makes immanent for historical critique. The niche he sought as a "cult" versus mainstream success tempted the worst possible fate for the book—that it would become obsolete, remembered only as being a literary fad. However, as Johnson also remarked, "I have always said that when the howling mob comes and the colored man sees that he has no chance but to give his life, he should sell that life at the highest possible price."[83] Placed on the market in a form that thrived on risk, *The Autobiography of an Ex-Colored Man* requires us to consider the kind of economies—literary, financial, and moral—that would operate according to such a death wish, one that would systematically devalue African Americans in such base terms.

In this regard, Johnson's novel does not make an unheralded point. Scholars of the "nadir," or the brutal regime of racism between Reconstruction's collapse and the U.S. entry into World War I, have long argued that murderous resonances can be traced between the popular culture of anti-black racism and the surge in lynchings that occurred in the 1890s and into the first decades of the twentieth century:

> To roll back the social, economic, and political clock . . . to 1860, American racists flooded the market with tens of thousands of the most heinous representations of black people, on children's games, portable savings banks, trade cards, postcards, calendars, tea cosies, napkins, ashtrays, cooking and eating utensils—in short, just about anywhere and everywhere a middle- or working-class person might peer in the course of a day.[84]

These fabrications of black life into deadened, commodity objects were invigorated by the corporeal aesthetics of minstrel reviews, freak shows, "coon" songs, plantation fiction, and early cinema—five lively arts that coarsened the already rough and ugly climate in which lynching flourished.[85] Written amid the consumption of such racial necrophilia, Johnson's novel might be said to survey this same social field.

The novel form of *The Autobiography of an Ex-Colored Man,* however, encourages the speculation that more than the fact of racism's commodification accounts for the nation's tolerance of the violence. In its purview, the internal logic of mass-cultural production harbors within it the need for and likelihood of a phenomenon like lynching to take hold as a social practice. As Johnson's turn to fictive discourse suggests, the violence of lynching specifies how mass culture levels out difference by establishing equivalences that confuse what counts (or not) as "real" experience.[86] For when we turn to the social world that *The Autobiography of an Ex-Colored Man* depicts, nothing appears to be what it in fact is. Disguise, deception, and secrecy are the modes of social intercourse in a world "organized as appearance"[87] within and across the color line. In the novel, machine-produced objects and their synthetic perfection set the standards for human activity and desires. Indeed, the public's craving for the unfamiliar and unique is so insatiable that replicas of objects, events, and even people satisfy the deepest needs of Americans' souls. Amid this "gas-light life" (*ECM,* 114), as the narrator describes his cultural milieu, lynching thrives in the world of the text as a virulently original act that can be reproduced in other modes on demand. Thus assuming a novel form of its own, lynching becomes the lens through which the narrator perceives and knows this world and its terms of existence. At once ubiquitous and singular, so quickly serialized but nearly unspeakable like the sublime, the violence is as Johnson knew it to be: the limit at which knowledge of the "real" and the history of American modernity found a terrifyingly powerful form.

Capital's Jubilee

The very first scene of *The Autobiography of an Ex-Colored Man* establishes this idea as the novel's premise. Recalling his earliest childhood memory, the narrator thinks back to the years just after the Civil War, during his early childhood in Georgia. Then, he remembers, he was fascinated by a phenomenon he did not understand: the front yard of his home was bordered by flower beds and "a hedge of varicolored glass bottles stuck in the ground neck down" (*ECM,* 4). This arrangement interests and confuses the boy, because he cannot tell which is the natural growth—the man-made containers or the plants. He learns the difference in a painful way. When he removes the glasses from the ground, the narrator receives a "terrific spanking" (*ECM,* 4) because he had unwittingly defiled what were sacred vessels containing the healing powers of light.

The narrator's decision to indulge his secular curiosity rather than preserve his family's spiritual investment in the bottles shows early hints of his acquisitive, selfish character, an episode that has been interpreted by critics to anticipate the ex-colored man's later "thefts" of black folk culture for his profit-driven use.[88] Readers can, however, concede that the narrator's boyish interest in the bottles is explicable, even forgivable. He was right to be drawn to the gleaming glass—its red, blue, green, and white light pulsed with energy that, to his child's eye, the monochromatic plants lacked. Why something manufactured could be more interesting and seem more "real" than what grows naturally is the question the ex-colored man intuits as a boy but cannot articulate. That he is beaten for seeking its answer teaches him that the pursuit of knowledge in this world of appearances can bring pain and that understanding what makes things "real" will hurt.

By depriving the narrator any awareness of the meaning of this African artifact, Johnson does not indict him for his cultural ignorance so much as place the character in historical time. Born after the Civil War, the ex-colored man lives through three periods simultaneously—black emancipation, the Gilded Age, and the era that Stephen Crane could not survive, "the incorporation of America"—and defines himself through the decisive development linking these eras: the consolidation of mass-cultural production. If he commits racial blasphemy by removing the bottles from the ground, the narrator does so because one meaning of freedom under corporate-commodity capitalism is that money can liberate him from the dictates of his black past. Just as it was for Ida B. Wells in Memphis, mass culture in this novel brings about the "shock of sameness" that historically allowed African Americans to leverage their citizenship rights in symbolic terms.[89] In this light, the ex-colored man recalls that he once linked his ideal of self-mastery to his consciousness of owning things:

> My mother and I lived together in a little cottage which seemed to me to be fitted up almost luxuriously; there were horse-hair covered chairs in the parlour, and a little square piano; there was a stairway with a red carpet on it leading to a half second story; there were pictures on the walls and a few good books in a glass-doored case. My mother dressed me very neatly, and I have developed that pride which well-dressed boys generally have. She was careful about my associates, and I myself was quite particular. As I look back now I can see that I was a perfect little aristocrat. (*ECM,* 7)

This is a tenuously enjoyed security, though, because what plush furniture, well-appointed rooms, nicely tailored clothes, and prudently selected friends meant to the narrator as a boy do not mean the same thing to him later as a man. The objects of comfort he and his mother prized as possessions "*seemed* . . . to be fitted up *almost* luxuriously," the narrator points out. Admitting the fallibility of his memory here at the novel's outset, the ex-colored man juxtaposes his adult skepticism with his youthful arrogance, suggesting that his ambitions over time (and the consequences that follow from them) have been shaped by more than his caste privilege as a light-skinned man of mixed race. Thus, as important to the course of the narrator's life history—and, so, to the writing of it as an "autobiography"—is what Jean-Christophe Agnew has called "acquisitive cognition," the habit of mind that encouraged Americans to view "social meanings as fungible things."[90]

The force of this relation is revealed more fully when, during his adult travels, the narrator settles briefly in Jacksonville, Florida and takes a job working in a cigar factory. Entering the trade as a "stripper," whose task it is to separate the tobacco leaves from their stems, the narrator admires a Cuban who occupies the rare post of the *regalía,* a master craftsman who rolls cigars by hand. The *regalía* can wrap the tobacco leaf about the shredded weed so deftly that none of the one hundred cigars he produces daily appears to be different from any other. Working alongside him, however, are men who operate machines that outpace him at the rate of four to one. But it is the *regalía*'s very physical incapacity to keep the pace of a machine—his humanity—that is the source of his cigar's worth as a market commodity. Working, as the ex-colored man marvels, "very carefully and slowly," choosing "each piece of filler and each wrapper . . . with care" (*ECM*, 70), the *regalía* creates an object whose originality mystifies the meaning of his labor and the cigar itself. Consumers smoke the cigars he makes precisely because his is a scarce talent; there are only so many bundles he can produce, and aficionados will pay a higher price for the luxury of this finite commodity. The workman's national citizenship further enhances the pleasure taken in smoking the cigars he rolls, and consequently their price as well. Because the *regalía* is a "real" Cuban, those who buy his cigars can indulge their fantasy that they are smoking "real Cubans" made by hand in the exotic city of Havana, renowned as the finest cigars in the world.

However, before readers can romanticize the *regalía* as a cultural icon—the authentic craftsman who resists the corrupting influence of mechanized labor—Johnson discloses that the man is leading a secret life. A political exile from Cuba, the *regalía* is chiefly interested in raising money and recruiting soldiers to liberate his homeland from foreign imperialist rule. The *regalía* successfully masks this political activism by leading a deceptively common existence: feigning a bare mastery of English, he toils at the factory and runs a boarding house with his wife. These disguises do not make the *regalía* a charlatan but, rather, a "personality" or the new social type Warren I. Susman finds to have emerged with the coming of corporate-commodity capitalism.[91] A man ready to make, unmake, and remake himself as the situation requires, the *regalía*'s true identity will only become known with the threat of violence, because whenever the planned coup occurs this artifice of simplicity will collapse (and since that moment never occurs in the novel, Johnson unnerves the reader even more because the *regalía*'s plan means America's war over Cuba is not over). The narrator's shock at the *regalía*'s duplicity—what he describes as that man's "eloquence" (*ECM*, 71)—is meant to be the reader's own. However unsettling the *regalía*'s deception may be, to dismiss him as a minor figure or a fraud would be to misunderstand his role in the novel's plot. In light of the history Johnson imagines for him, the *regalía* can be seen to embody the novel's concern with the relation between mass culture's definition of the "real" and the commission of violent acts.

As the *regalía*'s career suggests, in an age of mass manufacturing, authenticity and originality are no longer interchangeable definitions of the "real." In a commodity-driven market, objects assume an increasingly symbolic but highly volatile value, given the "ubiquity and liquidity of the commodity form." A cigar may be just a cigar, but in the social world of the novel the quality of the cigars made by the *regalía* also connotes the class aspirations of those who consume them. However, telling the difference between the cigars and the men who make them in this historic moment turns out not to be politically fraught because, as Johnson narrates them, acts of violence clarify the confusion produced by the socioeconomic commodity form. This dynamic foretells a central function for lynching in the novel. Ending with the final, unchangeable moment of existence—death—lynching's extreme violence offers a decisive check to the proliferations of meanings that "real" things like cigars and, even, books purportedly supply to the world.[92]

This cultural logic governs the narrator's social exchanges throughout the novel. For instance, on his way to Atlanta (the first stop on his adult journey) the narrator is rudely disabused of his unreal vision of this city. Like Henry Fleming in *The Red Badge of Courage* (who learned the art of war through the images he had seen in illustrated histories and magazines), the ex-colored man's fantasies of the South generally are dashed on direct contact with the place. The "luxuriant semi-tropical scenery" he hoped to see recedes before the "tough, scrawny grass, the muddy, struggling roads, the cottages of unpainted pine boards, and the clay daubed huts" (*ECM,* 52). This "burnt up impression" leaves him "extreme[ly] depressed" (*ECM,* 52), a bad mood that only worsens when he finally arrives in Atlanta. Sloshing through its unpaved streets, he finds lodging with the inhospitable, unhygienic "lower class" (*ECM,* 56) blacks who live there. Hoping that the Pullman porter who served him en route from Connecticut to Georgia will help him locate a better place to stay sets the ex-colored man up to be violated: the man robs him of his college tuition and his favorite store-bought necktie. Pilfered of his hoped-for cultural capital (the knowledge conferred by a college degree) and its commodified icon (the smartly styled necktie), the ex-colored man finds himself in a world in which no one's intentions are plain to see and no site's exterior appearance denotes its purpose directly. And again, only on contact with pain and violence do these hidden features become visible to both the narrator and the reader.

The North is no refuge from this welter of confusion, however. Roaming through New York's vice districts, the ex-colored man first has to learn how to interpret their obscure appearances. Nightclubs thrive behind the cover of Chinese restaurants, while gambling dens prosper inside the doors of ordinary row homes. Once behind those walls, the inversions revolve yet again. White vaudeville stars from Broadway frequent the hidden cabarets to plagiarize material from the black performers who work there; black minstrels, whose claims to fame come by caricaturing their racial identity, enact their dreams to be Shakespearean thespians in these secret spaces. The "Club's" subterranean locale is no accident; black vaudeville in New York City was, in fact, then being driven out of theater venues to make room for mass culture's emerging power—cinema.[93] Though underground and seemingly separate from the surface world's developments, the Club provides no refuge from the world's ways or history's unfolding legacies. Gamblers win and lose fortunes so rapidly that their revolving debt strips them of all they own (including their clothes), and their addiction to risk all but shackles them to the gaming tables, much like the chattel slaves their elders once were. Through the narrator's eyes, even the Statue of Liberty, the nation's totem of freedom and individuality, stands ready to execute the threat of death in the guise of her welcoming embrace:

> She sits like a great witch at the gate of the country, showing her alluring white face and hiding her crooked hands and feet under the folds of her wide garments—constantly enticing thousands from far within, and tempting those who come across the seas to go no further. And all these become the victims of her caprice. Some she at once crushes beneath her cruel feet; others she condemns to a fate like that of galley-slaves; a few she favors and fondles, riding them high on the bubbles of fortune; then with a sudden breath she blows the bubbles out and laughs mockingly as she watches them fall. (*ECM,* 89)

Johnson certainly means for readers to regard the statue as a surrogate for the state, just as he deliberately figures the statue's refusal to extend the rights of citizenship to be both capricious and brutal.[94] "Crushing," "condemning," and killing the unfavored, the nation acts under the guise of Liberty to reveal its principles of equality and mobility as the most unreal hope of all, though not because there is no telling how such injustice is dispensed. On the contrary, the novel carefully plots out how racial violence infuses the system of mass-cultural production as the means by which society at large can disavow the excesses to which its economy of progress and freedom is prone.

Knowledge, Pain, and the Mark of the Real

Abundance takes shape in the variety of people, places, and things the ex-colored man encounters on his life's journeys, in addition to the actual wealth made available to him through his relationships with monied white men (his estranged father and the patron of his music, the "millionaire"). As we have seen, though, that plenitude melds into indistinguishable forms, given the premium placed on the changeability or fungibility of things. In the world the novel imagines, violence and pain demarcate what is remembered and what is forgotten, what is true and false, what is real and what is a representation of reality; it is on these terms that narrative occurs within the text. As the ex-colored man explains:

> In the life of everyone there is a limited number of unhappy experiences which are not written upon the memory, but stamped there with a die; and in long years after, they can be called up in detail, and every emotion that was stirred by them can be lived through anew; these are the tragedies of life. (*ECM,* 20)

The narrator focuses on relating "unhappy experiences" (what we might otherwise call "traumas") certainly because they hold great weight for him personally. More importantly, by the narrator's measure the quality of the assaults' textuality lends them to representation in the first place. Tragedies can—and must—be narrated on the page because unlike "writing upon the memory," these events are stamped with a die whose cast does not break and whose ink does not (presumably) fade. This concept is remarkable, because it entrusts narrative production to the metaphor of the machine, an industrial allusion whose aptness links the novel's structure to the work of Frederick Winslow Taylor (who introduced his *Principles of Scientific Management* the same year *The Autobiography of an Ex-Colored Man* was published). But where Taylor's system of labor "attempted to instill confidence in machine rationality as the happy solution to the errors and irrationalities of the uncontrolled human element,"[95] Johnson's novel and its narrative economy recognize the coercive force of mechanized efficiency. As the ex-colored man explains, his narrative "stamping" machine creates a more authentic account precisely because it linguistically courts the prospect of death. The die process requires that the narrator revive his crises repeatedly, coming as close as possible to expiration without crossing the final line of mortality.[96] For the ex-colored man, then, what can be known and represented as "real" is not simply that which results from pain; what can be narrated as "realist" will be that which, using the modern techniques that Taylorism would endorse, figures death.

This relation between knowledge, pain, history, and their representation as realism mediates nearly every major scene of the novel and directs the narrative flow within the text. Spankings, scalding baths, humiliating exposures, shootings, fires, fatal illnesses, suicides, and stabbings are the "died" tragedies that the ex-colored man "stamps" into his story. Whenever he faces the threat of physical violence, the narrator moves from one locale to another, from one chapter to the next. In this way, the novel's nomadic and fragmented plot marks the threshold at which the dangers of mass culture become clear. If the narrative's conceit is that the ex-colored man has produced his autobiography himself and the theory of the "stamp" requires violence to be neither solely repulsive nor exclusionary, the many acts of physical wounding and moments of emotional severity that constitute his story require him to "die" in his effort to produce as precise an account of his experience as possible.

The die-process of racism generates the most efficient energy by which this principle operates. For example, the narrator's most devastating experience as a child occurs when he learns that he is "colored." It is a cruel lesson he learns in public, at school. On a visit to his classroom, the principal asks the white students to rise and the narrator heeds the instruction. Recognizing the boy's mistake, his teacher tells him to wait to be summoned with the black pupils. Humiliated by the command, he "sat down dazed," and "saw and heard nothing." "In a kind of stupor" (*ECM,* 16) he walks home, where he sequesters himself in his bedroom and studies his reflection in the mirror. Attempting to rehabilitate his self-image, he coaches himself through an unabashed exercise in narcissism:

> I had often heard people say to my mother: "What a pretty boy you have!" I was accustomed to hear remarks about my beauty; but now, for the first time, I became conscious of it and recognized it. I noticed the ivory whiteness of my skin, the beauty of my mouth, the size and liquid darkness of my eyes, and how the long, black lashes that fringed and shaded them produced an effect that was strangely fascinating even to me. I noticed the softness and glossiness of my dark hair that fell in waves over my temples, making my forehead appear whiter than it really was. How long I stood there gazing at my image I do not know. (*ECM,* 17)

The image of the ex-colored man mesmerized by his own beauty is certainly a striking feature of this scene and is arguably well explained by psychoanalytic models of identity formation. What is equally revealing, though, is the level of materialist exhortation in this self-portrait. Besides his immodesty, the reader sees the narrator for the first time; this is, perhaps, the most nuanced account of the narrator's body that appears in the novel. However, we come to know the color of his complexion, the shape of his mouth, the color of his eyes, eyelashes, and hair because of his humiliation at school. These physical details are not disclosed when he is whipped for removing the bottles from their sanctuary or when (in another occasion prior to the school rebuke) he receives a skin-chafing bath for playing in the crawl space beneath his house. In those incidents, the narrator does not describe himself or the situation as lucidly as on this occasion of narcissistic self-revelation. In accordance with the theory of the stamp, those episodes occur earlier in the narrative and are linguistically slight because they did not hurt the ex-colored man nearly as much as did his learning that he was not white.

In the novel's economy of pain, then, the whipping, scalding, and stabbing follow from one another, increasing the narrator's awareness of the world, even if those scenes of violence alienate him from the very knowledge he has suffered to obtain. However, if knowing one's "real" condition means knowing "race," and if knowing race entails being wounded, and, moreover, if a "died" account of one's experience is the most profound rendering a writer can muster, it should come as no surprise that the most heavily "stamped" passage in the book turns out to be the lynching scene that marks the climax of the novel's plot.

The Telltale Sign

The burning of a black man must be the most tragic of the ex-colored man's experiences, given the length of the passage and its degree of graphic specificity:

> Before noon they brought him in. Two horsemen rode abreast; between them, half dragged, the poor wretch made his way through the dust. His hands were tied behind him, and the ropes around his body were fastened to the saddle horns of his double guard. The men who at midnight had been stern and silent were now emitting that terror-instilling sound known as the "rebel yell." A space was quickly cleared in the crowd, and a rope placed about his neck, when from somewhere came the suggestion, "Burn him!" It ran like an electric current. . . . Fuel was brought from everywhere, oil, the torch; the flames crouched for an instant as though to gather strength, then leaped up as high as the victim's head. He squirmed, he writhed, strained at his chains, then gave out cries and groans that I shall always hear. The cries and groans were choked off by fire and smoke; but his eyes, bulging from their sockets, rolled from side to side, appealing in vain for help. Some of the crowd yelled and cheered, others seemed appalled at what they had done, and there were those who turned away, sickened at the sight. I was fixed to the spot where I stood, powerless to take my eyes from what I did not want to see. (*ECM,* 186–87)

The affected arrogance and distanced aestheticism that characterize the mirror scene give way in this passage to a feeling the ex-colored man seems to lack until this moment, a struggling-to-speak humility. "Fixed to [his] spot" and "powerless" to look away from the gruesome sight, the lynching forces the ex-colored man into another mode of narration. In his words, the victim is "half dragged," "squirms," "writhes," and "strains" in his captivity; the flames "crouch" and "leap" about the man's body; the crowd variously "yells," "cheers," or looks "appalled" and "sickened" at the sight of its deed. This use of strong, vivid verbs animates the scene, suggesting a degree of engagement from the narrator who (recalling the bottle and mirror scenes) typically recounts his tragedies from a posture of aloof impassivity. In the novel's economy of representation, the most tragic event ought to be the most graphically depicted in the text, and no other episode the ex-colored man relates matches the specificity of this one. Since the narrator "dies" to represent this moment, his "death" is unlike any other in the book and by that measure, the lynching is not a random event without a structural purpose. On the contrary, it is the central event of the narrator's life, the most "real" thing that happens to him.

And yet, the language of this scene invites the reader to question its realism. On the one hand, the narrator sees the black lynch victim physically annihilated and the text, in response, fills with stamp-like details: the high-rise of the sun in the sky as the time for murder crests at noon; the varying moods of the mob as the late night wanes, daytime arrives, and the ritual unfolds; the roaring of the flames as the oil combusts; the writhing of the victim as he convulses from the searing heat of the fire. On the other hand (and despite the length of the account), the narrator finds himself without words to discern the larger meaning of this event:

> Before I could make myself believe that what I saw was really happening, I was looking at a scorched post, a smoldering fire, blackened bones, charred fragments sifting down through coils of chain; and the smell of burnt flesh—human flesh—was in my nostrils. (*ECM*, 187)

The narrator's inability to express himself contrasts sharply with his notation of the murder's action that reads so diligently—the dust, the heat, and the screams are, perversely, details whose precision fastens the narrator's and reader's attention to the scene. This split image of the lynching occurs because the literal facts of the murder can be related and known; hence, the lengthy "died" account of the mob's deed. What those facts mean politically, culturally, morally, or philosophically, the ex-colored man cannot conceive. Hence, the "stamped" description of the victim's murder. Either way, lynching crosses a threshold beyond which real experience and realist aesthetics cease to adhere to socially familiar forms.

The narrator is unable to "make [him]self believe that what [he] saw was really happening" because what he assumes would be proof no longer has rhetorical force. Without a flesh-bearing corpse, he cannot rely on the victim's body to verify what occurred. Without the body's signs of life, he is left with the burnt post, the smoldering pyre, the ashy pile of bone fragments, and the smelted chain. And since these ruins elude evidentiary scrutiny—transient, they can be digested by the environment or removed from the site by souvenir seekers—the narrator confronts the death of discourse as well. Once the "smell of burnt flesh" permeates the air as the surest sign that the lynching took place, the murder warps the axis of space and time between the visible and invisible, the indelible and the ephemeral. Mimetic correspondence cannot bridge this gap. And so, the stamp's cast breaks. The machine of writing shuts down.

In the wake of his witnessing the lynching, then, the narrator's startling decision to pass for white is not made in order to escape that fate, but to historicize the violence as the central event in his life. By resolving to "neither disclaim the black race nor claim the white race; but [to] change his name, raise a moustache, and let the world take [him] for what it would" (*ECM,* 190), by declaring himself to be an "ex-colored man"—a thing broken and devoid of use or exchange value—the narrator emerges from this negative epiphany resembling no one as much as Walter Benjamin's angel of history, the avatar of destruction that comes in modernity's wake:

> His eyes are staring, his mouth is open, his wings are spread. . . . His face is turned toward the past. Where we perceive a chain of events, he sees one single catastrophe which keeps piling wreckage upon wreckage and hurls it in front of his feet. The angel would like to stay, awaken the dead, and make whole what has been smashed. But a storm is blowing from Paradise; it has got caught in his wings with such violence that the angel can no longer close them. The storm irresistibly propels him into the future to which his back is turned, while the pile of debris before him grows skyward. This storm is what we call progress.[97]

The violence that envelops the ex-colored man ought to propel him to act in forward-moving ways. At the very least, we would think that the lynching would shock him into declaring allegiance to the cause of civil rights if not to the Negro race itself. In fact, the tradition of "high realism" demands its protagonists make obviously "good" moral choices at a juncture such as this (and so Huck swears to liberate Jim; Silas Lapham refuses to swindle the English cartel; Isabel Archer decides to stay with Osgood and protect Pansy; and, as we saw in *The Monster,* Henry Johnson sacrifices his face to save Jimmie Trescott). But when Johnson's narrator repudiates the lynch victim individually and the black race generally as a class of people because the law regards them as "worse than animals" (*ECM,* 191), he descends to a depth of abjection from which he cannot recover and for which no adequate account of the "real" seems possible. A revision of realism's ideal subject, the narrator's renunciation cannot be interpreted as yet another role-switching exercise of his racial privilege.[98] It should be read instead as an effort to reclaim deep grief over the lynching murders committed in the midst of "this storm . . . we call progress," and as a lament for the inexpressibility of that sorrow as the condition for writing lynching's history in its fullest form.

Thus, when he thrice admits (like the disciple Peter) that his denial stems from "shame, unbearable shame" (*ECM,* 187–88), the narrator honors the pledge he makes at the outset of the book: "to divulg[e] the great secret of [his] life, the secret which for some years [he has] guarded far more carefully than any of [his] earthly possessions" (*ECM,* 3). More than the wealth and property he comes to amass, and more than the "sacred sorrows" (*ECM,* 49) of his mother's and wife's deaths, the lynching is the novel's structural secret because that event inaugurates and sustains the writing of the text, not the fact of the narrator's passing as white. Or as Ralph Ellison might explain Johnson's narrative choice, the lynching scene is "the dislocated beginning of the story and the time-present in which [history] is evoked out of the memory" of the novel's protagonist.[99] Because the story of a novel is not the same thing as its plot, however, we have to press further to grasp why Johnson would situate the lynching to confuse our perception of its actual significance in the text.[100]

A Man-Made Thing

That lynching both initiates and resolves the narrator's identity crisis suggests it is a singular event that does not recur in the narrative. However, variations on and early references to the scene proliferate throughout the plot, much like the other mass-produced phenomena that shape the ex-colored man's worldview. The lynching scene's interchangeability thus refines Johnson's critique of how mass culture enabled the violence to thrive because, in the novel's narrative economy, lynching turns into so many other forms besides itself, its textual proliferations making it ubiquitous and sparse, commonplace and rare, valuable and popular at once. Alluding to the violence metonymically rather than metaphorically, Johnson uses fire imagery to place the mob murder on a continuum of violence, one that spans the length of the novel. The differences between these instances of burning allow us to track lynching's mass appeal through its myriad forms. For instance, the scalding bath to which the narrator is subjected at the novel's opening is one such foreshadowing: "These tubs were the earliest aversion of my life," the ex-colored man complains, since in them his body was scrubbed raw with "strong, rank soap" that burned his skin and eyes (*ECM,* 4). Similarly, the whipping he received for defiling the sacred bottles left his flesh pink from the strikes of his mother's blows. These punishments anticipate the lynch victim's entire body being engulfed and destroyed by flames, casting the narrator's experience as different from, but related to, the brutality suffered by the novel's other unnamed black man.

Another scene of humiliating punishment prefigures the lynching scene even more precisely. The narrator recalls how, during an elementary school quiz, his white classmate "Red Head" is unable to correctly spell the word "fourth." The ex-colored man watches on as the other students taunt the child. This, like the lynching, is a scene of shame; as Red Head's embarrassment increases, so does the furious glee of the other children. They holler and dance, yelling for the teacher to call on one of them to answer the question. Under this pressure, Red Head's face brightens from the heat of his misery as if he wants to implode from his humiliation. "Slyly," the narrator whispers the answer to Red Head, who finally stammers out the correct spelling (*ECM,* 12). Only then does the persecution cease.

This memory serves as a chilling foreshadowing because Johnson takes particular care to make the spelling bee read like the lynching bee, except in miniature and in reverse.[101] Like the black lynch victim, the white boy is targeted for abuse by his social superiors. The classroom quickly degenerates into frenzy at the first sign of Red Head's otherness; like the adult mob, these children are schooled to interpret signs of difference in especially hostile ways. Crucially, the narrator looks on voyeuristically not because he can pass as white, but because his spelling skills allow him to blend into the crowd. The deferral of race in this scene does not disavow the importance of color to it, however. Unlike the black lynch victim, Red Head is not literally burnt to a pile of grey ash. And it is precisely the racial difference between the white boy and the black man that asserts the meaning of color as the leitmotif connecting these two scenes, for the pedagogy of the schoolhouse and the jurisprudence of the mob converge on two ideas. First, public scourgings are acceptable, productive measures of discipline in the North as well as the South; second, the dissemination of this idea occurs most efficiently through the use of mass-produced technologies—the standardized primer and the rapid transit of railroad trains. The little red schoolhouse in Connecticut where Red Head is belittled by his classmates could very well be set in the rural woods of Georgia, given the lack of difference and distance that Johnson's plotting asserts between lynching and literacy as American rites of passage.[102]

Similarly, emblazoned images serve as harbingers of destruction to forge the world the novel imagines. Atlanta's defeat by Sherman's guns and torches anticipates the annihilation of the black man in Georgia's woods, while a different explosion up North predicts the lynching that occurs in the South. When the sultry "white widow" who flirts with the narrator at the Club is shot in the throat by her jealous black lover, the "jet of blood" pulsing from the woman's wound inscribes an "indelible red stain" (*ECM,* 125) on both the narrator's memory and the novel's page because her murder makes the lynching narratively possible. Fleeing the scene of this crime, the narrator escapes to Europe but is eventually greeted with sensational news reports of lynching during his travels abroad. In Paris, the narrator is confronted by a man from Luxembourg who asks him to deny "an ugly rumor": "Did they really burn a man alive in the United States?" (*ECM,* 136). Writing about this exchange after witnessing the lynching in Georgia, the narrator knows this "rumor" is not just possible but true. However, by refusing to narrate this conversation retrospectively, the ex-colored man confronts why lynching permeates so many domains worldwide. Found everywhere but originating principally in one locale, the violence demarcates the meaning of difference, a function that, as the ex-colored man discovers, ensures death will be particularly (if perversely) valued as the most authentic experience anyone can ever have.

It is a cruel irony that the event the narrator wishes he did not know is the incident he cannot fully forget, that the most formative thing that happens to him turns out to destroy his sense of life and form altogether. When the actual lynching occurs, then, it sets the limits of writing a history of the violence because the mob murder and the narrator's witnessing of it comprise the amnesiac void the narrative itself is and tries to fill. These conditions of knowledge suggest why the novel begins with yet another foreshadowing of the lynching scene: "I know that I am playing with fire," the ex-colored man states in the first paragraph, and the thought of writing his story, he says, gives him "the thrill which accompanies that most fascinating pastime" (*ECM,* 3). Likening his pen to a flaming torch, this passage not only illumines the narrator's guilt for observing the white lynch mob perform its heinous deed, the opening paragraph also implies that the act of authorship—like the practice of lynching—calls into question the social order maintained by valuing "real" experience. For this reason, Johnson's critique of lynching's mass appeal achieves its full force when we study the narrative structure of the chapter where the actual lynching occurs. There, the plot's formal dependence on the mob murder as its generative source reveals lynching's thoroughgoing relation to mass culture and its modes of production.

Settling a Score

During a long and important phase of his career, the narrator earns his keep as a cabaret pianist in the secret after-hours Club, where he is introduced to ragtime music. A quick study, he becomes a fast star in the underground venue and is soon discovered by one of the many white interlopers who frequent the place, the morose "millionaire." The two strike a deal that obliges the narrator to perform whenever and for however long his patron wants. When the millionaire decides to tour Europe, he hires the narrator to accompany him as his valet, a self-abasing offer the ex-colored man resists through a fortuitous exchange with a German pianist. The white musician introduces the narrator to a clever idea: why not play classical music using ragtime arrangements and make a proverbial killing on the market? Anxious for fame and financial success, the narrator calculates the vast potential of this strategy. Based on his experience in the nightclub and his exposure to the monied classes through the performances commanded by the millionaire, he understands that Americans "were ever expecting to find happiness in novelty . . . [and] were always grateful to anyone who aided them in their quest" (*ECM,* 119).

Only in the United States would the narrator's ambiguous racial appearance add to the stock of this trade, though. Admitting that he "should have greater chances of attracting attention as a colored composer than as a white one" (*ECM,* 147), the ex-colored man decides to identify publicly as black in order to capitalize on promoting the music as authentic, or "real." A commercial savant, the narrator can justify this cultural exchange because America's mass-culture marketplace demands it, thriving as it does from both appropriation (the sacred bottles hung on the family's tree) and unprecedented raw creation (the *regalía's* handcrafted cigars). The ex-colored man feels further authorized to follow this plan because, as he exults, American literary culture needs fresh sources for its tropes. In the narrator's opinion, the market has exhausted the aesthetic potential of black culture by glutting the field with "dialect-speaking darkies" (*ECM,* 122), leaving him no choice (but with it, the fat chance) to fashion another alternative.

Convinced that his acquisitiveness not only reflects his economic acumen but also upholds a measure of cultural justice, the narrator returns to the United States and "strike[s] out into the interior" (*ECM,* 167) of the South, mining the Georgia backwoods for its musical ore. On the outskirts of Macon, the narrator finds a prize nugget, the week-long "Big Meeting." Attracting huge numbers of black evangelical worshippers, preachers, and song leaders, the revival provides the ex-colored man with an ample selection of sermons and slave songs to manufacture for his purposes: "[Having] made up my mind to go back into the very heart of the South, . . . I gloated over the immense amount of material I had to work with, not only modern ragtime but also the old slave songs—material which no one had yet touched" (*ECM,* 142–43). In those same environs, however, he discovers an equally deep vein of American folk culture—the ire that whites feel toward blacks living among them and the ends to which they will go to express their fear of and displeasure with them. The sequence these episodes follow is crucial to note: the lynching occurs in the chapter directly following the narrator's epiphany in Germany (chapter 9), while the revival and the lynching take place together in chapter 10, the latter immediately after the former. Because they inhabit the same narrative space, the lynching bears a logical relationship to the critique of originality and reproduction the ex-colored man's pursuit of wealth and distinction encompasses. Indeed, epitomizing the theory of the stamp, the lynching scene poses the problem of knowing the "real" as a complement to the narrator's philosophy of commercial trade, a juxtaposition that invites us to speculate how the novel's form might be symptomatic of lynching's mass appeal.

To begin with, the fictive murder is set in the rural woods where so many actual lynchings took place. Sparsely populated, only a railroad line connects the murder's site to the urban world beyond. In light of the allure of the cosmopolitan centers the narrator has frequented—Manhattan, Berlin, London, and Paris—this unnamed locale is barely known to exist. Indeed, it is so unremarkable that it lies beyond language; the town, the ex-colored man writes, is "of that kind which hardly requires or deserves description" (*ECM,* 184). However, the place is not a Rousseauian blank slate. Once the torture of the lynch victim begins, the clearing calls forth (precisely because it is so vacuous) the other sites and forms of modernity the narrator has encountered before. For instance, its narrative precedent is the Big Meeting, the location and fervor of which resemble the lynching in disturbing ways. Just as the black churchgoers make a special pilgrimage to attend the revival, so do the members of the white lynch mob journey to confirm their faith: by foot, horse, and rail the murderers travel to the appointed space, dedicated (as are the black evangelicals) to banish an evil spirit from their midst. Where the evocative sorrow songs take the black congregation back to the antebellum years of slavery, the "rebel yells" of the Confederate era remind the mob of its sufferings during the Civil War. Leading each service are men the communities acknowledge as their patriarchs. Father John Brown and Singing Johnson preside over the Big Meeting, while an equally select group of "fierce, determined men" (*ECM,* 185) usher the mob through its rites.

Sharing the textual space of the same chapter, the distinctions between these events are dangerously blurred, with lynching standing in too close relation to the spiritually elevated form of vernacular culture made all the more sacred by, for instance, the popular concerts of the Fisk Jubilee Singers. Linking the revival to the murder as its metonym is precisely Johnson's point, though. Juxtaposing one incident with the other to insist on their relation and interchangeability, Johnson demands that we contemplate the consequences of a cultural system that venerates the equivalence of kind without limits, that we query how such a system posits commensurabilities between events that ought to be regarded as distinct. What narrative cues signal us to embrace the Big Meeting and denounce the lynching? What, textually speaking, makes us prefer and promote one form of "folk" culture over another? Given the prevalence of duplicity in the world of the novel, on what grounds do we know one instance to be uncomplicatedly "good" and the other categorically "bad"? Obviously, the way we specify the meanings of these rituals forces us to acknowledge the role of violence in one and not the other. But that answer restates Johnson's theory of the stamp and encounters its same limit. For here, near the novel's end, lynching turns out to be terribly real because it is both reproducible and unique, commonplace and unprecedented in the terms of narration set forth by the novel.

For Johnson, lynching's special ubiquity extends beyond the rural South and the lower echelons of popular culture, though. *The Autobiography of an Ex-Colored Man* imagines that lynching infiltrates and, moreover, informs middle-brow culture in urban centers as well. That is, after all, the lesson of the ex-colored man's aborted folklore project. The narrator intended to sell the folk tunes he collected as sheet music and through concert hall recitals, but with Manhattan's Tin Pan Alley and Broadway as his likely venues of success, the ex-colored man's goal symbolically draws the nation's cultural capital into the orbit of lynching's violence.[103] Commodified as a parlor pastime or an evening out at the theater, his compositions would encourage northerners to consume his packaging of black culture differently from the "coon" shows, minstrel reviews, and "ol' darky" lithographs that were popular fare in the novel's time—or so the ex-colored man hoped: "I . . . felt stirred," he claimed, "by an unselfish desire to voice all the joys and sorrows, the hopes and ambitions, of the American Negro in classic musical form" (*ECM*, 147–48). However, the rhythms of his ragtime arrangements would spare northern audiences from musing about the world of violence that enveloped Big Meetings all across the South. As Stephen Crane envisioned in *The Monster,* Johnson's ex-colored man unhappily discovers the powers of commercial culture to turn seemingly innocent leisure hobbies like singing and concert-going (or writing and reading realist fiction) into potentially deadly pursuits, making of places like Port Jervis and New York City extensions of the killing fields in the South.

So far as the novel is concerned, though, lynching's seriality makes it a global phenomenon, a mode of modernity that draws its negative capabilities from the "high culture" precincts of Europe as well. In Paris—the famed City of Light—the narrator is enthralled with its grand boulevards because they teem with public displays of freedom and vice. Explaining his attraction to these scenes of drinking, illicit love affairs, and shameless parades of dandyism, the ex-colored man observes:

> I have thought, if some men will drink—and it is certain that some will—is it not better that they do so under the open sky, in the fresh air, than huddled together in some close, smoky room? There is a sort of frankness about the evils of Paris, which robs them of much of the seductiveness of things forbidden, and with that frankness goes a certain cleanliness of thought belonging to things not hidden. (*ECM,* 138–39)

Substitute the word "kill" for "drink" (as his U.S. train travels with a Texan no doubt inspired him to do) and this passage offers a powerful account of lynching's mass appeal in the United States. Were lynchings not committed "under the open sky" and "in the fresh air"? Was not the South being "frank" about its antipathies toward blacks? Did the South not "hide" its racism, unlike the North? This statement proposes a startling thought: the South is America's Paris. And if that is the case, as the syllogism of secrecy implies, then lynching is as enlightened, modernized, and rational a practice as are the habits—benevolent and bawdy—of the French.

Like Gallic street life, the "frankness" of the lynching in Georgia seeks to create a normalizing effect on the reader's perception of the violence within the novel's scheme of the modern and the "real." The lynch mob works with precision and decorum, as do the trains that ferry the murderers and their onlookers with efficient dispatch. Just as the ex-colored man enjoys the refreshing sight of the *boulevardiers* in Paris, the crowd in Georgia takes delight in the perversity marched before it. Then again, early modern Europe perfected the art of domination through torture, so that lynching's link to continental modernism is not an entirely implausible connection for Johnson to conceive.[104] Indeed, in *The Autobiography of an Ex-Colored Man,* lynching figures this transnational connection and is itself a product of it (given that Johnson wrote the novel while in Venezuela and Nicaragua, longing to go to France). There are the trains, of course. Those long-celebrated transformers of time, space, motion, and consciousness rush crowds of "fierce, determined men" and "a great many women and children" (*ECM,* 185, 186) to commit murder. The machines in Georgia's wilderness are no longer harbingers of sublime exuberance, as scholars of rail transport's cultural effects claim.[105] Here, in this world, the industrious speed of locomotion carries its passengers into an abyss of moral entropy. When, in a burst of classic American inventiveness, someone spontaneously calls out for the victim to be burned, Johnson describes the reaction provocatively: the idea ran through the group "like an electric current" (*ECM,* 186). Joining a recent discovery of modernity (electricity) to a traditional tool (the torch), the lynch mob appropriates the past in the present, and the residues of Old World Europe are folded into the emergent Eden that America historically aspired to be.

But what makes the ex-colored man's encounter with the lynching paradigmatically modern is that it occurs by chance. He happens to have met the millionaire, who happened to invite him to Europe, where he luckily meets the German, whose impetuous idea inspires him to return to rural Georgia, where he happened to be awake at a late hour of the night, when he was startled to hear the commotion of the mob's gathering and, to round out his wheel of misfortune: the ex-colored man just happened to be white enough to join the crowd and watch.[106] None of these contingencies and their consequences could have been predicted in advance, which makes their occurrence all the harder for the narrator to understand and unnerving in their effects on him. Exerting tremendous force against what can possibly be known and represented as history (let alone the "real"), the novel form of *The Autobiography of an Ex-Colored Man* not only confirms "the inability of all parts of the realist project to coalesce into a luminous whole," the book's craft also "reminds us of another and even larger story, . . . the story of a modernity in which connections weaken and links break."[107] As recompense against both realism's limits and lynching's mass appeal, writing for writing's sake therefore becomes for both the narrator and James Weldon Johnson what it was to Stephen Crane: an imperative to confront the "terribly real" dimensions of lynching's power.

Lynching's Denouement

Between 1908 and 1912, Johnson worked through at least four drafts of *The Autobiography of an Ex-Colored Man.*[108] Writing to his mentor, Brander Matthews, he complained that the conclusion posed special difficulties for him:

> Here is the M.S. of the last part of my book as I have re-written it. The job has been a fearful one. I feel that I have lost the spirit of the story, and I'm afraid that what I have just written is not up to the rest. I'm also afraid that I cannot write convincingly about love.[109]

Johnson's anxiety was with the earliest draft of the novel's conclusion, in which he was unable to determine what the consequences of the lynching scene should be. In that manuscript (like the published version), the narrator witnesses the lynching, flees the South, and relocates to New York City, where he passes as a white man. He then enrolls in business college, becomes a successful real estate investor, and marries a white woman. Significantly—and unlike the published ending—the ex-colored man does *not* tell his wife the truth about his racial identity.

A common criticism of realist novels is that they often conclude too neatly; as Harry E. Shaw explains, "the issue [is that they are] teleological in the sense that they culminate or eventuate in an ending, finding themselves directed by their endings or at least impelled toward them."[110] The early drafts of the novel's conclusion fell prey to this trap with the ex-colored man leading a successfully duplicitous life as a real estate tycoon, happily married with two children. That narrative's arc definitely lost "the spirit of the story," as Johnson fretted to Matthews. Once the character escapes the consequences of his actions—more specifically, if the ex-colored man feels no pain after the lynching—the novel's sequence of events does not make sense. The narrator must be deprived of leading a satisfying life, or else the "great secret" of the lynching loses its power of disclosure; the rationale of the plot collapses; and with each of those failings, Johnson's critiques of lynching, realism, and mass culture cannot be sustained by the novel's form. This creates the impasse Johnson described to Brander Matthews and he revised the ending to surmount the problem.

The final manuscript draft of the ending follows the basic outline of the earlier version. The narrator witnesses the lynching, moves North, passes as white, finds financial success, and meets the woman who is to become his wife. But Johnson alters the conclusion in two dramatic ways. First, he sharpens his account of the narrator's business career to enhance his withering critique of America's "money fever" (*ECM,* 194). Stressing the narrator's acquisitiveness as the ideal of whiteness, Johnson links the prime of the man's career to the early years of his youth, when the boy was obsessed with commodity objects. "I had made up my mind that since I was not going to be a Negro, I would avail myself of every possible opportunity to make a white man's success," crows the narrator, "and that, if it can be summed up in one word, means 'money'" (*ECM,* 193). With this turn of mind, the narrator identifies himself with his white father, a captain of industry and a husband of capital, ever devoted to nurturing his stock of investments.

Besides satirizing whiteness as crudely materialist, Johnson revised this section of the final chapter to ensure that the lynching scene retains its coherence as the central event defining the novel's structure and subject. In a passage that he added to the new ending, Johnson has the narrator smirk defensively about his wealth and the opportunities it affords him to wreak social havoc:

> The anomaly of my social position often appealed strongly to my sense of humour. I frequently smiled inwardly at some remark not altogether complimentary to people of colour; and more than once I felt like declaiming: "I am a coloured man. Do I not disprove the theory that one drop of Negro blood renders a man unfit?" Many a night when I returned to my room after an enjoyable evening, I laughed heartily over what struck me as a capital joke.[111]

The ex-colored man understands that his anomalous position results from two sources: his indeterminate complexion (that is, his race) and the determining influence money exerts on social relations (his class). As his tone of remorse reveals, though, these terms of white elitism and economic privilege are "stamped" as dear and cheap—so hard to come by if one is black or poor, but if white, so readily available that they can be bought. The consumerism of whiteness, its thorough dependence on capital to sustain its claims, is the joke the narrator finds bitterly amusing.

More profoundly than passing for white, though, lynching reveals mass-cultural acquisitiveness to be a life-denying force, given how Johnson revises one particular remark about the mob murder. In the 1912 edition of the novel, he recycled the most oft-repeated justification for lynching but with curious inflections: "From the *mutterings* [of the mob] we *vaguely* caught the *rumor* that some terrible crime had been committed. Murder! Rape!"[112] By 1927, the criminal charges were deleted from this passage. Keeping the accusations intact but calling them into question by the narrator's unreliable recollection (the charges are a "muttered," "vague" "rumor"), the 1912 edition recycles the sensationalized accusations in order to highlight their insufficiency as explanations, given the novel's systematic exposition of mass culture's role in sustaining lynching's violence in the world of the text.

However, a second major revision turned the "capital joke" against the ex-colored man by requiring him to pay an excruciating price for his privileged lot in life. Unlike the novel's first draft, wherein the narrator asks a white woman to marry him without reprisal, both published editions have him reveal his racial identity to her. Crucially, his beloved's reaction is punitive: she recoils with physical horror and refuses his proposal. The following passage, which does not occur in the earlier draft of the novel, shows the care Johnson takes to link the image of their wedding (the most coveted ritual in bourgeois culture) to the burning at the lynching pyre: "I felt her hand grow cold, and when I looked up, she was gazing at me with a wild, fixed stare as though I was some object she had never seen. Under the strange light in her eyes I felt I was growing black and thick-featured and crimp-haired" (*ECM,* 204). Before the "strange light" of his lover's stare, the narrator reenacts two pivotal scenes of debasement. "Black and thick-featured and crimp-haired," the ex-colored man is no longer the boy struggling to lose himself in his mirrored reflection. Here, in Johnson's revised conclusion, writing effects the destruction the novel predicts at its start, for the narrator sees himself as a brutish figure, torched like the man he watched burn to death as narrated in the preceding chapter.

From these new points of development, the narrator's shame can run its course, completing the novel's thematic and structural design. Though the woman eventually concedes her love and agrees to wed, the narrator imposes a crippling stipulation on himself as penance: he chooses to live in silence, refusing to tell his wife's family, their friends, and their children the truth of his racial identity. On bearing their second child, the wife dies, leaving the narrator to raise their daughter and son alone and the reader to wonder how yet another figure of reproduction fails in its function. Forsaking adult romance, the ex-colored man arrives at the end of his life story pondering whether, as the novel's final line mourns, he "sold his birthright for a mess of pottage" (*ECM,* 211). Forced to confront and pay for his cowardice in these final revisions, the narrator is humbled to the point where he hurts.

If these revisions exact more from the narrator emotionally, they remind us of the centrality of lynching to the craft of the story because a full sense of completion—the novel's "real" ending—occurs when the ex-colored man experiences punishment that brings him to the brink of death. Indeed, as the book ends and the narrator closes the lid to the coffin-styled box in which he keeps his sheet music notations, his "fast yellowing manuscripts" (*ECM,* 211) call to mind the destruction of the black lynch victim and that man's ashy remains. Though there are no corpses among the musical archives, many people lie dead among the leaves in the book that is the novel. Thus, with this closure and the revisions that lead to it, Johnson issues his final rebuke to commercial culture's terribly real relation to lynching. The intensity of this conclusion is satisfying to the degree that we accept the narrator's diminished view of the value of black life, a concession signaled by the "ex" that negates the colored man's name.

Writing in the Grooves of History

Ironically, the subsequent success of *The Autobiography of an Ex-Colored Man* only proved the force of Johnson's critique. The 1927 edition of the novel enjoyed wider attention and even better sales because the Harlem Renaissance had created a media swell that Johnson's publisher (Alfred A. Knopf) and chief promoter (Carl Van Vechten) exploited with aplomb.[113] In 1948, acting as Johnson's literary executor, Van Vechten arranged for *The Autobiography of an Ex-Colored Man* to be published by the New American Library, the nation's leading publisher of pulp fiction. The novel's strong sales as a paperback were no doubt helped by the thirty-five cent cover price, though its popularity did cheapen the book's integrity as fiction: *The Autobiography of an Ex-Colored Man* was billed as Johnson's own life story, stripping away the novel's analytic force in the name of making it popular.[114] Earlier though, in 1927 and at the height of the

Harlem Renaissance, the book was promoted as a scarce commodity, one that merited reissuing in Knopf's prestigious "Blue Jade Series" because it chronicled a bygone time during which lynching (so it was said) was a curious aberration:

> Jim Crow cars, crap shooting, and the cake-walk are inimitably described. Colour snobbery within the race is freely spoken of, together with the economic pressure from without which creates this false condition. There is a fine passage devoted to the celebration of the Negro spirituals and there is an excellent account of a Southern camp meeting, together with a transcript of a typical old time Negro sermon. There is even a lynching.

So Van Vechten promised in his introductory essay to the 1927 edition (*ECM,* xxxvii). Well into the twentieth century, as these reprintings of *The Autobiography of an Ex-Colored Man* suggest, the appeals of mass culture's abundance made the loss of black life a trivial pursuit.

By the end of his career with the NAACP, Johnson turned away from the critique of lynching that the history of *The Autobiography of an Ex-Colored Man* implies, adopting positions that were calculated to appeal without guile to the mass public. He organized "monster rallies" and silent protest marches, and lobbied Congress—unsuccessfully—to pass federal anti-lynching legislation. The NAACP's printing presses churned out pamphlets and special issues of *Crisis* that featured Johnson's reports on the organization's petition drives, and Johnson placed essays in the country's middlebrow magazines—*Century, Forum,* and *Current History*—in an effort to sway public opinion toward supporting the NAACP's agenda to criminalize lynching.[115] Notably, these writings reflected a new kind of argument against mob violence. Lynching did not eclipse the experience or sense of the "real" by mass culture's abundance. Nor should lynching be outlawed in order to end the unjust destruction of black people's lives and communities. Rather, lynching demanded action because the violence destroyed the moral fiber of white Americans. Or, as Johnson explained: "I believe it can be said that the more brutal aspects of the race problem involve the saving of the black American's body and white America's soul."[116] Working within the NAACP's interracial membership and distinctively bureaucratic structure, Johnson practiced the arts of negotiation and compromise, changing his positions to advance the group's legislative strategies to achieve racial justice. Ever a pragmatist but an imaginative thinker of the highest order, Johnson undoubtedly made these trade-offs because he understood that social change had to occur (if it was going to happen at all) both in the "real" time of literature and the "now-time" of history.

By imagining lynching's meanings through the possibilities of literature, Johnson was able to discern how the violence accrued sufficient staying power to last as long as it did, as virulently as it did, into the twentieth century. Racism alone could not—and did not—account for how thoroughly commonplace violence against black people had become. Attributing to mass culture's logic of production the significance of legitimating lynching's persistence, the novel form of *The Autobiography of an Ex-Colored Man* bravely issued what was then (and remains still) a stunning view of the ways in which racial violence made America modern. However, if readers today would claim *The Autobiography of an Ex-Colored Man* to be James Weldon Johnson's signature work, then we must confront how real an achievement it actually was.

FIVE

Through a Different Lens: Lynching Photography at the Turn of the Nineteenth Century

A photograph is a secret about a secret. . . . The more it tells you the less you know.

DIANE ARBUS, QUOTED IN SUSAN SONTAG, *ON PHOTOGRAPHY*

"Not a just image, just an image," Godard says. But my grief wanted a just image, an image which would be both justice and accuracy—*justesse:* just an image, but a just image.

ROLAND BARTHES, *CAMERA LUCIDA*

"I was, of course, intensely interested in what you told me the other evening about possibilities of making *The Autobiography of an Ex-Colored Man* into a picture; and I am today sending you the promised copy of the book," James Weldon Johnson wrote to Victor M. Shapiro, a production executive at Fox Film Corporation.[1] In a month, Johnson would retire from the NAACP and claim his endowed chair in Fisk University's English Department, but he remained alert for any niche in the nation's mass culture-market into which his book might fit. Having "heard so much about [the novel]," Shapiro replied promptly that he was eager to read it; on his next trip to Hollywood he promised to take his autographed copy of the book with him and, "if anything develop[ed]," Shapiro would "communicate directly" with Johnson.[2]

This bid was not the first time Johnson explored his career options in film, though. Soon after he returned to the United States after resigning his diplomatic post with the Consular Service—relishing *The Autobiography*'s headline-grabbing reviews in the stateside press but needing work—Johnson scouted his chances in Jacksonville's burgeoning cinema industry. By 1912, the industry's upstart companies of Kalem, Lubin, and Pathé had established studio centers in Johnson's hometown and, together with his wife Grace, Johnson shopped "a half-dozen short scenarios" among them, selling three that were adapted for the screen. Though satisfied with the fees he earned ($25 to $50 per script), Johnson was devastated to see how the final films came out. "We saw the exhibition of the first picture, and were so disappointed in it that we were actually ashamed of the others," he admitted in *Along This Way.*[3] Nevertheless, the chance to adapt *The Autobiography of an Ex-Colored Man* was no doubt intriguing, but Johnson and Shapiro never concluded a deal. And when the Ivan Kahn Agency sought to represent Johnson "on the sale of [his] book to motion pictures" in 1935, Johnson let the request go unanswered by letter.[4] The reasons why Johnson's novel was not adapted for the screen are worth exploring because the difficulties of translating the story to a different medium clarify the history of lynching the book aims to narrate as a function of its literary form.

The Autobiography of an Ex-Colored Man: The Movie would have posed a formidable challenge to Hollywood and "race movie" cinema of the 1930s. In an era of screwball comedies, Busby Berkeley musicals, legendary fables, grand romantic melodramas, and cautionary tales touting racial respectability, a novel as elliptical, morose, and violent as Johnson's would have had a hard time selling its nonnarrative virtues to this period's mass audience. First, the ways in which the book puns on the vagaries of fictive forms by masquerading as an autobiography would have required an especially inventive script and director because, in the novel, the narrator's authority derives from his anonymity and deliberate withdrawal of his corporeal self from the text. A story featuring (literally) no body as its star would have been a visual coup. Second, to represent the ex-colored man's life history in the terms that the novel suggests—not so much as a man who "passes" for white but who is dead to the world in which he lives—would have required feats of narration and image composition on a par with *Citizen Kane.* We will never know, however, because the film was never made.

Any cinematic adaptation of the novel that sought to be faithful to Johnson's text would be destined to fail in any event, precisely because the novel rejected theories of realism that presumed authenticity to be an aesthetic ideal worth achieving. Or, to put the central point of chapter 4 another way, *The Autobiography of an Ex-Colored Man: The Movie* would have had to find a visual vocabulary to convey Johnson's skepticism toward the real and the source of that deeply held conviction: his recognition of mass culture's seemingly unrestrainable role in spreading lynching's violence across the whole of American society and culture. As we learned in chapter 4, the novel posits lynching to be integral to the economic system that launched America's emancipation in the twentieth century: corporate-commodity capitalism. The material abundance that mass-cultural production made possible placed a perverse premium on death. When copies proliferated without end; when distinguishing between the original, rare, and commonplace was uncertain; when appearance sufficed as substance, making it increasingly difficult to tell reality from its representations—in such times as these, the singularity and finality of death could (and did, Johnson's novel bleakly reflects) create the fit that made lynching culturally logical.

Because the relation between the common and the unique becomes most palpable in death—it happens to everyone, but every death particularlizes the life it takes—lynching in *The Autobiography of an Ex-Colored Man* transforms the relation between individual and mass, self and society, and particular and universal into epistemologically discrete things that standardization otherwise confuses and conflates. The murders of black people allowed Americans to confront this implication of the market's changed character but to disavow their worries about it because African Americans' legal standing was so tenuous—like that of "animals," the ex-colored man mourns. That lynching codifies modern progress in such an insidious, demeaning way best explains why Johnson's narrator renounces his racial identity and lets "the world take him for what it will." To tell this story as the history of lynching and not passing as white, a film adaptation of *The Autobiography of an Ex-Colored Man* would have had to be more ingenious and daring than any other American film during the 1930s.[5] Perhaps Victor M. Shapiro, Gertrude B. Kahn, and Johnson realized that if a script embraced the novel's worldview as its own, the movie was probably better off not being made.

If *The Autobiography of an Ex-Colored Man* was not as cinematic as Hollywood producers and agents first thought, the novel nevertheless was immanently photogenic, and the narrative placement of the lynching scene suggests why this is so. As I pointed out in chapter 4, the murder seems to prompt the novel's close since it occurs near but not at the end of the book. Because the lynching actually incites the narrator to write in the first place, however, the lynching scene casts both the narrator and the reader in between "the grooves of history," where "the end is in the beginning," to recall Ralph Ellison's description of his novel's story telling.[6] Put another way, lynching's narrative force in *The Autobiography of an Ex-Colored Man* compels the narrator to tell his story backward, with the result that the novel develops according to a process akin to that of photography. This affinity makes sense if we think twice about a place like the "Club" and the historical moment it provides for our scrutiny, since it marks the displacement of vaudeville theater for nickelodeons and the coming of cinema in the United States. Exposing this shift not as a process but as a series of disparate but connected scenes and incidents, Johnson's account of American film history (and the role that black stage performers did not get to play in it) reads something like a Muybridge time-motion sequence, where the usually invisible actions that comprise history's events—the steps in the march of progress—are captured in fragmented succession, isolating a transformation that would otherwise be impossible for us to perceive.

Indeed, the whole of the novel becomes legible because the events it narrates follow the ex-colored man's theory of the "stamp"—the idea that the most representative and representable events of a person's life are those encounters that wound or lead one to the brink of death. Imprinted and bound between the book's covers, the words on the text's pages become visible through these negative contacts with violence, much like chemicals burn through coats of emulsion to bring photographic images to light. As the theory of the stamp predicts, the novel becomes clearer to the reader the more lethal the depicted violence becomes, so that the lynching scene is rendered for us as the sharpest, most detailed image-event in the text. Figuring the force of lynching in this way, the novel's photographic epistemology positions Johnson's narrator to move through the novel as if he is himself a camera. His eyes serve as lens; his ears and nose (especially at the lynching) as aperture settings, fine tuning all that can be sensed into a view. In his mind, memory pools like a chemical solution bathing his recollections, developing them into image-events that become visible on the novel's blank page.[7]

The Autobiography of an Ex-Colored Man's photo-cinematic possibilities are important to name because they reprise the problem that Ida B. Wells and Stephen Crane wrestled with in their writings about lynching. How does script-based language, fictive or not, make racial violence (and the consequences that follow from it) knowable, and on what terms? Even though, as Jane M. Gaines reminds us, "the printed page gives us *nothing to see,* really,"[8] Johnson, Crane, and Wells wrote with the reckless, brave hope that writing did matter in the world, that writing could change the world insofar as language could reveal those secret structures that made reality appear to be beyond artifice. Lynching would have us believe, through the sheer force of its viscerality, that African American life was so expendable and white supremacy so incontestable that the possibilities of deriving meaning from the violence were both endless and pointless. Dana B. Polan explains this anticognitive dimension of spectacles:

> The world of spectacle is a world without background, a world in which things exist or mean in the way they appear. . . . The image shows everything, and because it shows everything it can *say* nothing; it frames a world and banishes into non-existence everything beyond that frame. The will-to-spectacle is the assertion that a world of foreground is the only world that matters or is the only world that *is*.[9]

Following Polan, we might regard the writings of Wells, Crane, and Johnson as counterspectacles—that is, works in which lynching "says" so much about the "background" or secret histories that gave rise to the violence. In Wells's pamphlets, Crane's *The Monster,* and Johnson's *Ex-Colored Man,* lynching elucidates how modernity's best promises—individual freedom, wealth, rapid transit of information, pleasure, leisure, and the luxuries of abundant services and material objects—were kept at the expense of African Americans' lives. What, however, would their daunting accounts mean when other media forms rivaled literature? Could print narratives of the "real," which Wells, Crane, and Johnson crafted so ingeniously to define lynching's cultural logic, measure up to the challenges posed by photography and cinema once these media asserted their influence on public discourse? What would the spectacle of lynching mean once the nation's appetite for the printed word was sated instead by the rush of visual pictures that flooded the public sphere? What secret history about lynching's cultural logic would go untold?

Lynching in Black and White

If reading print narratives was the means by which Americans knew about anti-black violence throughout the nineteenth century, looking at images of mob murders was how Americans learned about lynching in the twentieth century once mass-produced visual imagery began to dominate public discourse about the violence around the years of World War I. Though the technology for half-tone photography was perfected for American newspapers and mass-market periodicals in 1899, this system (which set photographs and print text on the same page) was not routinely deployed until the late 1920s and 1930s in either the mainstream or African American popular press coverage of lynching.[10] The resistance on the part of the press regarding publishing lynching photographs prior to 1915 did not mean that pictures of the murders were not taken, though, and that forms one part of this chapter's investigation: who made or authored lynching photographs? How did those images circulate and what meanings did that "camerawork" (to recall Alfred Stieglitz's term) imply for the public's understanding of the violence?

That the traffic in lynching photographs runs parallel to the history of American photography's democratization at the turn of the nineteenth century is a convergence cultural historians and critics have not stopped to consider, partly because the racist construction of mass-media imagery has been defined through the infamous example of D. W. Griffiths's *Birth of a Nation* (1915). African American director Oscar Micheaux's *Within Our Gates* (1919) could also confound the issues at stake in analyzing lynching photographs precisely because Micheaux deliberately staged his film's lynching scene as a rebuttal to Griffiths's epic.[11] I do not, however, weave my argument through the critical debates concerning these films' depictions of lynching as founding moments in modern American cinema. Not because I believe photography and cinema are formally unrelated—in the course of the chapter I will pay attention to some of the earliest depictions of lynching on film, dating back to 1903. Rather, I want to bracket *Birth of a Nation* and *Within Our Gates* as the exceptions they are and to measure instead the visual rule by which lynching was represented to and known by the broader American public. That relation, I contend, was sustained foremost by the practices that defined American photography as the Victorian nineteenth century turned into the modern twentieth.

American pictures of lynching are important artifacts to study and read because, like literature, the photographs' formal composition can tell us more about how lynching's cultural logic operated in another cognitive register across historical time. As I did with newspapers and prose fiction in chapters 2 through 4, then, I assume that picture cards, stereographs, Kodak snapshots, and postcards figure lynching differently because each of these technologies of picture making implied distinctive aesthetic requirements for practitioners to negotiate. Tracing how the medium of photography, like the newspaper and novel, developed distinct formal practices that revolutionized the art of "light writing" around the turn of the nineteenth century, this chapter considers what lynching photographs strive toward as aesthetic statements. As Laura Wexler explains: "To be *seen,* photographs must be woven into other languages; otherwise, like the 'unexamined life' the 'unlinguistic image' will float off in an anarchy of unincorporated data. It follows that for photographs to communicate, the viewer must in turn be able to read and interpret them, like other languages and signs."[12]

To be sure, lynching photographs document the hard facts of mob violence and therefore convey important empirical information we cannot ignore: who was killed and how; who was present and, often, committed the murders; where the murders occurred. Coinciding historically with the police mug shot popularized during the 1880s and 1890s and anticipating the crime scene photography best known through the work of New York's Weegee during the 1930s, lynching photographs certainly must be viewed and read as evidence of death. For that reason, there can be no doubt that these images enacted the aims of white supremacy in the starkest terms possible. However heinous it is to contemplate, though, these photographs call out to be understood as Wexler suggests—namely, as aesthetic objects (not just historical documents) whose claims to intelligibility extend the manifest meanings of the murders in directions we cannot automatically predict. Thus, to ask why lynchings of African Americans are so scarce in stereographs but fecund in photographs and postcards; to trace how picture cards, stereographs, snapshots, and postcards circulated and were consumed as documentary art; to map the discursive spaces those modes occupied in late-nineteenth- and early-twentieth-century American culture—to read lynching photographs with these aesthetic lexicons in mind is to pose an entirely different kind of question about the "language" the images aspire to speak.

"Cameras did not simply make it possible to apprehend more by seeing . . . they changed seeing itself, by fostering the idea of seeing for its own sake," Susan Sontag tells us in her landmark study *On Photography.*[13] The very idea of what constituted vision was transformed in important ways at the turn of the nineteenth century, not least by the democratization of picture making into an amateur-oriented, popular pastime. But as Wells, Crane, and Johnson remind us, the most complex and potent formations of lynching's cultural logic take shape in the most widespread and common practices. Therefore, this chapter explores how the material production and pictorial rhetoric of lynching photographs linked the scene of racial violence to the new imperatives of visual literacy, or what Jonathan Crary calls "techniques of observation." As radical uses of (then) innovative visual technologies, these images defined the nature of sight and political subjectivity through depictions of mortally wounded black bodies. Making one phenomenon contingent on the other, these photographic discourses reinforced the scope of lynching's power to oppress by ordering the nation's knowledge in ways that, paradoxically, allowed Americans—both whites and blacks, in the South as well as throughout the country—to "remember to forget" the violence done to African Americans.[14]

This chapter explores this shift and its consequences in several ways. First, I sketch how the modalities of seeing and being seen became a central matrix of social experience at the turn of the nineteenth century, and I trace lynching's place in those "institutional reformations of vision."[15] Second, with lynching thus framed in its visual milieu, I consider the documentary details we can glean from the images. Paying special attention to lynching photographs' visual grammar—the recurring motifs of murders at railroads, light poles, and bridges; the look of the white mob-crowd; the visual attention paid to the victim's bodies—I explore how these patterns link the deadly exercise of white supremacy to the formations of modernity's dystopia, what Mark Seltzer aptly calls the "pathological public sphere."[16] Third, I analyze lynching's discursive spaces in photography. Studying the most popular and accessible styles familiar to the general public—picture cards, stereographs, Kodak snapshots, and picture postcards—I analyze their visual aesthetics, considering how their material production, pictorial form, and artifactual use (insofar as art historians have been able to ascertain private habits of consumption) may have produced their varied affects on likely viewers.

In the end, this is what we present-day viewers want to know most about these photographs: who took them, who looked at them, and why. But as my discussion of spectatorship suggests, identity politics do not explain either the rhetorical appeal or political force of these images as seamlessly as we might think. Thus, the chapter concludes with speculations about why lynching photographs are now (and undoubtedly were a century ago) so hard to look at. They are, to be clear, atrocious given the depiction of violent excess, of moral boundaries destroyed, of lives unjustly and cruelly ended. For precisely that reason lynching photographs are also sublime, given their capacity to awe us into silence—then, as well as now.

Undemocratic Vistas: Lynching's Visual Milieu

As fake cannon balls were fired across the bows of the ships safely anchored in the ocean off of Coney Island, the twelve thousand spectators crowded onto the benches erected on Manhattan Beach watched with bated breath: would the Spanish Armada's gunrunner be hit and sink to its oblivion, or would the U.S. boat go down first, leaving Cuba that much more vulnerable to the Spanish Crown's attack? If the "War of the Worlds" was not amusing to them, Coney Park's patrons could buy a cheap ticket to see the Johnstown (Pennsylvania) Flood of 1889 or the Galveston (Texas) deluge of 1900 restaged to see how the raging waters claimed the lives of twenty-two hundred or seven thousand victims, respectively, in those natural catastrophes. But "Fire and Flames" and "Fighting the Flames" were the most scintillating crises that parkgoers preferred to watch. Every day for nearly ten years, thousands of visitors would watch nervously as a crew of actor-firemen doused the flames that engulfed a four-story building scaled to size, and cheered with relief when those portraying the residents of the building leaped out of their windows to safety.[17]

Americans at the turn of the nineteenth century who spent some of their summers at Coney Island and other boardwalk leisure resorts throughout the country eagerly paid to see fires, shipwrecks, floods, and war battles recreated into entertainment extravaganzas. "During the first decade of the new century," film historians Andrea Stallman Dennett and Nina Warnke report, "historical re-enactments and disaster spectacles abounded in the popular entertainment industry."[18] However, these early incarnations of today's reality television shows commanded the nation's interest for more reasons than that they quickened some ancient sixth sense we might call "bloodlust." Explaining the appeal of Coney Island's fire-fighting dramas, Dennett and Warnke argue: "The lavishly staged disaster reenactments reaffirmed life by forcing the spectator to confront both his fears and fantasies by transforming an everyday activity into something extraordinary—dangerous and yet with a perpetual degree of safety."[19] The daily demands and risks that were part of living in crowded, multistoried tenement apartment buildings were fairly new experiences for most city-dwelling Americans, and they were certainly an anomaly to Coney Island's visitors from smaller, rural towns. Equally anomolous were the political conflicts stylized into visually riveting tableaux off Coney Island's shores: the incursions, imbroglios, and betrayals between governments that launched wars around the world were never made clear to the American public in quite the same way that Coney Island's spectacles managed to accomplish. Being able to see, firsthand, what historical change looked like was the underlying appeal of disaster spectacles.

And indeed, to burn and salvage buildings within half an hour, or to sink the ships of foreign governments in the waters separating

Manhattan, Brooklyn, and Queens was to do nothing less than to introduce those audiences to the vicissitudes of modern life. No sooner was the steel-plated *U.S.S. Maine* ripped open and sunk by an untraceable blast than the country waged war against Spain to start the new century as a global military power. The structures that Coney Island fires destroyed—"public spaces such as factories, hotels, theaters, and exhibition spaces"—revealed how tenuously established American civilization could, in fact, be.[20] If factories and tenement houses testified to our will to rationalize labor, manufacture at unprecedented rates, and inhabit the landscape in numbers that were unparalleled, how awesome it must have been to see that high level of planning thoroughly checked by nature's unpredictable force. In these recreations of historical events, the public confronted the fragility of progress as well as society's will to withstand nature's challenges to human power.

The threat never materialized in disaster spectacles is the one that lynchings delivered without fail, and never so forcefully as those murders where white mobs put African Americans to death by fire. Indeed, with the "theatricaliz[ation] . . . of destruction" emerging as a national pastime at the turn of the nineteenth century, it is an almost unspeakable shame but no wonder that burning black people became a popular tactic in the repertoire of lynching.[21] Emerging when the moral bounds of looking were so easily broken and crossed, lynching was unchecked throughout the late nineteenth and twentieth centuries, but not simply because fictionalized scenes of war and natural catastrophe dulled the public's horror of mob violence:

> By effacing the narrative frame [from the incidents they depicted, disaster spectacles] could evacuate the ethics of narrative; [they] could purify the sensation of cognitive complication. The spectacles, like the new amusement rides, could produce visceral reaction dislodged from moral(izing) teleology. In somewhat different words (the words of modernism), Coney Island realism had de-realized the content of disaster: subject matter as such had become the mere motivation of sensational effect.[22]

Lynching could thrive (however perversely) as a culturally logical practice because its violence enacted the premise that "Coney Island realism" depended on but did not fulfill—as the very essence of its appeal as a thrill—the spectacularization of death. On cue, the United States always sank the Spanish ship and the enemy's crew was captured alive, or the fire was always extinguished and the building's occupants were saved. With the restoration of safety and order guaranteed, the emergency dramatized by disaster spectacles—the source of the viewer's anxiety and interest—was invariably sutured shut.

Like the journalistic stunts that Ida B. Wells parodies in *Southern Horrors,* the prospect of seeing death actually occur was forestalled. But when a lynching ended, the victim was unmistakably dead. If he was burned to death, he perished from sight. And as James Weldon Johnson reminds us, if the victim survived he lived inside the space of death for the rest of his life. Because black people lacked the legal and social standing to be grieved for in the ways that disaster spectacles invited the public to do, their deaths determined the boundary toward which "amusements" like Coney Island's disaster spectacles were headed but did not dare to go. As such, lynching—even more than Coney Island realism—"demonstrated the . . . power of genuine liminality, wherein the structures of normalcy and everyday security break down."[23]

This new order of visual experience underscores why lynching was such a thoroughgoing form of racial domination at the turn of the nineteenth century. With Americans financially able to pay for and attend disaster spectacles as a matter of course, the violence of lynching was enveloped in a milieu that encouraged looking for its own sake, and that sanctioned the threat of mass injury or death to be a fun, leisure activity. Though the majority of mob murders occurred in the Deep South, lynching's "historical adjacency" to the visual practices redefining the nation's everyday life entrenched and normalized the violence, creating a social space where it could grow in its own festering way.[24] As such, lynching contributed to the late-nineteenth-century *zeitgeist* that fueled "the new stress upon visual sensations during these years."[25] Amid the rise of "amusement parks, world's fairs, urban theater districts and their White Ways, and circus extravaganzas"—together with the awe-inspiring constructions of elevated railways, underground subway systems, skyscraper buildings, and department stores—lynching was a vital link in this new order of display because the violence, like these other visual phenomena, heightened Americans' "consciousness about vision" in its own particular ways.[26] Indeed, lynching helped shape the experience and meaning of American "seeing" at the start of the twentieth century, just as those new modes of sight helped make lynching the distinctly visual phenomenon it was.

In early cinema, for instance—prior to either *Birth of a Nation* or *Within Our Gates*—lynching was a recurrent, organizing sight-event in American movies.[27] The "chase" film, which according to one early cinema scholar made "moving pictures really [able] to move," includes as one of its first examples *Avenging a Crime; Or, Burned at the Stake* (1903).[28] In it, a black man (or, rather, a white actor performing in blackface) commits a robbery that ends with his murdering a white shopkeeper. Suddenly, the film cuts to an open field; there, a mob has materialized on screen and fans out across the movie's frame in pursuit of the criminal. The hunt runs for several seconds before the black man is caught and the film ends as he is lashed to a pole and white smoke rises from the bottom edge of the screen.

The Whitecaps, a 1905 film directed by the pioneer director-producer Edwin S. Porter, recalls the antebellum history of lynching, as its anti-protagonist is an elderly white man who takes a younger white woman for his wife. Hooded vigilantes kidnap the man from his home and take him out to a secluded wood, where they tar-and-feather him as punishment. But in the film's final frames, the camera lingers on the moment when the man's body is colored black with tar. His hands bound with rope and tied to a tree, the man revolves in a glistening, 360-degree turn before the camera. This reference to lynching's modern mode gets erased when the victim's body turns its last time. Flocked with white feathers, the man becomes a thoroughly strange apparition whose formlessness compels the viewer's attention more than the transgression that placed him in such jeopardy.

Lynching figures astoundingly in one of Thomas Edison's films, *Electrocuting an Elephant* (1903). This live-action short—what film historians call an "attractions" movie—documents the execution of the animal at Coney Island's Luna Park. Led into the camera's view by a trainer, the elephant is directed to stand on a metal plate where, restrained by shackles and chains, the elephant cannot move. The film rolls on, fixed to this static scene, drawing the viewer's attention to the odd arrangement. Suddenly, the elephant's large-limbed body quivers, white smoke plumes rise from the soles of its feet, and it collapses into a heap on its side, at which point the film ends. Tom Gunning argues that *Electrocuting an Elephant* exemplifies how "the act of monstration," of showing things as a sight, was the point of filmic representation in early cinema. Specifically, this film "monstrates" the act of seeing itself since "the moment of technologically advanced death is neither . . . explained, nor dramatised."[29] But in the space of seeing created by the film's elision of the cause of death, we should recall Stephen Crane's critique of how monstrous realist representation could be. Because as it turns out, the elephant electrocuted in Edison's film was meant to be lynched.[30]

"Topsy" (no doubt named after the unruly black girl-child of Harriet Beecher Stowe's *Uncle Tom's Cabin*) had attacked a trainer who had stuffed lit cigarettes up its nose. Deeming the elephant too "wild" to be kept in captivity, Coney Island's managers decided to kill it. But as the home of disaster spectacles in America, park officials seized on the chance to turn the elephant's demise into an exhibit not just of their disciplinary power but of lynching-murder's commercial appeal as well: the animal was to be hanged as part of Luna Park's schedule of thrilling events. This first try at killing the elephant failed, though, because Topsy was too heavy for the scaffold. Electrocuting the elephant saved the show. Thomas Edison was commissioned to film the event, which he shot as a straight-forward documentary—the camera's view opens and stays fixed from one stable point, directly facing the elephant. The lynching that preceded "the moment of technologically advanced death" was indeed, as Stephen Crane predicted about techniques of realist representation and commercial culture's concern for black suffering, "neither . . . explained, nor dramatised."

An exhibitionist mode, the "cinema of attractions" (of which chase and disaster films were a part) thrived by providing viewers with novel things to see and with the idea of "looking" itself. To produce both effects, these films featured scenes of extremity that "invoke[d] the temporality of surprise, shock, and trauma" registered most viscerally through intensive close-ups and direct gazes from the actors on screen.[31] Concerned most with "the very pleasure of looking," attraction films emphasized "the phenomenon of motion itself" and encouraged spectators to "experience the thrill of intense and sudden changing sensations." As film historian Tom Gunning explains:

> The sudden flash (or equally sudden curtailing) of an erotic spectacle, the burst into motion of a terroristic locomotive, or the rhythm of appearance, transformation, and sudden disappearance that rules a magic film all invoke a spectator whose delight comes from the unpredictability of the instant, a succession of excitements and frustrations whose order cannot be predicted by narrative logic and whose pleasures are never sure of being prolonged.[32]

Such films as *Avenging a Crime, The Whitecaps,* and *Electrocuting an Elephant* revel in the visual intensities they create on screen. In them all, lynching murders occur but are foreshortened visually and temporally so that the death scenes revel in the act of display as an end unto itself. With their enforced curtailment (coming as the deaths do at the end of the film reel), the murders become "views" and seeing the violence encoded in these terms becomes the source of the unsettling surprise that Gunning describes. For lynching to be part of early cinema's visual vocabulary meant, then, that the public would regard the violence through the structures of seeing popularized by "attractive" movie making and watching.[33]

Thus, it is no small irony that one of the most disturbing lynching murders of the early twentieth century took place in a movie theater. In April 1911, in Livermore, Kentucky, Will Porter was accused of shooting a white man, Frank Mitchell, during a bar room fight. Shortly after his arrest, Porter was taken to the town's opera house, where he was murdered by a mob that had assembled to kill him. However, "the shooting of the negro was done in a weird scene," according to the *New York Times:*

> The negro was bound hand and foot and placed in the centre of the stage. Many of the lights when the current was turned on refused to burn, and in the semi-darkness the mob silhouetted against the theatre walls, awaited the signal of their leader. When it was given fifty guns fired in unison, one piercing scream was heard, and their work was over. The lights were extinguished, the curtain lowered, and the mob filed out.[34]

The NAACP's investigation of the murder uncovered an even more chilling turn of events. Porter had been removed from jail by Livermore's police officers and was taken to the opera house as the *Times* reported, but the mob did not simply lay in wait. "Those who bought orchestra seats had the privilege of emptying their six shooters at the swaying form above them, [while] the gallery occupants were limited to one shot," the NAACP claimed, noting that "the money taken in at the door went to the family of the white man the Negro had killed."[35]

Deliberately making Will Porter's murder a theatrical event led to its being reported on and denounced throughout the nation's press and around the world.[36] However, the interest stirred up by this lynching, its power of "attracting," derived not from the ideals of stage drama, but from those of cinema instead. In small southern towns like Livermore, Kentucky, the local opera house often served as a major venue for screening films.[37] Like modern movie palaces, opera houses devoted to film promoted "an ideal of polite order and elegant refinement significantly different from the working-class nickelodeons," according to cultural historian John F. Kasson.[38] By choosing to kill Will Porter on the stage of Livermore's institution of cultural sophistication, the mob selected the site where American modernity had taken root in their community, not to repudiate cinema's conventions, but to utilize them for all of their exhibitionary worth—from staging the murder in that space to charging the tiered price to see and shoot at Porter.

The ways in which cinema's structures of seeing mediated lynching's force and meaning can be traced one final step using the instance of mob murder with which this book began: the 1893 murder of Henry Smith in Paris, Texas. As I argued in chapter 1, the public display of the visual records of that lynching follows (if not anticipates) the course of American film history at the turn of the nineteenth century. Photographed and sound recorded at the murder scene, these reproductions were organized to resemble the kinetoscope that Thomas Edison was perfecting in Orange, New Jersey during the early 1890s. Unlike Edison's machine, the low-tech assemblage of the Seattle "screening" of Smith's murder actually advanced the progress of film technology, for that arrangement synchronized sight with sound nearly five years before Edison marketed such a system.[39] Indeed, by the time kinetoscopes had given way to the nickelodeon between 1894 and 1907, another film version of Henry Smith's death had been released, keeping his murder at the forefront of visual culture's modern development.

Booked at two separate venues on Manhattan's Sixth Avenue and in the Bowery in 1908, an extraordinary film featured "JOHN SMITH [*sic*] OF PARIS, TEXAS, BURNED AT THE STAKE. HEAR HIS MOANS and GROANS. PRICE ONE CENT!" African American film critic Lester Walton's surprise encounter with these screenings prompted his blistering essay published in the *New York Age,* "The Degeneracy of the Moving Picture Theatre."[40] Directing his outrage at the unconscionable commodification of black suffering, Walton would have certainly aimed his ire at the film's form, too, had he known about the conditions under which Samuel Burdett had seen Henry Smith's murder nearly a decade earlier. Its circulation across the country in growing urban centers; its screening taking place indoors at a movie palace instead of outdoors on a street corner; its cut-rate cost of a penny instead of a nickel for admission; its screening as a sound-tracked film instead of a photographically based kinetoscope projection—given all these factors, the lynching of Henry Smith heralded another transformative advance in visual culture. Jonathan Crary argues that once talking pictures became common, around 1927, the "full coincidence of sound with image, of voice with figure . . . was a crucial new way of organizing space, time and narrative, [and] it instituted a more commanding authority over the observer, enforcing a new kind of attention."[41] For that development to have been so thoroughly tested through the mob murder of Henry Smith, cinema's history points toward the ways in which the violence of lynching secretly shaped the experience of seeing in modern America.

Because its significance to the history of film begins with the photograph of Henry Smith's murder, the visual archive of that lynching demands that we turn our attention to the role that still, rather than moving, pictures played in shaping the nation's perception of the violence. At the turn of the nineteenth century, photography revolutionized public life. As Susan Sontag characterizes this shift: "It became clear that there was not just a simple, unitary activity called seeing (recorded by, aided by cameras) but 'photographic seeing,' which was a new way for people to see and a new activity for them to perform."[42] By contextualizing lynching photographs in this visual matrix—or, that is, by applying the rules of "photographic seeing" to them like any other image—we can discern more precisely why these depictions of the violence were oppressive at the turn of the nineteenth century and remain so to this day. If the promise of cinema was to make images move and through that motion to convey a sense of life, in photography the opposite was true. Making time stand still, photography promised to make memory possible by preserving that which could not keep its place in time. It is also true, though, that photography's images elude the fixity of documentary history; once taken, moments captured by still-camera pictures do not exist in the historical present. For lynching to be represented in this medium, then, made the violence easier to disavow because photography transformed it into a spectacle that would prove impossible either to ignore or to see. How could it be that photography could make lynching both appear and disappear in public?

In the Killing Fields: Picturing the Politics of Lynching

Throughout its history, photography has been shaped by the criticism that its mimetic capacities are both attenuated and enriched by its "predicament of comprehension"—namely, the ways in which the images it produces are, and are not, true to life.[43] Still, the medium's documentary impulse demands critical due and can shed light on lynching as a cultural practice and event. As Roland Barthes eloquently reminds us: "What the Photograph reproduces to infinity has occurred only once: the Photograph mechanically repeats what could never be repeated existentially. . . . It is the absolute Particular, the sovereign Contingency, . . . in short, what Lacan calls the *Tuché,* the Occasion, the Encounter, the Real, in its indefatigable expression."[44] Every lynching that ended in murder was its own "occasion" of or "encounter" with reality's final limit—death. And yet we believe that since there were so many lynchings, often carried out in the same general locale and in the same way (or so we presume), there are no unknown "sovereign Contingencies" that we need to identify; no "absolute Particulars" that still require definition and analysis; no existential questions that are worth raising about the deaths of African American people.

However, lynching photographs turn our attention to this relation between the common and the rare, the presumed and the unknown, the unimaginable and the image by yielding to us evidence that, first, specifies how the violence was particularly directed against African Americans. Second, the images show why the practice perfected the aims of white supremacy. As I explained in chapter 1, scholars agree that before the Civil War "lynching" generally referred to the corporal punishment of white men accused of violating social norms in frontier communities. By the end of Reconstruction, however, the nature and aim of lynching had changed perceptibly. What once had been an exacting and painful measure of social regulation became a mortal tactic of political terrorism, targeted to reverse the gains won by blacks because of emancipation. Importantly, photographs of mob murders help elucidate this shift. The earliest camera-made image captioned as a "lynching" (a stereograph, to be exact) dates back to 1878.[45] It and every subsequent photograph of a scene called "lynching" details the death of a mob's victim. Photography thus confirms the genealogical fact that, after the Civil War, the punishment inflicted in lynching's name was always lethal. However, what made lynching in late-nineteenth-century America different than in the antebellum era turns out to be, this visual archive confirms, an idiom for articulating racism's modern turn. For a close comparison of white lynching victims' bodies to those of African Americans in lynching photographs reveals how the intensity of violence, coupled with the techniques of picture making, accentuated the social vulnerability of blacks as visual subjects, and thus extended the political disfranchisement of African Americans in the public sphere.

The modern civil right denied to all victims of mob violence was one of the cornerstones of Reconstruction's radical policy of equality—the Fourteenth Amendment's guarantee of due process. But photographs of lynching victims prove how this right was not only denied but was exploited to negate the already tenuous claims of black freedmen and freedwomen as national citizens. Though trees, makeshift stakes, and bridge trestles were often the sites where the lessons of the scaffold were taught (so to speak) to black victims, many lynching photographs document murders that occurred in courtyards or other state-sanctioned spaces. Moreover, the masks that were typically draped over the legally condemned's head never appear in lynching photographs, suggesting that the victims were unfit to lay claim to the rituals of regular law. Third, distinguishing the mob from the crowd—that is, perpetrators from bystanders—in lynching photographs is often hard to do; the clear boundary separating the condemned from public spectators at legal executions appears to collapse at lynching murders.[46] Finally, whereas white men killed by vigilante mobs appear to be hanged with apparent dispatch and efficiency—most often fully clothed, their hands and feet are bound by rope or cloth and there are no visible marks of egregious harm having been inflicted on them—black men are photographed to display the extent of their wounding and humiliation to the fullest possible extent.[47]

In one utterly terrifying image printed in 1900, a man who has been bludgeoned to death is propped to sit upright in a chair. He has been tarred and feathered. His bloody, swollen face has been painted and both cheeks pasted with round disks to make him appear to be a battered buffoon. Defiling the man's body in these ways served the purpose of stripping him of the symbolic worth of his three-piece suit. That emblem of self-regard no doubt reminded the photograph's viewers that black achievement was a transgression punishable by death as much as any other crime.[48] Likewise, hanging murders are framed to show the victims' bodies dangling from tree limbs or bridge railings, typically facing the camera's lens. Their broken necks and mutilated bodies pressure the picture's foreground; their unsightliness proving both the unlimited range of the mob's rule and African Americans' perceived unfitness as citizens who deserve state protection.

As awful as they are to look at, lynching photographs were not exactly without precedent. Viewing pictures of the dead was not uncommon in nineteenth-century America. Haunted by death's frequency (the result of high infant-mortality rates, disease, and shortened life expectancy rates for adults), many Americans turned to photography as a consolation during their times of loss. Especially popular between the 1840s and 1860s, daguerreotype portraits brought special comfort because these jewel-boxed, palm-sized images performed a miraculous feat. With a flick of the wrist, the polished metal plate would illuminate the deceased's face, symbolically raising them back to life.[49] Taken after death, lynching photographs may technically qualify as postmortem images, but they generally do not seek to memorialize the dead as daguerreotypes did. More often than not (though there are rare exceptions, which I discuss shortly), lynching photographs figure the dead as signs of pure abjection who radiate no thought, no speech, no action, no will; who, through their appearance in the picture's field of vision, become invisible. Failing to restore positive bonds between the viewer and the dead, lynching photographs do not as a rule seek to summon the dead back to an imagined life. Rather, a particular kind of "scopic aggression" rages in lynching photographs, thwarting any such sympathetic identification between the viewer and the black (dead) subject.[50]

For example, photographers frequently etched their names onto the negatives of lynching photographs.[51] Though a practical reason explains this habit—small town and itinerant photographers worked under the pressure that competitors would reprint unauthorized copies of their work to sell, and they used this tagging system to assert their intellectual property rights—this defacement of the images belittles the dead in two ways that postmortem daguerreotypes never do. The signatures not only transformed the murders into a market commodity, the advertisement of the photographers' authorship underscored the nameless victims' anonymity, thereby enhancing the images' seeming visual homogeneity. By purposefully seeking not to distinguish African American victims of mob violence as particular individuals, scopically aggressive lynching photographs figure black victims of white mob violence as emblems of modernity, or indistinct parts of an interchangeable mass.

The photo archives of the U.S. Civil War provide another useful foil to lynching photographs because of the ways in which the former images memorialize the Union and Confederate dead as hallowed symbols deserving the nation's grief.[52] There is no need to consider them all—there are so many, too many, to choose from—so one of the more famous pictures will do. Sold first as a stereograph and then as a picture card, Alexander Gardner and Timothy O'Sullivan's "A Harvest of Death" sent the nation reeling with its depiction of the carnage at Gettysburg (figure 5.1). A seemingly endless field stretches back toward the picture's horizon. In the far distance stands a horse bearing a rider; Death has come to reap his due. Rising like mounds of earth, the fallen soldiers lie exposed atop the ground, soaking the soil with their blood. That the viewer cannot tell one side—North or South—from the other is the visual point the caption wishes us to conclude:

> A battle has been often the subject of elaborate description, but it can be described in one simple world, *devilish!* And the distorted dead recall the ancient legends of men torn in pieces by the savage wantonness of fiends. Swept down, without preparation, the shattered bodies fall in all conceivable positions. . . . Around is scattered the litter of the battle-field, accoutrements, ammunition, rags, cups and canteens, crackers, haversacks, etc., and letters that may tell the names of the owner, although the majority will surely be buried unknown by strangers, and in a strange land. Killed in the frantic efforts to break the steady lines of an army of patriots, whose heroism only excelled theirs in motive, they paid with life the price of their treason, and when the wicked strife was finished, found nameless graves, far from home and kindred.[53]

Figure 5.1. Timothy O'Sullivan, "Incidents of the War: A Harvest of Death, Gettysburg, July 1863." Photographs of the Civil War dead allow us to discern and evaluate the scopic aggression that characterizes the vast majority of anti-black lynching photographs. (Photo courtesy of Library of Congress, Prints and Photographs Division, Civil War Photographs, LC-B81814-7964-A.)

Seeing young American men killed "far from home and kindred" and buried in "nameless graves" was shocking for viewers of this image because, in Civil War America, an unattended death was a sacrilegious death. An unidentified body was a soul unredeemed, without hope of attaining eternal salvation. Through photography, however, both death and mourning could be made right again. In its allusion to the mythic angel of death and its compassionate caption extolling the soldiers' sacrifice, "A Harvest of Death" promises to lay the bodies it shows to proper rest. By contrast, scopically aggressive lynching photographs ruthlessly refuse black victims a "good death"; the images foreground the sacrilege done to them.[54] This defilement involved more than a visual emphasis on the corpse or evidence of mutilation, however. "In the 1900s it was traditional for African American communities to leave the casket open for viewing," Karla F. C. Holloway observes in her study of black mourning rituals *Passed On*. "A laying on of hands, touching, kissing, and expressing one's grief by viewing the remains . . . mattered deeply" to black communities, so much so that funerals were often a protest against lynching murders.[55] Given, then, the importance in African American death traditions of providing the dead a proper public memorial and natural shelter inside of the earth, lynching photographs robbed victims'

Figure 5.2. Lynching at a Texas [?] Courthouse, ca. 1905. Composed to emphasize the camera's distance from the lynching-murder scene, this photograph allows for critical viewing that scopically aggressive lynching photographs typically foreclose. (Photo courtesy of the Allen-Littlefield Collection.)

graves again and again, because the images continually disinterred the corpse for indiscriminate viewing.

Not every lynching photograph was scopically aggressive, though. Taken in 1905, the photograph in figure 5.2 documents a mob murder somewhere in Texas.[56] In the picture's foreground, a tall, narrow tree leans in from the right, its thickest limb bearing the weight of a black man hanging at the end of a rope. The corpse is fully dressed in a jacket, trousers, and shoes; his hands are bound from behind. The lower branches of the tree hold him at an angle that partly conceals him from the camera's lens. The victim is pictured in a partial profile; notably, his face is turned away from view. This studied avoidance of the victim draws the viewer's attention to what looms largest in the picture's frame. An empty scaffold stands sturdily erect on the other side of the picket fence that divides the image's foreground from its background. Shot with this long view, the photograph decisively joins the scene of lynching to the realm of civil society. For just behind the scaffold is the jail and courthouse, an imposing brick edifice that towers as high as the tree and whose double set of broad windows are fitted with iron bars. And behind those state buildings a church steeple points to the realm of God's law. These visual zones of the photograph compose an astonishing critique of lynching, if we trace the unbroken sight line that runs from the church's spire to the jail's top pair of windows, from those portals to the scaffold, and from the scaffold to the victim hanging from the tree limb. As the picture presents it, the denial of democracy's protections did not occur beyond the boundaries of the state but in the bright shadow of its authority, with its clear approval.

The camerawork in this image also draws our attention to the demography and politics of witnessing involved in lynching. As W. Fitzhugh Brundage points out in his careful typology of lynch mobs, the majority of murders were often clandestine, "private" events that only a select few white men (and boys) were allowed to attend. This particular photograph confirms Brundage's point.[57] Here, a tight cluster of six white men, dressed in suits and hats, stand leisurely off to the photograph's left edge, watching the victim calmly. Two young schoolboys stride past the adults so swiftly that the shutter speed cannot keep up with them, blurring their faces and torsos from clear view. Had the boys watched the grisly proceedings and were rushing away? Did they stumble on it unexpectedly and try to sneak past the backs of their elders?

The confusion created by the children's presence and quick departure locates the visual center of sight in the image. The photograph's third focal point is established by the lone man set apart from the small crowd. Standing before the fence that separates the courthouse from the lynching tree and interposed between the black victim and the empty stage of the scaffold, this man surveys the scene like no one else in the picture's field. He can look directly at the camera and return its gaze because he has experienced what the lens registers as its compositional point. With the murder scene juxtaposed against the backdrop of the state's agencies of power—the church, jail, courthouse, and scaffold—the violence of the law is revealed to be contingent on the violence of lynching. Indeed, they each make the other culturally intelligible as forms of punishment. That this man's look of repose depends on the black victim's death as both a citizen and subject finds its uncanny articulation in the metonymic link between the hat on his head and the bowler lying on the ground beneath the victim's feet. This sign of masculinity, prosperity, and civility may very well have graced the victim's head—much as the other men in the photograph, and none more than the mob's sentinel.

The solitary white man's right to watch over this scene, however, is belied by the visual cue of the bowler, precisely because the hat creates a visual connection between victim and observer that is at once unmistakable and inconspicuous. We can barely see it because of its location. Lying close to the tree, its round dome bobs up from the ground like a buoy, orienting the viewer's perception of the white man's grave stare and the black victim's broken neck. Along that filament of perception, the bowler draws attention to itself as a trope for how the "wages of whiteness" (to recall W. E. B. Du Bois's pungent term) were so wastefully misspent demeaning and destroying black life. But the bowler's presence and the studied composition of the image's field of vision also suggest how photography's powers of depiction could also rival the injustice of lynching.

Importantly, the photographer's distance from the scene makes the intricacies of this murder legible. As in "Harvest of Death," the photographer positions himself at a remove from which point his own relation to the scene can be marked and accounted for. Even though we cannot see it directly, the camera makes its distance discernible to the viewer, thus reminding us that the murder is being witnessed and recorded. It is this self-reflexivity that creates the space for political critique.[58] Lynching photographs that are scopically aggressive collapse this distance by allowing the camera to probe the victim's body, visually commanding its subjugation to the mob's power even further. Paradoxically, then, scopically aggressive lynching photographs often efface the suffering and death of black people through the camera's proximity to the victim's body. When pictured close up, lynching could be at once apprehended and disavowed, recognized and impugned, precisely because it was so near at hand.

In the first of three images, Frank Embree stands defiantly atop a buckboard wagon.[59] He is stripped nude and handcuffed; we do not know the crime he is accused of committing. Behind him, in crowded rows, white men gather around the makeshift stage. Not insignificantly, Embree shields his penis from their view and that of the camera to focus his own look on the photographer. Glaring directly into the camera's lens and rebuffing its gaze with his own indignant grimace, Embree's courage calls to mind the mob's readiness to exploit his vulnerability, the evidence of which is plain to see. In the first image, Embree's thighs and shoulders have been slashed and gouged by whips and knives. In the second image, with his back to the camera, the welter of wounds fills the picture's foreground because—like the crowd—the camera stands close to the wagon's edge. But Embree's refusal to flinch under the obvious duress of his wounds is captured not only by his stalwart stance, but by the response of visually prominent members of the mob. Several men turn away. Another, at first hidden, then revealed to be standing conspicuously to the left, drops his mouth open as if in awe of Embree's reserve of authority.

The fluidity between these two images is remarkable, suggesting how complicated the act of looking at lynching could be. However, the camera issues the final stroke of discipline in its figuration of Embree's death. In the last image of the sequence, he is pictured hanging from a tree, facing the camera again but with his head slumped back and his eyes cast blankly toward the sky. His hands bound and clasped behind his waist, with a long loin cloth covering his groin and the torture marks on his legs, the motive will Embree demonstrated in the first two images is arrested twice: first, by the death he has suffered; second, by the photograph's allusion to the crucifixion of Christ.[60] Though the photograph also reminds us of the profanity of its own rhetoric—the image shows the crush of men clustered around Embree's body, their hands gripping and groping the tree on which Embree hangs dead—the condition in which it and the other two were found underscores the photographer's political prescience: the three images had been "laced together with a twisted purple thread, so as to unfold like a map."[61]

As this discovery suggests, the binding of the photographs to resemble a devotional text creates two particularly insidious effects on the meaning of Embree's death. First, like the Christ imagery, the sacred binding (suggested by the purple thread) seeks to sanctify the mob's arrogant lawlessness as divine and biblically just. Second, the visual appeal to allegory removes the murder from the realm of secular history. At which point, "what [becomes] compelling about [such a] photograph derives partly from what it shares, as a composition, with [art history's traditions]. Indeed, the very extent to which [such a] photograph [becomes] unforgettable indicates its potential for being de-politicized, for becoming a timeless image."[62] Thus, the pictures of Frank Embree's murder urge viewers to disavow the violence of lynching, precisely because of the forms in which the dead appear before our very eyes.

The Studio's Punctum: Picture Cards of Lynching

The intelligence with which the photographs of Frank Embree's murder were composed is rivaled only by the ingenuity with which the images were preserved by their last owners. The apparent wish on the part of the photographer and the owner-viewer for these pictures to mean something more than Embree's death demands critical attention. That desire, legible through the visual conventions deployed in the images' composition and preservation, finds expression through the form in which these images in particular, and lynching photographs generally, were produced.

To appreciate why this is so, we need first to recall, as Jonathan Crary argues persuasively in *Techniques of the Observer,* that the optical devices used in nineteenth-century photography were not invented in cultural vacuums. Premised on "conceptual structures" that reflect "points of intersection where philosophical, scientific, and aesthetic discourses overlap with mechanical techniques, institutional requirements, and socioeconomic forces," photographic equipment also presupposes an ideal viewer—an observing subject—whose cultural privileges can be inferred from (and, consequently, conferred by) the ways in which a camera makes the world visible to human perception.[63] Thus, when considering lynching photographs and their social effects, we must approach them as artifacts that are more than transparent, self-evident documents of these events of racial murder. Indeed, lynching photographs encode more than the deadly operations of white racism. The images also inscribe how practices of racial violence were used to cultivate the experience and meaning of sight itself. For as a comparison between two separate lynchings taken by two studio photographers demonstrates, racial and regional allegiances were not the determining influences that shaped the cultural meanings of lynching photographs. The camerawork of J. L. Mertins (of Paris, Texas) and J. P. Ball (of Helena, Montana) captures how the conceptual structures of studio photography and the ubiquitous picture card that was the staple of that business trade could exacerbate and reinforce the wounds that lynching's violence sought to inflict.

After the daguerreotype but before the Kodak snapshot, Americans loved to collect picture cards.[64] Taken in the studio by a professional photographer, these palm-sized images were sturdily but cheaply made, the image being mounted on strong-ply cardboard instead of the exquisitely engraved glass and jewel-boxed frames of the daguerreotype. The heft of the card stock enabled the picture cards to be easily handled and readily exchanged; from photographer to sitter-clients, from sitter-clients to family, friends, and photo albums, picture cards made the rounds of a community, which only worked in favor of the photographer's business. Since the card mount was embossed with the studio's name and address, the keepsakes doubled as endorsements of the photographer's skill, advertising his service to possible future clients.

From the moment the agreement was struck for the photographs to be produced until the delivery of the finished images, the "currency" of picture cards—their value not just as commodities but as socially meaningful objects—depended on this open-ended exchange between the photographer and his clients.[65] With its bulky equipment, social protocols, and contractual obligations structuring the making of picture cards, it might seem that the conventions of studio photography would restrict its use at lynching murders. However, that was not the case. A significant number of lynching photographs were taken in the picture-card format. This cultural development was made possible by a purely technical advancement: by the 1880s, studio photographers could use gelatin dry-plate negatives instead of the cumbersome wet plates that had largely restricted them to indoor camerawork.[66] With this new film technology, studio photographers could make images outdoors, expanding their repertoires of picture card subjects. As William Stapp explains in his history of nineteenth-century American photojournalism: "Before the introduction of the gelatin dry plate, *photographs of events were necessarily images of aftermaths;* and until practical photomechanical reproduction techniques made the distribution of photographic images cheap, quick, and easy, photographic images were usually experienced only as original objects."[67] Able to produce images of social events as they unfolded in real time, studio photographers could turn their lenses to lynching murders as field assignments.

And Texas photographer J. L. Mertins did just that, having managed to capture on film one of the most spectacular lynchings of the nineteenth century, the 1893 murder of Henry Smith in Paris, Texas. Knowing his

Figure 5.3. "Avengers of Little Myrtle Vance, and the Villian [sic] Brought to Justice," J. L. Mertins (1893). By focusing on the mob's assembly at the lynching of Henry Smith in 1893, photographer J. L. Mertins captures modernity in action as a public sphere comes into visible being at the start of the twentieth century. (Photo courtesy of Library of Congress, Prints and Photographs Division, LC-USZ62-11549.)

trade as a professional should, Mertins took the precautionary step of depositing his work with the Library of Congress to ensure his copyright control over the images.[68] Elaborately captioned with copy, Mertins's twelve picture cards purport to narrate how "little Myrtle Vance was avenged." Spanning the time from when the infant girl's body was discovered to the capture, public parading, torture, and burning of her accused assailant, the series appears to follow a predictable arc of development. When examined closely, though, the images are not as transparent as the captions make them seem. Once Henry Smith enters into the image-narrative—when, as that picture card's caption tells us, "the fiend is paraded around the square"—he ceases to be the subject of the photographs' attention (figure 5.3). Instead, the picture cards' depth of field and detail evince a greater interest in the scene that swells around Smith: the rush of bodies in motion as the mob moves toward its goal to kill.

This focus occurs in part because of the technical requirements and limitations of the studio camera itself. Despite the more convenient film stock, the cameras were still bulky and required a tripod; lacking a shutter still made it difficult to photograph live action events. Taken from the rooftops of buildings surrounding Paris's town square and from an obviously elevated stage in the field where Smith was eventually killed, Mertins's picture cards are a testament to his dogged efforts to force his camera to do more than it was able. But what always does appear quite fully in the camera's view is the mob, though not so much as an entity *per se*. Rather, the mob's formation as a process of movement, flux, and action that the camera's long exposure time can capture becomes the printable, copyright-sanctioned image. Oddly enough, then, what the camera cannot bring into focus gets exchanged for another interest. What this picture depicts most clearly is how people move in space and time toward the thing they fear the most—death—while the ordeal of Henry Smith lays bare the goal of the Paris, Texas mob in a tangible, visible form.

To recall Mark Seltzer's theory of serial killing, Mertins's photographs of this lynching could be said to show us the "pathological public sphere" in formation. Taking "pathological" to mean what Seltzer suggests—that moment where "public and private spaces 'tear away' at each other . . . [where] intimacy is inseparable from the shock of contact with the public in ceaseless motion, with faceless crowds of strangers"[69]—we can see that Smith is not the focal point of the photograph. His subordination to the picture's interest does not free Smith from the power of Mertins's gaze. On the contrary, it renders him all the more vulnerable to it, precisely because the camera locates Smith's death as the nominal center of the picture's action only to render it invisible as the picture's focal point. With his death transformed into a spectacular secret, Smith becomes the vanishing point in Mertin's perspective on the lynching.

A series of four picture cards taken by J. P. Ball of the execution of William Biggerstaff in Helena, Montana provides a striking contrast to Mertins's photographic narrative. Accused, tried, and convicted of killing another African American, Dick Johnson, in June 1895, Biggerstaff claimed he acted in self-defense but was nevertheless sentenced to die for this crime.[70] A resident of Helena and former candidate for the post of county coroner, J. P. Ball was the most renowned African American studio photographer in nineteenth-century America; given his reputation and credentials, he was present to chronicle the event.[71] Though using the same technology as his counterpart in Texas, Ball deployed his camera differently, to memorialize Biggerstaff's death as one befitting a citizen wrongfully deprived of his life.

Of the three picture cards Ball printed, two were taken at the execution site; they show that Biggerstaff had been hanged in apparent accordance

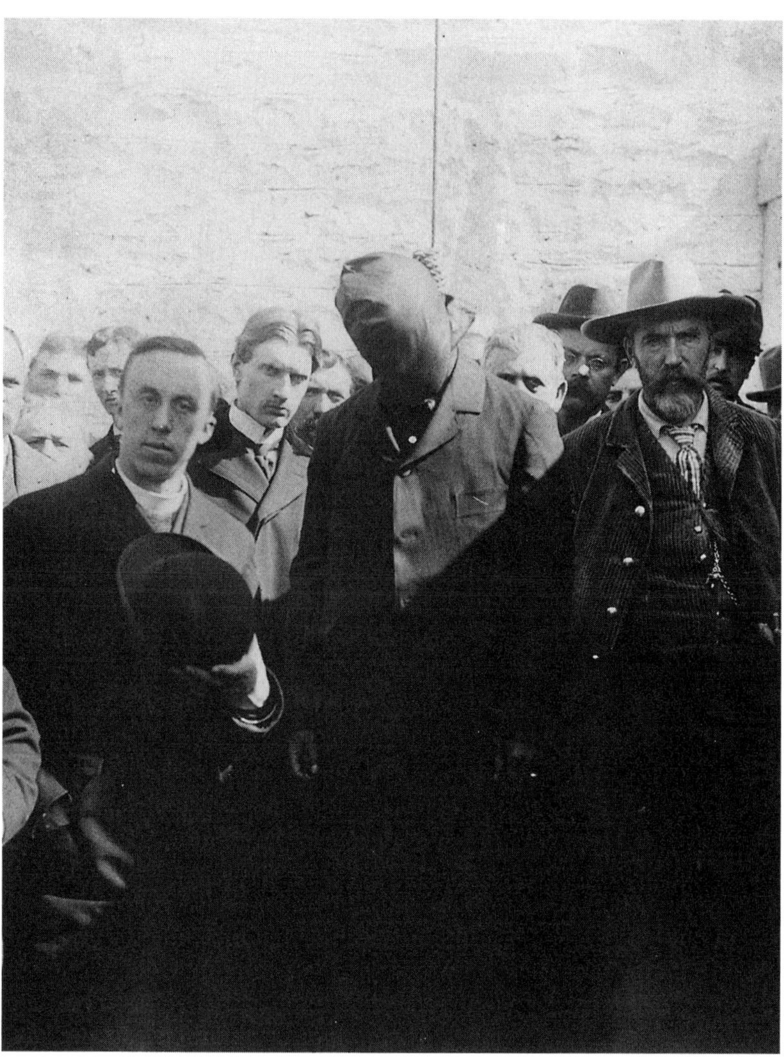

Figure 5.4. "Execution of William Biggerstaff," by J. P. Ball (1896). African American photographers did not shy away from making lynching photographs but often did so by fashioning them into framed narratives. Juxtaposing photographs of the murder scene with images of the victim alive or lying in state at his funeral, these series establish ethical boundaries within which looking at the murder becomes a mode of protest. (Photo courtesy of the Montana State Historical Society.)

with the protocols that defined state-sponsored death sentences (figure 5.4). Biggerstaff's face is veiled by a mask. Fully dressed in a black suit, he is flanked on either side by the town's minister and sheriff. A crowd stands behind, looking sober, grim, and dutiful. The frenzy of stares and hands groping at Frank Embree's body does not charge these scenes; rather, a different kind of intensity suffuses the visual rapport between Ball and the white witnesses. Indeed, the ease and calm demeanor with which the officials and onlookers return the camera's gaze is remarkable, given that the execution occurred in April 1896, the year the U.S. Supreme Court's ruling in *Plessy v. Ferguson* became federal law, and these white men were not bound to "abolish distinctions based on color, or to enforce social, as distinguished from political, equality, or a commingling of the races upon terms unsatisfactory" to them.[72] Nonetheless, the camera's unrelenting stare is returned by the white men, calmly trusting that their deed will be seen as the act of lawful justice they believed it to be. However, the crowd's presence (as opposed to its demeanor) in the picture card's frame recalls one of lynching photographs' telltale visual cues. The men and state officials who presided over and witnessed Biggerstaff's death press quite close to one another and to Biggerstaff's body. This proximity to the victim is particular to scenes of lynching, violating the decorum of distance usually maintained in state-sponsored executions. This is but the first of several visual cues that raise doubts about the proclaimed legality of Biggerstaff's death.[73]

Crucially, the death scene is preceded and followed by two other picture cards. At first glance, they are the stock fare of a prosperous commercial photographer like Ball—the indoor studio portrait and the postmortem memento. At some point before his lynching, Biggerstaff must have struck a deal with the photographer to make his portrait. Dressed well in a dark, snug-fitting suit (much like the one he was hanged in) Biggerstaff looks pensive and serene (figure 5.5). His right hand, thoughtfully propped under his chin, draws attention to his clean-shaven face; his hair is neatly parted down the middle and his moustache is evenly clipped. A flower blooms on his coat lapel. The folded corners of a white handkerchief peek out from his breast pocket. With only one of its buttons fastened shut, Biggerstaff's suit jacket opens to show the vest beneath.

Taken on its own, this portrait would appear to be but one of the hundreds Ball took over the course of his long career. If ever there was a type of photograph that encouraged the kind of moral lassitude that Roland Barthes defines as characteristic of the "studium" photograph, this would be it. Viewed as a single image, the portrait seems more like "a thing, [a]

Figure 5.5. "Portrait of William Biggerstaff," by J. P. Ball (1896). African American photographers did not shy away from making lynching photographs but often did so by fashioning them into framed narratives. Juxtaposing photographs of the murder scene with images of the victim alive or lying in state at his funeral, these series establish ethical boundaries within which looking at the murder becomes a mode of protest. (Photo courtesy of the Montana State Historical Society.)

taste for someone, a kind of general enthusiastic commitment . . . but without special acuity."[74] When examined in the context of Biggerstaff's death, however, this seemingly prosaic picture raises profound questions about the proceedings that led to the visually disturbing execution scenes. Who is this man—so obviously dignified and cultivated—and what kind of crude quarrel could have provoked him to kill Dick Johnson? He appears to be trustworthy; why wasn't his account of his fight with Johnson believed? Was his execution one in name only—was it in fact a lynching?

The image of a live and healthy Biggerstaff, a Biggerstaff who looks to be sober in thought and conduct, makes those last questions inevitable, especially when read against the photograph of the execution scene. In that picture card, Biggerstaff is unnerving to look at not simply because he is dead, but because of the manner in which the signs of legal sanction appear to abuse his body. What ought to be matter of decency—the black mask—seems instead to be improper. The mask fits too tightly about his face, as if it was pulled taut before the noose was placed around his neck, suggesting that he suffocated before his neck was broken. Likewise, Biggerstaff's body is not bound with the belts used to restrain the condemned during a hanging. According to the local news report, the last seven minutes and fifty seconds of his life were marked by his painful spasms at the end of the execution rope.[75] These images are in stark contrast to the peaceful scene of Biggerstaff at rest in his coffin, in the private quarters of the funeral parlor. This photograph of Biggerstaff underscores the cruelty of the execution itself. It may have been legal, but it was no less brutal or questionable than if he had been lynched.

In all three of these images, Ball's camerawork is notably still. Gone is the tumult that distinguishes Mertins's series depicting Henry Smith's murder. The absence of speed and movement, the insistence on steadiness, clarity, and focus makes these images radical photographs, because their reserve prompts us "to see . . . , feel, . . . notice, . . . observe, . . . think."[76] Ironically, the static quality of Ball's pictures transport them into the "subtle beyond" created by what Barthes calls the "punctum," because these images provoke us to ask questions about the facts which seem so certain, launching our desire to know more about Biggerstaff's death "beyond what [the images] permit us to see."[77] And in these photographs, "that item which pricks" most, which "suggests meanings other than the literal one," turns out to be the most domesticating of details: the absence and then presence of a wedding band on Biggerstaff's left ring finger.

Tracing through the series of photographs, the ring first appears in the least likely scene: it gleams brightly from the bottom left quarter of the execution photograph. A small curve of light, the ring stands out against the brown skin of Biggerstaff's hand, the dark cloth of his trousers and suit jacket, and the awful black mask drawn about his face and held fast by the rope around his neck. It appears next with Biggerstaff in the coffin. The ring is conspicuously missing from the studio portrait, though, where we would expect to see it most: his left hand rests prominently on the chair's armrest; his fingers are bare. Once again, the trajectory of Biggerstaff's life becomes the subject of the image. Who was he married to? Did he and his wife have any children? Who will survive him after his death? This question, in turn, provokes the interest in the photograph of Biggerstaff in his coffin. Who attended his funeral? Besides his family, what community mourned his loss? According to Helena's local newspaper, "100 colored people" lobbied Montana's governor to stay Biggerstaff's execution; certainly some (if not all) of these people attended the funeral service. Not surprisingly, one of Biggerstaff's final visitors and the leader of his clemency movement was none other than J. P. Ball.[78]

None of the above speculations are explicitly referenced in the images, of course. They emerge out of the picture cards' surfaces, puncturing (as Barthes predicts) the seemingly obvious proceedings of Biggerstaff's death. Raising the possibility that his viewers were being made privy to a murder, Ball's camerawork suggests that studio photography's visual conventions could be manipulated to tell a different history of lynching, one that allows us to see that the black people murdered by mobs were fully sentient, visible subjects, whose suffering was worthy to look at and mourn.

"Reckless Eyeballing"

Ball's execution series is not typical of lynching photographs. The trope of what we could call the "frame narrative"—printing images that depict the mob's victims before and after their deaths; paying empathetic visual care to the victims' bodies—appears to have been a distinctly black tradition in lynching photography.[79] Inviting viewers to imagine the life histories of black lynch victims as they look at the pictures, this aesthetic challenges the popular ideology of spectacle, which, as Dana B. Polan points out, depends on "a faith, virtually Rousseauist, in the purity of a cultural sight."[80] Indeed, sequenced around visual cues and temporal gaps that call William Biggerstaff's death into question, Ball's camerawork should remind us of Ida B. Wells's parody of lynching statistics in *A Red Record*. At the same time, though, Ball's photographs reveal how complex the act of looking at mob murders could be. Who was socially endorsed to make and view lynching photographs? How was that picture making, picture collecting, and picture viewing done? Or, put another way, can we talk—should we talk—about discrete "black" and "white" ways of viewing lynching photographs, or about "southern" ways contrasted to "northern" ways? In other words, how might we conceive an account of spectatorship when reading lynching photographs?

First, we must distinguish the act of viewing an actual lynching murder from that of reading a lynching photograph. As I have argued thus far, the documentary claims of photography generally and the specific conventions of studio-made cabinet cards are sufficiently different that they make the act of viewing lynching photographically its own endeavor. One reason is obvious: like a literary depiction, a photograph is a second-order representation and as such is materially unlike watching a murder occur. Nevertheless, lynching photographs imply their own specific relation between the viewer and the violence insofar as the images shape the meaning of the murders as historical events. Where an actual lynching takes place, from beginning to end, over the course of a measureable period of time, a photograph of that murder creates its own temporal order in which the violence remains visible indefinitely. Extended into a never-ending event, lynching murders—as photographs—placed viewers in a "sensory predicament" unlike James Weldon Johnson's "horror complex" and from which there was no easy escape.[81] Was the act of looking at lynching photographs a gesture of complicity with or resistance to anti-black mob violence? How was a person to handle such images if they came into his or her possession—keep and hide them? Keep and trade or sell them? Keep and deliver them to authorities? Destroy them?

To ask who it was that looked at lynching photographs and to surmise how they used and thought about them are, however, daunting tasks that can only be approached through speculation. Lynching photographs did not appear in and move through the public sphere the way, say, Jacob Riis toured the country using his magic lantern slides to show how the impoverished "other half" lived in New York City, or the way Lewis Hine published his portraits of child laborers in the pages of *Survey* magazine or for the bulletins and posters published by the National Child Labor Committee.[82] Nor did lynching photographs circulate as widely or freely as minstrel-themed chromolithographs and postcards. Published in lots of hundreds of thousands, so-called coon pictures carried their brazenly racist imagery (and equally offensive written messages) throughout the U.S. postal system and into the homes of white Americans without the threat of government censure or reprisal.[83] For example, the visual reproductions of Henry Smith's murder in 1893 can be traced from Paris, Texas to Seattle, Washington, D.C., Philadelphia, and New York City from 1893 to 1908, and from still photography to early cinematic projection. However, the wide circulation of the visual artifacts of Smith's murder is the exception that proves the rule: lynching photographs were fewer in number and moved more surreptitiously within the public sphere than did other types of photocards generally.

To appreciate how this dynamic fostered lynching's oppressive force, we must recall what distinguishes photography from other visual media. Walter Benjamin observed that the most wondrous (and troubling) feature about a photograph was its capacity to be easily reproduced on an unlimited scale.[84] Because photography's potential volume promised to spread visual experience to the greatest number of people for the lowest cost, an important source of the medium's aesthetic and social value derived from the ubiquity, accessibility, and portability of the images. If the medium is characterized by such abundance, however, lynching photographs violate that ideal; for instance, out of the 13.1 million photographs on deposit at the Library of Congress's Prints and Photographs Division, less than two hundred are classified as images of lynching.[85] When compared to the easy proliferation of other kinds of racist visual artifacts at the turn of the nineteenth century, lynching photographs are as hard to index and count accurately as lynching murders. That there could likely be more images of lynching murders "out there" waiting to be collected is neither a coincidence nor an accident.[86] On the contrary, the incomplete archive explains how the images were likely produced and used. Lynching photographs did not exercise their power to oppress through their promiscuous circulation as market commodities; rather, the scarcity of the images, their unpredictable appearance and disappearance from general circulation, enhanced their awful force.

Or, as I would contend, the secretion of the images into and out of the public sphere sustained the terrorist tendencies that animate lynching photographs as visual artifacts. The production and distribution of lynching postcards best exemplifies this dynamic (as does the near complete elision of anti-black lynchings from the popular medium of stereographs), and I detail those operations shortly. Conceived more generally, "secretion" first refers to the ways in which lynching photographs were produced and distributed by white photographers, but were then withdrawn from general view to be secretly exchanged among whites. The robust trade of "coon" postcards and stereographs suggests that, by comparison, lynching photographs and postcards were sold and exchanged in localized transactions whose restricted points of access favored whites' control over the circulation of the images. Rather than flooding the visual landscape, then, lynching photographs seeped into and out of the public sphere irregularly, which endowed them with their power to shore up white supremacist fantasies of dominance and to terrorize those who believed the violence was an unjust, indefensible practice. Understood doubly as a form of hidden knowledge and as an "enzyme" released to foster growth, the "secretion" of lynching photographs therefore details how the images were produced and released into the world at specific times, in particular forms, and in selected venues to produce certain kinds of political effects.

Most obviously, the secretion of lynching photographs was an explicit exercise of racial domination. If "reckless eyeballing"—looking at white women in a sexual way—could get black men killed by white lynch mobs, knowledge that photographs of those murders were circulating throughout the public domain no doubt terrorized black communities, especially those that had thus far been spared a lynching.[87] Indeed, the secretion of lynching photographs codified what was emerging at the turn of the nineteenth century as the civil right to look at and interpret the world in ways that perfected racism's hierarchies of privilege. For instance, though banned from viewing boxing films when those movies were first released and screened in the United States during the 1890s, white women often attended lynching murders, participated in them, and were frequent recipients of lynching photographs and postcards.[88] White men attended anti-black lynchings in droves; theirs are the faces in the crowds (and likely behind the cameras) in most lynching photographs. For African Americans, however, viewing photographic reproductions of mob murders was a nearly impossible choice to make insofar as they did not control how, when, or where the secretion of the images took place. But that was the point of restricting lynching photographs' reproducibility. "The right to see and be seen, in one's own way and under one's own terms" was the social ideal at stake in turning photography into a sequestered process that denied the medium's democratic promise to make visual experience (and, with it, visual knowledge) as broadly available as possible. Instead, like pornography, lynching photography functioned as "an enforcer, with the power to make [the violence] invisible just as surely as it . . . made [the violence] appear."[89]

This practice of releasing and withdrawing lynching photographs into and out of the public sphere points toward the ways in which their secretion suppresses the full range of meanings embedded in the images. The presumption that lynching photographs, because they are photographs, "can convey some kind of stable meaning [and] truth" about the murders they document is best tested when, like any other image, lynching photographs are contrasted against other kinds of visual statements.[90] When secreted in and out of view, though, lynching photographs remain hard to read because their social relation to other visual phenomena becomes obscured. What makes the images culturally logical, then, is that the violence "fit" the uses of photographic technologies and shaped emerging protocols of seeing at the turn of the nineteenth century; and yet, because secretion made them inaccessible and therefore inscrutable, lynching photographs were easy then (as well as now) to disavow as meaning anything other than what they manifestly show—the brutal, unjust murders of African American people. "No longer confronted by any image in relation to which it can mark itself, assert its special character, its scandal, its madness,"[91] lynching photographs wield assaultive power because they are phantasms of histories we need to know but cannot readily perceive.

But who actually looked at which lynching photographs, under what circumstances, and with what effects in the late nineteenth and early twentieth centuries? Owing to their mechanisms of concealment, secreted lynching photographs leave too few traces in public archives for us to detail how white viewers encountered the images.[92] On the other side of the color line, secretion worked best when lynching photographs emerged out of their shadowed economy into more readily accessible networks of visual culture where African Americans could be confronted with them. For this reason, we are able to evaluate the contexts in which black people saw and interpreted the images. However, we would be wrong to characterize their reactions as a unified "black" response. Members and supporters of the NAACP who intercepted such images forwarded them to the organization, expressing deep anger or fear.[93] For their part, NAACP officials wrestled with how to best use the lynching photographs that came into their possession. Though a bold provocateur when it came to marketing his novel about lynching, James Weldon Johnson, as the chief strategist of the NAACP's anti-lynching campaign, proceeded cautiously when faced with the choice to use secreted photographs as illustrations for the pamphlet exposés published by the organization.[94] Similarly, though W. E. B. Du Bois approved the reprints of secreted photographs in *Crisis* magazine, he did so only after carefully weighing whether his editorial decisions might reproduce the very violence the NAACP meant to check.[95] When he assumed Johnson's post as executive director in 1931, Walter F. White eagerly used the NAACP's publishing capacities to circulate lynching photographs as frequently as possible.[96] In doing so, White followed the path broken by Ida B. Wells, who welcomed the lynching postcard sent on to her by Albion W. Tourgée in 1892. She promptly published the image because, as she explained to Tourgée, the picture showed what even the most accurate statistics could not—how brutal and heinous lynching's violence could be.[97]

Much like the leaders of the anti-lynching movement, African Americans generally also responded to the secretion of lynching photographs in varied ways. Though the members of Helena, Montana's black community tried but could not save William Biggerstaff from his execution, they most likely attended his funeral, itself a visually conscious act of protest.[98] The thousands of subscribers to the NAACP's *Crisis* magazine paid an extra dollar for the special issue devoted to a photo-illustrated exposé, "The Waco Horror," that featured gruesome images of the 1916 burning-murder of Jesse Washington in Texas.[99] But it took Samuel Burdett ten years to write about his ordeal in viewing Henry Smith's murder because he felt immense guilt over his fascination with the technology that made the machine-display of Henry Smith's death possible. For the very reason Burdett succumbed to his curiosity, film critic Lester Walton refused to pay entrance into the Manhattan nickelodeon where a later film version of the Smith lynching had been booked in 1908. Turning a black man's murder into a cinematic "attraction" was, for Walton, a kind of racial violence he denounced by boycotting the film altogether. Not that looking at photographed scenes of anti-black murders became any easier as the century progressed; the prospect of viewing lynching photographs continued to be vexing for African Americans. For example, as I discuss in chapter 6, the murder of Emmett Till became a cause célèbre in 1955 because his mother shrewdly solicited the black press to publish photographs of her son's corpse. Almost half a century later, though, the sibling survivors of James Byrd Jr. refused to release the autopsy photographs of their brother's murder as their own kind of protest against the public dismemberment of his body; this countersecretion symbolized the family's wish to dignify Byrd's right to die a good death.[100]

As the range of these examples suggests, African Americans' responses to lynching photographs, even to the mere prospect of viewing them, were varied and unpredictable. Held in abeyance then released without warning, the images' secretion ensured this ambivalence because the process necessarily redefined what resistant or oppositional looking possibly involved.[101] Clearly, being deprived of the right to look at them urged countless African Americans to seek out lynching photographs. For exactly the same reason, others refused or otherwise restrained themselves from looking at them as a way to protest secretion's repressive force. This "spectatorial fluidity" points toward the fundamental condition that lynching photographs gave rise to in early-twentieth-century American life: namely, that the experience and meaning of seeing as such was importantly organized around the violence done to African American people.[102]

That the secretion of lynching photographs was so far-reaching a cultural practice is best gauged by considering why political cartoons about lynching were so prevalent in African American newspapers during this period and throughout the twentieth century. As I discussed in chapter 2, the black press covered lynching diligently—the mortal incidents of it, the nearly missed murders (such as the one James Weldon Johnson endured), and the protests—but these news reports were rarely illustrated by photographs of the murders. Instead, hand-drawn cartoons were featured prominently on newspapers' front, inner, and editorial pages. These visual depictions of mob violence were no less graphic than camera-made pictures; in fact, they were often quite gory and always explicit in their use of physical detail. But political cartoons differ from photographs in a crucial way. In their insistence on hyperbole and caricature, hand-drawn illustrations allowed viewers to see lynching's violence in ways that documentary photographs did not, because artists could use the drawing techniques of line, proportion, and point of view to determine what and how the viewer experienced the scenes staged in the cartoon's visual field. The inexplicable smiles and unseemly calm that often charge lynching photographs turn into curdled sneers and frenzied excitement in anti-lynching political cartoons. The complicity between state officials and the illegally constituted mob was drawn out for critique through cartoonists' use of sternly phrased captions and sure-handed allegory. Lynching's popularity as a distinctively and definitively American practice was often figured through the trope of the national map, marking the longitudes and latitudes of how widespread the violence was throughout the country.[103]

Reimagining the violence in these ways, African American cartoonists and black readers of the papers themselves could control lynching's signification more readily than even the most critically captioned lynching photograph. Indeed, the highly controlled excess of anti-lynching cartoons made clear how semiotically unruly documentary photographs of the murders could be. By offering explicit interpretations of the violence whose meanings deliberately rivaled those unleashed by lynching photographs, political cartoons restored both a moral certitude and a contemporary historicism to the act of seeing for the black news-reading public. No longer a timeless atrocity that bore no relation to (then) present-day cultural politics, lynching is figured as a symptom of modern American living in anti-lynching political cartoons, which is precisely the connection that secreted lynching photographs meant to obscure.

Viewed in contrast to each other, lynching photographs and anti-lynching cartoons anticipate what critic Barbie Zelizer argued concerning the heavily publicized, overcirculated photographs of the Holocaust's concentration camps: that the proof of wrongdoing documented in the most extremely literal images of atrocity do not ensure "the same kind of remembering."[104] Viewers bring "different kinds of knowledge—practical, national, cultural, aesthetic" to the act of looking at photographs, and they call on that knowledge to define the meaning of any given image.[105] Though any person can be fluent in reading visual artifacts in any number of ways, the secretion of lynching photographs made it impossible (and still does now, given the erratic emergence of the evidence into the public domain) to determine in advance whether looking at lynching photographs conferred power on white viewers and only deepened black social and political helplessness. Unfixing photographic meaning in this way—or, that is to say, "unbinding vision" from its usual coordinates of meaning production—secreted lynching photographs were "capriciously willful, . . . conforming to no fixed rule of principle of conduct, . . . erratic," and so "countered . . . what is reasonable." The images were, as the *Oxford English Dictionary*'s definition suggests, evidence of modernity's waywardness.

In the Realm of the Senses: Lynching's (Dis)appearance in Stereographs

Of all the photographic technology popularly available at the turn of the nineteenth century, stereographs encouraged wayward looking as a function of its viewing technology.[106] Equipped with a parallel set of short focal lenses, stereograph cameras produced double images of the same object or scene, reflecting the views of the right and left eyes, respectively. Mounted side by side on heavy stock paper, stereocards (as the images were called) eradicated point of view as it had been established in, for example, painting, sculpture, and daguerreotyping, because its viewing apparatus (the stereoscope) transformed the separate, flat images into a unified, three-dimensional field.

Originally invented in the 1830s to test theories of binocular vision (how do the left and right eye fuse what they see to create one image?), by the mid-nineteenth century "the chief object" of making stereocards evolved into creating "illusions of real things in real space," according to photography critic Alan Trachtenberg. The deepest pleasure afforded by the technology was to experience "the entire range of vision—unframed, unburdened, boundless, as if the eye were there before the very scene."[107] This fantasy was enabled by the looking apparatus itself and how the viewer had to position her body to see the images in the stereoscope's viewfinder. Bringing the binocular box to one's face and fitting the lenses to the sockets of one's eyes, the observer's body itself became an extension of the glasses protruding from the camera.[108] Entering its chambers of perception "in an ideal isolation," with their "own surrounds . . . the walls and floors . . . banished from sight," viewers could focus wholly on an image whose depth, perspective, and tactility created "a sense of reality that no other form of picture [could] remotely equal."[109] However, if the evocation of vicarious experience was the goal of making and looking at stereographs, we must ask why, in the forty or so "views" called "lynching," there are no more than five that depict the mob murders of African Americans.[110] Why is it that stereographs dated before World War I typically show the victims of mob violence to be white men killed in locales identified with the West?[111] What meanings of lynching do stereographs therefore aim to produce and why?

The experience of immersion and viscerality when looking through the stereoscope lens habituated the medium's most dedicated practitioners, the striving members of the northern white bourgeoisie, to regard the images and their connection to them as perpetually immediate and sensation-filled.[112] Precisely because looking at stereographs dilated the viewer's sense of time, the images' relation to history could be suspended (if not severed altogether) because in those moments of expansion, the illusion of presence could be confused with the materiality of looking itself, an effect that was intensified if the stereocard's setting was artificially staged to produce its view. Constituted in these terms by the stereograph's apparatuses, the sight of hotly contested political practices such as warfare, xenophobia, and imperialism became culturally tolerable because stereographs seduced viewers into regarding those events as deeply private encounters that need only be reckoned with through their personal experience. And indeed, the phenomenal production and sales records of "stereo views" of the Civil War, the Plains

Indians War, the Spanish American War, and the building of the Panama Canal (to name some ready examples) suggest this was the affective case.[113]

This dynamic of displacement through identification explains the overwhelming popularity of "coon" imagery in the stereographic archive, on the one hand, and the relative absence of anti-black lynching murders from those visual records, on the other. As "the most widely circulated images of African Americans in the late nineteenth century," the abundance of stereocards depicting black people in varied states of cultural regression is astounding.[114] An especially favored series evoked the pastoralism of the plantation past: in scene after scene, blacks toil ceaselessly in stereocards, stooping to perform the hard labor of harvesting cotton—picking the thorny balls by hand and heaping them into barrels for weighing. As the caption for "We's All Done 'dis Mornin' " (1899) reads:

> Every year thousands of travelers are drawn to the Hot Springs of Arkansas by the healing properties of their waters and the beauty of the surrounding country, but other sections of the state are equally charming. . . . The cotton fields, once the dread of the Virginia slave, have lost nothing of their picturesqueness with the abolition of slavery, and nowhere in the United States can primitive Negro life be better studied.[115]

Inviting viewers to tour the South—taking in the idea of hot spring baths against the sight of black laborers in "picturesque" cotton fields—the image would have us believe this scene to be a remnant of the slave past rather than evidence of the South's modern systems of tenant farming and sharecropping.

Other "views" are just as historically disorienting. In one stereograph, "Uncle Tom and Little Eva" (1895) pose in front of a squalid, ramshackle hut, whose scraggly thatched roof and unevenly planked walls enclose one room that yawns open into a dark and foreboding chasm. A heavy-set, matronly looking black woman sits across from "Tom" and "Eva," observing them. Where Stowe's novel thrived on depicting the interiors of homes as emblems of enlightened moral rectitude and order, this stereocard focuses our attention on the cabin's exterior, allowing the viewer to surveil and regulate the interracial contact between the young white maiden (Eva) and the older black man (Tom), domesticating the threat that lynchings were supposed to justify. Likewise, other stereocards encourage the fantasy of the white viewer's dominance over African American incompetence. Looking at a "Free Lunch" (ca. 1898), viewers peer on as black women absentmindedly breastfeed their children. Intellectually stunted from birth, such children were incapable of reason and skill: in "How de Debil Do Dey Make a Bicycle" (ca. 1891), a young black boy haplessly tries to assemble a bicycle while a white woman looks on in amusement. Reprising one of minstrelsy's best-known routines, countless stereocards depict black youth roaming the countryside stealing watermelons and chickens; but as "Dis' Am de Mos' Narrerest Escape Dis Chile Eber Had" (1897) implies, black thievery is always punished (even if the images do not stage such reprisals explicitly), because the white viewer's gaze puts the criminal in his place. Precisely because they flout the rule of law so easily, the "Fifteenth Amendment" (n.d.) cannot bring black men of any age into the realm of civic culture: in two different images bearing this caption, a group of boys clad in rags and cloth hats lazily stand barefooted beneath a pavilion's archway, while a man driving an ox-cart heaped with unbundled hay waits on a pier, seemingly unaware of how market society operates.

According to these stereocards, blacks still performed manual labor in an era of technology-driven industrialization. They lived off the land in the most "picturesque" and "primitive" conditions imaginable. Out of sync with the main currents of American life, they had no appreciation of the economic, political, and cultural transformations remaking the country and the world.[116] In stereovision, African Americans led such stunted lives not because the structures of racism thwarted their social opportunities; blacks lagged behind because they lacked the imagination, drive, and will to keep pace with modern progress. Thus, beneath their veneer of mirth, condescension, and derision toward their black subjects, "coon" stereocards enacted a form of scopic aggression all their own.

However, these images, together with the erasure of anti-black lynchings from the medium's archive, facilitated far worse habits of mind. First, by dissociating the murders of blacks by white mobs in the South from the category of "lynching" almost altogether, stereographs romanticized the violence as an unfortunate but exotic tradition of frontier society—a comforting illusion rooted even deeper into the nation's psyche by cinematic narratives about the settling of the West.[117] Second, and devastatingly, the surfeit of images in the one case and the paucity of pictures in the other meant that white aficionados could rest assured in the fantasy that stereograph technology promised: they need not regret nor feel responsible for things they could not see. Indeed, white people could pull away from their viewfinders eased by the thought that their ways of looking at the world had nothing to do with the murders and sufferings of African American people at all.

A Kodak Moment

Once they were introduced to the market in 1888, hand-held cameras made photographing lynching (and seeing the pictured results) a remarkably complex affair, given how George Eastman's Kodak No. 1 camera modernized visual experience. First, the size and weight of Kodak cameras made them portable. Palm-sized, weighing but two pounds, and installed with Eastman's dry roll mount film, the device quickly compared favorably with the sixty-pound box camera, bulky tripods, cumbersome wet plate negatives, and processing chemicals photographers had to transport to the locales of their shoots. The trim size and sheer simplicity of the camera's mechanics bolstered Eastman's second achievement: the deprofessionalization of the practice of photography. Specially skilled studio artists no longer ruled the province of camerawork because Kodak delivered on its promise to "remove all need for labor and photographic knowledge" from the picture-making process.[118] The task that intimidated amateurs most—developing negatives into cherished black and white images—was performed by technicians at the Kodak laboratories in Rochester, New York, and the cameras themselves were engineered to maximize use and minimize confusion. With the lens, aperture settings, shutter speed, and film stock calibrated at the factory, the complex science of composing a picture was distilled to a single gesture described by an easy-to-recall maxim: point and shoot.[119]

The "point and shoot" capacity of Kodak cameras made their third innovation possible: the rise of snapshot photography in American visual culture.[120] The photograph taken on the spur of a moment; the photograph taken inside or close to one's home; the photograph taken of family and close friends; the photograph taken of the possessions that hold special, particular meaning; the photograph taken of a monumental, life-defining incident; the photograph taken by oneself about the pleasures or hardships of one's own life—all these were suddenly made possible. Liberated from "the undeniable theatricality and bourgeois pretentions of the nineteenth-century [photographer's] studio," Americans were free to view themselves and their worlds as they desired, through the lens of accessibility provided to them by Eastman's technicians in upstate New York.[121]

Indeed, snapshots' credibility as authentic radiated from such notions of unprofessionalized simplicity, candor, and familiarity. However, their intimacy differed from that of the stereograph because of the ways in which snapshots "uproot vision."[122] Enabled by the camera's portability and capacity to take a series of shots rapidly, snapshot photographs promised the pleasures of spontaneity—the idea that the picture was not deliberately or consciously composed but unexpectedly happened. "The snapshot . . . offered a style of photography that was relatively rapid, serial, and instantaneous, in contrast to the individual plate exposures and carefully constructed tripod images that had characterized both amateur and professional photography to that time," cultural historian Nancy Martha West explains.[123] Unlike stereographs, whose temporal frame of vision was experienced primarily as ontological—that is, *being* in the scene—snapshots defined the observer in relation to time and space differently. Where stereographs fixed the viewer in one place and drew out his engagement with the image, the marvel of snapshot photography (according to Kodak's persuasive ad campaigns) was the camera's mobility and capacity to produce visual encounters instantaneously (figure 5.6). Furthermore, "shutterbugs" could take a rapid succession of photographs that divided movement and action into discrete visual moments.[124] But these technological advances did not mean that the snapshot camera's idiom of innocence could not be deployed in insidious ways. An informant for the NAACP filed the following report in 1915, writing from the killing fields where Thomas Brooks was lynched in Fayette County, Tennessee: "Hundreds of kodaks clicked all morning at the scene of the lynching. . . . Picture card photographers installed a portable printing plant at the bridge and reaped a harvest in selling postcards showing a photograph of the lynched Negro."[125] Snapshot photography's potential to promote harm and violence—its role in what historian Grace Elizabeth Hale calls the "deadly amusements" of American racism—is intriguingly probed in a series of snapshots that are, perhaps, the most remarkable photographs of lynching taken before World War I.

Taken in 1902, somewhere in the swamplands of Georgia's low coast, four images track the horrific burning of a black man.[126] From what the snapshots show, the immolation was finished, though not complete, for what remains of the victim's body is a startling, sickening sight. Headless, the man's charred torso has been hoisted into the air, suspended between two narrow-trunked trees. Standing below are leisurely dressed white men—their white shirt sleeves rolled up to their elbows and hats positioned to shade their eyes from the blinding glare of the sun. The fullest view of the murder scene, where the victim and culprits appear foregrounded, is rendered all the more chilling because of the inscriptions on the back of the photograph. Above the advertisement

Figure 5.6. Kodak snapshot of lynching (1902). Hand-held cameras revolutionized the politics of producing and consuming lynching photographs at the turn of the nineteenth century. With the invention of Kodak cameras in 1888, amateur photographers could take their own images and print them for their private uses. This development encouraged the secretion of lynching photographs, or the willed release and withdrawal of the pictures from open, public circulation. (Photo courtesy of the Allen-Littlefield Collection.)

for "WRIGHT'S KODAK FINISHING SHOP, 145 BALL STREET, SAVANNAH, GA.," written in ink, in a clear, steady hand, is the following message:

"Warning:
The answer of the Anglo-Saxon race to black
brutes who would attack the womanhood of
the South."

The unalloyed threat of the written message, together with the violence depicted in the photographs, demonstrates unequivocally how lynching photographs could be used to intimidate and terrorize viewers into silence—especially African Americans, to whom this note was no doubt addressed. However, the exercise of racial power that the written note seeks to confirm is made uncertain by the images themselves. First, for much of the company's early career, Kodak pursued an aggressive campaign to encourage picture taking as a delightful form of leisured play. Emphasizing "the sheer pleasure and adventure of taking photographs . . . [,] the delight of handling a diminutive camera, of not worrying about development and printing, of capturing subjects in candid moments, of recording travel to exotic places," Kodak ads featured the camera as a sign of cultured ease—at the tennis court, at the campground, on the sailboat, on the seashore, driving the car.[127] The working-class worlds of saloons, vaudeville halls, dance halls, nickelodeons, baseball games, amusement parks, and hunting trips were not envisioned as the "proper" domain for the camera, but these lynching snapshots suggest that some such venue was implicated. Indeed, these photographs hardly "delight" in the freedoms that the camera supposedly bestows on the photographer. On the contrary, these images are burdened by the camera's maneuverable ease. Photography's capacity to be mnemonic—to encode and incite memory—is shattered by the sight of the charred and mutilated corpse, whose violation and very presence defies description, suspends both attention and perception, stopping time before this sight of the victim's death.

That is why the size, lighting, and perspective of these Kodak snapshots contradict the written warning's assertion of racial and gender dominance most explicitly. When read as a self-reflexive confrontation with the medium of the snapshot, the composition of the images places in doubt whether photography (as opposed to writing) can answer the problems that the victim's death represents. What and where are the limits of (un)just action? And why does racial difference become the visible sign on which that limit is drawn?

But the diminutive size of these snapshots, 2-1/4 inches tall by 1-7/8 inches wide, places the burden of looking square on the viewer's shoulders.[128] Where stereographs were made legible by the binocular equipment that enlarged them for view, to see these snapshots the observer must move her face and eyes to the images themselves and concentrate intensively on the scenes they depict. With the observer's desire to see entangled with the mob's decision to kill, a complex commitment is then required for the observer either to continue looking or to extricate herself from the pictures' moral morass. However, the incorporation of such enormous, egregious violence within the scaled-down dimensions of the snapshot's visual field draws attention to the impossibility of this fantasy of control, because the snapshot camera's sequencing capacity demonstrates how tenuously the photographer regarded his place and power in the scene.

Kodak cameras' quick shutter action and prepackaged film roll allowed photographers to take a quick succession of snapped shots that, effectively, narrated the scenes depicted. In this way, the duration of action and lapse of time could be figured in the resulting prints. With each image in this series of lynching photographs, though, the camera recoils from entering the discursive space of the murder's unfolding.[129] The techniques of observation made possible by snapshot photography pressed this moral obligation to the fore, because one of the genre's innovations—its guarantee to the amateur—was the impossibility of making a technically "bad" picture. Between the camera's flexibility and the Kodak corporation's control over the printing process, "all possibility for error" was ostensibly removed from the picture-making process.[130] But in the snapshots of this lynching—and there were others like them, if we believe the NAACP's field agent's report—neither the camera nor its processes can "correct" the moral disarray generated by the violence. After all, the photographer's motives are not beyond question or reproach: he did travel some distance to attend the murder, and the warning inscribed on the back of one of the snapshots may very well have been written by him. Then again, since the snapshots' composition is tentative, we cannot infer the photographer's intent exactly. Indeed, because the images may be the only available forensic proof that the mob murdered the wrong man for the crime it sought to avenge, by what standards can we hold the photographer accountable for producing these images? What does accountability even mean in this case? Again, the bleak presence of the charred corpse demands an answer.

Photographed from the right, front, and back, always at a distance self-conscious of its measurement, it is as if the snapshots stammer in search of a language to fathom what possible justice the violence could have possibly served. In three of the images, the camera strikes harsh, disorienting angles from the ground up. From this view, we can see that the mob members look everywhere but at the victim's body. This position, however, also details the photographer's fixation on the cruelty done here, because the slant of the camera's lens opens the aperture to the wash of light that foregrounds the suspension of the victim's body in the air. Indeed, it is as if the images tremble from the power of access and mobility the camera permits, given how their point of view remains at the edges of the site. The story these images seem reticent to tell brings the incredulity of this lynching into sharp focus. What crime could have prompted this awful brutality? Why was the victim's body not completely cremated? Why rescue the corpse from the fire and display the body in this way? Why are there no images of the murder itself? Why are those moments missing?[131]

These questions surface and linger for two reasons. The first is technical: Kodak cameras of the types that probably produced these pictures (the Brownie) could take as many as a hundred exposures and had a depth of field that measured up to one hundred feet, according to Nancy Martha West.[132] Second, because the photographer could have taken many more pictures from any number of angles, we can never answer these questions to any degree of moral satisfaction because we cannot know if these are

Figure 5.7. Lynching of Lige Daniels, 3 August 1920. The breakthrough technology of "real-photo" postcards in 1910 made it possible for lynching murders to be quickly converted into visual artifacts and souvenirs. However, unlike large-scale commercial postcard manufacturers, real-photo postcards were more likely to be printed by local entrepreneurs in small-sized lots. While not flooding the marketplace, real-photo postcards nonetheless symbolized a daunting economy of visual power, precisely because the images were exchanged in more clandestine circuits that were easier to control. (Photo courtesy of the Allen-Littlefield Collection.)

the only images available to us. For that reason, snapshot photographs demand that we account for why we see what we see, the same as does every lynching murder.

A Penny for Your Thoughts: The Deadly Messages of Lynching Postcards

The looks of the white men and boys standing beneath (and slightly behind) the dangling feet of Lige Daniels radiate force in this 1920 real-photo postcard (figure 5.7), but for reasons we might not expect. The sober stares of some, the limp grins of others, the strained grunt of one, and the mirthful smile of another urge one important and necessary reading of their poses as a study of racial power. The building in the background was the courthouse in Center, Texas, and Lige Daniels had been tried and convicted of murder there. Unsatisfied with the jury's verdict, the mob pictured here—one thousand members strong—"stormed the . . . jail, battered down the steel doors, wrecked the cell, [and] chose a courthouse-yard oak" to murder this black man.[133]

Arrogating for themselves the state's jurisdiction over life and death, the mob's looks of satisfaction, content, and calm are not simply the first thing we see in this postcard. The faces of these white men and boys are almost all that we see, because of the photograph's composition of the murder scene. The geometrical lines gracing the courthouse's façade draw the building forward into the picture's plane, edging the mob closer to the front of the image. So close to the photograph's bottom border, the look of the men's and boys' eyes becomes the visual ground. All the while, hovering above, out of the viewer's immediate line of sight, lost in the sun's glare and the dappled light on the tree's leaves, hangs Lige Daniels whose life, this real-photo postcard suggests, is not even worth looking at.

There is a note on the back of this postcard (figure 5.8). Someone known to someone else as "Aunt Myrtle" wrote in a clear hand:

This was made in the court yard
In Center Texas
He is a 16 year old Black boy
He killed Earl's Grandma
She was Florence's mother.
Give this to Bud.

The appearance of Myrtle's note is as remarkable as those of the mob members because a palpable, visible degree of worry charges these brief

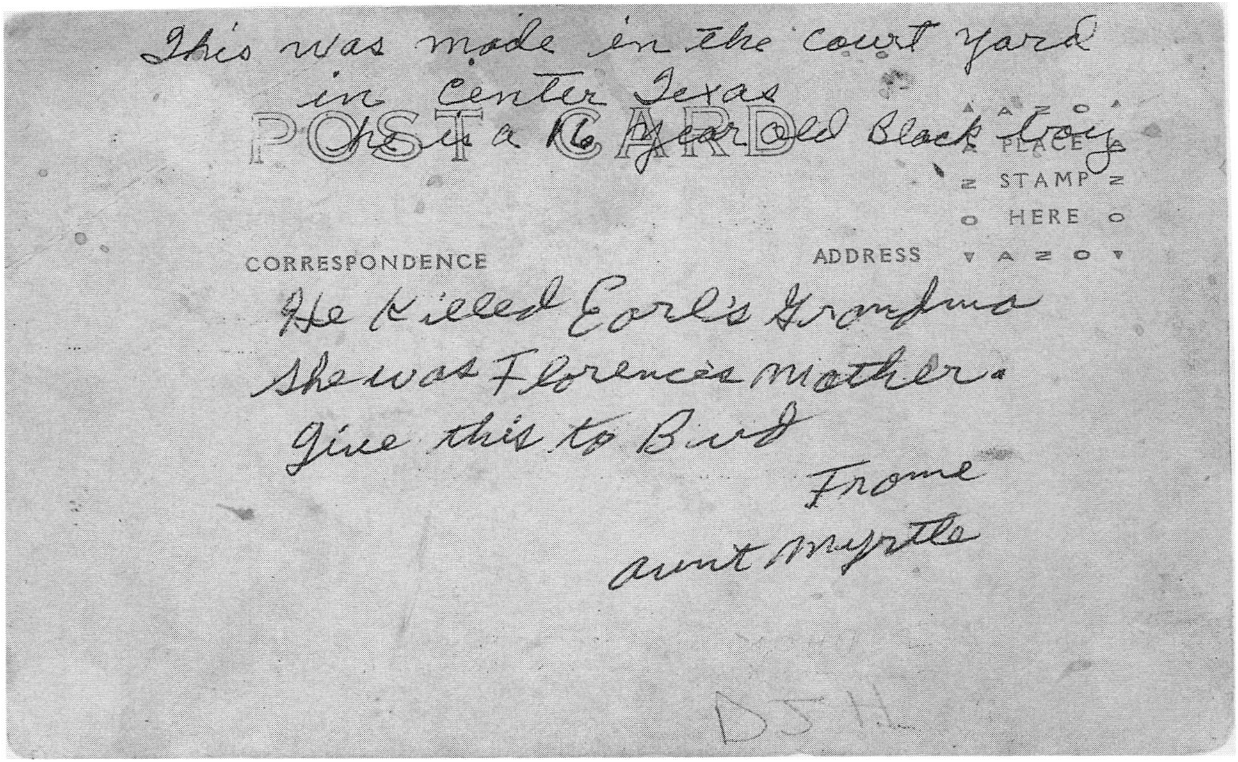

Figure 5.8. Verso of real-photo postcard depicting the lynching of Lige Daniels, 3 August 1920. The versos of lynching postcards often bear clues about the consumption and circulation of the images. Here, evidence of the manufacturer's name and production code, a postmark, postage stamp, and address are missing from the back of the card. These details confirm that a "real-photo" postcard machine was used to produce this artifact and that the postcard was exchanged directly or mailed inside of a sealed envelope. (Photo courtesy of the Allen-Littlefield Collection.)

lines. Though the card's verso has clearly designated spaces for Myrtle's message and the address of young Bud's confidante, she ignores the postcard's layout and writes her thoughts not down but across the back of the image. That Myrtle's note follows the horizontal rather than the vertical axis is no small slip, because the lines of her prose reorganize the visual planes of the photograph itself. At the top of the verso she composes her caption for the picture, her words nearly blotting out the stenciled insignia "POSTCARD." Blank space follows and lined beneath it, across the midsection of the card, Myrtle notes the facts of Lige Daniels's alleged crimes. He "killed Earl's Grandma" who was "Florence's mother." An "aunt" herself, Myrtle reminds her correspondent as well as herself that people they knew—women—lost their lives too, women who took care of others named Earl and Florence. Centering her relations as the primary focal point of the card's note, Myrtle's writing on the verso creates its own field of vision, not unlike how the look of the mob concentrates the front's point of view.

Nonetheless, Myrtle's note evinces clear struggle and the space between her captions figures her divided loyalties. Writing over the name of the object she has come to possess, Myrtle writes against the commodification of this "16 year old Black boy['s]" death. The raised place of Myrtle's caption elevates her remarks to a tone of incredulity and disbelief at what she sees: "a 16 year old Black boy" killed, with perverse ceremony from both the mob and postcard photographer that her note, at least, will not join. There is no evidence of a stamp having been affixed to this postcard: no gummed residue, no tiny shafts of torn paper. Myrtle either mailed this card inside an enclosed envelope or delivered it personally to her correspondent. That she cares for Daniels more than the mob—or, that is, more than her possession and secreted trade of the card might suggest—finds expression in her remarkable choice to capitalize the "B" in "Black."

The regard implied by her spelling convention strongly suggests that Aunt Myrtle may very well be "Black" herself—or Mexican, or (less likely) white. What kind of woman in 1920, living in or near Center, Texas, would dignify a despised people with this script salute? The chance that Aunt Myrtle may be African American alters how her recitation of the case facts read to her correspondent and, now, to us. In 1920, in or near Center, Texas, in the wake of violence such as this, would a black woman refer to white people through their kin and using their first names? Were "Earl's Grandma" and "Florence's mother" also black? Why, then, would a white mob go to these murderous lengths for Earl's and Florence's sakes? Against whom and on whose behalf were these murders committed?

These questions cast Myrtle's admonition to her correspondent in a different light. "Give this to Bud" cannot be read as the same, strange entitlement to see the world that the young white boys in the picture were led to claim watching this lynching occur. Instead, Myrtle's note may have been a caution rather than a license for Bud to beware violence like this. Disciplined to recognize through sight that he lacked the prerogatives of mastery and immunity that these white boys and men violently claimed for themselves, Bud would receive this real-photo postcard as an emblem of his chances to survive in a world that accommodated the misrule of law in places like Center, Texas. Signifying the most profound kind of estrangement and alienation between Myrtle and Bud as kin, this postcard sends a chilling, deadly message to them both. Like young Richard Wright or young Lige Daniels, Bud may be a small black boy about to get the sternest lesson of living "the ethics of Jim Crow" that he would ever receive.

Then again, given the secreted, wayward trail of this postcard, we cannot know Aunt Myrtle's racial identity for certain, or where she lived, or how she came to possess this card, or who she sent it to in the name of entitling or protecting "Bud." The material construction of this postcard as a visual artifact does leave clues to trace, however. That the card was "made in the court yard" but delivered surreptitiously; that there was statutorily defined space for Myrtle to write on the verso; that the card bears the machine-made imprint of manufacture but lacks the trademark code of a large-scale, national publishing firm; that the picture's image is not color tinted but appears instead in black and white: these technical specifications made postcards a particularly modernist medium through which lynching was represented and, so, made known as a cultural phenomenon.

Surprisingly, the history of postcard production and use in the United States is a history about radical change.[134] The policy innovations required to make it possible for Americans to send note cards through the mail transformed the nation's communication networks. Setting the price of stamps at a penny ended the government's monopoly on the trade and led it to cooperate with European administrations (most notably in Germany and England) to establish global standards for a transatlantic market. The significance of 1898 to the American Century redoubles with this crucial domestic policy shift: in that year Congress established Rural Free Delivery, plugging the most far-flung and sparsely populated communities into the national grid of mailed communication. Once it became legal to write notes on the backs of postcards (another congressional decree passed in 1907), "a short simple message could be carried across the entire country within a few days' time for less than a penny."[135] And, because of agreements struck by the United States with postal agencies abroad, that year a penny postcard could be sent anywhere around the world.

With as many as 677,777,798 postcards moving through the U.S. mail system,[136] Americans clearly wanted to surf this early version of today's Internet. For those who preferred to collect cards as part of their personal archive, postcard emporia, exchange clubs, and subscription lists facilitated easy trading of cards to build their lines of visual interest.[137] So long as it could be photographed, nearly anything could be made into a picture sized to fit the 3-1/2″ × 5-1/2″ card stock, bringing far-away and foreign sights close up. Channeling exotica into the realm of daily life to anyone who could afford the cost of the card and penny stamp, postcards made it possible for Americans to believe they had seen the world without having left their parlors. This prosthetic vision no doubt stoked the fantasies of mobility, freedom, autonomy, and power that (as we now well know) virtual reality technologies are bound to excite. As the e-mail and Palm Pilots of the day, however, picture postcards liberated communication by abbreviating the cognitive processes ordinarily enacted to select, obtain, and use a "view." And it would be this capacity for attenuation and abridgement, curtailment and contraction—what Frederic Jameson calls "representational containment"—that would make lynching postcards so rare to find then and so hard to look at now.[138]

The reproduction of a black-and-white lynching photograph (figure 5.9) into a color-tinted postcard (figure 5.10) exposes how the postcard's manufacturing process could strip history's force from the photographic image, rendering the murders pictured below into a spectacle of meaninglessness. Virgil Jones, Robert Jones, Thomas Jones, and Joseph Riley were murdered in Russellville, Kentucky on July 31, 1908. The men had dared to organize black sharecroppers to resist the physical abuse their landowning bosses inflicted on them as part of their labor contracts.[139] Arrested for "disturbing the peace," they were hauled out of jail by a mob of a hundred men and lynched on what appears to be the borderlands adjacent to a farm.

As a photograph, starkly vivid clues about the murders arrest our attention. The sharp-edged tints of light and dark foreground the binding and knotting of the ropes about the men's wrists, suggesting how intent the mob was to kill them. The two men clad in white underwear prompt us to wonder what happened to their clothes. Why are they half-dressed? The color of their garments draws our attention to the chest of the dead man at the far right of the picture's frame—is the blotchy white glare on

Figure 5.9. Lynching of Virgil Jones, Robert Jones, and Joseph Riley, 31 July 1908. (Photo courtesy of the Allen-Littlefield Collection.)

Figure 5.10. Lynching of Virgil Jones, Robert Jones, and Joseph Riley, 31 July 1908. Color-tinted images increased the price of lynching postcards but often distorted the accuracy of the original black-and-white photograph, as is the case in this reproduction. The ropes binding the victims' hands are blurred so as to obscure how the mob worked to tie them up; a "warning" is added onto one victim's chest; a horse is airbrushed out of the picture's right edge; and a caption is added that mythologizes the murders as a nonracist act. (Photo courtesy of the Allen-Littlefield Collection.)

the bib of his overalls an odd spot of light or a note fastened to his chest? The onlookers at this murder scene are ones rarely pictured in lynching photographs: two black men. One stands behind the bush that fills the sightline between the murder tree's farthest right trunk and the body of Joseph Riley; to the farthest right, holding onto the handlebars of a bicycle, is the other man (standing to that man's right is a bridled but untethered horse). What made these men come to look? What did they actually see? What did they do once they saw the bodies? Did anything violent happen to them for being present at the murder scene? This lode of detail is a load to anyone troubled by what this photograph shows. Given its specificity and clarity, as well as its focus on the presence of the dead, the living, and their relations to one another, the black-and-white image lends itself much more readily to a fluid reading than does the color-tinted postcard.

Because of their bolder tones and brighter palette, color-tinted postcards were a high-priced novelty; on the verso of this card the owner recalls paying the extraordinary sum of fifteen cents for this copy of the card. This would not have been an unusual price, though, because manufacturers passed on the labor-intensive costs expended to produce these kinds of cards to the purchasing public. Unlike color lithographs (stone-engraved images that could be inked and stamped by machine) color-tinted postcards were produced individually by hand. At the nation's leading firms, hundreds of boys and young women mixed and applied as many as ten shades of blue, green, red, and yellow dyes in carefully calibrated formulas to each image on a sheet of photographed cards.[140] The dyeing process effected an astounding change to the black-and-white photograph that served as the template. "Each . . . image was subdivided into individual areas to which particular colors were applied," Howard Woody explains. "[This] in effect fractured each image into successive arrangements of color shards."[141]

Since only a dull wash of yellow-green colors the grass and tree leaves in this postcard, it was likely produced by a smaller firm, and the photograph was probably not decomposed as fully as it ordinarily might have been as part of this image remaking process. Nonetheless, the low-tech dye job applied here shatters the coherence that the black-and-white image may be read to possess. The details of the murder scene that stand out more decisively in the photograph appear drab in the color-tinted card's picture field. For instance, since the intricate knots of the ropes cannot be seen as readily, the cruel care with which the mob bound these men before murdering them is lost in this view of the crime scene. Though the black witnesses still stand watch, their facial features—barely visible but legible in the photograph—are smudged into a dark gray blankness. If the effacement of their presence recalls Stephen Crane's description of Robert Lewis's murder in *The Monster,* the acuity of that novella's point explains the outrageous piece of writing grafted onto Joseph Riley's chest. What was an inexplicable, illegible rub of white in the photograph becomes, in the postcard's view, a bluntly drawn "WARNING." This threat, insisting arbitrarily that its meaning is self-evident, calls attention to the missing horse: summarily removed from the scene, the horse was a critical cue to the murder scene's location and the politics that led to the men's deaths.

In rural Kentucky of 1908, a horse would have been as common on a farm as a modestly clothed working-class black man would have been riding a bicycle. With the animal's link to locomotion and husbandry missing from the picture (as opposed to automation and factory work, economic systems that the black man on the bicycle brings to mind), the reason why Virgil Jones, Robert Jones, Thomas Jones, and Joseph Riley were murdered can be air-brushed from the postcard's image as well, which is precisely what the caption printed on the card's right-hand side attempts to do:

"TAKEN FROM DEATH," LYNCHING AT RUSSELLVILLE,
LOGAN COUNTY KENTUCKY, JULY 31, 1908.
HANGED ON THE OLD PROCTOR LYNCHING TREE. THIS IS
A MULTIPLE CEDAR TREE AND THESE FOUR MAKE A
TOTAL OF NINE MEN LYNCHED ON THIS TREE. SOME
WERE WHITE MEN. THIS TREE IS AN OLD LANDMARK AND
WAS AN OLD CEDAR TREE, EVEN IN THE YOUNGEST DAYS
OF THE OLDEST SETTLERS.
RUSSELLVILLE IS ONE OF THE PIONEER TOWNS OF
KENTUCKY AND WAS SETTLED IN A CANE BRAKE.
THIS IS AN EXACT PHOTOGRAPH TAKEN AT DAWN AUG. 1'08.

The tree—no less than five times does the caption salute the cedar, as if it needs to be "taken from death." However, by glorifying "Old Proctor's" long life as foundational to Russellville's settlement and growth as a "pioneer town," the caption's language mystifies the violence pictured here, remaking these murders into something else. Racism has nothing to do with these black men's murders; after all, the legend explains, nine nameless men have been killed by the strength of this "landmark," even "some white men." Consequently, the tree stands as a timeless totem of equality's persistence in Russellville, rather than a historically specific place where nature was turned into an instrument of political and racial oppression.

The person who purchased this postcard knew that the town's and the region's history was more complicated than the red-lettered caption insists, however. He wrote: "I read an account of the night riders' affairs where it says these men were hung without any apparent cause or reason whatever." Importantly, this note uncouples the murders from Ku Klux Klan terrorism because it refers to a contemporary crisis in Kentucky's political history. Though known to recycle the symbols and rituals of the Klan (wearing black masks instead of white hoods and white shoulder sashes instead of robes; speaking in arcane tongues), the "night riders" involved in this lynching were bands of tobacco farmers who escalated what were known as the "Black Patch Wars" to new, deadly heights between 1905 and 1920. Outraged by the efforts of tobacco manufacturers to suppress prices for this globally popular crop, white farmers rallied into vigilante posses to coerce small-scale tobacco growers and tenant farmers in Kentucky and Tennessee into joining their Planters Protective Association.[142] Undoubtedly, Virgil Jones, Robert Jones, Thomas Jones, and Joseph Riley were killed as a result of these struggles. And yet, the labor history effaced by the postcard owner's note still does not capture the full force of the postcard's cultural meanings and effects. From the image's recomposition into color from black-and-white to the euphemistic rhetoric of its caption, the postcard both documents and mystifies how far-ranging the murders' cultural logic actually extends.

The stakes of the Black Patch Wars clarified that the South's economy was increasingly embedded in both national and global formations of corporate capitalism.[143] "The emergence of the American Tobacco Company and the corresponding monopolization of the tobacco industry brought the new industrial order squarely into the social and economic fabric of life in America's tobacco regions," historian Tracy Campbell explains in his account of this turmoil. "Farmers in Kentucky and Tennessee who relied on tobacco as their cash crop consequently found themselves up against the world: a debilitating financial system, an unresponsive political structure, and one of the most effective industrial monopolies in American history," Campbell stresses.[144] Viewed in this context, the postcard image, its caption, and the owner's notations link these lynchings to the murder of Robert Lewis in Port Jervis, New York and Stephen Crane's novella based on that case, *The Monster,* discussed in chapter 3. That is, while the black men murdered in Russellville, Kentucky faced working conditions that were unjust, exploitative, and lethal because tenant farming was particular to the South, their lives and deaths as laborers were also shaped by the greater shift in the nation's economy from an agrarian-industrial capitalist order to a more fully corporate-commodity system. An artifact of that change, the postcard archives the ways in which these lynching murders were symptomatic of American modernization. However, precisely because the postcard's color tint is so underdeveloped and its caption focused exclusively on the lynching tree's local origins, the murders mean nothing beyond their immediate time and place in Kentucky. These tensions reveal the double force of lynching's cultural logic to be endemic to the process of seeing itself, for the national (and even global) implications of these murders get diminished to the degree that the picture's "view" is made visible to us.

The owner of the postcard knew that the account it offers is not germane; hence his countercaption on the verso. But the text on the card's back side hints toward another counterhistory offered by the image, a history obscured by the photographic spectacle of the men's deaths. Remarkably, the handwritten annotation mirrors the electrotyped one, with its use of the vertical space on the verso's left side. The owner's note is not addressed to someone else—there is no stamp, and the "space for address only" is left conspicuously blank. Why? The message describes how this card was secreted into the owner's possession: "I bought this in Hopkinsville. 15 each. *They are not on sale openly. I forgot to send it until just now I ran across it. . . . A law was passed forbidding these to be sent thru the mail or to be sold anymore*" (emphasis added). As the writer realizes, the surreptitious marketing of this card circumvents the law's authority to regulate this traffic in images. Even though the town, city, county, or state where the owner of this card lived had forbidden its citizens from sending lynching postcards through the mail, it would be impossible for any official auditor to ascertain if the public obeyed the rule since, as this person divulges, "I forgot to send it until just now I ran across it."

And yet, remembering he forgot to send the card when it was legal to do so (since it cannot be done "anymore" implies there was a prior time when such exchanges could be conducted through the mail), the owner could just as well forget the law applies and send the card anyway, because the law could not remember its duty either. In the millions of pieces of mail it inspected and confiscated on behalf of the federal government between 1877 and 1915, the New York Society for the Suppression of Vice never banned or removed lynching postcards from circulation as part of its annual purity drives.[145] With the state's malfeasance as precedent, this postcard owner could justify any decision he wished to make in this instance. That we cannot know for certain what he chose to do with the card—to mail it, keep it, swap it—is not, then, simply a problem of paper trails turning cold or empty. Our ignorance is a frightening corroboration of how postcards' nonuse also defined how lynching's history could be known.

Lynching postcards' economy of scale made their nonuse possible. Large publishing firms like the Teich Company in Chicago and the Detroit Publishing Company kept as many as 40 million cards in their active stocks and could print orders for any line of views at the rate of nearly three hundred sheets (with one hundred images to a sheet) per hour.[146] Though this superabundance was possible in only the most fully industrialized and capitally solvent firms, even subcontractors and midlevel publishing firms dealt in staggering volumes of cards. For instance, the Rotograph Company of Manhattan, which promised to print "Postcards from Your Own Photographs," required its customers to order at least three thousand cards (at $9.00 per thousand, or $27). With the bonuses of color-tinting and electrotyped captions included in the price, the next level of service might have enticed customers into buying an even larger shipment; for $2 less in unit costs, a client could buy five thousand views for $35.[147] A customer could not receive her postcards immediately, though, because the company's system processed orders slowly, taking three to five months to deliver the goods. It is precisely this glut of time and product that the system used to produce lynching postcards aimed to avoid.

That method was known in the trade industry as the "real-photo postcard," a technique developed by George Eastman and his staff at Kodak.[148] In 1902 the company joined the gold rush in postcard publication by manufacturing and selling postcard-sized printing paper onto which a snapshot negative could be directly printed. For the second tool in this kit, Eastman and his staff designed a new style of camera; in 1903, the Kodak No. 3A hit the market. At the affordable price of $2.00, this camera could make negatives that were postcard-sized contact prints. Crucially, in 1910, one of Kodak's subsidiaries, the Rochester Optical Company, introduced the "R.O.C. Postcard Printer." "Practically impossible to get out of order," this device was marketed to "the man who desires an inexpensive, yet rapid and trustworthy machine for printing and developing-out postcards," the ads gushed. Anyone with $7.50 to spend could purchase the printer at list price, but professional photographers were given a 40 percent discount on the device, suggesting they were the principal target market.[149] For postcard collectors not interested in the technology of their production, Kodak offered its usual expertise. By 1906, customers who sent their film to be processed in the Rochester labs could have their snapshots turned into postcards on request.[150]

These "innovations in cameras, film, and printing stock made it possible for almost anyone to produce his own personalized picture postcard," visual historians Paul N. Vanderwood and Frank J. Samponaro rightly claim.[151] For every American who thrilled at the hand-held sight of Niagara Falls or the Eiffel Tower, there was someone else who was interested to see his own environs represented as a "view." Visually akin to the snapshot, the real-photo postcard chronicled the events of daily life in local places. Unlike the snapshot, real-photo postcards were printed serially, one image repeated for as few as one but as many as five thousand times, and were sold publicly in local stores and regional postcard emporia.[152]

Downsizing the scale of the production process, the entrepreneurial manufacture of real-photo postcards was no less modernized than the operating systems of the large corporate postcard publishers. Using machinery that could nearly instantly produce as few or as many images as the photographer needed, and with supplies that could be purchased at steep discounts, the makers of real-photo postcards mastered the challenges of an advanced process that was marked by flexibility and speed. While we cannot rule out that many thousands of lynching postcards were produced by large- or medium-sized publishing firms, the available evidence suggests that real-photo postcards dominated the trade precisely because the distinctly supple character of the technology maximized the maker's and consumer's control over the production–consumption cycle. This seemingly lower-tech option offered the more sophisticated exercise of visual power: publishing real-photo postcards on a narrower scale truncated and privatized the paper trail of these images, making them too hard to trace. Paradoxically, the smaller ambit of the real-photo postcard's trade concentrated and magnified the power of the images to do harm, meaning that the production and possession of them resignified lynching's violence into the most spectacular secret in the world.

As a secret(ion), lynching postcards exact the most damage and exert maximal power precisely because we cannot tell where they are, who owns them, or when they will be released for public view. This mystification of their existence makes lynching postcards a particularly power-charged souvenir, especially if we conceive their discursive space as cultural theorist Susan Stewart suggests. The souvenir, she explains, "distinguishes experiences. We do not need or desire souvenirs of events that are repeatable. Rather we need and desire souvenirs that are reportable, of events whose materiality has escaped us, events that thereby exist only through the invention of narrative."[153] Stewart's is a remarkable idea: souvenirs do not "report" on events we wish to remember; souvenirs enable the "invention of narrative" about the event, whose status as such can no longer be assured since their "materiality has escaped us." Souvenirs, in other words, embody not the absence of memory but a lack of memory. In which case, souvenirs are not symbols. They are not even metaphors, since either of those tropes derives its identity and rhetorical function from its full correspondence to the other object (or objects) it stands for. As James Weldon Johnson understood the historicism of the realist novel, Stewart argues that souvenirs are metonyms because they are not supposed to replace the event or experience they represent. They "never entirely recoup" the moment they signify because, if they did, souvenirs would "erase [their] own partiality, that partiality which is the very source of [their] power."[154] A final look at a postcard suggests how Stewart's conception can transform how we read lynching postcards as souvenirs of white power over the lives and deaths of black people.

The front of this postcard is horrific (figure 5.11). Suspended from what must have been an unusually long chain is a destroyed human form. Burnt into a weirdly familiar pose—the remains of his head erect, his torso fixed rigidly upright, both arms raised as if to flex his biceps, a white cloth draped around his groin, his legs missing below the knees—Jesse Washington was hoisted high on the bullet-riddled pole that served as the stake on which he was burned to death for the crowd of over ten thousand in Waco, Texas, to see.[155] One white man, dressed in a workman's cap and overalls, leans against the pole as if asleep: his eyes are closed, his mouth drawn into a quietly sealed line of silence. Standing immediately behind him a crowd of men and boys face the camera, eyes wide open, mouths shut in grim glares. To the far right edge of the postcard's picture another white man stands guard before Washington's body. But unlike the sleeping sentinel (whose cap is pulled forward to shade his brow), this man's bowler is tipped to the very back of his head, showing him to be wide awake and alert to this scene.

"This is the barbecue we had last night," the note on the back of the postcard begins. "My picture is to the left with a cross over it [*sic*] your son Joe." Though the "x" that marked Joe's spot is now blurred, we can still locate him in the picture: he appears in the lowest left-hand corner, standing directly to the side of the man leaning against the pole. Joe's hat and shirt suggest how young he is—soft brim curled down, his shirt collar puckering up—as does his sense of incredulity: the left corner of his lip drawn up slightly, Joe looks to be drawing in a long, low breath, summoning the strength he presumes belongs to him now that he's seen "the barbecue." Joe's stare of wonder, paired with the guards'

Figure 5.11. Lynching of Jesse Washington, 16 May 1916. (Photo courtesy of the Allen-Littlefield Collection.)

studied avoidance of Jesse Washington's body (the one sleeps; the other looks away from the body), is a compelling focal point for critical attention. However, Jesse Washington's body deserves our first look, and we can transform our view of him if we contemplate Stewart's definition of souvenirs. Joe's written note seeks to fix the violence done to Washington depicted in the postcard, but does his narrative complete its task? What history of this event does his writing invent?

Signing with the salutation "your son," Joe intended this postcard for one of his parents. It may have been his father; it could have been his mother (interestingly, one hat in this postcard appears to be a woman's—the straw hat with a single cord of ribbon tied about the cap and a brim so wide it shades the wearer's face and shoulders; two hats to the left of the alert watchman, the woman's head is cast downward, her hand placed on her cheek). But the stamp is missing from the place where the card calls for one. Nor is the card formally addressed to his parents: the space under "NAME AND ADDRESS HERE" is blank. Like Aunt Myrtle and the (wo)man from Hopkinsville, Joe likely delivered the postcard in person or mailed it in a sealed envelope, presenting the image to his parent(s) not as evidence of Washington's murder but as proof of his distinction as an adult white man. Fearing that his parents would not recognize him in the crowd, Joe points himself out by creating a legend for himself on the card. "X" marks his spot, placing himself at the center of this murder, where his writing suggests he most wished to be.

Since Joe's note suggests that the mob's sadistic power is not the point of his interest in the postcard image so much as asserting his individuality within the scene (not unlike J. L. Mertins's visual attraction to the murder of Henry Smith), it would seem that Stewart's construct of the "exotic" souvenir describes Joe's example best:

> Removed from its context, the exotic souvenir is a sign of survival—not its own survival, but the survival of the possessor outside his or her own context of familiarity. Its otherness speaks to the possessor's capacity for otherness: it is the possessor, not the souvenir, which is ultimately the curiosity.[156]

However, what also turns "other" is the figure of writing itself here. After nearly one hundred years since Washington's murder, Joe's "x" has all but faded away, while his note on the verso strained then (and does so now) to sound a properly ironic tone. His writing, unlike Aunt Myrtle's, is steeped in the cruel banality Hannah Arendt defined in *Eichmann in Jerusalem*.[157] But where Arendt ascribes the violence of totalitarianism to the bureaucratization of violence, lynching postcards and the writing on them point to the commodification of violence as the source of racism's institutionalized malevolence. In this regard, the postcard, as image and artifact, fetishizes the violence in the way not of Freud, but of Marx. Congealing and concealing the labor that goes into the work of killing black people, the photograph figures the violence as a sight to be looked at instead of the choices and acts that the murder actually involved.

Though the charred, brutalized remains of Jesse Washington's corpse are intimidating to look at, we would be wrong to conclude that the postcard and Joe's writing on it completes the mob's domination over Washington, over other black men and women, and over us as viewers. To the extent that it is a souvenir in the sense Susan Stewart defines, this postcard (and, by extension, all lynching postcards) represents its maker's and consumers' lack of control and the impoverished state of their power. We need not fear these images because they strike us today as revolting. Instead of calling them "souvenirs" with rage, we can invoke the term to critique how our received histories of photography have taught us to look at but not see the deaths of black people as paving the way for America's turn to modernism.

Lynching and the Injuries of Time

What Americans at the turn of the nineteenth century expected photographs to be, mean, and do turned out to generate the force with which images of lynching extended the scope of mob violence. More than anything else, photographs test our faith in—and hope for—their archival capacities to represent and memorialize the facts, events, and people that make up our worlds, to document and prove that things exist. We think that photographs offer certainty when, it must be said—and lynching photographs provide us the occasion to confront this epistemological truth—they do not. The "records" we think we are looking at are not reality *per se* but a *subjectively construed* interpretation of reality, one that is imposed upon us *formally*—through composition, framing, lighting, exposure, angle. Even when the photographs are "relatively undiscriminating, promiscuous, or self-effacing"—even when, as Susan Sontag complains, they lack a sense of style as so many lynching photographs *seem* to do—scopically aggressive images nonetheless act on us with the kind of awesome power that more distinguished looking art elicits when we stand before it. They compel our attention.[158] And it is for this reason that we struggle over whether we should choose to see or turn away from photographs of the violence.

But the pictures compel us in ways that newspapers and novels do not. Photography is unique as a system of representation because of its relation to the passage of time and to the things it depicts. Where writing and other plastic arts (painting, sculpture, or sketching, for instance) do not require referents, photography does so of necessity. James Weldon Johnson did not have to have nearly been killed by a mob in order to write about one. Stephen Crane did not see the murder that took place in front of his brother's house; still, he managed to give us *The Monster.* Even if Ida B. Wells had not endured a symbolic murder by the Memphis mob, she may have sojourned on to lead her crusades against lynching. But for even the most unskilled photographer, the referent is, as Roland Barthes explains, "the founding order of [the medium]" because it is "not optionally the real thing to which an image or sign refers but the necessarily real thing which has been placed before the lens, without which there would be no photograph." Therefore, what photographs evince and confirm, what they authenticate with certainty, is not juridical but metaphysical: they certify that "what I see has indeed existed."[159] But what do photographs do, what proof do they offer, if what they depict defies our notions of existence? What are we to make of photographs that depict what should not have been?

To put these questions another way: if reference is "the founding order of Photography"; if "the nature—the genius" of photography is to "compel me to believe its referent had really existed,"[160] then we must conclude that lynching photographs bring the medium to the brink of nonsense because the violence of lynching disrupts and disproves the certainty that photographs are presumed to confer. Before images of lynching, we cannot believe that what we see actually happened. We do not want to admit that what we see existed. Those traits of reader-response encourage us not to acknowledge the damage that has been done to black people. In that abyss, lynching photographs become unbounded by history and, as John Berger so astutely argues, politics, too. Because "the reader who has been arrested by the photograph[s] may tend to feel this discontinuity as his own personal moral inadequacy, as soon as this happens even his sense of shock is dispensed [and the violence depicted in the image] is effectively de-politicized. The picture becomes the evidence of the general human condition. It accuses nobody and everybody."[161]

Tragically, atrocity photographs can become banal through the kind of studied, earnest overlooking that Berger describes. Our familiarity with an image—or, rather, a sort or type of image—can keep us from "seeing" it and its contingencies precisely because a surfeit of such images can "mak[e] the horrible seem ordinary . . . familiar, remote ('it's only a photograph'), inevitable."[162] The look of lynching photographs seems inevitable to us today—they all show the same thing the same way, we suppose. However, at the turn of the nineteenth century—when visual catalogs were becoming vast and when our repertoire of cultural images was growing ever more quickly—lynching and the photographs of that violence refined the norms by which Americans looked at and saw the world before them. Linking the unimaginable to the imagined as the image, lynching photographs from the turn of the nineteenth century until today, early in the twenty-first, define what we think of as (un)sightly and (un)seeming—indeed, of what it means to see at all. Before the photographs' gruesome tableaux of death, vision becomes legible as a cultural operation, one premised on this truth about how knowledge of the modern world was obtained, and what objects would constitute that knowing.

The ways in which African American people would serve photography's function so obviously, and yet have that relation remain historically marginalized, brings us to the problem of the unspeakable, and suggests that lynching photography may be related to—and so, understood through—the discursive space of the sublime. That may seem like an untoward, even unethical, claim to make about such atrocious images and the "lower" orders of visual culture from which they come—especially after claiming at the chapter's outset that the photographs extend lynching's power to oppress. If, however, we recall that the sublime describes more than the grand, beautiful, or exalted; if we admit to being equally awed by the horrific and the degraded—if we agree that "the sentiment of the sublime . . . develops as a conflict between the faculties of a subject, the faculty to conceive of something and the faculty to 'present' something"—the unspeakableness of these photographs describes lynching's deepest enigma: why the violence could command the public's attention and yet will the nation to a collective silence; why Americans remember to forget lynching, when—and if—they recall its history at all.[163]

SIX

In the Mind's Eye

Some things you forget. Other things you never do. . . . Places, places are still there. If a house burns down, it's gone, but the place—the picture of it—stays, and not just in my rememory, but out there in the world. What I remember is a picture floating around out there in my head. I mean, even if I don't think it, even if I die, the picture of what I did, or knew, or saw is still out there. Right in the place where it happened.

TONI MORRISON, *BELOVED*

The "sublime," the "terrible real," "indifference," and "dynamitic"; "cultural logic," "spectacular secret," and "modern": over the course of the previous chapters I have developed these terms to test whether I could coin a term to replace "lynching" as the one we ordinarily use to summarize the history of mob violence directed against African Americans. Even though I have stressed "cultural logic" more than the others and do believe that it offers an interpretative range whose usefulness I say more about below, I have come to the conclusion that the history of lynching poses too great a burden for one word to carry. Given the virulence of the violence, on the one hand, and the protean forms it assumed across the late nineteenth and twentieth centuries on the other, I have used "cultural logic" and its collateral terms more as indices to ways of knowing what "lynching" means than as an alternative lexicon *per se*.

And yet, as I have argued throughout the book, formalist aesthetics allow us to situate lynching as an historical phenomenon more decisively than we might ordinarily expect.

For instance, Stephen Crane's pecuniary turn to the novella with *The Monster* implicates lynching in the history of contracts and corporate capitalist development at the end of the nineteenth century. The cameras that trained Americans to see the world through a viewfinder transformed what it meant to document historical events, but with lynching photography's "uprooting" of vision, I explained in chapter 4, the medium reinforced the oppressive aims of the violence by habituating Americans to see the deaths and sufferings of African American people as a disturbing but tolerable sight. Why turn to racial violence to determine the boundaries of freedom in a secularized society? Ida B. Wells's parodies of news writing about anti-black mob murders exposed how lynching facilitated the rationalization of knowledge in public life. Lynching's persistence was not a fad, nor was it a fluke; the violence occurred under any number of guises because its popularity sated Americans hungry for "real" or authentic experience—or so James Weldon Johnson proposed in the novel *The Autobiography of an Ex-Colored Man*.

As these late-nineteenth- and early-twentieth-century cases make clear, the issues that define the trajectories of lynching's cultural logic—its fit into history's milieu together with our disavowal of those connections—were embedded in the developments that marked America's march of progress. In the preceding chapters, I have argued that lynching's cultural logic allows us to disavow those historical contingencies because the citizenship rights of African Americans were actively nullified by the state, making lynchings not as "extralegal" as the word encourages us to suppose. But after considering the histories of lynching made available to us by Ida B. Wells, Stephen Crane, James Weldon Johnson, and (as we shall soon see) Gwendolyn Brooks, I have come to another conclusion about the significance of this process. Lynching's cultural logic works so effectively because, over time, we have become invested in knowing certain kinds of historical accounts. Writing about the Holocaust, James E. Young observes that what we might call legendary thinking often organizes survivors' narratives about their experiences under the Nazi regime and in the death camps. In these narratives, "survivors retell actual events parabolically, even didactically, around pre-existing cultural axioms." Because the events they recount may or may not have actually happened, legends are valuable because, as allegories, they offer "insight into the humane . . . apprehension of the most inhuman times"—that is, such tales archive a community's understanding of its experience with terror.[1]

Regarded in "legendary" terms, lynching has been easier to disavow as central to the nation's past, because the violence can then be causally linked to more fathomable problems (white supremacy; caste, class, and gender discrimination; agrarian economics) in one locale (the South), in response to one social transgression (rape), involving just two races (white and black), following from one cultural condition (anti-modernism). Admittedly, the alternative is bleak. It is unsettling to think that it was not only the Ku Klux Klan that killed African Americans *en masse,* that lynching did not just happen in front of thousands of people, or that anti-black mob murders did not always involve castration. "As long as lynchings are interpreted as a ritualized expression of the values of united white communities the task of explaining both the great variation in the form and the ebb and flow of lynching across space and time will remain incomplete," historian W. Fitzhugh Brundage cautions in his landmark study *Lynching in the New South.*[2]

Though I agree with this assessment, the literary histories of Ida B. Wells's anti-lynching pamphlets, Stephen Crane's *The Monster,* and James Weldon Johnson's *The Autobiography of an Ex-Colored Man* counter the tendency Brundage describes. These works and the lives of their authors require us to confront what is, to my mind, one of the most insidious consequences of ritualizing our telling of lynching's history.

Once we let ourselves consider that lynching could happen anytime to any black person (witness Robert Lewis and James Weldon Johnson), or that mobs were often led by businessmen and other officers of civic order (remember who razed the offices of the *Free Speech* in Memphis), then we would have to face the terrifying reality that led Chicago's Anti-Lynching Bureau to ignore Ida B. Wells's request for political and financial support in 1902: that violence directed against African American people had become so entrenched a practice that it was a normal routine in national life. Lynching's cultural logic reveals the stakes of our fixation on the extremities of the practice, as does literature that grapples with its dynamics, both of which free us to imagine lynching's history as broadly as it demands.

If academic and popular historiographies of the violence have resisted acknowledging lynching's relations to national culture, cultural studies of American modernity have neglected to consider lynching as one of the signal events that changed the world sometime around 1910, as

Virginia Woolf famously prophesied.[3] Anti-black mob murders certainly revolutionized the worlds of Ida B. Wells, Stephen Crane, James Weldon Johnson, and this survivor of the 1919 "Red Summer" race riot in Washington, D.C.:

> The Washington riots gave me the thrill that comes once in a lifetime. I was alone when I read between the lines of the morning newspaper that at last our men had stood like men, struck back, were no longer dumb, driven cattle. When I could no longer read for my streaming tears, I stood up, alone in my room, held both my hands high over my head and exclaimed, "Oh, I thank God, thank God!" When I remember anything after this, I was prone on my bed, beating the pillow with both fists, laughing and crying, whimpering like a whipped child, for sheer gladness and madness. The pent-up humiliation, grief and horror of a lifetime—half a century—was being stripped from me.[4]

Notice how this woman's "thrill" of recovery depends on two severe breaks with reality: the loss of her senses and self-control. She falls unconscious. She goes blind and falls mute. She infantilizes herself through figurative abuse ("whimpering like a whipped child"; "being stripped"). History turns the woman into a hysteric because, as she narrates it, her existence prior to and in this moment of revelation disorients her so profoundly that public time ("half a century") cannot guarantee order, just destruction and devastation. Broken by an unbearable-to-remember past, an impossible-to-inhabit present, and a still-volatile future, this woman has endured freedom—which for others would be the ticket to advancement and achievement—as the "horror of a lifetime." If, as theoreticians of modernity tell us, the events and inventions of the late nineteenth and early twentieth centuries ushered in new ways of experiencing, conceiving, and knowing the self, world, and history—if, as these scholars argue, modernity changed nothing less than the contours of experience and structures of thought itself—then by these measures lynching rates as a cultural development that shaped the modern mind, which this woman's recollection confirms.[5]

An experience such as this, however, is rarely encountered in accounts of modernity in World War I-era America. And yet, by the criteria scholars have defined, the survivor's reverie—together with the riot-murders themselves—should be construed as a "modernist" experience precisely because the woman's response distinguishes between the impact of technological progress and the states of consciousness those advances were supposed to produce. As Jonathan Crary reminds us: "Modernity in whatever age it appears, cannot exist without a shattering of belief, without discovery of the 'lack of reality' . . . together with the invention of other realities."[6] Her grasp of reality breaks down from its known coordinates to reassert potentially new social linkages, because literature mediates her encounter with lynching in a radical way: the woman "reads between the lines" of a newspaper to gloss the historical significance of the Washington, D.C. riots. Since news writing both enables and threatens her sense of self, time, and space so profoundly, lynching's literary history underscores how our periodization of the modern era is insufficiently conceived. As such, we must consider lynching's power to dominate from this vantage point as much as any other arguments we already know.

That said, the new modernism that lynching's history suggests need not reproduce canonical accounts. Indeed, lynching's modernist ethos introduces four conceptual-political contributions that distinguish its force and meaning as such. First, given its cultural logic—its fit with the contemporary milieu and the public's collective disavowal of those relations—lynching calls into question how we define modernity in the first place, not in terms of chronology, or when periods begin and end, but why we presume modernity necessarily means "progress" that promotes human liberty and happiness. "Racial terror is not merely compatible with occidental rationality but [is] cheerfully complicit with it," theorist Paul Gilroy observes about slavery's function in transforming the world during the eighteenth and first half of the nineteenth century.[7] Because lynching's spectacular secrecy fomented so many key developments in U.S. national culture at the start of the twentieth, its history challenges us to look, in Gilroy's words, "more deeply into the relationship of racial terror and subordination to the inner character of modernity."[8] Second, the provisionality of constructing periods also means that by calling lynching "modern" and its effects "modernist" we can resist the tendency to overpsychologize causation of social formations. Because they are concepts based on the idea of lynching's contingent (rather than inevitable) relation to history, cultural logic and modernism both allow us to talk about human agency critically, which is to say that we can then better comprehend how American society negotiates the complexities of cultural change at any given point in historical time.

Third, to call lynching "modern" shifts the scene where modernity is supposed to occur. If modernization and modernity are distinct processes, the metropoles of the Northeast have southern counterparts in the rural countryside. Then, the concept of "newness" might find another correlate—nostalgia—that is no longer regarded as reactionary or atavistic. Consider this testimony from a Georgia clergyman in 1899:

> I was on my way to preach in another part of the city [Atlanta] just as the trains were pulling out to take the yelping mob to [the] execution of Sam Holt [*sic*]. On one side of the street a crowd had gathered for preaching—some were praying and singing while all around them newsboys were crying as loud as they could "All about the capture of Sam Holt!" People were excited, cars blocked, and wild confusion reigned. . . . As I came back from preaching matters were even worse. Newsboys were running in every direction with a second extra crying "All about the burning of Sam Holt!"[9]

In a scene that recalls Samuel Burdett's street encounter with Henry Smith's murder in 1893, Reverend Leonard G. Broughton stands witness to a maelstrom of activity. For all its malevolent tumult, though, time unfolds precisely. The trains come and go according to schedule. The wire reports are updated. The newsboys' cries pierce through actions that may be said to hold history still—praying and traffic jams. As Broughton's testimony suggests, the South's infamous tendency to "look away" is not always an anti-modern gesture. Longing for a world without such "wild confusion" is not to retreat from the present-day but to mark instead the place where the "new" takes hold in contemporary life. Or, as Georgia-born novelist and anti-lynching activist Lillian Smith remarked, the south "walked backward into its future."[10] Seen from this perspective, with our evaluative categories tipped to the south, open to the rural, and cognizant of the unsettling paradox that anti-black mob violence helped shape modern American life, we can then appreciate lynching's fourth challenge to the meaning of modernity: how to value black death as central to our processes for building a nation.[11]

More than anything else, lynching and its cultural logic signal how little Americans care for the deaths of black people. This morbid association was not unique to late-nineteenth-century and early-twentieth-century America, though. That the deaths of African Americans were expendable to the nation's definition of citizenship follows from the dehumanizing norms perfected under chattel slavery, a condition that Emancipation did not end or transform, as lynching attests. Before this history of "political necrophilia," denial and retreat seem to relieve us from feeling too complicit in the culture of death that lynching's racism promoted.[12] However, the long-term effects of lynching's place in modern U.S. society becomes an especially daunting thought when one ponders history's ironic turn wherein, freed to kill one another with impunity, today's gang-bangers conduct drive-by shootings that read too much like lynch mob raids and "rescues" a century ago. For all of the life-affirming change it brings, for all the advances it creates, modern progress, lynching's history teaches us, can be strange and terrifying indeed.

This conundrum sets the stage for lynching's signal development during the twentieth century. After World War I, the numbers of reported anti-black mob murders steadily declined to the point where contemporary observers and scholars declared lynching to have disappeared. Echoing the conclusion drawn by historians and sociologists for nearly a century, W. Fitzhugh Brundage specifies 1950 as the end of an era: "As the number of lynchings declined sharply during the 1940s, the tradition of mob murders by mass mobs, with their attendant public rituals, virtually came to an end."[13] Arguments as to why this is so vary little. The main position holds that modernization waved its wand across the region with beneficent results. With the mechanization of agriculture, the industrialization of manufactured goods, the broader spread of wealth and market commodities, and the liberalization of politics and culture (for example, the extension of the vote to women and blacks, increased acceptance of federal power, the growth of a progressive intellectual class, and the secularization of popular culture), the tensions that incited the vast majority of lynching murders were relaxed, thus releasing southern whites from their murderous ways.[14]

Though the reported numbers of anti-black mob murders decreased, the anxiety that haunted late-nineteenth-century observers and activists did not wane: did the reported cases account for all instances of lynching murders? Because we can never answer that question for sure, we can ask another question about lynching's decline that proponents of the modernization thesis fail to consider. If that violence did indeed disappear, what can explain the steady rise during the twentieth century of other incidents of racist aggression in the forms of race riots, longer incarceration rates in the nation's prisons for black men compared with whites, and the infamous "legal lynchings," epitomized by the Scottsboro Trial of the 1930s?[15] And we need only to study the NAACP's photographic archive from the 1940s and 1950s to know that lynching remained a clear and present danger to African Americans. In addition to images of brutalized black corpses, the visual records in the organization's anti-lynching files are full of scopically sympathetic pictures (photographed at a remove, with the victim-subjects facing the camera's eye) that depict lynching's reappearance in blindings, amputations, and other corporeal mutilations that southern "progress" was supposed to have made obsolete.[16]

Lynching did not disappear. Rather, James Weldon Johnson's prophetic insights into lynching's mass appeal came about. What distinguished lynching's contagion in the twentieth century, compared to the late-nineteenth-century discourse concerning its spread, was this broader ubiquity. With more than one way to deny African Americans their rights as citizens, there was less reason for whites in the North or South to resort to lynching as a means to dominate black people. As Ralph McGill, editor of the *Atlanta Constitution,* pointed out in 1955: "In Mississippi a Negro got up and urged integration before the governor's committee. All he lost was his bank credit. Think of what he might have lost ten years ago."[17] Nonlethal assaults such as this were both easier to inflict and harder to decry because such forms of social discrimination were not physically extreme like lynching murders (the lesson James Weldon Johnson learned a half-century before). But since the thoroughgoing disfranchisement of African Americans did not "look" like lynching murders, the kinds of social deaths black people endured could be disavowed in the name of modernity once again.

My methodological approach to drawing such historicist conclusions takes its cues from reading the formalist aesthetics used to depict lynching's violence. Which texts in particular, you might ask, lead me to critique the disappearance-thanks-to-modernization thesis? So many of them do (and I will discuss them shortly) because of the paradox their proliferation suggests. Both the production and acuity of literary depictions of the violence rose sharply when the empirical evidence indicates actual lynching murders were in decline. Why the outburst of literary inventiveness in the wake of the violence's waning? In works like William Faulkner's *Light in August* (1932), Richard Wright's "Big Boy Leaves Home" (1938), or Angelina Weld Grimke's *Rachel* (1916), lynching is not only a direct threat to the protagonists' lives; the violence exerts itself as a contemporary force in the narratives' present tense (this relation explains why Joe Christmas is castrated by the Nazi sympathizer Percy Grimm; Faulkner aligns southern racism with German fascism to map the global reach of lynching's mass appeal). Jean Toomer's *Cane* (1923), Claude McKay's "The Lynching" (1922), Countee Cullen's "Black Christ" (1929), and Langston Hughes's "Aug. 19th . . ." (1939) do not set lynching in the distant past like Mark Twain's novels of the 1880s and 1890s. Instead, these works figure lynching as a phenomenon of formlessness, the threat of which remains keen because it does not disappear but instead assumes varied shapes.

"They charged. I saw him stagger, fall / Beneath a mill of hands, feet, stares," Cullen's narrator intones solemnly while recounting the murder of his brother Jim. "His spirit in smoke ascended to high heaven. / His father, by the cruelest way of pain, / Had bidden him to his bosom once again; / The awful sin remained still unforgiven," the priest-like speaker proclaims sadly to open "The Lynching." Though much can be said about Cullen's redemptive vision compared with McKay's nihilism (in the closing sestet of "The Lynching," the speaker observes impassively as white women "throng to look" at the victim's body while children "danced round" the corpse "in fiendish glee"), I want to stress instead the poets' shared distrust of the empiricist claim that lynching murders were relics of the past. McKay's turn to the sonnet and Cullen's to the dirge implies that lynching has not disappeared; the violence endures—transformed into other, long-lasting forms. Inventing a new visual icon to symbolize lynching's persistence, McKay and Cullen figure the black victims to be the crucified (and, for Cullen, the risen) Christ, an allusion that resignifies the destruction of black life from a meaningless rite in a godless world to be a sacred loss that cannot be annulled by the passing of secular time.[18]

The generic fluidity of Jean Toomer's *Cane* calls critical attention to the history of lynching's disappearance in two profound ways as well. First, the text stages lynching's passage from being a literal threat to a malaise that infuses the whole of American institutions from the cane fields of Georgia to the university metropolis of Chicago. Tracing the paths of the Great Migration, *Cane* begins in the South where the book's short story and verse cycles chillingly remind us of lynching's omnipresence. As the workday ends in "Georgia Dusk," the "feast of moon and men and barking hounds" leave the sawmill factories in search of black flesh "for the night's barbecue," while "Portrait in Georgia" (whose verse is structured to read like an exercise in psychoanalytic free association) observes the scene of lynching as a composite of the mortification of black flesh and the sanctification of white femininity: "Hair—braided chestnut, / coiled like a lyncher's rope, / Eyes—fagots, / Lips—old scars, or the first red blisters." These poems foreshadow the climax of the short story "Blood Burning Moon," which narrates the doomed efforts of Tom Burwell to best his white rival for the love of black Louisa; killing Bob

Stone in a jealous rage, Burwell meets an awful death at "Georgia Dusk's" setting, a sawmill factory where he is burned to death:

> A great flare muffled in black smoke shot upward. The mob yelled. The mob was silent. Now Tom could be seen within the flames. Only his head, erect, lean, like a blackened stone. Stench of burning flesh soaked the air. Tom's eyes popped. His head settled downward. The mob yelled. Its yell echoed against the skeleton stone walls and sounded like a hundred yells. Like a hundred mobs yelling. Its yell thudded against the thick front wall and fell back. A ghost of a yell slipped through the flames and out the great door of the factory. It fluttered like a dying thing down the single street of the factory town.[19]

As Toomer describes it here, Burwell's suffering is difficult to contemplate because it is, simply, physically awful; hence, the declarative phrasing and tone of the passage. The scene is startling, however, because it insists on the contemporaneity, the "now-ness" of lynching not as a southern atavism but as a form of culture that knows no bounds. For the "ghost of the yell" that slips out and "flutter[s] like a dying thing down the single street of the factory town," calls into question whether the scene stops or launches lynching's violence. To be "like a dying thing" does not mean the mob's yell is dead. Moving down the street, the sound can be carried away to other places, instead of settling on the ground where the murder occurs.

And indeed, the text moves forward from this scene to northern cities, carrying lynching's death spirit with it. Immediately following the demise of Tom Burwell is the story of "Rhobert," a man so burdened by the weight of capitalism's greatest promise—property ownership—that "he is way down. . . . He is way down. He is sinking. His house is a dead thing that weights him down" (40). Toomer does not exaggerate Rhobert's predicament to imagine it is as life-crushing as Tom Burwell's burning: many twentieth-century race riots began as conflicts over blacks owning homes in white neighborhoods in the urban North.[20] In these ways, *Cane* traces lynching's dissipation into social forms and institutions that crippled African American lives.[21]

According to the literary history of the period, then, what makes lynching modern in the twentieth century is how the rhetoric of disappearance compounded the intensity of lynching's cultural logic. On the one hand, from the 1920s forward, there is finally public recognition of lynching's fit within the cultural milieu, a tide that turns for three reasons: (1) African American writers were always among the first to analyze lynching as a national phenomenon, and with the ranks of black authors growing steadily between the two world wars, those critiques gained a more amplified telling; (2) the Communist Party took up the "Negro Question" and lynching in particular to advance its agenda of radical political change; and (3) the emergence of southern-based liberal intellectuals whose published critiques actively linked the conflicts generated by the region's split-labor market to national economic developments and policies.[22] On the other hand, the persistent disfranchisement of African Americans' civil rights was redoubled by the disappearance thesis, whose basic premise and conclusion made it necessary, even, to disavow that the violence existed.

Of the twenty-nine poems he wrote to protest lynching, Langston Hughes struggled to understand this transformation of lynching's cultural logic in three particularly powerful works.[23] Echoing the title of Toomer's poem, "Georgia Dusk" (1935) searches for lynching in the landscape but cannot detect its presence: "Sometimes there's a wind in the Georgia dusk / That cries and cries and cries / Its lonely pity through the Georgia dusk / Veiling what the darkness hides." Unable to trust his senses to distinguish between the empty sound of nature (the crying wind) and the noise of culture's violence (the murders hidden under cover of darkness), the speaker cannot read signs innocently anymore; the blood-red streaks of the sunset that closes the poem could be just color or bloodshed—"A crimson trickle" belonging to "everyone." As late as 1957, Hughes's anxiety over lynching's elusiveness—captured in the neat couplets of the poem "Expendable"—is stark and formidable, while "August 19th . . . ," a poem written in 1938 on behalf of Clarence Norris, one of the nine "Scottsboro Boys" sentenced to death for allegedly raping two white women in Alabama in 1931, draws out the full measure of Hughes's understanding of lynching's formlessness as the matrix of its cultural logic in the twentieth century.

Perfectly exemplifying how legal lynchings operated, the Scottsboro case and Clarence Norris's death sentence epitomized the fallacy of arguing lynching's disappearance. First mandated by the court to die in 1933, Norris won a first appeal to the U.S. Supreme Court that led to a second trial in 1935. Two years passed before that court date arrived, only to see Norris sentenced to death again. Appealing to Alabama's governor for clemency, Norris won the reprieve of having his death penalty commuted to a life sentence in June 1938, just two months before he was scheduled for execution.[24] The law's capacity to move Norris in and out of this space of death (and through its officialdom, to make the public complicit in the violence) opens Hughes's poem: "August 19th is the date. / Put it in your book. / The date that I must keep with / death." Speaking for himself but directly to the reader, Norris spares no room to equivocate about the stakes of his predicament.[25]

As the poem makes clear, all of American society colludes with the law to make Norris's death possible. Equally important to notice is the condition of knowledge this legal lynching produces, because the poem captures the modernism of lynching's violence. When Norris ponders how he is supposed to die, he envisions instead an image of freedom: "August 19th is the date. / The electric chair. Swimmers on cool beaches / With their bodies bare." Knowing he will be strapped to a man-made device meant to burn his body's fluids from the inside out, Norris thinks of naked flesh caressed by sand and sun, perfectly modulated ("cool") to do no harm. For Norris to maintain the equanimity he does while contemplating the thought of his own demise is the modern predicament the poem fathoms through its seemingly didactic form. Lest readers miss the complexity of this point, Hughes provided these Brechtian suggestions to readers and performers:

> Read this poem aloud, and think of young Clarence Norris pacing his lonely cell in the death house of Alabama, doomed to die on August 18. When used for public performances, the last two verses punctuate the poem with a single drumbeat after each line. AUGUST 18TH IS THE DATE [*sic*]. During the final stanza, let the beat go faster, and faster following the line, until at the end the drum goes on alone, unceasing, like the beating of a heart.[26]

If we have created narrative fetishes to control our trauma over lynching's history, literature—or much of it, as Hughes's stage directions suggest—proceeds along another route toward experimentation. Ironically, lynching urges writers to broach new depths of creativity because, I think, they need to explore the limits of literary form to express what the violence means to them. Put another way, I have come to think that lynching's cultural logic is most movingly explored parodically, if we think of parody not as a reactive but an experimental mode that offers more than critical distance as a refuge. Parody that tests the boundaries of form(lessness) and seeks to estrange us from the familiar histories we know registers the trauma that lynching produces. In the works of Ida B. Wells, Stephen Crane, and James Weldon Johnson—together with the other twentieth-century writers I have discussed so far—parody functions to express anguish of the deepest sort. In this way, writers' interest in literary form is not a resistance to affect but an articulation of it, one that registers how much lynching's history hurts. To close this discussion, I examine a poem that takes its interpretative measure from the lynching that arguably hurt the nation the most. Writing about the murder of Emmett Till, Gwendolyn Brooks parodies the ballad once again, to teach us how lynching's far-reaching violence shaped the nation's cultural life.

Of the more than three thousand lynching murders that have occurred in the United States since Reconstruction (and among the uncounted who survived near-death mob assaults), a select few we remember by name: Leo Frank; the Scottsboro Boys; Rodney King; Reginald Denny; James Byrd Jr.; Matthew Shepard; even Clarence Thomas. But one victim has proven to be especially hard to forget: Emmett Till.[27]

The bare facts of Emmett Till's death shed some light on why his lynching murder haunts our national conscience. Just fourteen years old, on summer vacation in Money, Mississippi from his home in Chicago, Till was killed for allegedly flirting with a white woman. As, perhaps, the sternest lesson of "living Jim Crow" that generations of African Americans had to learn during the second half of the twentieth century, the senselessness of Till's death has had the paradoxical effect of making us think about his murder more.[28] But the sheer terror of his case only begins to explain why this lynching has disturbed us like no other.

His is, perhaps, the one instance where the synchronicity of lynching's cultural logic runs in astoundingly precise order. For instance, Till's murder marked the start of the school year following the Supreme Court's ruling in *Brown v. Board of Education,* thus linking the transformation of American education to the loss of his life.[29] In an era consumed with nuclearity—from the idea of the perfectly parented suburban home to the underground bunkers that housed nuclear war missiles—the murder of Emmett Till heated up Cold War debates about the limits to democratic politics and capitalist development. His death exposed how unexceptional and necessarily violent the "American" way of life was in daily practice. Because his murder invaded the space and ideological sanctity of "home," domestic politics in the United States were never the same after this lynching. Indeed, many historians now argue that the modern civil rights movement was inspired by the protests that erupted across the country in the wake of Till's murder.[30]

We might think Till's lynching to be so memorable because of his age. Till was just a boy when he was killed, but as other black children had been murdered by white lynch mobs, an appeal to childhood's innocence is not sufficient to explain why Till's lynching was, and remains, so significant.[31] African Americans who lived during the time of Till's murder, however, often speak of a photograph that jolted them into recognizing the historic importance of lynching's cultural logic.[32] They refer to the photograph of Emmett Till's corpse that his mother, Mamie Bradley, agreed to let the black press publish.

In these final pages of the book's text, I explore the ramifications of Mamie Bradley's choice to "make the whole world see" (as she put it) what white supremacist violence looked like when enacted on the body of her child. Specifically, it is the idea of "looking"—together with the attendant practice of "seeing" that Bradley appealed to—that I propose to analyze, because Bradley's shrewd choice foregrounds how lynching importantly organized American ways of seeing and how those mechanisms furthered the power of the violence to oppress black people. What would "the whole world" know that it couldn't comprehend otherwise without the aid of a photograph? Why would writing be a compromised mode of representation in this instance (and, perhaps, by extension, in any other instance of lynching)? What discursive shifts had occurred, what new cultural value had photography acquired, for Bradley to insist on technologies of seeing and sight as the most effective way to express moral outrage and to mount political action to redress her loss? My approach to answering these questions is by way of a poem that directly confronts Till's murder, Mamie Bradley's decisive response, and the capacities of poetry and photography to serve as archives of lynching's history.

Gwendolyn Brooks's "The Last Quatrain of the Ballad of Emmett Till" grieves the loss of Till's life and is charged by a sad fury at the irreparable loss endured by Mamie Bradley.[33] I argue, however, that the poem grieves something else too. Naming and working through the politics of making language visible—weighing the risks and gains implicit in Mamie Bradley's decision—are, I contend, the constitutive energies of Brooks's poem. The poem finds its form through its restless need to express in words what so many were finding compelling about photographic representations of lynching. In "Last Quatrain," Brooks struggles to understand the public's trust in the visual image as much as she seeks to express her anger at Till's death. What she grieves in this poem, then, is the tenuous authority that poetry can claim as a mode of social engagement.

"Last Quatrain" relates the meaning of Emmett Till's murder (and that of lynching generally) to questions of epistemology and the struggles black people waged to claim as true not just what we know, but how we know what we know. For as the poem envisions it, writing and seeing—poetry and photography—are equally deficient when it comes to recounting the hardest history of all: the record of experience that is ignored, that remains unregarded, and that exists as a cultural secret despite the fact that its force changes the world around it. Although the ballad structure and line movements of Brooks's poem draw our attention to how poetry and photography narrate and circulate history in equally limited ways, writing and seeing prove to be, in "Last Quatrain," equally necessary to the task of describing the violence of lynching for what it was: the sternest example of (as well as the strongest rebuke possible to) America's claim to be the avatar of all things modern.

The modernization of the black press is pivotal to the full story of the Emmett Till case not only because it made Mamie Bradley's decision possible but also because it recalls Ida B. Wells's critique of how journalism produced the nation's common sense about lynching. Since Chicago was Emmett Till's hometown, Bradley had ready access to perhaps the most technologically sophisticated and market-minded press networks in the nation. The *Chicago Tribune* had long been a paper of national importance, but from the 1930s through the 1950s, the city became a major media outlet for African America.[34] Collaborating with the NAACP, Bradley was able to mobilize its resources and those of the *Chicago Defender,* along with *Jet* and *Ebony* magazines, to publicize across the nation and around the world the court case arising out of her son's lynching.[35]

The media coverage of Emmett Till's murder trial was, therefore, unprecedented in the history of lynching for this and two other reasons. First, there was the very scope of news coverage given over to the case. Sixty to seventy newspaper reporters covered the proceedings from Sumner, Mississippi, while all three television networks flew film footage to New York for broadcast on the national news because mass-media outlets were wired to produce information in print and picture nearly instantaneously. Between the investigative serials published by Chicago's black press and the white media's nascent advocacy of African Americans' civil rights, the editorial bias of the coverage was finally weighted toward the victim—there was near unanimous agreement that Emmett Till did not deserve to die and, further, that the alleged defendants were guilty of the crime.[36] Second, the alliance among Bradley and the editors and journalists of *Crisis, Defender, Jet,* and *Ebony* evinced their savvy understanding of the cultural moment that defined their position and opportunity. As the founder of Johnson Publications put it: "The great Negro weekly newspapers—and the great White dailies—had by this time reached their peak and were giving way to the blitzkrieg of the photograph . . . and then . . . television."[37] With more than half of the American public plugged into television networks and just as many pursuing photography on their own or in magazines devoted to that art, Bradley and the black press understood that, in 1955, they and the rest of the nation were living in what Heidegger called "the age of the world picture."[38]

Precisely because it is so expansive, the visual archive chronicling this case makes clear that the murder of Emmett Till coincided with that moment when "instead of just recording reality, photographs . . . bec[a]me the norm for the way things appear to us, thereby changing the very idea of reality, and of realism."[39] The logic of this "pictorial turn"—the strong emergence of visual media as a mode of cognition that contends equally with print literacy—is apparent in figure 6.1, which depicts a design layout from the *Chicago Defender*'s coverage of the case. This shift is also captured in the striking image in figure 6.2, whose composition provides the figurative and political grounds of Brooks's poetic concerns in "Last Quatrain."[40]

Figure 6.2 is a photograph that was never published in any newspaper or magazine, most likely because the busy background would be hard to crop out to feature the portrait of the trial's presiding judge, Curtis L. Swango.[41] But the figures crowding the visual field—those young white men wearing their blindingly white shirts—are important to this picture's meaning insofar as they function in a way that the still photograph alone cannot: they are filming the courtroom. Juxtaposing these modes of seeing this way, the photograph posits image making as a cultural "other" to writing (figured here by the thick, leather-bound books sitting atop Judge Swango's bench). More than just a "bad" or "wasted" picture, this visual statement suggests how photography was central not just to informing the public about the case, but to structuring the experience of lynching's meaning itself, as a cultural consequence of Emmett Till's death.

Living and writing as a poet when the world "was not merely represented by pictures," but was increasingly understood to be "actually constituted and brought into being by picture-making," Gwendolyn Brooks bore witness to this discursive shift in mid-twentieth-century American life.[42] Brooks was attentive to this transformation because she lived in Chicago and was an avid reader of the *Chicago Defender,* the *Chicago Tribune,* and *Jet Magazine.* Moreover, she was especially enamored of photography, an affinity that she cultivated if not all her life, then certainly for the longest part of it.[43] Her interest in the photogeneity of life primed

Emmett Till Funeral Saddens City, Nation

Throngs pass bier of Chicago youth whose death turned the spotlight on Mississippi shame

Figure 6.1. With its technological capabilities more fully modernized, the African American press deployed photography in ways that not only catalyzed national protests against Emmett Till's murder in 1955, but that, by the production of those images, also transformed the meaning of lynching from the mid-twentieth century forward. (Reprinted by permission of *Chicago Defender*.)

Figure 6.2. Judge Curtis L. Swango. This unpublished photograph delineates the cultural developments at stake in the trial of Emmett Till's murderers. The South's rule of law, conspicuously figured by the thick tome on Judge Curtis L. Swango's bench, was challenged by the court of public opinion, which made its form and force felt through the media of photography and cinema. (De-accessioned photo from Corbis/Bettmann Archives.)

her to appreciate that the new cultural interest in seeing would prove to be so important to the meaning of Emmett Till's murder.

But being a poet who studied the literary history of her craft, Brooks had to have known that by being preoccupied with the mass media as she was and titling her poem "The Last Quatrain of the Ballad of Emmett Till," she would link her interests to those that William Wordsworth described as the "high" tradition of the genre (compared to "Pearl May Lee's" popular genealogy).[44] If, for the romantics, the emergence of mass-produced print technologies threatened poetry's hegemony as the arbiter of critical judgment, in Brooks's day visual apparatuses like photography and television (and, particularly, the novel channels of the photo-essay and live broadcast) instituted a comparable change worth worrying about.[45] Insofar as the visual telling of Emmett Till's murder moved broadly and instantaneously throughout society—inciting discussion, sparking speech, and urging the public to assume the risks of toppling the racial status quo—the production and circulation of photography about the case did as much as (if not more than) a ballad poem could ever hope to achieve in the way of fostering critical judgment and moral action. So, to call a poem memorializing the case a "ballad"—or, more precisely, "the last quatrain" of a ballad—summons a Wordsworthian mood only to dash it in the same breath. As the "last quatrain," the poem signals that its embodied theory of poetry writing does not work in this modern circumstance, and that the romantic ideal of the ballad and its transcendent relationship to politics have met their end.[46]

As I noted in the introduction, like all of the poems Brooks wrote about lynching (and not unlike anti-lynching dramas by women playwrights), "Last Quatrain" recalls the afterlife of the violence, describing the worlds of hurt inhabited by those who survive lynching's deadly assaults. Thus, though he is the titular subject, the poem does not speak of Emmett Till directly. Rather, his mother, Mamie Bradley, is the focal point, which means the poem is not quite what it declares itself to be. As such, the poem questions the idea of reference itself because, if the poem we have before us is the "last" quatrain, where is the ballad that precedes it and justifies it? The absence of that text renders the unspeakability of Emmett Till's murder into the form of the poem, as the condition of the poem's expression.

Indeed, what is immediately remarkable about the poem is the quietness that suffuses the depiction of Bradley's grieving the loss of her son. Near-rhymes finish each of the poem's eight lines ("taffy," "coffee," "sorry," "prairie") and the alliteration within each line draws us into a zone of silence:

Emmett's mother is a pretty-faced thing;
   the tint of pulled taffy.
She sits in a red room,
   drinking black coffee.
She kisses her killed boy.
   And she is sorry.
Chaos in windy grays
   Through a red prairie.[47]

The scenes that enclose Bradley within the poem's purview contrast sharply with the public, visual record of Bradley's public demeanor as an activist-survivor and as a woman overcome by the loss of her only son (figure 6.3). The aim and achievement of "Last Quatrain" is to scale Bradley's hypervisibility as a photographic subject down to a

Figure 6.3. "Funeral for Emmett Till." Emmett Till's mother, Mamie Till Bradley, pauses at the casket at A. A. Raynor Funeral Home. Note the snapshots of her son lining the casket lid. (Photo reprinted with special permission from the Chicago Sun-Times, Inc. © 2003. Published May 26, 2002.)

less iconic, more human form by the rhetorical structure of the poem. Hence, the poem's first announcement ("After the murder / After the burial.") marks a time zone where there are no cameras, no reporters, no rallies, no trials, no open caskets, no graves.

In this space of timelessness, new sights emerge into view. To see the "tint of pulled taffy" in Bradley's complexion the speaker is, perhaps, standing directly before the woman. In the blood-colored "red room," the speaker must be sitting close enough to peek into Bradley's cup and know she drinks her coffee "black." In the antechamber that has become the poem (and assured of their intimacy in this space), the speaker can witness what was an excruciatingly beautiful moment of love—watching as Bradley "kisses her killed boy" and knowing "she is sorry." Privy to the primacy of this act, the speaker claims the right to address Bradley using terms of endearment and the diminutive—"Emmett's mother is a pretty-faced thing." The colloquialisms indicate the intensity of their bond, which the context and form of the poem allow. Precisely because they are precious turns of phrase, the references counter the perception that figured Bradley to be knowable only as a picture, an image-object

Figure 6.4. The African American press riveted the nation's attention on Emmett Till's murder case long after the trial had ended with exclusive features such as this interview with Mamie Till Bradley in 1956. (Reprinted by permission of *Chicago Defender*.)

detachable from her self, as a *Chicago Defender* ad unwittingly suggests (figure 6.4).[48]

By comparison, the close-up views afforded within the frame of "Last Quatrain" recall the uprooted vision of a hand-held camera. Unlike the Kodak snapshot sequence of the lynching murder discussed in chapter 5, the poem's pictures of Bradley mean to reveal the secret of her private suffering rather than to secret(e) that knowledge beyond our view.[49] Arguably, though, paying homage to Bradley in this way diminishes her public achievements and all but erases her place in social history. She is placed in scenes whose locales we cannot exactly place on a map. Left speechless in every line and at every turn, all she is in this poem "is sorry."

The privatization of her experience does not, however, diminish the power or meaning of her loss. On the contrary, the poem's canny choice of lyric over folk balladry, publicity over privacy, universality over locality—all to level the cultural field separating writing from seeing—grants Bradley leave to do what the news coverage did not allow her to do: to grieve. And grieve privately. Once it became newsworthy as a "political event" and a "moral cause"—or, to regard this point in light of Anne Cheng's *The Melancholy of Race*, once the case became enmeshed in and defined through its politics of grievance[50]—Till's lynching murder ceased to be what it was, at its start and in its end: a murder. A boy's murder. A black boy's murder. A loss of life that was as unwarranted as it was irreparable. "Last Quatrain" gracefully rummages through poetry's literary history to find a mode in which the violence that disorders black family life—lynching—can be seen and understood for all the unendurable pain it inflicts.

The "news" that the "Last Quatrain of the Ballad of Emmett Till" carries forth, then, is that black life is invaluable and the loss of it irremediable. Hence, the poem's chilled (and, on a first gloss, seemingly inscrutable) ending: "Chaos in windy grays / Through a red prairie." If poetry can lead us to this insight, if poetry can help us see this as a dimension of lynching's power to oppress—the ways in which the violence enrages us into silence—then a poem like "Last Quatrain" urges yet another set of questions to address: can a photograph ever attain poetry's depth of field in its vision of the world? Can a photograph really get to the "inside" of an event? Does poetry, for that matter? If one can and the other cannot—or, worse yet, if neither medium is capable of the task—what can we then claim (or hope) to know?[51]

According to their memoirs and interviews, this was the ambition of the photographers and journalists who covered the Till murder case. Looking again at figure 6.2, the juxtaposition of the law and visual media suggests another reading: in mid-twentieth-century America, the faith in photography's power to picture the truth was such that it could be used to try the case in the court of public opinion. However, when confronted with the questions concerning knowledge and referentiality implied by "Last Quatrain," photography's limitations as a sign system become apparent and the certitude the medium promises buckles beneath the weight of its own truth claims.

Without inducing any doubt whatever, the visual archive of Emmett Till's lynching tells us that the trial occurred in Sumner, Mississippi. Countless photographs verify that present at all the proceedings were Mamie Bradley, Carolyn Bryant (the woman reputed to have been flirted with by Till), the defendants, jury and judge, onlookers and reporters, and funeral crowds and protest marchers. The photograph of Till's battered and water-logged body proves that he died.[52] However, there are no photographs of Till's encounter with Carolyn Bryant inside the grocery store. There are no photographs tracking when and how Roy Bryant and J. W. Milam drove Till to the shack where they beat and shot him to death. There are no photographs that catch Bryant and Milam towing and dumping Till's body (barbed wired to a cotton gin fan) in the Tallahatchie River. None of these photographs exist in the visual archives of the case.

The images that do exist forestall the hard fact that a missing one points toward, which is that photography's capacities to document the real are not indisputable, and that the medium is more fully capable of *depicting* (not documenting) "what must be imagined, what can[not] be actually seen—what can[not], in any verifiable way, be known."[53] When we look at the photographs having to do with Emmett Till's murder, then, what we see is what we can never get. What we see is what we can never know for sure. In the midst of such ambiguity, caught in the "chaos of windy grays," we grieve the loss of Till's life as keenly as we do—and for as long as we have—because of the impossible knowledge that photography produces for us.

Making photography's logic of visibility the subject of its scrutiny, "Last Quatrain" reminds us of the fallibilities of it and any other system of representation before the chaos created by lynching. Even so, "Last Quatrain" would be a vividly visual poem if we only paid attention to its color scheme. The "tint of pulled taffy" brightens boldly to the shock of a "red room," whose stark planes dissolve into a pool of "black coffee," which swirls out to a lesser tone of itself, only to summon the horror of blood again in the poem's final line: "Chaos in windy grays / Through a red prairie." Studiously avoiding the literalist denotations of black-and-white photography, Brooks applies her words to the page like a painter might stroke her canvas, a gesture that calls on the tradition of ekphrasis to make its point.

Involving the verbal representation of graphic representation, ekphrastic poems aim to "speak" the language of the visual other that incites their poetic encounter. Ekphrastic poems do not seek to look like a photograph, painting, or sculpture, though, as much as they try to comprehend the aesthetic terms of the other form and to represent the effort to make language visible between the two media.[54] When abstracted into the expressions of race and racism in American society, politics, and culture, color was the deadliest form of imagination. However, published in an era when painting aspired to abstract color from the domain of politics, "Last Quatrain" stages the confrontation between writing and seeing as one where tropes of color figure the terrain of lynching's violence.[55] And as the palette of the poem's canvas-text reveals through the one drop of "pulled taffy" confusing and contaminating the poem's otherwise orderly visual scheme, the damage wreaked by a lynching murder like Emmett Till's proved America's fetish for color to be a deadly pursuit that would always be mired in historical circumstance.

But Brooks also believed that "a little more should be required of the poet than perhaps is required of the sculptor or painter" because, she explained, "the poet deals in words with which everyone is familiar." The task of poetry in relation to the visual arts involved "do[ing] something with those words so that they will 'mean something,' will be something that a reader may touch."[56] The haunting force of Emmett Till's absence from a poem meant to memorialize his death leaves its trace on the text in another way as well, referring (as its "colored" words do) to the history of modernism and the literary movement of imagism. Red, black, and gray: William Carlos Williams's "The Red Wheelbarrow," Ezra Pound's "In a Station of the Metro," and Wallace Stevens's "The Gray Room" come promptly to mind when reading "Last Quatrain." Why?[57]

The spare but concentrated focus on the subjects of these poems—for Williams, the toy wagon; for Pound, the black tree bough; for Stevens, the diffident woman who resists the speaker's attention—treasures them as warranting sustained attention precisely because they can be made subject to poetic contemplation (that is why "so much" could depend on looking at a red wheelbarrow, from Williams's point of view). As deployed in her poem's color scheme, Brooks embraces the radical possibilities of imagism's commitment to discerning the extraordinary in ordinary life,[58] though for her lynching's poetic potential was defined through a distinctive political economy:

> In Chicago we have had spirited conversations about whether a black poet has the right to deal with trees, to concern himself with trees. And one of the things that I've always said was, certainly, certainly a black poet may be involved in a concern for trees, if only because when he looks at one he thinks of how his ancestors have been lynched thereon.[59]

And indeed, the murder of Emmett Till was a compelling subject for an imagist poem insofar as it presented nothing less than "an intellectual and emotional complex in an instant of time."[60] But in its veneration of perception as singularly significant, by making a virtue out of isolating the subjects of poems from their social surround, imagism (in its Pound-driven, high modernist mode) could not let Brooks say what she needed to say about this case, much like the photography of the trial could not let the public see what it actually needed to know most.

It is fitting that Brooks closes "Last Quatrain" by summoning the legacy of Carl Sandburg, for the prairie poet wrote one of the most powerful accounts of the race riot that ripped apart Chicago in the "Red Summer" of 1919.[61] In that instance, another black boy's life was placed in death's way. After crossing an imaginary line that divided the waters of Lake Michigan into racially segregated spaces, Eugene Williams was hounded down by white swimmers who beat and clubbed him to death. That assault led to a week of violence during which twenty-three black people were killed and 342 more injured.[62] As perspicacious as her verse could be, Brooks probably would not have preferred that her poem's concerns with the (in)visibility of black suffering and grief foretell the anxieties that would grip the nation in the wake of Rodney King's beating by the rogue squad of Los Angeles Police Department officers in 1992. For that case should have solved the problem photography produced in Emmett Till's murder: George Holliday's video camera recorded those awful moments when the assault occurred. Indeed, in our age of surveillance where every public space is monitored by visual technologies, the evidentiary gap that made Emmett Till's murder so awful to contemplate was filled by proof from Holliday's footage.[63] And yet this evidence was rendered meaningless by the Simi Valley jury's reading of it. It would seem that from 1955 to 1992—and back a century to 1892 and the protocinematic display of Henry Smith's murder—lynching has provided an "American grammar book" (to recall Hortense J. Spillers's phrase), forging our cultural fluency in modernity through the suffering and deaths of black people.

"Chaos in windy grays / Through a red prairie." This nod to Sandburg's poem "Fog" and its vision of the feral character of violence nonetheless points back to Pound's "In a Station of the Metro" because Brooks leaves out the predicate that might make her poem's most enigmatic line make ready sense, too. Does chaos "blow" through the red prairie? How do the windy grays move toward the frontier—do they "swirl," "ravage," "sweep"? That we do not know, that we *cannot* know, reprises the critique of representation that "Last Quatrain" enacts through its verse form; though here, at the poem's end, Brooks insists on a different emphasis. In the gap where the predicate ought to be, and where the diacritical mark that punctuates every other line in the poem is missing from its expected space, writing ceases to finish its statements. And, so, writing fails to clarify the scene it depicts. Before that void, Brooks leads us to this truth: that understanding lynching may mean "understanding the limits of understanding."[64] Composing the "last quatrain," then, Brooks's own poetic practice appears to meet its limit too. However, to admit our frailty before an experience as large, vast, and ugly as lynching is to know the full measure and character of the violence, which is the humbling paradox Brooks's poem attempts to explain.

———

"Last Quatrain" can constantly renew our anguish over the murder of Emmett Till because the poem's form does not reduce or seek to contain the enormity of the loss of Till's life. And indeed, literature that engages with lynching's power in all its subtlety and complexity urges us to think again about how we remember history—where it occurs and who makes it happen, toward what ends and with what consequences. As James E. Young points out, literature "makes a case for an essentially reciprocal relationship between the truth of what happened and the truth of how it is remembered. . . . Together, what happened and how it is remembered constitute a received history of events."[65] What we think we know about lynching is so small, too small, to do justice to the lives lost in anti-black mob murders. But by admitting the power of the violence in all its terrible, fearsome authority, the literature that engages lynching (unlike the handwriting on the back of lynching postcards) saves us from misunderstanding why the violence has lasted for as long as it has, in as many guises as it can manage. Through its subtle intimations of aesthetic form, literature performs what Brooks (in her other ballad about Emmett Till's murder) called the "sew-work" of history. Joining together and describing for us the causes that would otherwise remain beyond our grasp to comprehend, literature imagines the terrible acts and consequences of lynching as racism's modern life form, to remind us of the lives we could save if only by remembering the many thousands gone before.

Acknowledgments

I have lived with this book for a very long time, as have others whose intellectual, collegial, or financial support have sustained me over these years. For guiding me to this project, I am glad to thank my advisors and instructors at Yale University's American Studies Program: Robert Stepto, Richard Brodhead, Jean-Christophe Agnew, Ann Fabian, Matthew Jacobson, Wai-Chee Dimock, Alan Trachtenberg, Hazel Carby, Nancy Cott, Michael Denning, John Blassingame, and Vera Kutzinski. Both in the classroom and in their writings, they have all been inspiring models of scholarship.

The evolution of *A Spectacular Secret* was similarly influenced by the University of Chicago Press. Alan Thomas is an excellent editor. He believed in this project from the start and supported it enthusiastically, not least through his choice of readers to evaluate the manuscript. I owe deep thanks to those scholars for their frank, sometimes tough, but always insightful criticisms of the book's argument and methods. Likewise, I thank my manuscript editor, David Bemelmans, for his thoughtful work to ensure that my prose matched what I meant to say. And I am grateful to Randy Petilos and Monica Holliday for steering the book through the production process so efficiently.

Several institutions and foundations awarded me fellowships to support my research and writing, and I am glad to have the opportunity to acknowledge their aid. A nontenured faculty research grant from Cornell University's Society for the Humanities (1998–99) supported archival fieldwork for chapter 3; likewise, a Kate B. and Hall J. Peterson fellowship from the American Antiquarian Society (summer 2000) funded my research into "coon" stereocards, which I discuss in chapter 5. Winning a NEH fellowship to spend as a scholar in residence at the New York Public Library's Schomburg Center for Research in Black Culture (2000–1) provided a tremendous lift for the overall project. In the company of the other fellows—Robin Kelley, Genna Rae MacNeil, Kim Butler, Kali Gross, and Cecelia Green—I was inspired to read more widely and draft two new chapters that received rigorous feedback from this stellar group of historians. I am gladly indebted to them for their support, as I am grateful to the Schomburg's director, Howard Dodson, its chief manuscript curator, Diana Lachatanere, and the scholar-in-residence program's director, Colin Palmer, for fostering such a productive work year. A year's leave from teaching while on an Andrew W. Mellon fellowship for career enhancement (administered by the Woodrow Wilson National Fellowship Foundation [2002–3]) made it possible for me to complete the manuscript. For that year I was required to exchange my work with a senior scholar; Farah Jasmine Griffin proved to be an exemplary mentor, generously offering her time to read the manuscript in-progress during the course of my fellowship.

At the University of Chicago I met my match in colleagues who have read every word, line, paragraph, and chapter in this book with rigor and stunning care, and whose tough criticisms always presumed I was capable of crafting a stronger arguments. I appreciate the collective wisdom of my English department colleagues, but I also want to offer a special salute to those who read my full drafts more than once and who took particular time to discuss with me whatever conceptual concerns about the project they may have had: Lauren Berlant, Bill Brown, Jim Chandler, Bradin Cormack, Frances Ferguson, Elaine Hadley, Miriam Hansen, Elizabeth Helsinger, Janice Knight, Carla Mazzio, Lisa Ruddick, Eric Slauter, Jacqueline Stewart, Richard Strier, and Ken Warren. Crucial, too, were my department chairs, Jay Schleusenser and Elizabeth Helsinger, and Deans Janel Mueller and Danielle Allen, who cleared the bureaucratic paths for me to accept my fellowships at the Schomburg and from the Mellon Foundation. I am deeply grateful to them all for supporting my work.

I am also indebted to other precision-minded colleagues who helped me rethink the terms of my argument and who took time to critique chapters then still in progress: Lois Brown, Joan Jacobs Brumberg, Gabrielle Foreman, Sharon Holland, Toni Irving, Carolyn Karcher, Dominick La Capra, Rachel Lee, David Levin, Elizabeth McHenry, Dorothy

Mermin, Debbie Nelson, Franny Nudelman, Mary Panzer, Danilyn Rutherford, Shirley Samuels, Hortense Spillers, and Laura Wexler. I also previewed chapter drafts to audiences at the University of Oregon, Fairfield University, University of Illinois-Chicago, the Race and Reproduction of Racial Ideologies Workshop, and the Franke Institute for the Humanities at the University of Chicago. I am grateful to Shari Huhndorf, Susan Tomlinson, Dwight McBride, the Center for the Study of Race, Politics, and Culture, and Jim Chandler for inviting me to share my ideas with those communities.

In my final two years of revising the manuscript, Yvette Piggush proved to be a superb research assistant. Whether tracking down photograph cites from state historical archives or persuading county clerks to copy century-old court records for me, Yvette completed every assignment perfectly and on time. I could not have completed the manuscript without her help. Yvette also helped me train and supervise a group of undergraduates who (encouraged by my colleague, political scientist Melissa Harris-Lacewell) enthusiastically volunteered to comb the archives of late-nineteenth-century newspapers during Winter Quarter 2003. I am grateful to Joon Jeon, Hubert Lee, Margo Miller, Kristin Niver, Francine O'Bun, Oluseyi Oyenuga, and Carla Robinson for their diligent assistance. The same thanks are owed to Cheryl Beredo and Annette Portillo, my former students at Cornell University. Eileen Fitzsimons helped steady the project during its most crucial phase. With grace, wit, and patience, she undertook the mammoth task of typing and proofreading intermediate drafts of the manuscript. But Eileen did more than turn out fresh pages of copy; she talked through the ideas of the chapters with me, cajoled me to stay focused, and encouraged me to get the job done as sanely as possible. I am truly grateful for her camaraderie during that long winter of 2004.

Portions of chapter 4 appeared in different form in "'Keeping the Secret of Authorship': A Critical Look at the 1912 Edition of James Weldon Johnson's *The Autobiography of an Ex-Colored Man*," in James P. Danky and Wayne A. Wiegand, *Print Culture in a Diverse America* (Urbana: University of Illinois Press, 1998). Portions of chapter 6 appeared in different form in "The High and Low-Tech of It: The Meaning of Lynching and the Death of Emmett Till," *Yale Journal of Criticism* 9(2) (Fall 1996). I am grateful to the University of Illinois Press and The Johns Hopkins University Press for granting me permission to reprint from these works.

I am also grateful to have received permission to cite materials from the following archives: Columbia University Rare Book and Manuscript Library, for use of materials from the John Franklin Crowell Papers, the

Stephen Crane Papers, the Cora Crane Papers, and the Harper & Bros. Archive; the Minisink Valley Historical Society, for use of materials from its case files of the murder of Robert Lewis; the Beinecke Rare Book and Manuscripts Library at Yale University; Dr. Sondra Kathryn Wilson, executor of the estate of James Weldon Johnson, for use of materials from the James Weldon Johnson Memorial Collection; Brooks Permissions for the consent to reprint "Ballad of Pearl May Lee" and "The Last Quatrain of the Ballad of Emmett Till," by Gwendolyn Brooks; and Pixel Press on behalf of the Allen-Littlefield Collection for use of photographs reprinted in chapter 5.

Notwithstanding all the support I have received from those colleagues and others mentioned above, any and all mistakes herein are mine and mine alone.

Since labor alone did not get this book done, I wish to thank the people who brought joy, pleasure, and fun to my life. These friends welcomed me when I had time to spare but were amazingly patient and forgiving when I had to disappear for weeks (or sometimes months) at a time to focus on writing: May Pat Brady, Kate McCullough, and their daughter Ana Luisa; Lois Brown; Joan Jacobs Brumberg, and David Brumberg; Joan Bryant; Gabrielle Foreman; Lisa Freeman; Michel Gelobter; Sharon Holland and Jennifer Brody; Kellie Jones; Cynthia Young; George Chauncey and Ron Gregg; Debbie Nelson and Adrienne Hiegel; Elizabeth McHenry; Tina and Chris Meltesen; Judith Peraino; Joseph Peterson, Rachel Amdur, and their daughters Anna and Lily; Reverend Juan Reed and the congregation at St. Martin's Episcopal Church; Shirley Samuels; Beryl Satter; Eric Slauter, Stephanie Brooks, and their children Nora and George; Jacqueline Stewart, Jake Austen, and their daughter Maiya; Trysh Travis; Connie Yowell, Jennifer Fleming, and their sons Sam and Jake.

More than anyone, my family has coped lovingly with my silences and disappearances. My sisters, Sharon Barnett and Stacy Goldsby, my brother-in-law, Victor Barnett, and my father, Mack Goldsby, have believed in me and this project for such a long time, always offering me unconditional support for the work I do, and I treasure that trust more than I can say. My life partner, Cybele Raver, and our daughter, Natalie, have lived with this book for far longer than they imagined or certainly wanted. One of the great joys of finishing this book will be to "celebrate every day" (as Natalie puts it) the magic of our love for one another.

Finally, I dedicate this book to the memory of my mother, Lois Marie Glenn Goldsby. Her lifelong involvement in public culture as a librarian, city government secretary, adult education teacher, and lover of the arts taught me to care about literature, history, and social justice as much as I do. She is the very best teacher I ever had.

Notes

INTRODUCTION

1. Gwendolyn Brooks, "Ballad of Pearl May Lee," in *Blacks* (Chicago: Third World Press, 1994), ll. 1–7.
2. The death statistic and time period I cite follow Philip Dray, *At the Hands of Parties Unknown: The Lynching of Black America* (New York: Modern Library, 2002), iii. Dray's tally is based on data tabulated from the Tuskegee Institute's Lynching Clippings Files. For an important critique of this source material, see Stewart E. Tolnay and E. M. Beck, *A Festival of Violence: An Analysis of Southern Lynchings, 1882–1930* (Urbana: University of Illinois Press, 1995), appendixes A (259–63) and B (265–67).
3. Black newspapers often covered the aftermath of lynching murders: the pogroms visited on the locales where the victim's family lived; the sermons delivered at memorial services and funeral rites; the rebuilding and relocation projects waged after the mob's killing and damage were done. The *Chicago Defender* is often cited for its archive of such information, but the *Richmond Planet* is another valuable source because the paper covered the events of the 1890s and early 1900s, before the *Defender* started publishing.

   Oral histories are harder to find as intact archives, though important repositories do exist: the testimonies gathered during the 1871 congressional inquiries into the Ku Klux Klan; the autobiographical narratives collected in William H. Chafe et al., eds., *Remembering Jim Crow: African Americans Tell about the Segregated South* (New York: Free Press, 2001). More recently the reparations movements in Rosewood, Florida; Tulsa, Oklahoma; Duluth, Minnesota; and Moore's Ford, Georgia have yielded state commission transcripts, news articles and interviews, magazine essays, and books that contain testimonies of still-living survivors.

4. For discussions of the "push-pull" thesis, see James R. Grossman, *Land of Hope: Chicago, Black Southerners, and the Great Migration* (Chicago: University of Chicago Press, 1989), chaps. 1–3; Tolnay and Beck, *A Festival of Violence,* chap. 7; Farah Jasmine Griffin, *"Who Set You Flowing?": The African American Migration Narrative* (New York: Oxford University Press, 1995), chap. 1.
5. On lynching's literary history as the absent referent in blues lyrics, see Adam Gussow, *Seems Like Murder Here: Southern Violence and the Blues Tradition* (Chicago: University of Chicago Press, 2002), esp. chaps. 1–3. Like blues lyrics, female-authored anti-lynching plays during the 1920s and 1930s grappled with the problem of adequately representing the violence and its aftermath for survivors' families. Compared with the widows and orphaned children in plays like Angelina Weld Grimké's *Rachel* (1916), Mary Powell Burill's *Aftermath* (1919), Georgia Douglas Johnson's *Safe* (1929), and Ann Seymour Link's *Lawd, Does You Undahstahn?* (1936), Pearl May Lee's rage at Sammy is unparalleled. The works just mentioned are collected in Kathy A. Perkins and Judith L. Stephens, eds., *Strange Fruit: Plays on Lynching by American Women* (Bloomington: Indiana University Press, 1998). To my knowledge, only Alice Walker's short story "Advancing Luna—and Ida B. Wells" (1981) broaches the topic as Brooks envisioned it in 1945.
6. Though feminist critiques draw careful attention to the triangulation of power that privileges white men, white women, and black men as analytic subjects over black women in lynching's cultural politics, those studies tend not to feature black women's contempt for black men's alleged sexual betrayals as an effect to historicize. See, for instance, the ground-breaking work of Hazel V. Carby, "'On the Threshold of Woman's Era': Lynching, Empire, and Sexuality in Black Feminist Theory," *Critical Inquiry* 12 (Autumn 1985): 262–77; Jacquelyn Dowd Hall, "'The Mind That Burns in Each Body': Women, Rape, and Racial Violence," in Ann Snitow, Christine Stansell, and Sharon Thompson, eds., *Powers of Desire: The Politics of Sexuality* (New York: Monthly Press, 1983); Darlene Clark Hine, "Rape and the Inner Lives of Black Women in the Middle West: Preliminary Thoughts on the Culture of Dissemblance," in Ellen Carol DuBois and Vicki L. Ruiz, eds., *Unequal Sisters: A Multicultural Reader in U.S. Women's History* (New York: Routledge, 1990); Sandra Gunning, *Race, Rape, and Lynching: The Red Record of American Literature, 1890–1912* (New York: Oxford University Press, 1996).
7. For a comprehensive definition of the genre, see the "ballad" entry in *The Princeton Encyclopedia of Poetry and Poetics*, ed. Alex Preminger (Princeton: Princeton University Press, 1974), 62–64. On African American poets' appropriations of the genre, see Gary Smith, "The Black Protest Ballad," *Obsidian II* 1(3) (Winter 1986): 54–67, and "The Literary Ballads of Sterling A. Brown," *CLA Journal* 32(4) (June 1989): 393–409; Maria K. Mootry,

"'Chocolate Mabbie' and 'Pearl May Lee': Gwendolyn Brooks and the Ballad Tradition," *CLA Journal* 30(3) (March 1987): 278–93; Gladys Williams, "The Ballads of Gwendolyn Brooks," in Maria K. Mootry and Gary Smith, eds., *A Life Distilled: Gwendolyn Brooks, Her Poetry and Fiction* (Urbana: University of Illinois Press, 1987).

8. According to W. Fitzhugh Brundage, "the scholarly study of lynching waned" during the mid-twentieth century because "the rate of lynching declined" during these decades. Thus, Brooks's poem bears witness to an actual, material void. See Brundage, "Introduction" to *Under Sentence of Death: Lynching in the South* (Chapel Hill: University of North Carolina Press, 1997), 9.
9. Influential studies that have shaped common discourse in these terms include Walter F. White, *Rope and Faggot: A Biography of Judge Lynch* (New York: Knopf, 1927); John Dollard, *Caste and Class in a Southern Town* (New Haven: Yale University Press, 1937); W. J. Cash, *The Mind of the South* (New York: Knopf, 1941). For a rich, evaluative survey of the critical legacies spawned by these (and other) works, see Brundage, "Introduction," *Under Sentence of Death*, 1–14.
10. Though I consider modernism's closeted relation to racial violence in chapter 6, cultural logic's resonance with queer theory's notion of the "open secret" is a comparison I do not draw out in the earlier chapters. Nonetheless, I thank Frances Ferguson and Michael Warner for calling that relation to my attention.
11. Walter Benjamin, "Theses on the Philosophy of History," in *Illuminations*, ed. Hannah Arendt, trans. Harry Zohn (New York: Schocken Books, 1969), 255.
12. As histories of the U.S. anti-lynching movement make clear, organized protests succeeded on three main fronts: raising public consciousness about the violence, funding publication of a vibrant literature of resistance, and mobilizing select sectors of the national public for mass political action. However, with the exception of Ida B. Wells's anti-lynching campaigns between 1893 and 1895 (which brought in their wake the passage of state-based anti-lynching laws; I discuss this development in chapter 2), anti-lynching organizations never did win their main goal—to outlaw lynching as an actionable crime—until 1964. I draw this conclusion based on the following studies: Mary Jane Brown, *Eradicating This Evil: Women in the American Anti-Lynching Movement, 1882–1940* (New York: Garland, 2000); Claudine Ferrell, *Nightmare and Dream: Antilynching in Congress, 1917–1922* (New York: Garland, 1985); Donald L. Grant, *The Anti-Lynching Movement, 1883–1932* (San Francisco: R & E Research Associates, 1975); Jacquelyn Dowd Hall, *Revolt against Chivalry: Jessie Daniel Ames and the Women's Campaign against Lynching*, rev. ed. (New York: Columbia University Press, 1993 [1985]); George C. Rable, "The South and the Politics of Anti-Lynching Legislation, 1920–1940," *Journal of Southern History* 51:2

(May 1985): 201–20; Robert L. Zangrando, *The NAACP Crusade against Lynching, 1909–1950* (Philadelphia: Temple University Press, 1980).

13. For an excellent study of lynching in avowedly white supremacist texts, see Mason O. Stokes, *The Color of Sex: Whiteness, Heterosexuality, and the Fictions of White Supremacy* (Durham: Duke University Press, 2001).
14. See the web site www.blackholocaustmuseum.org. See also Cameron's searing memoir of his near-death experience, *A Time of Terror: A Survivor's Story* (Baltimore: Black Classics Press, 1994).
15. On Tulsa, Oklahoma: "Panel Calls for Reparations in Tulsa Race Riot," *New York Times*, 1 Mar. 2001, A12, col. 4; Brent Staples, "Unearthing a Riot," *New York Times Magazine*, 19 Dec. 1999, 64. On Rosewood, Florida: "Florida Panel Backs Compensation in Riots," *New York Times*, 24 Mar. 1994, A17, col. 1. On Duluth, Minnesota: "It Did Happen Here: The Lynching That a City Forgot," *New York Times*, 4 Dec. 2003, A22, col. 1; "A Lynching Memorial Unveiled in Duluth," *New York Times*, 5 Dec. 2003, A38, col. 1; "Duluth Lynching Anniversary," *All Things Considered*, National Public Radio broadcast, 8 June 2001. On Moore's Ford, Georgia: www.mooresford.org; www.georgiahistory.com/moore's.htm. On Scottsboro, Alabama: "Marker Is Planned for Landmark Case," *New York Times*, 13 Jan. 2004, A23, col. 1.
16. For compelling histories of the song, see Joel Katz's documentary film *Strange Fruit* (2002); David Margolick's *Strange Fruit: Billie Holiday, Café Society, and an Early Cry for Civil Rights* (Philadelphia: Running Press, 2000). On the "Without Sanctuary" photo exhibit, see "An Ugly Legacy Lives on, Its Glare Unsoftened by Age," *New York Times*, 13 Jan. 2000, E1, col. 4; "A Quest for Photographs He Could Barely Look At," *New York Times*, 13 Jan. 2000, E8, col. 1.
17. Michel-Rolph Trouillot, *Silencing the Past: Power and the Production of History* (Boston: Beacon Press, 1995), 99.
18. Christopher Waldrep traces the political etymology of lynching's name in "Word and Deed: The Language of Lynching, 1820–1953," in *Lethal Imagination: Violence and Brutality in American History*, ed. Michael A. Bellesiles (New York: NYU Press, 1999). James E. Young's *Writing and Re-Writing the Holocaust: Narrative and the Consequences of Interpretation* (Bloomington: Indiana University Press, 1988), especially informs my point here. According to Young, the Jewish lexicon of catastrophe provided three terms to describe the Nazis' genocidal campaign. *Churban* (a Hebrew term for the destruction of the First and Second Temples); *Sho'ah* (adopted to specifically refer to the unprecedented nature of the destruction of Jewry); and "*Holocaust*" (an English-language cognate meant to translate the idea across the world in the wake of World War II's end). As Young argues: "As one of the first hermeneutical moves regarding an event, its naming frames and remembers events, even as it determines particular knowledges of events" (87–88).

19. Philip Dray discusses the anomalies of excluding Reconstruction-era violence from lynching statistics in *At the Hands of Parties Unknown,* 36–47. On the particular forms of lynching that African American women suffered, see Crystal Feimster's important discussion in "Ladies and Lynching: The Gendered Discourse of Mob Violence in the New South, 1880–1930" (Ph.D. diss., Princeton University, 1998), chap. 5, esp. 237–38.
20. On the fatalities amassed under these regimes, see Pete Daniel, *The Shadow of Slavery: Peonage in the South, 1901–1969* (Urbana: University of Illinois Press, 1972); Edward L. Ayres, *Vengeance and Justice: Crime and Punishment in the Nineteenth-Century South* (New York: Oxford University Press, 1984), chap. 6; David M. Oshinsky, *"Worse Than Slavery": Parchman Farm and the Ordeal of Jim Crow Justice* (New York: Free Press, 1996), chaps. 6 and 9.
21. On this concept, see Roland Barthes, "The Rhetoric of the Image," in *Image, Music, Text,* trans. Stephen Heath (New York: Hill and Wang, 1977), 39.

CHAPTER ONE

1. This description summarizes details found in two contemporary pamphlets about the Smith lynching: R. C. O. Benjamin's "Southern Outrages: A Statistical Record of Lawless Doings" (n.p., 1894), in D. A. P. Murray Pamphlet Collection (microfilm), Library of Congress; J. M. Early's "Eye for an Eye or, The Fiend and the Fagot" (Paris, Texas: n.p., 1893). Quotes from Early, 40; Benjamin, 41.
2. Early, "Eye for an Eye," 31.
3. See, e.g., *Chicago Tribune,* 2 Feb. 1893, 5, col. 2; *New York Times,* 2 Feb. 1893, 1, col. 2; *Atlanta Constitution,* 2 Feb. 1893, 1, col. 1; *Kansas City (Kansas) American Citizen,* 10 Feb. 1893, 1, col. 2; *Louisville Courier-Journal,* 2 Feb. 1893, 1, col. 2. For a compendium of British response, see Charles F. Aked, "The Race Problem in America," *Contemporary Review* 65 (June 1894): 818–27.
4. On the publicity garnered for the murder, see Joel Williamson, *The Crucible of Race: Black-White Relations in the American South since Emancipation* (New York: Oxford University Press, 1984), 185–86; Grace Elizabeth Hale, *Making Whiteness: The Culture of Segregation in the South, 1890–1940* (New York: Pantheon, 1998), 207–9. Mertins's photographs can be found in the Library of Congress's Division of Prints and Photographs, lot 2839F. For Mertins's marketing plan, see his ad in Early, "Eye for an Eye," 73.
5. Quotes from Samuel Burdett, "A Test of Lynch Law: An Exposé of Mob Violence and the Courts of Hell" (Seattle: n.p., 1904), 17, in D. A. P. Murray Pamphlet Collection (microfilm), Library of Congress.

6. For Burdett's description of the display, see "Test of Lynch Law," 17–19. Burdett's account matches the series of photographs documenting the lynching on deposit at the Library of Congress, Prints and Photographs Division, lot 2839 F. Since the images were copyrighted by the Paris, Texas-based photographer J. L. Mertins, and because Mertins intended for the collection to be sold as a set, I assume that these photographs were the ones Burdett viewed in Seattle. About the gramophone, see Frederick William Wile, *Emile Berliner: Maker of the Microphone* (Indianapolis: Bobbs-Merrill, 1926), chap. 18; Friedrich A. Kittler, *Gramophone, Film, Typewriter*, trans. Geoffrey Winthrop-Young and Michael Wutz (Palo Alto: Stanford University Press, 1993), chap. 2.
7. Burdett, "Test of Lynch Law," 17–18. The detailed description of the recording and images is graphic and devastating; see ibid., 17–19.
8. For these biographical details, see ibid., 45. According to Burdett, the Seattle-based council was a secret society that took an unusual approach to anti-lynching politics. Instead of emphasizing protests based on moral suasion or constitutional due process, the council planned a more mercenary approach, offering $500 retainers to detectives and lay lawyers to investigate and prosecute lynch-mob members. As Burdett explained sanguinely: "Man will go to the ends of the earth for money, . . . therefore, what appeals to sentiment and love of right and justice will not secure, money will" (46).
9. For statistics see appendix C, table C-3 in Stewart E. Tolnay and E. M. Beck, *A Festival of Violence: An Analysis of Southern Lynching, 1882–1930* (Urbana: University of Illinois Press, 1995), 271–72. These figures only summarize lynchings in the Deep South; they do not reflect anti-black lynchings in the West or North. Nonetheless, I cite Tolnay and Beck's inventory because their data amend the errors of duplication in the news clippings files of the National Association for the Advancement of Colored People (NAACP) and the Tuskegee Institute, as well as the necrology tables published by the *Chicago Tribune*. On the limitations of these sources, see Tolnay and Beck, appendix A, 259–63.
10. W. Fitzhugh Brundage, "Introduction,"*Under Sentence of Death: Lynching in the South* (Chapel Hill: University of North Carolina Press, 1997), 4.
11. The James quotation is from Gail Bederman, *Manliness and Civilization: A Cultural History of Gender and Race, 1880–1917* (Chicago: University of Chicago Press, 1995), 73. The periodical literature on lynching at the turn of the nineteenth century is rich and underexamined by scholars. I cite these sources throughout; for more on their archival obscurity, see note 69.
12. As historians have argued, books such as Phillip Alexander Bruce's *The Plantation Negro as Freeman* (1898), Frederick L. Hoffman's *Race Traits and Tendencies of the American Negro* (1896), and Robert W. Shufeldt's *The Negro: A Menace to Civilization* (1907), provided important ideological backing for

post-Reconstruction racial violence. See Williamson, *Crucible of Race*, chap. 4; Lawrence J. Friedman, *The White Savage: Racial Fantasies in the Postbellum South* (Englewood Cliffs, N.J.: Prentice-Hall, 1970); George M. Frederickson, *The Black Image in the White Mind: The Debate on Afro-American Character and Destiny, 1817–1914* (Middletown, Conn.: Wesleyan University Press, 1987), esp. chaps. 8 and 9; Mason Stokes, *The Color of Sex: Whiteness, Heterosexuality, and the Fictions of White Supremacy* (Durham: Duke University Press, 2001), esp. chap. 3. On the other side of the color line, nonfiction works such as T. Thomas Fortune's *Black and White: Land, Labor, and Politics in the South* (1886), Mary Church Terrell's "Lynching from a Negro's Point of View" (1904), and Kelly Miller's "Open Letter to Thomas Dixon" (1916) were widely known in black reading circles.

13. For a succinct survey of the legal definitions of lynching, see Philip Dray, *At the Hands of Parties Unknown: The Lynching of Black America* (New York: Modern Library, 2003), iii.
14. Howell Colston Featherston, "The Origins and History of Lynch Law," *Green Bag* 12 (1900): 150.
15. Informative surveys of the pre-Civil War traditions include James E. Cutler, *Lynch Law: An Investigation into the History of Lynching in the United States* (Montclair, N.J.: Patterson Smith, 1969 [1905]), chaps. 1–4; Richard Maxwell Brown, *Strain of Violence: Historical Studies of American Violence and Vigilantism* (New York: Oxford University Press, 1975), chap. 2; Bryan D. Palmer, "Discordant Music: Charivaris and Whitecapping in Nineteenth-Century North America," *Labor/Le Travailleur* 3 (1978): 5–62; W. Fitzhugh Brundage, *Lynching in the New South: Georgia and Virginia, 1880–1930* (Urbana: University of Illinois Press, 1993), 4–7; Christopher Waldrep, "Word and Deed: The Language of Lynching, 1820–1953" in *Lethal Imagination: Violence and Brutality in American History*, ed. Michael Bellesiles (New York: NYU Press, 1999), 230–39.
16. Brown, *Strain of Violence*, 97.
17. On the exceptional cruelties inflicted at these executions, see Dray, *At the Hands of Parties Unknown*, 26–27.
18. Some historians date this shift as early as the late 1830s, once "lynching" is used to categorize increasingly harsh and deadly attacks on anti-slavery activists. The pivotal event in these accounts is the murder of abolitionist editor Elijah Lovejoy, whose murder by a proslavery mob in Alton, Illinois prompted Abraham Lincoln's famous 1838 speech "On the Perpetuation of Our Political Institutions." See Dray, *At the Hands of Parties Unknown*, 28–29. Christopher Waldrep points out that abolitionists quickly seized on this shift to advance their political cause. Exercising editorial control over anti-slavery newspapers, abolitionists were able to "redefine lynching" as executions of anti-slavery activists. "By 1840," Waldrep observes, "the abolitionist press had succeeded in changing the meaning of lynching from a whipping to an action resulting in death" ("Word and Deed," 236).

19. Featherston, "Origins and History of Lynch Law," 151; Walter Fleming, "An Investigation of Lynching in the United States," *Dial* 39 (1905): 34–36.
20. On this first wave of Klan violence, see David M. Chalmers, *Hooded Americanism: The First Century of the Ku Klux Klan, 1865–1965* (Garden City, N.Y.: Doubleday, 1965), 1–21; Herbert Shapiro, *White Violence, Black Response: From Reconstruction to Montgomery* (Amherst: University of Massachusetts Press, 1988), 11–30; Eric Foner, *A Short History of Reconstruction, 1863–1877* (New York: Harper and Row, 1990), 184–91.
21. The single best account of this reversal remains Rayford W. Logan's *The Betrayal of the Negro: From Rutherford B. Hayes to Woodrow Wilson* (London: Collier Books, 1965).
22. Because the Court's ruling upheld the right of corporations to coerce smaller business competitors out of a market, the *Slaughterhouse* cases established a theory of collective action that could be interpreted to protect mobs from federal prosecution. In *Cruikshank*, the Court held that blacks could not raise armed self-defense as a right protected by the Fourteenth, First, and Second Amendments. Rescinding the Civil Rights Acts of 1875 affirmed the practice of Jim Crow segregation in public accommodations and transportation. *Plessy* upheld the "separate but equal" doctrine that remanded African Americans to second-class citizenship. Claudine Ferrell provides the most succinct summary of these and other court cases and congressional floor debates that shaped the legal legitimation of lynching; see *Nightmare and Dream: Anti-Lynching in Congress, 1917–1922* (New York: Garland, 1986), 16–34.
23. Dray, *At the Hands of Parties Unknown*, 109–11.
24. For more on the congressional debates, see Ferrell, *Nightmare and Dream*, 210–30; Robert L. Zangrando, *The NAACP Crusade against Lynching, 1909–1950* (Philadelphia: Temple University Press, 1980), 19–20. Philip Dray offers an insightful explanation of why the Sixth Amendment was never used as a constitutional support for federal anti-lynching legislation. Though that provision ensures citizens fair trials, in the early twentieth century "the federal judiciary had still never inserted itself to try to enforce that guarantee in a state criminal case" (Dray, *At the Hands of Parties Unknown*, 154).
25. Featherston, "Origins and History of Lynch Law," 152.
26. Winthrop Sheldon, "Shall Lynching Be Suppressed, and How?" *Arena* 36 (1906): 225.
27. Frederick Douglass, "Lessons of the Hour" (n.p.), in D. A. P. Murray Pamphlet Collection (microfilm), Library of Congress, 3.
28. Thomas Nelson Page, "The Lynching of Negroes: Its Causes and Prevention," *North American Review* 178 (January 1904): 136.
29. Kelly Miller, "The Attitude of the Intelligent Negro toward Lynching," *Voice of the Negro* 2(5) (May 1905): 307.

30. On the denominational schism, see Mary Louise Ellis, "'Rain Down Fire': The Lynching of Sam Hose" (Ph.D. diss., Florida State University, 1992), 182 n. 42.
31. Sheldon, "Shall Lynching Be Suppressed, and How?" 229. Also see Zangrando, *NAACP Crusade against Lynching,* 15. Sheldon's specification of the State of the Union address as the index of a president's political commitment to outlaw lynching is shrewd, because that standard calls into question the strategy devised by Benjamin Harrison and Theodore Roosevelt, and continued by others, to use unofficial channels such as closed meetings with anti-lynching activists or personal correspondence on the topic to manage the public discourse about the violence.
32. Boston's branch of the Colored National League drafted this letter and, according to historian Mary Louise Ellis, published it as a pamphlet following an anti-lynching rally in October 1899; see Ellis, "Rain Down Fire," 224. As both Ellis and Glenda Gilmore point out, McKinley stonewalled this and other petitions from African American activists in order to shore up his Republican base in the South. See ibid., 217–26; Glenda Gilmore, *Gender and Jim Crow: Women and the Politics of White Supremacy in North Carolina* (Chapel Hill: University of North Carolina Press), 87–88, 113, 115.
33. Ida B. Wells, *Crusade for Justice: The Autobiography of Ida B. Wells*, ed. Alfreda Duster (Chicago: University of Chicago Press, 1970), 299. As she remarked about this display of what appeared to be general apathy: "The fact that nobody seemed worried was as terrible a thing as the riot itself."
34. Sheldon, "Shall Lynching Be Suppressed, and How?" 227.
35. Classic studies of lynching's roots in negrophobia include Walter F. White, *Rope and Faggot: A Biography of Judge Lynch* (New York: Knopf, 1929); W. J. Cash, *The Mind of the South* (New York: Knopf, 1941); Lillian Smith, *Killers of the Dream* (New York: Norton, 1949). More recently, Orlando Patterson threads this line of argument throughout his analysis in *Rituals of Blood: Consequences of Slavery in Two American Centuries* (Washington, D.C.: Civitas, 1998), chap. 5.
36. Two important exceptions to this trend are Grace Elizabeth Hale's *Making Whiteness*, which explores lynching's modernity in relation to the emergence of consumerism in the late-nineteenth- to early-twentieth-century South, and Nancy MacLean's study of Leo Frank's lynching in 1915, which, she demonstrates, was driven by the processes of industrialization and gendered labor reform in early twentieth-century Atlanta. See "The Leo Frank Case Reconsidered: Gender and Sexual Politics in the Making of Reactionary Populism," *Journal of American History* 78 (December 1991): 917–48.
37. So many lynchings were performed at light poles and bridges that we forget electrification and rail transportation were harbingers of modernity at the

turn of the nineteenth century. Ida B. Wells describes how, in 1899, Lee Walker's corpse was used in a macabre football game; see *Crusade for Justice,* 186–87. On the modernity of football's brutality, see Bill Brown, *The Material Unconscious: American Amusements, Stephen Crane, and the Economics of Play* (Cambridge: Harvard University Press, 1996, chap. 3). I discuss the use of photography at lynching murders at length in chapter 5.

38. On the dehumanizing discourses of white supremacy at the turn of the nineteenth century, see note 12; see also Forrest G. Wood, *Black Scare: The Racist Response to Emancipation and Reconstruction* (Berkeley: University of California Press, 1968); Jacquelyn Dowd-Hall, *Revolt against Chivalry: Jessie Daniel Ames and the Women's Campaign against Lynching*, rev. ed. (New York: Columbia University Press, 1993), 145–57; Bederman, *Manliness and Civilization*, esp. chap. 1.
39. Sheldon, "Shall Lynching Be Suppressed, and How?" 228.
40. Burdett, "Test of Lynch Law," 39. Willard B. Gatewood compiles similar observations in "*Smoked Yankees and the Struggle for Empire: Letters from Negro Soldiers, 1898–1902* (Urbana: University of Illinois Press, 1971). Also see Amy Kaplan, "Black and Blue on San Juan Hill," in *The Cultures of U.S. Imperialism*, eds. Donald E. Pease and Amy Kaplan (Durham: Duke University Press, 1993).
41. For contemporary comparisons between U.S. lynching and genocidal violence abroad at the turn of the nineteenth century, see Maxey, "Mob Rule," *Arena* 30 (July/December): 377; Mark Twain, "King Leopold's Soliloquy: A Defense of His Congo Rule," in *Following the Equator and Anti-Imperialist Essays* (New York: Oxford University Press, 1996).
42. *Americus (Georgia) Times-Recorder*, 24 Apr. 1899, quoted in Ellis, "Rain Down Fire," 153.
43. Maxey, "Mob Rule," 377; Edward L. Pell, "The Prevention of Lynch-Law Epidemics," *American Monthly Review of Reviews* 17 (March 1898): 321.
44. I refer, of course, to the great financial panic of 1893. For lucid accounts chronicling its effects, see Nell Irvin Painter, *Standing at Armageddon: The United States, 1877–1919* (New York: Norton, 1987), 116; Alan Trachtenberg, *The Incorporation of America: Culture and Society in the Gilded Age* (New York: Hill and Wang, 1982), chaps. 3 and 7. On the cotton market's particular vulnerability to the panic's run, see C. Vann Woodward, *Origins of the New South, 1877–1913* (Baton Rouge: Louisiana State University Press, 1991), esp. 185–86, 305–6, 351. For examples of market-based analyses of lynching, see Tolnay and Beck, *Festival of Violence*, chap. 5; E. M. Beck and Stewart E. Tolnay, "A Season for Violence: The Lynching of Blacks and Labor Demand in the Agricultural Production Cycle in the American South," *International Review of Social History* 37(1) (1992): 1–24; Jay Corzine et al., "The Tenant Labor Market and Lynching in the South: A Test of Split Labor Market Theory," *Sociological Inquiry* 58(3) (Summer 1998): 261–78.

45. On the kinetoscope's history, see Lary May, *Screening the Past: The Birth of Mass Culture and the Motion Picture Industry* (Chicago: University of Chicago Press, 1983), chap. 2. The earliest film depicting the lynching of African Americans dates back to 1903, *Avenging a Crime; Or Burned at the Stake*, dir. Paley and Steiner, in Library of Congress, Motion Picture, Broadcast, and Recorded Sound Div., FLA 4486. I discuss these developments and their relation to lynching's cultural logic in chapter 5.
46. The following studies undergird my understanding of the period: Trachtenberg, *Incorporation of America;* Painter, *Standing at Armaggedon;* Robert Wiebe, *The Search for Order, 1877–1920* (New York: Hill and Wang, 1967); Richard Slotkin, *Gunfighter Nation: The Myth of the Frontier in Twentieth-Century America* (New York: Harper Perennial, 1992), esp. chaps. 1–6; John Higham, *Strangers in the Land: Patterns of Nativism, 1860–1925* (New Brunswick: Rutgers University Press, 1988), and Higham, "Re-Orientation of American Culture in the 1890's," in *Writing American History: Essays on Modern Scholarship* (Bloomington: Indiana University Press, 1970); Peter Gay, *The Cultivation of Hatred: The Bourgeois Experience, Victoria to Freud* (New York: Norton, 1993); T. J. Jackson Lears, *No Place of Grace: Antimodernism and the Transformation of American Culture, 1880–1920* (New York: Pantheon, 1981); Steven Kern, *The Culture of Time and Space, 1880–1918* (Cambridge: Harvard University Press, 1983); Steven J. Diner, *A Very Different Age: Americans of the Progressive Era* (New York: Hill and Wang, 1998); Adam Hochschild, *King Leopold's Ghost: A Story of Greed, Terror, and Heroism in Colonial Africa* (Boston: Houghton Mifflin, 1998).
47. A. P. Dennis, "Political and Ethical Aspects of Lynching," *International Journal of Ethics* 15 (1904/1905): 150.
48. On these pursuits and their emergence at the end of the nineteenth century, see Thomas Schlereth, *Victorian America: Transformations in Everyday Life* (New York: Harper Collins, 1991), 223–24; Brown, *Material Unconscious,* 130; Bederman, *Manliness and Civilization,* 16–23, 170–96, 218–32.
49. Sinclair's novel becomes all the more damning when read with William Cronon's account of the meat-packing industry in *Nature's Metropolis: Chicago and the Great West* (New York: Norton, 1991), chap. 5. Cronon's analysis not only confirms the brutalities involved in the meat-packing process, it also makes clear how that violence was central to the modernization of an important American corporate business practice and way of thinking about commodities: the "annihilation of space" in transporting perishable goods.
50. Haygood, "The Black Shadow across the South," *Forum* 16 (September 1893): 168–69. Haygood's order of horrors is biased, no doubt. But this essay's phobic racism is remarkable for its turn from Haygood's famous paternalist treatise *Our Brothers in Black* (1885).
51. Northen quoted in Williamson, *Crucible of Race*, 289. A public opponent of mob violence, in 1893 Northen was among the first state governors to pass

an anti-lynching bill. Unfortunately, that law did not stop white mobs in Georgia from murdering 423 African Americans between 1882 and 1930. On Northen's anti-lynching politics, see ibid., 287–91; Brundage, *Lynching in the New South*, 195, 201, 214. For Georgia's lynching rates, see Tolnay and Beck, *Festival of Violence*, appendix C, table C-4, 273.

52. John Franklin Crowell, "Lynching—II," [1], box 1, folder 4, typescript ms., in John Franklin Crowell Papers, Rare Books and Manuscript Library, Columbia University, New York. A graduate of Yale Divinity School (1885) and president of Trinity College (now Duke University) from 1887 to 1894, Crowell entered Columbia's Ph.D. program in sociology in the fall of 1894 with the apparent intent to write either a seminar essay or, perhaps, his doctoral thesis about the emergence of lynching at the turn of the nineteenth century, given the scope of the papers contained in Columbia's collection. On Crowell's life and early career, see his memoir *Personal Recollections of Trinity College, North Carolina, 1887–1894* (Durham: Duke University Press, 1939).

53. I refer here to historical studies that suggest U.S. modernization and modernity can be traced back to the turn of the nineteenth century: Wiebe, *Search for Order;* Higham, "Reorientation of American Culture"; Trachtenberg, *Incorporation of America;* Lears, *No Place of Grace;* Diner, *A Very Different Age;* Thomas L. Haskell, *The Emergence of Professional Social Science: The American Social Science Association and the Nineteenth Century Crisis of Authority* (Urbana: University of Illinois Press, 1977). The following literary histories of the era also revise modernization's history in the United States: David E. Shi, *Facing Facts: Realism in American Thought and Culture, 1850–1920* (New York: Oxford University Press, 1995); Amy Kaplan, *The Social Construction of American Realism* (Chicago: University of Chicago Press, 1988); Miles Orvell, *The Real Thing: Imitation and Authenticity in American Culture, 1880–1940* (Chapel Hill: University of North Carolina Press, 1989); Mark Seltzer, *Bodies and Machines* (New York: Routledge, 1992); Martha Banta, *Taylored Lives: Narrative Productions in the Age of Taylor, Veblen, and Ford* (Chicago: University of Chicago Press, 1993); Bill Brown, *Material Unconscious*; Donna M. Campbell, *Resisting Regionalism: Gender and Naturalism in American Fiction, 1885–1915* (Athens: Ohio State University Press, 1997); Kate McCullough, *Regions of Identity: The Construction of America in Women's Fiction, 1884–1914* (Stanford: Stanford University Press, 1999).

54. On residual and emergent forms, see Raymond Williams, *Marxism and Literature* (New York: Oxford University Press, 1977), chap. 8. Though Frederic Jameson coined the phrase "cultural logic," Williams's theory of residual/emergent culture more directly informs my use of the term. His notion captures the play between historical epochs and the cultural developments that occur within them. Jameson, on the other hand, characterizes cultural logic as a rigid norm that, though it changes over

time, establishes an unbroken horizon against which human invention and action occurs: "It was only in the light of some conception of a dominant cultural logic . . . that genuine differences could be measured and assessed. . . . If we do not achieve some general sense of a cultural dominant, then we fall back into a view of present history as sheer heterogeneity, random difference, and coexistence of a host of distinct forces whose effectivity is undecidable." In my view, cultural logic refers to lynching's contingent relation to modernity. It is not a necessary, compulsory, or arbitrary one, as Jameson's concept would have it. See Frederic Jameson, "The Cultural Late Capitalism," in *Postmodernism or the Cultural Logic of Late Capitalism* (Durham: Duke University Press, 1999), 6.

55. Guy Debord, *The Society of the Spectacle*, trans. Donald Nicholson-Smith (New York: Zone Books, 1995 [1967]), 12–13, thesis 5, emphasis added. My use of the term differs from the two most important treatments of the concept in lynching historiography, Brundage's theory of "mass mobs" as explained in *Lynching in the New South*, 19, 36–37, and that found in Hale, *Making Whiteness*, 203–9.
56. This (ab)use of the black body to "analogically verify" large-scale cultural shifts has been defined broadly by Elaine Scarry in *The Body in Pain: The Unmaking and Making of the World* (New York: Oxford University Press, 1985), 13–14. Ralph Ellison describes the African American case with his usual acuteness in "Twentieth Century Fiction and the Black Mask of Humanity," in *Shadow and Act* (New York: Vintage, 1995 [1964]), 28–29. These explications have informed my understanding and use of the term "cultural logic" as well.
57. Michael Rogin, "'Make My Day!': Spectacle as Amnesia in Imperial Politics," *Representations* 29 (Winter 1990), 103. Amy Kaplan studies how the spectacularization of white male dominance in historical romance fiction from the late nineteenth century anticipates the political amnesia Rogin describes as a postmodern (i.e., 1980s) phenomenon; see Kaplan, "Romancing the Empire: The Embodiment of American Masculinity in the Popular Historical Novel of the 1890s," *American Literary History* 2(4) (Winter 1990): 659–90.
58. Toni Morrison, *Playing in the Dark: Whiteness and the Literary Imagination* (Cambridge: Harvard University Press, 1990), 17.
59. "Negro Rule" reprinted with permission of North Carolina Collection, University of North Carolina Library at Chapel Hill. On the legend of the incubus and its adaptation for the Democrats' 1898 political campaign in Wilmington, North Carolina, see Gilmore, *Gender and Jim Crow*, 85.
60. See ibid., chap. 4.
61. Examining testimony transcribed during Congress's inquiry into Ku Klux Klan violence in 1871, Hodes concludes that black men's political activities and bids for social power were often coded as acts of sexual transgression (e.g., the desire to vote or own property would lead to interracial marriage)

in order to justify Klan assaults. See Martha Hodes, "The Sexualization of Reconstruction Politics: White Women and Black Men in the South after the Civil War," *Journal of the History of Sexuality* 3(3) (January 1993): 402–11; Lisa Cardyn, "Sexualized Racism / Gendered Violence: Outraging the Body Politic in the Reconstruction South," *Michigan Law Review* 100(4) (February 2002): 675–867.

62. "The Vulture's Roost" (LC-USZ62-063063), reprinted with permission of Library of Congress, Prints and Photographs Division.

63. For instance, Hoke Smith, editor of the *Atlanta Journal* and a gubernatorial candidate in Georgia's 1906 election that led to the Atlanta riots of that year, exhorted voters to fear corporate wealth and to lynch black men in, literally, the same breath during his stump speeches. See Williamson, *Crucible of Race*, 212. A more coherent argument linking corporate capitalism's dominance to the specter of African American emancipation was Rebecca Latimer Felton's 1897 speech, "Woman on the Farm." In it, the first female U.S. senator called for "a thousand lynchings a week" to defend white women against the supposedly criminal threat posed by roving masses of unemployed black men. But, as Felton explained her case, black men were masterless and white women vulnerable to sexual assault because white male political leaders had neglected the "inner life" of the family farm to pursue industrial and foreign trade policies that plunged the region into deep debt. For a fascinating analysis of Felton's argument, see Lee Ann Whites, "Rebecca Latimer Felton and the Problem of 'Protection' in the New South," in *Visible Women: New Essays on American Activism*, eds. Nancy A. Hewitt and Suzanne Lebsock (Urbana: University of Illinois Press, 1993); Whites, "Rebecca Latimer Felton and the Wife's Farm: The Class and Racial Politics of Gender Reform," *Georgia Historical Quarterly* 76(2) (Summer 1992): 354–72.

64. "Next!" (1899) and "What Stands a Snowball's Chance in ___" (n.d.) are both reprinted with permission of the Library of Congress, Prints and Photographs Division (LC-USZ62-49513 and LC-USZ62-26205, respectively). On the national distemper toward bureaucracy and its relation to lynching, see Brundage, *Lynching in the New South*, 99–101; Dray, *At the Hands of Parties Unknown*, 146–50.

65. Herbert L. Stevens, "Casuistry of Law," *Nation* (24 Aug. 1916), 174; Winfield T. Durbin, "The Mob and the Law," *Independent* 55 (30 July 1903), 1790.

66. Mary Church Terrell, "Lynching from a Negro's Point of View," *North American Review* 178(6) (June 1904): 862–63.

67. For contemporary commentaries evaluating anti-black lynching rates in light of the revival of capital punishment, see Walter Clark, "The True Remedy for Lynch Law," *American Law Review* 28 (1894): 801–7; Charles J. Bonaparte, "Lynch Law and Its Remedy," *Yale Law Journal* 8 (May 1899): 335–43; Henry Bischoff, "The Law's Delay No Excuse for Lynching," *Albany Law Journal* 65 (1903): 337–41; James E. Cutler, "Capital Punishment and

Lynching," *American Academy of Political Science Annals* 29 (January/June 1907): 601; J. W. Garner, "Crime and Judicial Inefficiency," *American Academy of Political Science Annals* 29 (January/June 1907): 601–18. According to Tolnay and Beck, 1,977 African Americans were legally executed in the Deep South between 1882 and 1930, while only 451 white men were sentenced to death during that same period. When combined with the rates of lynching murders, Tolnay and Beck conclude that "an African American was put to death somewhere in the South on the average of every four days." See Tolnay and Beck, *Festival of Violence*, 100.

68. "The progress of mob-law in many states invites, if it does not compel, a serious inquiry into the constitutional question of federal power to put an end to it," Albert E. Pillsbury argued in "A Brief Inquiry into a Federal Remedy for Lynching," *Harvard Law Review* 15 (May 1902): 707. For an explication of Pillsbury's point, see Mark Curriden and Leroy Phillips Jr., *Contempt of Court: The Turn-of-the-Century Lynching That Launched a Hundred Years of Federalism* (New York: Anchor, 2001).

69. Now that the major magazines of the late nineteenth and early twentieth centuries are digitized and keyword searchable, "lynching" draws double the citations I was able to locate by my low-tech methods using print indexes and bibliographies. For instance, Cornell University's database for "The Making of Modern America" (www.cdl.library.cornell.edu/moa/moa_search.html) elicits 285 matches to "lynching" as a keyword. *American Periodicals Series Online, 1740–1900* produces 512 references. For the years 1882–1930, Pro Quest Historical Newspapers reports 13,808 references to lynching in the *Chicago Tribune, New York Times*, and *Washington Post.*

70. Brooks's complete cycle of lynching ballads includes "Southern Lynching" (1937); "Ballad of Pearl May Lee" (1945); "A Bronzeville Mother Loiters in Mississippi. Meanwhile, a Mississippi Mother Burns Bacon" (1960); "The Last Quatrain of the Ballad of Emmett Till" (1960); and "The Ballad of Rudolph Reed" (1960). All of these poems can be found in *Blacks* (Chicago: Third World Press, 1994) except "Southern Lynching," which is not collected in any of Brooks's published volumes of verse. I discovered it in the June 1937 edition of the NAACP's *Crisis* magazine.

71. My focus on genre differentiates my study of lynching's literary-historical canon from Trudier Harris's *Exorcising Blackness: Historical and Literary Lynching and Burning Rituals* (Bloomington: Indiana University Press, 1984), and Sandra Gunning's *Race, Rape, and Lynching: The Red Record of American Literature, 1890–1912* (New York: Oxford University Press, 1996). Where Harris considers literary form as a means to "exorcise" or banish the threat of lynching from African Americans' social milieu, I examine how narrative aesthetics archive or retain authors' perceptions of the violence as sources to understand the persistence of anti-black violence over time as "modern." In Gunning's view, literary depictions of lynching narrate how national debates about racial, gender, and class formations made anti-black mob

murders politically possible at the turn of the nineteenth century. While I too am concerned with lynching's centrality to American life during that time period, I am more specifically interested in how literature imagines lynching's imbrications with the politics of modernity rather than identity *per se*.

72. Wai-Chee Dimock, *Residues of Justice: Literature, Law, Philosophy* (Berkeley: University of California Press, 1996). Dimock's earlier essays strongly influence my thinking as well. See "The Economy of Pain: Capitalism, Humanitarianism and the Realistic Novel," in *New Essays on The Rise of Silas Lapham*, ed. Donald E. Pease (New York: Cambridge University Press, 1991); and "A Theory of Resonance," *PMLA* 112 (October 1997): 1060–71.
73. In *Blood Talk: American Race Melodrama* (Chicago: University of Chicago Press, 2003), Susan Gillman takes up many of these texts, analyzing their typically "excessive" (5) depictions of lynching (and other forms of anti-black violence) as heralds of a modernist temperament. In her reading, lynching serves as a modernist trope because the violence takes its thematic and narrative cues from the "fundamentally protean" (5) character of racial identity, temporality, and history writing at the turn of the nineteenth century.
74. This gruesome lynching scene drives chapter 30, "The Tragedy of the Manor House," in Mark Twain, *A Connecticut Yankee in King Arthur's Court*, ed. Bernard L. Stein (Berkeley: University of California Press, 1983 [1889]), 290–300. While the episode's premise depends on Hank Morgan's acutely felt class consciousness, the turn of events (as Morgan relates them) reads exactly like the cases of so many black sharecroppers whose disputes with field bosses and land owners often culminated in their deaths at the hands of white lynch mobs. Morgan's historical amnesia may be a turn of irony on Twain's part, but his protagonist's memory block strikes me as symptomatic of Twain's persistent difficulty writing about lynching's modern-day "black" form.

    This same problem—Twain's brave commitment to champion African Americans' civil rights being reversed by his novels' narrative structures—persists in his nonfiction writing about lynching as well. Twain had planned to write a book-length study of lynching, but never managed to finish it or to publish the essay he composed to start the project, titled "The United States of Lyncherdom" (1901). He did summon and sustain his brilliant wit to finish and publish "King Leopold's Soliloquy" (1905), a blistering screed against the Belgian monarch's genocidal invasion of the African Congo. Where Twain could barely bring himself to write a steady, calm passage describing lynching murders in the United States, he boldly narrated Leopold's crimes against black humanity, going so far as to reprint photo-postcards showing the mutilated bodies of the victims of Leopold's imperialist project.

75. An interesting comparison would be to read Grimké's fiction together with Du Bois's "Of the Coming of John" (1903) on the one hand, and E. A. Rogers's utopian fantasy *Light Ahead for the Negro* (1908), on the other. "Blackness" and "Goldie" can be found in *The Selected Writings of Angelina W. Grimké*, ed. Carolivia Herron (New York: Oxford University Press, 1991). All page cites are noted parenthetically in the text.
76. Grimké noted the Turner case as her inspiration in a letter accompanying the manuscript to the magazine; see Herron, *Selected Writings of Angelina W. Grimké*, 417–18. For details on Turner's murder, see Dray, *At the Hands of Parties Unknown*, 245–46.
77. *Rachel* is reprinted in *Strange Fruit: Plays on Lynching by American Women*, eds. Kathy A. Perkins and Judith L. Stephens (Bloomington: Indiana University Press, 1998). For information on *Rachel*'s stage productions, see ibid., 23–25 and 25 n.1. References to the play script from this source are noted parenthetically in the text.
78. Two perceptive analyses of *Rachel*'s ruptured speech patterns (for both voice and performative body language) are William Storm, "Reactions of a 'Highly Strung Girl': Psychology and Dramatic Representation in Angelina W. Grimké's *Rachel*," *African American Review* 27(3) (1993): 461–71, and Daylanne K. English, *Unnatural Selections: Eugenics in American Modernism and the Harlem Renaissance* (Chapel Hill: University of North Carolina Press, 2004), chap. 4.
79. Burdett, "Test of Lynch Law," 18. Subsequent page cites are noted parenthetically in the text.
80. Irenas J. Palmer, "The Black Man's Burden; or, The Horrors of Southern Lynchings" (Olean, New York: Olean Herald Print, 1902), 31.
81. Toni Morrison, "Friday on the Potomac," in *Race-ing Justice, En-gendering Power: Essays on Anita Hill, Clarence Thomas, and the Construction of Social Reality*, ed. Toni Morrison (New York: Pantheon, 1992), xvi.

CHAPTER TWO

1. My summary of this lynching murder draws from Ida B. Wells-Barnett, *Crusade for Justice: the Autobiography of Ida B. Wells*, ed. Alfreda Duster (Chicago: University of Chicago Press, 1972), chaps. 6–8, hereafter referred to as *Crusade* parenthetically in the text; Patricia A. Schecter, *Ida B. Wells and American Reform, 1880–1930* (Chapel Hill: University of North Carolina Press, 2001), 75–79; Linda O. McMurry, *To Keep the Waters Troubled: The Life of Ida B. Wells* (New York: Oxford University Press, 1999), chap. 7; Philip Dray, *At the Hands of Parties Unknown: The Lynching of Black America* (New York: Modern Library, 2003), 61–65.
2. For insightful discussions of small grocery and dry goods stores as sources of race and class tensions, see Grace Elizabeth Hale, *Making Whiteness: The Culture of Segregation in the South, 1890–1940* (New York: Pantheon, 1998),

172–73; Edward L. Ayers, *Promise of the New South: Life after Reconstruction* (New York: Oxford University Press, 1984), chaps. 3 and 4.

3. These details about the murder can be found in *Crusade*, 50–51, and Schecter, *Ida B. Wells and American Reform*, 75–76.
4. On the style and politics of "scooping" in the late nineteenth century press, see Frank Mott, *American Journalism, A History: 1690–1960*, 3d ed. (New York: Macmillan, 1962), 89–90; Michael Schudson, *Discovering the News: A Social History of American Newspapers* (New York: Basic Books, 1978), 95–96; Hazel Dicken-Garcia, *Journalistic Standards in Nineteenth-Century America* (Madison: University of Wisconsin Press, 1989), 89–90; Christopher P. Wilson, *The Labor of Words: Literary Professionalism in the Progressive Era* (Athens: University of Georgia Press, 1985), 26–28, 35–37.
5. Wells voiced this critique in *Southern Horrors: Lynch Law in All Its Phases* (1892), in *Selected Writings of Ida B. Wells-Barnett*, comp. Trudier Harris (New York: Oxford University Press, 1991), 31. Further references to this pamphlet are abbreviated *SH* and noted parenthetically in the text.
6. According to Wells, residents migrated to the place Ralph Ellison extols in his essays as the freest place for black people in America: Oklahoma; see *Crusade*, 56–58. According to Schecter, four thousand blacks left Memphis during the period between the murders and Wells's editorials (78).
7. For the *Commercial Appeal*'s crude comments, see Schecter, *Ida B. Wells and American Reform*, 81. Wells tried to file slander suits but dropped her case on the advice of the liberal, white jurist-novelist, Albion W. Tourgée, because "a win was far too unlikely and a loss far too devastating for her cause and reputation to sustain" (ibid., 91).
8. It is important to remember that Wells was not the only one threatened by this assault. Her coeditor J. L. Fleming fled to Detroit for safety. Over the years, he grew to resent Wells for jeopardizing his career with this editorial. See *Crusade*, 67.
9. Schecter, *Ida B. Wells and American Reform*, 18. As I suggest in the introduction and chapter 1, the anti-lynching movement prior to World War I met with limited success, which makes Wells's efforts all the more commendable. I mark the boundaries of Wells's influence with the rise of the NAACP, whose style of bureaucratic, legalistic activism quickly outpaced Wells's single-handed, personality-driven approach to political leadership. Patricia A. Schecter treats this comparison with great skill and insight.
10. See Wells's pamphlets *Southern Horrors* (1893) and *A Red Record* (1895) for these analyses. Her multilayered examinations of racism, sexism, class inequality, sexuality, and imperialism in lynching's violence anticipate what black feminist theory now calls "intersectional" critique. See Hazel V. Carby, "'On the Threshold of Woman's Era': Lynching, Empire, and Sexuality in Black Feminist Theory," *Critical Inquiry* 12 (Autumn 1985): 262–77; Paula Giddings, *When and Where I Enter: The Impact of Black Women on Race and Sex in America* (New York: William Morrow, 1984), 24–30; Gail

Bederman, "'Civilization,' the Decline of Middle-Class Manliness, and Ida B. Wells' Anti-Lynching Campaign (1892–94)," *Radical History Review* 52 (Winter 1992): 5–30; Vron Ware, *Beyond the Pale: White Women, Racism, and History* (London: Verso, 1992), chap. 4; Sandra Gunning, *Race, Rape, and Lynching: The Red Record of American Literature, 1890–1912* (New York: Oxford University Press, 1996), chap. 3.

11. Wells acknowledges her mentor relationship with Douglass in *Crusade*, 72. In his political valedictory address "The Lessons of the Hour" (1891), Douglass discusses at great length the "forms of the charge" used in public discourse to define lynching's cultural logic.
12. W. E. B. Du Bois invokes the phrase "great human experiment" to describe the significance of black emancipation in *Black Reconstruction in America, 1860–1880* (New York: Free Press, 1992 [1935]), 583.
13. Beginning with the disestablishment of the church and its constitutionally mandated separation from the state during the early national period, secularization is argued to have crystallized at the end of the nineteenth century as a result of the rise of huge, centralized bureaucracies that governed national life; the emergence of the college-trained professional-managerial class and the cult of expertise; the invention of scientific theories and protocols to diagnose and cure the interior workings of the human body; the rivalry among museums, nickelodeons, libraries, amusement parks, and the like as they vied for Americans' growing leisure time; and, above all, the transformation of the economy from an agrarian-based market to a corporate-monopoly financial order. For accounts of these developments, see Ann Douglas, *The Feminization of American Culture* (New York: Knopf, 1977); Thomas L. Haskell, *The Emergence of American Social Science: The American Social Science Association and the Nineteenth-Century Crisis of Authority* (Urbana: University of Illinois Press, 1977); Lawrence W. Levine, *Highbrow/Lowbrow: The Emergence of Cultural Hierarchy in America* (Cambridge: Harvard University Press, 1988); Michael Warner, *The Letters of the Republic: Publication and the Public Sphere in Eighteenth-Century America* (Cambridge: Harvard University Press, 1990); Richard Ohmann, *Selling Culture: Magazines, Markets, and Class at the Turn of the Century* (London: Verso, 1998); T. J. Jackson Lears, *No Place of Grace: Antimodernism and the Transformation of American Culture 1880–1920* (Chicago: University of Chicago Press, 1994 [1983]); John Higham, "The Re-Orientation of American Culture during the 1890s," in *Writing American History: Essays on Modern Scholarship* (Bloomington: Indiana University Press, 1970); Stephen Kern, *The Culture of Time and Space, 1880–1918* (Cambridge: Harvard University Press, 1983).

    In *Righteous Discontent: The Women's Movement in the Black Baptist Church, 1880–1920* (Cambridge: Harvard University Press, 1993), Evelyn Brooks Higginbotham offers an important corrective to this theory of national progress. As she argues, secularization in African America was not premised on the idea of separating church authority from the state, precisely because the black church was often the only institution willing to provide African Americans the services that both the state and the private sector denied them. For this reason, Higginbotham contends, black churches and the process of secularization are best characterized as "protean" forces that "tend[ed] to blur the spiritual and the secular, the eschatological and the political, the private and the public" (16). As I hope this chapter makes clear, Ida B. Wells's life, writings, and critique of lynching's cultural logic pose an interesting counterexample to both Higginbotham's and the traditional accounts of secularization.

14. Because I contend that the mass media's styles of representation were evolving during the 1880s and 1890s, my interpretation of newspaper depictions of lynching differs from those offered by Hale, *Making Whiteness*, 203–8, who contends that the "lynching narrative" promulgated by the white press was impermeable to narrative change.
15. Christopher P. Wilson's excellent analysis of the "re-presentation" of news discourse in "Stephen Crane and the Police," *American Quarterly* 48 (June 1996): 273–315, and Linda Hutcheon's *A Theory of Parody: The Teachings of Twentieth-Century Art Forms* (Urbana: University of Illinois, 2000 [1983]), most heavily influence my thinking about Wells's parodic strategies. I do not invoke either Henry Louis Gates Jr.'s theory of signifying or Mikhail Bakhtin's concept of parody in my reading of Wells's work for two reasons. First, since Gates's *The Signifying Monkey* regards late-nineteenth-century African American literary production as reductively mimetic (what Gates calls "the mockingbird school" of black writing), an author like Wells would not know how to "signify" under Gates's interpretation. See *Signifying Monkey: A Theory of African-American Literary Criticism* (New York: Oxford University Press, 1988), 113–18. Second, as Bakhtin defines it most lucidly in "The Problems of Dostoevsky's Poetics, in *The Bakhtin Reader*, ed. Pam Morris (London: Edward Arnold, 1994), parody depends on the novel's cultural primacy for its explanatory power. Because Wells decisively abandons fiction, I prefer an account of parody flexible enough to embrace news writing as a generative literary form; hence my reliance on Wilson and Hutcheon.
16. Hutcheon, *Theory of Parody*, 85.
17. Since I rely on Wells's diaries and memoir extensively throughout my discussion, I should note that each source is biased by its discursive construction of Wells's life, the diaries being a daily chronicle meant for her private perusal, while the memoir was prepared explicitly for the reading public. Then, too, these sources stand in tension with one another because the private writings were composed during Wells's years in Memphis (1885–92), while her memoir retrospectively recalls those years from the perspective of a future the diaries could not narrate. Throughout, I rely on the published compendium of Wells's diary, *The Memphis Diary of Ida B.*

Wells, ed. Miriam DeCosta-Willis (Boston: Beacon Press, 1995), hereafter abbreviated *MD*.

18. *MD*, 16 July 1887, 150. My summary of Wells's childhood years draws on her account in *Crusade* and from McMurry, *To Keep the Waters Troubled*, chap. 1, and Schecter, *Ida B. Wells and American Reform*, 11–13.
19. On the political volatility of Holly Springs during Reconstruction, see McMurry, *To Keep the Waters Troubled*, 5–11.
20. In 1878, a yellow fever epidemic swept through the Mississippi Valley and into Wells's hometown of Holly Springs. Her parents and one sibling died from the disease, leaving Wells and five other children orphaned. Refusing the help of her father's friends, Wells raised the children largely on her own (*Crusade*, 10–17). The following diary entries capture her struggles in the face of this responsibility: *MD*, 13 Jan. 1886, 28–29; 29 July 1886, 93; 2 Aug. 1886, 95–96; 9, 12, and 14 Sept. 1888, 103–6; 4 Dec. 1886, 121–23.
21. *MD*, 16 July 1886, 151.
22. Schecter astutely places Wells's career struggles in this context of professionalism, which inspired much of my argument in this chapter.
23. Higginbotham, *Righteous Discontent*, 47.
24. Ibid., 14.
25. My account of Memphis and its "New South" economy is based on Schecter, *Ida B. Wells and American Reform*, 39–43; McMurry, *To Keep the Waters Troubled*, 18–22; DeCosta-Willis, "Introduction," *MD*, 1–16; Thomas Holt, "The Lonely Warrior: Ida B. Wells-Barnett and the Struggle for Black Leadership," in *Black Leaders of the Twentieth Century*, eds. John Hope Franklin and August Meier (Urbana: University of Illinois Press, 1982), 40, 41, 45; Kenneth W. Goings and Gerald L. Smith, "Unhidden Transcripts: Memphis and African American Agency 1862–1920," *Journal of Urban History* 21(3) (March 1995): 379–80; Ayers, *Promise of the New South*, 73–74.
26. According to McMurry, the Memphis Race Riot of 1866 caused widespread death and damage to the city's black community; see *To Keep the Waters Troubled*, 19–20. Herbert Shapiro notes the gendered brutality of the pogrom: "[A]t least five black women were raped by the mobsters." See Shapiro, *White Violence, Black Response: From Reconstruction to Montgomery* (Amherst: University of Massachusetts Press, 1988), 6–7.
27. Goings and Smith, "Unhidden Transcripts," 379–80.
28. Schecter, *Ida B. Wells and American Reform*, 39–43.
29. See *MD*, 11 Mar. 1886, 51–53; 28 Nov. 1886, 119–20; 21 Dec. 1886, 124–25; 11 Apr. 1887, 140–41; 29 July 1887, 151–52.
30. On Wells's theater-going, see *MD*, 29 Dec. 1885, 123–26; 21 Jan. 1886, 31; 24 Jan. 1886, 33–34; 8 Feb. 1886, 40–43; 18 Feb. 1886, 45–46; 25 Feb. 1886, 48; 6 May 1886, 64–65; 4 July 1886, 84–85; 3 May 1887, 145–46. According to Schecter (20), Wells's own dramatic flair led a New York City agent to Memphis to scout her talents. During the last decades of her life in

Chicago, Wells supported the development of black movie theaters in the Windy City (see *Crusade*, 34).

31. *MD*, 29 Dec. 1885, 26; 11 Apr. 1886, 59; 29 Apr. 1886, 63.
32. Hale, *Making Whiteness*, 128.
33. *MD*, 29 Apr. 1886, 63.
34. Wells's biographers interpret these tensions as evidence of the strength of Wells's piety. Though my reading differs from McMurry's and Schecter's on this point, I do not doubt Wells's faith or practice of religion. Rather, I mean to explore how she wrestled with the world's seductions and how those struggles informed her anti-lynching activism.
35. *MD*, 15 June 1886, 80.
36. Schecter, *Ida B. Wells and American Reform*, 50. The central theme in McMurry's biography concerns the role strain that Wells endured trying to reconcile her ambitions with the cultural mores of the black middle class.
37. As both Wilson J. Moses and Henry Louis Gates Jr. have shown, the "New Negro" is not an invention of the Jazz Age of the 1920s. Rather, the phrase and figure emerges from the era of Reconstruction, especially the 1890s. See Moses, "The Lost World of the Negro, 1895–1919: Black Literary and Intellectual Life before the 'Renaissance,'" *Black American Literature Forum* 21 (Spring-Summer 1987): 61–84; Gates, "The Trope of the New Negro and the Reconstruction of the Image of the Black," *Representations* 24 (Fall 1988): 129–55. For important explorations of New Negro culture, see Elsa Barkeley Brown, "Negotiating and Transforming the Public Sphere: African American Political Life in the Transition from Slavery to Freedom," in *The Black Public Sphere*, ed. Black Public Sphere Collective (Chicago: University of Chicago Press, 1995); Kevin Gaines, *Uplifting the Race: Black Leadership, Politics, and Culture in the Twentieth Century* (Chapel Hill: University of North Carolina Press, 1996); Higginbotham, *Righteous Discontent.*
38. For a brief social history of this conundrum, see James Oliver Horton, "Freedom's Yoke: Gender Conventions among Antebellum Free Blacks," *Feminist Studies* 12 (Spring 1986): 55. Hortense J. Spillers explores the psychic ramifications of this dilemma in "Mama's Baby, Papa's Maybe: An American Grammar Book," *Diacritics* 17(2) (Summer 1986): 65–81.
39. For an astute analysis of the masculinist bias promoted by racial uplift ideology, see Gaines, *Uplifting the Race,* 12–13, 78–79, 112–16, 135–43.
40. *MD*, 12 June 1886, 77–78.
41. *MD*, 30 Jan. 1886, 37–38.
42. *MD*, 28 June 1886, 83; 29 Apr. 1886, 64.
43. One of Wells's more ardent suitors, I. J. Graham, was a school principal in Memphis. As public figures, their lovers' quarrels became the subject of city gossip; at its worst peak, Wells and Graham were nearly fired from their posts for "immoral conduct." On Graham and this turn of events, see De Costa-Willis's head notes in *MD*, 26, 110. For Wells's entries about this scandal, see *MD*, 13 Jan. 1886, 28; 2 Oct. 1886, 112–14. For similar

controversies with other male suitors, see *MD,* 13 Jan. 1886, 28–30; 30 Jan. 1886, 37–38; 29 Apr. 1886, 62–64; 15 June 1886, 81–83; 13 July 1886, 88–89; 2 Oct. 1886, 112–14; 12 Oct. 1886, 114–15; 28 Dec. 1886, 126–27; 1 Feb. 1887, 130–31; 20 Feb. 1887, 133–34. A particularly cruel accusation leveled against Wells charged that her youngest sister Lily was her daughter, the offspring of an illicit affair with an older white man. On this rumor and Wells's response to it, see *MD,* 12 Oct. 1886, 115; *Crusade,* 17.

44. On the emergence of "New Women" among the white bourgeois and elite class, see Carroll Smith-Rosenberg, "The New Woman as Androgyne: Social Disorder and Gender Crisis, 1870–1936," in *Disorderly Conduct: Visions of Gender in Victorian America* (New York: Knopf, 1985). Kathy Peiss best describes this transformation among working-class white women in *Cheap Amusements: Working Women and Leisure in Turn-of-the-Century New York* (Philadelphia: Temple University Press, 1986). According to John D'Emilio and Estelle B. Freedman, the social trend levels out in the 1930s; see *Intimate Matters: A History of Sexuality in America* (New York: Harper and Row, 1988), chaps. 5–8.
45. Glenda Elizabeth Gilmore, *Gender and Jim Crow: Women and the Politics of White Supremacy in North Carolina, 1896–1920* (Chapel Hill: University of North Carolina Press, 1996), 95–96. As Nancy MacLean argues in her study of the Leo Frank lynching case in 1915, white women's increased employment in industrial factories created the cultural tensions that led to the Jewish factory manager's murder in Georgia. However, Gilmore's evidence from North Carolina suggests that industrialization's effects on southern gender roles took hold significantly earlier than the Frank case, and may have played an underexamined role in the rise of lynching during the 1890s.
46. Felton quoted in Lee Ann Whites, "Rebecca Latimer Felton and the Wife's Farm: The Class and Racial Politics of Gender Reform," *Georgia Historical Quarterly* 76 (Summer 1992): 356.
47. Historian Crystal Feimster contends that southern New Women leveraged their public power to participate in lynching; see "Ladies and Lynching: The Gendered Discourse of Mob Violence in the New South, 1880–1930" (Ph.D. diss., Princeton University, 1998), chap. 2, esp. 92–93, 96–97, 102.
48. Joel Williamson, *The Crucible of Race: Black–White Relations in the American South since Emancipation* (New York: Oxford University Press, 1986), 115.
49. Gail Bederman, *Manliness and Civilization: A Cultural History of Gender and Race in the United States, 1880–1917* (Chicago: University of Chicago, 1995), 14.
50. Ibid., 15, 220.
51. In these three decades, 1,640 African Americans were reported as murdered by white lynch mobs. This figure represents 66 percent of the 2,462 blacks killed between 1882 and 1930. For these figures, see Stewart E. Tolnay and E. M. Beck, *A Festival of Violence: An Analysis of Southern Lynchings,*

1882–1930 (Urbana: University of Illinois Press, 1995), appendix C, table C-3, 271.

52. Thomas Nelson Page, "The Lynching of Negroes—Its Causes and Prevention," *North American Review* 178 (January 1904): 33–48.
53. *Atlanta Journal*, quoted in Dray, *At the Hands of Parties Unknown*, 164.
54. This cultural fetishization of the medieval past was a national fad, especially during the 1890s. See Lears, *No Place of Grace*, chap. 4; Amy Kaplan, "Romancing the Empire: The Embodiment of American Masculinity in the Popular Historical Novel of the 1890s," *American Literary History* 2(4) (Winter 1990): 659–90. In the South, this sensibility was bolstered by the region's feudalistic cult of honor. For a contemporary view of this influence, see Nathaniel Southgate Shaler, "The Peculiarities of the South," *North American Review* 151 (1890): 477–88. Historians Jacquelyn Dowd-Hall and Crystal Feimster chart how the chivalric mystique and the language of racial degeneracy shaped lynching discourse from the 1890s until the 1930s. See Dowd-Hall, *Revolt against Chivalry: Jessie Daniel Ames and the Women's Campaign against Lynching*, rev. ed. (New York: Columbia University Press, 1993), chap. 5, esp. 150–57; Feimster, "Ladies and Lynching," chap. 2, esp. 64–65, 69–70. For a different interpretation of the semiotics of medieval ritual and purity discourse in lynching murders, see Orlando Patterson, *Rituals of Blood: Consequences of Slavery in Two American Centuries* (Washington, D.C.: Civitas, 1998), chap. 2, esp. 188–224.
55. Women activists like Jane Addams and Susan B. Anthony—both of whom Wells knew personally and debated these ideals with over the course of her career (*Crusade*, 235)—deliberately chose to remain unmarried and childless in order to serve as the nation's "public mothers."
56. Wells did take up other political issues over the course of her career. In 1891 she advocated for temperance. The drive for women's suffrage occupied her throughout her career but she became more intensely involved after 1913. A guiding force in the black women's club movement from its official inception in 1896, she remained active in that movement well into the 1920s. Still, compared to her female contemporaries, Wells's focus on anti-lynching politics was uniquely single-minded. Only James Weldon Johnson would match her zeal as a public leader, though the bureaucratic organization of the NAACP would cloak his intensity from view.
57. *Crusade*, 31. This is a remarkable confession for Wells to make because by 1931 she had four children of her own and an impressive legacy of organizing kindergartens in Chicago. For a useful discussion of the racialization and feminization of the teaching profession in Memphis, see Schecter, *Ida B. Wells and American Reform*, 40–45.
58. Between 1827 (the year when *Freedom's Journal*, the first black-run newspaper in the United States, was founded in New York City) and the end of the Civil War, an estimated fourteen black newspapers existed across the country, though largely in northern states where slavery had been

abolished. The first decades of freedom—the 1870s, 1880s, and 1890s—saw a boom in black newspaper publishing. During these years, more than 154 weeklies were established in the South, the Midwest, and the Far West, locales where freedwomen and freedmen relocated after Reconstruction. Rising literacy rates among blacks created the audience necessary for these journalistic enterprises, as did black church organizations, which provided access to print technologies and political autonomy needed to emancipate the press from its earlier dependency on the patronage of white abolitionists. For the figures charting the growth of the black press, see I. Garland Penn, *The Afro-American Press and Its Editors* (New York: Arno Press, 1969 [1891]), chap. 15. On the role of black churches in fostering African American print culture generally speaking, see Elizabeth McHenry, *Forgotten Readers: Recovering the Lost History of African American Literary Societies* (Durham: Duke University Press, 2002); Frances Smith Foster, "Introduction," in *Minnie's Sacrifice, Sowing and Reaping, Trial and Triumph: Three Rediscovered Novels by Frances E. W. Harper* (Boston: Beacon Press, 1994), xxiv–xxvii; Higginbotham, *Righteous Discontent*, 11, 76.

59. For a list of newspapers in which Wells published during the early years of her career as a journalist, see *Crusade*, 33–34.
60. *New York Freeman*, 12 Dec. 1885, quoted in Schecter, *Ida B. Wells and American Reform*, 37.
61. See *Crusade*, 32; Penn, *Afro-American Press*, 408.
62. Wells noted in her diary the theme of her 1887 address: "to urge the young women to study & think with a view to taking places in the world of thought and action" (*MD*, 12 Aug. 1887, 153). On her purchasing a managing share of *Free Speech*, see *Crusade*, 35; David M. Tucker, "Miss Ida B. Wells and Memphis Lynching," *Phylon* 32 (Summer 1971): 113–17.
63. Gilmore, *Gender and Jim Crow*, 45; Rodger Streitmatter, "Economic Conditions Surrounding Nineteenth-Century African American Women Journalists: Two Case Studies," *Journalism History* 18 (1992): 33–40. Where Wells relates her apprentice years (when she was most dependent on male patronage) with guarded detail in her memoir, her diaries candidly reveal the conflicts with her male peers and editors. See, e.g., *MD*, 29 Dec. 1885, 23; 5 Jan. 1886, 27; 28 Jan. 1886, 36; 26 Aug. 1886, 100; 28 Nov. 1886, 120; 2 Dec. 1886, 125; 18 Jan. 1887, 128; 14 Mar. 1887, 136; 12 Aug. 1887, 153.
64. According to Wells, this case ended disturbingly. After one of the teachers continued her affair against the wishes of her family, a quarrel ensued between the woman and her brother-in-law and the woman committed suicide. See *Crusade*, 35–37.
65. On the censorship of sexuality from public discourse in black politics at this time, see Hazel V. Carby, "Policing the Black Woman's Body," *Critical Inquiry* 18(4) (Summer 1992): 738–55.
66. A year later, in 1892, this social formation would be tested even further by a controversial lesbian murder case that rocked Memphis. See Lisa Duggan's

Sapphic Slashers for a social history of this event and its implications for the construction of gender identities and sexualities, and for the demarcations between the public and private spheres. *Sapphic Slashers: Sex, Violence, and American Modernity* (Durham: Duke University, 2000).

67. I base this number on the women journalists profiled in Penn, *Afro-American Press*, 367–427.
68. *MD*, 28 Jan. 1886, 35–36; 11 Mar. 1886, 51–52. Wells was quite smitten with "Charlie boy," as she called him. Though Morris was younger than Wells and their age difference concerned her, he clearly understood the way to her heart was to take her writing seriously, as she admits in this rare expression of passion: "He writes a good letter & I feel my scepter departing from me, before him as before no other & it is somewhat humiliating" (*MD,* 35).
69. Since her draft outlines are not extant, all that remains of the novels are the notes Wells records in her diaries: *MD*, 18 Feb. 1886, 45–46; 22 Aug. 1886, 99; 4 Sept. 1886, 101.
70. *MD*, 4 Sept. 1886, 101. An admirer of Charles Dickens and Louisa May Alcott (*Crusade*, 21), Wells probably had their standards of social realism in mind when she judged Morris's effort. In her diaries, she writes intelligently of her reading tastes in fiction. See *MD*, 29 Dec. 1886, 25–26; 11 Mar. 1886, 52; 20 Apr. 1886, 60; 29 July 1887, 151–52.
71. *MD*, 18 Feb. 1886, 46.
72. *MD*, 1 Sept. 1886, 101. During this burst of fiction-writing Wells did manage to finish and publish two short stories. "A Story of 1900" appeared in the *Fisk Herald* (April 1886), while "Two Christmas Days: A Holiday Story" ran in the *A.M.E. Zion Church Quarterly* (January 1894).
73. These citations are drawn from the following diary entries (in order): *MD*, 3 June 1886, 74; 30 Jan. 1886, 38; 1 Feb. 1886, 38–39; 8 Feb. 1886, 41.
74. *MD*, 26 Aug. 1886, 100.
75. *MD*, 4 Sept. 1886, 102. Compare this entry with Wells's sorrow about lynching murders she does not write about, in ibid., 18 Mar. 1886, 54–55.
76. *Crusade*, 169.
77. According to Crystal Feimster, 162 African American, Latina, and white women were murdered by lynch mobs between 1880 and 1930. In many instances, the victims were accused of poisoning white women for whom they worked or encountered in some relation of social dominance, much like the case Wells cites in her diary. On this demographic pattern, see "Ladies and Lynching," 237, 257–61.
78. On the conservatism of black women's anti-lynching activism, see ibid., chap. 4, esp. 167–69, 186–93, 201–22.
79. *MD*, 8 Feb. 1886, 41–42. Cooper's eloquence when describing lynching in *A Voice from the South* (1896) is striking compared to Wells's more blunt, less circumspect depictions. Where Wells lingered for pages on the gruesome details of mob murders, the scenes of lynching in Harper's *Minnie's Sacrifice* (1869) and *Iola Leroy* (1892) are pivotal but brief (and it must be noted that

Harper's use of Wells's pen name in the title of her second novel begs to be read as a chastisement for breaching Harper's preferred methods of protest). Matthews's dramatization of lynching in her short story "Aunt Lindy" (1893) turns into an oblique but powerful commentary about lynching's traumatic effects on women survivors. Wells, by contrast, described lynching murders in such graphic detail that her pamphlets themselves arguably were an ordeal to read.

80. Wells's excitement is in keeping with her attraction to the character of Lady Macbeth, whose soliloquies she performed in dramatic recitals sponsored by her lyceum. See *MD*, 21 Jan. 1886, 31–32. For a contrasting view of Wells's gendered style of writing, see Gunning, *Race, Rape, and Lynching*, 84–85.
81. On this development, see Christopher P. Wilson, *Labor of Words*, 17.
82. Dicken-Garcia, *Journalistic Standards*, 221. For my purposes, the term "journalism" refers primarily to newspapers.
83. Contemporary observers of black journalism were adamant about the need to keep current with these developments. See, e.g., Penn, *Afro-American Press*, chaps. 23 and 24, and contributor Gertrude Mossell's recommendations for the field's progress, 487–91.
84. As I remark in chapter 1, there is to my knowledge no single published book or monograph devoted to a comparative analysis of lynching's discursive formation in the U.S. press. As a step toward correcting the situation, Richard M. Perloff offers "The Press and Lynchings of African Americans," *Journal of Black Studies* 30(3) (January 2000): 316, 326–27. Perloff, however, draws his examples from secondary sources. My own claims here are only provisional, since I tackle this unwieldy archive through targeted case studies and selective comparative analysis between the mainstream and African American press. I also examined the newspaper accounts compiled in Ralph Ginzburg's *One Hundred Years of Lynching* (New York: Lancer Books, 1962) and the NAACP Papers (microfilm), Anti-Lynching Campaign, 1912–1955, part 7, series A, reels 5–7. Ginzburg's survey spans the period from 1880 to 1961; the NAACP's records date from 1885 to 1937.
85. For example, see the *New Orleans Picayune*, "Charles Killed after Slaying Four Others," 25 July 1900, 1; and the *Atlanta Constitution*'s elaborately illustrated story, "New Orleans Is Now Guarded by Special Army of Police," 29 July 1900, 3. I discuss the case these reports describe—Robert Charles's siege of New Orleans—at the end of this chapter.
86. Neal's was a particularly heinous murder, not least because the lynching was publicized in advance by Florida newspapers and radio stations along the East Coast. See Dray, *At the Hands of Parties Unknown*, 344–53.
87. See "Negroes Hunted All Night by Mobs Made Up of Boys," *New Orleans Picayune*, 26 July 1900, 1, 7.
88. For instance, the Manhattan-based coverage of the 1892 lynching of Robert Lewis in Port Jervis, New York reflected this third strategy over the month it took for the incident to unfold. I discuss this case at length in chapter 3.

89. These headlines are drawn from Ginzburg, *One Hundred Years of Lynching,* recounting reports on the murders of Zachariah Walker (1912, in Coatesville, Pennsylvania), 73, and Mary Conley (1916, in Arlington, Georgia), 110. Lisa Duggan discusses the cloaking effects of sensationalized news reporting in *Saphhic Slashers*, 35–36, 62.
90. Penn profiles these writers (except Alexander Manly) in *Afro-American Press.* Also see Emma Lou Thornbrough, "T. Thomas Fortune: Militant Editor in the Age of Accommodation," in *Black Leaders;* Ann Field Alexander, "Black Protest in the New South: John Mitchell, Jr. and the Richmond *Planet*" (Ph.D. diss., Duke University, 1972); W. Fitzhugh Brundage, "'To Howl Loudly': John Mitchell, Jr., and His Campaign against Lynching in Virginia," *Canadian Review of American Studies* 22 (Winter 1991): 325–41; Peter Gilbert, ed., *The Selected Writings of John Edward Bruce: Militant Black Journalist* (New York: Arno, 1971). On Manly's volatile tenure at the *Daily Record,* see Gilmore, *Gender and Jim Crow,* 105–7.
91. Writing about the burning-mutilation murder of Sam Hose in Georgia, the *American Citizen,* a black newspaper published in Kansas City, Missouri, ran this headline: "White Cannibals Burn a Negro!" 28 Apr. 1899, 1. The *Wisconsin Weekly Advocate,* published in Madison, turned the accusation of irrationality onto the white lynchers by describing the mob that tortured Hose as "thoroughly maddened." See "Burned at the Stake," 27 Apr. 1899, 1.
92. *Richmond Planet,* 1 Feb. 1890, 2.
93. "He Defended His Home," *Richmond Planet,* 22 Feb. 1890, 3.
94. See, e.g., "Butchered in Race War," 4 Jan. 1890, 3; "Eight Colored Men Shot," 4 Jan. 1890, 3; "The Hub," 15 Feb. 1890, 4; "Barnwell—Detailed List of Suffering Survivors," 22 Mar. 1890, 3, all in the *Richmond Planet.*
95. *Richmond Planet,* 4 Jan. 1890, 3.
96. Lead paragraph to the *Planet*'s "Eight Men Shot," 4 Jan. 1890, 3.
97. White quoted in Dicken-Garcia, *Journalistic Standards,* 221.
98. This discussion follows from Schudson, *Discovering the News,* 40–43, 97–98, 102; Amy Kaplan, *The Social Construction of American Realism* (Chicago: University of Chicago Press, 1988), chaps. 1 and 3; Alan Trachtenberg, "Experiments in Another Country: Stephen Crane's City Sketches," in *American Realism: New Essays,* ed. Eric J. Sundquist (Baltimore: The Johns Hopkins University Press, 1982). On the sacralizing functions of newspaper reading and the spiritual symbolism of newspapers' corporate headquarters; see David T. Z. Mindich, "Building the Pyramid: A Cultural History of 'Objectivity' in American Journalism, 1832–1894," Ph.D. diss., New York University, 1996, 147–48, 150–60.
99. Benedict Anderson, *Imagined Communities: Reflections on the Origin and Spread of Nationalism,* rev. ed. (London: Verso, 1991), 24–36.
100. Edwin L. Shuman, *Steps into Journalism: Helps and Hints for Young Writers* (Evanston: Correspondence School of Journalism, 1894), 23.

101. On the complex debates about simultaneity at the turn of the nineteenth century, see Kern, *Culture of Time and Space*, 67–68, 81, 88. In African American journalism, ephemerality was not a goal of newspaper publishing during the first half of the nineteenth century. On the rhetoric and practice of "durability" in black news writing and reading during the antebellum era, see McHenry, *Forgotten Readers*, 113–15, 134–39.
102. As Linda Hutcheon explains in *A Theory of Parody*, the proper "context" in which to analyze parodic art is its "enunciative" surround (24), which requires evaluating "the text and the 'subject positions' of encoder [author] and decoder [reader], but also the various contexts (historical, social, ideological) that mediate their communicative act" (108).
103. *Crusade*, 78. Brooklyn-based journalist Victoria Earle Matthews and settlement house worker Maritcha Lyons organized this testimonial fundraiser to sponsor Wells's return to news publishing. The rally accomplished this goal and more: feminist historians agree that this meeting launched the club movement among African American women into national prominence.
104. For the translation of "Mizpah," see Schecter, *Ida B. Wells and American Reform*, 19.
105. Rising literacy rates would have been crucial to the formation of *Southern Horrors*'s enunciative contexts because, as Linda Hutcheon observes, "historians of parody agree that [it] prospers in periods of cultural sophistication that enable parodists to rely on the competence of the reader (viewer, listener) of the parody" (*A Theory of Parody,* 19).
106. In *Crusade*, Wells notes that the newspaper exposé on which *Southern Horrors* was based (what she calls "the first inside story of Negro lynchings" [71]) had a print run of ten thousand copies. Though she cites no figures for the sales of the pamphlet, it seems fair to project the booklet's circulation was widespread as well, based on the initial report's success.
107. Importantly, Douglass does not revive the oppressive politics that defined antebellum slave narratives, wherein white patrons used their endorsements to control the autonomy of black narrators and their narratives. He deferred to Wells's understanding of lynching: "I have spoken, but my word is feeble in comparison" (*SH*, 15).
108. My typology and periodization of the stunt draws from Mott, *American Journalism*, 416–21, 436–39, 442, 575–78; Schudson, *Discovering the News*, 69; Wilson, *Labor of Words*, 17, 27–28, 37; Jean Marie Lutes, "Into the Madhouse with Nellie Bly: Girl Stunt Reporting in Late Nineteenth Century America," *American Quarterly* 54(2) (June 2002): 217–53.
109. The word "spice" in this context comes from William Dean Howells's novel about the changes that revolutionized the news profession, *A Modern Instance* (Boston: Houghton Mifflin, 1957 [1882], 212). Interestingly, Howells uses the word when the amorally ambitious Bartley Hubbard and

the old-style editor Ricker debate whether lynching should be included in their coverage of the news.

110. Lutes, "Into the Madhouse," 227.

111. Ibid., 225–26.

112. See Stephen R. Fox, *The Guardian of Boston: William Monroe Trotter* (New York: Athenaeum, 1970), 49–58.

113. For discussion of this episode in Mitchell's fascinating career, see Alexander, "Black Protest in the New South," 150–51; Brundage, "To Howl Loudly," 329.

114. On Wells's lawsuit, see *Crusade*, 18–20; *MD*, 11 Apr. 1887, 140–41; Schecter, *Ida B. Wells and American Reform*, 43–44; McMurry, *To Keep the Waters Troubled*, 30. In 1891 she also toured the Mississippi Delta, Tennessee, and Arkansas, selling subscriptions for the *Free Speech* and drafting local residents to serve as correspondents for the paper. "It was quite a novelty to see a woman agent who was also editor of the journal for which she canvassed," Wells recalled (*Crusade*, 41). As these two examples and my discussion of *Southern Horrors* should make clear, I disagree with Jean Marie Lutes's claim ("Into the Madhouse," 248) that stunt journalism was irrelevant to and unused by African American journalists as a news-writing tactic.

115. On Barber's exile from Atlanta, see Brundage, *Lynching in the New South*, 205–6.

116. Manly's case is terrifying because of the ways in which the editorials in question were recycled over time. The following accounts detail the violent trail left by the wire-reprint system that was being perfected at the nineteenth century's end: Williamson, *Crucible of Race*, 195–201; Gilmore, *Gender and Jim Crow*, 105–7; Gunning, *Race, Rape, and Lynching*, 63, 90; Eric J. Sundquist, *To Wake the Nations: Race in the Making of American Literature* (Cambridge: Harvard University Press, Belknap Press, 1993), 413–17.

117. Benjamin's wounds are described in the preface to his pamphlet "Southern Outrages" (1894), in the Daniel Alexander Payne Murray Pamphlet Collection, microfilm, Library of Congress. An attorney in Lexington, North Carolina, Benjamin was eventually murdered. In 1900, a white poll worker killed him for trying to register a group of black men to vote. See Gilmore, *Gender and Jim Crow*, 125 n. 39, 277.

118. For an insightful analysis that links Wells's syntactic experiments to African American practices of collage and call-and-response together with Bakhtin's theory of dialogism, see Simone Davis, "The Weak Race and the Winchester: Political Voice in the Pamphlets of Ida B. Wells-Barnett," *Legacy* 12 (1995): 77–97.

119. Shuman, *Steps into Journalism*, 98–99. This rule was based on the *Chicago Tribune*'s "Instruction to Country Correspondents" (98). Of course, these standards were violated regularly in cases involving white-on-white sex crimes.

120. As Sandra Gunning and Patricia A. Schecter rightly contend, Wells's anti-archival approach recovers the otherwise lost histories of black women's sexual abuse, producing a fuller record of evidence to debate the politics of lynching. Though I agree, *Southern Horrors*'s parody of the stunt specifies the role that literary genres can play in creating the conditions necessary for the public to imagine such exclusions as legitimate in the first place.
121. Anticipating the rise of muckraking journalism nearly a decade before that genre became a popular writing style, Wells was largely excluded from publishing in the mainstream venues of investigative journalism. On this point, see Herbert Shapiro, "The Muckrakers and the Negroes," *Phylon* 31 (Spring 1970): 78; Maureen Beasely, "The Muckrakers and Lynching: A Case Study in Racism," *Journalism History* 9 (Autumn-Winter 1982): 86–91.
122. According to Patricia A. Schecter, this work began in May 1892 and ended in June 1895. Wells traveled between Chicago and London for three- to six-month tours, following a vigorous schedule of lectures and newspaper editorial writing across England and Scotland. My summary here draws from Wells's personal account in *Crusade,* chaps. 11–26; Schecter, *Ida B. Wells and American Reform,* 23, 91–120; Bederman, *Manliness and Civilization,* chap. 1; Bederman, "Ida B. Wells' Anti-lynching Campaign"; and Ware, *Beyond the Pale,* chap. 4.
123. Interestingly, Wells's strategy recalls the work of black abolitionist Sarah Parker Remond, who toured England in 1859 and also exhibited a style of refinement that stressed an impersonal command of knowledge. Remond makes an illuminating foil to Wells in this regard. See Carla L. Peterson, *Doers of the Word: African American Women Speakers and Writers in the North, 1830–1880* (New York: Oxford University Press, 1995), 137–45.
124. *New York Times,* 24 July 1894, quoted in Floyd W. Crawford, "Ida B. Wells: Her Anti-Lynching Crusades in Britain and Repercussions from Them in the United States," unpublished typescript in Ida B. Wells Papers, box 5, folder 10, Special Collections Research Center, University of Chicago (1958): 18–19.
125. Schecter, *Ida B. Wells and American Reform,* 106.
126. Wells herself claimed and scholars generally agree that the impact of the British tour marked a watershed moment in the history of the anti-lynching movement; from that point (1894) on, the consensus is that lynching became a topic of national discourse. See *Crusade,* 180–90; Giddings, *When and Where I Enter,* 90–92; Bederman, *Manliness and Civilization,* 69–71; Schecter, *Ida B. Wells and American Reform,* 109–10, 122–23.
127. My discussion of this pamphlet relies on the edition included in *Selected Works of Ida B. Wells-Barnett,* comp. Trudier Harris (New York: Oxford University Press, 1991). Subsequent citations of this pamphlet are abbreviated *RR* and noted parenthetically in the text.

128. On the fetishization of empirical evidence in late-nineteenth-century American life and literature, see Seltzer, *Bodies and Machines* (New York: Routledge, 1993), 91–118; Shi, *Facing Facts: Realism in American Thought and Culture, 1850–1920* (New York: Oxford University Press, 1995), chap. 9. On the use of statistics in journalism, see Schudson, *Discovering the News*, 71–75. As Mott points out, sociological studies and monographs were routinely used by journalists as background source materials for their stunts; see *American Journalism*, 436–39, 442, 522–23, 573–74.
129. On Chicago's importance to sociology's disciplinary development, see Helene Silverberg's introduction to *Gender and American Social Science: The Formative Years* (Princeton: Princeton University Press, 1998), 13.
130. Smalls quoted in Haskell, *Emergence of Professional Social Science*, 209. Published in 1895, Smalls's "The Era of Sociology" is exactly contemporaneous with *A Red Record.*
131. On this concept of "interdependence," see Haskell, *Emergence of Professional Social Science*, 12–13, 15, 199.
132. For more on this convergence, see Brundage, "Introduction," in *Under Sentence of Death: Lynching in the South,* ed. W. Fitzhugh Brundage (Chapel Hill: University of North Carolina Press, 1997), 6; James E. Cutler, *Lynch Law: An Investigation into the History of Lynching in the United States* (New York: Longmans, Green, 1905), the most influential sociological study of lynching before 1922.
133. Wells's interest in sociology was undoubtedly well informed. As Evelyn Brooks Higginbotham points out, black Baptist reformers quickly adapted sociological analysis as part of their activist methods during the 1890s; see *Righteous Discontent*, 172.
134. On the varied disciplines of scientific racism, see Dray, *At the Hands of Parties Unknown*, 98–103; Williamson, *Crucible of Race*, 199–224; George M. Frederickson, *The Black Image in the White Mind: The Debate on Afro American Character and Destiny, 1817–1914* (Hanover, N.H.: University Press of New England for Wesleyan University Press, 1987 [1970]), chaps. 8 and 9; Bederman, *Manliness and Civilization*, 46–53; Gaines, *Uplifting the Race*, 70–76. For instance, the renowned Harvard anthropologist Nathaniel Southgate Shaler defended lynching in publications directed toward a national lay audience. See, e.g., "The Future of the Negro in the South," *Popular Science Monthly* 57 (June 1900): 147–56; "The Peculiarities of the South," *North American Review* 151 (1890): 477–88.
135. On the masculinization of American sociology in 1890s Chicago, see Silverberg, "Introduction," in *Gender and American Social Science*, 3, 5, 12–15, 22.
136. *RR,* 150. The *Tribune* began publishing lynching statistics in 1882. Printed on New Year's Day until 1904, the information was promoted as part of the paper's retrospective of the year past. That this "necrology table" (as the

Tribune named it) helped to popularize statistical collection strategies suggests how racial violence was used to figure the problematic nature of social progress. Christopher Waldrep discusses the cultural symbolism of the *Tribune*'s use of lynching statistics in "Word and Deed: The Language of Lynching, 1820–1953," in *Lethal Imagination: Violence and Brutality in American History*, ed. Michael A. Bellesiles (New York: New York University Press, 1999), 243–44.

137. Wells reprints a woodcut engraving copied from an 1893 photograph (*RR*, near 170) and an electrotype of a lynching postcard, front and verso (*RR*, near 197). The formal distinctions between these images is of no small consequence; I define and discuss the genre conventions of lynching photographs and postcards at length in chapter 5.

138. Du Bois's traumatic encounter with the lynched remains of Sam Hose in 1899 is the more famous example of Wells's point. On his epiphany to abandon academic sociology for public activism, see *Dusk of Dawn: An Essay toward an Autobiography of a Race Concept* (New York: Harcourt, Brace, 1940), 67.

139. According to Floyd W. Crawford, anti-lynching bills introduced by the governors of Louisiana, Tennessee, and Virginia all failed, while measures presented in North Carolina and Georgia (1893), South Carolina and Ohio (1896), and Kentucky and Texas (1897) all passed. United States Representative William Henry Blair (R-New Hampshire) introduced a bill calling for federal investigations of mob violence as a result of Wells's 1894 crusade, though that initiative failed to move past committee to a floor vote. See Crawford, "Ida B. Wells: Some American Reaction to Her Anti-Lynching Crusade in Britain," 13–23, lecture delivered at Le Moyne College, 2 Mar. 1963, typescript, in Ida B. Wells Papers, box 5, folder 10, Special Collections Research Center, University of Chicago.

140. For examples of club women's defense of Wells, see Feimster, "Ladies and Lynching," 195; Higginbotham, *Righteous Discontent*, 143, 152; McHenry, *Forgotten Readers*, 191–92, 195, 215; Schecter, *Ida B. Wells and American Reform*, 103–4; McMurry, *To Keep the Waters Troubled*, 233. John "Grit" Bruce's 1901 pamphlet *A Blood Red Record* most obviously borrows from Wells's 1895 work.

141. For these rebukes, see Schecter, *Ida B. Wells and American Reform*, 106, 115, 106, respectively. Also see McMurry, *To Keep the Waters Troubled*, 217–18, 231–35, 244–51.

142. *Lynch Law in Georgia* (Chicago: Ida B. Wells, 1899), in the Daniel Alexander Payne Murray Pamphlet Collection, microfilm, Library of Congress. Citations to this pamphlet are hereafter abbreviated *LL* and noted parenthetically in the text. *Lynch Law in Georgia*'s print run was financed through donations solicited at two rallies organized by the Chicago branch of the Afro-American Council, to which Wells and her husband Ferdinand

Barnett belonged. For more on the provenance of the pamphlet, see Mary Louise Ellis, "Rain Down Fire: The Lynching of Sam Hose" (Ph.D. diss., Florida State University, 1992), 199–202.

143. The details I cite here are drawn from Hale, *Making Whiteness*, 209–15; Brundage, *Lynching in the New South*, 34, 82–84; Herbert Shapiro, *White Violence, Black Response: From Reconstruction to Montgomery* (Amherst: University of Massachusetts Press, 1988), 63. Mary Louise Ellis's case study "Rain Down Fire" provides the most complete investigation of all three lynchings. On the Palmetto Nine, see the following coverage in the *Atlanta Constitution:* 16 Mar. 1899; 19 Mar. 1899; 21 Mar. 1899; 23 Mar. 1899; 25 Mar. 1899.

144. Ellis, "Rain Down Fire," 147.

145. Ibid.

146. For the transformative impact of telegraph technology on news writing and newspaper production, see Richard A. Schwartzlose, *The Nation's Newsbrokers: The Rush to Institution, from 1865 to 1920,* vol. 2 (Evanston: Northwestern University Press, 1990), 145–47; Mindich, "Building the Pyramid," 100, 166–69. James W. Carey offers the most theoretically compelling account of the technology's revolutionary impact; see his thought-provoking "Technology and Ideology: The Case of the Telegraph," *Prospects* 8 (1993): 303–25.

147. On this process, see Schwarzlose, *Nation's Newsbrokers,* 2:112–22; Wilson, *Labor of Words*, 34, 37, 59, 149, 199; Schudson, *Discovering the News*, 77–84; Kaplan, *Social Construction*, 110–17. For contemporaneous descriptions, see Shuman, *Steps into Journalism*, 18–21, 60.

148. Because it turned the collection and dissemination of news into a market commodity, wire reporting arguably democratized access to information for the nation's news readers. However, rural and small-town newspapers often could not afford the service fees, which frustrated the ambitions of some among the black press to offer broad-based coverage to its readers. Even so, the black press rejected as biased the wire-report coverage of racial politics, and tried often to acquire the resources to launch its own wire service. For more about these efforts during the 1890s, see Penn, *Afro-American Press*, chap. 28.

149. Since I have not been able to obtain a run of the *Atlanta Journal*, I rely on the case coverage in the *Atlanta Constitution* as a reference to gauge the point of Wells's critique.

150. Quoted in Schwartzlose, *Nation's Newsbrokers*, 1:122.

151. Grant Milnor Hyde, *Newspaper Reporting and Correspondence: A Manual for Reporters, Correspondents, and Students of Newspaper Writing* (New York: Appleton, 1912), 4. Hyde explained this method was a "new form" of news writing, "as different and individual as any other form of expression" (36). However, as early as 1894, Edwin L. Shuman featured the style in his

manual *Steps into Journalism* (22–92). Journalism historian David Z. Mindich dates the practice earlier than Shuman, tracing it back to the Civil War dispatches of the Lincoln administration; see "Building the Pyramid," chap. 3.

152. Hyde, *Newspaper Reporting*, 127.
153. On the problems posed by news report "hoaxes" and "fakes," see Shuman, *Steps into Journalism*, 120–22; Schudon, *Discovering the News*, 79–80; and Wilson, *Labor of Words*, 35–37.
154. Shuman, *Steps into Journalism*, 125.
155. In this way Wells's parody surpasses the criticisms delivered against the wire report system in either Theodore Dreiser's "Nigger Jeff" (1901) or Charles W. Chesnutt's *The Marrow of Tradition* (1900). While compelling and complex, those fictional accounts focus more on the field aspects of wire reporting—how stringers were pressed to "see" the angle of a story (Dreiser), or how editors planned to saturate news networks with their staff reports (Chesnutt). *Lynch Law in Georgia* penetrates the bureaucratization of the writing process itself.
156. In its coverage of the murder, the *Atlanta Constitution* corrected this reporting error the next day following its initial wire dispatch; compare "Nine Negroes Shot Down at Palmetto, Ga. This Morning," *Atlanta Constitution,* 16 Mar. 1899, 1, with "Scenes and Incidents at Palmetto, Ga.," *Atlanta Constitution*, 17 Mar. 1899, 1.
157. The recommended protocol for reporting catastrophic death was as follows: "When the number of dead or injured reaches any significant figure it is customary to make a table of the dead and injured. This table is usually set into the story close after the lead, but very often the list is put in a 'box' and 'slipped' in above the story." Hyde, *Newspaper Reporting*, 63.
158. It is important to note that *Lynch Law in Georgia* closes with another white man's report. Wells hired Chicago detective Louis P. Le Vin to investigate the lynching cases and commissioned him to summarize his findings in writing. Using his race to his advantage, Le Vin moved freely about the white and black communities in Newnan and Palmetto, interviewing local residents firsthand. His investigation revealed that Hose did indeed kill Alfred Cranford but in the heat of a fight over Hose's wages and work contract. Further, their fatal fight occurred outside in the farm yard, not in the Cranford house; and, according to Le Vin, Hose did not rape Mattie Cranford. Though historian Mary Louise Ellis disputes Le Vin's report as the work of an amateur and political sycophant (see Ellis, "Rain Down Fire," 79–80), *Lynch Law in Georgia*'s parody comes full circle with Wells's editorial gesture because she uses Le Vin's report not simply to contradict Daniel's account but to stress how arbitrary the perspectives of field reporters and in-house editors could be.

159. *Mob Rule in New Orleans,* in *Selected Works,* 254. Hereafter this pamphlet is abbreviated *MRNO* and page citations are noted parenthetically in the text.
160. For the definitive account of Charles's life and death, see William Ivy Hair, *Carnival of Fury: Robert Charles and the New Orleans Race Riot of 1900* (Baton Rouge: Louisiana State University Press, 1976).
161. On the saturation of news coverage in New Orleans, see ibid., 202–3. For examples of national coverage, see *Atlanta Constitution,* 25 July 1900, 2, cols. 5 and 6; 26 July 1900, 2, cols. 2 and 3; 27 July 1900, 1, cols. 3 and 7, and 2, col. 7; 29 July 1900, 1, cols. 1–4, and 3, cols. 2–6; 29 July 1900, 3, cols. 1–4; 30 July 1900, 1, cols. 1–5; 31 July 1900, 3, col. 1; *Chicago Tribune,* 27 July 1900, 1, col. 2; 28 July 1900, 1, col. 1, and 5; 29 July 1900, 6, col. 3; 29 July 1900, 38, col. 3; *New York Times,* 26 July 1900, 1, col. 4; 27 July 1900, 1, cols. 1–3; 28 July 1900, 1, cols. 1 and 2; 29 July 1900, 29, cols. 1 and 2; *Richmond Planet,* 28 July 1900, 5, col. 1; 4 Aug. 1900, 4, cols. 1 and 2.
162. *New Orleans Picayune,* 25 July 1900, 1.
163. Though she often affiliated herself with them, Wells's tenure with newspapers was inconsistent. See *Crusade,* 63 (*New York Age*), 125 (*Chicago Inter-Ocean*), 242–43 (*Chicago Conservator*).
164. Mott, *American Journalism,* 523–24.
165. Hyde, *Newspaper Reporting,* 132–33.
166. See the *New Orleans Picayune* for Charles's escape, 25 July 1900, 1, cols. 1–5; on the random assaults against black men, see 26 July 1900, 1, cols. 1–5. Remarkably, the white posses are indexed by squad number, commander, and enlistees; see ibid., 27 July 1900, 3, col. 3.
167. The line-engraved portrait I describe here was (according to the caption) based on a photograph of Charles. See *Times-Democrat,* 25 July 1900, 1. The *Picayune* published the same illustration on its front page on 27 July 1900, but two days earlier had printed a different image. Though neatly drawn, Charles is dressed in casual attire above an inflammatory caption that reads: "ROBERT CHARLES, the surly Black who committed the Double Murder." See *New Orleans Picayune,* 25 July 1900, 1, col. 5. For more on the variations of Charles's portraits in the New Orleans and national press coverage, see Hair, *Carnival of Fury,* 97–98.
168. According to case historian William Ivy Hair, Charles migrated to New Orleans in 1894 and worked as a manual laborer throughout the city. For more on Charles's biography, see Hair, *Carnival of Fury,* chaps. 1–4, 6. Interestingly, Hair conjectures that Charles was interested in Bishop Henry M. Turner's emigration movement because of his likely knowledge about the lynching of Sam Hose the previous year (107–8).
169. For a fascinating analysis of *Mob Rule*'s symbolic projection of Charles as an ideal of black Christian masculinity, see Schecter, *Ida B. Wells and American Reform,* 116–17.
170. See Hair, *Carnival of Fury,* chaps. 8 and 10.
171. Ibid., 185.

172. Ida B. Wells, Letter to the Anti-Lynching Bureau, 1 Jan. 1902, in D. A. P. Murray Pamphlet Collection (microfilm), Library of Congress. Emphasis added.
173. Wells stayed active as a political leader, both in Chicago and on the national scene. However, her biographers are clear (as is Wells herself in the final chapters of *Crusade*) that her scope of influence narrowed significantly after 1909 once the NAACP, National Urban League, and National Association for Colored Women became entrenched as the main institutions of political reform in black communities.
174. In this way, Wells's parodies anticipate Stuart Hall's insight that, "if the media functions in a systematically racist manner, it is not because they are run and organized exclusively by active racists; this is a category mistake. This would be equivalent to saying that you could change the character of the capitalist state by replacing its personnel. . . . The media, like the state, have a *structure*, a set of *practices* which are *not* reducible to the individuals who staff them." Hall, "The Whites of Their Eyes: Racist Ideologies and the Media," in *Silver Linings: Some Strategies for the Eighties*, ed. George Bridges and Rosalind Brunt (London: Lawrence and Wishart, 1981), 46.
175. For the most detailed analysis of white women's active participation in lynching murders, see Feimster, "Ladies and Lynching," chaps. 2–3.
176. Wells's influence on the course of American thought and debate about lynching is confirmed by W. E. B. Du Bois's ungenerous remarks upon her death in 1931. Though she deserved "more than an ordinary obituary," he refused to write it for the NAACP's *Crisis* magazine and belittled her achievements instead. Praising her as a "'pioneer'" in anti-lynching activism, Du Bois followed with this false lament: "'[She] has been easily forgotten because [her work] was afterward taken up on a much larger scale by the NAACP and carried to greater success.'" Du Bois quoted in Schecter, *Ida B. Wells and American Reform*, 249.
177. Schecter, Giddings, and Wells herself regard these appropriations as evidence of the NAACP's bad-faith gender politics, which saw the organization marginalize black women from its leadership ranks. See Schecter, *Ida B. Wells and American Reform*, 121–23, 135, 138, 141–42, 165; Giddings, "Missing in Action: Ida B. Wells, the NAACP, and the Historical Record," *Meridians* 1(2) (2001): 1–17.

CHAPTER THREE

1. The sources for these accounts are "Lynched," 3 June 1892, in Lynching Scrapbook, file cabinet row 1, drawer 4, "Port Jervis Lynching—Bob Lewis, June 1892" file at Minisink Valley Historical Society (MVHS), Port Jervis, N.Y. My account of Lewis's murder is based on the local news clippings in this source and the following newspapers: *Orange County (N.Y.) Times-Press, New York Tribune, New York World, New York Times, Chicago Tribune, Atlanta*

Constitution, *Richmond Planet*, *Indianapolis Freeman*. My account also relies on Peter F. Osborne III, "Robert Lewis Accused of Brutal Assault on Young Lady," 22 Apr. 22 1985, "Mary Jane Clarke Key Witness in Lynching Inquiry," 29 Apr. 1985, and "Foley Stands Trial," 13 May 1985—all from the *Port Jervis (N.Y.) Tri-State Gazette*, located in MVHS Lynching file.

2. "Lynched," 3 June 1892, MVHS Lynching Scrapbook.
3. "Port Jervis Lynching," *Richmond Planet*, 11 June 1892, 2, col. 5. This same report appears in the *Indianapolis Freeman* along with "The New York Lynching: A Scene That Would Make a Savage Shamefaced," 25 June 1892, 3, col. 4.
4. The *New York World* reported that Lewis's body was hanged for more than three hours before being cut down. See "Lynched in Port Jervis," *New York World*, 3 June 1892, 1. Tying knots precisely was no small detail to botch; it was one of the issues cited in debates against reviving capital punishment, on the one hand, and a persuasive reason for advocating the electric chair as an alternative method for dispensing death sentences, on the other. See James Barr, M.D., "The Mechanics of Hanging," *Popular Science Monthly* 27 (1885): 503.
5. See "Lynched at Port Jervis," *New York World*, 3 June 1892, 1.
6. Useful accounts of post-Civil War politics that link these trends to anti-black violence during the 1870s to 1890s include George M. Frederickson, *The Inner Civil War: Northern Intellectuals and the Crisis of Union* (New York: Harper and Row, 1965); Nina Silber, *The Romance of Reunion: Northerners and the South, 1865–1900* (Chapel Hill: University of North Carolina Press, 1993). Based on my review of Port Jervis's local newspapers, though, the racial peace was kept largely because African Americans were regarded in paternalist, patronizing ways. See the Port Jervis *Evening Gazette* and *Union*, 1877–90, for the tenor of the town's postwar politics.
7. Excluding fatalities from race riots, lynching murders have been reported in the following northern locales: Coatesville, Pa.; Detroit, Mich.; Omaha, Neb.; Wilmington, Del.; Duluth, Minn.; Marion, Ind.. New York State's history of lynching dates back to the eighteenth century. Africans and African Americans were summarily hanged by mobs during the riots in 1741 and 1863, and were killed and suffered lethal injuries in the race riots of 1900, 1935, and 1943.
8. See "The New York Lynching," *Atlanta Constitution*, 6 June 1892, 4, col. 5.
9. See "The Port Jervis Lynching," *Richmond Planet*, 11 June 1892, 2, col. 5; "The New York Lynching," *Indianapolis Freeman*, 25 June 1892, 3, col. 4.
10. Foley's pact with Lewis is reported in all of the newspaper sources I consulted except the *Atlanta Constitution*. Lewis's captors recounted his alleged confession at the subsequent coroner's inquest. See Testimonies of Seward B. Horton and Sol Carley, Coroner's Inquest Transcript, Orange County (N.Y.) Superior Court, 10 June 1892.
11. "The Port Jervis Horror," 6 June 1892, in MVHS Lynching Scrapbook.

12. "Additional Particulars," 3 June 1892, in MVHS Lynching Scrapbook.
13. "What Is Said of It," 3 June 1892, in MVHS Lynching Scrapbook.
14. "More of Foley's Case" 15 June 1892, in MVHS Lynching Scrapbook.
15. Two separate legal inquires were held following the lynching. A coroner's jury was impaneled to present the mob leaders for grand jury indictments. This proceeding was held 3–10 June 1892. Later that month, John McMahon filed larceny charges against Peter Foley for using their private correspondence "to make certain exposures" about Lena McMahon public. The blackmail case was pursued to hold Foley legally accountable for his role in the alleged rape. A grand jury assembled and issued an indictment against Foley, but he was acquitted at trial. For news coverage of that inquiry, see MVHS Lynching Scrapbook; *New York World,* 4 June 1892, 15 June 1892, 23 June 1892; *New York Daily Tribune,* 15 June 1892, 21 June 1892; *Orange County (N.Y.) Times-Press,* 21 June 1892, 24 June 1892, 28 June 1892.
16. Once McMahon's father filed criminal charges against Peter Foley, the reports of the metropolitan papers reports shifted in emphasis, placement, and length: from mid-June to July 1892, Foley's trial is remanded to the regional news page and is lain out on the bottom half of the page with about an inch of column copy allotted to it. See sources in note 1.
17. See all news clippings in MVHS Lynching Scrapbook and *Orange County Times-Press,* June–July 1892. Neither the *New York Times* nor the *New York World* used invectives against Lewis, referring to him most frequently as "the negro" and by the town's nickname for him, "Bob" Lewis.
18. *New York World,* 15 June 1892, 1, col. 3.
19. I discuss the sociology of the "crowd" and its relation to lynching in chapter 1. On psychiatry's focus on autonomous subjectivity during this era, see Lisa Duggan, *Sapphic Slashers: Sex, Violence, and American Modernity* (Durham: Duke University Press, 2000), 102–3.
20. For illuminating analyses of sexology's development and its dependencies on theories of race and racism, see Siobhan Somerville, *Queering the Color Line: Race and the Invention of Homosexuality in American Culture* (Durham: Duke University Press, 2000); Mason Stokes, *The Color of Sex: Whiteness, Heterosexuality, and the Fictions of White Supremacy* (Durham: Duke University Press, 2001).
21. Crane's finances were strained throughout his career but especially during the final years of his life, 1897–1900. At that point, he was so mired in debt that he placed himself in what amounted to receivership, where his literary agents and attorney garnished his earnings and arranged his creditors' payments for him. Since Crane's biographers and critics tend to treat his money woes with bemusement (for his presumed youthful, bohemian ineptitude) or dread (for the hackwork his poverty gave rise to), throughout the chapter I turn to primary sources to explore this dimension of Crane's literary career and its relation to lynching's cultural logic.

22. The correspondence between Stephen and his eldest brother William suggests that the residents of Port Jervis were distressed to read *The Monster* and pressured William to demand an account if not an apology from Stephen for his indiscretion. See Stephen Crane to William Howe Crane, 2 Mar. 1899, in *Correspondence of Stephen Crane,* ed. Stanley Wertheim and Paul Sorrentino (New York: Columbia University Press, 1988), 2: 446–47.
23. There was no denying the strong resemblance between the novella's principal characters and Port Jervis residents involved in the lynching. Henry Johnson's occupation as a coachman made him an obvious double for Robert Lewis. Whilomville's pillars of propriety, Dr. Ned Trescott and Judge Denning Hagenthorpe, decide the fate of the injured Henry Johnson, much like William Crane and the physician W. H. Illman determined how Robert Lewis died when they decided to abandon him to the lynch mob in Port Jervis. The alleged rape victim, Lena McMahon, appears briefly in Crane's story as "an Irish girl" who "thr[ows] a fit" when she encounters the disfigured Henry Johnson on the street. The girl's shocked cries cause "a sort of riot" that incites "a big crowd [to] chas[e] him, firing rocks"—a scene quite like what happened to Robert Lewis six years earlier. That Crane created a different cause than rape to explain the "Irish girl's" fright was the final and most damning clue readers in Port Jervis needed to know that *The Monster* was based on the lynching of Robert Lewis in 1892. Making Henry Johnson innocent of any transgression and subjecting him to the horrific ordeal of having his face burned away, Crane seized on the very symbol—fire—that Port Jervis leaders had used to describe the town's desire to atone for the mob's deed.
24. It took exactly 102 years for American literary and cultural critics to conceive of *The Monster*'s symbolic debts to the history of lynching. From 1899 to the early 1960s, critics typically analyzed the novella as an American revision of Mary Shelley's gothic classic *Frankenstein,* or as a humanist rebuke of the petty cruelties common to small-town life. Henry Johnson's race and Whilomville's racism were not motivating categories of analysis in these discussions. See the reviews and essays on *The Monster* in Richard M. Weatherford, ed., *Stephen Crane: The Critical Heritage* (London: Routledge and Kegal Paul, 1973), 259–67.

    The mid-1960s through the early 1980s saw critics stress the intricacies of *The Monster*'s narrative form, the better to link the novella to Crane's naturalist philosophies of agency, free will, and determinism. See, e.g., Thomas A. Gullason, "The Symbolic Unity of The Monster," *Modern Language Notes* 75(8) (December 1960): 663–68; Charles W. Mayer, "Social Forms versus Human Brotherhood in Crane's 'The Monster,'" *Ball State University Forum* 14(3) (Summer 1973): 29–37; Robert A. Morace, "Games, Play, and Entertainment in Stephen Crane's 'The Monster,'" *Studies in American Fiction* 9(1) (Spring 1981): 65–81; Michael D. Warner, "Value,

Agency, and Stephen Crane's 'The Monster,'" *Nineteenth-Century Fiction* 40(1) (June 1985): 76–93.

From the mid-1980s to the present day, critics have examined the cultural politics of *The Monster* more consistently, analyzing the significance of racial difference to the structure of the story's plot and tracing those dynamics to late-nineteenth-century social formations. Some interpret those formal dynamics as allegories of the Republican Party's collapse as the defender of African Americans' civil rights; see Malcolm Foster, "The Black Crepe Veil: The Significance of Stephen Crane's 'The Monster,'" *International Fiction Review* 3(2) (July 1976): 87–91; Lee Clark Mitchell, "Face, Race, and Disfiguration in Stephen Crane's 'The Monster,'" *Critical Inquiry* 17(1) (Autumn 1990): 174–92.

The anomie produced by commercial mass culture in small-town America is examined by John Carlos Rowe, *Literary Culture and U.S. Imperialism: From the Revolution to World War II* (New York: Oxford University Press, 2000), chap. 7. The novella's interest in the rise of scientific racism against the waning legacy of liberal philanthropy is explained by Price McMurray in "Disabling Fictions: Race, History, and Ideology in Stephen Crane's 'The Monster,'" *Studies in American Fiction* 26(1) (Spring 1998): 51–72.

Perhaps the best-known reading of the novella is Michael Fried's "Stephen Crane's Upturned Faces," in *Realism, Writing, Disfiguration: On Thomas Eakins and Stephen Crane* (Chicago: University of Chicago Press, 1987). Fried likens the trope of the "upturned face"—usually of a corpse or otherwise mutilated figure in Crane's fiction—to the "scene of writing" wherein the wounded face elicits and represses representation, thus signaling the limits of writing itself. As attentive as it is, Fried's gloss of Henry Johnson's burned visage refuses to regard *The Monster*'s allusions to race or racial violence substantively at all.

25. The statistic accounts for the lynching murders of African Americans in Deep South states. See Stewart E. Tolnay and E. M. Beck, *A Festival of Violence: An Analysis of Southern Lynchings, 1882–1930* (Urbana: University of Illinois Press, 1995), 271, table C-3.
26. Ralph Ellison was the first to note *The Monster*'s likely reflection of the cultural politics of lynching. In "Stephen Crane and the Mainstream of American Fiction" he writes: "'The Monster' places us in an atmosphere like that of post-Civil War America, and there is no question as to the Negro's part in it, nor to the fact that the issues go much deeper than the question of race. Indeed, the work is so fresh that the daily papers tell us all we need to know of its background and the timeliness of its implications." See Ellison, *Shadow and Act* (New York: Vintage, 1995 [1964]), 75. Exactly thirty years later, Ellison's cryptic suggestion was confirmed by Stanley Wertheim and Paul Sorrentino's publication of select news articles concerning Robert Lewis's murder in their documentary history of Stephen

Crane's life *The Crane Log: A Documentary Life of Stephen Crane* (New York: G. K. Hall, 1994), 71–73. Since then, Elaine Marshall, Price McMurray, and now I read *The Monster* as decisively based on Lewis's lynching; how each of us interprets the significance of Crane's interest differs considerably. See Marshall's "Crane's 'The Monster' Seen in Light of Robert Lewis' Lynching," *Nineteenth-Century Literature* 51 (September 1996): 205–24; McMurray, "Disabling Fictions." In contrast, while she acknowledges the event and its resonances in the novella and Crane's early work, biographer Linda Davis all but dismisses the relevance of the Port Jervis lynching to *The Monster*'s narrative concerns; see *Badge of Courage, The Life of Stephen Crane* (Boston: Houghton Mifflin, 1998), 45–46.

27. This apt phrase comes from Kelly Miller, "The Attitude of the Intelligent Negro toward Lynching," *Voice of the Negro* 2(5) (May 1905): 308.
28. "Souvenir of Port Jervis, New York: 1900," typescript ms. in MVHS Port Jervis History File, file cabinet row 1, drawer 1, 1. Subsequent references to this text are abbreviated PJ and cited parenthetically in the text. These additional sources inform my limited summary of Port Jervis's cultural history: Peter Osborne III, *The Gilded Age of Port Jervis* (Port Jervis: Port Jervis Historical Commission, 1991; Malcolm A. Booth, *A Short History of Orange County, New York* (New York: Greentree, 1975); D. B. Raynor and R. B. Coler, *Where the Rivers Meet* (Port Jervis, N.Y.: Port Jervis Golden Jubilee Corp., 1957).
29. For these details about Port Jervis's economy, see Osborne, *The Gilded Age,* 17–24. On the distinction between raw and finished goods in the southern economy, see C. Vann Woodward, *Origins of the New South: 1877–1913* (Baton Rouge: Louisiana State University Press, 1991); Edward L. Ayers, *Promise of the New South: Life after Reconstruction* (New York: Oxford University Press, 1992), chaps. 4–5.
30. On Port Jervis's manufacturers, railroad development, and economic prosperity, see Osborne, *The Gilded Age*, 17–20, 22–24; Booth, *Short History of Orange County*, 36–45.
31. For his unsparing account of the region's "cultural famine," see Woodward, *Origins of the New South*, 429. Du Bois also regarded the southern elites of this era to have been culturally profligate; see *Black Reconstruction in America, 1860–1880* (New York: Free Press, 1998 [1935]), 34–37, 45, 53–54. Ayres tempers these assessments in *Promise of the New South,* esp. chaps. 5, 7, 8, 13, 15.
32. Osborne, *The Gilded Age*, 11–12.
33. According to Booth's *Short History of Orange County*, Griffith shot his films at nearby Cuddeback from 1906 to 1915 (30).
34. According to Osborne, white immigrants hailed mainly from eastern and southern Europe (Poland, Holland, Ukraine, Germany, and Italy); see *The Gilded Age,* 28. Blacks most likely migrated west from New Jersey (Robert Lewis's place of birth) and north from Manhattan and Philadelphia. United

States Census Reports for 1890 and 1900 confirm the small numbers of racial minorities in Port Jervis: sixty men and sixty-six women were counted under "total colored," a category that, in 1890, included "persons of negro descent, Chinese, Japanese, and civilized Indians." In 1900, the census tracked each group separately, reporting 119 persons (male and female) as Negroes, seven as Chinese, and none as Japanese or Indian.

35. Alan Trachtenberg, *The Incorporation of America: Culture and Society in the Gilded Age* (New York: Hill and Wang, 1982), 5–7.

36. Osborne recounts the social conflicts that Rev. Crane faced in *The Gilded Age,* 28–29. On the town's saloon culture, see Wertheim and Sorrentino, *Crane Log,* 14–15. For discussions of Jonathan Crane's theological critiques of commercial society and leisure culture, see ibid., 9–10, 12; John Berryman, *Stephen Crane: A Critical Biography,* rev. ed. (New York: Cooper Square Press, 2001 [1950]), 7–12; R. W. Stallman, *Stephen Crane: A Biography* (New York: Braziller, 1968), 2–7; Christopher Benfey, *The Double Life of Stephen Crane: A Biography* (New York: Vintage, 1994), chap. 3; Brown, *Material Unconscious,* 29–30. For a day-to-day chronicle of Rev. Crane's ministry (and particularly that of his temperance-activist wife Mary, who worked extensively with Port Jervis's African American community), see Wertheim and Sorrentino, *Crane Log,* chaps. 1 and 2.

37. On Crane's travels between Asbury Park, Manhattan, and Port Jervis during these years, see Wertheim and Sorrentino, *Crane Log,* chaps. 1–5.

38. For biographical background on William Crane, see MVHS, "Stephen Crane Remembered: A Walking Tour, Port Jervis, NY," [6]; Wertheim and Sorrentino, *Crane Log,* chaps. 1–2, 5–7; Stallman, chaps. 1–5, 17–18, 25–27, 28–33; Joseph Katz, "Stephen Crane: Metropolitan Correspondent," *Kentucky Review* 4 (Spring 1983): 40; Paul Sorrentino, "Stephen and William Crane: A Loan and Its Aftermath," *Resources for American Literary Study* 11 (Spring 1981): 101–8.

39. Bill Brown's characterization of Asbury Park's "economy of play" provides a useful foil against which I interpret William's choice; see *Material Unconscious,* 34–67.

40. On William's early fortunes in Port Jervis, see Wertheim and Sorrentino, *Crane Log,* chaps. 1–3.

41. On William's strategy to build Hartwood, see Charles A. Campbell, *Traditions of Hartwood* (Winter Park, Fla.: Orange Press, 1930), 29–41; Edward J. Dimock, "Stephen Crane and the Minisink Valley," typescript speech delivered to MVHS, 23 Feb. 1953, 8; Wertheim and Sorrentino, *Crane Log,* 47, 83, 108.

42. In his letter to Stephen's wife Cora, William insisted Port Jervis was suitable for his ambitions; see William Howe Crane to Cora Crane, 22 Dec. 1899, in Stephen Crane Correspondence, Butler Library, Columbia University, microfilm reel 1. In 1901 William did leave to head a mining corporation headquartered in Manhattan, finally settling into his post as president in

Alta, California, the site of the mine. On William's arc out of Port Jervis, see MVHS, "Stephen Crane Remembered" [6].

43. Crane's correspondence describes his fretful relationship with the celebrity brought on by his best-selling novel. See his letters, in *CSC*, to Curtis Brown, 31 Dec. 1896 [1895], vol. 1, 161; Ripley Hitchcock, 7 Jan. [1896], vol. 1, 175; Willis Brooks Hawkins, 27 Jan. [1896], vol. 1, 187; Nellie Crouse, 5 Feb. [1896], vol. 1, 197–99.
44. Crane's other trips can be gleaned from Wertheim and Sorrentino, *Crane Log*, 34, 63, 65, 75, 79–80, 180–9, 111, 112, 113.
45. Personal communication with Peter F. Osborne III, MVHS archivist, 9 Nov. 1996. Also see Wertheim and Sorrentino, *Crane Log*, 150–51.
46. According to Wertheim and Sorrentino (*CSC*, vol. 1, 72 n. 2), Louis Carr, J. Frederick Lawrence, and Louis Senger Jr. were the upstate friends who inspired the characters of the "Little Man," "Pudgy Man," and "Tall Man" in these stories.
47. On the "Pike County Puzzle" and the local press's support for it, see Wertheim and Sorrentino, *Crane Log*, 112; Davis, *Badge of Courage*, 90. The praise is cited in the *Crane Log* from the 7 September 1894 review by the *Port Jervis Union*.
48. The infamous "Dora Clark" columns were published in the August–September issues of the *Port Jervis Evening Gazette*. For critical accounts of this conflict, see Wertheim and Sorrentino, *Crane Log*, 201, 202, 204, 205–14; Davis, *Badge of Courage*, 155–67; Benfey, *Double Life*, chap. 8; Christopher Wilson, "Stephen Crane and the Police," *American Quarterly* 48(2) (June 1996): 273–315.
49. Trusts were legal entities that facilitated corporate mergers. On the revision of this cultural ideal and the protests it wrought, see Trachtenberg, *Incorporation of America*, 80–86; Martin J. Sklar, *The Corporate Reconstruction of American Capitalism, 1890–1916* (New York: Cambridge University Press, 1988), 177–79, 188–89; Alfred D. Chandler, *The Visible Hand: The Managerial Revolution in American Business* (Cambridge: Harvard University Press, Belknap Press, 1977), 319–20; Gabriel Kolko, *The Triumph of Conservatism: A Reinterpretation of American History, 1900–1916* (New York: Free Press, 1963), 17–25, 64–65; Steven J. Diner, *A Very Different Age: Americans and the Progressive Era* (New York: Hill and Wang, 1998), chaps. 1 and 2.
50. Crane defined his ideals of sincerity and commitment in letters to Willis Brooks Hawkins, [8 Nov. 1895], vol. 1, 136–37; John Northern Hilliard, Jan. 1896[?], vol. 1, 195–96; Nellie Crouse, 11 Feb. [1896], vol. 1, 201–2, all in *CSC*.
51. See Stephen Crane to Willis Brooks Hawkins, [7 Jan. 1896], vol. 1, 175; 31 Mar. [1896], vol. 1, 219–20, both in *CSC*.
52. One such moment occurred in 1893 when Stephen was unable to pay his typist for the finished manuscript of *Maggie;* instead of a loan or gift,

William offered to purchase Stephen's share of their mother's stock in a Pennsylvania mine. Another occasion involved the $500 loan William extended to help Stephen fend off his English creditors in 1899; for that favor, William sent his daughter Helen to live with Stephen and Cora.

53. For population data on Port Jervis, see Osborne, *The Gilded Age,* 27–28.
54. Robert Wiebe, *The Search for Order, 1877–1920* (New York: Hill and Wang, 1967), chaps. 1–3.
55. For a full account of Port Jervis's modernized infrastructure, see Osborne, *The Gilded Age*, 17–27.
56. Ohmann, *Selling Culture: Magazines, Markets, and Class at the Turn of the* Century (New York: Verso, 1998), 119.
57. Briefly, Haskell argues that different phases of capitalist development produce particular modes of thinking about the self's relation to money and society that furthers the aims and processes of those markets at any given time in history; see Haskell, "Capitalism and the Origins of Humanitarian Sensibility, Part I," *American Historical Review* 90(2) (April 1985): 339–61, and Part II, *American Historical Review* 90(3) (June 1985): 547–61.
58. Lee Ann Whites, "Rebecca Latimer Felton and the Wife's Farm," *Georgia Historical Quarterly* 76 (Summer 1992): 369.
59. Sklar, *Corporate Reconstruction*, 26.
60. My analysis differs from arguments positing that economic modernization quells lynching. I contend that in Port Jervis, economic development promoted anti-black mob violence. For two excellent case studies that follow from the modernization-as-constraint thesis, see J. William Harris, "Etiquette, Lynching, and Racial Boundaries in Southern History: A Mississippi Example," *American Historical Review* 100(2) (April 1995): 404–10; Dennis B. Downey and Raymond M. Hyser, *No Crooked Death: Coatesville, Pennsylvania and the Lynching of Zachariah Walker* (Urbana: University of Illinois Press, 1991). Nancy MacLean brilliantly analyzes how modernization enabled lynching; see "The Leo Frank Case Reconsidered: Gender and Sexual Politics in the Making of Reactionary Populism," *Journal of American History* 78 (December 1991): 917–48.
61. Far from being a reputable office-bound bureaucrat, Foley allegedly plied his white-collar looks to swindle Port Jervis residents into bogus insurance policies and to seduce female lovers. On these charges, see "Additional Particulars," 3 June 1892; "Foley Tells His Story," 8 June 1892; "Foley Writes McMahon," 23 June 1892, in MVHS Lynching Scrapbook.
62. Testimony of Seward B. Horton, Coroner's Inquest Transcript, Orange County (N.Y.) Superior Court, 6 June 1892. Also see ibid., testimony of Sol Carley. These details are not referenced in any news accounts that I have read.
63. My interpretation of Foley and Lewis's deal is shaped in significant part by Mark Twain's novella *Those Extraordinary Twins* (1894), which uses the

burlesque conceit of Siamese twins (Luigi and Angelo Capello) to explore the cultural limitations of joint action and behavior.

64. Testimony of William Howe Crane, Coroner's Inquest Transcript, Orange County (N.Y.) Superior Court, 8 June 1892.
65. Ibid.
66. "Lynchers Not Revealed," 10 June 1892, in MVHS Lynching Scrapbook. Also see *New York World*, 4 June 1892, 8 June 1892, 11 June 1892; *New York Daily Tribune*, 7 June 1892, 10 June 1892, 21 June 1892; *Orange County Times-Press*, 10 June 1892, 14 June 1892, 21 June 1892, 24 June 1892.
67. "The Coroner's Inquest," 7 June 1892, in MVHS Lynching Scrapbook.
68. Yaples also contested William Crane's version of the murder, implying that the judge exaggerated the extent of his intervention with the mob. As the policeman recalled, Crane "spoke a few words . . . [and] then disappeared." See Testimony of Simon Yaples, Coroner's Inquest Transcript, Orange County (N.Y.) Superior Court, 6 June 1892.
69. "Crane and Carr Testify," 9 June 1892, in MVHS Lynching Scrapbook.
70. See each man's testimony in Coroner's Inquest Transcript. I describe them as working class based on the occupations they report in their testimonies.
71. Quotes from the *Advertiser* and *Times* quoted in "Lynchers Not Revealed," 10 June 1892, in MVHS Lynching Scrapbook.
72. The phrase comes from Herbert Stewart, "The Casuistry of Lynch Law," *Nation*, 24 Aug. 1916, 174.
73. "Echoes of the Lynching," 4 June 1892, in MVHS Lynching Scrapbook. As another report put it, "the tree will soon be killed if it doesn't have police protection." See "The Port Jervis Horror," 6 June 1892, in MVHS Lynching Scrapbook.
74. On the culture of landscaping in Port Jervis, see Osborne, *The Gilded Age*, 5.
75. "The Port Jervis Horror," 6 June 1892, in MVHS Lynching Scrapbook.
76. *Port Jervis Union*, 9 June 1892, quoted in Peter Osborne, "Foley Never Stands Trial," *Tri-State Gazette*, 13 May 1985, in MVHS Lynching file.
77. Taylor's sermon is quoted in "The Port Jervis Horror," 6 June 1892, in MVHS Lynching Scrapbook.
78. Verdict, Orange County (N.Y.) Coroner's Inquest Transcript, 10 June 1892. Also see "Bob Lewis' Death," 11 June 1892, in MVHS Lynching Scrapbook.
79. Though biographer Linda Davis contends that Crane "was apparently back in New York" when the lynching murder occurred (*Badge of Courage*, 46), Dimock ("Stephen Crane and the Minisink Valley," 7–8), and Wertheim and Sorrentino (*Crane Log*, 75) point out that Crane signed the Hartwood Club's guest register on 17 May 1892. Since his stays upstate ran as long as six months, it is just as reasonable to assume that Crane remained in town until, or just past, June 2.
80. "Additional Particulars," 3 June 1892, MVHS Lynching Scrapbook.
81. The *New York Tribune*'s coverage of the case ran from 4 June to 29 June 1892. The "Sullivan County Tales" appeared between February 21 and

July 31, 1892, according to the publication history detailed in *The Works of Stephen Crane*, ed. Fredson Bowers (Charlottesville: University of Virginia Press, 1979), vol. 8, 847–61.

82. See, e.g., Joseph J. Kwiat, "The Newspaper Experience: Crane, Norris, and Dreiser," *Nineteenth-Century Fiction* 8 (September 1953), 103–6; Thomas A. Gullason, "A Stephen Crane Find: Nine Newspaper Sketches," *Southern Humanities Review* 2 (Winter 1968): 1–37; Gullason, "The 'Lost' Newspaper Writings of Stephen Crane," *Syracuse Library Associates Courier* 21 (Spring 1986): 57–87; and Wilson, "Stephen Crane and the Police."
83. In 1892, Crane was working as a stringer reporter for his brother Townley's Associated Press wire news agency. His sketches detailing the summer season at Asbury Park appeared in the *New York Tribune* from July 2 to September 16, 1892, soon after the lynching in Port Jervis. On this phase in Crane's career, see James B. Calvert, *Stephen Crane* (San Diego: Harcourt, Brace, 1984), 32–47; Stallman, *Stephen Crane,* chap. 4; Kwiat, "Newspaper Experience"; Brown, *Material Unconscious*, chap. 1.
84. "Parades and Entertainments" appeared in the *New York Tribune*, 21 Aug. 1892.
85. Publisher Whitelaw Reid fired Crane from his job as the paper's New Jersey stringer because Reid was courting the endorsement of the Junior Order of United American Mechanics to support his nomination as the vice-presidential candidate on the Republican ticket in 1892. On this conflict, see Wertheim and Sorrentino, *Crane Log,* 77–80; Stallman, *Stephen Crane*, 53–57; Davis, *Badge of Courage*, 49–50; Benfey, *Double Life*, 78; Brown, *Material Unconscious*, 60–61.
86. "The Port Jervis Horror," 6 June 1892, in MVHS Lynching Scrapbook.
87. Frank Bergon mentions this missed opportunity in *Stephen Crane's Artistry* (New York: Columbia University Press, 1975), 103. Wertheim and Sorrentino also cite it in *Crane Log,* 79. Unfortunately, neither source explains why Crane's southern tour did not materialize.
88. At the coroner's hearing, William Crane and Simon Yaples recount this moment during Lewis's ordeal in nearly exact terms; see their testimony in the Coroner's Inquest Transcript (Crane, 8 June 1892; Yaples, 6 June 1892).
89. In chapter 5 of *Material Unconscious*, Bill Brown also argues that Crane's intrigue with race is fundamental to his modernism and that *The Monster* is the text where this aesthetic finds expressive form. Where Brown vests his reading in Crane's fascination with visual culture and the figures of black minstrels and freaks, I argue that Crane's engagement stems from his subjugation by corporate-monopoly capitalism's practice of contracts and his interest in an equally spectacular figure: the lynched body of Robert Lewis.
90. On Crane's sketch-writing style and its place in American journalism's literary history at the end of the nineteenth century, see Trachtenberg, "Experiments in Another Country: Stephen Crane's City Sketches," in

American Realism: New Essays, ed. Eric J. Sundquist (Baltimore: The Johns Hopkins University Press, 1982); Wilson, "Stephen Crane and the Police"; Kwiat, "Newspaper Experience"; Thomas A. Gullason, "Stephen Crane's Private War on Yellow Journalism," *Huntington Library Quarterly* 22 (May 1959): 201–8; Michael Robertson, *Stephen Crane, Journalism, and the Making of Modern American Journalism* (New York: Columbia University Press, 1997), chaps. 2–3.

91. Stephen Crane to Joseph Conrad, 11 Nov. [1897], *CSC*, vol. 1, 310. Crane's remark is part of his praise for Conrad's draft of Jimmy Waite's death in the *Nigger of the Narcissus* (1897). Crane's awe at the black man's passing is telling, given his work on *The Monster* at the same time: "The simple treatment of the death of Waite is too good, too terrible. I wanted to forget it at once."
92. For a related but different reading of Crane's elision of a race riot from his Asbury Park sketches, see Brown, *Material Unconscious*, 63–66.
93. This phrasing of Crane's debt comes from his letter to J. Herbert Welch in late April or early May 1896, *CSC*, vol. 1, 232.
94. The structural features of this shift included the consolidation of the printing, distribution, and marketing of books along vertical lines; the rise of mass-market magazines and "story papers" to sell and promote serialized and book-length fiction; and the establishment of hierarchical bureaucracies required for these fiction factories to function profitably. On these developments, see John Tebbel, *A History of Book Publishing in the United States: The Expansion of an Industry, 1865–1919*, vol. 7 (New York: Bowker, 1975); Daniel Borus, *Writing Realism: Howells, James, and Norris on the Mass Market* (Chapel Hill: University of North Carolina Press, 1989), esp. chap. 5; Susan Coultrap-McQuin, *Doing Literary Business: American Women Writers in the Nineteenth Century* (Chapel Hill: University of North Carolina Press, 1990); Michael Denning, *Mechanic Accents: Dime Novels and Working Class Culture in America* (London: Verso, 1987); Richard Ohmann, "Where Did Mass Culture Come From?" in *The Politics of Letters* (Middletown, Conn.: Wesleyan University Press, 1987); James L. W. West III, *American Authors and the Literary Marketplace since 1900* (Philadelphia: University of Pennsylvania Press, 1988); Christopher P. Wilson, *The Labor of Words: Literary Professionalism in the Progressive Era* (Athens: University of Georgia Press, 1985); Nancy Glazener, *Reading for Realism: The History of a U.S. Literary Institution, 1850–1910* (Durham: Duke University Press, 1997).
95. "Vertical" holdings allowed corporations to own those entities whose separate market functions combined to make one product, as opposed to "horizontally" held properties, which involved owning companies that manufactured the same exact product. On publishing's adaptation of this corporate business model, see Borus, *Writing Realism*, chap. 5; Wilson, *Labor of Words*, chap. 1.

96. McClure quoted in Borus, *Writing Realism*, 42–43; Ohmann, *Selling Culture*, 250.
97. My summary of the professionalization of late-nineteenth-century American writing is drawn from Wilson, *The Labor of Words;* Amy Kaplan, *The Social Construction of American Realism* (Chicago: University of Chicago Press, 1988); and Richard H. Brodhead, *Cultures of Letters: Scenes of Reading and Writing in Nineteenth-Century America* (Chicago: University of Chicago Press, 1993).
98. From the time he launched his professional career, Crane was beset by his inabilities to conform to the industrialized expectations of publishers and editors. With a few exceptions, all of his published correspondence chronicles these struggles in rich detail. Since they are too numerous to cite individually, see Crane's correspondence with his literary agents, Paul Reynolds and James B. Pinker, from 1897–1900, as well as his exchanges with Willis Brooks Hawkins between 1895 and 1896 in *CSC,* vols. 1 and 2. For revealing discussions of how Crane's sloppy accounting of his work affected his literary estate, see the following exchanges from Reynolds to Cora Crane: 6 Sept. 1900; 22 Sept. 1900; 29 Sept. 1900; 23 Oct. 1900; 14 Dec. 1900; 28 Dec. 1900. These unpublished letters can be found in the Correspondence of Stephen Crane, Columbia University, New York, microfilm reel 2.
99. Crane to William Howe Crane, 29 Oct. [1897], *CSC,* vol. 1, 301.
100. Crane to editor of the *Critic,* 15 Feb. 1896, *CSC,* vol. 1, 205.
101. Crane to S. S. McClure, 27 Jan. [1896], *CSC,* vol. 1, 192. For vivid accounts of the sluggishness that attended Crane's pace of writing, see Davis, *Badge of Courage,* 35–36, 41, 53–54, 60–61, 71–72, 74, 105, 311. In "Stephen Crane's Upturned Faces," Michael Fried offers a provocative analysis of Crane's uneconomic style of writing; see *Realism, Writing, and Disfiguration,* 137, 145–47.
102. Crane's chief writing rivals, the novelist Frank Norris and the reporter Richard Harding Davis, did not conceal their indignation at Crane's work and personal habits; see Wertheim and Sorrentino, *Crane Log,* 302 (Norris); 253–254, 299–302, 325–326 (Davis).
103. On these authors' work strategies, see Borus, *Writing Realism,* 70–72; Brook Thomas, *American Literary Realism and the Failed Promise of Contract* (Berkeley: University of California Press, 1997), 232.
104. Crane to Paul Revere Reynolds, 14 Jan. [1898], *CSC,* vol. 2, 327. On his brief try at typewriting, see Davis, *Badge of Courage,* 297.
105. On the publishing industry's standards, see Tebbel, *History of Book Publishing,* 172.
106. Crane to Nellie Crouse, 5 Feb. [1896], *CSC,* vol. 1, 198. By the time Crane refocused his energies on long novel projects (after 1898), his efforts were too late to recoup his earlier losses. As a saddened Cora Crane observed: "[Stephen's] great difficulty is the lack of that machine-like application

which makes a man's work steady." Cora Crane to Edward Garrett, [first week of Jan. 1899], *CSC*, vol. 2, 413.

107. The rates paid to Crane's contemporary Richard Harding Davis are instructive. For his novels, Davis was paid 11.8 cents per word, while his Sunday Supplement features on the Spanish-American War commanded as much as $3,000 per story. Crane, on the other hand, received just $20 per column for his battle dispatches. I draw this information from Davis, *Badge of Courage*, 297; Borus, *Writing Realism*, 43, 55 n. 22, 259; James A. Stronks, "Stephen Crane's English Years: The Legend Corrected," *Papers of the Bibliographic Society of America* 57 (July–September 1963): 340–49; J. C. Levenson, "Introduction," in *Works*, vol. 3, xxxii–xli; xliv–li. Also see Crane to Paul Revere Reynolds, 21 Oct. [1898], 24 Oct. [1898], [25–28 Oct. 1898], in *CSC*, vol. 2, 381–85. On Crane's wartime pay, see Calvert, *Stephen Crane*, 136–37; Crane to Paul Revere Reynolds, 24 Oct. [1898], *CSC*, vol. 2, 382. Davis's contracts in the business archives of Harper and Brothers show that he enjoyed a favored status there as well, earning more lucrative royalty rates and advances than did Crane; see Harper and Brothers Archives, Contract Books, vol. 10, 1896–1900, reel 4 at Butler Library, Special Collections, Columbia University, New York.
108. Frederick A. Stokes to Crane, 23 Sept. 1899, *CSC*, vol. 2, 522. For a fascinating analysis of Crane's predilection for shorter literary forms and the short story's affinities with "the irrationality of the American economic system," see Brown, *Material Unconscious*, 102.
109. Crane to Willis Brooks Hawkins, quoted in Davis, *Badge of Courage*,143.
110. Crane to Ripley Hitchcock, 27 Jan. [1896], *CSC*, vol. 1, 191. Also see Crane to Hitchcock, 26 Mar. [1896], *CSC*, vol. 1, 217.
111. Crane to William Howe Crane, 29 Oct. [1897], *CSC*, vol. 1, 301. Crane exiled himself to England in the late spring of 1897 for three reasons, each of which could have generated the "unkindness and envy" of which he speaks. First, he was accused by Amy Leslie of absconding with money she had entrusted to Crane for safekeeping (Davis, *Badge of Courage*, 170; Wertheim and Sorrentino, *Crane Log*, 217, 233). Second, while on assignment to cover the Spanish-American War, Crane took as his common-law wife Cora Stewart, who ran the bordello where they met in Jacksonville, Florida (Colvert, *Stephen Crane*, 102). Third, since Crane's earning power as a writer was diminished in the United States, it was wise to relocate to England, where critics held him in high esteem and publishing venues offered a fresh chance to earn his due (Davis, *Badge of Courage*, 197).
112. This sketch can be found in *Stephen Crane: Poems and Literary Remains*, vol. 10 of *Works* (1975). Editors date its composition to early or mid-1892. Interestingly, there are two versions of the allegory. In the second draft, the mob violence erupts more frequently and graphically because Crane re-casts his naïf as a boy who travels unchaperoned to meet "King Publico."

113. See Eric Lott's important study, *Love and Theft: Blackface Minstrelsy and the American Working Class* (New York: Oxford University Press, 1995).
114. Trying to encourage his college classmate Armistead Borland to venture out for sexual companionship while touring the South, Crane wrote: "Just read these next few lines in a whisper: —I—I—think black is quite good—if—if—it is yellow and young." Crane to Borland, 16 Feb. 1892, *CSC*, vol. 1, 44. Also see John Northern Hilliard to Thomas Beer [1922], *CSC*, vol.1, 200–1. Crane's lapses into racist caricature occur throughout his journalism and fiction; for stern critiques of this aesthetic, see Rowe, *Literary Culture and U.S. Imperialism,* chap. 7; Amy Kaplan, "Black and Blue on San Juan Hill," in *Cultures of United States Imperialism*, eds. Donald E. Pease and Amy Kaplan (Durham: Duke University Press, 1993); Adam Zachary Newton, *Narrative Ethics* (Cambridge: Harvard University Press, 1995), chap. 5.
115. On the turn of events that led Crane into this Faustian bargain, see Levenson, "Introduction," in *Works*, vol. 3, xlv–xl; Davis, *Badge of Courage,* 196; Colvert, *Stephen Crane,* 106.
116. Crane to Paul Revere Reynolds, 14 Jan. [1898], *CSC,* vol. 1, 327.
117. Crane to Paul Revere Reynolds, [Oct. 1897], *CSC,* vol. 1, 305. For evidence of Crane's strained relationship with McClure, see the following in *CSC*: Crane to Nellie Crouse, 12 Jan. [1896], vol. 1, 180–83, and 26 Jan. [1896], vol. 1, 184–88; Crane to J. Herbert Welch, [late Apr.-early May 1896], vol. 1, 231–33; Crane to Paul Revere Reynolds, 9 Sept. 1896, vol. 1, 254, and 14 Jan. [1898], vol. 1, 327–28.
118. For Crane's plea, see Crane to Paul Revere Reynolds, 14 Jan. [1898], *CSC,* vol. 1, 327.
119. Crane to John Phillips, [Oct. 1897], *CSC,* vol. 1, 307.
120. Thomas C. Holt, *The Problem of Race in the Twentieth Century* (Cambridge: Harvard University Press, 2000), 69; *Richmond Planet,* 9 Apr. 1892, 2, col. 3. Crystal Feimster discusses the incidence of black women lynched over labor disputes in "Ladies and Lynching: The Gendered Discourse of Mob Violence in the New South, 1882–1930" (Ph.D. diss., Princeton University, 2000), 262, 268.
121. Crane to Paul Revere Reynolds, 20 Dec. [1897], *CSC,* vol. 1, 318. I interpret this phrase differently from Wertheim and Sorrentino, who suggest that it refers to the equestrian parlance "to take a fall." However, since the term also surfaces in stories where Crane offers hard-hitting critiques of the exploitative relations between capitalists and laborers (the 1894 sketches "An Experiment in Misery" and "In the Depths of a Coal Mine"), I take "come a cropper" to be more about Crane's labor crises than his leisure activities.
122. My discussion about contracts is indebted to Thomas, *American Literary Realism and the Failed Promise of Contract,* and Saidiya V. Hartman, *Scenes of Subjection: Terror, Slavery, and Self-Making in Nineteenth-Century America* (New York: Oxford University Press, 1997), chap. 4.

123. Wertheim and Sorrentino, *Crane Log,* 268.
124. From the time he began work on *The Monster* in June 1897 until its book publication in December 1899, Crane refers obsessively to the manuscript's word count. See the following in *CSC:* Crane to Edmund B. Crane, 9 Sept. [1897], vol. 1, 296–97; Crane to William Howe Crane, 29 Oct. [1897], vol. 1, 301; Crane to John Phillips, [Oct. 1897], vol. 1, 307–8; Crane to Paul Revere Reynolds, [Oct. 1897], vol. 1, 305–6, 20 Dec. [1897], vol. 1, 317–18, 7 Feb. [1898], vol. 1, 36–37, 19 Jan. [1899], vol. 2, 418–19.
125. Crane to Paul Revere Reynolds, [Oct 1897], *CSC,* vol. 2, 305. Predictably, though, McClure did not cede his claim so quickly. The publisher delayed his decision on *The Monster* but promptly agreed to publish the briefer—and cheaper—"Bride Comes to Yellow Sky." Still obligated to McClure's but released from the first-look requirement with *The Monster,* Crane then submitted the manuscript to Harper's.
126. Stephen Crane, *The Monster,* in *Works* (1969), vol. 7, 9. Further citations are abbreviated *Monster* and noted parenthetically in the text.
127. Brown, *Material Unconscious,* 88.
128. For a psychoanalytic reading of Jimmie's oedipal anxiety and of Henry Johnson's role as the fetish that restores the white father and son's filial bond as "masculine individualism," see Joseph Church, "The Black Man's Part in Crane's *The Monster,*" *American Imago* 45(4) (Winter 1988): 375–88.
129. Richard H. Brodhead defines this phenomenon and its antebellum roots in "Sparing the Rod: Discipline and Fiction in Antebellum America," *Representations* 21 (Winter 1988): 67–96.
130. For arguments that hone in on this dynamic, see John R. Cooley, "The Monster—Stephen Crane's Invisible Man," *Markham Review* 5 (Fall 1975): 10–14; Michael D. Warner, "Value, Agency, and Stephen Crane's 'The Monster,'" *Nineteenth-Century Fiction* 40(1) (June 1985): 76–93; Lee Clark Mitchell, "Face, Race, and Disfiguration in Stephen Crane's *The Monster,*" *Critical Inquiry* 17(1) (Autumn 1990): 174–92; Anthony Mellors and Fiona Robertson, "Introduction," in *The Red Badge of Courage and Other Stories* (Oxford: Oxford University Press, 1998); Marshall, "Crane's 'The Monster,'" 220–22.
131. Harry E. Shaw, *Narrating Reality: Austen, Scott, Eliot* (Ithaca: Cornell University Press, 1999), 115–16.
132. Rowe, Marshall, and Newton regard the iconicity of the black figures in less forgiving terms than I do; see Rowe, *Literary Culture and U.S. Imperialism,* 154–55, 162 n. 56, 237; Marshall, 221–22; Newton, *Narrative Ethics,* chap. 5.
133. Brown, *Material Unconscious,* 229.
134. As James Nagel points out, "Henry's decision to enter the burning building is the key moral choice in the story, the one with the most at stake, the one with the most dire consequences." See Nagel, "The Significance of Stephen Crane's *The Monster,*" *American Literary Realism, 1870–1910* 31(3) (Spring 1999): 55.

135. As Ronald K. Giles observes, the narrator in *The Monster* "is selectively omniscient in his technique, sometimes specifying exactly what happens, sometimes refusing to do so." See "Responding to 'The Monster,'" *South Atlantic Review* 57(2) (May 1992): 45–65. Where Giles regards this slippage as an opportunity for the narrative to elicit the reader's ethical interest and response, I understand it to be where the narrator's choice of comprehension functions to disavow the need to make critical judgments about Henry Johnson's fate at all.

136. For more than a century, Ned Trescott has been lauded as a moral hero for his actions on Johnson's behalf. James Nagel's most recent tribute fairly characterizes this consensus: "Trescott is amazingly free of internal turmoil, for he never hesitates in his embrace of Henry, never wavers in his resolve. . . . Henry has saved Jimmie, and Henry must be helped at all costs. It matters not to Trescott that Henry is black; the opposition of the neighborhood does not figure into the doctor's calculations [. . .] Trescott 'goes about his business with the calm assurance of one who never doubts the truth or validity of his own values.'" See Nagel, "Significance of Stephen Crane's *The Monster*," 52.

137. For an early interpretation of mass culture's (un)natural forms and meanings in Whilomville, see Charles W. Mayer, "Social Forces versus Human Brotherhood in Crane's 'The Monster,'" *Ball State University Forum* 14 (Summer 1973): 29–37. John Carlos Rowe usefully updates Mayer's critique through broader critiques of market relations and commodity fetishism at the core of corporate-monopoly capitalist development; see Rowe, *Literary Culture and U.S. Imperialism*, 148–51, 154–55, 167.

138. On the corporate meaning of the veil, see Thomas, *American Literary Realism and the Failed Promise of Contract*, 239.

139. Roosevelt objected to the end of "One Dash—Horses" (1896): "Some day I want you to write another story of the frontiersman and the Mexican Greaser in which the frontiersman shall come out on top; it is more normal that way!" Roosevelt to Crane, 18 Aug. 1896, *CSC*, vol. 1, 249.

140. Frank Norris, "Stephen Crane's Stories of Life in the Slums: Maggie and George's Mother" in *The Literary Criticism of Frank Norris*, ed. Donald Pizer (Austin: University of Texas Press, 1964), 164.

141. As his biographer Linda H. Davis gushes, the novella offers "a near-perfect tale," "beautifully crafted, with a strong sense of place and vivid characterizations" (*Badge of Courage*, 215–16). Like many twentieth-century readers, Davis lauds *The Monster* as a mature work, evidence of the promise cut short by Crane's death at age 29. My claim here is that the romance of his thwarted genius has kept critics from considering how anomalous the work is in his canon.

142. For more than a century scholars have claimed Crane to be a jack-of-all-writing trades, accomplished in the idioms of realism, naturalism, impressionism, regionalism (Campbell), and modernism.

Joining in that controversy lies beyond the scope of my aims here, but I would like to contribute two points. First, Crane's defiance of easy categorization is said to add to the romance and mystification of him as a Promethean figure, a writer whose work remains unsullied by cultural politics, an opinion with which I disagree. Second, like J. C. Levenson, I believe that Crane sincerely believed himself to be conversant with realism's propositions and aims. How he executed that belief was a different matter altogether. See Levenson, "Introduction," in *Works*, vol. 3, xi–xxiv.

143. Crane to Lily Brandon Munroe, [Mar.-Apr. 1894], *CSC*, vol. 1, 62.

144. Crane to John Northern Hilliard, [Feb. 1895], *CSC*, vol. 1, 99.

145. Howells, *Selected Criticism of William Dean Howells*, ed. Ulrich Halfman, Donald Pizer, and Ronald Gottesman (Bloomington: Indiana University Press, 1993), 3:222.

146. The discussion that follows here is based on Roland Barthes, *The Rustle of Language*, trans. Richard Howard (Berkeley: University of California Press, 1989), esp. "The Discourse of History," "The Reality Effect," and "Writing the Event." Also see Mieke Bal, *Narratology: Introduction to the Theory of Narrative*, 2d ed. (Toronto: University of Toronto Press 1998 [1985]) 36–43.

147. In Barthes's words: "Such notations [. . .] correspond to narrative *luxury*, [. . .] offering many 'futile' details and thereby increasing the cost of narrative information" ("Reality Effect," 141).

148. Ibid., 143.

149. Ibid., 147.

150. Ibid., 148.

151. An equally astounding example surfaces in Crane's praise for Joseph Conrad's *The Nigger of the Narcissus* (1897). See their exchange in *CSC:* Crane to Conrad, 11 Nov. [1897], vol. 1, 310; Conrad to Crane, 10 Nov. 1897, vol. 1, 312–13; Conrad to Crane, 24 Dec. 1897, vol. 1, 319; Conrad to Crane, 16 June 1898, vol. 1, 328.

152. Published as a short story in 1898, "The Open Boat" was based on two earlier news sketches about the sinking of the *Commodore* in 1897, the first of which ("Stephen Crane's Own Story") featured an extraordinary scene as its climax. While the shipwrecked survivors row away from the sinking boat, they make a fateful decision to cut the lifeline linking their dingy to a black crewman. Described explicitly in Crane's news report, the man's drowning appears nowhere in the subsequent fictive accounts of the event. In "Flanagan's Filibustering Adventure" (1897), the man and the moment are transmogrified into a Spanish gunboat that is smashed by the American steamer; in "The Open Boat" the black crewman's drowning is completely elided from the text.

153. The phrase "sacrifice of relation" comes from James's preface to *The American*, where he distinguishes between the historicism of realism and the romance; see James, *Art of the Novel* (New York: Scribner's, 1934). My discussion of Jamesian aesthetics follows from *The Art of the Novel* and

Dorothy J. Hale's *Social Formalism: The Novel in Theory from Henry James to the Present* (Palo Alto: Stanford University Press, 1998).

154. James, *Art of the Novel*, 122–23.
155. Catherine Gallagher and Stephen Greenblatt, *Practicing New Historicism* (Chicago: University of Chicago Press, 2000), 188.
156. Ibid., 167, 168–69.
157. Ibid., 195. Gallagher and Greenblatt praise this outcome as a positively construed "skepticism" that elevates the literary imagination to be as "trustworthy an organ of perception for [historical] phenomena as any other," with the politically salutary chance of "not necessarily affect[ing] the veracity of the experience" (195). Indeed, they go so far as to argue that there can be no "ideological effect" to speak of, since that assignation of social consequence is but mere "speculation" on a critic's part (170). My reading of *The Monster* leads me to disagree with Gallagher and Greenblatt's claim that the distinction between imagination and recollection is "irrelevant." At the very least, Crane's novella suggests that the imagining and recalling are deeply intertwined and bound by ethical-political consequences of the severest sort.
158. Some might challenge my claim here by citing what critics have taken to be Crane's remark against politicized writing: "Preaching is fatal to art in literature. I try to give readers a slice out of life; and if there is any moral or lesson in it I do not point it out. I let the reader find it for himself. As Emerson said, 'there should be a long logic beneath the story, but it should be carefully kept out of sight.'" Crane to Editor of *Demarest's Family Magazine*, [late Apr.-early May 1896], *CSC*, vol. 1, 230. I would agree that Crane rejects propaganda as art, but he is not claiming that art necessarily is or should be apolitical. Rather, he makes the careful exception that his "theories and pet ideas" not "be seen in [his] writing."
159. In order, see Price McMurray, "Disabling Fictions," 66; Newton, *Narrative Ethics*, 190; Brown, *Material Unconscious*, 241. In *Realism, Writing, Disfiguration,* Michael Fried makes the thematization of writing in this scene available for scrutiny. However, John Carlos Rowe emphatically rejects readings that venerate this moment in any way; see his discussion in *Literary Culture and U.S. Imperialism*, 151–55.
160. Fried, *Realism, Writing, and Disfiguration*, 151–55.
161. Kirkegaard quoted in Newton, *Narrative Ethics*, 170.
162. *The Monster* finally appeared in *Harper's Magazine* in August 1898. Harpers and Brothers then purchased and published the short story collection *The Monster and Other Stories*, which was available to American readers in 1899 and posthumously to the British reading public in 1901.
163. Crane to Paul Revere Reynolds, 7 Feb. [1898]: 336–57. In this edition, *The Monster* was paired with "The Blue Hotel" and "His New Mittens."
164. For a useful analysis of these western stories, see John Feaster, "Violence and the Ideology of Capitalism: A Reconsideration of Crane's 'The Blue

Hotel,'" *American Literary Realism, 1870–1910,* 25 (Fall 1992): 74–94. The London edition also included "An Illusion in Red and White," a chilling study of how a father conceals the murder of his wife from their children by creating false memories of her disappearance.

165. Crane to Paul Revere Reynolds, [19 Jan. 1899], *CSC*, vol. 2, 418–20.
166. Crane to James B. Pinker, [1 Feb. 1899], *CSC*, vol. 2, 425.
167. William Crane assumed control over his brother's literary estate in a bold legal move. Filing the necessary papers with the Orange County Surrogate's Court, William had himself appointed executor, refusing to honor Stephen's informally stated wish (through letters) to have Cora Crane serve in that capacity. This is, perhaps, the last testament to Stephen's profound alienation from the culture of corporate-monopoly capitalism and its chief instrument of power negotiation, the contract. See Davis, *Badge of Courage,* 171, 212, 324, 336; Cora Crane to Alfred T. Plant, 9 July 1905, and William Howe Crane to Cora Crane, 21 Aug. 1900, in Stephen Crane Correspondence, microfilm reel 1, Butler Library, Columbia University, New York.
168. See Edna Crane Sidbury, "My Uncle, Stephen Crane, As I Knew Him," *Literary Digest International Book Review* 4 (1926): 248–50. Interestingly, too, Edna added that William understood himself to be Stephen's model for Ned Trescott: "He always claimed that the characterization flattered him" (ibid., 248).
169. See, e.g., Davis, *Badge of Courage*, 217–18; Stallman, *Stephen Crane*, 193.
170. Crane to John Norton Hilliard, [Jan. 1896?], *CSC*, vol. 1, 195–96.
171. According to town archivist Peter Osborne III: "Even to this day, the incident is spoken about in hushed tones" (*The Gilded Age,* 20).
172. Wells's *A Red Record* is included in *Selected Works of Ida B. Wells-Barnett*, comp. Trudier Harris (New York: Oxford University Press, 1991).

CHAPTER FOUR

1. The accident occurred near Wicasset, Maine on June 26, 1938. For additional details see the following news reports: *New York Age*, 9 July 1938, 1; *Pittsburgh Courier*, 9 July 1938, 5; *Chicago Defender*, 9 July 1938, 1; *Baltimore Afro-American*, 2 July 1938, 1, and 9 July 1938, 6; *New York Herald Tribune*, 1 July 1938, 16; *New York Times*, 1 July 1938, 19.
2. During the 1930s, American universities began offering endowed professorships to creative artists. Johnson (hereafter referred to in notes as JWJ). On this point, see JWJ, *Along This Way* (New York: Viking, 1933), 407–9; Eugene Levy, *James Weldon Johnson: Black Leader, Black Voice* (Chicago: University of Chicago Press, 1973), 290–91; JWJ Scrapbook, Fisk University, box 4, folder 7, JWJ Memorial Collection, Beinecke Rare Book and Manuscript Library, Yale University, New Haven, Conn. All

unpublished archival materials pertaining to JWJ and *The Autobiography of an Ex-Colored Man* come from this repository.

3. News reports in the black press headlined JWJ's funeral attire. They also attribute the decision for the outfit and the selection of *God's Trombones* to his wife Grace. See note 1.
4. JWJ, *The Book of American Negro Poetry* (San Diego: Harcourt, Brace, and Jovanovich, 1959 [1922]), 41–42.
5. Throughout this chapter, I refer to the following edition of the novel: *The Autobiography of an Ex-Colored Man*, intro. by Henry Louis Gates Jr. (New York: Vintage, 1989). Citations are abbreviated as *ECM* parenthetically in the text.
6. On JWJ's central importance to the NAACP's organizational history and anti-lynching crusades, see Charles Flint Kellogg, *NAACP: A History of the National Association for the Advancement of Colored People, Vol. 1, 1909–1920* (Baltimore: The Johns Hopkins University Press, 1967); Robert L. Zangrando, *The NAACP Crusade against Lynching, 1909–1950* (Philadelphia: Temple University Press, 1980); Claudine L. Ferrell, *Nightmare and Dream: Anti-Lynching in Congress, 1917–1922* (New York: Garland Publishing, 1986).
7. W. E. B. Du Bois, "JWJ Dinner," typescript, in JWJ Scrapbook, "JWJ Testimonial Dinner," box 3, vol. 5. For all quotes from this text, see the unpaginated typescript in this scrapbook.
8. News clippings from the *New York Amsterdam News* saved in JWJ's Scrapbook highlight Du Bois's disclosure with a tone of marked surprise, suggesting that this episode in JWJ's career was not commonly known. See "Laud Career of J. Weldon Johnson at the Hotel Pennsylvania" in "1936: Miscellaneous Clippings," box 7.
9. As defined by Glazener, "high realism" refers to "promotions of realism based in *Atlantic*-group magazines that emphasized some combination of philanthropy and national citizenship and connoisseurship, values whose . . . major U.S. spawning ground was Boston." See Glazener, *Reading for Realism: The History of a U.S. Institution, 1850–1910* (Durham: Duke University Press, 1997), 43. Kenneth H. Warren, *Black and White Strangers: Race and American Literary Realism* (Chicago: University of Chicago Press, 1993).
10. Just as Frank Norris had set the growth of western agribusiness as the backdrop of his important "wheat trilogy" (*The Octopus* [1901], *The Pit* [1903], and *The Wolf* [planned but cut short by Norris's death in 1903]), Du Bois intended to draw attention to the South's cultivation of cotton as part of the drama unfolding in the development of corporate capitalism at the start of the twentieth century.
11. The phrase "moral spectacle" comes from William Dean Howells's *The Rise of Silas Lapham* (1885). Interestingly, Howells could not conceive of lynching as a fictional subject but did sign on as a charter member to the NAACP's call for members in 1909.

12. Based on his unpublished notes and manuscripts, JWJ's literary concern with lynching dates back to 1897, when he began to write verses whose images were haunted by figures of rape ("Art versus Trade") and immolation (the 1899 poem "The Smoker's Dream"). For these items, see JWJ Notebook 5, JWJ MSS 369. Another unpublished work in this vein is his chilling tirade "A Texas Carnival" (*ca.* 1922), which implicates modern technology, mass culture, and the urban reader in the scene of murder. See JWJ, "Clippings of Poetry by Negro Authors," box 6.
13. JWJ's accounts bear out the pattern that lynchings decreased in numbers but intensified in cruelty (particularly after World War I), and that race riots became more prevalent after the turn of the century, especially in locales outside of the South. See *Along This Way* at 84–85, 114–15, 145, 157–58, 166–70, 202, 314, 317–18, 319–20, 321–24, 329–30, 334, 341–43, 361, 362–72. JWJ also highlights other kinds of incidents involving violence and corporal punishment, ranging from the whippings he received from his mother (14–15) to the atrocities committed by the U.S. Marines during the occupation of Haiti in 1915 (344–46, 358–60). In this regard, *Along This Way* is a book deeply engaged with the relations among violence, progress, and personal identity.
14. *Black Manhattan* (New York; Arno Press, 1968 [1930]) remains a standard reference for historians of black musical theater in New York. For the framing effects of JWJ's discussions of violence, see the following: on the 1712 and 1741 uprisings, 3–11; on slave insurrections, 33–38; on the New York City Draft Riots of 1863, 51–53; on the Race Riot of 1900, 126–30; on the Silent Protest March of 1917, 236–38.
15. "Brothers" is preceded by "O, Southland!," "The Black Mammy," and "Father, Father Abraham," which establish the themes of loss and (dis)loyalty. "Fragment," "The White Witch," and "Mother Night" follow "Brothers," narrowing the frenetic mood of the lynching down to a disquieting calm. The realignment of these poems, together with the revision of "Brothers" in *St. Peter Relates an Incident* (1935), clarifies the poetic order of *Fifty Years.*
16. Typically, *The Autobiography of an Ex-Colored Man* has been interpreted as a roman à clef, a shrewd parody of black autobiography, or as a proto-modernist text whose achievements remain, nonetheless, overshadowed by Jean Toomer's *Cane* and Richard Wright's *Black Boy.* Most recently, critics have become intrigued by the narrator (and JWJ's) possibly queer sexuality. Amid the attention, however, the novel's relation to late-nineteenth- and early-twentieth-century American realism remains unexplored by critics.
17. Henry James, *The Art of the Novel*, ed. R. P. Blackmur (New York: Scribner's, 1934), 66.
18. See Grace Elizabeth Hale's *Making Whiteness: The Culture of Segregation in the South, 1890–1940* (New York: Pantheon, 1998), esp. chap. 5, for a bold but

differently focused account of lynching's imbrications with mass consumer culture.

19. All further references to this work are abbreviated *ATW* and noted parenthetically in the text.
20. Also see Levy's treatment of JWJ's public career prior to 1912 in *Black Leader*, chap. 3, and "Ragtime and Race Pride: The Career of James Weldon Johnson," *Journal of Popular Culture* (Spring 1968): 357–70.
21. I suspect the correspondent was Victoria Earle Matthews. She worked as a freelance journalist and did publish a profile of Jacksonville in the 11 May 1901 edition of the *Washington (D.C.) Bee*. My thanks to Lois A. Brown for bringing Matthews's article to my attention.
22. For an insightful examination of how the "violence of the law" denies black women juridical standing under statutory definitions of rape, see Saidiya V. Hartman's *Scenes of Subjection: Terror, Slavery, and Self-Making in Nineteenth-Century America* (New York: Oxford University Press, 1997), chap. 3. Susan Gillman proposes a different view of melodrama's potential as a source of liberation for black writers than JWJ suggests here; see "The Mulatto, Tragic or Triumphant? The Nineteenth-Century Race Melodrama," in *The Culture of Sentiment: Race, Gender, and Sentimentality in Nineteenth-Century America*, ed. Shirley Samuels (New York: Oxford University Press, 1992).
23. On JWJ's pivotal role in this political project, see *ATW*, chap. 35. The 1921 bid—as did all of the NAACP's efforts—passed in the House but failed in the Senate because of the filibustering tactics of southern Democrats.
24. Cathy Caruth, *Unclaimed Experience: Trauma, Narrative, and History* (Baltimore: The Johns Hopkins University Press, 1996), 4. Further references are noted parenthetically in the text.
25. On JWJ's interest in psychoanalysis and its "sex factors," see his concluding remarks about his own near-lynching in *ATW*, 170. Two of his pocket diaries are obsessed with sexuality's unruly psychic charge; see JWJ Notebooks 3 (MSS 367) and 4 (MSS 368).
26. See Hartman, *Scenes of Subjection*; Thomas C. Holt, "Marking: Race, Race-Making, and the Writing of History," *American Historical Review* 100(1) (February 1995): 1–20; J. William Harris, "Etiquette, Lynching, and Racial Boundaries in Southern History: A Mississippi Example," *American Historical Review* 100(2) (1995): 387–410. Two earlier works also detail how quotidian practices contributed to lynching's normalization at the end of the nineteenth century: Rayford W. Logan, *The Betrayal of the Negro: From Rutherford B. Hayes to Woodrow Wilson* (New York: Collier, 1965); Bertram Wyatt-Brown, *Southern Honor: Ethics and Behavior in the Old South* (New York: Oxford University Press, 1982).
27. As Miller's "vicarious" burden makes clear, class divisions within African American communities made some groups of men and women more (or less) vulnerable to violation. See Kelly Miller, "The Attitude of the

Intelligent Negro toward Lynching," *Voice of the Negro* 2(5) (May 1905): 307–12. W. Fitzhugh Brundage thoughtfully interprets how their silence in public records encodes working-class black communities' response to the daily threats and events of lynching in "The Roar on the Other Side of Silence," in *Under Sentence of Death: Lynching in the South* (Chapel Hill: University of North Carolina Press, 1997), as does Adam Gussow in his ingenious excavation of blues musicians' autobiographies in *Seems Like Murder Here: Southern Violence and the Blues Tradition* (Chicago: University of Chicago Press, 2000), chaps. 1 and 3.

28. Hartman, *Scenes of Subjection*, 145.
29. Arnold quoted in Gilmore, *Gender and Jim Crow: Women and the Politics of White Supremacy in North Carolina, 1896–1920* (Chapel Hill: University of North Carolina Press, 1996), 132.
30. Miller, "Intelligent Negro," 309. As Miller's "vicarious" burden makes clear, class divisions within African American communities made some groups of men and women more (or less) vulnerable to violation. W. Fitzhugh Brundage thoughtfully interprets how their silence in public records encodes working class black communities' response to the daily threats and events of lynching in "The Roar on the Other Side of Silence," in *Under Sentence of Death: Lynching in the South* (Chapel Hill: Univ. of North Carolina Press, 1997), as does Adam Gussow in his ingenious excavation of blues musicians' autobiographies in *Seems Like Murder Here*, chaps. 1, 3.
31. Wells in Bettina Aptheker, ed., *Lynching: An Exchange of Views* (American Institute for Marxist Studies, 1977), 33.
32. My thanks to Robin D. G. Kelley, Genna Rae MacNeil, Colin Palmer, Kali N. Gross, Josefina Arroyo, and Cecilia Green, who challenged me to recognize this shortcoming of prevailing trauma models. I'm especially grateful to Robin Kelley for calling Thomas Holt's essay to my attention.
33. These archived books are thick and numerous. See Book 2: Scraps, box 1, vol. 1; Scrapbook 3, box 2; Scrapbook: Miscellaneous, 1929–33, box 2; Scrapbook: 1915–17, box 5; Du Bois Scrapbook, box 5; Magazine Articles: A–J, box 6; Magazine Articles, K–O, box 6.
34. This number of those murdered by mobs is from Stewart E. Tolnay and E. M. Beck, *A Festival of Violence: An Analysis of Southern Lynchings, 1882–1930* (Urbana: University of Illinois Press, 1995), appendix C, table C-3, 271.
35. Hartman, *Scenes of Subjection*, 35. For more on the wounding effects of racism's normalization, see David L. Eng and Shinhee Han, "A Dialogue on Racial Melancholia," in *Loss: The Politics of Mourning*, eds. David L. Eng and David Kazanjian (Berkeley: University of California Press, 2003).
36. The account that follows is based on the following sources: *ATW*, chaps. 23–27; Levy, *Black Leader*, chap. 5; Jacqueline Goldsby, "'Keeping the Secret of Authorship': A Critical Look at the 1912 Edition of James Weldon Johnson's *The Autobiography of an Ex-Colored Man*," in *Print Culture in a Diverse*

America, ed. James P. Danky and Wayne A. Wiegand (Urbana: University of Indiana Press, 1998).

37. Needless to say, the discrimination he faced and the agenda he enacted during his time in Venezuela, and especially later in Nicaragua, schooled JWJ in the ways of U.S. imperialism. See n. 49 below.
38. For JWJ's genteel but embittered account of his tenure with the Consular Service, see *ATW*, chaps. 23–27. In correspondence with his wife Grace, he expressed his frustrations more candidly. See their exchanges in Family Correspondence, series III, box 40–41.
39. The phrase "aristocrat of color" is from Willard B. Gatewood, *Aristocrats of Color: The Black Elite, 1880–1920* (Bloomington: Indiana University Press, 1990).
40. An alumnus of Atlanta University, George A. Towns kept the campus community abreast of JWJ's ambitions in the Consular Service; see JWJ to Towns, 26 June 1912, in Miles M. Jackson, "Letters to a Friend: Correspondence from James Weldon Johnson to George A. Towns," *Phylon* 29 (Summer 1968): 186–89. For Washington's machinations, see the following correspondence in Louis R. Harlan and Raymond W. Smock, eds., *The Booker T. Washington Papers,* vols. 9–11 (Urbana: University of Illinois Press, 1977): Charles W. Anderson to Washington, 27 May 1907, vol. 9, 274–77; Anderson to Washington, 30 Nov. 1910, vol. 10, 495–96; Washington to Ralph Waldo Tyler, 1 Dec. 1911, vol. 11, 379–80.
41. JWJ to Grace Nail Johnson, 31 Aug. 1912, Family Correspondence, series III, box 41, folder 23.
42. JWJ to Grace Nail Johnson, 10 Sept. [1912], Family Correspondence, series III, box 41, folder 23.
43. The account of this turmoil in *ATW* does not mention these symptoms, though JWJ's distress about his position is clear. Only to Grace does he confide the physical signs of his stress: JWJ to Grace Nail Johnson, 17 Aug. 1912, folder 22; 31 Aug. 1912, folder 22; 10 Sept. [1912], folder 23; 16 Nov. [1912], folder 23, all in Family Correspondence, series III, box 41.
44. JWJ was humiliated for this same reason when, in 1935, President Franklin D. Roosevelt refused to back his nomination to the WPA's Labor Policy Board after JWJ's candidacy had been touted in the national press. See JWJ's obituary report in the *Baltimore Afro-American*, 2 July 1938, 14.
45. Gilmore, *Gender and Jim Crow*, 21. Gilmore's point and JWJ's example help predict the emergence of "returning vet" lynchings following World Wars I and II. In these cases, black servicemen were targeted and killed by white mobs for wearing their uniforms in public, a symbolic declaration of their state-based citizenship. For case studies, see: Harris, "Etiquette," 398–400, 404–10; Dray, *At the Hands of Parties Unknown*, 247–48, 369–76; and Shapiro, *White Violence, Black Response*, 146–47, 305–10.

46. August Meier, *Negro Thought in America, 1880–1915: Racial Ideologies in the Age of Booker T. Washington* (Ann Arbor: University of Michigan Press, 1963), 164–65; Joel Williamson, *The Crucible of Race: Black–White Relations in the American South since Emancipation* (New York: Oxford University Press, 1986), 356–58; Lawrence Friedman, *White Savage: Racial Fantasies in the Postbellum South* (Englewood Cliffs: Prentice-Hall, 1970), 152.
47. For an especially poignant statement of this point, see JWJ's summary of the Consular Service's clean sweep of black men from its ranks in *ATW*, 300–10.
48. For his letter of resignation, see JWJ to William Jennings Bryan, 1 Sept. 1913, series I, box 4, folder 71. For JWJ's assessment of his "duel" with the secretary of state, see *ATW*, 293. Saidiya V. Hartman astutely explains how "the pleasant path" of power extends the domain of racialized violence in *Scenes of Subjection*, 42–47.
49. On the National Guard's founding and the roles it performed to ensure the market's transition to a corporate-monopoly model of capitalism, see Richard Hofstadter and Mike Wallace, eds., *American Violence: A Documentary History* (New York: Knopf, 1970), 18, 142–43, 160–61. JWJ's diplomatic positions in Venezuela and Nicaragua testify to the global ambitions of U.S. foreign policy between the Spanish-American War and World War I. For his opinions on American imperialism in Latin America and the Caribbean, see *ATW,* 288–89, 344–60; William E. Gibbs, "James Weldon Johnson: A Black Perspective on 'Big Stick' Diplomacy," *Diplomatic History* 8 (Fall 1984): 329–47.
50. The phrase comes from Nell I. Painter's *Soul Murder and Slavery* (Waco, Tex.: Baylor University Press, 1995).
51. For JWJ's account of his anti-lynching activism with the NAACP see *ATW*, 308–74. For useful secondary histories, see Zangrando, *NAACP Crusade against Lynching*, 53–84; Kellogg, *NAACP*, esp. chap. 10.
52. Spingarn made this comment at JWJ's resignation dinner from the NAACP in 1931; see Spingarn, "Resignation Speech," typescript, in JWJ Scrapbook, "JWJ Testimonial Dinner," Scrapbooks, box 3. Also see Spingarn's memorial tribute to JWJ in *Crisis* (September 1938): 292–93.
53. See JWJ's *New York Age* columns reprinted in Sondra Kathryn Wilson, ed., *Selected Writings of JWJ,* vol. 1 (New York: Oxford University Press, 1995); JWJ typescripts of his NAACP speeches in Notebook 10 (MSS 374).
54. JWJ, "Lynching—America's National Disgrace," *Current History* 19 (January 1927): 598.
55. Judith Butler, *The Psychic Life of Power: Theories in Subjection* (Palo Alto: Stanford University Press, 1997), 6–10. Further references are noted parenthetically in the text.
56. The concept of "passionate attachment" is useful insofar as (like Caruth's theory of trauma) it allows me to avoid analyzing JWJ's encounters with lynching as an ahistorical fixation or obsession, and to explore how lynching produced JWJ's subjectivity as a citizen and author. But the

reasons why JWJ's turn to art both provides and denies him relief from the force of lynching's violence will make clear why both models are limited.

57. I am not trying to say that "prior" power is necessarily or expressly just and good. Indeed, fully considered accounts of racial trauma would consider the ways in which "home" societies enact malfeasance and violence against people of color as well, tracing how those experiences of domination (and the efforts to resist it) bear on the formation of racial subjectivity in the United States. For a searching discussion of how this longer view might shape our understanding of racial traumas, see Eng and Han, "Dialogue on Racial Melancholia," 352–58.
58. On the psychic and political value of social recognition as a counter-traumatizing act, see ibid., 363–65; Eric L. Santner, *Stranded Objects: Mourning, Memory, and Film in Postwar Germany* (Ithaca: Cornell University Press, 1990), 24–26, 155; Dominick LaCapra, *Representing the Holocaust: History, Theory, Trauma* (Ithaca: Cornell University Press, 1994), 193–94, 199–200, 215–18. Anne Anlin Cheng considers this idea more cautiously; see Cheng, *The Melancholy of Race: Psychoanalysis, Assimilation, and Hidden Grief* (New York: Oxford University Press, 2001), esp. 11–20, and her distinction between grief and grievance in chap. 6.
59. Zangrando, *NAACP Crusade against Lynching*, 19.
60. E. E. Hoss, "Lynching: Its Cause and Cure," *Independent* 46 (February 1894): 130. According to Hoss, a jury in Kansas awarded this paltry amount in 1894. Before World War I, eleven states had anti-lynching statutes on their books that, among other provisions, allowed black families to file wrongful death suits in civil courts against cities and counties (though not against individual mob members). According to James H. Chadbourn's *Lynching and the Law* (Chapel Hill: University of North Carolina Press, 1933), these statutes allowed juries to award from $1,000 (Nebraska) to $10,000 (Pennsylvania) to the victim's survivors (48). Two-dollar awards could be considered, then, a kind of jury nullification. In addition, it is important to note the slight implied by such suits being actionable as a matter of civil instead of criminal law. The distinction effectively exonerated the state from liability by remanding the violence into the realm of private torts instead of public policy. This evasion of jurisdiction is noteworthy in light of Nan Goodman's analysis of the era's concern with questions of liability and negligence in tort law; see Goodman, *Shifting the Blame: Literature, Law, and the Theory of Accidents in Nineteenth-Century America* (Princeton: Princeton University Press, 1998).
61. On reparations paid to Italy, see Marco Rimanelli, "The 1891–92 U.S.–Italian Diplomatic Crisis and War Scare," in *U.S.–Italian Relations: A Look Back*, ed. Marco Rimanelli and Sheryl L. Postman (New York: Peter Lang, 1992), 255; Walter F. White, *Rope and Faggot: A Biography of Judge Lynch* (New York: Knopf, 1929), 208. On payments to China, see James Elbert Cutler, "Proposed Remedies for Lynching," *Yale Review* 13 (August

1904), 206–7. Regarding both examples, see E. W. Huffcut, "International Liability for Mob Injuries," *Annals of the American Academy of Political and Social Science* (1891): 77–84. To be sure, many more Chinese, Mexicans, and white ethnic immigrants were lynched without official recognition. But these precedents underscore not just U.S. malfeasance but the state's complicity in normalizing this brutal punishment against its black citizens under the cover of lynching's supposed "extralegality."

62. Sharon P. Holland, *Raising the Dead: Readings of Death and (Black) Subjectivity* (Durham: Duke University Press, 2000), 15–16.
63. Butler, *Psychic Life of Power*, 13.
64. This is why Mark Twain's Roxana cannot sustain her wickedly brilliant plan to topple the white patriarchy that governs the world of *Puddn'head Wilson* (1894). Once she becomes "the dupe of her own deceptions," her plot can be exposed and its course checked (though not completely reversed) by David Wilson's scientific "fads." The same might be said for the force of law as it impales Babo's "cunning hive of subtlety" in Melville's *Benito Cereno* (1855).
65. JWJ to George A. Towns, 5 Oct. 1906, in Jackson, "Letters to a Friend," 184.
66. JWJ, "Autobiography of an Ex-Colored Man," MSS 141.
67. See ibid., "Working Draft," chap. 10, 22. Also see the verso of page 4 in chap. 2 for a remarkable foreshadowing of the scene.
68. JWJ Notebook 3 (MSS 367). Though there is one late entry dated 1919, the bulk of entries appear to have been written between 1909 and 1911.
69. See "Art" in JWJ Notebook 4 (MSS 368). He wrote two other "essayettes" on this theme, "The Dilemma of the (New) Poets," and "Clothes and Words" also in Notebook 4. JWJ probably developed these ideas in light of his literary studies with Brander Matthews at Columbia University. For more than forty years, Matthews wielded considerable influence in the development of American literary studies as an academic discipline. He taught Columbia's first survey course in American literature and authored a best-selling textbook on American literary history, *An Introduction to the Study of American Literature* (which sold 250,000 copies in 1896). Matthews wrote voluminously in and about realism, publishing some ten works of fiction and over a dozen essay collections. One of the first presidents of the Modern Language Association (1910–11), a founder of the forerunner to the American Academy of Arts and Sciences (the National Institute of Arts and Letters, 1912–14), and confidante to President Theodore Roosevelt, Mark Twain, and William Dean Howells, Matthews was a key figure in the literary debates about realism's foundational strength as a national literature at the turn of the century. For an illuminating study of Matthews's career, see Lawrence J. Oliver, *Brander Matthews, Theodore Roosevelt, and the Politics of American Literature, 1880–1920* (Knoxville: University of Tennessee Press, 1992).

70. Harry E. Shaw, *Narrating Reality: Austen, Scott, Eliot* (Ithaca: Cornell University Press, 1999), 29. Further references are noted parenthetically in the text.
71. For an illuminating discussion about the historicist possibilities and limitations of metaphors, see James E. Young, *Writing and Re-Writing the Holocaust: Narrative and the Consequences of Interpretation* (Bloomington: Indiana University Press, 1988), chap. 5.
72. JWJ to Grace Nail Johnson, 26 June 1912, series III, box 41, folder 22. Also see JWJ to George A. Towns, 10 Aug. 1912, in Jackson, "Letters to a Friend," 189–90.
73. JWJ's correspondence with Grace clearly states his investment in the novel's "secret" success as recompense for his humiliation; I discuss this dimension of the novel's publication in my essay "Keeping the Secret of Authorship."
74. I mean "arrogant" in the sense Ralph Ellison describes: "Arrogance aids the novelist in attacking the enormity of his task, which is that of reducing a society—and through the agency of mere words—to manageable proportions; to proportions which will reflect one man's vision, one man's sense of the human condition, and in such volatile and eloquent ways that each rhythm, each nuance of character and mood . . . becomes expressive of *his* sense of life and, by extension, that of the reader." See "On Initiation Rites and Power: Ralph Ellison Speaks at West Point," in *Going to the Territory* (New York: Vintage, 1995), 54. For a provocative analysis of how "capitalism underdeveloped" the black novel during the antebellum era, see Carla L. Peterson, *Doers of the Word: African American Women Speakers and Writers in the North, 1830–1880* (New York: Oxford University Press, 1995), chap. 6.
75. For recent analyses of this relation, see Dwight A. McBride, *Impossible Witness: Truth, Abolitionism, and Slave Testimony* (New York: NYU Press, 2001); Jeanine De Lombard, "'Eye-Witness to the Cruelty': Southern Violence and Northern Testimony in Frederick Douglass' 1845 *Narrative*," *American Literature* 73(2) (June 2001): 245–75; Ann Fabian, *The Unvarnished Truth: Personal Narratives in Nineteenth-Century America* (Berkeley: University of California Press, 2000), chap. 3.
76. The cultural backdrop of abolition's engagement with pain and sentiment is now voluminous. I draw on the following works to make this point: Hartman, *Scenes of Subjection*; McBride, *Impossible Witness*; Marcus Wood, *Blind Memory: Visual Representations of Slavery in England and America, 1780–1865* (New York: Routledge, 2000); Lindon Barrett, "African American Slave Narratives: Literacy, the Body, Authority," *American Literary History* 7 (Fall 1995): 415–42; Karen Sánchez-Eppler, "Bodily Bonds: The Intersecting Rhetorics of Feminism and Abolition," *Representations* 24 (Fall 1988): 28–59; Lauren Berlant, "Poor Eliza," *American Literature* 70(3) (September 1998): 635–68; Cynthia J. Davis, "Speaking the Body's Pain: Harriet Wilson's *Our Nig*," *African American Review* 27(3) (Fall 1993): 391–404. From the field of cultural history, see Elizabeth A. Clark, "The Sacred Rights of the Weak:

Pain, Sympathy, and the Culture of Individual Rights in Antebellum America," *Journal of American History* 82 (September 1995): 463–93; Karen Halttunen, "Humanitarianism and the Pornography of Pain in Anglo-American Culture," *American Historical Review* 100 (April 1995): 303–34.

77. JWJ Notebook 3 (MSS 367).
78. Ralph Ellison, "Society, Morality, and the Novel," in *Going to the Territory*, 244.
79. M. M. Bakhtin, "The Dialogic Imagination," in *Theory of the Novel: A Historical Approach*, ed. Michael McKeon (Baltimore: The Johns Hopkins University Press, 2000), 328. Bakhtin's theory of novelization sheds crucial light on a work like *The Autobiography of an Ex-Colored Man*. William L. Andrews provides such a reading in his 1990 essay, "The Novelization of Voice in African American Literature," PMLA 105 (January 1990): 23–34. However, by stressing Bakhtin's notion of laughter, I hope to explore the tensions novelization risks masking—the interplay between the genre form, authorial will, and narrative effect—because I wish to explain why the realist novel in particular would be both the best possible and most inadequate medium for Johnson to contemplate the violence of lynching.
80. Ibid.
81. I detail these aspects of JWJ's publicity campaign in "Keeping the Secret of Authorship." On the cultural politics of the rare book trade, see Charles Chesnutt's brilliant short story "Baxter's Procrustes" (1904), as well as Lawrence Rainey, "Cultural Economy of Modernism" in *The Cambridge Companion to Modernism*, ed. Michael Levenson (Cambridge: Cambridge University Press, 1999).
82. JWJ discloses his name change in correspondence with George A. Towns, 5 Feb. 1913, in Jackson, "Letters to a Friend," 191.
83. JWJ quoted in *Baltimore Afro-American*, 2 July 1938, 14.
84. Henry Louis Gates Jr., "Preface," in *Black Male: Representations of Masculinity in American Art*, ed. Thelma Golden (New York: Whitney Museum of American Art, 1994), 11–12.
85. For a provocative analysis linking minstrelsy and "coon" material culture to lynching, see Susan Gubar, *Racechanges: White Skin, Black Face in American Culture* (New York: Oxford University Press, 1997), chap. 2.
86. On this transformation in late-nineteenth-century America, see Miles Orvell, *The Real Thing: Imitation and Authenticity in American Culture, 1880–1940* (Chapel Hill: University of North Carolina Press, 1989); T. J. Jackson Lears, *No Place of Grace: Antimodernism and the Transformation of American Culture, 1880–1920* (New York: Pantheon, 1981), esp. chaps. 2 and 3.
87. Jonathan Crary, "Spectacle, Attention, Counter-Memory," *October* 50 (Fall 1989): 107.
88. Reminding us that this display of the bottles is a West African tradition to capture the spirits of the dead, Robert Stepto offers a nuanced version of

this critique in *From behind the Veil: A Study of Afro-American Narrative*, 2nd ed. (Urbana: University of Illinois Press, 1991 [1979]), 100–101.

89. On this point, see Hale, *Making Whiteness*, 137, 145. Also see Michael O'Malley, "Specie or Species: Race and the Money Question in Nineteenth-Century America," *American Historical Review* 99 (April 1994): 364–95.
90. Jean-Christophe Agnew, "The Consuming Vision of Henry James," in *The Culture of Consumption: Critical Essays in American History, 1880–1980*, eds. Richard Wightman Fox and T. J. Jackson Lears (New York: Pantheon, 1983), 67.
91. On the transformation of the American ethos of self-making from "character" to "personality," see Susman, "Personality and the Making of Twentieth Century American Culture," in *Culture as History: The Transformation of American Society in the Twentieth Century* (New York: Pantheon, 1984).
92. For this reason, *The Autobiography* uncannily anticipates the outbreak of anti-labor lynchings in Florida's cigar factories during the 1930s. See Robert P. Ingalls, *Urban Vigilantes in the New South: Tampa, 1882–1936* (Gainesville: University Press of Florida, 1988). On fungibility, see Agnew, "Consuming Vision," 68.
93. This cycle in the culture industry's development ran between 1909 and 1916, according to Anna Everett and other film historians. See Everett's discussion of this phase in *Returning the Gaze: A Genealogy of Black Film Criticism, 1909–1949* (Durham: Duke University Press, 2001), chap. 1.
94. This passage recycles—or, we could say, refabricates—one of JWJ's poems about lynching, "The White Witch," which was composed during the same time as *Ex-Colored Man* and published in *Fifty Years and Other Poems* (1913).
95. Martha Banta, *Taylored Lives: Narrative Productions in the Age of Taylor, Veblen, and Ford* (Chicago: University of Chicago Press, 1993), 13.
96. A third meaning of "die" resurrects the world of gambling in the novel: the racial coding of dice—black dots on ivory white cubes—summons the specters of violence and death, because the language of the gambling den is morbid. "Fate me!" "Shoot me two!" "Gimme the bones!" (*ECM*, 93) are the cries heard during a game of craps.
97. Walter Benjamin, "Theses on the Philosophy of History," in *Illuminations*, ed. Hannah Arendt, trans. Harry Zohn (New York: Schocken, 1969), 257–58.
98. Compared to earlier scholarship that found fault with the ex-colored man's shame, anti-essentialist identity critiques have given rise to more flexible readings of the narrator's renunciation. See, e.g., Paul Gilroy, *The Black Atlantic: Modernity and Double Consciousness* (Cambridge: Harvard University Press, 1993), 130–33; Kenneth W. Warren, "Troubled Black Humanity in *The Souls of Black Folk* and *The Autobiography of an Ex-Colored Man*," in *The Cambridge Companion to American Realism and Naturalism: Howells to London*, ed. Donald Pizer (New York: Cambridge University Press, 1995), 273–76.

99. Ellison, "Society," 270.
100. On the distinction between the story and plot of a novel, see E. M. Forster, *Aspects of the Novel* (San Diego: Harcourt, Brace, 1955 [1927]), chaps. 2 and 5; Seymour Chatham, *Story and Discourse: Narrative Structure in Fiction and Film* (Ithaca: Cornell University Press, 1978), chap. 2.
101. See the initial description of this scene in an early draft of the novel; JWJ, "Autobiography of an Ex-Colored Man," MSS 142, 15.
102. Interestingly, JWJ's draft marginalia note how he envisioned the ex-colored man's white schoolmate: "Redhead a Southerner." See ibid., 13.
103. Anticipating Zora Neale Hurston's publishing plan for her anthropological studies, the narrator aims to collect his rural sources and then set up a writing shop in "some city like Nashville to begin my compositions and at the same time earn at least a living by teaching and performing before my funds gave out" (*ECM*, 173). From there the narrator would, presumably like Hurston (or, better, like Ida B. Wells), head North to Manhattan where he could sell and distribute his art nationally.
104. Studies by George Rudé, Natalie Zemon Davis, and Peter Linebaugh are suggestive in this regard. See, e.g., Rudé, *The Crowd in History: A Study of Popular Disturbances in France and England, 1730–1848* (New York: Wiley, 1964); Davis, *Society and Culture in Early Modern France: Eight Essays* (Palo Alto: Stanford University Press, 1975); and Linebaugh, *The London Hanged: Crime and Civil Society in the Eighteenth Century* (Cambridge: Cambridge University Press, 1992).
105. On railroads and modernity, see Stephen Kern, *The Culture of Time and Space, 1880–1918* (Cambridge: Harvard University Press, 1983), chap. 8; Wolfgang Schivelbusch, *The Railway Journey: The Industrialization of Time and Space in the Nineteenth Century* (Berkeley: University of California Press, 1986); and Hale, *Making Whiteness*, 128–37.
106. For an insightful discussion of chance as modernist, see Bill Brown, *The Material Unconscious: American Amusement, Stephen Crane, and the Economies of Play* (Cambridge: Harvard University, 1996), chap. 2, esp. 94–102.
107. Shaw, *Narrating Reality*, 97.
108. JWJ, "The Autobiography of an Ex-Colored Man," MSS 141, 142, 143, 144.
109. JWJ to Brander Matthews, [ca. 1908], series I, box 13, folder 315.
110. Shaw, *Narrating Reality*, 109. Amy Kaplan makes a sterner claim in this regard; see Kaplan, *The Social Construction of American Realism* (Chicago: University of Chicago Press, 1988), 160.
111. *ECM*, 197. Compare the early draft JWJ, "Autobiography of an Ex-Colored Man," MSS 141, with the final draft JWJ, "Autobiography of an Ex-Colored Man," MSS 143. JWJ adds the dependent clause in the second sentence ("and more than once I felt like declaiming"), inserts the phrase "when I returned to my room" in the third sentence, and from the end of the final sentence strikes the phrase "I was playing." These changes indicate his

concern with the narrator's identification and sense of agency in the face of his deception, which JWJ causally relates to the lynching.

112. Emphasis added. This published line matches JWJ phrasing in the typescript draft; see JWJ, "Autobiography of an Ex-Colored Man," MSS 143, 162.

113. See publicity ads and Knopf's catalogs in JWJ Scrapbook: Autobiography of an Ex-Colored Man, 1927. Van Vechten's support of JWJ republishing the novel was both generous and troubling. See their correspondence in Carl Van Vechten, Letters from Blacks, JWJ to Van Vechten, folder 1925–26; and JWJ Correspondence, Van Vechten to JWJ, series I, box 21, folder 497.

114. New American Library (NAL) published JWJ's novel under its Mentor imprint, adding it to a list that included Richard Wright's *Uncle Tom's Children*, Lillian Smith's *Strange Fruit*, and, interestingly, Ruth Benedict's *Patterns of Culture*. Remarkably, NAL promoted *Ex-Colored Man* as part of a campaign to organize black reading clubs, hiring an African American community activist, Ellen Tarry, to lead a pilot campaign in Harlem. See Arabel J. Porter to Carl Van Vechten, 29 Nov. 1948, JWJ Correspondence, series I, box 21, folder 506.

115. See, e.g., "The Washington Riots: An Analysis" (New York: NAACP, 1919); "Lynching—America's National Disgrace," *Current History* 19 (January 1924): 596–601;"Lynching," *Forum* 77 (February 1927): 308–9; "The Practice of Lynching: A Picture, the Problem, and What Shall Be Done About It," *Century* 115 (November 1927): 65–70. Also see JWJ's editorial columns published in the *New York Age* in Sondra Kathryn Wilson, *Selected Writings of JWJ*, vol. 1.

116. JWJ traces this idea to the gruesome aftermath of Ell Parson's lynching murder in 1917; see *ATW*, 317–18. He first commits the idea to print in "The Black Man's Body and the White Man's Soul," *The Classmate* (October 1928), in JWJ Scrapbook, 1917–30, box 2, vol. 3.

CHAPTER FIVE

1. James Weldon Johnson (JWJ) to Victor M. Shapiro, 27 Apr. 1931, JWJ Memorial Collection, Beinecke Rare Book and Manuscript Library, Yale University. Correspondence, series I, box 18, folder 431.
2. Victor M. Shapiro to JWJ, 28 Apr. 1931, JWJ Correspondence, series I, box 18, folder 431.
3. JWJ, *Along This Way* (New York: Viking, 1933), 298. On Jacksonville's importance to early American cinema, see Jane M. Gaines, *Fire and Desire: Mixed Race Movies in the Silent Era* (Chicago: University of Chicago Press, 2000), 95.
4. A dutiful correspondent, JWJ usually answered letters within two days of receipt. However, I could find no follow-up exchanges between him and Shapiro, nor was there a reply to the Kahn agency's query. See Gertrude B. Kahn to JWJ, 21 Oct. 1935, JWJ Correspondence, series I, box 12, folder 260.

5. For instance, though the 1936 version of Fannie Hurst's *Imitation of Life* would draw its own parallels between the tragedies of racial renunciation and mass-cultural production, neither the novel nor its film adaptation linked its concerns to the popularity of racial violence as did JWJ.
6. Ellison, *Invisible Man* (New York: Vintage, 1980 [1952]), 571.
7. To the extent his wanderings make his range of vision possible, the narrator's affinity with precinematic forms confirms his literary kinship with the flâneur. Vanessa R. Schwartz's critical review of flânerie suggested this connection to me; see Schwartz, "Cinema Spectatorship before the Apparatus: The Public Taste for Reality in Fin-de-Siecle Paris," in *Viewing Positions: Ways of Seeing Film*, ed. Linda Williams (New Brunswick, N.J.: Rutgers University Press, 1994).
8. Jane M. Gaines, *Fire and Desire: Mixed Race Movies in the Silent Era* (Chicago: University of Chicago Press, 2001), 148.
9. Dana B. Polan, "'Above All Else to Make You See': Cinema and the Ideology of Spectacle," in *Postmodernism and Politics*, ed. Jonathan Arac (Minneapolis: University of Minnesota Press, 1986), 61.
10. On the half-tone process, see Robert Taft, *Photography and the American Scene: A Social History, 1839–1889* (Minneola, N.Y.: Dover Press, 1964 [1938]); David Phillips, "The Birth of Mass Photography, Half-Tone Technology, Illustrated Magazines, and the Social Transformation of American Print Culture, 1880–1950," *Textual Studies in Canada* 10/11 (Winter 1998): 5–16. My research shows that the Associated Press archives contain no photos of anti-black lynching murders used to service its wire accounts prior to 1929. However, this finding does not exclude the possibility that individual photographers sold such images directly to newspapers. Mainstream magazines exploited half-tone technology as early as 1905 to publish lynching photographs, apparently relying on the freelance-itinerant market to supply such images; see the illustrations to Ray Stannard Baker, "What Is a Lynching? A Study of Mob Justice, South and North," *McClure's Magazine* 24 (January 1905): 299–314. Though the first lynching photographs circulated by the African American press were part of Ida B. Wells's *A Red Record* in 1895, those images were reproduced through engraving and electrotype techniques. Half-tone lynching photographs first appeared in the black media's most widely read publications, the *Chicago Defender* newspaper and *Crisis*, in 1915 and 1916, respectively. On the *Defender*'s illustration record, see Philip Dray, *At the Hands of Parties Unknown: The Lynching of Black America* (New York: Modern Library, 2003), 224–25. For *Crisis*, see all issues from 1910–14.
11. See, e.g., Gaines, *Fire and Desire*, 165.
12. Laura Wexler, *Tender Violence: Domestic Visions in an Age of U.S. Imperialism* (Chapel Hill: University of North Carolina Press, 2000), 50. In addition to Wexler, the following studies shape my approach to interpreting lynching photographs: Alan Trachtenberg, *Reading American Photographs: Images as*

History, Mathew Brady to Walker Evans (New York: Hill and Wang, 1989); Jonathan Crary, *Techniques of the Observer: On Vision and Modernity in the Nineteenth Century* (Cambridge: MIT Press, 1992 [1990]); John Tagg, *The Burden of Representation: Essays on Photography and Histories* (Minneapolis: University of Minneapolis Press, 1993).

13. Sontag revised the principal claims of *On Photography* (New York: Anchor Doubleday, 1990 [1977]) in *Regarding the Pain of Others* (New York: Farrar, Strauss and Giroux, 2003).
14. This phrase is taken from Barbie Zelizer's study of Holocaust photography and the production of popular memory, *Remembering to Forget: Holocaust Memory through the Camera's Eye* (Chicago: University of Chicago Press, 1998).
15. Jonathan Crary, *Suspensions of Perception: Attention, Spectacle, and Modern Culture* (Cambridge: MIT Press, 1999), 289.
16. Mark Seltzer, "Serial Killers, II: The Pathological Public Sphere," *Critical Inquiry* 22(1) (Autumn 1995): 122–49.
17. Andrea Stulman Dennett and Nina Warnke, "Disaster Spectacles at the Turn of the Century," *Film History* 4 (1990): 103–7; Bill Brown, *The Material Unconscious: American Amusement, Stephen Crane, and the Economies of Play* (Cambridge: Harvard University Press, 1996), 116–17. Also see John Kasson, *Amusing the Millions: Coney Island at the Turn of the Century* (New York: Hill and Wang, 1978), esp. 65–82.
18. Dennett and Warnke, "Disaster Spectacles," 110.
19. Ibid., 107.
20. Ibid., 106.
21. The phrase "Coney Island Realism" comes from Brown, *Material Unconscious*, 116. "Theatricalization . . . of destruction" is coined by Dennett and Warnke, "Disaster Spectacles," 110.
22. Brown, *Material Unconscious*, 116–17.
23. Ibid., 123.
24. In *Suspensions of Perception*, Crary distinguishes between levels of causality when he separates empirically "demonstrable links" between historical phenomena from "historically adjacent" or coincident events (343). While it would be irresponsible (and untrue) to argue that disaster spectacles "caused" lynching murders, it is worthwhile to consider the consequences of their temporal relatedness as cultural phenomena. In this regard, Philip Fisher's concept of "co-visibility" informs my thinking here as well; see Fisher, "Appearing and Disappearing in Public: Social Space in Late-Nineteenth-Century Literature and Culture," in *Reconstructing American Literary History*, ed. Sacvan Bercovitch (Cambridge: Harvard University Press, 1986), 177.
25. Patricia McConnell, "American Early Modern Artists, Vaudeville, and Film," in *On the Edge of Your Seat: Popular Theater and Film in Early Twentieth-Century American Art*, ed. Patricia McConnell (New Haven: Yale University Press,

2002), 26. Though it offers a persuasively argued account of the late-nineteenth century's visual milieu, both McConnell's fine essay and the volume overall fail to consider the South as a field for visual culture studies.

26. Ibid.
27. In addition to the films I discuss, see *Indiana Whitecaps* (1902); *Tracked by Bloodhounds; or, Lynching in Cripple Creek* (1904); *The Horse Thief* (1905); *The Black Viper* (1908); *The Black Sheep* (1912); *Colored Villainy* (1915); *The Cheat* (1915); *A Close Call* (1912); and *The Lion's Claws*, part 2 (1917). All of these films are on deposit at the Library of Congress, Motion Picture, Broadcast and Recorded Sound Division.
28. David Levy quoted in Miriam Hansen, *Babel and Babylon: Spectatorship in American Silent Film* (Cambridge: Harvard University Press, 1990), 46. According to early cinema scholars, the chase films' popularity peaked between 1903 and 1906, exactly when *Avenging a Crime* was released.
29. Tom Gunning, "An Aesthetic of Astonishment: Early Film and the (In)credulous Spectactor," *Art and Text* 34 (Spring 1999), 37.
30. In *Amusing the Millions,* John Kasson asserts that the park managers tried to kill the elephant with poisoned carrots (71). But the PBS documentary *Coney Island* (dir. Ric Burns, 1993) argues that the elephant was to be hanged.
31. Attraction movies typically featured "current events (parades, funerals, sporting events); scenes of everyday life (street scenes, children playing, laborers at work); arranged scenes (slapstick gags, a highlight from a well-known play, a romantic tableau); vaudeville performances (juggling, acrobatics, dances); or even camera tricks (Mèliés-like magic transformations)." See Tom Gunning, "Now You See It: The Temporality of the Cinema of Attractions," *Velvet Light Trap* 32 (Fall 1993): 4.
32. Gunning, "Now You See It," 10–11.
33. In addition to chase and disaster narratives, cinematic depictions of executions can be counted as part of lynching's visual genealogy. On execution films' popularity, see Hansen, *Babel and Babylon*, 31.
34. *New York Times* report quoted in George C. Wright, *Racial Violence in Kentucky, 1865–1940: Lynchings, Mob Rule, and "Legal Lynching"* (Baton Rouge: Louisiana State University Press, 1990), 117.
35. Ibid., 118.
36. Ibid., 165.
37. On the prominence and role of opera houses as cinema venues, see Gregory A. Waller, *Main Street Amusements: Movies and Commercial Entertainments in a Southern City, 1896–1930* (Washington, D.C.: Smithsonian Institution Press, 1995), 46–52; Robert C. Allen, "Which Modernity? Whose Modernity?" lecture delivered at Weisman Art Center, April 2002. Tensions between local exhibitors and national distributors were often centered on the use of opera house space; see Hansen, *Babel and Babylon*, 43–44, 98–101.
38. John Kasson, *Rudeness and Civility: Manners in Nineteenth-Century Urban America* (New York: Noonday Press, 1990), 255.

39. As Gregory A. Waller notes, "entirely mechanical entertainments" that coordinated record playing with the projection of stereopticon slides were routinely staged as early as 1897 (8, 34). However, in *Slow Fade to Black: The Negro in American Film, 1900–1942* (New York: Oxford University Press, 1993 [1977]), Thomas Cripps points out that Edison "had hoped to use minstrelsy in a test reel which was to synchronize sound-on-cylinders with film" (12), a plan that was realized in the first talking film, *The Jazz Singer* (1927), starring Al Jolson. Put differently, black abjection seemed to be the story through which filmmakers wanted to test the powers of sound.
40. Anna Everett details Walton's encounter and critique in "Lester Walton's Écriture Noir: Black Spectatorial Transcodings of Cinematic Excess," *Cinema Journal* 39 (Spring 2000): 41–43, and in *Returning the Gaze: A Genealogy of Black Film Criticism, 1909–1949* (Durham: Duke University Press, 2001), 19–21.
41. Jonathan Crary, "Spectacle, Attention, Counter-Memory," *October* 50 (Fall 1989), 103.
42. Sontag, *On Photography*, 88–89. In contrast, Sarah Greenough argues that the "contagion" of photography insulated vision from a distinctly social character or purpose. See "The Curious Contagion of the Camera," in *On the Art of Fixing a Shadow: 150 Years of Photography*, eds. Sarah Greenough et al. (Washington, D.C.: National Gallery of Art, 1989), 130.
43. Trachtenberg, *Reading American Photographs*, 6.
44. Roland Barthes, *Camera Lucida: Reflections on Photography*, trans. Richard Howard (New York: Hill and Wang, 1981), 4.
45. "View of the Remains of Ketchum and Mitchell," Library of Congress, Prints and Photographs Division, LC-USZ62-117499.
46. These observations follow from my reading of Louis P. Masur, *Rites of Execution: Capital Punishment and the Transformation of American Culture, 1776–1865* (New York: Oxford University Press, 1989); Edward L. Ayers, *Vengeance and Justice: Crime and Punishment in the Nineteenth-Century American South* (New York: Oxford University Press, 1984); and Lawrence Friedman, *Crime and Punishment in American History* (New York: Basic Books, 1993).
47. The following plates in James C. Allen et al., *Without Sanctuary: Lynching Photography in America* (Santa Fe: Twin Palms Press, 2000), depict the lynching murders of white men: 1, 5, 7, 8–9, 13, 33, 35, 73, 90. For exhibits of exceptional, excessive violence committed on the bodies of white men, see plates 68, 69–70, 80.
48. Ibid., half-title page. Also see plate 93.
49. On daguerreotypes and their use in nineteenth-century mourning rituals, see Jay Ruby, *Secure the Shadow: Death and Photography in America* (Cambridge: MIT Press, 1995), 52–60; Nancy Martha West, *Kodak and the Lens of Nostalgia* (Charlottesville: University of Virginia Press, 2000), 139–42; Franny Nudelman, *John Brown's Body: Slavery, Violence, and the*

Culture of War (Chapel Hill: University of North Carolina Press, 2004), 103–5, 110–13; Trachtenberg, *Reading American Photographs,* 13.

50. Wexler, *Tender Violence*, 200.
51. For examples of this authorship practice, see the following in Allen et al., *Without Sanctuary:* plates 1, 4, 5, 7, 22, 28, 35, 37, 38, 46, 49, 51, 94. Of these photographs and postcards, three (plates 5, 7, and 35) depict the murders of white men. Sybil Miller's "Hard Roads, Easy Money: Itinerants at Work," *Exposure* 24(4) (Winter 1986): 27–52, provides a helpful context to consider this motif.
52. My discussion is informed by Taft, *Photography and the American Scene*, chap. 13; Trachtenberg, *Reading American Photographs*, chap. 2; and Drew Gilpin Faust, "The Civil War Soldier and the Art of Dying," *Journal of Southern History* 67(1) (February 2001): 3–38. Franny Nudelman offers a strikingly different account of Civil War battlefield photographs, and their reception and function in 1860s America; see Nudelman, *John Brown's Body*, chap. 4.
53. Alexander Gardner, *Gardner's Photographic Sketch Book of the Civil War* (New York: Dover, 1959 [1866]), "Harvest of Death," plate 36. It is crucial to recall that Gardner staged the composition of "Harvest of Death." As Franny Nudelman points out, the photographer used the same corpses in that image and another, "Field Where General Reynolds Fell." See Nudelman, *John Brown's Body*, 119–21. The artifice of "Harvest of Death" does not invalidate the comparison I mean to draw here, though. On the contrary, the indeterminacy of Gardner's image underscores two points central to my discussion. First, like "Harvest of Death," lynching photographs are complex depictions, not transparent documents, of the violence. Second, Gardner's rearrangement of the corpses and his use of picture captions to produce different meanings for the images confirm that he meant to elicit the viewer's identification with the dead—precisely the opposite effect that scopically aggressive lynching photographs seek to create.
54. Drew Gilpin Faust's exploration of Civil War death rituals informs my discussion. See "The Civil War Soldier and the Art of Dying," *Journal of Southern History* 62 (February 2001): 3–38. I am grateful to Professor Faust for sharing a copy of her essay with me.
55. Karla F. C. Holloway, *Passed On: African American Mourning Stories, A Memorial* (Durham: Duke University Press, 2002), 25. W. Fitzhugh Brundage describes lynching funerals as protests in "The Roar on the Other Side of Silence," *Under Sentence of Death: Lynching in the South,* ed. W. Fitzhugh Brundage (Chapel Hill: University of North Carolina Press, 1997), 274. The most famous funeral protest occurred in Chicago in 1955, following the murder of Emmett Till, a case I discuss in chapter 6. As Ashraf Rushdy points out, black communities also refused to bury the dead as a way to protest lynching murders; see Rushdy, "Exquisite Corpse," in *The Best American Essays: 2001*, ed. Kathleen Norris (Boston: Houghton Mifflin, 2001), 262.

56. For this information, see provenance note to plate 2, in Allen et al., *Without Sanctuary,* 166.
57. W. Fitzhugh Brundage, *Lynching in the New South: Georgia and Virginia, 1880–1930* (Urbana: University of Illinois Press, 1993), 28–33.
58. My reading is influenced by Barbie Zelizer's brilliant analysis of depth of field as moral space in *Remembering to Forget,* 100–10.
59. The murder of Frank Embree in Fayette, Missouri in 1899 was staged for white adult men only, according to the photographs of the incident; see Allen et al., *Without Sanctuary,* plates 42–44 and provenance note 181. A reading of the homoerotic tensions produced by the crowd's relation to Embree's body could explain the power dynamics involved in his murder. I concentrate instead on the ways in which the camera works to figure Embree's subjection through his erasure as a visual subject.
60. See *Without Sanctuary,* plate 44. This is not an uncommon trope in lynching photographs, as plates 12, 28, 36, 78, and 85 attest. Interestingly, African American poets reclaimed this symbolism during the 1920s and 1930s. I discuss this reversal in chapter 6.
61. Allen et al., *Without Sanctuary*, notes to plate 42, 81.
62. Sontag, *On Photography*, 107.
63. Crary, *Techniques of the Observer,* 118, 8.
64. On the popularity of picture cards, see Taft, *Photography and the American Scene*, chap. 18; Trachtenberg, *Reading American Photographs*, chap. 2; Stapp, "Subjects," 5.
65. Tagg, *Burden of Representation*, 165–75.
66. On the difficulties of photographic fieldwork with wet-plate cameras, see Taft, *Photography and the American Scene*, 364–76; Trachtenberg, *Reading American Photographs*, 72-73; William Stapp, "'Subjects of Strange . . . and of Fearful Interest': Photojournalism from Its Beginnings in 1839," in *Eyes of Time: Photojournalism in America*, ed. Marianne Fulton (Boston: Little, Brown, 1988), 5.
67. Stapp, "Subjects," 5–6 (emphasis added).
68. Mertins' photographs are collected in Lot No. 2839 at the Library of Congress's Division of Prints and Photographs.
69. Seltzer, "Serial Killers, II," 125.
70. For local news coverage of Biggerstaff's execution, see *Helena (Mont.) Daily Herald,* 6 Apr. 1896, 1.
71. On Ball's career, see Deborah Willis, ed. *J. P. Ball: Daguerrean and Studio Photographer* (N.Y.: Garland, 1993), xiv–xix.
72. Justice Brown for the majority in *Plessy v. Ferguson*, in Henry Steele Commanger, ed., *Documents of American History*, 7th ed. (New York: Appleton-Century-Crofts, 1963), 628.
73. Ball's photographs of the execution of William Gay, a white man hanged for murder a month later, provide a foil to the visual evidence of Biggerstaff's proceedings. See Willis, *J. P. Ball*, plates 4.69–4.72.

74. Barthes, *Camera Lucida,* 26.
75. For a description of Biggerstaff's death, see *Helena (Mont.) Daily Herald,* 6 Apr. 1896, 1.
76. Barthes, *Camera Lucida,* 21.
77. Ibid., 59.
78. *Helena (Mont.) Daily Herald,* 6 Apr. 1896, 1. According to local news reports, J. P. Ball headed Biggerstaff's clemency committee. See *Helena (Mont.) Daily Herald,* 13 Apr. 1896.
79. Besides Ball, see the camerawork of H. C. Anderson in *Separate but Equal: The Mississippi Photographs of Henry Clay Anderson* (New York: Public Affairs, 2002), 120–35. The images produced by African American photographers in the Emmett Till case are, probably, the best known black-authored lynching photographs. I discuss those images and their cultural logic in chapter 6.
80. Polan, "To Make You See," 63.
81. Jeanine DeLombard coined the phrase "sensory predicament" in "'Eye-Witness to the Cruelty': Southern Violence and Northern Testimony in Frederick Douglass's 1845 *Narrative,*" *American Literature* 73(2) (June 2001), 254. By stressing the optical dimensions of witnessing lynching, I do not mean to dismiss the equally powerful dynamics at work in nonoptical encounters with the violence. As the ex-colored man's experience suggests, all of a person's senses—smell, touch, taste, and hearing as well as sight—are subject to their own "predicaments" as well. For testimonies of such effects, see David Margolick, *Strange Fruit: Billie Holiday, Café Society, and an Early Cry for Civil Rights* (Philadelphia: Running Press, 2000), 80–81, 89; James Cameron, *A Time of Terror* (Baltimore: Black Classics Press, 1994); W. E. B. Du Bois, *Dusk of Dawn: An Essay toward an Autobiography of a Race Concept* (New York: Harcourt Brace, 1940), 67; Anna Deveare Smith, *House Arrest: A Search for American Character in and around the White House, Past and Present* (New York: Dramatists Play Service, 2003), 92–99.
82. On Riis and Hine, see Trachtenberg, *Reading American Photographs,* chap. 4.
83. Brooke Baldwin, "On the Verso: Postcard Messages as Key to Popular Prejudice," *Journal of Popular Culture* 22(3) (Winter 1988): 15–17.
84. Benjamin's admiration of the medium's democratizing potential posed its own dilemma, though, because the mass reproduction of camera-made pictures destroyed the images' "aura" as singular and aesthetically powerful. See Benjamin, "The Work of Art in the Age of Mechanical Reproduction," in *Illuminations,* ed. Hannah Arendt, trans. Harry Zohn (New York: Schocken Books, 1969), 220–26.
85. For the Library of Congress's data, see its web site (www.loc.gov) and use "lynching" as a subject keyword to search the Prints and Photographs Division's online catalogue. In my own survey of state archives across the nation (conducted in the summer of 2002), I located 169 lynching photographs available through these collections. The only publicly acknowledged archive devoted to lynching photographs, the

Allen/Littlefield Collection, consists of 184 images that detail the practices of lynching photography in the United States from as early as 1878 to 1960. Taken together (and disregarding the possibility of image duplication across these collections), this body of evidence cannot prove that lynching photographs swept across the nation in massive waves of popularity. There are simply not enough extant photographs to substantiate such a claim.

86. James C. Allen provides an important glimpse into this world of exchange. See his afterword to Allen et al., *Without Sanctuary*, 205–8, where he outlines his movements through these sales networks as a cultural "picker."
87. Though its exact origins are unclear, "reckless eyeballing" usually refers to the illicit looks that black men would give to white women and that would lead to so many lynching murders. I intend to use the phrase more broadly, to consider the ways in which lynching photographs helped organize the experience and meaning of seeing during the late-nineteenth and early-twentieth centuries.
88. Miriam Hansen cites the gender ban at boxing films in *Babel and Babylon*, 1. For a remarkably archived analysis of white women's attendance and participation at lynching murders, see Crystal Feimster, "Ladies and Lynching: The Gendered Discourse of Mob Violence in the New South, 1880–1930" (Ph.D. diss., Princeton University, 2000), chap. 3, esp. 120–63.
89. Wexler, *Tender Violence*, 299.
90. Sontag, *On Photography*, 106.
91. Barthes, *Camera Lucida*, 118.
92. Such evidence strikes me as the truly original contribution of the Allen/Littlefield collection of lynching photography—to map the networks in which the images were (and still are, obviously) secreted, exchanged, and released for arbitrary view. On this point, see Allen's afterword in Allen et al., *Without Sanctuary*, 204.
93. As early as 1912 the NAACP's *Crisis* magazine reprinted lynching postcards found by its readers. For one such remarkable discovery, see *Crisis* (March 1912): 209.
94. Judging from the pamphlets published under his name or explicit direction, Johnson preferred text to be free of illustration (see, e.g., *The Washington Riots* [New York: NAACP, 1917]), or to organize stately public protests like the Silent Protest March (1917) and the prayer vigils and fasts performed by the women's auxiliaries of the NAACP.
95. David Levering Lewis begins *W. E. B. Du Bois: The Fight for Equality and the American Century, 1919–1963* (New York: Henry Holt, 2000), with a moving account of Du Bois's qualms over publishing lynching photographs (1–11).
96. Walter F. White's interest in lynching's photogeneity is easy to trace, based on the editorial debates he fostered on the use of the images in the NAACP's anti-lynching campaign during the 1930s; the "Art against Lynching" gallery exhibit he organized in 1934; and his own spectacular career passing as white to investigate lynching murders more thoroughly.

For examples of White's visual commitments, see his correspondence with Earl Brown, 26 Jan. 1937; New York City news editors, 3 Feb. 1937; and Thurgood Marshall, 15 Feb. 1937 in Papers of the NAACP, part 7, Anti-Lynching files, reel 5. On the art exhibition, see Marlene Clark, "Lynching and Anti-Lynching: Art and Politics in the 1930s," *Prospects* 18 (1993): 311–56. Lastly, on White's infiltration of white supremacist networks, see *A Man Called White: The Autobiography of Walter White* (New York: Viking, 1948), 39–59.

97. See Wells's correspondence with Albion W. Tourgée on this point: Wells to Tourgée, 10 Feb. 1893 and 23 Feb. 1893, in Ida B. Wells Papers, box 10, folder 6, Special Collections Research Center, University of Chicago Library.

98. According to the *Helena (Mont.) Daily Herald* (6 Apr. 1896, 1), Biggerstaff spent the hours before his execution surrounded by supporters. "The jail was crowded with visitors and more were coming every minute," the paper reported. Given this show of concern, it is reasonable to assume that Biggerstaff's community attended his funeral as a final refusal of the death sentence. It is also quite possible that members of this group purchased copies of J. P. Ball's picture card series to make the same point.

99. See "The Waco Horror," *Crisis* 12 (July 1916): 1–8. On the supplement's compilation, see the following case histories: James M. SoRelle, "'The Waco Horror': The Lynching of Jesse Washington," *Southwestern Historical Quarterly* 86(4) (April 1983): 535–37; Grace Elizabeth Hale, *Making Whiteness: The Culture of Segregation in the South, 1890–1940* (New York: Pantheon, 1998), 215–22. I discuss the secreted photo postcards manufactured of this murder at the end of this chapter.

100. I discuss the politics of visibility at work in the Till case in chapter 6. On the lynching of James Byrd Jr. and his family's decision to restrict the circulation of the postmortem photographs, see Rushdy, "Exquisite Corpse."

101. As defined by Elizabeth Alexander, Jacqueline Bobo, Manthia Diawara, and bell hooks, resistant or oppositional spectatorship comes close to being a natural habit of mind for African Americans. See Alexander, "'Can You be BLACK and Look at This?': Reading the Rodney King Video(s)," in *Black Male: Representations of Masculinity in Contemporary American Art*, ed. Thelma Golden (New York: Whitney Museum of American Art, 1994). In *Black American Cinema*, ed. Manthia Diawara (New York: Routledge, 1993), see the following essays: Bobo, "Reading through the Text: The Black Woman as Audience"; Diawara, "Black Spectatorship: Problems of Identification and Resistance"; and hooks, "The Oppositional Gaze: Black Female Spectators." Useful revisions of this visual politic that inform my discussion include Kobena Mercer, "Reading Racial Fetishism: The Photographs of Robert Mapplethorpe," in *Welcome to the Jungle: New Positions in Black Cultural Studies* (New York: Routledge, 1994); James A. Snead, "Spectatorship and Capture in King Kong: The Guilty Look," in *Representing Blackness: Issues in Film and Video*, ed. Valerie A. Smith (New Brunswick: Rutgers University

Press, 1997); Jacqueline Stewart, "Negroes Laughing at Themselves?: Black Spectatorship and the Performance of Urban Subjectivity," *Critical Inquiry* 29 (Summer 2003): 650–77.

102. I borrow the phrase "spectatorial fluidity" from Stewart, "Negroes Laughing," 659.

103. See, e.g., John Henry Adams, "Woman to the Rescue!" *Crisis* (May 1916): 43; "Moonlight Antics of an Effete Southern Chivalry," *Indianapolis Freeman*, 16 June 1894; "Map Shows Jonah in Memphis," *Chicago Defender*, 16 Aug. 1913, 1.

104. Zelizer, *Remembering to Forget*, 155.

105. Barthes, "Rhetoric of the Image," in *Image, Music, Text*, trans. Stephen Heath (New York: Hill and Wang, 1977), 210.

106. My analysis of stereographs is informed by Crary, *Techniques of the Observer*, 116–24; Trachtenberg, *Reading American Photographs*, 16–20; Taft, *Photography and the American Scene*, 167–74; Rosalind Krauss, "Photography's Discursive Spaces," in *The Contest of Meaning: Critical Histories of Photography*, ed. Richard Bolton (Cambridge: MIT Press, 1989), 290–93.

107. Trachtenberg, *Reading American Photographs*, 17.

108. Some stereograph viewers were hand-held or table-top devices; others were mounted on body-sized pillars and posts. With any model, the viewer would slip the stereocard into the clip stand affixed to the base of the lens mount, and then peer through the pair of binocular lenses to see the images on the card.

109. Krauss, "Discursive Spaces," 290; Taft, *Photography and the American Scene*, 167.

110. I have discovered six stereograph images of lynching. All of them are dated before 1910; five of them depict the mob murders of white men. See "And Speedily the Punishment Fits the Crime" (1901; LC-USZ62–76918); "The Higgins Lynching Part and the Hanging of Louis Higgins" (1907; LC-USZ62-26560); "The Lynching of MacManus" (1882; LC-USZ62-2462). Two others lack accession numbers: "A Necktie Party" (1898), and "Hanging of Jos. Lewis Brassell and George Anderson Brassell" (1878). All are at the Library of Congress, Prints and Photographs Division. According to the provenance note for "View of the Remains of Ketchum and Mitchell" (LC-USZ62-117499), the victims were African American; see Allen et al., *Without Sanctuary*, note to plate 69, 191–92.

111. In Allen et al., *Without Sanctuary*, see plates 5, 7, 33, 68, 73, 89.

112. Thomas J. Schlereth, *Victorian America: Transformations in Everyday Life, 1876–1915* (New York: Harper, 1992), 197–99.

113. On the use of stereographs as political propaganda for U.S. expansionist policies at home and abroad, see ibid., 195–97; Trachtenberg, *Reading American Photographs*, chaps. 2 and 3; Taft, *Photography and the American Scene*, chaps. 13–15.

114. Hale, *Making Whiteness*, 154.

115. One of the 482 stereocards I examined in the American Antiquarian Society's "Negro" stereograph collections, "We's all done 'dis mornin'" is typical of the "View of the South" that were largely published between 1891 and 1906. These images would be significant if only because they archive the legacy of minstrelsy in shaping anti-black racism into the twentieth century. The stereocards are doubly important, as I hope to show, because their pictorial rhetoric and archival abundance explain why anti-black lynchings are hardly depicted in the medium.

116. As photographers and consumers, African Americans sought to counter the effects of both minstrel-themed stereocards and lynching photographs by popularizing what visual historians now call "New Negro" photography. On this countertradition, see Wexler, *Tender Violence*, chap. 4; Deborah Willis, *Reflections in Black: A History of Black Photographers 1840 to the Present* (New York: Norton, 2000), 35–48; Shawn Michelle Smith, *American Archives: Gender, Race, and Class in Visual Culture* (Princeton: Princeton University Press, 1999), chap. 6.

117. Justice in the West was necessarily "rough," these stereograph images imply, because the disciplinary institutions of American civil society—government, law, prison, school, church—had yet to be established and to take root in such locales. Cinema (before and after *Birth of a Nation*) reinforces this regionalization of the violence by using lynching as a central plot device to resolve plot conflicts about land claims and mistaken identity during the nation's westward expansion.

118. Quoted in Nancy Martha West, *Kodak and the Lens of Nostalgia* (Charlottesville: University of Virginia Press, 2000), 49.

119. In 1892, Kodak's advertising campaign to promote daylight film loading pledged, "You Press the Button, We Do the Rest." For a comprehensive analysis of the company's instructional rhetoric, see West, *Kodak and the Lens of Nostalgia*, esp. chap. 1.

120. When Kodaks first appeared on the market in 1888, the steep price ($25) depressed sales and only 3,250 cameras were manufactured. Once the price dropped to $5 and then $1, sales soared: 25,000 in 1895, then a staggering 1.2 million in 1900. See West, *Kodak and the Lens of Nostalgia*, 23–24, 41.

121. West, *Kodak and the Lens of Nostalgia*, 77. For a different critique of the cult of professionalism that characterized turn-of-the-century American photography, particularly its hegemony over the "visual sphere of cultural production" and the management of racial conflict, see Wexler, *Tender Violence*, 177–79.

122. Crary, *Techniques of the Observer*, 113.

123. West, *Kodak and the Lens of Nostalgia*, 62.

124. Ibid.

125. Quoted in Leon W. Litwack, "Hellhounds," in Allen et al., *Without Sanctuary*, 11.
126. Notes to plates 59–61, in Allen et al., *Without Sanctuary*, 185–86.
127. West, *Kodak and the Lens of Nostalgia*, 13.
128. Given their size, these images were most likely the products of Kodak's Brownie camera. On its technical specifications, see West, *Kodak and the Lens of Nostalgia*, 23–24, 74–75.
129. The recoil becomes clear when these images are compared to two other sets of snapshots; see Allen et al., *Without Sanctuary,* plates 20 and 77.
130. West, *Kodak and the Lens of Nostalgia,* 50.
131. To understand how uncertain and indeterminate these images are, compare them to the photographs and postcards of the murder of Jesse Washington in 1916. See plates 24–26 in Allen et al., *Without Sanctuary*, and the following ten images in the Library of Congress collection: LC-USZ62-102806; LC-USZ62-102808; LC-USZ62-35740; LC-USZ62-36635; LC-USZ62-33786; LC-USZ62-38918; LC-USZ62-38917; LC-USZ62-38539; LC-USZ62-102807; and LC-USZ64-4647.
132. West, *Kodak and the Lens of Nostalgia*, 74.
133. Allen's provenance note to plate 54 in Allen et al., *Without Sanctuary*, 184
134. The following postcard histories inform my discussion in this section: Richard Carline, *Pictures in the Post: The Story of the Picture Postcard and Its Place in the History of Popular Art*, 2nd ed. (Philadelphia: Deltiologists of America, 1972 [1959]); Christraud M. Geary and Virginia Lee Webb, eds., *Delivering Views: Distant Cultures in Early Postcards* (Washington, D.C.: Smithsonian Institution Press, 1998); Hal Morgan and Andreas Brown, *Prairie Fires and Paper Moons: The American Photographic Postcard, 1900–1920* (Boston: David R. Godine, 1981); Paul J. Vanderwood and Frank N. Samponaro, *Border Fury: A Picture Postcard Record of Mexico's Revolution and U.S. War Preparedness, 1910–1917* (Albuquerque: University Press of New Mexico, 1998). The following articles shaped my thinking as well: T. J. Brady, "Postcards as History," *History Today* 19(12) (December 1969): 848–55; Kelly Henderson, "The Art of the View: Picture Postcards of Virginia, 1900–1925," *Virginia Cavalcade* 40(2) (Autumn 1990): 66–73; Kim Keister, "Wish You Were Here," *Historic Preservation* 44 (March-April 1992): 54–61; Jeffrey L. Meikle, "A Paper Atlantis: Postcards, Mass Art, and the American Scene," *Journal of Design History* 13(4) (2000): 267–86; Frank T. Morn, "Postcards from the Past: Pictures, Prisons, and Popular Culture," *Material Culture* 31(3) (1999): 53–70; David Prochaska, "Thinking Postcards," *Visual Resources* 17 (2001): 383–99; John W. Ripley, "The Art of Postcard Fakery," *Kansas Historical Quarterly* 38(2) (Summer 1972): 129–31.
135. Roger L. Welsch, "Bigger Than Life: The Tall Tale Postcard," *Southern Folklore Quarterly* 38(4) (1974): 311.

136. Henderson provides this estimate of postcards' global circulation rates in "The Art of the View," 66.
137. For a revealing account of these systems, see Howard Woody, "International Postcards: Their History, Production, and Distribution (circa 1895 to 1915)," in *Delivering Views*, ed. Geary and Webb, 13–14 and fig. 22, 31. The South's public network of postcard outposts needs further research, given the medium's tendencies toward secretion, discussed above.
138. Jameson quoted in Robert Rydell, "Souvenirs of Imperialism: World's Fair Postcards," in Geary and Webb, *Delivering Views,* 53.
139. Allen, provenance note to plate 76, Allen et al., *Without Sanctuary,* 195–96.
140. Color tints were the "signatures" of large firms, and publishers patented their dye formulas to protect the value and integrity of their images in a highly competitive market. On these practices, see Carline, *Pictures in the Past,* 45; Woody, *International Postcards,* 25.
141. Woody, *International Postcards*, 18.
142. This summary of the Black Patch Wars is drawn from Tracy Campbell, *The Politics of Despair: Power and Resistance in the Tobacco Wars* (Lexington: University Press of Kentucky, 1993), chap. 5, esp. 90–93; Wright, *Racial Violence in Kentucky*, 134–43. As Campbell points out, the turn to vigilantism was a late development in the trajectory of the wars, peaking between 1906 and 1909 (96). Prior to those years, the Planters Protective Association followed the footsteps of nonviolent workers' movements such as the Greenbacks and Populists, organizations that stressed voluntarism and cooperative economic equity as the bases of their activism. For more on this angle, see *Politics of Despair*, chap. 3.
143. Ibid., chaps. 1–3, 9.
144. Ibid., 2.
145. According to historian Andrea Friedman, demeaning or pornographic depictions of black people were never considered to be in need of federal protection policies or practices so far as anti-obscenity politics were concerned. See Friedman, *Prurient Interests: Gender, Democracy, and Obscenity in New York City, 1909–1945* (New York: Columbia University Press, 2000), 10.
146. On Detroit Publishing Company, see Woody, "International Postcards," 23; on Teich, see Meikle, "Paper Atlantis"; Keister, "Wish You Were Here."
147. This information comes from a postcard Rotograph published to advertise its services. See Woody, "International Postcards," 27, fig. 17.
148. For discussions of real-photo postcards, see Morgan and Brown, *Prairie Fires,* xiii–xiv, 105–13; Vanderwood and Samponaro, *Border Fury,* 3–6.
149. See the advertisement for the Kodak No. 3A, reprinted in Vanderwood and Samponaro, *Border Fury*, 6.
150. Ibid., 4.
151. Ibid., xiv.

152. For the production levels of the R.O.C.-styled printer, I draw from Vanderwood and Samponaro's case study of the archives of Walter Horne, an itinerant postcard photographer. See Vanderwood and Samponaro, *Border Fury,* chaps. 2 and 3.
153. Susan Stewart, *On Longing: Narratives of the Miniature, the Gigantic, the Souvenir, the Collection* (Durham: Duke University Press, 1993), 136.
154. Ibid.
155. For background analyses of this World War I-era murder, see SoRelle, "The Waco Horror," 517–37; Hale, *Making Whiteness*, 215–22; Dray, *At the Hands of Parties Unknown*, 215–19.
156. Ibid., 148.
157. Hannah Arendt, *Eichmann in Jerusalem: A Report on the Banality of Evil* (New York: Penguin, 1994 [1963]).
158. Sontag, *On Photography*, 7.
159. Barthes, *Camera Lucida*, 77, 76, 82.
160. Ibid., 77.
161. Berger quoted in Zelziner, *Remembering to Forget*, 208–9.
162. Sontag, *On Photography,* 21.
163. Jean-François Lyotard quoted in Crary, *Techniques of the Observer,* 143 n.15. On the negative force of the sublime, see Hayden White, "The Politics of Historical Interpretation: Discipline and De-Sublimation," in *The Content of the Form: Narrative Discourse and Historical Representation* (Baltimore: The Johns Hopkins University Press, 1987), 66–70.

CHAPTER SIX

1. James E. Young, *Writing and Re-Writing the Holocaust: Narrative and the Consequences of Interpretation* (Bloomington: Indiana University Press, 1998), 40, 42. For a different account of lynching's "legendary" effects in contemporary African American poetry and fiction (specifically the "redress" function of abjection in blues literature), see Adam Gussow, *Seems Like Murder Here: Southern Violence and the Blues Tradition* (Chicago: University of Chicago Press, 2002), chap. 3.
2. W. Fitzhugh Brundage, *Lynching in the New South: Georgia and Virginia, 1880–1930* (Urbana: University of Illinois Press, 1993), 13.
3. Woolf quoted in Stephen Kern, *The Culture of Time and Space: 1880–1918* (Cambridge: Harvard University Press, 1983), 183.
4. This unnamed survivor's testimony is quoted in Steven J. Diner, *A Very Different Age: Americans of the Progressive Era* (New York: Hill and Wang, 1998), 252.
5. The literature on U.S. modernization, modernism, and modernity is vast and I am surely reducing the complexities of its long-standing discourses and debates. Three texts that have clarified the overarching thematics and archives for me are Kern, *Culture of Time and Space;* David Harvey, *The*

Condition of Postmodernity: An Enquiry into the Origins of Cultural Change (Oxford: Blackwell, 1989); Leo Charney and Vanessa R. Schwartz, eds., *Cinema and the Invention of Modern Life* (Berkeley: University of California Press, 1995).

6. Jonathan Crary, *Techniques of the Observer: On Vision and Modernity in the Nineteenth Century* (Cambridge: MIT Press, 1990), 143 n.15.
7. Paul Gilroy, *The Black Atlantic: Modernity and Double Consciousness* (Cambridge: Harvard University Press, 1993), 56.
8. Ibid., 70–71. Other useful studies of racism's constitutive relations to modernity and modernism include Houston A. Baker Jr., *Modernism and the Harlem Renaissance* (Chicago: University of Chicago Press, 1987), and *Turning South Again: Re-Thinking Modernism, Re-Thinking Booker T.* (Durham: Duke University Press, 2001); Homi K. Bhabha, *The Location of Culture* (London: Routledge, 1994).
9. *Atlanta Constitution*, 25 April 1899, quoted in Mary Louise Ellis, "Rain Down Fire: The Lynching of Sam Hose" (Ph.D. diss., Florida State University, 1992), 174.
10. Lillian Smith quoted in Dray, *At the Hands of Parties Unknown*, 368. My thinking here is informed by Nancy Martha West's treatment of nostalgia's forward-leaning potential; see *Kodak and the Lens of Nostalgia* (Charlottesville: University Press of Virginia, 2000), 154–55.
11. For incisive analyses of death's relation to black subjectivity, see Sharon P. Holland's *Raising the Dead: Readings of Death and (Black) Subjectivity* (Durham: Duke University Press, 2000); Karla F. C. Holloway, *Passed On: African American Mourning Stories: A Ritual* (Durham: Duke University Press, 2002).
12. The phrase "political necrophilia" comes from Russ Castronovo, *Necro-Citizenship: Death, Eroticism, and the Public Sphere in the Nineteenth-Century United States* (Durham: Duke University Press, 2001), 6. My thinking here is also influenced by Holland, *Raising the Dead;* Gilroy, *Black Atlantic*, chap. 2, esp. 63–70.
13. Brundage, *Lynching in the New South*, 292. According to Stewart E. Tolnay and E. M. Beck's inventory of lynching, between 1920 and 1930, the reported numbers of anti-black lynchings dropped steadily, totaling 219 in that decade; see Tolnay and Beck, *Festival of Violence: An Analysis of Southern Lynchings, 1882–1930* (Urbana: University of Illinois Press, 1995), app. C, table C-3, 272. According to statistics compiled by the Tuskegee Institute (and covering years that Tolnay and Beck's inventory does not), between 1930 and 1968 177 African Americans and whites were reported murdered by lynch mobs. Of those, 160 were black victims. This represents a decline from one hundred lynching murders per year during the 1880s and 1890s to four per year. For these figures, see Robert L. Zangrando, *The NAACP Crusade against Lynching, 1909–1950* (Philadelphia: Temple University Press, 1980), table 2, 7–8.

14. Brundage points out that the modernization thesis dates back to the 1930s and was popularized by southern social scientists associated with the liberal activist group, the Commission on Interracial Cooperation; see *Lynching in the New South*, 246–48. Recent studies that argue such positions include Philip Dray, *At the Hands of Parties Unknown: The Lynching of Black America* (New York: Modern Library, 2000), 406–7, 459–61; Tolnay and Beck, *Festival of Violence*, chap. 7, esp. 213–33; Brundage, *Lynching in the New South*, 249–51, 257–58; Edward L. Ayres, *Vengeance and Justice: Crime and Punishment in the Nineteenth-Century South* (New York: Oxford University Press, 1984), 270, 275–76.
15. For a compelling critique of linking anti-black mob violence to bureaucratized "legal lynchings," see Brundage, *Lynching in the New South*, 255–57.
16. For instance, see the following images in the Library of Congress's Prints and Photographs Divisions, Visual Materials from the NAACP Records: LC-USZ62-116733; LC-USZ62-128327; LC-USZ62-131170; LC-USZ62-128328.
17. McGill quoted in *Jet* (26 May 1955), 30. For more on the bureaucratization of racial violence by municipal and federal government agencies, see Mary L. Dudziak, *Cold War Civil Rights: Race and the Image of American Democracy* (Princeton: Princeton University Press, 2000), 149–50.
18. To appreciate how complementary McKay's and Cullen's visions are, compare these poems to Langston Hughes's "Christ in Alabama" (1931), where the profanity-laced invocation of the lynching victim as divinity is, I think, the bleakest homage to the sanctification of martyrdom in this canon of American literature.
19. All citations regarding Toomer are to *Cane* (New York: Norton, 1975), 13, 25, 34–35.
20. The 1925 trial of Ossian Sweet draws the starkest portrait of this trend. For recent accounts of the case, see Dray, *At the Hands of Parties Unknown*, 283–92; Kevin Boyle, *Arc of Justice: A Saga of Race, Civil Rights, and Murder in the Jazz Age* (New York: Henry Holt, 2004).
21. Rhobert's demise (which ends with a mob-like crowd egging him on in his folly) leads us into the deep ennui of "Avey," "Beehive," "Theater," "Box Seat," and "Bona and Paul," where the black elites in Washington, D.C. and Chicago, the two meccas for the first great wave of migration before World War I, find that the city, arts, and education turn their passions for life into "slim," "diluted" versions of force, leading them to "die" (51, 46) quiet deaths of social impotence. By the time *Cane* closes with the novella-length "Kabnis," lynching reappears in the text, this time more symbolically charged because the "yell's" northern echoes transforms the practice and meaning of the violence in the South.
22. The U.S. Communist Party popularized its critiques of lynching most effectively when its legal affairs unit, the International Labor Defense,

represented the Scottsboro Boys at trial during the 1930s. Case studies that explore the party's analysis include Dan T. Carter, *Scottsboro: A Tragedy of the American South* (Baton Rouge: Louisiana State University Press, 1979); James Goodman, *Stories of Scottsboro* (New York: Pantheon, 1994). For representative scholarship authored by southern liberals of the 1930s, see Arthur Raper, *The Tragedy of Lynching* (Chapel Hill: University of North Carolina Press, 1933); James Chadbourn, *Lynching and the Law* (Chapel Hill: University of North Carolina Press, 1933); John Dollard, *Caste and Class in a Southern Town* (New Haven: Yale University Press, 1937). Jacquelyn Dowd-Hall's *Revolt against Chivalry: Jessie Daniel Ames and the Women's Campaign against Lynching*, rev. ed. (New York: Columbia University Press, 1993 [1979]) remains the best book-length study of southern white women's activism during the 1930s.

23. All of the following poems can be found in Arnold Rampersad and David Roessel, eds., *The Collected Poems of Langston Hughes* (New York: Knopf, 1994): "Song for a Dark Girl," "Gal's Cry for a Dying Lover," "Magnolia Flowers," "Flight," "Scottsboro," "Christ in Alabama," "Open Letter to the South," "The Town of Scottsboro," "A Negro Song," "Revolution," "One More 'S' in U.S.A.," "Ballad of Ozzie Powell," "August 19th . . .", "Song for Ourselves," "Southern Mammy Sings," "The Bitter River," "Ku Klux," "Broadcast to the West Indies," "Beaumont to Detroit: 1943," "The Ballad of Margie Polite," "Freedom [2]," "Blue Bayou," "Will V-Day Be Me-Day, Too?" "Silhouette," "Third Degree," "Georgia Dusk," "Mississippi," "Expendable," and "Three Songs about Lynching."
24. Rampersad and Roessel, *Collected Poems*, 647.
25. Printed in bold black and juxtaposed against the comparably banal activities of the reader's life—attending church, baseball games, and jazz concerts—the death sentence "August 19th is the date" becomes a chant that intones, visually and aurally, how routine it had become to take black life and to leave those deaths unmourned in 1930s America.
26. Hughes provided these instructions with the poem's first publication in the Communist Party's news organ *The Daily Worker*, 28 June 1938. See Rampersad and Roessel, *Collected Poems*, 647.
27. Until this year, the one book-length study devoted to the case, Stephen Whitfield's *A Death in the Delta: The Story of Emmett Till* (New York: Free Press, 1988), proposed the debatable thesis that Till's murder is best understood as an exceptional outburst of southern white racist etiquette, violence that Whitfield refuses to recognize as lynching. With the release of *The Untold Story of Emmett Louis Till* (2004), documentary filmmaker Keith Beauchamp brings more facts to light that will complicate our understanding of the case, since his investigations located more men who were involved in the murder. Survivors from that time now testify that, remarkably—sadly—two other black men, employees of Roy Bryant

and J. W. Milam, helped murder Till. See Rick Bragg, "A Hate Crime That Refuses to Give Up Its Ghosts," *New York Times*, 1 Dec. 2002, sec. 4, 1, 7.

28. See Jacqueline Goldsby, "The High and Low-Tech of It: The Meaning of Lynching and the Death of Emmett Till," *Yale Journal of Criticism* 9(2) (Fall 1996): 247. Also see Marianne Hirsch, "Projected Memory: Holocaust Photographs in Personal and Public Fantasy," in *Acts of Memory: Cultural Recall in the Present*, ed. Mieke Bal, Jonathan Crewe, and Leo Spitzer (Hanover, N.H: University Press of New England, 1999), 10–16, for a fascinating analysis of why children figure so prominently in atrocity photographs.
29. The *Brown* case is explored in Dudziak, *Cold War Civil Rights*, 113–14.
30. Many historians now contend that Till's lynching murder galvanized working-class black people to rise up against their oppression in the South. They point to the connection between the end of the murder trial and the start of the Montgomery bus boycott as contingent events rather than mere coincidence, stressing that the courage required to sustain the year-long protest was stoked by the grief and rage black people felt over Till's death. The PBS video documentary series *Eyes on the Prize* (dir. Henry Hampton, 1992) launched this revisionist interpretation of the case. See the first episode, "Awakenings."
31. Till's murder resonates more fiercely than the lynching murder of two other fourteen-year-old black boys, Charlie Lang and Ernest Green, for instance. According to Jahan Ramazani, these children were "lynched together beneath the Shubarth Bridge over the Chicasawhay River, in Mississippi, October 12, 1942." See *The Poetry of Mourning: The Modern Elegy from Hardy to Heaney* (Chicago: University of Chicago Press, 1994), 170. Though Langston Hughes memorialized their deaths in his 1943 poem "The Bitter River," these boys' names remain unfamiliar to us as emblems of lynching's history.
32. Exemplary memoirs include Muhammad Ali, *The Greatest: My Own Story* (London: Hart-Davis, MacGibbon, 1976), 34; Baker, *Turning South Again*, 2–4; Holloway, *Passed On*, 132–33; Charlayne Hunter-Gault, *In My Place* (New York: Farrar, Strauss, and Giroux, 1992), 116–17; Anne Moody, *Coming of Age in Mississippi* (New York: Dell, 1968), 121–29. I highlight black-authored testimonies here because, as I point out in this chapter's discussion, the photograph in question was published exclusively in the African American press.
33. First published in *The Bean Eaters* in 1960, "Last Quatrain" is one of a pair of elegies Brooks contributed to the public's mourning of Till's murder. In the interests of space, I do not discuss "A Bronzeville Mother Loiters in Mississippi. Meanwhile a Mississippi Mother Burns Bacon," because it is a very long poem that deserves a close reading of its own. Ultimately, it and "Last Quatrain" ought to be analyzed together as the diptych they are

meant to be. By focusing instead on the shorter, eight-line verse, I want to highlight "Last Quatrain's" complex rapport with mid-twentieth-century America's preoccupation with seeing and the consequences of that fascination for lynching's late history.

34. On the centrality of Chicago to black media culture during this period, see Robert Bone, "Richard Wright and the Chicago Renaissance," *Callaloo* 28 (Summer 1986): 460–61; Bill V. Mullen, *Popular Fronts: Chicago and African American Cultural Politics, 1935–1946* (Urbana: University of Illinois Press, 1999), chaps. 2, 4–5.
35. Although it is important to note the NAACP's vital role in supplying funds and research to the black press's efforts, it is equally crucial to trace the historical trajectory back to the turn of the nineteenth century insofar as this achievement fulfilled Ida B. Wells's hope that the black press would be sufficiently independent in both its opinion and technological capabilities to mount this kind of public consciousness campaign.
36. Goldsby, "The High and Low-Tech of It," 255–61.
37. John H. Johnson, with Lerone Bennett Jr., *Succeeding against the Odds* (New York: Warner Books, 1989), 153, 155.
38. Goldsby, "High and Low-Tech," 255–59.
39. Susan Sontag, *On Photography* (New York: Anchor, 1990 [1977]), 87. When reading the memoirs of journalists who covered this case—David Halberstam, Dan Wakefield, John Chancellor, and Simeon E. Booker among others—it is clear that reporting Till's death shaped their political coming of age and their sense of ethical duties as journalists committed to democratic politics. These autobiographies and the "norm" to which Sontag refers resonate interestingly with Barbie Zelizer's account of the journalists, particularly photographers, who covered the liberation of the concentration camps in Nazi Germany. It is interesting to speculate what visual work that cohort of men and women produced when they returned to the United States, if Bernice Abbott's 1951 essay "Photography at the Crossroads" is any indication: "Today, we are confronted with reality on the vastest scale mankind has known [and this puts] a greater responsibility on the photographer" (Abbott quoted in Zelizer, *Remembering to Forget: Holocaust Memory through the Camera's Eye* [Chicago: University of Chicago Press, 1998], 120). I would wager that some of those journalists wound up covering the American South (or training others to do so), and were very likely some of the photographers who covered the Till case so diligently. For Zelizer's discussion of this group, see 61–63.
40. W. J. T. Mitchell describes the "pictorial turn" that characterizes modern visual culture in *Picture Theory: Essays in Verbal and Visual Representation* (Chicago: University of Chicago Press, 1994), chap. 1, esp. 11–16.
41. I first located this photograph at the Bettmann Archives in New York City in 1995. At that time it was catalogued in the Bettmann's "Emmett Till" photo file. In my research of mainstream and African American press

coverage of the case and murder trial, I never came across this image in print. As of 2005, this photograph is no longer catalogued with the Till case file at what is now the Corbis/Bettman Archives. According to the firm, the image is "no longer... in our possession." E-mail correspondence with Gina Calderon, 30 June 2005.

42. See Mitchell, *Picture Theory*, 41. As attractive as it is as an explanatory device, Mitchell's concept of the "pictorial turn" is elusive because it remains unclear just when the world "turned" this way. He claims the idea describes "contemporary culture" (109), but is imprecise as to just when that period starts or ends. Judging from the examples Mitchell cites and discusses, the shift took hold sometime around 1964 and characterizes visual experience ever since, but that periodization disallows so central an event as the murder of Till and the public registering of it.
43. These biographical points are easily inferred from Brooks's memoirs and across the expanse of her poetic practice. Indeed, we might say that what the concept of collage was to Romare Bearden the idea of snapshots was to Gwendolyn Brooks: a way of scaling public history down to manageable, malleable, accountable size.
44. As a member of the South Side Poetry Group, Brooks read the poetic canon and its attendant criticism diligently, as well as subscribing to *Poetry* magazine. See her memoir *Report from Part One* (Detroit: Broadside Press, 1972), 66.
45. On the romantic embrace of "phonocentrism," see Mitchell, *Picture Theory*, 114–20. According to John Dos Passos, "the visual habits of Americans as a group [had changed]. From being a wordminded people, we became an eyeminded people." And, of course, Dos Passos would acknowledge this shift by inventing the "camera eye" as a point of view in novel writing; see his *USA* trilogy. Dos Passos quoted in Miles Orvell, *The Real Thing: Imitation and Authenticity in American Culture, 1880–1940* (Chapel Hill: University of North Carolina, 1989), 262.
46. Jahan Ramazani calls "Last Quatrain" "one of the most desolate and bitter [examples] of the modern lyric" canon. See *Poetry of Mourning*, xii. I find Ramazani's claim powerful but not completely persuasive because he classifies all lynching poems as blues-informed (if not styled). Langston Hughes may very well be the most skilled practitioner of the blues-elegy "lynch poem," as Ramazani understands it. But Robert Hayden's "Night, Mississippi," any of Brooks's five lynching ballads, Paul Laurence Dunbar's "The Haunted Oak," Angelina Weld Grimké's "Tenebris," Jean Toomer's "Portrait in Georgia," or Richard Wright's "Between the World and Me" (among others) do not follow this pattern as neatly as Ramazani claims (if they do so at all). For his full discussion of the genre, see *Poetry of Mourning*, chap. 4, 167–75.
47. "Last Quatrain of the Ballad of Emmett Till" is reprinted in its entirety with the kind permission of Brooks Permissions.

48. As James E. Young points out in his discussion of how news reports of the Holocaust distorted the public's perception of (and feeling for) the substance of loss, "newsreels, newspapers, and radio . . . create public figures and icons not by using them as figures so much as saturating the imagination with them." See *Writing and Re-Writing the Holocaust,* 121.
49. Bradley faced the near-impossible task of being called on (as the circumstance demanded) to perform the role of the aggrieved mother/savvy political activist. For an astute analysis of the sources and stresses she encountered negotiating this role, see Ruth Feldstein, "'I Wanted the Whole World to See': Race, Gender, and Constructions of Motherhood in the Death of Emmett Till," in *Not June Cleaver: Women and Gender in Postwar America, 1945–1990,* ed. Joanne Meyerowitz (Philadelphia: Temple University Press, 1994).
    For a different take on Bradley's plight, see my discussion in "The High and Low-Tech of It," 261–64.
50. "Grief" and "grievance" are central to Cheng's theory of racism as an incitement to melancholia, because they pose two potential responses to the kinds of losses that make racial subjects feel melancholic and/or mournful. As she explains in *The Melancholy of Race: Psychoanalysis, Assimilation, and Hidden Grief* (New York: Oxford University Press, 2001), grievance can be understood as "the social and legal articulation of grief" (x). Where grievance can be expressed in language amenable to public discourse such as political protest marches, trials, or legislative acts, grief struggles to find its form. That is because grief speaks "in a different language—a language that may seem inchoate because it is not fully reconcilable to the vocabulary of social formation or ideology but that nonetheless cuts a formative pattern" (x). However, because the language of grievance is not that of grief and, for that reason, fails to do justice to the grief for which it is supposed to speak, Cheng is quite exacting in her critique of grievance-driven politics. For her full explication of this idea, see *Melancholy of Race,* 169–95.
51. In *Figural Realism: Studies in the Mimesis Effect* (Baltimore: The Johns Hopkins University Press, 1999), Hayden White cites Gertrude Stein's 1936 lectures titled *Narration* to explore this point. As Stein understands it, history is hard to understand because writing is no longer a sufficient condition of knowledge. In Stein's words, history "is not real enough for writing, real enough for seeing, almost real enough for remembering but remembering in itself is not really an important enough thing to really need recalling, insofar as it is not seeing, but remembering is seeing and so anything is an important enough thing for seeing" (Stein quoted in White, "The Modernist Event," in *Figural Realism,* 84). It is hard to say if Brooks read Stein's volume; though, since the lectures were delivered at the University of Chicago, Brooks may very well have attended the talks herself. The possible link is noteworthy because of Brooks's and Stein's

shared concern for how we know what we know about history by way of print and visual culture. According to White, Stein argues throughout these lectures that events are "unreal" compared to "things which have really existed" because events are "'an outside without an inside'" (Stein quoted at ibid., 82). Stein's critique of journalism (compared to modernist prose) is that the news reifies things and events because journalism doesn't get the "outside inside." This strikes me as the concern animating "Last Quatrain"—and all of Brooks's lynching poems: they seek an "inside" to the "outside" of the murder.

52. Incredibly, the defendants' chief argument was that the body pulled from the Tallahatchie River was not Till's. I discuss the implications of this claim and its particular mediation by the news photographs of the case in "The High and Low-Tech of It," 261–64.
53. Wendy Lesser, *Pictures at an Execution* (Cambridge: Harvard University Press, 1993), 142–43.
54. See James Heffernan's useful explanation of this technique in "Ekphrasis and Representation," *New Literary History* 22(2) (Spring 1991): 297–316; Mitchell, *Picture Theory*, chap. 5.
55. The signal practitioner to cite alongside Brooks in this regard is Jacob Lawrence, whose work in gouache painting struck the perfect balance between the indeterminancy of color and the social structures that would limit physical shapes and meanings. But I can think of at least three stunning exceptions to Brooks's approach in "Last Quatrain"—Langston Hughes's short story, "Home," Toni Morrison's passage devoted to the 1917 Silent Protest Parade against Lynching in *Jazz*, and Elizabeth Catlett's dizzying linotype "I Have a Special Fear for My Loved Ones." These works suggest that the effort to represent lynching ekphrastically generates different pairings of aesthetic encounters, between prose writing and music (which is the case with Hughes and Morrison) and between sculpture and sketching (which structures the tensions in Catlett's work). Put differently, the extremities of lynching seem to demand a rethinking of ekphrasis's scope and expressive forms. Karla Holloway's citation and discussions of Morrison's and Catlett's work inspire my thinking here; see Holloway, *Passed On*, 70, 74. For an equally intriguing critique of ekphrasis as impossible for African American poetic practice, see Stephen Henderson, *Understanding New Black Poetry: Black Speech and Black Music as Poetic References* (New York: Morrow, 1973), 28–29.
56. Brooks, *Report from Part One*, 148.
57. My thanks to Jim Chandler for suggesting that I follow this connection, and to the students of Susan Tomlinson's introduction to African American literature class at Fairfield University for letting me try these ideas out in our seminar discussion in April 2002. The discussion that follows here is informed by Gertrude Reif Hughes, "Making It Really New: Hilda Doolittle, Gwendolyn Brooks, and the Feminist Potential of Modern Poetry,"

American Quarterly 42(3) (September 1990): 375–401; Ramazani, *Poetry of Mourning,* 171–72; Glen Hughes, *Imagism and the Imagists: A Study in Modern Poetry* (Palo Alto: Stanford University Press, 1931); John T. Gage, *In the Arresting Eye: The Rhetoric of Imagism* (Baton Rouge: Louisiana State University Press, 1981).

58. Though I disagree with her characterizing Brooks's visual sense as "mimetic, less stylized" ("Making It Really New," 192), Gertrude Reif Hughes offers an astute analysis of Brooks's work in these terms, especially her reading of "A Bronzeville Mother Loiters in Mississippi" as a critique of imagism's ahistoricism. See ibid., 193–94.
59. Brooks, *Report from Part One,* 166. In this same interview, Brooks explained why a tree is not just a tree in African American poetry. "It is possible, but if a black person looks *long* enough, he might think of other things that a white person might not . . . especially if you've seen some of the pictures in *Jet* magazine of what has happened on some of those trees—horrific" (ibid.).
60. Pound, "A Few Don'ts by an Imagiste," *Poetry* (March 1913), 200.
61. See Sandburg, *Chicago Race Riots, July 1919* (New York: Harcourt, Brace, and Howe, 1919). For an illuminating but stern critique of Sandburg's account, see C. K. Doreski, "From News to History: Robert Abbott and Carl Sandburg Read the 1919 Chicago Riot," *African American Review* 26(4) (Winter 1992): 642–48.
62. White casualties were steep too: fifteen died and 178 were injured. For discussions of this pogrom, see Allen H. Spear, *Black Chicago: The Making of a Negro Ghetto, 1880–1920* (Chicago: University of Chicago, 1967), 215–19; James R. Grossman, *Land of Hope: Chicago, Black Southerners, and the Great Migration* (Chicago: University of Chicago Press, 1989), 179.
63. The essays collected in Robert Gooding-Williams, ed., *Reading Rodney King, Reading Urban Uprising* (New York: Routledge, 1993) address this development. For a brilliant analysis of how George Holliday's videotape was misrepresented at the first trial of King's assailants, see Elizabeth Alexander, "Can You Be BLACK and Look at This?: Reading the Rodney King Video(s)," in *Black Male: Representations of Masculinity in Contemporary American Art,* ed. Thelma Golden (New York: Whitney Museum of American Art, 1994), 106–8.
64. Cheng, *The Melancholy of Race,* 194.
65. James E. Young, "The Holocaust as Vicarious Past: Art Spiegelman's *Maus* and the Afterimages of History," *Critical Inquiry* 24 (Spring 1998): 698.

Index

Page numbers in italics refer to figures.